Strange Bird

NEW DIRECTIONS IN NARRATIVE HISTORY

John Demos and Aaron Sachs, Series Editors

The New Directions in Narrative History series includes original works of creative nonfiction across the many fields of history and related disciplines. Based on new research, the books in this series offer significant scholarly contributions while also embracing stylistic innovation as well as the classic techniques of storytelling. The works of the New Directions in Narrative History series, intended for the broadest general readership, speak to deeply human concerns about the past, present, and future of our world and its people.

Strange Bird

The Albatross Press and the Third Reich

Michele K. Troy

Yale
UNIVERSITY PRESS
New Haven & London

Yale University Press books may be purchased in quantity for educational, business, or promotional use. For information, please e-mail sales.press@yale.edu (U.S. office) or sales@yaleup.co.uk (U.K. office).

Set in Bulmer type by Integrated Publishing Solutions.
Printed in the United States of America.

Library of Congress Control Number: 2016948025
ISBN 978-0-300-21568-7 (hardcover : alk. paper)

A catalogue record for this book is available from the British Library.

This paper meets the requirements of ANSI/NISO Z39.48-1992 (Permanence of Paper).

10 9 8 7 6 5 4 3 2 1

For the generations:

Virginia and Bart Troy
Tess, Isabella, and Theodore Robinson

I have always imagined that paradise will be a kind of library.
—Jorge Luis Borges

Lock up your libraries if you like; but there is no gate, no lock, no bolt that you can set upon the freedom of my mind.
—Virginia Woolf, *A Room of One's Own*

Contents

Acknowledgments

The moment scholars yearn for is the one we most often see depicted in police detective shows: someone—a woman, say—races into a basement archive, rifling through box after box, file after file, the intensity building as she runs her hands through her hair, jotting down notes, until finally her face lights up. The answer is there, within reach. The music builds as the information seeker seizes upon the file that will deliver answers that have long evaded her. Yet research trips are also filled with mishaps: the wrong file that arrives during the last hopeful minutes of a research day because an archivist read the researcher's "7" as a "1" (she forgot to draw a line through it as they do in Germany); the box that no one can locate, even though it is not checked out; the realization, on arriving in Berlin, that she should be in Leipzig instead because the Nazi regime relied heavily on regional organizations for its bureaucratic daily work; the clock ticking the days down to zero, when she returns home without her questions answered, yet again.

So I am immensely grateful to the archivists who guided me on my research journey at the two dozen archives that provided the foundation for this book, among them Carola Wagner at the German Federal Archives in Berlin-Lichterfelde, Lucia van der Linda of the Political Archive in Berlin, and Barbara Koschlig at the City Archive in Hamburg. Special thanks go to Monique Leblois-Pechon at the French National Archives for digging into a file slated for transit; Carola Staniek, Director of the German Book Museum at the German National Library, for answering my ongoing and obscure book-trade questions; and Thekla Kluttig of the City Archive of Leipzig for leading me in an inspired behind-the-scenes file hunt and for creating time when I thought I had none left. Not to be forgotten is a staff member at the French National Archives, whom I know only by his first name, Thierry, who tracked down the mysteriously missing, all-important, Box 1006 on my very last day in Paris. Without the patience and persistence of people like these, this book would not be here.

Funding for this project comes from multiple sources. I thank the Harry Ransom Center at the University of Texas, Austin, for a Mellon research fellowship in 2005; the Bibliographic Institute of America for a grant to work at New York area libraries in 2006; the German Academic Exchange Service (Deutsche Akademische Austausch Dienst) for a 2012 grant to explore German archives; and most of all, the University of Hartford, where the Provost's Office provided sabbatical time and travel funds, and the Faculty Senate gave me Coffin Grants and summer stipends. David Goldenberg, my dean at Hillyer College, not only gave me a crash course in money laundering—useful when writing about Holroyd-Reece's fast-and-loose financial dealings—but has also been a tireless fundraiser and supporter of my work. Thanks to his efforts, the Jay Camp Fellowship and the Gareau Fund offered additional travel monies and time.

Scholars need many things to write a book, especially one that requires so much research abroad: access to information; a place to rest their heads; and, if they're lucky, the chance to exchange ideas with convivial, open-minded people over hearty meals after days spent in the company of old files (which, however entrancing, are not particularly adept at dinner conversation). I have been immensely fortunate to have found all of these. Jean-Dominique Fabrega scanned for me Holroyd-Reece's thirty-page Christmas card for 1938, which I discovered on his blog "Histoires d'Histoire"; Yvette Vibert shared documents from her father's days with the Pegasus Press; Geneviève Latour shared memories of the German Occupation of Paris and led me to Denys Ghiel, the daughter of the French Albatross managing director Jean-Louis Bricaire. Both she and Michel Ollendorff, the son of Holroyd-Reece's right-hand man, Wolfgang Ollendorff, opened their homes and family albums to me. Editor Marc Jaffe told me of his early days with Kurt Enoch and Victor Weybright at the New American Library. Heike Schrammer and Gabriella Hemmersbach let me stay with them in Berlin, as did Reinart Feldmann and Hilde Koller in Leipzig. Michael Schwab played detective at the British National Archives before I could get there myself, and Sebastian Pannwitz sent me leads from the German Collection in Moscow's National Archive. My uncle, "Onkel" Dick Troy, helped me wade through Nazi spreadsheets to uncover the story behind them. Helen Rozwadowski and Daniel Hornstein gave me a writer's refuge in New London, Connecticut, as did Eric

Martinson, in Wellfleet, Massachusetts. Dorothea Hauser, the lawyer-scholar who managed the Warburg Archive in Hamburg, spontaneously offered her guest bedroom in Berlin, and her outside-the-box thinking about my research. Joachim Gerdes, with his polished Italian, helped me navigate the Mondadori Fondazione archive in Milan, though it had been two decades since we had seen one another in Germany. He and his wife, Mariarosario, and their son, Dario, also gave me a home away from home in Genoa. Special thanks to Albatross-Tauchnitz collector Alastair Jollans for sharing his knowledge of these series and contributing so many images from his collection, and to Hauke Voss for his friendship, his company on bicycle forays to Albatross-related spots in Hamburg, and a standing room at the "Pension Voss."

No book of this scope is built on air. I am grateful for the thoughtful networks of scholars, and for their meticulous and groundbreaking scholarship, which have offered me a solid base for my own research. The University of Hartford's History Reading Group—Katherine Owens, Avi Patt, Michael Robinson, and Bryan Synche—first suggested that I break away from the traditional academic history, and Erin Striff was a motivating writing partner for a string of Saturdays. Marie Françoise-Cachin, in Paris, has graciously introduced me to international scholars. Pascal Fouché met with me to discuss French publishing during the German Occupation. Alan Steinweis not only informed my research through his work at the intersection of economics and culture in the Third Reich but also emailed me research suggestions and supported my grant applications though we had never even met. In Jan-Pieter Barbian, I encountered both an expert, author of many books on Nazi literary politics, and a generous spirit; whether responding to my "cold emailing" with research suggestions, meeting to talk Nazi literary politics behind the New York Public Library, or writing letters of recommendation, Dr. Barbian has been an important sounding board. In a time when everyone seems increasingly busy, these scholars have offered a model of generosity which I highly value.

I have been stunned, too, in other ways at the sheer openness of strangers who, when I arrived at their doorsteps, shared stories of decades past in response to my questions about their family members. Lady Elisabeth Schiemann, Holroyd-Reece's stepdaughter, spoke at length with me, and—in a moment of great suspense—sifted through boxes in her attic to send me materials that have found their place in these pages. Thomas Wegner made the trip to the Cologne train station to share his memories of his uncle, the Albatross cofounder Max Christian Wegner. Charles Enoch took time from his hectic job at the International Monetary Fund to talk about his father's cousin, the Albatross distributor Kurt Enoch, and to scan images for my book.

Friendships have also sprung up along the way. Ruth and Peter Gruenthal, Enoch's daughter and son-in-law, opened their door to me over lunches and brunches and even for Ruth's marvelous ninetieth birthday celebration, and Ruth has sent me many a necessary clarification. At the home of Markus Wegner, Wegner's son from his third marriage, I have memories of eating berries and cream after sifting through the sepia tones of old photographs; Markus, a true historical and legal researcher, has also informed my book through his writings about his father's military career and his insights into his father's imprisonment. Matthias Wegner, Wegner's son from his second marriage, unwittingly supplied me with my detective-show "Ah ha!" moment. Opening his hall closet, he pulled several thick binders from well-organized shelves, and the next thing I knew, I was walking across Hamburg, carrying bags of correspondence between his parents from the 1930s and 1940s. For the trust he has placed in me and for our illuminating, hours-long conversations over Earl Grey tea in his library, or over Hefeweizen at Tiefental, I am deeply appreciative. Fiona Brewster, Holroyd-Reece's daughter, arrived late in my research scene, yet has taken up a lively and informed place within it. In providing anecdotes and photographs of her father, and in welcoming both me and my family into her little corner of France with amazing hospitality, she has become like extended family. Besides which, she is the only person in the world to call me "darling."

This book has fortunately had many eyes upon it. I am grateful to Chris Rogers, former editorial director and history editor at Yale University Press, who pushed me to look at my story from ten thousand feet, and to Aaron Sachs, co-editor of Yale's New Directions in Narrative History series, who advised me how to get there from the ground up. Dr. Sachs, in particular, brought his excitement about the project and his constructive criticism to the fore, both of which helped me push the book into its final form. Also at Yale, Erica Hanson and Clare Jones guided me through permissions and Senior Editor Susan Laity brought her amazing patience and careful eye for detail to this book, making it stronger with each query. Bevin Rainwater, at the University of Hartford, helped me generate production-ready images. My sister and brother, Christine and David

Troy, volunteered to be my "urban readers," offering their feedback at different stages. My friend, the writer-editor Rand Richards Cooper, deserves special mention (and a gold medal for patience) for willingly taking on the role of book surgeon when I needed to cut out a massive portion of my original manuscript. Any surgery is painful, but I would not have trusted anyone else to take this one on with such humor, grace, and precision.

Thanks to my in-laws, Lucille and Bob Robinson, in Maine—who passed away in April 2016—for believing in me. I especially thank Bob, a Second World War veteran of the Army Corps of Engineers, who, in true Robinson fashion, always made me feel I had accomplished more than I had. My dream team of critical thinkers and friends includes Ruth Hofstatter, for guidance in a dark time; my colleagues Mary Fister and Marcia Seabury, for their optimism and the occasional hallway dance; Molly Cooper, for knowing the power of a good talisman; Emilee Bozic, for emotional rescue bracelets; Karin Peterson, for making me laugh loud and long; Catherine Blinder, for her kitchen stool reality checks and inspired gatherings; Meg Staley, for being wacky and wise; Hebe Guardiola-Díaz, for keeping my gaze trained forward; Christine Troy, my sister, for feisty, pirate-mouthed tirades against those who stood in my way; Virginie L'Homme Fontaine, one of my oldest and dearest friends, for taking up the adventure with me; and my aunt, the painter Susann Minton, for living on in my heart ten years after her death, reminding me how lucky we are to be here, even in our confusion, and what a challenge and gift it is to bring something creatively to life.

There are, finally, the people I do not know how to thank. This list begins with my parents, Virginia and Bart Troy. Again and again, they have given the greatest gift of all: their time. They have flown in from Illinois to be super-hero grandparents to my three children, and the memory of them all squeezed in one bed with my parents reading to my children or playing games always leaves me with a smile. Coming from their world of order, they have tolerated our mess, even making dinner from behind the clothesline strung across our kitchen when our dryer broke. I hold for them a fierce love and appreciation and great gratitude that they taught me that our best shot at happiness lies in following our curiosity where it takes us.

My children—Tess, Isabella, and Theo—have grown up with this book, sometimes in the background and sometimes in the foreground. They have given me hugs and songs and cards on bad days, as on good. Day by day, they have rocked my world, teaching me a lesson beyond the scope of any research project: the reminder, as E. M. Forster once said, that "next to the Everlasting Why there is an Everlasting Yes." I am in awe of the people they are becoming.

And finally, Michael Robinson, my husband of twenty years, has been my partner in this book as in my life. He was there to catch my first excitement about the topic, there to read draftier drafts of chapters than anyone should have to tolerate, and there to help me pull out the narrative thread that would keep the story moving forward. Now he—my love, despite and because, forever and always—will be there for the celebration, too, for which I am deeply grateful.

At one point when I was struggling with the arc of the story, a writer acquaintance of ours gave me a hopeful thought. "One day," he said, "you will find yourself writing the last word of all." And. Here. It. Is.

Strange Bird

INTRODUCTION

Behind the Door

WILLY HOFFMAN STRODE through Paris in June 1941 bearing special orders from Germany. His journey took him to a set of massive doors at 12 rue Chanoinesse, a noble address on the Île de la Cité in the middle of the Seine. When he opened these doors, heavily carved with rectangles and arcs in the shape of a Roman soldier's breastplate, he found himself propelled back to an earlier time, long before Nazi flags waved over Paris. Beyond the entryway, wide and high enough to accommodate a horse-drawn wagon, lay a medieval courtyard with a carved stone well hearkening back to the city's earliest days. At the back of the courtyard, he found what he had come looking for: the abandoned office of the Albatross Press, a publisher well known and well loved for producing British and American paperbacks in English that had been selling across continental Europe since 1932.

Hoffman was a bureaucrat, not a soldier. A lawyer by trade, he worked in Paris by authority of the Reich Commissioner for the Handling of Enemy Property. Ever since the German army had occupied northern France the year before, the Reich Commissioner had sent German professionals to turn French, Jewish, and enemy firms in the Occupied zone to Germany's advantage. Hoffman was just one in this legion of "enemy property custodians." He arrived at Albatross's door knowing that Albatross was an anomaly. Though the publisher produced books in English, it was technically a German firm, listed as the Albatross Verlag in the German registry of commerce. Albatross had maintained a Parisian office throughout the 1930s—a toehold closer to London and New York from which it had wooed British and American authors for its popular Albatross Modern Continental Library. Albatross's international ties raised suspicions among Nazi officials, and with some reason. From the finance president in Leipzig, Hoffman gathered that Albatross had transferred substantial funds every month from Germany to Paris until the war broke out. Armed with this information, Hoffman had one specific task: to determine whether Albatross had illegally funneled these monies out of Germany and, if so, whether the Reich could recoup its losses.[1]

As Hoffman soon found, his assignment required a good deal of sleuthing. He knew the head of the French office was a certain John Holroyd-Reece. Beyond that, German intelligence was not very helpful. The head of the Propaganda Office in Paris offered only the haziest clues: that "Holroyd-Reece played a role in the beginnings of the Albatross Press that could not exactly be assessed" and that he reigned over a number of "correspondence enterprises" whose "exact influence and interlocking relationship could not be ascertained."[2] Other reports on Holroyd-Reece—described by Nazi propaganda officials in Paris as "a nauseating *belle-mondain* German emigrant" heading a "foreign Jewish clique"—did not add much clarity. Nor could Hoffman ask Holroyd-Reece himself.[3] He had fled Paris before the Germans marched into the city.[4]

Albatross turned out to be no less of a mystery. Although registered in Germany, it was financed largely by British-Jewish money through a holding company in Luxembourg. After sifting through this tangle of alliances, the Reich Commissioner had declared Albatross enemy property in Germany some months after the onset of war in September 1939. But Albatross's foreign ties and multiple incarnations made its operations in Paris hard to track.

So it was that, a stone's throw from Notre-Dame cathedral on this island in the Seine, Hoffman set to work to resolve the confusion. He rifled through files in the silent office. He questioned the two former Albatross employees he could track down: Max Christian Wegner, the German cofounder of Albatross, and Sonia Hambourg, a British Albatross editor who had remained in Paris during the war, and who, unbeknownst to Hoffman, was half Jewish. Hoffman steeped himself in the intricacies of French and German law, disentangling the financial threads that linked the German Albatross office to its French counterpart, and Albatross to the Reich. That Hoffman took his job seriously is clear from the seventeen-page report he sent to the chief finance president of Leipzig, with its nearly forty pages of attachments.[5]

Far more interesting than his report, though, is how and why Hoffman found himself in front of that door at 12 rue Chanoinesse in the first place—there, in the heart of Paris, getting to the bottom of a German firm with British and Jewish ties that sold English books and was accused of having swindled the Reich out of foreign currency for the better part of a decade. In the end, Hoffman is important less for the conclusions he reached than for the position he occupied. He was just one in a long line of Nazi administrators through the 1930s and into the war who struggled to make sense of Albatross's financial and legal ties so they could bend the firm to Germany's ends. Contact with the Albatross Press seemed to breed confusion. For years, Albatross had hidden in the open. Obfuscation was, in the end, its best defense against the Nazi bureaucracy, the strategy that had enabled it to keep Anglo-American books in front of German eyes even as the strident cries of Hitler's Germany mounted around it.

*

On the surface, it is hard to see why Nazi officials would have been interested in the Albatross Press except as a target of censorship. This was my first thought as I mused over *The Albatross Book of Short Stories,* the silvery volume I had called forth from the massive stacks at the French National Library in Paris. The graphics were pleasingly simple: a series of rectangles, one inside the other, tracing the periphery of the volume, with the title in block letters at the top and the silhouette of a bird in flight near the bottom. I sat in the imposing reading room, a space bounded by concrete walls and softened only by the oak tones of wooden tables and persimmon carpets. I had long been researching the reputations of British authors in Europe, from the well to the little known: James Joyce,

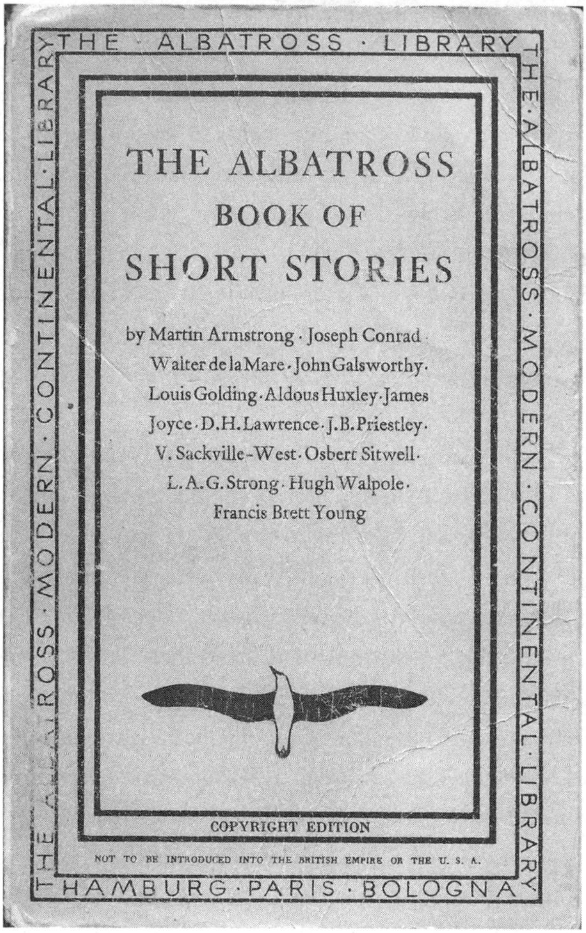

Cover of *The Albatross Book of Short Stories* (Courtesy of the Collection of Alastair Jollans)

D. H. Lawrence, Virginia Woolf, May Sinclair, among others. I knew that many continental publishers in the 1920s and 1930s had eagerly translated the work of British and American authors then in vogue for their own reading publics. And what I expected when I opened this volume was what I had seen before: translations of English literature into French. Instead, I saw a sea of words in English. But the copyright page stated clearly that the book had been printed in Germany in 1935. And two clues indicated that it was a book designed for readers in continental Europe: the words "The Albatross Modern Continental Library" running up and down the sides of the cover, and the warning across the bottom, "Not to be introduced into the British Empire or the U.S.A."

Even the most casual reader of history cannot help but spy the contradiction. Albatross began printing its books in Germany in May 1932. Hitler came to power on 30 January 1933. I knew that Nazi censors had banned certain books by authors listed on the cover I had before me. Aldous Huxley's *Brave New World* had certainly not been a Nazi favorite, nor James Joyce's *Ulysses.* The Jewish author Louis Golding was not translated into German within Reich borders in the 1930s, and his complete works ended up on the Nazi censorship list, the *Index of Damaging and Undesirable Literature.* As I later discovered, D. H. Lawrence's *Lady Chatterley's Lover* was deemed so offensive that authorities banned the book not only in German but also in English, just to be on the safe side.

The more I researched, the more I found that Albatross made its name not in the trade of mild classics but in edgy, modern British and American books. And these books became visible soon after Albatross broke into the market. As the British author Wyndham Lewis wrote after a trip to Berlin in 1934, "The Albatross editions I saw everywhere."[6] If we imagine ourselves, like Lewis, as railway travelers in 1930s Europe, we might well have seen fellow tourists paging through the colorful, well-designed books of the Albatross Modern Continental Library as they huddled in train compartments or leaned against posts in railway stations. These books were packaged to please, with captivating covers in kelly green, acid yellow, sprightly orange, robin's egg blue, red, and magenta, each color for a different genre. Even by today's standards, Albatross's streamlined covers convey a forward-looking elegance.

In its heyday, from 1932 to 1939, Albatross brought continental readers reprints of nearly five hundred titles at roughly six thousand venues across continental Europe. Albatross books were affordable as well as accessible. For a modest price—12 francs, 9 lira, or 1.80 Reichsmarks—readers could acquire the most recent English and American literature. The Albatross Crime Club and Albatross Giants series kept European readers supplied with English and American tales of mystery and biography. Albatross formed a subsidiary, Odyssey Press, solely to reprint *Ulysses* and *Lady Chatterley's Lover*—hot sellers for sure, in part because they were banned in England and the United States. The Albatross Modern Continental Library included an array of so-called middlebrow fiction, as well as cutting-edge modernist texts that provoked curiosity abroad, among them, Lawrence's *The Rainbow,* Woolf's *To the Lighthouse,* Forster's *A Passage to India,* and Ernest Hemingway's *The Sun Also Rises.*

That Albatross printed and sold such books both in and from Hitler's Germany flies in the face of what we know, or think we know, about the Nazi regime's crackdown on foreign culture.[7] In the popular imagination, the subject of books in Hitler's Germany conjures up a host of repressive scenes: heaps of books aflame in May 1933, when student groups set fire to books "against the German spirit"; soldiers ransacking bookshops and confiscating stacks of volumes on censorship lists; mountains of "undesirable" books rotting away in warehouses; and, most disturbing of all, the regime's exclusion of Jewish or anti-Nazi publishers and authors from the literary landscape, and, ultimately, its threat to their very lives. These images have staying power because of the undeniable historical truth they illustrate: the Nazi regime repressed freedom of thought and censored or destroyed books that encouraged this practice.

Against this backdrop, Albatross should have raised the hackles of German authorities at multiple levels. From its titles to its packaging, Albatross projected a cosmopolitan ethos at odds with German nationalism. Lists of its offices in France, Germany, and Italy paraded across its covers. Brief summaries in English, French, German—and, early on, Italian—occupied the inside fly leaf. These précis in multiple languages were just one sign that Albatross reached for its clientele beyond English-speaking travelers who hungered for reading material abroad. Seizing on continental curiosity about Anglo-American culture and the English language that had surged during the 1920s, Albatross sought a new coterie of readers: educated Europeans who did *not* have English as their mother tongue but who were able to read it. With its inexpensive books, Albatross encouraged these readers to cross the bridge from translations into the magical, modern world of British and American books in English.

Such a welcome into British and American literary terrain might not have seemed so threatening to the Reich if books were merely books. But as the British publisher Geoffrey Faber aptly reminded the chancellor of the exchequer early in the Second World War, "Books are not mere merchandise. Books are a nation thinking out loud."[8] From a propaganda perspective, Albatross books sent British and American ideals streaming across Europe on the eve of war. Seen in this light, Albatross might have had a German base, but it remained for Hitler's regime a potential enemy. Indeed, many Nazi officials openly dismissed

Albatross as a "notorious foreign firm." Its British funding and French editorial office put portions of Albatross operations outside German control, as did its partnerships with the prominent Scottish and Italian publishers William Collins and Arnoldo Mondadori. Nazi officials staggered through this labyrinth of affiliations. But it was especially the nature of Albatross's connections that tripped them up. Albatross was, in their words, "influenced by Jewish circles." Not only was the principal British financier Jewish; so were two of the firm's three leaders.[9]

It is here that the crux of the curious relationship between the Albatross and the Third Reich is laid bare. For how was a British-funded publisher of English-language books with Jewish ties allowed to print and sell its books within the nationalistic climate of 1930s Germany? This question, which beats at the heart of this book, baffled not only the German book trade but the president of the Reich Literary Chamber himself. The fact remains that in the late 1930s, sales in a Germany that was smothered in Reich propaganda made up a third of Albatross's market. Even after the onset of war, German readers still reached for Albatross titles. In 1941, the Albatross enemy property custodian informed his superiors that Albatross sales in Germany and elsewhere were mounting, with the demand "so large as to guarantee profits in the near future." Continental readers remained eager for books in English; indeed, the German Foreign Office envied Albatross its reach, wanting German books to have the same appeal to European readers. So when German Occupation authorities in Paris took the logical step of seizing Albatross's office on the rue Chanoinesse as British enemy property, higher authorities in Berlin ordered them to stand down, declaring instead, "The Reich is interested in this enterprise."[10]

Twining together such anecdotes, what remains to be told is how and why Nazi officials saw an opportunity rather than a liability in the burgeoning market for Anglo-American books. National Socialism openly harnessed culture to promote the German nation. Yet Nazi officials, in the midst of their headlong push to glorify all things German, also covertly cultivated the continental market for English editions—to the point where they badgered Albatross to sell still *more* English-language books. This is not a classic story of the regime banning foreign books. Nor does it fit the profile of German publishers under surveillance. For Albatross was of the nation and beyond it; it was simultaneously an economic insider, whose printing and distribution were firmly lodged in the German economy, and a complete cultural outsider to the Third Reich. Ultimately, its position made Albatross suspect, but also useful, to certain factions in Hitler's Germany. And Albatross used its precarious status for its own ends, as well; it repeatedly exploited vagaries in German law and power differentials between cultural and financial wings of the Nazi bureaucracy to win a place for Anglo-American culture in the twentieth century's most violent regime. Albatross was, as my title indicates, a strange bird.

*

This book, then, is the story of what happened when a resolutely cosmopolitan, multinational publishing house became entwined with the most destructively nationalistic culture of modern times. It is, at one level, a book about books and how they came to mean something beyond themselves in a politically charged time. But far more, it is a book about the lives that Albatross drew into its orbit, about the firm's attempts to keep Anglo-American books before continental eyes, and about a world that has disappeared. The more I researched Albatross's story, the more I wondered how Albatross had so quickly become the largest purveyor of English-language paperbacks in 1930s Europe and then vanished, leaving so little trace.

Perhaps because Albatross fell across national lines rather than within them, it has fallen outside the scope of popular national memory. Historians have traced in great detail the maneuvers of Hitler's armies across national borders, but even the most nuanced histories of publishing and censorship tend to stop at those borders. It is hard to know what to do, historically, with a firm that in vociferously nationalistic Germany was both British and German—and neither—at a time when the two powers staked out their positions against one another.[11] Recovering Albatross's story, we recover, then, other lost pieces of European and Anglo-American history that cut across national lines: how Anglo-American modernism gained ground in continental Europe; how quality mass market paperbacks became propaganda tools for both the Allied and Axis powers; how international trade regulations and economic realities swayed Nazi cultural policy and censorship; and how Hitler's regime was forced to confront an international threat that was both amorphous and concrete: the growing popularity of Anglo-American culture and the English language in continental Europe, and even in the heart of the Reich itself. Only if we follow the actions of the press through the 1930s does the larger picture of Anglo-American books under the rise of fascism begin to cohere. And only by tracking the flight of Albatross books across national borders can we gain insight into the migration of Anglo-American culture—and the dynamics of Nazi propaganda and censorship against it—in prewar and wartime Europe.

While Albatross's story arcs over literary, cultural, and political history, those who remember it are few and widely scattered. Some older Europeans I met recounted how they had once purchased Albatross volumes or seen copies on their parents' coffee tables. One middle-aged French bookseller pointed his finger at me questioningly, cocking his head: "They were collaborators, weren't they?" Were they? I was not sure. Younger European friends of mine told me of discovering a few battered English paperbacks in buoyant colors on their grandparents' bookshelves—Thornton Wilder's *The Bridge of San Luis Rey* (green) or Katherine Mansfield's *The Garden Party* (magenta), among others—and wondering why these bright offerings in English were wedged among books in their native tongue.

And so, though its books once circulated in the hands of many continental readers, Albatross has been relegated to the annals of the nearly invisible. What remains visible, mostly to historians of publishing, is not Albatross's role as a firm, but its position as a forebear. In 1934, Allen Lane used Albatross as the model for Penguin Books, a move that set Penguin on its path to success. Publishing lore even has it that a secretary at Lane's enterprise, overhearing a debate about which animal to use as an icon for a series to compete with Albatross, popped his head over an office divider and chirped, "What about a Penguin?" The next day, Lane shuttled the illustrator off to the zoo to sketch, and the rest, as they say, is history—Penguin's history.[12] Even within literary history, Albatross is little known, despite its contracts with so many luminaries of the 1930s. Yet for many Anglo-American authors seeking to extend their continental reputations, Albatross became the publishing house of choice.

It has not helped Albatross's legacy that it lacks something many publishers have: a standing archive devoted to its history. Only two boxes of Albatross documents survived the Occupation in France; the German hub in Leipzig was destroyed in the Allied bombing raids of December 1943; and Russian troops made off with Reich Economics Ministry files, which are still held in Moscow. Since few secondary sources about Albatross exist, I have pieced together the firm's story by tracking its vast, dispersed correspondence with two distinct groups: British and American publishers, authors, and agents, on one hand, and

Nazi officials and bureaucrats, on the other.[13] This book is largely born of the archive, or, rather, of a host of over two dozen archives in the United States and Europe.

There is a human story here, too, tucked away in these archives, of choices individuals made for survival or advancement. "How did people live, survive, or disappear under the Third Reich?" the longtime historian of the Nazi regime Pierre Ayçoberry has asked, calling this question "every bit as fundamental as the [question] . . . why did it happen?" We could ask this of Albatross, too. Yet we can understand how Albatross "survived" only by exploring the actions and inactions of a rich and complicated cast of characters across the political spectrum: authors, agents, Albatross partners, and government officials. For this reason, my book is both a biography of a publisher and the story of the individuals whose decisions shaped its direction.[14]

In this story of survival against the odds, the survival of this firm, its personalities, and the market for English-language books in the face of Nazi aggressions were all intertwined. Decisions about Albatross's survival became entangled with questions of personal survival. (The functioning of a British-funded firm, supported by Jewish money, in the heart of Nazi Germany gave new meaning to "life-or-death" decisions.) Albatross punched above its weight as a cultural institution, its path often driven by the passionate attitudes of its leaders rather than the dispassionate workings of macroeconomics. For example, the audacious decision to expand Anglo-American publishing in 1931—against the backdrop of the Great Depression and the rise of European fascism—made little sense according to any rational business model. Yet it made perfect sense to Albatross's three principal agents. Survivors of World War I, hyperinflation, and political turmoil, they had all made names for themselves exactly through finding opportunities in the improbable. While other publishers hunkered down, Albatross soared.

The narrator of W. G. Sebald's novel *Austerlitz,* retracing the steps of his lost childhood years after the Nazi era, offers us another way of understanding why such layers of research are meaningful. Looking around an old fort, furnished only with the detritus of bygone wartime days, he is thrown into contemplation. "Even now, when I try to remember them . . . ," he says, "the darkness does not lift but becomes heavier as I think how little we can hold in mind, how everything is constantly lapsing into oblivion with every extinguished life, how the world is, as it were, draining itself, in that the history of countless places and objects which themselves have no power of memory is never heard, never described or passed on."[15] The books of the Albatross Press are tied in with the story of a particular time and place. This story begins in 1931 with the aggressive optimism of the firm's cofounders. It moves through the realities of censorship and red tape and Nazi aggression against the Jews, and ends in a grim postwar world where the discernible outlines of Albatross's prewar market—and the lives of so very many people not yet ready to finish living—had been obliterated. In this sense, Albatross books, with their elegant, rainbow array of covers, all point to a far darker and more splintered history than their appearance would lead us to believe. They are all, in Sebald's words, "objects which themselves have no power of memory." Here, in this book, are the stories they tell.

ONE

Tauchnitz Has a Rival

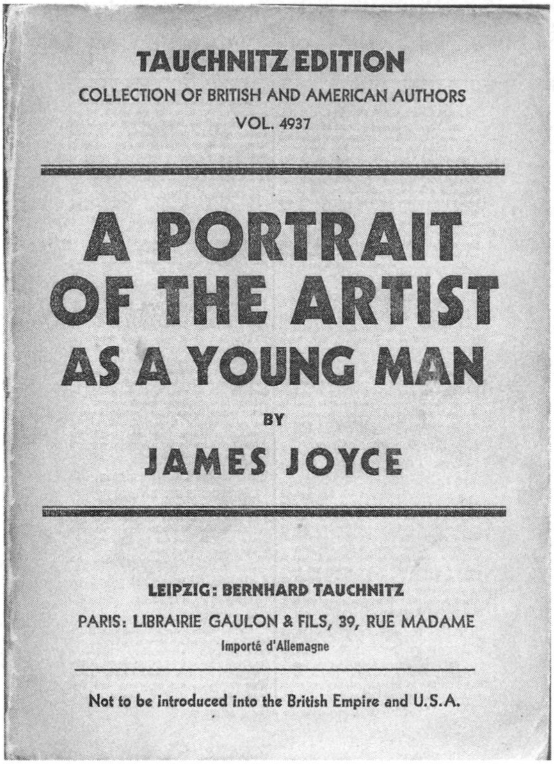
TAUCHNITZ EDITION
COLLECTION OF BRITISH AND AMERICAN AUTHORS
VOL. 4937
A PORTRAIT
OF THE ARTIST
AS A YOUNG MAN
BY
JAMES JOYCE
LEIPZIG: BERNHARD TAUCHNITZ
PARIS: LIBRAIRIE GAULON & FILS, 39, RUE MADAME
Importé d'Allemagne
Not to be introduced into the British Empire and U.S.A.

BY THE TIME Nazi officials started scrutinizing Albatross and its books, books in English had been part of the German economy for nearly a century. It was, remarkably, not an enterprising British or American publisher but a German firm—Bernhard Tauchnitz—that had seized on the idea of selling inexpensive paperbacks in English throughout continental Europe. As the 1930s began, readers across Europe knew and revered the Tauchnitz name. Tauchnitz had invented its specialized market for English books in 1841, and had dominated it ever since: the tell-tale ivory books of the Tauchnitz edition, with their stark black block-print lettering, had become synonymous with English literature on the continent.

So when Dr. Hans Otto, the head of the Tauchnitz board, first heard rumors of the Albatross Press in late October 1931, he paid attention. Word of Albatross wended its way to his office at Dresdnerstraße 5, a prominent corner address at the entrance to the "Graphic" quarter of Leipzig, where many printers and publishers had set up shop. Otto was alarmed. Tauchnitz had a legacy to defend. Learning that a newcomer was poised to invade its market unsettled him. The continental niche for such books was not big enough for two.[1]

How a German firm cornered the market for English books on the continent is an odd story, leading back to a Leipzig merchant with a good idea. In the early 1840s, one Christian Bernhard, Freiherr von Tauchnitz, learned that British authors and publishers were frustrated because literary pirates were hawking illegal reprints of their titles on the continent. With international copyright law decades away—it was not passed until 1895—they could do little to fight back. Von Tauchnitz drafted an inspired plan. He offered to pay British publishers a modest fee to reprint their books in Leipzig; in return, his English editions, sold across continental Europe, would secure them the copyright protection they desired. British publishers were both intrigued and worried. They wanted protection, surely, but were nervous about losing profits if von Tauchnitz sold his cheap paperbacks in the British Empire, a move that would undermine sales of their expensive hardcover editions. They agreed to the baron's plan on one condition: that he sell his editions outside the British Empire. Under these terms, in 1841, the Tauchnitz "Collection of British Authors" was born, and with it the market for so-called "continental English editions." Tauchnitz added American books over time, rechristening its series the "Collection of British and American Authors" in 1914.[2] Each book bore the mark of this debate in the words "Not to be introduced into the British Empire and the U.S.A." stamped on its cover.

Over nine decades, the little ivory books spread across Europe, earning von Tauchnitz a distinguished reputation as the protector of Anglo-American authors and the savior of many a traveler. "If you love me, send me something to read," pleaded D. H. Lawrence to one friend as he traveled through Austria in 1912. "I can't get Tauchnitz any longer." The Nobel Prize–winning American writer Sinclair Lewis recounted a more successful tale of emotional rescue, remembering "a hundred hotels . . . in which the possibility of getting back home by way of buying a Tauchnitz has saved my life."[3] In more formal tributes, books commemorating the Tauchnitz silver, gold, and diamond anniversaries cited authors from Charles Dickens to George Bernard Shaw expressing gratitude to the firm for forging a path for English books on the other side of the English Channel.

By 1931, when Otto heard his first rumors about Albatross, Tauchnitz editions had grown into a thriving sector of the international book trade. That same year, Tauchnitz had published its five thousandth volume and reported sales of over forty million copies since its beginnings—a pile of books later humorously imagined to stretch between London and New York, or to reach "eighty times as high as Mount Everest." And as one German journal pointed out, Tauchnitz showed no sign of losing its influence: "In the smallest German spa-town, in the most remote Italian village, on the faraway Dalmatian Coast, on the Canary Islands as on the Balearic Islands, when everything else is missing, the newest Tauchnitz is there at hand." Appearing "everywhere," as it were, Tauchnitz was even credited with popularizing the English language. Little did the baron know what he had started.[4]

For readers familiar with Tauchnitz's eminence, Otto's worry might, then, have seemed unwarranted. The firm's headquarters in Leipzig, stretching a full block, were as impressive as its international reputation. The neoclassical stone mansion housing its head office conveyed an aura of staid grandeur, as if to advertise that rivals stood little chance. Tauchnitz had history on its side: not only had the German firm invented the market for continental English editions; it had ostensibly fought off forty-two competitors in the decades since.[5]

Yet in October 1931, Otto did not act like a man reassured by Tauchnitz tradition. Anxious about Albatross, the first serious challenger to Tauchnitz's de facto monopoly in years, he dispatched one associate to London and another to Paris to gather intelligence. But they returned with more questions than answers, as the highly tentative language of Otto's report to the Tauchnitz board made clear: "The new enterprise will probably start under the name 'The Albatross' on 1 January 1932, namely, with its base in Paris, probably also with a special base in Germany, which, however, is not yet certain. . . . In London, it could not be determined with certainty who is financing the enterprise, although discussions about it are hovering about. . . . In general, there was very little and almost nothing that could be determined in Paris."[6]

These circumlocutions expressed only one thing well: Tauchnitz knew almost nothing about its rival. "We must, with all intensity, take advantage of the lull in the wind that remains to us before 1 January 1932 to get ahead," Otto declared to his colleagues. He dispatched one colleague to visit influential distributors in Switzerland, Italy, Vienna, and Prague, and another to England to shore up Tauchnitz's ties to authors and publishers. Back home in Leipzig, he sought covert intelligence. On 4 November, he hired lawyers from Hamburg to verify his meager leads and to investigate whether Albatross was entered in the registry of commerce there. Forty marks later, he was no wiser. He could not have been. Albatross was first registered in Hamburg on 12 November 1931.[7] Encircled by rumors, Otto was one week early. Albatross was an imminent threat that did not yet officially exist.

Albatross sent Otto into such a flurry partly because he took his task personally. He had his family name as well as Tauchnitz tradition to uphold. His brother Dr. Curt Otto had shepherded Tauchnitz from the dawn of the century until his death in 1929. Under his watch, Tauchnitz had solidified its reputation as a cultural link among peoples, and only his clever maneuvering had kept Tauchnitz alive in the Great War, when its volumes were treated as politically laden pawns speaking for Germany's enemies.[8]

In 1931, Hans Otto faced different challenges entirely. He had been grappling to keep Tauchnitz liquid amid the global financial calamity the American Depression had spawned abroad. The British and American tourists who were Tauchnitz's bread and butter were staying home. Germany, Tauchnitz's largest market, was lodged in its own devastating financial crisis. And British publishers were bucking at Tauchnitz's dominance. On a recent business trip to London, Otto had caught the edges of a wave of anti-Tauchnitz sentiment rolling through the boardrooms and men's clubs in which British publishers did their business. With sales of Tauchnitz editions rising dramatically in the late 1920s, he wondered how long British publishers would let a German firm reap the continental rewards.[9]

So Otto made haste. Yet one reason for his anxiety over Albatross trumped all others. If rumors were true, this new enemy had on its side a secret weapon whose potency Otto knew all too well: Max Christian Wegner, known as "Christian," the thirty-seven-year-old publisher Otto had fired from Tauchnitz the year before, who was armed with insider knowledge of Tauchnitz and ready for a fight.

*

Wegner made for an unnerving nemesis. Even as an ally, he had been a formidable presence, an outsized personality who strode fearlessly into a room.[10] A quick study, he was ambitious and had pushed Tauchnitz to modernize. As Tauchnitz's former managing director, he had an intimate knowledge of the firm's strengths and weaknesses—everything from its marketing strategy and sales figures down to the firm's financial liabilities and the personal quirks of the Tauchnitz family members. And he had left Tauchnitz in a rage.

Not even a year into his tenure, Wegner had violated a principle that Tauchnitz leadership held sacrosanct: he had started selling *Cimarron,* a novel by the American author Edna Ferber, before the original edition had completed its six-month run in the British and American markets—and, as was eventually revealed, before Ferber had even signed a contract. What emerged was not just a disagreement over rules but a clash of cultures between the old publishing world and the new. The Tauchnitz leadership concurred that Wegner had not merely violated one contract; he had insulted the most important silent partner in the firm: Tauchnitz tradition. Witness the indictment of Freiherr von Tauchnitz: "If anyone knows my grandfather and father . . . ," he wrote to Otto in an agitated state, "he knows that the whole interaction with English authors was built on correctness and trust." The great irony underlying it all, which Otto discerned only in hindsight, was that Wegner might never have met the British connections who helped him mount an opposition to Tauchnitz had Tauchnitz not sent him to England in the first place.[11]

Though Otto could never have anticipated it, Albatross found its beginnings in the moment when he fired Wegner. Wegner was suited to this oppositional role—"rash, certain, and goal-oriented," as one army comrade remembered him. The eldest of five sons born to a doctor from Kiel, Ernst Paul Wegner, and his wife, Anna Adelheid Kippenberg, Christian Wegner dropped out of university to join the German army in August 1914, just before his twenty-first birthday. Initially an infantryman fighting in the trenches, he was wounded and promoted to lieutenant, and he later volunteered as a pilot in Germany's first Luftwaffe. By August 1918, he had run 105 air missions into enemy territory in the Halberstadt

Max Christian Wegner, taken in Paris in 1933 (Courtesy of Dr. Matthias Wegner)

CL IV—the kind of fighter plane now featured in flight shows, where co-pilots sat in two buckets, exposed to whipping winds and the deafening roar of the engines. Wegner emerged from the war with a host of awards: the Iron Cross First Class, the Hamburg Hanseaten Cross, and the Knight's Cross of the House Order of Hohenzollern with Swords. The nomination for the final, and highest, of these distinctions noted his unusual ability to take clear-sighted risks in the confusion of battle, calling him an "an exemplary and riveting example of reckless grit."[12]

After the war, Wegner channeled his boldness into a career in publishing. His mother counted among her siblings a brother, Anton Kippenberg, who together with his wife, Katharina, had built the Insel Verlag into a respected publisher of belles-lettres by the time their nephew, the young Christian, was fishing around for a vocation. Wegner had attended one of the most distinguished schools in Hamburg, the Johanneum, and while his transcript remained mediocre, he showed from early on a love of literature and poetry. His father wrote a poem to Anton Kippenberg for Christmas 1909 titled "The Book Uncle with a Portrait of the Younger Sons" that identifies each of the five sons by one trait—including "Max Christian, the future publisher." Wegner was then sixteen. In his year at university he had snapped up literary seminars from prominent professors Albert Köster and Georg Witkowski. In training for the Great War, he was said to have squeezed discussions about Hugo von Hofmannsthal and Rainer Maria Rilke into his company's exercises, between the commands "Lie down!" and "Jump up, march, march!"[13]

So in September 1930, when Otto informed Wegner he would probably be fired, he was tangling with a very determined man's lifelong dream. Wegner "admitted without delay that he had handled the case . . . in an entirely inappropriate and outrageous way." Yet he also reassured Otto that he had "resolved the situation on all sides in England with the greatest elegance" and "was entirely convinced the case had been forgotten" by Ferber and her agent—one of the most prominent in London—Curtis Brown. Wegner's defense aside, the meeting ended badly. A disbelieving Wegner kept repeating, "Is it then possible that this publishing house values so little all I have accomplished so far—that it can ignore everything that I have done for them, . . . and that it is putting me on the street simply because of this one case!" A week later, Otto informed Wegner that he would be fired as of 30 December, unless his case was "cleared up." With the watchful eyes of the Tauchnitz board upon him, Wegner labored on, while Otto traveled to London to assess the damage to Tauchnitz's name.[14]

Otto regretted this impasse. Even through the haze of his anxiety that Wegner had irreparably damaged Tauchnitz's reputation, he recognized that Wegner offered "great assets that one could not and would not find" in others, among them his antenna for up-and-coming authors. Confronted with Wegner's outburst, Otto also hit on a critical insight: Wegner had not intentionally acted against Tauchnitz. Instead, Otto reflected, "Mr. W. is a person who is constantly trapped in an egocentric mentality, who, perhaps in the best sense, thinks first of himself" but also "identifies himself with the publishing house." Otto was correct on this score: Wegner assumed that situations were right and fair if they were right and fair for him, a narcissistic quality he carried with him throughout his life. A simple example goes a long way. When Wegner's mother-in-law from his third marriage visited Hamburg in 1948, she brought with her a large pumice stone. "What a stone!" Wegner exclaimed, or something to that effect, no longer used to seeing such an item in postwar Germany, which lacked all but basic supplies. He took the stone, cracked it in two pieces and handed the smaller piece back to his mother-in-law.[15] Otto had seen versions of this behavior: so long as Wegner met his goals, he expected others to deal with the consequences. Only this time Wegner was left holding the smaller piece of the stone. And Otto did not realize what kind of enemy he had created.

In his career, as in school, Wegner followed only those rules he chose to. This habit had landed him in trouble at Insel, in a "row" with his aunt that had led to his leaving, and then again at Tauchnitz.[16] (Years later, this blinkered quality would also nearly land him in front of a Nazi firing squad.) Yet whatever his liabilities, Wegner had amassed sixteen years of experience at Insel before Tauchnitz wooed him to become its managing director in 1929. So when he found himself on the outs with Tauchnitz, he took his talents to the unlikeliest of allies: Curtis Brown, the agent of the very author whose book Wegner had printed without permission. Far from antagonizing Brown, Wegner had won his esteem, and Brown helped him find a business partner to mount an opposition to Tauchnitz.[17] To Otto's chagrin and alarm, Wegner would now wield his German know-how for an upstart, seemingly British, rival. He was a man of ideas and initiative and pragmatism. He was full of energy and daring. And he had returned to confront Otto, wielding larger, more formidable weapons.

*

Otto got his first look at those weapons in early December 1931. After weeks of strategizing against a rival he could not see, there it was, in the *Börsenblatt für den deutschen Buchhandel*, the German book-trade journal: a full-page announcement for the Albatross Modern Continental Library. Otto scrutinized the details. Suspended across the top was an inviting mixture of text and image. The name, "The Albatross," stretched, mantra-like, in capital letters over the words "Hamburg—Paris—Milan," directly above an eye-catching bird hovering in flight. Of particular interest to him was the phrasing underneath the Albatross icon: "The Albatross is a German publishing enterprise, born of the collaboration of two publishers and friends, one German, Max Christian Wegner, and one Englishman, John Holroyd-Reece. The headquarters of the enterprise is in Hamburg, where the sole distribution rests in the hands of the Oscar Enoch

Publishing Firm (with the exception of Italy, for which the firm A. Mondadori, Milan, has charge of distribution)."[18]

The announcement told a tale of many nations working in harmony to found a great new enterprise. Germany and England were the anchors, with Wegner and Holroyd-Reece joining forces across the North Sea. But there was Italy. And France, too, with the advertisement disclosing that the editorial office operated from the bustling, intellectual center of Paris's 14th arrondissement. What worried Otto most, however, was Albatross's appeal to the German trade. Albatross invited this trade—the same distributors and booksellers with whom Tauchnitz had held court for nine decades—to stock their shelves with the "most outstanding works of modern British and American [authors] in technically consummate form for an inexpensive price." Otto circled back to the opening phrase: "Albatross is a German publishing operation."[19] In what way, exactly, Albatross was German, Otto was not sure. And then there was the enigmatic unknown of Wegner's partner.

Holroyd-Reece had blown into Tauchnitz's world without warning nearly a month earlier in the form of a letter that marked the firm's first direct communication from Albatross. In it Holroyd-Reece took on the guise of the knightly competitor preparing for a casual joust. "Gentlemen," he opened,

> It is a time-honoured English practice for the latest arrival in the publishing field to call upon his senior colleagues, and I am particularly sorry that the urgency of my private affairs will make it impossible for me to offer you this courtesy at the moment I would normally have chosen—namely the day previous to the first public announcement of the Albatross.
>
> I will nevertheless come to Leipzig at the earliest moment—in about a fortnight. . . . In the very special circumstances in which I have come to engage in the Albatross venture, I would be especially happy to answer any questions you might care to put to me, to inform you frankly of the principles of friendly rivalry upon which I am determined and to discuss, should you desire it, such measures as may be beneficial to our mutual interest.
>
> Hoping that you will understand the courtesy I intend in the

spirit in which it is offered and looking forward keenly to the pleasure of making the personal acquaintance of your directors,

I remain,
Gentlemen,
Yours very truly,

JOHN HOLROYD-REECE

The courteous phrasing provoked skepticism among the Tauchnitz leadership—and some alarm. Otto knew Albatross had a French office, so could presume Holroyd-Reece was fluent in French. A second letter requested that Otto write Holroyd-Reece at his house in Italy, which suggested connections there. And a third, postponing his trip to Leipzig, was written in impeccable German. Holroyd-Reece also sent a German Albatross prospectus, noting with a veneer of gallantry that he "would like at least to take care to see that you receive this from me before it reaches the book trade."[20]

The man himself finally made an appearance on 9 December, after a month of leaving Tauchnitz to wonder about its competition. Otto and his colleagues, Dr. Hauff and Mr. Keller, met with him for three hours, and Holroyd-Reece made an impression. "We have come to know Herr H.R. as someone to be taken seriously," Otto relayed with some pathos and urgency, "who is in literary and business matters fighting fit, and, in addition, a cosmopolitan in the truest sense of the word. . . . I believe him, [when he says] that he has strong and influential relationships to the London circles that are determinative for us. To put it briefly . . . he would actually have been the man we needed."[21]

Otto's appraisal touched on a theme that had troubled him since Wegner had blazed out of Tauchnitz: the search for "der leitende Mann," literally, "the leading man," someone to take the firm forward. With the continental market increasingly entrenched along nationalistic lines—and with British publishers accusing Tauchnitz of usurping their terrain—Otto needed a leader with the skills that had enabled his brother to piece Tauchnitz together after the Great War. "One must know the British and their attitude against Germany," he had stressed to the Tauchnitz board the year before. The "leading man" must know how to impress them, a skill "that can never be learned," and that requires "an un-heard-of

John Holroyd-Reece in the 1920s (Courtesy of Lady Elisabeth Schiemann)

engagement with the British mentality . . . , the most precise diplomatic and . . . international tact."[22]

Holroyd-Reece truly was, even more than Otto feared, a man who nimbly crossed national and cultural boundaries. "When in the mosque, take your shoes off," he insisted to his daughter in the 1940s, an impulse reflected far earlier in his work as a translator in the 1920s. He received accolades for exquisitely rendering an eclectic array of titles into English—among them groundbreaking works by the German Jewish art scholar Julius Meier-Graefe, whose biographies of van Gogh, Degas, and Cézanne positioned these artists at the vanguard of early-twentieth-century movements. In the early 1920s, he became a Paris correspondent for the *Christian Science Monitor,* writing articles on everything from Czechoslovakian ceramics to Lalique crystal. In 1923, he built up publishing connections across national lines, selling books as a continental agent for the British publisher Ernst Benn. In 1927, he turned publisher himself in Paris, founding the Pegasus Press (Les Éditions Pégase), which specialized in luxurious art books.[23]

He also struck out on a bold publishing project, linked with Pegasus, which provided a model for Albatross's international structure. Teaming up with the German publisher Kurt Wolff, he produced the Pantheon Series, two hundred volumes tracking the "history of the development of European culture." Each volume was to be written by a connoisseur and translated into three to five languages. "The publisher wants to be international," declared the Pantheon prospectus, "in the deeper sense": to plumb "the conjoined destiny, which despite all the races and folks, in attraction and oppositions, . . . has also left its deep and fertile trace on the creative, artistic life of the individual nations." Pantheon's structure was as international as its philosophy. The German typographer Hans Mardersteig produced most of the books at his Officina Bodini in Florence. Wolff handled distribution in Germany, Holroyd-Reece's Pegasus Press in France and England, Harcourt Brace in the United States, and Gili in Spain.[24] These connections formed a web in which Holroyd-Reece hoped to ensnare Tauchnitz.

In this sense, cosmopolitanism was not just Holroyd-Reece's philosophy; it was his business plan. To plant a seed of fear in Otto, or to convince agents to sign authors with Albatross, it was exceedingly practical for him to identify what his audience valued and to abide by their values, if only for the moment. Not incidentally, Holroyd-Reece earned a reputation as a master talker. The novelist Radclyffe Hall deemed him "rather a soldier of fortune perhaps, but a man who knows more about most things than anyone I have ever come across." The agent Graham Watson called him "one of the most engaging talkers I have ever listened to," and marveled at the way Holroyd-Reece held others captive. "You would mention that you were visiting Rome. He would at once explain that in a remote street behind the Spanish steps there was a shop specializing in making silk pyjamas and all you had to do to enjoy this good fortune was to mention his name. In Venice there was that little restaurant behind the Academia where the mushrooms were marvelous (but not on Wednesday when the chef was away). In New York it was essential to go and see Joe on Eighth Avenue and Thirty-Third Street who knew a girl. . . . What was so sickening about these tips was that he was always right."[25]

It was quickly dawning on Otto that the British publishing establishment would not—not yet, at least—be Tauchnitz's most dangerous threat. Albatross, the brainchild of two men who had consciously broken with the publishing traditions of Leipzig and London, would instead put Tauchnitz in peril. That such outsiders rose against Tauchnitz, a pillar of the German publishing world so visible abroad, seemed to Otto a cruel twist of fate.

*

Wegner and Holroyd-Reece were an intimidating duo. Yet they needed one thing Paris could not offer them: a German base. Germany was the largest market for continental English editions, worth a critical one-third of sales; to survive, Albatross needed to beat Tauchnitz on its home ground. Wegner, with his longstanding German ties, was the obvious man for the job. Yet he lacked capital, and a clause in his original Tauchnitz contract barred him from launching a competitor from the publishing centers of Munich, Berlin, or Leipzig for two years after leaving the firm.[26] Tauchnitz's ire against him made it contentious for him to take the lead role in Germany, anyway. Albatross needed a cleaner start.

The bustling port of Hamburg held the solution in the up-and-coming publisher Kurt Enoch. The thirty-six-year-old Enoch had run his family business in the heart of the downtown since 1921: a publishing house, the Gebrüder Enoch Verlag, and a newspaper distribution wing, the Grossohaus Enoch.[27] This combination was critical to Wegner and Holroyd-Reece. They sought a partner to round out their leadership, someone with know-how across arenas of publishing who could promote books aggressively in Germany but also organize distribution across Europe.

Hamburg was a propitious location, not only because it fell outside the list of German cities verboten to Wegner. It had been a thriving port for more than eight centuries, its location fifty miles down the Elbe River from the North Sea earning it the nickname "Gateway to the World." By the time Holroyd-Reece and Wegner invited Enoch to join Albatross, Hamburg was also widely known as "the Anglophile city," a propitious coincidence for a firm proposing to send English-language paperbacks flying across Europe. With London and Hamburg an easy ship's journey apart, British and German merchants had first traded goods, and then family members, as wealthy families from one port of call sent their children to foreign lands to enhance their educations.[28] The Albatross partners needed Hamburg to be for them what it had been for merchants centuries

Kurt Enoch in the 1920s (Courtesy of Charles Enoch)

before: the seat of international alliances that could facilitate sales of their goods across Europe.

When Enoch set up his publishing and distribution business at Schauenburgerstrasse 14, he had all manner of worlds within reach. His office was in the middle of things. From one end of his street he could access the so-called "business office" quarter; from the other, he could reach the Chamber of Business or the Rathaus. Unlike the Rathaus—a neo-Renaissance confection distinguished by a central tower and ornamented with sculptural detail and earnest statuary—Enoch's five-story warehouse was spare and modern, with a flat front and expansive windows that let in natural light. In five minutes, he could walk to the lively cafés downtown, or in ten to the central train station and the edge of the "warehouse city" that was Hamburg's claim to fame. Here, in the heart of this German provincial capital, he agreed to orchestrate the distribution of Albatross's books across continental Europe.

While Otto suspected that Enoch's firm was merely a "dummy" firm or postbox address for Albatross in Germany, Enoch actually offered Wegner and Holroyd-Reece a full-fledged partnership that worked for both sides. Like his partners, he was a publishing outsider, building his business in a city not known for publishing. Like them, he wanted to encourage innovation across national lines. When he took over the Gebrüder Enoch Verlag from his father in 1921, he borrowed money from his wife's uncle, a banker in London. "Being young myself," he recounted, "I wished to become a publisher of the new writers whose works gave expression to or reflected the spirit of the post-war generation, its new life style, new ideas and new concepts of our society." Enoch landed Klaus Mann, the novelist son of Thomas Mann. He translated works by Maurice Bedel and Panait Istrati from the French and Edna Ferber and Margaret Kennedy from the English. He became known for his attention to detail. A book on ski methods by Hannes Schneider was among the first to use reprints of movie reel sequences to teach skiing technique. He tracked down recognized artists to design his book covers, as with a book of satirical poems by Christian Morgenstern illustrated by Hans Reiersback, later known as H. A. Rey, author of the *Curious George* books.[29]

Temperamentally, Enoch was also an interesting match for his Albatross partners. "Enoch was not lacking in confidence," acknowledged one fellow publisher years later. Nor was he lacking in curiosity or independence. The stories he recounts of his early years stress these qualities, suggesting they were critical to his self-fashioning. Enoch was born in Hamburg in 1895 to a liberally educated family that expected diligence from its offspring—his father regularly quizzed him on school readings—but also encouraged independence. As a boy, he rode his bicycle far and wide, "eagerly exploring what his modern world had to offer": the "first flickering movies," and the "first crystal radio receivers." He played competitive tennis and soccer and tramped through the woods with a youth group, overnighting in barns or fields. At twelve, he sailed his dinghy back and forth across the Alster. Largely bored by school, he was nonetheless drawn to books whose heroes inspired his own exploits, including classics by James Fenimore Cooper, Robert Louis Stevenson, Jules Verne, Jack London, and Mark Twain—"in particular *Tom Sawyer* and *Huckleberry Finn.*" Much like Twain's two irreverent but clever protagonists, Enoch sought what adventures he could find. Fascinated by the zeppelins he and his brother watched for hours at the airport, the two boys had the wild idea of testing their own glider prototype—by jumping from the second story of their house. Disaster was averted when their mother discovered their plans.[30]

Like his two brash partners, Enoch had worked hard and did not easily cede ground. His studies at the Technical University of Berlin were interrupted when, at the age of nineteen, he was drafted into the German army. For much of his first year, he was assigned to an observation post in a trench one hundred yards beyond the front lines. Through a periscope, he reported on enemy positions and directed gunfire all winter long, with only a small coal stove to warm the freezing bunker. He lived close to danger, recalling, "I will never forget the sharp swishing sound of rifle bullets passing close to my head," and he admitted his "increasing horror and revulsion when seeing death at such proximity." Yet his remembrances also suggest a temerity akin to that of his partners: "Whether it was unconscious suppression or a kind of blind confidence I do not remember having felt fear for myself."[31]

In December 1918 Enoch returned to a Hamburg impoverished by war. Roughly forty thousand young soldiers from the city had been killed. British blockades had created food shortages. Random violence and crime were on the rise: gangs roamed the city, Communist factions rioted and raided warehouses for food, and the right clamored for order. In the midst of this chaos, Enoch sought a way forward. The war had left him with an Iron Cross for valor, an incomplete education, and a formidable drive for success. He studied economics at the University of Hamburg. His engagement to Hertha Rehse Frischmann in 1921 pushed him to finish his doctorate in economics and commit to publishing, which to him presented "an ideal combination of creative opportunity and socially useful and intellectually satisfying work along with the prospect of achieving a decent standard of life." Enoch's brother, meanwhile, had finished his doctorate in engineering and become engaged to Hertha's older sister.[32] So at the end of 1921, degree in hand, a double wedding in place, Enoch became the financial anchor of his family.

He was quickly thrust into the crisis of hyperinflation. With the astronomical price of raw materials, it cost more to produce books than Enoch could sell them for. So he adapted. "I remember that every night after the closing of the office—or even during the day by telephone—I made strenuous efforts to convert all the cash into new inventory or new material and that I quite frequently went on the night train to Berlin or Leipzig to buy as many books as possible from wholesalers or publishers wherever I could find them." His parents' well-being, as well as that of his growing family—his first daughter, Ruth, was born in 1922, and his second, Mirjam, in 1923—depended on his success, and he, indeed, succeeded, becoming visible enough as a publisher that Wegner and Holroyd-Reece approached him in 1931.[33]

*

With the threat the Albatross trio posed to Tauchnitz, the advantage would seem to have been all theirs. Yet it is impossible to understand the weight of Wegner and Holroyd-Reece's decision to establish a base in Hamburg, or Enoch's decision to join them, without stressing that Albatross faced one potentially insurmountable problem: it was not the most auspicious moment to launch a continental press with a German base. In the fall of 1931, when Albatross took flight, the German economy became so perilous that any foreign investor putting money into the country needed a well-honed plan to retrieve it. In the late 1920s, the German government had been dependent on foreign, and especially American, capital to make wartime reparations and meet its foreign debts. This overreliance on American loans meant that the U.S. stock market crash in October 1929 quickly flattened the German economy. American and other foreign creditors came knocking, needing to be repaid. Businesses could not pay their workers or afford raw materials. Industrial production fell, along with wages. By January 1930, roughly 14 percent of the "working-age" population—3,218,000 people—was unemployed, the figure rising to over 4.5 million, including part-time workers.[34] With each passing month, the German economy plunged ever more disastrously, along with the liberal climate that had made Hamburg such an ideal center for English-language books.

This economic devastation gave Hitler's National Socialist Party the opportunity it had been seeking. In December 1929, the American reporter Karl Wiegand—the first American correspondent to have interviewed Hitler, years earlier in 1922—sought him out to gauge his reaction to the crisis. "The public mind of the German people is in utter confusion," declared Hitler in Wiegand's article for the *New York American,* complaining about rising bankruptcies, burgeoning unemployment, and the inability of German politicians to stem the tide. Hitler vowed to "save Germany from being economically enslaved to foreign powers on the one hand and on the other hand from being utterly bolshevized and falling into disorganization and demoralization." On the basis of such appeals, his party won astounding gains in the election of September 1930, rocketing from 2.5 percent of the vote just two years earlier to 18.3 percent, from only 12 seats in the Reichstag to 107.[35]

While this political shift made Hitler's party the second largest in the Reichstag, it did not inspire confidence in foreign investors. Hitler's victory sparked a massive capital flight that ate up one-third of Reichsbank reserves. Germany's onerous reparations debts from the Great War, meanwhile, had become a matter of fierce international debate, with German officials pushing for reduced payments. As these discussions wore on, Germany lost hundreds of millions more Reichsmarks in foreign exchange. In the first half of 1931 alone, Berlin's largest banks lost roughly 2.5 billion RM in foreign assets, with an additional 2.7 billion RM of capital streaming out of Germany. Looking back decades later, Enoch summarized the effects on Germany's economy and people. "The flow of loans—the life-blood of Germany's economic recovery—came to a halt," he wrote. "Repayments of past loans became due. Rapidly diminishing foreign trade cut industrial production almost in half. As a consequence, businesses went bankrupt by the thousands, factory doors closed, and millions of people were thrown out of work. . . . The German people began to panic and despair."[36]

These economic blows were more than Germany could take. In July 1931 the economy cracked open, in a crisis brought on most directly by the Reichsbank's dwindling foreign currency reserves. Germany owed 1 billion RM in reparations, plus an additional 1.2 billion RM in interest, but had an active balance of only 450 million RM. To pay the difference, the government offered 1.7 billion RM from its gold and foreign currency reserves, nearly exhausting its supply. To staunch further leakage of capital, the Reichsbank initiated emergency regulations on 15 and 18 July, severing its currency from the gold standard. Two weeks later, on 1 August, it instituted a radical law stating that the Reichsbank would thenceforth control all foreign currency outlays, determining who could access currency and how much each could claim. A new office in Berlin, the Reich Center for Foreign Exchange Control (Reichsstelle für Devisenbewirtschaftung), was charged with keeping the nation's export gains higher than its import expenditures; smaller Foreign Exchange Offices (Devisenstellen) monitored intake and output of foreign currency in each region and reported results to this centralized agency. These controls largely kept Germany from hemorrhaging foreign capital, apart from hefty interest payments on its international debts. But they also had palpable consequences for Germans working or studying abroad, and for the businesses, small and large, that bolstered its economy. Import businesses were restricted by year's end to 75 percent of their previous allocation of foreign currency, which threatened their ability to purchase the raw materials abroad—leather, silk, and paper, among others—on which their production relied. Ordinary Germans could no longer exchange Reichsmarks for foreign currency on the open market. The Reichsbank, in a desperate bid to get its hands on foreign currency, even required Germans to convert their own foreign currency holdings into Reichsmarks.[37]

It was this straitjacketed climate that had pushed Wegner into the arms of British, rather than German, investors; he could find no German partners to mount capital for a campaign against Tauchnitz. In fact, because of the German crisis, his plan to rival Tauchnitz had almost ended before it began. "The German crash has also crashed the Albatross scheme for the present," announced Curtis Brown's agency to prospective authors and publishers. Wegner's plan regained momentum only when Curtis Brown introduced him to Holroyd-Reece, who, in turn, put his powers of persuasion to work on Sir Edmund Davis, a Jewish copper magnate known for his philanthropic contributions to the arts. As a Jew, Davis may have appreciated the liberal-minded spirit of an enterprise that promised to disseminate modern Anglo-American books across a Europe rumbling with nationalism and narrow-mindedness. "Edmund Davies [*sic*] is behaving splendidly," wrote Holroyd-Reece, confirming his investment of £5,000.[38] Splendidly, indeed. Otto may have wanted to keep Albatross out of Germany, but the German government welcomed foreign investment with open arms: any money was good money, and foreign money was better than German. Albatross broke into Germany with the weight of British sterling behind it.

The invitation to join forces with Albatross must have suited Enoch on multiple levels, speaking to his desire to achieve something out of the ordinary. For Enoch, running a family business that was prey to the whims of the German crisis, the Albatross opportunity also came along at the right time. His businesses suffered in tandem with the economy, and his personal life was difficult, at best. His wife had contracted tuberculosis and sought treatment at a sanatorium in Switzerland, with their daughters boarding at a school nearby, while he stayed in Hamburg. His letters from the early 1930s show that he worried about earning enough money to support them all. Hamburg had been especially hard hit by Black Friday. The city had contracted hefty loans from American banks, and when these banks demanded repayment, many companies declared bankruptcy, international trade dropped, and unemployment rose to nearly 40 percent, leaving the city's welfare resources stretched beyond their limits. Enoch recognized that challenging Tauchnitz was "a daring undertaking." But a small investment would place him center stage in a multinational concern with good prospects. Enoch accepted Albatross's offer.[39]

And so on 12 November 1931, Wegner set a cornerstone of Albatross's international structure in place, signing the Albatross Verlag into the Hamburg Registry of Commerce and making Albatross a legitimate firm under German law. In Paris, Wegner and Holroyd-Reece selected authors, signed contracts, and edited the series; in Hamburg, Enoch oversaw marketing and distribution, and became "a participant in the overall management and policy decisions."[40] To economize on overhead, Enoch's office became Albatross's German home, existing alongside his family businesses. This arrangement gave Albatross ties to a German publisher who could work the German market from the inside; in turn, it gave Enoch security against the fluctuations of the German economy, since his income would largely be generated by the two-thirds of Albatross sales predicted in markets abroad.

Albatross changed Enoch's path. It enabled him to travel to London and Paris, throwing himself into the time-consuming work of building a distribution network for Albatross stretching across the continent. Back in Hamburg, at the end of each day he could hop the train home, his roughly forty-five-minute commute whisking him away from the bustle of downtown, past the workers' quarters in Altona, the elegant Jugendstil villas of Ottensen, and suburban single-family homes to his idyllic, woodsy hillside perch in Blankenese. From the large windows of this retreat, he could look out over the Elbe River and the meandering traffic of sailboats and cargo ships below. From that line of sight, the future must have looked bright, at least for a time.

But Kurt Enoch was Jewish. And even as he sealed his contract with Albatross, the debilitating state of the German economy was tangibly altering the political climate. Following the National Socialist Party's triumph in 1930, party membership rose dramatically across Germany—so much so that the Nazi bureaucrats issuing membership cards could not keep up with demand. Even in Hamburg, which traditionally tilted left, the Nazis gained ground with each election. The party secured 26.2 percent of the vote in September 1931, and in 1932 won fifty-two seats in the state parliament.[41] Albatross had found its footing in Germany, prepared to overtake its German rival. Yet the ground it stood upon was already shifting, changing the terms of the bargain Albatross had struck.

T W O

Spies for England

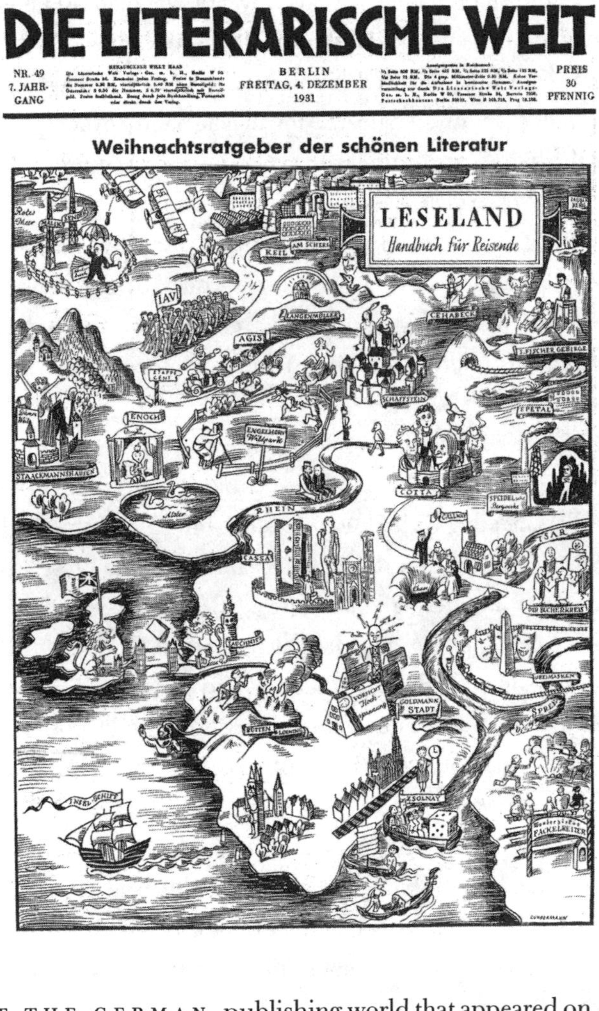

DIE LITERARISCHE WELT

NR. 49
7. JAHRGANG

BERLIN
FREITAG, 4. DEZEMBER
1931

PREIS
30
PFENNIG

Weihnachtsratgeber der schönen Literatur

A M A P O F T H E G E R M A N publishing world that appeared on 4 December 1931—one day after Albatross's first advertisement in the *Börsenblatt*—showed no sign that the publishing industry was suffering any economic woes at all. To boost book sales in the critical weeks before the Christmas season, *Die literarische Welt,* a progressive journal that kept German readers up to speed in world literature, had concocted a special issue inviting fifty German publishers to offer gift recommendations to readers. Albatross received mention in the inner pages, but failed to make the cover, which featured the most prominent publishers.[1] The Samuel Fischer Verlag, publisher of Thomas Mann, inhabited its own mountain range in the top right corner, which peaked in a "magic mountain" humorously riffing off of Mann's famous novel of that name. The Insel Verlag—where Wegner had once worked under his uncle Anton Kippenberg—had published Rainer Maria Rilke and Stefan Zweig, among others. On the map, it sailed its ships through placid waters in the lower left-hand corner, perhaps seeking repose after the hard work of translating D. H. Lawrence, Aldous Huxley, and Virginia Woolf into German. Even the Tauchnitz lions, facing one another mid-page and guarding the gates of this distinguished publisher, amused themselves, lobbing a book back and forth over London's Tower Bridge. Only the Communist-inclined Malik Verlag, in the upper left corner, reflected a dark sign of the times: a man raising a tiny umbrella in futile protest against bombardments launched from airplanes etched with swastikas.

The Gebrüder Enoch Verlag also made an appearance, tucked away behind Alster lake in the center of Hamburg; Albatross, in contrast, was not yet on the map. And his meeting with Holroyd-Reece on 9 December had fired Otto's resolve to keep it this way. But the map also inadvertently illustrated a problem that Otto had been pondering and Holroyd-Reece's visit had crystallized for him: Tauchnitz occupied an imaginary England in Germany. "The shortest, cheapest crossing over the English Channel and the [Atlantic] Ocean is still to be found with the tried-and-true shipmasters Bernhard Tauchnitz," proclaimed Tauchnitz's entry inside the special pre-Christmas edition of *Die literarische Welt.* Yet this benefit suddenly carried with it a potentially insurmountable liability: Tauchnitz had no physical presence in London, no office, let alone a British agent who could keep his nose to the ground. Otto saw too clearly that Albatross filled the vacancy Tauchnitz had left open. To tend the continental market from Leipzig had made sense earlier, but times had changed. Albatross, he worried, "can make a mere cat's leap from Paris and work at the source against us, without us noticing anything at all or first noticing when it's too late."[2]

Otto still hoped to find a British partner—a Holroyd-Reece of Tauchnitz's own—who could restore Tauchnitz's blighted finances and protect it from such surprise attacks. Yet he also knew that the continental English editions market was struggling. Following the American stock market crash, more Americans were returning home each year as their inheritances or savings dried up. "The continued fall of the dollar is creating a more and more confused atmosphere, and France is rapidly emptying itself of Americans," wrote the Parisian agent William Bradley to his author Sinclair Lewis. The British, caught up in the ripple effects of the American crash, flocked back across the Channel, too. For Tauchnitz, this drought of tourists was devastating, especially with Albatross looming. From Austria and Italy in the weeks before Christmas, booksellers echoed the same refrain: "There are absolutely no sales of English books, since the English and Americans are completely missing!"[3]

Otto could see only one way to proceed: to play up Tauchnitz's German loyalties in hopes of keeping its German readers from defecting to Albatross. What he could not yet fathom was the power of the model his adversaries were adopting in Paris, one in which thinking along strict national lines no longer mattered. Otto's response to the Albatross threat showed him to be many things: a clear-sighted strategizer, a vindictive detective, a leader by turns condescending and supportive. Not least among these personas was the deeply emotional man, agitated to his core by the fear that Tauchnitz could face, under his leadership, its end. In this sense, Otto was not unlike many Germans in the 1930s, anxious at the threat of impending financial ruin and grasping at solutions.

*

Otto logically felt that Tauchnitz had been outwitted by a foreign power and plotted his defense along nationalist lines. He aligned Tauchnitz with the German economy and urged his colleagues to realize that "at least for the moment, the English have a strong national orientation economically, and for this reason, will easily give the new British enterprise the advantage over the German enterprise, regardless of the great qualities we may have." He could not know that the British publishing establishment would have no greater love for Albatross, when it learned of the new series months later, than for Tauchnitz. Seeing, instead, "how easily the authors had veered" to Albatross, he concluded that "we must oppose [Albatross] with strong *decisive* work."[4]

Albatross's *Börsenblatt* advertisement of 3 December gave Otto his first opportunity. He lodged a complaint with the Leipzig District Court that Albatross had falsely represented itself as "a German publishing company." On 10 December, one day after Holroyd-Reece's visit, Otto won his injunction. In a full page in the *Börsenblatt,* Tauchnitz advertised its claim: Albatross was not German at all, "since its capital and its shareholders are foreign, its managing director and chairman of the board—the latter an English citizen—live in Paris, where they maintain their own little specialty shop, whereas the operations and distribution in Germany are run through a third-party publishing house, the Oscar Enoch Verlag in Hamburg." The court forbade Albatross to describe itself as German. For each violation, its owners faced a fine of "unrestricted magnitude" or up to six months in prison.[5]

Albatross capitulated, and just after Christmas 1931 solicitously ceded to Tauchnitz's demand to print a retraction. "We regret that the framing of our advertisement conveyed a meaning that did not match our intention," read its apology. "A veiling of the facts or a consequent heightened competition lay entirely far from our intentions." To prevent future "misunderstandings," Albatross laid bare its national makeup, acknowledging that its capital was in "British hands"—but still underscoring that it was officially registered in Germany and that "German capital also played a role in the enterprise."[6] Otto welcomed the apology. Tauchnitz had forced Albatross into the book trade equivalent of retreating on bended knee, embarrassing the firm at the moment it sought to present itself in a positive light.

At one level, Otto's tactic was no different from that invoked by the British book trade when it urged readers to "Buy British." Yet at another, the underlying logic of his campaign against Albatross was, intentionally or not, drawn from the threads of conservative nationalist assumptions that had been woven into the fabric of the German political scene since the end of the First World War. The Weimar era had brought with it changes that many resented. The generation defeated in the war felt bitter about the price Germany was forced to pay at the hands of foreign powers. Many conservative Germans, seeking to justify their nation's losses, succumbed to the "stab in the back" myth: the idea that Jews, like a fifth column, had undermined Germany's victory from the inside. Many also sensed that the modern world, with the heightened exchange of liberal ideas from abroad, had destabilized daily life; they sought a return to *völkisch* values, rooted historically in German tradition, as a means of reinvesting their world with order. While the National Socialist Party had come to dominate the German right by 1931, the political field was rife in the 1920s with what one scholar has called "a complex amalgam of political parties, economic-interest organizations, patriotic associations, paramilitary combat leagues, and young conservative salons."[7]

Otto's campaign against Albatross, as he grasped at ad hoc solutions, seemed less informed by any one group than by the undercurrent of malaise and blame that sustained them all. The economic catastrophe of 1931 had only exacerbated the convictions of the German right that Germany had grown weak in its dependence on foreign money, and that the solution was for Germans to reunite in a *Volksgemeinschaft*—a people's community—purified of foreign influence. If national renewal was dependent on a return to the Volk, then, too, anti-Semitism became a kind of cultural code for expressing generalized dissatisfaction with forces beyond German control. For the Pan-German League, which sought to expand German empire and suppress foreign influence, for instance, "'The Jew'—the homeless and rootless international and cosmopolitan Ahasver—embodied all of that which in the modern age was subverting inherited traditions and values."[8]

Tauchnitz had, like Albatross, begun as a firm with cosmopolitan impulses, yet Otto increasingly defended it in the way the German right defended the Volksgemeinschaft, reducing complex issues to the simplest explanation at hand: Albatross was a Jewish, foreign firm poised to stab Tauchnitz in the back. Otto decided that presenting Albatross as anti-German was Tauchnitz's best hope of survival. Early in 1932, when Albatross advertisements began appearing more frequently, Tauchnitz launched a campaign to convince German readers to align themselves with German tradition. "Those who read English buy Tauchnitz!" ran its slogan in gothic, curlicued German script. Otto hit the theme of national betrayal especially hard with the German book trade. He spread word that under all its bright, shiny marketing, Albatross was built on Wegner's betrayal of Tauchnitz, and thus rotten to its core. Early response boded well. "Everyone is pleased with Tauchnitz," one colleague reported. "In Frankfurt and Munich people find it pathetic that Wegner is acting as a trade spy for the British."[9]

Perhaps encouraged by such response, Otto tried to further undermine Wegner's credibility. In late December, he luxuriously summarized for the head of the German Publishers Union Wegner's misdeeds and requested that his membership be revoked. "Mr. Wegner," he wrote, is "with all consciousness and all intention making use of his Germanness, and his belonging to the German Publishers Union, to create inroads into Germany for a foreign firm that he spurred on and is managing to the disadvantage of a German publishing firm."

Albatross used its German address at Enoch's firm, he claimed, simply "to block out or veil the foreign character of the company to gain easier entry into the German market" In fact, said Otto, "The whole business and spiritual achievement of the firm (the direction and editorial functions) lie in Paris." Holroyd-Reece had admitted that Albatross was British. The books were printed in Milan, with the publisher Arnoldo Mondadori, who doubled as president of the Albatross board. It was clear, Otto concluded, that "the financial plunder of the firm does not even come to German advantage, but instead travels through the tax Eldorado of Luxembourg out to foreigners." He ultimately had to drop the matter. Tauchnitz could sue Wegner for unethical behavior, ruled the union. But Otto should be sure Tauchnitz was not merely trying to damage its nascent competition.[10]

With this accusation lingering in his ears, Otto turned his attention to Holroyd-Reece. He found his start in a rumor a Tauchnitz shareholder had overheard that Holroyd-Reece was not British but had been born under the name Riess to an English mother in Dresden. Hiring a lawyer in Munich, he dug into Holroyd-Reece's past. "That the man is a Jew appears to me, given his personal circle, seemingly clear," he wrote. When he learned that Holroyd-Reece's late father had declared himself a Protestant, Otto pronounced the name Riess "decidedly Jewish," and pushed for verification. "This British man already looks different, when one only knows him in the future as Johann Hermann Riess, son of the private tutor Dr. Max Magnus Riess."[11]

In England, as in Germany, Otto set out to prove that Holroyd-Reece was not what he seemed. When the British Home Office confirmed that Holroyd-Reece was indeed a citizen, Otto plotted how even this news might undermine Albatross. "No one from the German book trade circles speaks or will speak for Herr Johann Hermann Riess," assumed Otto, "since he has given up his German citizenship in this manner and is now scrounging for business in Germany." Conversely, he concluded that "the noble British authors would not enthusiastically take in their arms such a German as the British citizen he pretends to be." Otto suggested that Holroyd-Reece's fluctuating national loyalties were only one sign of his deviation from social norms. The lawyer had also discovered that Holroyd-Reece, just thirty-five, was married to a fifty-three-year-old widow, with whom he had lived lavishly in a large house with a butler, cook, and chauffeur.[12]

Otto grasped at such details. In March 1932, as Albatross began selling its books, he castigated himself for "not taking enough advantage of this dirty 'Reece.'" To a Dr. Silex, a potential British connection for Tauchnitz, he presented Holroyd-Reece as "undoubtedly a very clever, talented and world-oriented man," but one over whom "hovers a certain darkness" and "cosmopolitan superficiality." Soon he propagated a more sinister theory—that if Wegner had acted as a trade spy, Holroyd-Reece had perhaps been an *actual* spy for England in the Great War. Otto's German lawyer in London passed on a report from his trusted diplomatic source: "R. entered the Cavalry Cadet Corps in 1916. After further education, he was sent to Egypt. . . . In 1917 he was sent back to England, as an officer in the Intelligence Service, that is to say, in the Information and Secret Service. His naturalization followed on 4 February 1919."[13]

The deeper Otto dug, the more enigmatic Holroyd-Reece seemed. And in fact, many of his suspicions about his adversary's origins were correct: in 1897 Holroyd-Reece had been born Johann Hermann Riess, to a British mother and German father in the utopian artistic community of Hellerau, near Dresden. His father died in 1908, when Holroyd-Reece was eleven; two years later, his mother sent him to England for a "proper" education, and there he had remained. In 1919 he became a British citizen, married an Englishwoman, and anglicized his name. But in France, as Otto determined, Holroyd-Reece had once operated under the name Recci.[14] And German authorities later called him Riess, his birth name, but also Reiss, Rease, Riese, Riis, Reeze, or even Rieze. This slippage between names was strangely befitting his personality. He was hard to pin down, and even the shortest descriptions identify this quality in him.

The story of how this German youth transformed himself into John Holroyd-Reece, British publisher, is little known. One researcher described him as "undoubtedly one of the most colorful personalities among 20th century publishers," while the literary agent Graham Watson framed him as the protagonist of a nearly untellable tale, noting, "I doubt whether a tenth of the mystery of an undoubtedly mysterious man has yet been revealed." Pieces of this mystery are, fortunately, stored in two files at the British National Archives. When Holroyd-Reece's mother sent him to England at thirteen, she found him an eccentric guardian, the director of the London School of Dalcroze Eurhythmics, and a traditional boarding school, Repton. By the time Holroyd-Reece tried to enter King's College, Cambridge, the Great War was under way, and he found himself neither German enough to be an enemy nor British enough to make it through the university's doors; his file claims he was turned away "owing to difficulties on account of his nationality."[15]

This was not the last time that his straddling of cultures cost Holroyd-Reece a kind of belonging. Perhaps to avoid such consequences, he threw himself into the task of becoming British. "With regard to naturalization I cannot conceive of anyone who could have a better claim to it, if to be thoroughly English in tastes, ideas and sympathies forms the ground on which such claim is based," wrote his housemaster at Repton. The headmaster concurred: "His sympathies and his 'Spiritual home' are in England." With war everyone's priority, however, his application got stalled. By 1919, he was twenty-two years old and over the age where he could gain citizenship because his mother was British-born. His guardian intervened. "His habits of thought and action are essentially English and I am convinced that it is not only just to him, but also in the public interest, that he be granted the status of a British subject."[16]

Indeed, Holroyd-Reece had become so much an Englishman in his manner and accent that he fought for the British in World War I while still a German national. Otto was right on this score, too. Records state that Holroyd-Reece joined the British Army on 12 December 1916, served until January 1918, and was posted to the Dorset Yeomanry until February 1919. "This youth's career is among the most remarkable that the war has produced," exclaimed one official, noting, "He started as a Repton schoolboy, . . . [was] then interned for staying out late at night & finally served as a British Cavalry officer, being an enemy alien all the time." Even his military superiors did not know his origins. "My legal position is entirely unknown to everyone in my regiment," Holroyd-Reece explained to one official when he sought citizenship in 1919, "and . . . you would be doing me a great kindness by asking my Colonel for the required certificate without referring to the purpose for which it is required."[17]

Holroyd-Reece also carefully handled another fact Otto had ascertained: his father was Jewish. He resembled his fair-skinned, round-faced mother more than his wiry, dark-bearded father. As a young teenager, he looked every bit the plump British schoolboy in his corduroy jacket, long shorts, and tweed cap, sitting cross-legged reading his book in a field. He grew into a rather rotund Englishman, who reveled in hearty food and a good smoke.[18] By appearance and name, then, he could downplay his Jewish ties to avoid scrutiny in the anti-Semitic, upper-crust circles of London. Or he could reveal them, as perhaps he did to Sir Edmund Davis, who became Albatross's primary investor and a friend to Holroyd-Reece, as well.

A German-born man who lived in France and cultivated business ties in Italy, Holroyd-Reece developed a chameleon-like ability to change his identity to protect and advance his aims. On his visit to Leipzig in December 1931, he could easily have stressed his German roots. Instead he had so convincingly presented himself as an Englishman born and bred that it took Otto weeks to realize that his rival held a knowledge of German language and culture as intimate as his own.

By April 1932, realizing he had been played, Otto had deployed every tactic in his arsenal—some logically sound and others merely catty or racist—against the wily Holroyd-Reece. In his defense, it must be said that his concerns were more economic than political, and that his anxiety fueled his attacks. With Tauchnitz finances in such bad shape that board members had to forgo their monthly income, Otto capped his campaign by requesting information from the German Embassy in Paris to protect Tauchnitz, "a pure German firm," from Albatross's advance. Holroyd-Reece was probably a spy, he informed embassy officials, "since I find it highly unlikely that [the British] in the war regularly used Germans on the front, especially those who had mastered perfectly both English and German." Otto also warned that Holroyd-Reece operated under "the most varied names" and probably still held German identity papers. Donning one mask after another, presenting himself as a "full-blooded Englander" when he had German roots, Holroyd-Reece was, like the firm he had helped create, just the kind of foreign, slippery threat Germany could ill afford.[19]

Putting these pieces together, Otto framed Wegner and Holroyd-Reece as partners in deceit. Wegner had betrayed his nation, while Holroyd-Reece belonged fully to *no* nation. Yet Otto's tactic of slandering his rivals had limited success. Some big names in the German book trade did take pro-Tauchnitz measures. Koehler and Voelckmar, one of Germany's largest distributors, even handed over to Otto its correspondence with Albatross, rejecting an Albatross contract until the two firms had resolved their differences.[20] Yet in the end, as the Publishers Union had warned, there was no law against rivals entering the field. Still, Otto's attacks, made on the cusp of Hitler's seizing power, resonate awkwardly back into Germany's history and the anti-Semitism that had wormed its way through German society in the late nineteenth century, and forward to the coming era when the Nazis would insist that Germany be purified of foreign influences so German culture could reach its true and glorious pinnacle.

*

Otto's inability to stop Albatross was indicative not only of his limited vision but, in a sense, of his limited horizons. What he presented as Albatross's failure in Germany—its lack of loyalty to one nation—Wegner and Holroyd-Reece saw as the germ of Albatross's success. They waged their pan-European publishing war from a most unlikely seat of battle: a charming two-story house at 37 rue Boulard in the fourteenth arrondissement—a hotbed of literary activity near the Latin Quarter and the Sorbonne. Rue Boulard cut down the triangular wedge of Albatross's neighborhood, abutting the Montparnasse Cemetery on one side, and bisecting a busy market street rimmed with cafés and shops. The picturesque house, preserved only in a photograph, seems an oddly domestic locale for the cutting-edge conglomerate that Albatross aspired to be. But there Holroyd-Reece and Wegner plugged away at creating their ideal library, leaving Otto to strategize against them in Leipzig as he might.

Paris offered special advantages for any publisher. When the British publisher Jonathan Cape landed in court over the lesbian overtones in Radclyffe Hall's novel *The Well of Loneliness,* for instance, it was to Holroyd-Reece in Paris that he shipped the book plates in September 1928. Within weeks, Holroyd-Reece had printed an edition and tried to sneak it past British customs. Writing to Richard Aldington to secure his novel *Death of a Hero* for Albatross, Holroyd-Reece did not care a whit that it had been banned. "I naturally do not want to use the expurgated edition," he wrote, "and being a continental publisher I should like to take advantage of the fact that I am not restricted by English prudery."[21]

It was this sentiment that had made Paris flush with publishers and writers—writers Albatross hoped to pluck for its series. Expatriate authors from Edith Wharton to Ernest Hemingway to Ford Madox Ford had chosen Paris as their home away from home. Numerous exile presses had set up shop along its winding streets: Sylvia Beach's Shakespeare and Company, Robert McAlmon's Contact Editions, Harry and Caresse Crosby's Black Sun Press, Laura Riding and Robert Graves's Seizin Press, Edward Titus's Black Maniken Press, Gertrude Stein and Alice B. Toklas's Plain Edition Press, Jack Kahane's Obelisk Press. Their proliferation signaled that Anglo-American literature could be at home in Paris.[22] Holroyd-Reece followed suit, housing Albatross at his Pegasus office, hanging up one more shingle, as it were, for Anglo-American books in the backstreets of Paris.

Yet there was at least one difference between Albatross and these publishers: Albatross wanted to make money, and a lot of it. Albatross planned to produce 48 titles per year, with a hoped-for sale of 11,000 copies per title over a three-year run, with sales after the third year "anticipated to exceed 528,000 copies." In a Europe plagued by economic crisis, this proposal was resplendently ambitious. Italian booksellers gave Albatross little chance of success, "since people would not want to burden themselves with unknown things, especially since Tauchnitz is known in the entire world."[23] And to be sure, with Tauchnitz mired in debt, what business did the arriviste Albatross have flying headlong into the same furious economic gale?

The answer, from the Albatross perspective, lay in its cosmopolitan approach. From Paris, Holroyd-Reece and Wegner detected what Tauchnitz, lodged in Leipzig, had not: the continental market for Anglo-American books was ripe for change. No amount of cajoling would lure British and American travelers and expatriates with depleted bank accounts back to the continent. It was high time to turn elsewhere, and that elsewhere was everywhere to be found. Ever since the First World War, with the influx of British and American soldiers, Anglo-American culture had been seeping into continental Europe—through jazz, film, Coca-Cola, detective fiction, and other literature in translation—and with these, a growing curiosity about the English language itself. If Tauchnitz had envisioned Anglo-American travelers on Grand Tour as its clientele, Albatross reached out to foreign readers who sat fireside, reading English against the backdrop of whatever language was intoned from the radio.[24] Out of the least auspicious of times, sandwiched between economic depression and the Nazi takeover of Europe, Albatross wagered everything on a most auspicious idea: that English was the current to carry continental readers aloft into the future. Albatross was British, certainly, but it wanted to be German, French, and Italian, too.

One key to Albatross's gamble lay inside its covers: a chart in English, German, French, and Italian explaining the color system for identifying the genres of Albatross books, as well as summaries in the first three languages. As Enoch remarked, the publishers "expected that the multi-national character of the new enterprise would favor the acceptance of our books abroad," and "help in sales and selection by booksellers and readers who were not too familiar with the English language." Holroyd-Reece further outlined Albatross's international strategy to *Publishers Weekly* in April 1932. "The market for English books on the continent . . . is by no means restricted to the English-speaking tourists," he explained. "It includes intelligent readers of France, Germany, and other countries. After four years of collecting facts on distribution in various countries, I came to the conclusion that most English and American publishers have acted as if that market did not exist."[25]

Continental curiosity about Anglo-American culture was growing, Holroyd-Reece intimated. And it was true. A British Publishers Association survey of continental bookstores in 1931 revealed "an almost unanimous opinion that the sales both of English fiction and of Tauchnitz editions was increasing on the Continent." And the 1920s and 1930s spawned a wealth of surveys, essay collections, and monographs about Anglo-American literature, especially in Germany and France, Tauchnitz's largest markets. The French minister Abel Chevalley described his own tome, *The Modern English Novel* (1927), as a "travel guide" through contemporary literature. Some such volumes circulated only in the ivory towers. Yet even academics—such as Bernhard Fehr, whose *The English Literature of the Nineteenth and Twentieth Century* (1923) set a high bar—often published surveys written more cogently for students or the literarily curious. In France, for instance, René Lalou's *Panorama of Contemporary English Literature* and Paul Dottin's *English Literature* paved the way for French readers' understanding of Anglo-American culture; in Germany, Karl Arns's *Youngest England* and Ernst Vowinckel's *The English Novel of the Most Recent and Present Time* filled the same need. For obvious reasons, Tauchnitz also encouraged German readers to read Anglo-American books, and compiled a guide—in German—to lead them through the vast reaches of Tauchnitz terrain.[26]

Increasingly, European reviewers also featured Anglo-American books in the literary sections of metropolitan newspapers, so that authors "of the moment" in New York or London found themselves much discussed in Paris or Berlin. In Germany, periodicals such as *Die Literatur* and *Die literarische Welt*—the latter with print runs of twenty thousand in 1930—catered to readers curious about foreign literature. Others, like *Der Querschnitt, Der Bücherwurm,* and *Die neue Rundschau,* regularly included articles and cartoons about Anglo-American authors. In his research, the scholar Anselm Schlösser noted that more than 25 German journals and newspapers regularly discussed Anglo-American literature between 1895 and 1934, with up to 128 periodically including articles on the subject. German translations of Anglo-American works nearly doubled between 1920 and 1930. Initially, Anglo-American literature had mostly been popularized via translation, yet he also credited English editions: "The volumes of the Tauchnitz Edition inhabit a middle ground that has surely in many cases significantly furthered the renown [of Anglo-American literature] in Germany."[27]

Anecdotes from the French market reveal similar enthusiasm. In the 1920s, numerous firms translated contemporary English and American books; Plon, Albin Michel, Fayard, Hachette, and the Librarie Stock, for instance, all inaugurated series including English and American authors. Sylvia Beach's legendary bookshop Shakespeare and Company became a Parisian hub for books in English. Approximately half of Beach's customers were French. In her memoir, Beach conjured up André Gide, who "always carried some English book or other in his pocket," and a group of French intellectuals who "were pinning their hopes on *Ulysses* to enlarge [their English vocabulary]." (Her notebooks document the moment when Albatross broke into Tauchnitz's market, as lists of "A"s collide with "T"s down the right side of each page.) The American Library in Paris, created to funnel English-language books to British and American soldiers in World War I, remained a growing force for titles in English.[28]

To *Publishers Weekly*, Holroyd-Reece explained the beauty of Albatross's pan-European plan. British publishers had ceded the continent to Tauchnitz, he contended, because it was cost-prohibitive to distribute books from England: "In the past there has not been what we should call a proper contact between the publishing interests of Leipzig, New York and London." With this implied dig at the British publishing establishment and Tauchnitz alike, he noted that Albatross had struck out in a new direction, exploiting "a centralized and mobile organization" that married "thorough continental knowledge, and English capital and connections." To maximize its efficiency, Albatross organized its operations around a host of centers rather than one: Paris, which allowed for quick contact with authors, as the editorial center, with Verona and Hamburg offering advantages for production and distribution.[29]

Holroyd-Reece had also carefully selected Albatross's partners to increase sales in distinct markets. Hachette, holding a near monopoly over distribution in France, handled Albatross books, as did Messaggerie Italiane in Bologna. The more successful Albatross proved, the more profits would be passed to these partners, who held a vested interest in creating a climate favorable to Anglo-American books. Holroyd-Reece did not so much grant a contract as compel an obligation from his partners; for the privilege of winning the Albatross contract, for instance, Messaggerie Italiane was obligated to sell at least six hundred copies of each title. Holroyd-Reece had promised in his business proposal to exploit the untapped bounty of Italy, a market which already produced a higher proportion of foreign literature in translation than either France or Germany.[30] If language summaries were one means of boosting Albatross's success, these tactics were another.

Holroyd-Reece and Wegner also wasted no time in seizing on that most modern asset of the book trade—the literary agent—to help them fulfill their international ambitions. "[Ralph] Pinker has been frightfully good to the Albatross," said Holroyd-Reece, Pinker's agency having handed him Katherine Mansfield and Aldous Huxley, among others. Curtis Brown's agents urged authors to sever ties with Tauchnitz and sign with Albatross. "The new company's agreements are such as to give indications already of excellent Continental sales," Brown's office explained to the author Joseph Hergesheimer in June 1931, "and I think they will increase considerably the number of distinguished English and American authors sold this way on the Continent."[31] Word of mouth spread that Albatross was boldly staking out its claim.

This brave new publishing world required vision, money, experience—and a degree of mettle with which Holroyd-Reece and Wegner were more than well-equipped. They made a formidable team despite, or perhaps because of, their status as outsiders. As Tauchnitz fought to keep its hold on the continental market, and British publishers strategized ways to break into it, Albatross flew straight between national interests. Not beholden to tradition or a single national arena, Albatross's cofounders were free, not just to invade the continental market for English books, but to re-envision how it might work.

*

Looking back, we might argue that Albatross gathered up all the liberal notes that fell by the wayside when Germany was overtaken by nationalistic strains. In one sense, this was not surprising. Wittingly or unwittingly, the Albatross series blended beautifully into emerging British propaganda agendas. And whether or not Holroyd-Reece had worked as a British intelligence officer during the Great War, as Otto's diplomatic source claimed, his activities for Albatross put him at least two steps ahead of the British government in promoting British culture abroad. In 1931, this was not difficult. The British were miserably behind in the game of self-promotion. Before the First World War, when the sun never set on the British Empire, there seemed little reason to engage in propaganda. Yet while Britain rested on its laurels, its European counterparts had launched propaganda initiatives: for the Germans, the Verein für das Deutschtum im Ausland in the 1880s; for the French, the Alliance Française since 1883; and for the Italians, the Dante Alighieri society, founded in 1889. In contrast, the British Council, the first true equivalent for promoting British culture and the English language abroad, was not established until December 1934.[32]

British distaste for the idea of propaganda, seen as a dirty, tacky business suitable to more desperate nations, finally gave way during World War I, when the Foreign Office offered compelling evidence that German propaganda was badly eroding the British image abroad. During the war, the British created a bevy of offices to handle propaganda: a Press Bureau, to censor news items; the Foreign Office News Department, to liaise with foreign journalists and spread British news abroad; and the War Propaganda Bureau, to create pro-British illustrated periodicals and pamphlets for dissemination abroad. But these efforts ended with the war. The Ministry of Information was liquidated on the last day of 1918, and its most important areas of oversight transferred to the News Department of the Foreign Office. During the 1920s, officials categorized propaganda in three arenas—political, commercial, and cultural—disagreeing over which should be prioritized. In April 1919, Foreign Office officials pushed to privilege cultural propaganda; yet the Treasury disagreed so strongly—arguing that such propaganda did not yield measurable results—that it put an embargo on funding cultural propaganda that remained in place through the 1920s. As a result, by 1930 Britain had many organizations for commercial propaganda yet few devoted to promoting British culture and the English language per se. As Clifford Norton, a Foreign Office affiliate who became the wartime British ambassador to Switzerland, once quipped, "We may tell foreigners about our aeroplanes and our coal strikes, but not about our poets and painters. We may, in fact export bacon but not Bacon." In 1930, the Foreign Office got wise. It had immense ground to make up. By 1934, the French and German governments were estimated to be spending over a million pounds annually on cultural propaganda, with the Italians allocating 0.3 percent of their budget toward it. The British Council, in contrast, had only five thousand pounds in its inaugural month in January 1935 to start "projecting" England before other governments did the job for them.[33]

So when Holroyd-Reece spent the last months of 1931 trying to out-Tauchnitz Tauchnitz, he inadvertently advanced the work of the British Council —before it even existed. It is striking, in fact, how closely his philosophy for Albatross anticipated British propaganda policy. In 1934, when Sir Reginald Leeper—the future intelligence chief—laid the groundwork for the council, he insisted that the Foreign Office determine policy but that propaganda itself "should so far as possible be conducted through private organisations, which should be encouraged to stand on their own feet." He also took a quality over quantity approach reminiscent of Holroyd-Reece's own, establishing as a guideline that "propaganda defeats its own end unless you propagate what is really worth propagating." And among the goals the British Council articulated in 1935 were some couched in the same language that Holroyd-Reece used to promote Albatross: "To make the life and thought of the British peoples more widely known abroad," "to promote a mutual interchange of knowledge and ideas with other peoples," and "to encourage the study and use of the English language."[34] In this way, Albatross was born of its cultural moment: a privately funded, commercial publisher that, consciously or not, held the promise of fulfilling British propaganda aims.

In the summer of 1931, however, British propaganda officials and Holroyd-Reece also had at least one other thing in common: they were both broke. The British Treasury had approved a modest budget of £2,500 for cultural propaganda in 1930, only to rescind it in a budget crisis in August 1931. That same month, Wegner had joined with Holroyd-Reece hoping to find funding through his connections abroad; within a matter of weeks, Arnoldo Mondadori offered, and then suddenly withdrew, his backing for several Holroyd-Reece ventures: Pegasus, Pantheon, and Albatross. "Taking all the cash at the various bank accounts together . . . we have not got one thousand francs," Holroyd-Reece admitted in late September to his friend, the printer Hans Mardersteig. "In order to live until today—the business and ourselves—I have had to make private debts. . . . I have no money to pay the salaries at the end of the month unless A.M. [Arnoldo Mondadori] who said that he would advance Lit. 50.000 will send telegraphically the 20.000 lit. I have asked for." Even with the funding from Sir Edmund Davis, which he confirmed in the same letter, Holroyd-Reece sketched a bleak picture. "Now if A.M. leaves us in the lurch . . . it will also be impossible for me to go on with the Albatross for which everything is going so splendidly (the contracts of most of the best authors are already signed now)." Holroyd-Reece laid out only one solution: that Mondadori would have "to run a certain risk—or lose heavily himself at once and smash me."[35]

Fortunately, Holroyd-Reece was a talented propagandist. There is in French a verb his daughter used to describe his way with people: *embobiner,* literally, "to spool a thread onto a bobbin." Holroyd-Reece spent much of his adult life reeling friends and investors in for this or that plan. Just as Otto had been taken in by his prowess, so, too, were many whom he left, baffled, in his wake, as he pursued his next great idea. If anything, Holroyd-Reece was nearly bankrupt in the fall of 1931 because he juggled too many schemes his finances and time constraints could not support. As his Albatross partners were soon to find out, Holroyd-Reece could not keep up with himself. Nor, really, could others keep up with him. He traveled so much that his stationery held two addresses: the rue Boulard in Paris and the Casa Beata in Rapallo. Suspended between the two was the phrase "Please reply to," from which he drew an arrow to the address of the week. Perpetually suspended between residences, he lived in the rhythm of infinite deferral and could, often rightly, claim he had been elsewhere. As the French printer Marius Audin fumed, Holroyd-Reece postponed payment "in hiding behind a curtain of smoke consisting of superficial correspondence, unforeseen voyages necessitated by his numerous affairs abroad, and *mea culpa* of the genre, 'I am a monster, it's true—but despite myself.'" "There is not the slightest justification for anybody at any time ever thinking that there is a shadow of intent to deceive, or to impose upon anybody," the printer Stanley Morison, one business associate, reflected. "I think that Reece's mind is so saturated with Romance that he often fails to realize that for the execution of his plans a prosperous world is a necessary condition."[36]

Considering the state of the international economy and his own fiscal near-demise, Holroyd-Reece's successes by November 1931 were many and enviable. While British officials sat like so many lame ducks, their funding for cultural propaganda eradicated, Holroyd-Reece convinced Mondadori to stay his course. In several months Holroyd-Reece had won from Sir Edmund Davis and Mondadori roughly ten thousand pounds to fund Albatross. Not until the 1936–37 budget would the British government put this level of resources at the disposal of the British Council.[37] Holroyd-Reece was thus not only financially five years ahead; politically he gave British interests a toehold in two nation states where British propaganda officials were clamoring to extend the reach of British culture. In fascist Italy, he ensured that Mondadori had a stake in Albatross's success by granting it a contract to print the first eighteen volumes. And in Germany, teeming with National Socialist sympathies, he nestled Albatross into Hamburg. Playing with Albatross's identity as he had played with his own, he won British interests a vantage on zones of political turmoil while minimizing obvious British presence.

In Albatross, in fact, Holroyd-Reece achieved one of his best disappearing acts ever. On paper the details are tedious, but the pay-off was spectacular. German officials were eager to encourage foreign investment and did not question too closely Albatross's relationship to its investors abroad. Start-up capital for the Albatross Verlag in Hamburg was a mere 21,000 RM, far too little for an enterprise with high-flying ambitions and estimated start-up costs of 383,000 RM. To cover this gap, on 15 November 1931, Holroyd-Reece's French firm, Pegasus, granted the Albatross Verlag a one-time loan of £10,000 at 8 percent interest. In exchange, the Albatross Verlag "hired" Holroyd-Reece's Pegasus for a substantial monthly fee to act as its "sole managing agents" to handle all contracts, royalties, and the editorial development of the series. Looking past the dry details and considering German financial instability, this scheme was a stroke of brilliance. On paper, it appeared that Albatross and Pegasus were two separate firms, with Wegner attached to one and Holroyd-Reece to the other.[38] This solution allowed Holroyd-Reece to reassure investors that their money would not simply disappear into the gurgling sinkhole of the German economy. All told, among the 6,000 RM monthly "fee" that Albatross would pay Pegasus for managing its affairs in Paris, monies for royalties, and interest payments on the loan, he guaranteed that sums approximating a German professor's annual salary would be transferred from Albatross in Germany to Pegasus in Paris each month.

Holroyd-Reece's scheme also cleverly masked the power structure behind Albatross. From the outside, it looked like a German firm. But anyone peeking inside its shell would have discovered another entity hiding inside: a publishing holding company, based in Luxembourg, whose financing came from England. This holding company owned the Albatross shares and was, in turn, financed by two other holding companies, financed by Sir Edmund Davis. Holroyd-Reece owned 400 of the 1,080 regular shares of this publishing holding company, as well as 200 of the preference shares, which gave him majority control over votes in the company; in addition, he was its director. As owner of Pegasus, he was Albatross's sole managing agent and the sole creditor for the loan to Albatross in sterling. Holroyd-Reece was everywhere and nowhere: everywhere in Albatross's power structure, nowhere in the German paperwork that left traces for the authorities to follow.[39]

It is somewhat disarming to overlay the image of Holroyd-Reece as aggressive businessman with the weathered photographs from the album that documents his earliest days at the utopian community at Hellerau, outside Dresden. In one picture, Holroyd-Reece is perhaps five or six, still young enough to wear the smock dress typical for boys of the day. He stands bending over a wooden schooner elaborate enough to feature two masts with a mainsail, topsail, and jib gracefully extended across its length. He holds his hand carefully on top of the mast to guide its movement. But there is one problem he seems not to see or care about: the boat has hardly anywhere to go. It floats in a basin barely twice its length. Such, in later years, was the liability that earned Holroyd-Reece the nickname "The Lord High Romantick": his visions of grandeur were too grand to sail as far and as wide as he wished in the real world.[40] With Germany on the cusp of the not yet predictable National Socialist takeover, only time would tell whether Albatross was the most foolish or most brilliant of schemes.

THREE

Winning the Continent

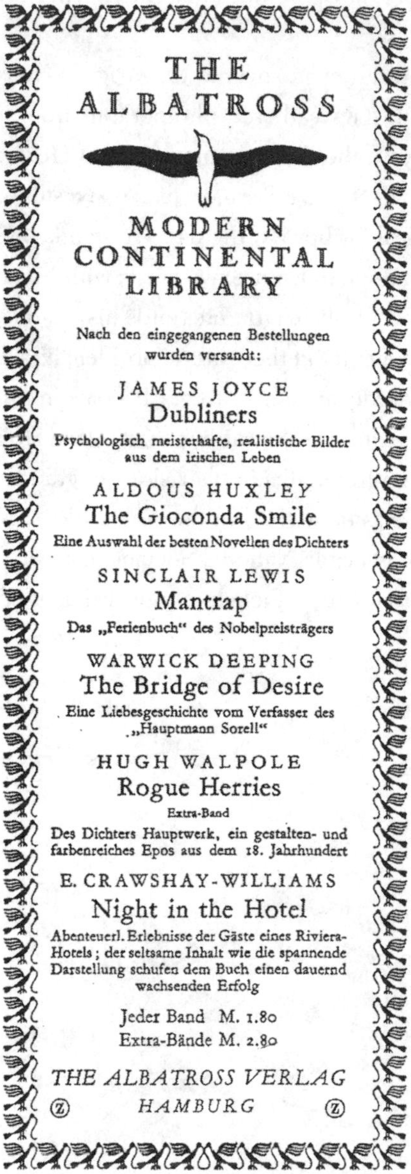

ON 15 FEBRUARY 1932, flying in the face of the economic turmoil raging in Europe, Albatross began with optimism. In a half-page advertisement in the *Börsenblatt,* the firm introduced the first six volumes of the Albatross Modern Continental Library to booksellers in the German-speaking world. The impressive array spanned a range of reading tastes: James Joyce's "psychologically masterful" *Dubliners;* the short stories of Aldous Huxley, well known for his satirical social commentary; lighter fiction from Sinclair Lewis, who had won the Nobel Prize for Literature in 1930; Warwick Deeping's *The Bridge of Desire,* whose heady romantic title reached out to female readers; a classic, historically rooted family saga from Hugh Walpole; and E. Crawshay-Williams's *Night in the Hotel,* which promised readers the "adventurous experiences of the guests of a hotel on the Riviera."[1]

Even this relatively short list meant that the exhausting work of the previous year had come to fruition: securing funding, testing printers, creating a look for the series, selecting the titles, and persuading authors, agents, and publishers to throw over Tauchnitz for Albatross. Early 1932 had been a hectic time for the Albatross team. They had launched production and distribution from Italy while staffing offices in Hamburg and Paris and averting further publicity smears about the firm's national allegiances. Wegner and Enoch had traveled between Hamburg and Paris, and Holroyd-Reece had crossed borders between England and France and Germany and Italy so many times that his partners could hardly keep track of him. Tauchnitz might have a name stretching back ninety years, but in less than one year Albatross had created a brand. Now the directors would see what their grand experiment would yield.

It was, all in all, an enormous risk. Politically, Tauchnitz already dominated Albatross's largest potential market, which was also being consumed by conservative nationalist interests. Commercially, too, Albatross's idea of a modern library was in one sense nothing new. Nineteenth-century French publishers had cultivated the model of the *bibliothèque idéale,* a collection of books curated by an editor whose education and taste were presumed to rub off on readers. In Germany, the "little yellow books" of the Reclam Verlag's Universal Bibliothek offered one precedent in paperback, while Tauchnitz offered another. British and American publishers generally preferred hardcover series, both to lend an aura of prestige to their ventures and to garner higher profits per volume. Albatross needed to wedge itself between these extremes, to edge out Tauchnitz and to protect itself from British publishers increasingly keen to maximize hardcover sales on the continent. Its challenge—its innovation, really—was to establish itself as a publishing house of distinction despite its inexpensive paperbacks and entrepreneurial aims.[2]

To win the continent—including the increasingly nationalistic German market—Albatross chose to be modern, whereas Tauchnitz had been genteel. As its business proposal stated, it strove to win "a better standard of book" and to "avoid the very dull appearance" of the Tauchnitz volumes. Wegner knew that although Tauchnitz had surpassed its five thousandth volume, it had not kept pace with contemporary literature. As Sylvia Beach recalled, "They didn't go much further than Kipling and Hardy in those days." In 1923, the German reviewer Max Meyerfeld noted, for instance, that D. H. Lawrence's books were rare commodities despite the author's growing word-of-mouth fame. "I had long endeavored in vain to get my hands on one of his books," he explained, grateful that a German friend finally loaned him a copy of *Sons and Lovers.* Tauchnitz had not yet published the novel, though it had come out eight years earlier. Similarly, James Joyce's *Portrait of the Artist as a Young Man* had remained buried in a Tauchnitz file from 1920 until someone brought it to Curt Otto's attention in 1928. Finally, under Wegner's management, it appeared as Tauchnitz Volume 4937. As late as July 1931, Richard Aldington's editor at Chatto and Windus dismissed Tauchnitz out of hand. "And what a bone-yard the Tauchnitz Library is!" he remarked, dissuading Aldington from selling his rights.[3]

In pursuing a modern agenda, in fact, Albatross was trespassing on the terrain of the British publishing establishment. For the surest way to get hot-off-the-press books in English in 1931 was to order expensive editions from England or the United States through specialized continental booksellers. Yet as Beach contended, this was not a realistic option for most native Europeans: "Our moderns, particularly when pounds and dollars were translated into francs, were luxuries the French and my Left Bankers were not able to afford." Albatross filled this gap, catering to literary explorers with modest means. While Albatross books in France cost double the 6-franc French series launched by top publishers including Éditions de France, Baudinière, Stock, and Albin Michel in 1931, they were, until Penguin editions appeared in 1935, the least expensive English books around. Beach's meticulous daily journal documented that they could be had for the price of a dozen oranges or a haircut. And in Germany, Albatross books—

sold for 1.80 RM—cost less than the average German book, and two to four times less than translations. The Insel Verlag, owned by Wegner's aunt and uncle, sold translations of Huxley, Woolf, and Lawrence in the early 1930s, for instance, for between 4 and 8 RM. Albatross played up this benefit in the pre-Christmas issue of *Die literarische Welt* in 1931. "Many of your friends surely enjoy reading English books," it acknowledged, striking a colloquial tone. "But you think about how expensive the original English editions are and how difficult it is to obtain them and pay in foreign currency. There, the Albatross Modern Continental Library can help you procure the most valuable books of modern English and American literature at inexpensive prices in exquisite form."[4]

And exquisitely packaged they were. If clothes made the man, as the Albatross leaders' eye toward their own dapper *habille* attested, Albatross's bright covers and jackets distinguished them from the average paperback. While at Tauchnitz, Wegner had introduced a key marketing advance: color-coded bands on each book to identify its genre. Designer Hans Mardersteig followed this lead, saturating each Albatross book in its own vibrant hue. Readers racing for a train, seeking a dip into murder and mayhem, could grab a red book for "a story of adventure or crime." Those craving stories "of travel and foreign peoples" reached for a green one, while lovers of short stories or humor might prefer the orange, and aficionados of biography or history would opt for purple. Blue covers for love stories and yellow for "a psychological novel or essays" rounded out the array. For foreign readers with varying competence in English the color system eased selection. Plus, as Holroyd-Reece told booksellers, "The various colors . . . combine most interestingly in a window display," helping the books market themselves; Mardersteig's elegant icon added to their appeal.[5]

Holroyd-Reece had long been particular about appearances, and he counted on Albatross's appearance to lure readers away from Tauchnitz. He loved the beautiful thing, especially the beautiful thing one could take in the hand and touch. His mother had served daily tea in ancient Chinese porcelain cups. As he grew older, he collected fine tapestries and intricate ceramics. He wore hand-tailored silk shirts and leather shoes sewn to size in Italy, and ordered enormous bound volumes containing sketches of the collections of other collectors: furniture, bibelots, books.[6] The exquisite books of the Pegasus Press bore this mark of tactile refinement: leather bindings smooth in the hand, thick ivory paper, printing worthy of the queen.

Holroyd-Reece held to this ideal of aesthetic pleasure when he turned to paperbacks—in contrast to much of the British publishing establishment, which looked down its nose at even the cheaper hardcover editions. Indeed, in his *Publishers Weekly* interview, he defined Albatross as a publisher that stood on the side of taste. "It is a cardinal mistake to try to exploit cheap quality in cheap books," he remarked. "The public does not want a low price; it wants quality at a low price. The public hates to spend money on books; but it loves to get, for its money, a better-looking book than it had expected." He lingered upon the minutiae of the Albatross Modern Continental Library with the delight a connoisseur might show at the acquisition of a rare etching. "We had to have it," he noted of the precise font, paper, and "five separate editorial readings," even if quality came at a cost. With nothing breeding success like success, Holroyd-Reece wove his words as the tapestry makers of old had threaded golden filaments through half-finished scenes of pilgrimage and conquest, creating for Albatross the victory over Tauchnitz he envisioned in a tale yet just begun.

By his account, Albatross's winning appearance turned its fortunes around. After the trade's initial reticence—"Reaction, nil"—he sent twenty-four travelers shooting out from Paris and Hamburg and Milan, deeper into Tauchnitz territory each day. He had instructed them to show booksellers Albatross volumes without mentioning the price. "The almost universal comment was 'beautiful, but, of course, too expensive.'" Then came the moment of astonishment, as the travelers flipped over the books, revealing the low prices. Sales leapt forward, more than doubling their initial estimate. Holroyd-Reece attributed this feat "even more to the appearance of the books than to the excellence of the list, for the list itself did not sell the series sight unseen." To underscore Albatross's unique vision, the article included a photo of a hand reaching into a lovely patterned box holding the first six Albatross titles, each in a different color, inviting readers to touch this rainbow display in their own lives.[7]

*

Still, this ideal library was not launched into an ideal world. Albatross's fate was far from secure. While Holroyd-Reece acted as the public face of Albatross, cultivating contacts, and Enoch secured orders with booksellers far and wide, Wegner manned the shop in Paris. "The first stressful day here is over," wrote Wegner to his second wife, Annemarie, on 11 March 1932. He had taken the train to Paris from Germany a day or two earlier. He had since met with Enoch—

in Paris for the sales launch—and one printer, and would be meeting with another the next day. Because of new German regulations, Albatross was considering transferring printing from Italy to Germany. "I'm almost at the end of my strength," Christian admitted after a day piled high with work. But at least Paris was decked with snow: "Lovely!"[8]

His world was aswarm with details. The first six volumes had made it to stores, with Volumes 7 and 8, Virginia Woolf's *To the Lighthouse* and A. A. Milne's *Two People,* not far behind. Numbers defined his days, as he tracked sales and weighed print runs of twelve thousand copies against production prices of 43 pfennig per volume. "Today Enoch had roughly 300 new orders!" he wrote Annemarie on 12 March, thrilled by a number that high less than two weeks after the sales launch. His letters reveal the rush of these early days, as if he were swept up in love. He bought raincoats in matching colors for himself and Annemarie, "so we can run around like twins." He wrote of Albatross tenderly, as "our shared Albatross bird," as if it were a child they had brought into the world together. Albatross was, in a way, their baby. They were newly married, and she, like he, poured her effort and care into the firm. She worked tirelessly for the Albatross cause, writing letters, fielding phone calls, billing accounts, and keeping her cool when the exacting personalities running the firm—especially Holroyd-Reece—exacted too much from her.[9]

For Christian Wegner, the annoyances were worth it. To live with and for books fed him. He did not own the business, yet he could run it as if he did, for Holroyd-Reece was often elsewhere. Albatross was his chance to prove his merits after the Tauchnitz debacle, and he threw himself into all areas of the business. By mid-July, sales were zooming. Wegner worked through searing tooth pain, which had emerged on his trip back to Paris from Germany—in Cologne he had "quickly visited bookstores," he wrote, "& found Albatross everywhere." Arriving in Paris, he won partial relief from a dentist before racing back to the rue Boulard to meet with Paul Léon, James Joyce's agent, to negotiate rights for a continental, uncensored edition of *Ulysses.* Even the still-throbbing tooth could not quell his excitement at Albatross' success: "Sales until 11 July already 5,976 copies!"[10]

While Wegner worked determinedly on day-to-day details, he remained keenly interested in Albatross's larger prospects. He gravitated toward cutting-edge books as a reader, and so was especially interested in the series' critical success. He helped Albatross land important authors, just as he had won Radclyffe Hall, Virginia Woolf, and Aldous Huxley for Tauchnitz in his brief time there. Joyce's agent, for instance, described Holroyd-Reece rather dismissively: "Reddish whiskers, a tie tied twice round a very open collar, a very clean shaven face, fattish face, a talk implying 'I am the important person in this house' all this you will admit is not very attractive hence I had a kind of distrust and kept very quiet." In contrast, he seemed reassured by Wegner: "He seems a very energetic and competent person." In late September 1932, after much deliberation about whether to forsake the highbrow world of special editions for the mass market, Joyce decided to "go into this Albatross cage together" with Sylvia Beach, who had bravely taken on the first publication of *Ulysses* a decade earlier. Wegner was elated. "*Ulysses* is turning into a big deal," he wrote Annemarie. Albatross had landed one of the most controversial works of the age—less a book than a literary landmark. To protect itself from unwanted lawsuits, it printed *Ulysses* under a separate imprint, the Odyssey Press, in Hamburg. The first continental paperback edition in English went on sale in December 1932, with a backdrop of international voices singing its praises, just in time for Christmas. In the first six months of 1933, the Odyssey edition of *Ulysses* sold 5,158 copies, more than the Shakespeare and Company edition had sold in two years.[11]

By the time of this magnificent literary coup, several things had crystallized for the Albatross partners. The first was a realization about Tauchnitz. If they could weaken Tauchnitz, they wanted to purchase it, so Albatross could borrow from Tauchnitz's name recognition; the Albatross leaders could then run two series distinct in flavor, Tauchnitz for classics and Albatross for more contemporary titles. "It looks like we're going to clinch the Tauchnitz deal. We'll find out more in the next few days," Christian Wegner wrote to Annemarie. "In any case, Otto has been pushed out!" he added, savoring the thought that his former nemesis had been ousted from power. The second realization was more fraught: although their ambitions to take over Tauchnitz were in sync, Wegner and Holroyd-Reece had their differences about how to manage the financial bottom line.[12]

This difference showed itself most immediately in a terse debate about how Albatross should handle its relationship with Mondadori. The Italian publisher had produced the first eighteen Albatross volumes and expected to remain Albatross's printer, but Albatross's choices were soon circumscribed by both its British backers and German government restrictions. At the end of 1931, the German government had imposed a 10 percent reduction in prices for books produced in Germany to jump-start flagging domestic sales and exports; Tauchnitz accordingly reduced its prices, forcing Albatross to follow suit to stay competitive. To cut costs, Wegner turned from Italy to Germany. He took bids from printers in Leipzig, the German book trade capital, which could ship books more cheaply to their destinations in Albatross's largest anticipated market than Mondadori. In the first week of March 1932, only five days into Albatross's first week of sales, Holroyd-Reece broke the bad news to Mondadori, explaining that German regulations had forced Albatross's hand.[13]

Yet there was more to the shift than Albatross's financial bottom line. In May 1932, Mondadori offered to match the lowest German bid if he could keep production in Italy. Wegner declined, leaving Mondadori—who had seen Albatross through the difficult fall of 1931—nursing feelings of ill-will. With Tauchnitz campaigning against it, Albatross sought a stronger toehold in the German market. Wegner secured a Leipzig distributor, R. Streller, and took bids from two of the largest Leipzig printing firms, Hag-Drugulin and Oscar Brandstetter.[14] Brandstetter not only undercut the competing bid by at least a third but also printed the Tauchnitz series, a not incidental advantage, since Albatross hoped to seize control of Tauchnitz and it would be handy to gather accounts with one printer. With Enoch organizing Albatross distribution from Hamburg, and Brandstetter printing Albatross books in Leipzig, Tauchnitz's primary public argument against Albatross would lose force. Many ties to the German economy, in this case, were better than one—or so, at least, the Albatross partners thought.

In the summer of 1932, it remained an open question whether moving production to Germany would help Albatross trounce Tauchnitz. Albatross entered the competition with exuberance and fresh funds, Tauchnitz with experience and reputation. The German economic crisis, which affected both firms, continued to eat away at the book trade. In 1932, the number of first print runs for books produced in Germany had dropped 10.9 percent over the previous year alone. The average price per book fell from 6.16 to 5.08 RM.[15] Albatross and Tauchnitz prices of 1.80 RM per copy were inexpensive enough to remain appealing. The question was whether readers would gravitate toward tradition or novelty.

As the year wore on, Albatross leaders had reason to be reassured. Press response was almost uniformly glowing. In Italy, Albatross invaded Tauchnitz terrain with a powerful ally in Messaggerie Italiane. "The Albatross Collection offers the best works of modern English and American letters," the distributor proclaimed in *L'Avvisatore settimanale,* its trade catalogue. "The collection has obtained, at its first appearance . . . , a success surpassing all expectations," it added in early June, amply quoting Holroyd-Reece and noting foreign booksellers' delight at Albatross's inexpensive price but polished appearance.[16]

This review struck on a theme reiterated across the continent: Albatross's books offered more value than readers expected—more, at least, than they had learned to expect from Tauchnitz. On 17 March, the Dutch paper *Het Vaderland* openly privileged Albatross over Tauchnitz. "We all know the Tauchnitz edition, the small, inexpensive English books, printed in Germany," it began. "Once one has kept the books a few years in the bookcase, they look unsightly: the paper has turned yellow and they no longer preserve their allure." Albatross offered a solution. "The appearance of their books is excellent and much better than the Tauchnitz edition," ruled the review, and "printed on good paper in a handy format." The article also applauded the selection, concluding, "Whoever is interested in English literature cannot fail to take this particular new library into account." Holroyd-Reece himself could not have not penned a more ringing endorsement.[17]

Albatross also won points for its international model. The newspaper *Allgemeen Handelsblad* commended its cosmopolitan reach: "An English-German publisher that includes, among other things, an office in Paris, and has its books printed in Italy. . . . The Albatross has quite an international character." The April 1932 issue of *Die literarische Welt* similarly welcomed Albatross editions because they exposed German readers to other cultures. "Today, a mutual intellectual understanding between peoples is a necessity," the article opened, implying that the series offered a timely antidote to rising nationalist sympathies. "How important it is to make foreign literature popular in its original form in Germany." Certain Albatross titles had already been translated into German, the writer admitted, yet many readers would welcome the chance to read the original versions in English.[18]

And many did. Albatross insinuated its way into Germany, the birthplace of continental English editions and its most fertile ground. In mid-September, six months into a fierce Albatross-Tauchnitz rivalry, one *Frankfurter Zeitung* reporter with twenty-six Albatross volumes lined up before him praised the "charming play of color in a stiff cardboard cover, durable and easy to hold, with fine typesetting on splendid paper." He ribbed Albatross for claiming to produce only the "best" books, noting, instead, the wildly varying quality of its offerings. "We find all types of 'stars' among the represented authors," he wrote, "beginning with the 'highbrow stars,' for whom, in English opinion, there can only be a tiny reading public of four thousand, down to the 'lowbrow stars,' who only laboriously give their works a literary veneer; among these belong detective novels, with the mention of a cigarette every third page on average." Yet he also highlighted Albatross's German ties, noting that "printing, paper, and binding are all sourced by different major firms in Germany."[19]

Still, Albatross's presence in Germany was not without conflict. Two weeks earlier, *Die literarische Welt* had praised Tauchnitz as the lifeblood of English editions in a special "England" issue lit up by "highbrow stars" which included an opinion piece by Aldous Huxley; a Katherine Mansfield story, "The Wind Blows," translated into German; and an excerpt from James Joyce's *Finnegans Wake.* "The oldest and most important enterprise of this type is that of Tauchnitz," claimed one reviewer, apparently reluctant to see the firm undermined. "For over ninety years, it has produced English authors in impeccable form at very cheap prices," its influence "extraordinarily great, yet still too little recognized." The firm had long rescued "less well-off readers, who first through this edition were put in a position to become acquainted with the English classics," and helped scholars and critics stay abreast of new releases. Albatross, in contrast, earned lackluster commentary, as a "trusty imitation of the Tauchnitz Collection."[20]

In December 1932, in its annual Christmas issue, *Die literarische Welt* listed both Albatross and Tauchnitz book recommendations, one indication in the month before Hitler's rise to power that German readers remained curious about modern literature in English. Albatross's entry rattled off an impressive list: Katherine Mansfield, Aldous Huxley, D. H. Lawrence, Virginia Woolf, James Joyce, Hugh Walpole, Sinclair Lewis, Louis Bromfield, Thornton Wilder. As lighter fare, it offered detective novels by Ellery Queen and Barnaby Ross, as well as Dashiell Hammett's soon-to-be-filmed *Maltese Falcon.* Many of these authors—including Mansfield, Huxley, Lawrence, Woolf, and Joyce—Albatross had plucked from Tauchnitz, just as it hoped to pluck Tauchnitz readers. "The Albatross books decked out in their colorful envelopes will make an appealing complement to the German coffee table for Christmas," the Albatross entry declared. "On the inside and the outside they fulfill all expectations one has of the beautiful book of today." The Tauchnitz entry was titled "Rule Britannia!"—a phrase suggesting deeply rooted ties to British culture. Tauchnitz appealed to its longstanding "friends" with a list of new titles, as well as "a little guidebook on the best books of our publishing house . . . from which the discerning reader can make his choice with ease." Yet records suggest that it was too late for such appeals. Tauchnitz sold 494,000 volumes in 1932, down from 662,141 just two years before—barely enough to keep it from folding outright.[21]

The Albatross partners had rightly sized up their competition. Yet they could not foresee the consequences of striking their roots deeper into Germany. Once Albatross moved to print its books in Leipzig, it became something more than an international firm financed by British interests; it transformed itself into a German exporter. From a cultural perspective, its books were, and would always remain, Anglo-American goods. But they would count in international trade circles from this moment forward as products of German labor. Albatross, like Tauchnitz before it, would earn either hard currency or trade credits for the German trade balance with each little paperback it sold abroad. In throwing over Mondadori—in cultivating hopes of taking over Tauchnitz—the Albatross partners had inadvertently locked themselves into a track taking them ever deeper into Nazi Germany.

On 11 January 1933, in the midst of negotiations for D. H. Lawrence's *Lady Chatterley's Lover*—banned in Britain and the United States for leading readers from the parlor into the heart of the boudoir—Holroyd-Reece left for Germany. This would be his last trip to a democratic Germany for over a decade. On 26 January, he landed his much coveted contract for "Lady C."[22] Four days later, Adolf Hitler seized power, opening the Albatross partners to a world of compromise and contention.

FOUR

Un-German Literature

Stre Vom **Albatross Verlag** in Hamburg erbitte von der Alleinauslieferung
Oscar Enoch, Hamburg:

Albatross Modern Continental Library sowie **Odyssey Press**

1. James Joyce: Dubliners
2. Huxley: The Gioconda Smile
3. Sinclair Lewis: Mantrap
4. Deeping: The Bridge of Desire
5. Hugh Walpole: Rogue Herries *
6. E. Crawshay-Williams: Night in the Hotel
7. Virginia Woolf: To the Lighthouse
8. A. A. Milne: Two People
9. Edgar Wallace: The Man at the Carlton
10. Sinclair Lewis: Dodsworth *
11. Lord Gorell: Gauntlet
12. C. Mackenzie: Buttercups and Daisies
13. Hergesheimer: The Limestone Tree
14. L. Lewisohn: The Golden Vase — Roman Summer
15. W. B. Seabrook: The Magic Island
16. L. A. G. Strong: The Brothers
17. Kathleen Norris: The Love of Julie Borel
18. van Dine: The Bishop Murder Case
19. Susan Glaspell: Ambrose Holt and Family
20. Dashiell Hammett: The Maltese Falcon
21. P. Bloomfield: The Traveller's Companion
22. Katherine Mansfield: The Garden Party
23. de Kruif: Microbe Hunters
24. Huxley: Antic Hay
25. Ostenso: The Waters under the Earth
26. Rosamond Lehmann: Dusty Answer
27. Barnaby Ross: The Tragedy of X
28. Louis Bromfield: A Modern Hero *
29. Thornton Wilder: The Bridge of San Luis Rey
30. Hilaire Belloc: Richelieu
31. D. H. Lawrence: Apocalypse
32. D. H. Lawrence: The White Peacock
33. Jos. Conrad: The Arrow of Gold
34. Phil Stong: State Fair
35. Kitchin: The Sensitive One
36. Frank Harris: Bernard Shaw
37. Louis Golding: Magnolia Street *
38. Queen: The Greek Coffin Mystery
39. Sinclair Lewis: Free Air
40. Michael Arlen: Young Men in Love
41. Walpole: Judith Paris *
42. B. Worsley-Gough: Public Affaires

43/44. James Joyce: Ulysses *

45. de Kruif: Men against Death
46. Ronald Fraser: Marriage in Heaven
47. Aldous Huxley: Brave New World

48 Francis Iles: Before the Fact

49. Beverley Nichols: Evensong
50. G. B. Stern: Little Red Horses *
51. Earl Derr Biggers: Charlie Chan Carries On
52. Katherine Mansfield: Journal
53. Liam O'Flaherty: Skerrett
54. Julian Duguid: Tiger-Man
55. The Albatross Book of Living Verse *
56. Lawrence: Lady Chatterley's Lover *
57. Charles Morgan: The Fountain
58. Bromfield: The Strange Case of Miss Annie Spragg
59. Evelyn Waugh: Black Mischief
60. Lawrence: The Virgin and the Gipsy

Jeder Band kartoniert (1.80)
* = Extrabände (2.80)

Vorzugsangebot bis 31. 3. 33:

50 Bände gemischt je 1.05 (Extrabde. 1.63)

100 Bände gemischt je 1.— (Extrabände 1.55)

The Albatross Almanac.
Kart. (—.80). Rabatt 50%.

Neue vollständige Verzeichnisse.

Ort und Datum: Firma:

JUST AS ALBATROSS was setting out to restructure the literary-political world in Europe, this world began shifting shape. Years later, Enoch recalled how quickly life in Germany changed. "Like cockroaches out of the walls, Nazis in brown and black uniforms appeared all over the place," he reflected. "An orgy of parades and mass meetings jammed streets and public places; jubilant or violent oratory and martial music filled the air; Nazi uniforms, flags, banners and streamers appeared everywhere transforming the colors of the city environment; names of the streets, places, and official buildings were changed to glorify Nazi heroes and officials, and the Nazi greeting with the raised arm and the words 'Heil Hitler' became an almost universal gesture."[1] For Enoch, a German Jew, Hitler's rise to power hit a strong personal nerve, putting his life and that of his family at risk.

But in the early days, Enoch was more anxious about his business than his safety. Albatross's status under the new regime was precarious enough to worry all its directors. In their favor was Albatross's legal standing as a German firm, registered under and protected by German law, as well as its German ties: Wegner as managing director, Brandstetter as the printer, and Enoch as the distributor. Yet Nazi officials might also treat Albatross as a foreign firm, financed by the British, which produced foreign books, had its editorial offices in Paris, and gave decision-making power to foreign partners. Or they might seize on Albatross's "Jewish influence"—the phrase of choice for Nazi officials—given Enoch's prominent role and the sotto voce awareness that Albatross was financed by a Jewish magnate, Sir Edmund Davis. Whether Albatross and its titles survived the groundswell surging around Hitler depended on the results of political infighting, as multiple government factions struggled for control of the cultural arena.

Within its first month, Hitler's regime sent out two decrees that alarmed many German publishers. On 4 February 1933, the Reich President, Paul von Hindenburg, set in place the Decree for the Protection of the German Volk, which stated that "publications the content of which is apt to endanger the public safety and order" could be confiscated and removed from circulation. The law implicitly granted officials carte blanche to decide which books posed this threat, and the Gestapo, Criminal Police, Interior Ministry, and local authorities, among others, all took advantage of this freedom to raid libraries and bookshops unannounced. Then, several weeks later, after the Reichstag mysteriously went up in flames, Hitler outlawed free speech and public gatherings via the Decree of the Reich president for the Protection of the People and State. This new order dissolved Weimar-era protections of the rights of free expression and free speech in "word, writing, imprint, image, or in any other manner." Hamburg authorities were among the first to act on these laws; city officials quickly threw Communist Party functionaries in prison.[2]

The changes to German law did not bode well for Albatross or its management. Yet their fears did not prevent them from pushing forward. On 1 March, little over a month after Hitler claimed power, Albatross took out a two-page *Börsenblatt* advertisement celebrating the firm's first anniversary. It presented a business-as-usual approach, confidently promoting its cutting-edge list of books. The first page covered Albatross's newest volumes—which included *Lady Chatterley's Lover.* The ad featured high praise from the German translator Paul Lerbs, who stressed Albatross's "selection of contemporary English and American literature made with sure taste and lively flexibility" as one mark in its favor, and as another its production at the Brandstetter plant in Germany. The ad's second page was no less triumphant. In its first year, it proclaimed, the Albatross Modern Continental Library had achieved "rising sales" around the world and carved out "a secure place" among booksellers.[3]

By all appearances then, Albatross was thriving, even as tolerance for the kind of literature it produced was dwindling. As of 1 March 1933, its order forms included Huxley's *Brave New World* (Volume 47) sandwiched between *Ulysses* (Volumes 43–44) and *Lady Chatterley's Lover* (Volume 56). The Joyce and Lawrence books were so controversial they had been banned in the United States and the United Kingdom, and Huxley's dystopian challenge to a world where individual voices were suppressed in favor of the collective seemed, suddenly, dangerously prescient.

As March drew on, Albatross leaders watched with dismay the further erosion of the democratic structures that had made Germany the perfect home for their books. After the Reichstag election of 5 March, for which he had prepared a savage campaign against the Communist Party, Hitler consolidated his power. Having won a near majority of 44 percent in the election, he made a deal which granted him and the Nationalist Socialist Party the ability to make unilateral decisions. Little more than a week later, on 13 March, Reich President Hindenburg appointed Joseph Goebbels head of the Reich Ministry of Enlightenment and Propaganda. Previously, individual German states had maintained control over cultural matters. But this new ministry—with its departments for the press, radio, film, theater, and propaganda (which included literature)—effectively stripped the states and other government divisions of control over these arenas and centralized it in Goebbels's hands. Hitler passed the Act for the Removal of Distress from People and Reich—the so-called Enabling Act—several weeks after the election, a law which gave him the right to declare any emergency legislation he felt necessary without parliamentary approval.[4]

Albatross's leaders assumed the worst. Wegner traveled from Paris to Hamburg to strategize with Enoch. He arrived on 31 March 1933, hours before the regime's first official boycott of Jewish stores, planned for the first of April. That night, he wrote to Annemarie back in Paris, describing the "mind-boggling" scene: "The whole of Hamburg resembles an agitated swarm of bees. . . . Everyone is telegraphing all the regions of the world, so that this, for heaven's sake, might stop, yet the question is whether it is of any use. On top of everything else, everyone wants to throw Jews out of all administrative offices and schools, etc. It is not clear at all to what medieval conditions everyone is reverting." Looking around in dismay, Christian claimed that it was "as if we've stumbled into a madhouse." What transpired the next day stunned him. Soldiers patrolled with signs reading "Germans protect yourselves. Don't buy from Jews." In some neighborhoods, clusters of Germans discouraged others from buying at Jewish stores. With his sister-in-law, Wegner broke through the lines. "In front of the big Jewish businesses stood Nazi guards; nevertheless, with Elisabeth on my arm, I wormed my way—simply out of protest—through the slavering crowd that spat epithets at us and bought something, in fact, a white, short-sleeved blouse for you."[5]

For Enoch, as for all German Jews, the new regime altered his very way of living. He soon found himself affected by what he called the "ominous" regulations that hindered Jewish participation in public life. On 7 April, on the heels of the boycott, the state announced the Civil Servant Statute, which outlawed state funding of Jewish employees. Initially, roughly 2,500 of 5,000 Jewish career civil servants lost their livelihoods. The statute then spurred similar regulations in other domains: more than half of Jewish doctors were forced out of their positions by mid-1933, as were teachers, professors, and court employees. Overall, roughly 5 percent of the approximately 240,000 Jews listed in the 1933 census were pushed out of their jobs. Enoch's family suffered directly from this legislation. Enoch himself was barred from his position as a lay judge in the Hamburg Labor Court, though his publishing businesses were, for the moment, protected in the private sector. His older brother, Otto, in contrast, was soon cut from his position as an engineer. With the help of letters from Enoch's friend Erich Warburg of the prominent Hamburg Jewish banking family, Otto looked for a post abroad. Enoch's sister, Ilse, was fired from her job as a chemist, her doctorate rendered useless, so Enoch granted her signing authority in his business. Enoch's cousin Hans spent a year in the Fuhlsbüttel jail in northern Hamburg; a promising scientist who later contributed to the development of penicillin, Hans Enoch was "denounced by a disgruntled former employee who wanted to ingratiate himself with the Nazi authorities."[6]

These travails were distressing. Yet by Enoch's account he was most deeply offended by the daily indignities of being Jewish in a Germany overrun with scuttling forces beyond his control. "There were many situations that were more annoying or emotionally upsetting than touching on any vital interests," he explained in his memoir, "such as the legal obligation during office hours to have my employees, including Jews and myself, listen to Hitler's radio speeches, or the necessity of swallowing direct or indirect insults in order to avoid consequences of a more serious nature."[7]

Wegner found himself in a strange position. Albatross was selling well, with "very sizable deliveries" in hand for April. Yet the boycott signaled bigger problems. "It will make us a lot of trouble," he wrote to Annemarie. He alternated between awareness and denial. He found the racist behavior of his fellow Germans both surreal and abhorrent, and feared that fascism was already spiraling out of control. As he wrote to Annemarie, "The whole thing here looks a damn sight like bolshevism, with somewhat different portents; in any case the movement is escaping from the Berlin Führer's hands, whereto, who knows." Yet rather than reacting against these larger, irrational forces by relocating Albatross, Christian Wegner's instinct was to stay put. He made his gesture against the boycotts—buying the blouse from the Jewish store—and then narrowed his sights, attending to business as usual. He monitored finances, keeping tabs on sales and payments and noting Enoch's newest account statement with pleasure: "April is certainly starting off well."[8]

Yet the pragmatism that made Wegner a superb organizer also blinkered him to potential dangers. His letters reveal an interesting disconnect. He proudly reported crossing boycott lines, yet also envisioned the benefits that this political friction might open up for him. "I have considered with Enoch all the precautionary measures that we want to follow in the worst-case scenario," he wrote to Annemarie on the eve of the boycott: "transfer of the whole warehouse to Switzerland, transfer of the Enoch publishing house to me, etc." This last-ditch solution—the "transfer" of Enoch's publishing house to himself—he sketched only vaguely. But the idea stirred in him a moment of optimism. "You see with which possibilities I, and not just I alone, am reckoning."[9]

Three days after the boycott, Wegner waited eagerly for word on whether Tauchnitz had finally capitulated to Albatross. "I am dying to know what Wildhagen will tell [us] of Tauchnitz," he exclaimed, suggesting that he saw no reason to derail the plan of overtaking their German rival. He also needed to track down Holroyd-Reece, who was, as always, missing in action. "I have important things to discuss with him, . . . truly frightening things. It is difficult to predict [what will happen]!" Above all, though, he was eager to leave the tense scene in Germany behind. "Yesterday & today a lot again at Enoch's," he wrote Annemarie, "on top of which is the earthshaking political situation—I will be happy when I am back with you again."[10]

*

In the spring of 1933, no one yet knew how starkly the regime would draw lines to protect German culture from perceived foreign invasion, or to police books that expressed sentiments counter to National Socialist ideology. As of 1 March 1933, Albatross's order form advertised many authors whose works might be read as direct challenges to National Socialist mores. Huxley and Lawrence were represented with multiple titles. Rosamond Lehmann had earned a succès de scandale with *Dusty Answer* (Volume 26), which one British reviewer had damned as the "outpourings of a sex maniac" because its heroine pursued affairs with both men and women.[11] Katherine Mansfield's first volume of stories, *In a German Pension* (1911), had proffered trenchant critiques of German high society; Albatross published her second, *The Garden Party* (Volume 22). Ludwig Lewisohn, author of *The Golden Vase* (Volume 14), was a well-known advocate for Judaism in the United States, and Louis Golding, also Jewish, warmly portrayed Jewish family life in his critically acclaimed *Magnolia Street* (Volume 37), as did G. B. Stern in *Little Red Horses* (Volume 50).

Yet among Albatross's most unpredictable authors was Sinclair Lewis, catapulted into the international spotlight in 1930 when he became the first American to win the Nobel Prize for Literature. Lewis's works tilted to the left—and he was disinclined to show diplomacy in this, or any other, environment. Famously bumptious, he had once managed to pick a fight at a banquet for Nobel laureates. (As one journalist wryly remarked, "Sinclair Lewis paid tribute to the memory of the inventor of dynamite by exploding in his honor.")[12] Not surprisingly, Lewis quickly got irritated by Nazi Germany and the publishers who sold his books there. In fact, he became as controversial in Germany by the end of 1933 as he had been popular before it.

Unlike most Albatross authors, Lewis received eyewitness accounts of German upheaval from a recognized expert, Dorothy Thompson, who happened to be his wife. A feisty journalist, Thompson had interviewed Hitler in 1931 for the *New York Evening Post,* causing a minor sensation with her book *I Saw Hitler!* "He is formless, almost faceless, a man whose countenance is a caricature, a man whose framework seems cartilaginous, without bones," she declared. "He is the very prototype of the Little Man." Even his ascent to power did not alter her opinion. On 12 May 1933, two days after Nazi sympathizers burned books in public squares across Germany, she went on record with the *New York Times:* "I still believe [Hitler] is a little man, but I see that he is really a great demagogue who believes in all this stuff."[13] Such public declarations earned her no friends among the Nazi elite.

Ironically, Lewis chose the last week of January 1933—the week Hitler seized power—to launch his own grand international publicity stunt for *Ann Vickers,* his first novel following the Nobel Prize. His American agent, Ann Watkins, had joked in July 1931 that Lewis had "been asleep at the switch as far as foreign rights are concerned and is just now beginning to see that they should be dug up." Once he realized that sales of American books were escalating on the continent, he orchestrated a marketing feat of derring-do. So it happened that on 25 January, five days before Hitler's coup, Lewis released *Ann Vickers* simultaneously in seventeen countries and thirteen languages.[14]

The novel portrayed a forward-thinking suffragist turned prison reformer —hardly a woman adhering to Nazi ideals. When Ann Vickers becomes pregnant from her first sexual experience, with a Jewish man she finds alluring, she has an abortion. When stuck in a loveless marriage, she has an extramarital affair with a judge (so much for the morals of government representatives), gets pregnant again, and decides to raise her son. Feminist through and through, she juggles family life and an ambitious career in which she fights to improve prison conditions. Lewis had based his protagonist loosely on his wife, as critics recognized. And Thompson despised the Nazi movement. "Fascism is the rule of the top sergeant and the half-educated," she wrote in her diary; "national socialism is the sick affirming their health—a lot of wavy-haired bugger boys talking about woman's function in bearing SONS for the state."[15]

Lewis's continental reputation had blossomed in the late 1920s, especially in Germany, and with the Nobel Prize pushing his sales to dizzying heights, publishers across Europe scrambled to win *Ann Vickers* for their lists. Wegner and Holroyd-Reece muscled in on the action. Albatross had already secured *Mantrap* (Volume 3), *Dodsworth* (Volume 10), and *Free Air* (Volume 39). Lewis's European agent encouraged him to publish *Ann Vickers* with Albatross by sending him Albatross's fall list, "so that you will see in what company you will find yourself: your own!" Nelson Doubleday gleefully anticipated sales of one hundred thousand in the first year in the United States alone, and in the weeks after its release reported average sales of four thousand copies per day. By the end of August 1933, Lewis had sold twelve thousand copies in French for Librarie Stock, with year-end predictions of fifteen thousand or higher. Sales were nearly twice that for his German publisher, Ernst Rowohlt, who had solidified Lewis's popularity in Germany when he offered four of his novels in translation between 1928 and 1931.[16]

In short, Lewis had been selling a free-thinking worldview and making his publishers very happy. But to anyone reading the signs, the German market for such liberal-minded literature was en route to disappearance. In the months after Hitler's takeover, Thompson wrote despairingly to Lewis of changes to the country she loved so well. "The roster of names of the writers and scientists who have left Germany reads like the German Who's Who," she wrote in early March from Santa Margherita, Italy, where she had observed an influx of prominent refugees, including the playwright Franz Werfel, the pacifist writer Fritz von Unruh, and Gerhard Hauptmann, winner of the 1912 Nobel Prize in literature. "There's not a single important writer there any longer. Thomas and Heinrich Mann, Alfred Döblin, Feuchtwanger . . . Did you ever hear of anything more fiendish than the blackmailing of the whole world, by holding the German Jews as hostages? I lie awake nights thinking what one could do."[17]

Thompson reported that the literary world had shrunk within weeks. On 15 February, under pressure from Bernhard Rust, the Prussian minister for cultural affairs, Heinrich Mann stepped down as president of the Literature Section of the Prussian Academy of the Arts. On 13 March—the same day on which Hitler appointed Goebbels Reich Propaganda Minister—the author Gottfried Benn urged writers belonging to the Prussian Academy to sign a declaration of loyalty to the regime. His insistence cracked open a fault line in the literary landscape when many of Germany's most prominent liberal authors refused and were kicked out of the academy: among them Alfred Döblin, Ricarda Huch (vice president), Thomas Mann, Rudolf Pannwitz, Alfons Paquet, René Schickele, and Jakob Wasserman. Even some writers willing to sign the declaration were later barred after Nazi authorities gathered information on them: Fritz von Unruh and Bernhard Kellermann because of their political orientations, and Leonhard Frank, Ludwig Fulda, Georg Kaiser, Alfred Mombert, and Franz Werfel because they could not hold state-funded positions as "non-Aryans."[18]

National Socialists also quickly marginalized other literary organizations that ran counter to the party's interests. On 10 March 1933, the largest and most politically important writers union, the League of German Writers (Schutzverband deutscher Schriftsteller), with more than 2,400 members, was brought under National Socialist control and its leader, Arnold Zweig, driven out. Just one month later, on 9 April, the executive council of the German branch of the international PEN club resigned in protest; within two weeks government officials had slotted into these positions writers friendly to National Socialist ideals—Hans Hinkel, Hanns Johst, and Rainer Schlösser—all of whom would take up important roles in the Nazi cultural bureaucracy. The nationalization of the German section of the PEN Club was oxymoronic; the British author Catherine Amy Dawson Scott had founded it in 1921 explicitly to forge international understanding among writers rather than to promote one nation's exclusive interests. In Hamburg, where Enoch continued to organize sales and promotion for Albatross, several newspapers were shut down: on 29 April, the *Hamburger Echo,* and both the *Hamburger Nachrichten* and *Hamburgische Correspondent,* shortly thereafter. Other papers and radio stations opposing the regime were either shut down or taken over by new leaders willing to toe the party line.[19]

On the day of Benn's declaration, while Lewis basked in the afterglow of *Ann Vickers,* Thompson conveyed to him the scene unfolding in Germany. "It is really as bad as the most sensational papers report. . . . Hitler gets up and speaks about German unity and German loyalty and the new era, and the S.A. [Sturmabteilung, Storm Trooper] boys have simply turned into gangs and beat up people on the streets . . . and take socialists and communists and pacifists & Jews into so-called 'Braune Etagen' [brown floors] where they are tortured," she reported. "Italian fascism was a kindergarten compared to it. It's an outbreak of sadistic and pathological hatred. Most discouraging of all is not only the defenselessness of the liberals but their incredible (to me) docility. And, my dear, in Berlin suddenly the old shop-worn ideas of civil liberties, democratic sanctions etc. seemed pretty good to me. I wanted to go around reciting the Gettysburg address."[20]

The death of civil liberties took many forms in 1933, nowhere more symbolically apparent than in the book burnings of 10 May. Following the boycotts of Jewish stores and the Civil Servant Statute, university students, inspired by National Socialist ideology and supported by the Press and Propaganda Section of the German Student Union, developed their "Twelve Theses Against the Un-German Spirit." Playing on Martin Luther's historical protest against the Catholic Church centuries earlier, these statements venomously defined as "un-German" anyone who was Jewish, who sided with Jews, or who shared in "Jewish intellectualism." From this toxic logic was born the fourth thesis, "Our most dangerous adversary is the Jew and those enslaved by him," and the fifth: "A Jew can only think Jewish. If he writes German, then he is lying. A German who writes German but thinks un-German is a traitor." By the end of April, student groups had developed their own black list, culling titles from lists developed by Alfred Rosenberg's Combat League for German Culture and national organizations for librarians. From libraries and bookshops students hauled out titles that embodied "un-German" ideals, challenging others to help them "overcome Jewish intellectualism and the consequent liberal decay of the German spirit."[21]

Berlin was the metaphoric heart of this strike. Frederick T. Birchall, a *New York Times* reporter, painted the scene as forty thousand onlookers waited in the drizzle at the public square between the opera house and the university where students had built up a "funeral pyre of crossed logs, some twelve feet square and five feet high." Roughly five thousand students marched in a torchlit parade, amid borrowed trucks and cars loaded with books, to Opera Square, where "a Nazi band had striven to keep up enthusiasm," and failed, in Birchall's opinion. Only when Goebbels appeared did the crowd's energy revive. "The age of an overly refined Jewish intellectualism has come to an end, and the German Revolution has made the road clear again for the German character," he began. He roused listeners to take action against a situation in which "the libraries became filled with trash and filth from Jewish *asphalt-litterateurs,*" and urged Germans to "consign the unclean spirit of the past to the flames," insisting that "the new will arise from the flame of our own hearts."[22]

Students threw into the flames the works of several Nobel Prize winners, including Thomas Mann and the pacifist author Bertha von Suttner. "What saved Sinclair Lewis may never be revealed," wrote Birchall, "but many other 3,000,000 volume sellers became sacrifices, beginning with Erich Maria Remarque's *All Quiet on the Western Front.*" The 160 authors whose books were burned were mostly Germans, including Lion Feuchtwanger, Arnold and Stefan Zweig, and Walther Rathenau, the previous German foreign minister, who had been assassinated by National Socialist thugs. But some American authors were targeted, too, including Upton Sinclair, Helen Keller (for her 1912 essay "How I Became a Socialist"), Jack London, and Theodore Dreiser. Birchall's tone was resigned. "A lot of the old German liberalism—if any was left—was burned tonight."[23]

The German book trade did not change overnight. But calls to "purify" it grew stronger. Goebbels made a point of appearing at the annual Cantate Sunday gathering of the German Publishers' and Booksellers' Association (Börsenverein der deutschen Buchhändler), the central book trade organization, in Leipzig the following week. His speech called on the trade to reject "internationalism, pacifism, and the democratic constitutional state"—the ideals that had previously set the tone for the German book market—and to join the "national revolution." The book trade, he argued, had brought "un-culture" into Germany, publishing what would sell best, rather than taking up the "historic mission" of books "to convert the spirit." Goebbels's speech was received with "rapturous applause," one more sign that the trade would continue to fall in line with the new order. The librarian Wolfgang Hermann, who had shared his own black list with students plotting the book burnings, defined for book trade professionals the genre of literature they should most arm themselves against: "Asphalt literature, which is predominantly written for urban readers, to reinforce their lack of connection to the environment, to the Volk, and to any community, and to fully uproot them." On 13 May, three days after the book burnings, the German Publishers' and Booksellers' Association listed on the front page of the

Börsenblatt twelve German authors whose works were considered "damaging for Germany's reputation" and should be pulled from sale.[24]

Back in Paris, Wegner and Holroyd-Reece could draw only meager comfort from their geographical distance from such cries. Enoch lay exposed in Hamburg, in an increasingly virulent, anti-Semitic climate. Their printer, Brandstetter, had tens of thousands of Albatross books stored in Leipzig. And after the book burnings, no one knew exactly how Nazi authorities would expand the definition of "un-German" literature. What role could Albatross have in this Germany? Easily half of its list could be defined as the cosmopolitan "asphalt" literature which the flames had reduced to ash.

Lewis would have none of it. He was one Albatross author who protested German intolerance, although he typically kept away from Nazi politics. The subject fatigued him. His wife surrounded herself with journalists and politicians who talked of little but Hitler. But if Lewis was frustrated by politics—or jealous at the attention his wife gave to it—he was fired up by threats to literary freedom. The publisher William Morrow printed statements against the book burnings by Lewis and four other American authors, cited in newspapers across the United States. "Throughout the ages many of the greatest scientists and theologians have been uncomfortably honored by being burned at the stake," asserted Lewis. "Apparently the Nazis are paying the same kind of honor to the noblest books that have been produced in Germany in the last twenty years. The authors should feel nothing save satisfaction at receiving this unintentional tribute from an organized mob. I trust that this action will serve to spread their reputation and glory in every land outside Germany, and that America, among other countries, will mark down for reading whatever books may be burnt."[25]

Surprisingly, this outburst did not get Lewis into trouble with Nazi authorities. The real threat to his work came in the fall of 1933. Klaus Mann, the son of Thomas Mann, had launched a journal called *Die Sammlung,* "The Collection," in Amsterdam with the Querido Verlag—a press that published German refugee writers opposed to Hitler. With the backing of no less than André Gide, Aldous Huxley, and Klaus's uncle Heinrich Mann, the journal attacked the Nazi regime through writers with broad international appeal. Two Albatross authors, Huxley and Ernest Hemingway, offered their writings, and Mann had approached Lewis to secure his endorsement. Lewis did not grant his permission, but he might as well have. On the masthead of the first issue in September 1933, Mann listed Lewis's name as a "Mitarbeiter."[26]

The consequences were swift. The *Börsenblatt* published an article in mid-October against exile newspapers like *Die Sammlung*. Rowohlt, Lewis's German publisher, urged him to distance himself from Mann's journal or to claim he was unaware of its intentions. "*Your* books will no longer be sold in Germany," Rowohlt insisted. He also conveyed his sympathies for the regime—if not for all its methods—as if to sway Lewis. Citing the ruined economy and over-abundance of Jews in leadership positions, he concluded, "It is without a doubt, and the election on 12 November will prove it, . . . that arguably three quarters of the German Volk will side with Hitler's government."[27]

Yet Lewis had made up his mind. He had never granted Klaus Mann permission to include his name, he insisted to Rowohlt. But he nonetheless denounced the efforts of the German book trade to censor his books if he had done so. He considered such actions akin to blackmail, and if the Nazis were censoring his books, Lewis warned, he would censor Germany. Two days later, he wired his Parisian agent not even to try to publish his next book with a German publisher.[28]

The consequences for Albatross were potentially grave. Lewis had just signed his contract for *Ann Vickers*. He liked the series and the men running it. Now his agent, confused by his telegram, wrote to verify Lewis's stance. "The Albatross Presse being a German house although they publish their books in English, we surmise that the above applies to them also and abstain from communicating proofs to them in spite of the interest they have already expressed in your new book." Again, the question raised its head: What nationality was Albatross, exactly? Holroyd-Reece might frame it as British in British quarters, but if the continental public—including Lewis's agent—saw it as German, Albatross could face backlash. Fortunately for Albatross, Lewis backed down. He abided by his contract. And he let Rowohlt translate his next novel, *The Work of Art,* though he threatened to sever their relationship for all time if Rowohlt tried to censor him again.[29]

Over time, Lewis grew intent on becoming even more notorious in Nazi Germany, while on 25 August 1934, Dorothy Thompson became one of the rare foreign journalists to be expelled from the country. But in 1933, *Ann Vickers* sold largely unhindered. Once Rowohlt assured authorities that Lewis was not writing for Mann's journal, they allowed Lewis's reformist feminist protagonist to make her way to German coffee tables. Yet either from market saturation or fear of repercussions, sales of the German edition dropped from roughly thirty thousand in 1933 to four thousand in 1934. Royalty receipts, however, show that German readers considered Lewis's work suspect enough that a third of those who purchased the German translation of *The Work of Art* from Rowohlt in 1934 returned it to stores.[30]

*

Throughout the summer of 1933, Albatross continued to sell books from Germany. Enoch kept his head down, cultivating a few core friendships and pouring himself into work. His memoirs of this time radiate a muted melancholy, especially at the sundering of trusted relationships. "Suddenly appearing in new Nazi uniforms or wearing the Nazi insignia, were people whom I knew well, had been friendly with." These included some of his best customers and employees, many of whom, to his surprise, "remained friendly and loyal." But he was also stung by former colleagues, including fellow soldiers from the trenches, who sacrificed their friendship as they scaled the party ladder. "Talk in public became hushed and guarded and looking around at who was near you became a familiar gesture." So Enoch pulled in his horizon. "Except for the vigorous pursuit of my work, which under the precarious circumstances demanded my full energy and attention, my private life had become quiet and isolated," he explained. "Theater, movies, concerts, . . . offered little that was untainted by political influences," and he wanted, whenever possible, "to avoid the possibility of unpleasant encounters."[31]

Enoch's professional world had shrunk around him, leaving him ever less room to maneuver. The German Publishers' and Booksellers' Association had passively accepted the book burnings. Its leaders had not even protested when students invaded private bookshops, confiscating books. The organization had tied its own hands. On 11 and 12 of April, one month before the book burnings, its board had met in Leipzig and struck a deal with the Reich Ministries of Economics and the Interior, agreeing to support the regime if the regime promised to subsidize the trade. The resulting deal, the so-called Immediate Program of the German Book Trade, made membership in the association mandatory for all who produced or sold books, centralizing the board's hold over the trade. It cannot have inspired confidence in Enoch or his partners when the association published its revised bylaws on 3 May. Declaration 10 explicitly left the "Jewish question" to Reich authorities: "With respect to the Jewish question, the board places its trust in the leadership of the Reich government. It will carry out government instructions for its own area of influence without reservation."[32]

Enoch found his freedom further curtailed when Goebbels, already the Reich Propaganda Minister, pushed through the formation of the Reich Chamber of Culture (Reichskulturkammer) on 22 September 1933 and installed himself as its president. On the surface, the chamber looked to be merely an efficient system for handling questions of culture. It had seven subchambers, one each for literature, the press, theater, music, fine arts, film, and broadcasting, with Goebbels-approved leaders heading each of these divisions. Yet de facto, this system operated as a massive censorship machine, giving Goebbels and his underlings control over who could produce culture and what that culture would be. No one could practice a cultural profession in Germany without securing membership in one of the chamber's seven divisions. Such centralization had been unheard of in the Weimar era, when an abundance of larger and smaller trade institutions had always coexisted to pursue the interests of their members. Now, suddenly, anyone who violated National Socialist principles could be denied membership, losing his or her livelihood overnight. This threat was enough to keep most publishers in check.[33]

Yet Albatross was not, as it happened, "most publishers." At exactly the moment its leaders might have been expected to flee a book trade so starved of democratic freedoms, they drove their cosmopolitan roots deeper into German soil. This impulse was counterintuitive, to say the least. Yet in the fall of 1933, Tauchnitz was finally buckling, both to internal financial problems and to external competition. The time was ripe for Albatross to purchase its rival. Albatross leaders were faced with an economic opportunity and a moral choice. Perhaps their ambitions trumped their growing uneasiness at the increasingly restrictive climate. Perhaps, too, the tacit approval that Nazi authorities had given Albatross —bestowing upon it the status of "valuable foreign currency earner"—made the three men confident they could work around obstacles as they arose. This catchphrase meant one thing above all: if Albatross's books sold well abroad, bolstering Germany's international trade balance, Albatross could expect special treatment from the Reich Literary Chamber, the subchamber of the Chamber of Culture which would, hereafter, oversee its operations in Germany.

At first, conditions for the Albatross-Tauchnitz deal seemed promising. As Enoch remembered decades later, the Tauchnitz heirs put out feelers to see if Albatross wanted to purchase their shares. By Holroyd-Reece's account, Albatross sealed the deal. Yet Nazi authorities soon unsealed it. With the Chamber of Culture and its subchambers established, they had moved a giant step closer to their goal of *Gleichschaltung*—their desire to wrench every institution of German society into alignment with National Socialist aims. Holroyd-Reece recalled the fears of the leading Tauchnitz shareholder, Count Dohna von Finckenstein, "that his friends, the Nazis, would disapprove of his selling what he described as a 'German cultural institution' to foreigners, i.e. to British owners, particularly because most of the financial backing of the Publishing Holding Company was in the hands of my friend Sir Edmund Davis . . . who was a Jew." The Reich Literary Chamber indeed laid down its law. Characterizing Albatross as a "pure foreign firm," Nazi officials announced that "the authorities will not allow such an important enterprise to be taken over by foreign owners." Tauchnitz would remain in German hands.[34] Albatross had overstepped its bounds, learning a new lesson: it would be allowed license in Nazi Germany until it was not.

FIVE

Made in Britain?

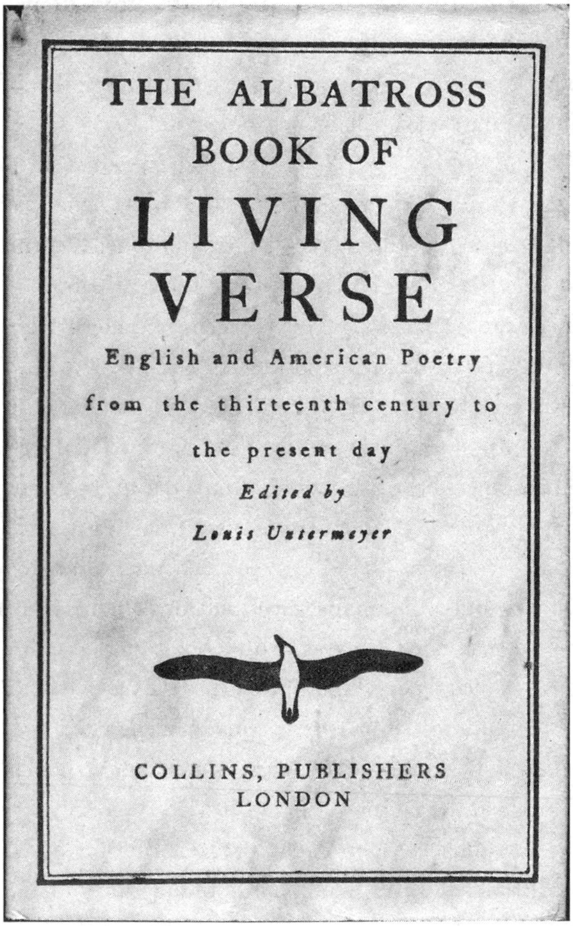

THE ALBATROSS
BOOK OF
LIVING
VERSE
English and American Poetry
from the thirteenth century to
the present day
Edited by
Louis Untermeyer

COLLINS, PUBLISHERS
LONDON

FROM OTHER QUARTERS, too, Albatross faced resistance, some less and some more serious. The American poet Ezra Pound, for one, was never known for mincing words, and he did not spare Holroyd-Reece his visceral detestation of *The Albatross Book of Living Verse.* "Also that ass Reece has sent Albatross FILTHY anthology an' a l'er [letter] wich purrmits me to tell him *exactly* WHAT kind of a bum he IZ," he declared to his long-time mistress, Olga Rudge, "an' I have done it. *Fully.*" Edited by the Pulitzer Prize–winning poet Louis Untermeyer and published for Albatross's first anniversary, the seven-hundred-page anthology contained poems spanning the ages, from thirteenth-century lays to verse from a hundred or so contemporary poets. Pound was included in its cadre of living bards. A year earlier, he had permitted Albatross to include his poem "The Ballad of the Goodly Fere." At the time he had also happily taken the check of £5.5.0 that Wegner had mailed to him—five times more than Tauchnitz had paid him to include the same poem in its *Anthology of Modern English Poetry* two years earlier. Pound did not complain about that part. Instead he let loose on Holroyd-Reece a vituperative stream of invective in his own, grammatically inventive, inimitable style, describing the distasteful, stomach-turning experience he found *The Albatross Book of Living Verse* to be. He framed it as lowest-common-denominator verse, a literary excrescence he alternately called "Untermeyer's last fahrt," and "The Eng/ shitition of Livink Worse."[1]

Pound was merely doing what he did so well: complaining about editors' taste, or more to the point, carping that they had overlooked the poems *he* would have selected had others been sage enough to pay *him* for *his* advice. His aversion to the mass market was legendary—apart from wanting to sell his own poems to as many readers as possible, of course. And so he accused Holroyd-Reece of being lazy and cheap in his selections for Albatross, claiming that the publisher "was not interested in giving people better stuff at 10 lire per volume." Pound protested against Tauchnitz, and Albatross's projected takeover of Tauchnitz, on the same grounds. "Albatross has just amalgamated with Tauchnitz/ I have explained carefull why he ought to be poisoned, I mean explained TO him," complained Pound to the editor-writer Ford Madox Ford, not yet aware that Nazi authorities had blocked the Tauchnitz sale. "But mebbe you cd/ manage him/ He seemed worried by my telling his step/daughter I intended to assassinate him. I explained WHY/ but he is VERY resilient. I doubt if grief wd sink very deep."[2]

*

With political changes in Germany threatening to destabilize Albatross, Holroyd-Reece had so much to take seriously in 1933 that he relished the chance to joust with the cantankerous poet. "I have just returned from a lengthy and tedious trip, to my new abode," he wrote in mid-September from a house he had rented in southeastern France, "and learn on arrival . . . that you wish to assassinate me." He sent Pound "a block on which to chop off my head"—a copy of the maligned anthology—and wryly noted his "real cause" for writing: "If you can express yourself in terms that will not obliterate the printer's ink, the Albatross will be very glad to have a letter of 'appreciation.'" Knowing Pound would resist supplying any kind of endorsement, Holroyd-Reece left the door open for repartee, signing, "With kindest greetings and in the happy anticipation of my imminent assassination by your very own hand." Pound's "appreciation" was, in fact, so colorful that Holroyd-Reece joked that his office had not forwarded it to him "for fear lest its content might burst into flames."[3]

Yet beneath the banter, Holroyd-Reece had serious intentions about this little volume and the mass market experiment it represented. "However little you would believe it," he responded to Pound, "the ALBATROSS is interested in supplying the best stuff which it can market. The ALBATROSS on the whole is particularly fortunate because, so far, broadly speaking, the best stuff has, contrary to the experience of most publishers, found the best market for us." Holroyd-Reece priced the anthology, unapologetically, to sell. He defended it to Pound as a "remarkable feat"—"the first occasion on which a book of such scope is brought within reach of a public that has looked with longing on such publications as the 'Oxford Book of English Verse' but cannot afford the higher price."[4]

Fortunately for Albatross, not everyone felt the same loathing for the volume, or for Albatross's mass market ambitions. One Scandinavian critic welcomed the book for its "discriminating selection," praising its section of twentieth-century lyrics as far stronger than the corresponding section of the more expensive Oxford volume. On the last day of 1933, the anthology received special mention in the "Books of the Year" column of the London *Observer.*[5] In the same issue, eight pages farther in, appeared a column-long interview with Holroyd-Reece not incidentally titled "Albatross: British Authors on the Continent." For anyone wondering about Albatross's allegiance at the end of this, the first year of Hitler's regime, the article gave one answer: Albatross was British, through and through. *The Albatross Book of Living Verse,* printed by William Collins and Sons in Edinburgh rather then the Brandstetters in Leipzig, was one tactical pawn to prove it. To protect Albatross's aims abroad, Holroyd-Reece needed to convince its British opponents, more successfully than he had done so far, that Albatross had British rather than German interests at heart, and that Albatross's mass market paperbacks were the best means of serving those interests.

*

From its inception, Holroyd-Reece had publicly framed Albatross as British, much to the ire of the British publishing establishment. Albatross books were "Printed in Germany," as each copyright page advertised, and its covers evoked its continental affiliations—"Hamburg, Paris, Bologna"—with no "London" anywhere to be found. Yet Albatross's sympathies were, Holroyd-Reece claimed, indubitably British. In March 1932, introducing Albatross as the "English Tauchnitz" for the London *Times,* Holroyd-Reece had touted Albatross's Britishness to woo British readers away from the German-produced Tauchnitz editions they knew from their travels abroad. Yet in 1933, with Hitler looming over the horizon, his insistence on Albatross's Britishness served a more targeted purpose: to distance Albatross from Germany. Already, there were rumblings in British papers about what it meant, morally, to buy Tauchnitz books on the Nazis' watch. One reader of the *Observer* wrote a letter to the editor in July 1933, whose title, "Why Tauchnitz?," summed up his stance. "The bulk of the Continental English-reading public is compelled to buy English books in the Tauchnitz Edition," he complained, adding, "Most of us, I think, dislike having to do this, especially since Hitler came into power." The letter writer proposed a very pro-British solution: "English publishers and English writers should co-operate with a view to supplying the Continental English-reading public with books published in Great Britain."[6]

In fact, in the wake of Albatross's meteoric rise, British publishers were intensely preoccupied by precisely this question of how to get more British-produced books onto the continent. In May 1932, two months after Albatross entered the market, the British book trade journal featured an article titled "British Books Abroad." The gist was clear: British publishers needed to increase their stake in British books on the continent, and fast. There were cultural reasons: "It is generally agreed that books are the best silent ambassadors that can be found. It is from the books of a country that the picture of the life and opinions of its people has to be obtained by the majority." There were economic reasons, too, best summed up in the British publisher Stanley Unwin's pithy phrase: "Trade follows the book." The Department of Overseas Trade so strongly wanted to infuse the continental market with more British-produced books that it even developed a memo on the subject, with recommendations for publishers.[7]

Of course, while British publishers and the Department of Overseas Trade had been pondering how to wrangle British books into the continental market, Tauchnitz, and then Albatross, had done it. And for decades, the British Publishers Association had nursed a certain animosity against such continental editions. In the early twentieth century, British publishers feared that Tauchnitz was endangering its domestic profits when travelers enamored of the little ivory volumes smuggled them back into England. Beginning in 1911, British customs officers were instructed to search travelers' luggage for Tauchnitz volumes; one man was rumored to have been so fond of Tauchnitz that he lumbered through customs with his greatcoat weighted down by volumes sewn into its lining. By the early 1930s, with continental sales of Anglo-American books on the rise, the Publishers Association was faced with a new worry: Tauchnitz and Albatross might undermine their profits abroad. In November 1931, the Publishers Association surveyed its members to determine what percentage of their sales derived from the continent. It also gathered evidence from booksellers, which all too trenchantly underscored the association's fears. One bookseller in Budapest requested fifteen copies of Aldous Huxley's *Brave New World* with the caveat, "When it appears in Tauchnitz within three months, send only five copies." A Berlin bookseller similarly requested that Chatto and Windus supply him with twelve copies "as long as no continental edition like Tauchnitz, The Albatros[s] or Crosby will be published in . . . four months time."[8] This random sampling pointed in one direction: as soon as readers heard that a cheap edition was on its way, they folded their wallets and snapped their purses closed.

Not yet ready to embrace the mass market model that Tauchnitz and Albatross espoused, the Publishers Association fought back. By spring 1933, when Holroyd-Reece published *The Albatross Book of Living Verse,* it had transformed its once polite campaign against continental editions into a full-blown rebellion. In *The Author,* the journal of the Society of Authors, the association declared that "the Continental market has become of such importance that no English publisher of standing dare neglect it." The association directly dissuaded authors from signing with Tauchnitz and Albatross; it urged them instead to preserve a tiered continental market, selling expensive editions first to an educated elite, with cheap editions following two years later. If authors stuck with them, the association argued, higher-priced editions could enjoy their full run, and authors would reap higher royalties. Harold Raymond of Chatto and Windus summed up this disagreement best: "What then is the object of selling 2/- Tauchnitz rights at a time when the English 3/6 rights are in swing and a 2/- edition in the offing? It almost looks like an anti-Buy-British campaign, a determination to give a German firm a start on the English publisher."[9]

If British publishers had thought Tauchnitz was privileging German economic interests to their detriment, Albatross—with its modern books and clever advertising—was perceived as an even greater threat. With its claim to be British, Albatross was also seen as an insult to English goodwill. British publishers could identify no British loyalties in Albatross beyond the accident of its investors, and, indeed, saw Albatross's surprise attack on their flank in 1932 as reason enough to treat it as another continental usurper. Raymond took particular umbrage at Albatross's claim—published in the London *Times* on its first day of sales in March 1932—that Albatross was "produced by British labour." Much as Otto before him had protested all the way to court that Albatross could not call itself German, Raymond teamed up with publishers Kenneth Potter of Longmans Green and Wren Howard of Jonathan Cape to draft language for a memo to be circulated to the British trade noting that Albatross printed its books in Italy, and so did not serve the British economy.[10]

It did not help that Albatross's aggressive business model was also seen as a gauche violation of British propriety. In December 1933, for instance, even James Joyce's French agent, Paul Léon, warned Joyce's British agent to be cautious when discussing the much-coveted prize of a British *Ulysses.* "No offer should ever be communicated to the Albatross," he insisted, "since they can always behind our back approach the offering firm and cut the grass from under our feet by abolishing the competition." When John Lane/Bodley Head publishers made an offer as 1933 turned into 1934, Léon was pleased. "I think John Lane as a firm is a much more reputable firm to deal with [than] some newcomer to England. Don't you think so?"[11]

No longer content to watch from the sidelines while Albatross and Tauchnitz wreaked havoc on their profit margins and book trade etiquette, many British publishers pressured their authors to decline Albatross contracts. Chatto and Windus informed authors of potential royalty losses, yet let them reach their own decisions—as in the case of Huxley, who evidently heeded his agent instead, and reprinted a dozen titles with Albatross between 1932 and 1939. Jonathan Cape took a harder line, threatening to revoke authors' contracts if they signed with Albatross. Even the hot-headed Sinclair Lewis backed down. Despite Wegner's persuasive tactics—which were many and well grounded—and Lewis's own liking for Albatross's books, Lewis refused Albatross the option on all his future books. Cape also rejected an option to publish a limited edition of *Ulysses* for subscribers with the logic: "The book is now obtainable in Albatross Editions, is it not?" He then added, "P.S. A good many copies will come into England, as always happens with these continental editions."[12]

The seething resentment of the British publishing establishment posed a true threat to Albatross. Albatross could not afford to alienate the British and American publishers who allowed it to reprint their authors abroad, any more than it could risk running afoul of the German bureaucrats who monitored its production and sales. And Albatross's obvious legal ties to Hitler's Germany only complicated the question of its Anglo-American loyalties. Authors and agents alike had, in fact, begun complaining about the hidden cost of business with Albatross: the difficulty of getting royalties out of Germany. Albatross controlled the money it paid to the Reichsbank but had little sway over when the Reichsbank transferred payments to Britain or the United States. "We had to pay in marks to the Central Bank all sums due abroad (i.e., advances, royalties, overheads, etc)," explained one Albatross employee to a disgruntled agent, "and the Central Bank then provided us with the necessary foreign exchange as and when it became available. This was a slow and cumbrous procedure and explains why payments were subject to delay." Lewis was so irked that his royalties were locked up in Germany that he refused to pay the required German income tax. His German publisher should pay it instead, he insisted, and if his publisher refused, he quipped, the Nazi regime would have to turn to God for it instead—an unlikely outcome, since the Nazis had, in his view, done away with God.[13]

With these political and economic challenges, Holroyd-Reece had more than one reason to enhance the firm's ties to the British economy. Hence, Holroyd-Reece's partnership with the Scottish publisher William Collins and Sons of Edinburgh, forged in April 1933. To those who suggested that Albatross fed the German, and not the British, economy, Holroyd-Reece pointed to *The Albatross Book of Living Verse*. Albatross's partnership with Collins signaled a new trajectory for the publisher, which also planned two other series printed in

Edinburgh: the Crime Club series, and a "special series of classics illustrated by the Old Masters."[14]

Here, as Holroyd-Reece explained to the *Observer* on the eve of 1934, was a uniquely British solution to continental books (and, as he did not say, a response to British publishers' complaints): books produced "by British labour," for sale first in the British market, and then on the continent.[15] Holroyd-Reece held up Albatross's British side for view, listing only Sir Edmund Davis and himself as founders of the Albatross Publishing Company—true as far as it went, since Wegner and Enoch played little role in the Luxembourg parent company. He touted Albatross's top-notch British authors, including those who had penned the *Observer*'s "four outstanding novels of 1932": Charles Morgan's *The Fountain,* Aldous Huxley's *Brave New World,* L. A. G. Strong's *The Brothers,* and Louis Golding's *Magnolia Street.* He explained how Albatross's innovative color coding of covers helped continental readers identify genres and take risks on books in English. "The result has been," he declared, "that the Albatross has definitely secured for its authors a new market and an increased interest among Continental publishers in translating the best modern works from the English language." Albatross did yeoman's service spreading British culture across Europe in a politically charged time; as proof, Holroyd-Reece cited the French diplomat Phillippe Berthelot: "The work of Albatross represents one of the most valuable and distinguished forms of pacific British propaganda, because it leads people of all nations to understand the British mind and temperament."[16]

As Holroyd-Reece saw it, idealism was good business and good politics; selling the best books for the cheapest prices to the most people was the whole point in 1930s Europe, financially, culturally, politically. Riding the coattails of the mass market, Albatross could bypass the "Not to be introduced inside the British Empire or the U.S.A." stamped on each cover, becoming both British and continental, with all the advantages that lay therein. In propelling this strategy forward, Holroyd-Reece was a visionary, leading a sea change in publishing toward mass market paperbacks, which the more traditionally inclined Publishers Association still rejected. In fact, one Arthur Chichester, who had followed the assault on Tauchnitz and Albatross in *The Author,* urged the association to wise up, arguing in an August 1933 letter to the editor that British publishers should learn a thing or two from their continental competitors. "The number of continental buyers of expensive English editions is any case small in comparison with the mass of potential buyers of popular editions from the bookstalls," he asserted.[17] The continental market had changed in hard economic times. British publishers could either fight or embrace it. If they could not see Albatross as their ally, then let them take action to make Albatross truly their foe. For the moment, the best, because most accessible, ambassador for British books on the continent as 1933 came to a close was this nascent publisher whom the British book trade did not even recognize as British and whose books could not be legally brought onto British soil because the British Publishers Association feared they would undermine British sales of the same titles.

*

In the short term, the Albatross Crime Club was perhaps the most interesting test case for the idea that mass market books produced in Britain for the British market might double as Anglo-American propaganda abroad. Detective fiction was a fine distraction, an excuse for readers to escape reality and test their wits against those of a host of shrewd gumshoe protagonists. Even Ezra Pound had something good to say about it. Holroyd-Reece wrote him, astonished, "I note with mixed feelings that the result of your buying and reading—an uncommon combination—some Albatross Crime Club titles, causes you feelings of clemency towards me," he mused. "I feel I should either arrange to prevent your booksellers from selling you any more, or offer to present you with a few titles at your choice. The decision is left to you. I believe good temper is going to be one of your virtues."[18]

Albatross introduced the series to the German book trade two months after Hitler seized power. A full-page *Börsenblatt* ad on 29 March 1933 laid out the welcome mat to German booksellers and readers, inviting them to join a circle of twenty-five thousand members worldwide who enjoyed the "best detective and crime tales . . . painstakingly selected by a committee of experienced experts for the Crime Club Ltd. in London." Albatross touted its ties to Collins, which helped it deliver the hottest crime novels a mere two months after they appeared in England.[19] For continental readers, this time frame was unheard of: they usually waited six months or a year or more for titles in English. In this small way, the Crime Club promised foreign readers a sense of belonging to something bigger than themselves. For Albatross wanted to sell more than suspense; as Holroyd-Reece got in the habit of repeating as fascism took hold in Germany, Albatross held the door open for readers to identify with Anglo-American culture—

an identification he claimed as increasingly important the more violently the Nazi regime forced German sympathies into National Socialist channels. Whether a sales pitch or his true philosophical aim, this logic fit its time.

How, exactly, the Crime Club would lead "people of all nations to understand the British mind and temperament," as Holroyd-Reece claimed, was unclear. Certain, however, was that crime novels in translation were all the rage in Germany by the time Hitler took power. Hands down, as Kate Sturge, an expert on translation in the Nazi era, documents, the British writers who had the most books translated into German during the 1920s and 1930s were those spinning detective tales, which filled a gap in German literature: diverting, light-hearted, and suspenseful reads. The genre solidified its hold when a Munich-based publisher, Wilhelm Goldmann, began translating the work of Edgar Wallace in 1927. Wallace churned out novels at breakneck speed, often dictating them in three to four days, while chain-smoking cigarettes and downing pots of tea. He wrote twelve novels in 1929 alone. German readers devoured them. Of the 166 titles Goldmann had translated from English up to 1934, 84 were Wallace titles. Indeed, the number of Wallace's editions—including first, special, and reprint editions combined—totaled 195, with Arthur Conan Doyle coming in a close second at 175. One-third of fiction translated into German from English, in fact, was detective fiction; in 1934 and 1938, the percentage rose to just under half.[20]

Yet the detective novel was despised by Nazi ideologues as much as it was loved by German readers. Many authorities were suspicious of reading solely for entertainment; National Socialism cultivated the more serious ideal that German culture in general, and German literature in particular, should feed the nation's soul. On this score, British detective fiction, which had grown popular during the last years of Weimar, embodied for many cultural leaders the amoral frivolity of an era whose values they wanted to extinguish. As Sturge contends, "Literary and librarians' journals attacked its embeddedness in the city, its playfulness and, especially, its association with Anglo-American rationalism." Nazi officials' distaste for this breed of foreign invasion did little until the start of war to stem the tide. The genre remained so popular that German authors began producing their own detective novels, adopting British settings—as in Willy Reese's *Ein Kabel an Scotland Yard* [A Cable to Scotland Yard] (1939)—and even British-sounding pseudonyms—as in Percy Brook's *Der Fall Westminster Abbey* [The Case of Westminster Abbey] (1937).[21]

The Albatross Crime Club series played to this trend, dishing up for German readers all the suspense they desired in over twenty titles published in 1933. Some, like Colin Ward's *House Party Murder* or Agatha Christie's *Lord Edgware Dies,* let readers glimpse an upper-crust milieu. Readers could wander the British landscape in Joseph Farjeon's *Dead Man's Heath* or enter the sideshow with Anthony Abbot's *Murder of the Circus Queen.* Most of all—something Nazi officials vocally protested behind the scenes—readers could identify with British or American detectives, those "good guys" whose diligent efforts and incisive logic led them to quash evil and restore society once more to order. Seen in this light, the Crime Club might have inadvertently been among the most popular propaganda Albatross disseminated in Hitler's Germany—despite, or perhaps because of, the evil-doers and tongue-in-cheek attitude woven through its plotlines.

At a larger level, the entire undertaking of a cloak-and-dagger series put forth by Albatross resonated with ironies. With a German CEO, a German office and head of distribution in Hamburg, and a German printer in Leipzig, the firm was deeply entwined with the German economy. Yet it retained a British outlook, British funding, and a British identity. This duality was strategically important for business purposes—and for Albatross's goal of maintaining a strong presence in the German market. With Hitler's regime overseeing roughly one-third of the market for continental English paperbacks, and ratcheting up its control over literature with each season, Albatross volumes were poised to become something more than just books: they operated as efficient little covert agents, more easily finding a foothold in the Reich than other Anglo-American books because so many Albatross titles had never even crossed German borders.

SIX

The Scissors in Their Heads

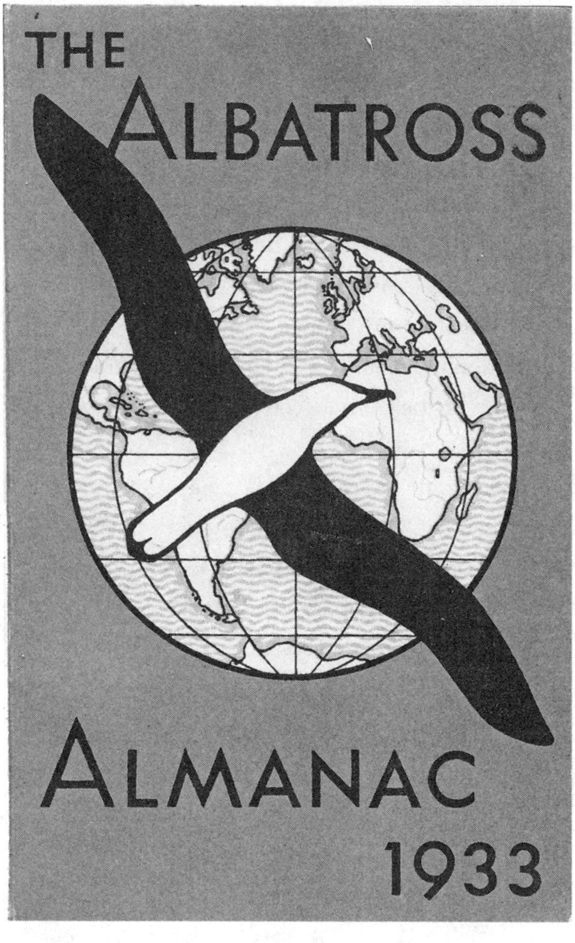

IF IN BRITAIN, ALBATROSS armed itself against enemies it could largely see, in Germany, it faced a more insidious threat: the unpredictable nature of Nazi censorship. Throughout 1933, Aldous Huxley had followed the Nazi takeover with despair from Sanary-sur-Mer, a haven in southern France to which he and his wife, Maria, had retreated. In the wake of Nazi restrictions, most of the literary and political elite critical of National Socialism had taken flight, debilitating Germany's once innovative and vigorous literary scene. Four times more authors emigrated from Germany in the first six months of Hitler's regime than in all the years that followed. By the summer of 1933, a number of these prominent refugees, Jews and non-Jews alike, had made their way to Sanary, bringing the "Barbarous German news," as Maria called it, with them. "I have never more passionately felt the need of using reason *jusqu'au bout,*" wrote Huxley to one friend, describing Europe in 1933 as seething with "the awful sense of invisible vermin of hate, envy, anger crawling about looking for blood to suck. And reason in the midst . . . waiting to be devoured, not by rats, but bugs."[1]

Yet despite the frightening events unfurling alongside thousands of Nazi flags, 1933 had turned into a year of strange momentum for Albatross. Its books glided from Germany to other markets without impediment, much like the bird circling the globe with wings outstretched on its first *Albatross Almanac.* Along with George Bernard Shaw, James Joyce, Katherine Mansfield, Sinclair Lewis and others, the almanac included British-Jewish authors Louis Golding and G. B. Stern. Albatross had secured these authors in the last, more tolerant months of the Weimar Republic; their contributions would now be printed and sold from Nazi Germany.[2]

One choice at a time, Albatross's leaders adjusted to the anomalous situation they faced: they had chosen to produce one of Europe's most cosmopolitan series from its most virulently nationalistic hub. How long they could push their luck, they did not yet know. The start of 1934 found the German book trade uncertain how to proceed under conditions set by Hitler's cultural henchmen. The book burnings had sent a clear message about "un-German" books reverberating from booksellers to publishers and authors, on one hand, and to readers, on the other: books trending against National Socialist ideals, in German or any other language, had no place in Hitler's Germany. On the surface, the book trade took its lead from the speech Goebbels gave the day piles of books flamed skyward. Hitler urged the development of "eternal German" tendencies in the arts and railed against modernist experimentation for its decadence and transience.[3] Pro-German rhetoric suffused the *Börsenblatt,* ousting its more liberal impulses, and implying that books in Germany fell into clear categories: those that might pass scrutiny and those that would not.

In truth, however, the censorship machine in the early years of Hitler's regime was far less organized and efficient than popular stereotypes would have it, with no all-encompassing censorship or control of books, German or foreign. While Goebbels remained a powerful figurehead, especially for foreign literature, censorship lists sprouted like mushrooms, as multiple figures tried to sway the role books might play in the new political order. The minister of the interior had traditionally made decisions about culture. Bernhard Rust—the Prussian minister of cultural affairs until Hitler appointed him minister of science, education, and national culture in June 1934—controlled lists sent to lending libraries, while Robert Ley, head of the German Labor Front and the Strength Through Joy movement, handled censorship of small private libraries. Alfred Rosenberg, founder of the Combat League for German Culture, cracked down on books that undermined National Socialist goals and character. And because each province had its own say over cultural issues, the police in each region exerted control over books—for example, the Bavarian police had cultivated a list of 6,834 titles from 2,293 authors by 1934. One frustrated Berlin author and publisher, William Jaspert, complained to the Propaganda Ministry in December 1933 that Hitler's first year in power had provoked absolute mayhem. By his count, more than twenty-one censoring bodies had confiscated or banned over 1,000 publications. By another count, forty different agencies had developed competing censorship lists by 1934. Not only was the Nazi literary bureaucracy inefficient; it functioned in a state historians have come to call "authoritarian anarchy."[4]

Yet for all of this infighting and disarray, German publishers held little doubt about the power of governing agencies over their literary output. Inundated with official lists and brash proclamations about literature as the protector of the German soul, the book trade was steeped in fear. It was not that all books suddenly expressed National Socialist loyalties or that all foreign books were banned. German authors still penned plenty of middle-of-the-road romances, family sagas, and tales of struggling doctors, soldiers, and the working class. German publishers still sought out foreign authors with a reputation for strong sales. But not knowing when the next crackdown might come, publishers operated on the defensive. Jan-Pieter Barbian, a historian of Nazi literary politics, has put it best: "It was vital for [publishers] to keep constantly updated on political developments, create and cultivate personal contacts within the apparatus of literary policy, remove 'undesirable' authors from their lists, compromise on revising new editions, and insist on their authors keeping a low political profile. . . . The question was not whether these strategies were applied but how skillfully, and how far a publisher succeeded—despite all the concessions—in preserving intact the core of what he or she saw as professional ethics and values." Previously broad-minded publishers scrutinized their offerings to put them beyond reproof. They suddenly looked twice at authors who might bring them unwanted attention, whether as Jewish, Communist, foreign, liberal, or experimental in subject or style.[5] The era of self-censorship had begun, slowly altering the niche for foreign books in Germany, and Albatross's importance within it.

Not surprisingly, modern Anglo-American books were one target in German publishers' strategy to tame their offerings. While there were no blanket bans against such English-to-German translations, publishers had little guidance, apart from forbidden titles periodically listed in the *Börsenblatt.* Between early November 1933 and January 1934, the German Publishers' and Booksellers' Association sent to all booksellers a circular—developed by a "working committee" of propaganda and book trade experts—of mostly German titles that should be pulled from circulation. "Supplying and distributing the works named is undesirable for national and cultural reasons," stated the circular, and publishers not abiding by the guidelines would be expelled from the association and left unable to practice their professions. Hardest hit by these secret bans, which were, not incidentally, to be kept "strictly confidential," were publishers who specialized in experimental forms such as naturalism and expressionism, but also in modern translated literature.[6]

No accident, then, that the regime's aggression cast a temporary pall over such books. Herberth Herlitschka, the translator of a veritable *Who's Who* of modern British authors, warned one agent in January 1934 of his difficulties securing contracts. "The truth is that for a long time it seemed indeed very uncertain," he wrote, "whether translations generally and that kind of English literature, for which I was going in particularly would have any further chance in Germany." Translations from the English had enjoyed a vogue in Germany, their numbers rising throughout the 1920s, higher than translations from all other source languages. Yet their numbers fell sharply in 1934. Kate Sturge offers this rationale: "It appears that this was a year where the most visible source of translation was approached with the greatest caution by publishers, who later regained their confidence, altered their programme, or both."[7]

Publishers of more liberal-minded foreign books walked the knife's edge between political sanction and economic ruin. After authorities banned H. G. Wells in 1935, Zsolnay was forced to withdraw from sale thirty thousand copies of his books, the firm's best-selling translations. Rowohlt, the German publisher of Sinclair Lewis and Ernest Hemingway, had lost roughly a half million Reichsmarks from banned and confiscated books in his stock by 1936 alone.[8] The smart political choice—taming their offerings into submission—might save their books from confiscation, yet their books in translation were often strong sellers. Publishers watched and waited, calculating their risks. Many sought advice from the Reich Literary Chamber—which was busily ratcheting up scrutiny of contracts for foreign books.

No longer could publishers secure contracts with foreign authors in the way they wished. Instead, they had to submit a welter of paperwork: the translation itself, a summary, a sample of the translation, information about the author's "racial" background, and insight into how the translation might aid German understanding of the foreign culture in question.[9] Herlitschka, wishing to publish the late Katherine Mansfield, all the rage for her dark short stories in England, received a request from the Literary Chamber for a précis "showing the 'literary, national and ethical qualities' of the author."[10] A bohemian at heart, Mansfield had loved impulsively, her romantic path including lesbian affairs, a pregnancy from premarital sex, a marriage with an older man whom she abandoned on the day of their wedding, a miscarriage, and a tumultuous relationship with the editor John Middleton Murry—whom she married, and cheated on, once her divorce was finalized. Fortunately, the censors were not aware of these details—which represented for Nazi ideologues the worst excesses of the Weimar era—nor did they recall the anti-German sentiment rampant in her collection *In a German Pension,* which had launched her fame in 1911. Several of Mansfield's volumes were translated into German in the 1930s, and published in Albatross editions, as well.

The arbitrary standards invoked in censorship made Anglo-American books a gamble; publishers had to pay for translations before knowing if they would be approved. In the late Weimar years, they had often purchased rights from well-known authors before their manuscripts were even finished. Now, caution crept in. Robert Graves, for instance, readily took in stride that his books might need to be censored. "If you can sell German translation rights of 'I, Claudius,' do so," he wrote to his British agent. "If there is any retrospective high-treason against Germany in it, the translator can tone it down: the prejudice against Germany was not mine, but Claudius's own—his beloved father & brother being convinced German-killers." The Deutsche Verlags-Anstalt thought it over. Yet because Graves was writing a sequel, *Claudius the God,* the firm was hesitant to make any decision until it could verify the "quality" of the second book.[11]

Within the miasma surrounding foreign books, those published in the original language were an odd category, prone to less scrutiny than German translations because they would reach fewer readers. Having its editorial office in Paris, moreover, gave Albatross additional freedom. Yet Wegner and Holroyd-Reece nonetheless faced a dilemma. Albatross had always embraced cutting-edge authors, but they did not know how long it could keep selling the modern books that distinguished their series from the "Tauchnitz bone-yard."

*

As it happened, Wegner and Holroyd-Reece had in their hands a manuscript that brought the question to a crisis—Aldous Huxley's caustic *Beyond the Mexique Bay.* "The Zeitgeist is a most dismal animal and I wish to heaven one c[oul]d escape from its clutches," Huxley wrote to one friend in October 1933, in the midst of finishing his book, in which he not only lamented the Zeitgeist but declared in no uncertain terms why the Nazi regime was to blame for it.[12] Huxley and his brash social commentary had been a hot ticket in Germany during the late 1920s and early 1930s, with German translators barraging his agent with requests for rights to his works. The new work was an account of his journey along the Mexican coast; a travelogue in name, in truth it was a philosophical critique of authoritarian structures of government and tradition, masked as a *rocambolesque* sojourn from one quaint Central American town to the next.

By chance, Huxley's German publishers were none other than the Kippenbergs of the Insel Verlag, Wegner's aunt and uncle. In June 1934, Wegner discovered that Huxley had disappeared from the Insel catalogue. Rightly assuming that Insel was running scared, Wegner uncovered an opportunity for Albatross: while the Kippenbergs had "no intention of dropping Mr. Huxley and [were] still keeping his books on sale and on their lists" they were "willing to resign their rights" in *Beyond the Mexique Bay,* "because even if they were to publish it without the offending passages, which are openly directed against the Nazi-government, somebody would be sure to denounce them on account of those passages in the original."[13] For Insel, which had published translations of six Huxley novels between 1929 and 1932, this rejection of a Huxley book was unprecedented. And true to Herlitschka's prediction, not a single German publisher published *Beyond the Mexique Bay* in translation, leaving Huxley without a way to reach his German readership in German.

Wegner and Holroyd-Reece seized the moment. If Huxley was barred from publishing his book in German, he could still publish it in English. The Albatross Modern Continental Library had listed six Huxley volumes between 1932 and 1934, including *Brave New World* as Volume 47 in 1932. Slated for 1935 were his novels *Brief Candles* and *Music at Night.* Eager to keep Huxley on their rolls, Albatross signed up *Beyond the Mexique Bay.* Wegner and Holroyd-Reece excised obviously offensive passages before censors could get to them, and in 1935 the book took on new form as Albatross Volume 269 in bookshops across continental Europe, including Hitler's Germany.

Given Huxley's pointed attacks against fascism throughout *Beyond the Mexique Bay,* it is a wonder that Albatross was allowed to publish the book in any form. It was a political bomb between paper covers, engineered to shake readers out of their complacency by describing the horrifying erosion of democracy in Europe. Albatross expunged two lengthy sections, in particular, that featured scathing anti-Hitler sentiments that would have invited trouble for any other publisher daring to print them on German soil. In one, Huxley compared Germans to Roman hordes enthralled by the violent spectacle of people ripped apart by lions. "It is noteworthy," Huxley wrote in the original version, "that all the Nazi leaders have been particularly eloquent about the necessity of being 'hard,' of 'learning once more to punish.' Their followers have gleefully obeyed them, and large sections at least of the general population have undoubtedly approved their brutality." Like a prosecutor, Huxley continued, "The beating, kicking, shooting, starving of Jews and Communists in Germany goes on because a majority (so it seems) of German people desires it to go on."[14]

Another, equally potent section which Albatross cut from the book framed National Socialism as a movement that capitalized on people's baser instincts—hatred and stupidity—as well as their "[hunger] for certainty." Huxley condemned "the newly fashionable idea of nationalism," whose followers he called "the New Stupid" for their blind adherence to nationalism's most virulent forms. "Nationalism is not the theory of a God whom nobody has seen," he wrote. "It is a theory of some actual country and its flesh-and-blood inhabitants. The theory is demonstrably untrue; but that does not matter. What matters to the New Stupid is that the subject of their there is real." Huxley also crowned the two kings of the New Stupid: "Mussolini and Hitler have restored to the New Stupid some of the substantial pleasures enjoyed by the Old Stupidity. Can these pleasures be restored in some other and less pernicious name than that of collective hatred and vanity?"[15]

There was nothing subtle, then, about Huxley's condemnation of Nazi ideology. The Albatross editors, wanting to see the book in print, fell into line with all editors in Germany: they deployed "die Schere im Kopf"—the "scissors in their heads"—and sheared away the book's most aggressive passages. Gone was Huxley's eighteen-page exposé of nationalism and "the New Stupid." Gone, too, was his stinging accusation that the Nazi regime was propelling Germany into barbarism, that "its leaders are doing their best to transform Modern German society into the likeness of a primitive tribe." And gone, finally, was the scathing sarcasm of his denunciation of Nazi demagoguery. "The duty of all Germans is, in Hitler's own words, 'not to seek out objective truth in so far as it may be favourable to others, but uninterruptedly to serve one's own truth,'" Huxley had written. "An ethic of head-hunters is to be justified by a philosophy of paranoiacs. The result promises to be extremely *gemütlich* [cozy]."[16]

The Albatross edition of *Beyond the Mexique Bay* remains a fascinating document for the fact that it appeared at all. Throughout the late 1930s, Holroyd-Reece and Wegner expunged far less damning references to German culture and Nazis as they saw fit. They lopped off bits of a story in Hugh Walpole's *The Inquisitor* (1936), in which one character refers ironically to the Nazis as an "army of angels" worshipping Hitler as its Christ. They removed an entire essay, "After the Steppe Cat, What?" from James Thurber's *Let Your Mind Alone! And Other More or Less Inspirational Pieces* (1938), for its criticisms of National Socialism. Hugh Walpole's *Head in Green Bronze, and Other Stories,* from April 1939, included one story, "The German," in which a London dachshund tracks his British family's growing awareness of German atrocities. "Every day brought fresh horrors. No one was safe in Germany," read one pointed line—which the Albatross editors carefully excised.[17]

These calculations were part and parcel of producing Albatross books, each book its own experiment. Indeed, Albatross's self-censorship remains both a troubling sign of the firm's willingness to bend to the regime's wishes and compelling evidence of its persistence in testing the limits of Nazi tolerance. For as Wegner and Holroyd-Reece learned, officials took their own pragmatic attitude, even toward the rabble-rousing Huxley. And so, German readers were able to ponder Huxley's reflections on "mob irresponsibility" and nationalism just ten pages into *Beyond the Mexique Bay.* Huxley posed a philosophical question fitting for his time, as he wandered Central American fruit plantations, observing how the owners peddled damaged fruit by making it seem better than it was. What kind of marketing magic, he wondered, would it take for scientific inquiry to persuade consumers to privilege peace over hatred? Whatever it might be,

> it must first persuade the consumer that being able to buy harvests and live in peace is better than being able to indulge in hatred for the foreigner, pride of race, national and class exclusiveness. Men do not live by bread or bananas alone: they also live by their passions—their good passions and, still more, their evil passions. Which sort of fun does this consumer like best—the fun of being at peace and so able to consume and to create? Or else the fun of boasting, the fun of hating and despising, the fun of mob-intoxication and mob-irresponsibility, and of sobbing, in chorus, over the final scenes of *Cavalcade*?[18]

The Albatross editors had cut only one phrase from this passage: Huxley's original had followed "the fun of mob-intoxication and mob-irresponsibility" with "the fun of yelling *Deutschland, Deutschland über alles.*" Albatross sacrificed this detail, while leaving intact many of Huxley's still trenchant critiques of what he called "nationalistic hatreds and hysterias." Albatross's 1935 edition sold out its original print run of twelve thousand and the publisher launched a second printing in 1937, even as the "hatreds and hysterias" unloosed by Hitler's Germany mounted around Albatross and its books.

*

Oddly enough, Nazi authorities did not crack down on this or other Albatross books in 1933, nor did it otherwise privilege the German-owned Tauchnitz over the British-owned Albatross. In fact, the year Hitler seized power became the best year to that time for the production of English-language books in Germany. The hard numbers are striking. For the four decades between 1894 and

1934—not including the Great War years, when production slumped—Tauchnitz had published roughly forty volumes a year. In 1933, the number of new continental English editions in Germany more than doubled, to eighty-eight. Albatross and Tauchnitz, in fierce competition, introduced more Anglo-American authors to the German market between them than ever before. In 1933 alone, their rivalry yielded thirty-three authors new to Germany.[19] This surge ran entirely counter to nationalistic calls to suppress "asphalt" literature and "un-German" books, as did the seeming indifference of Nazi officials to this potentially liberal influence in their midst.

Yet it was no accident that Albatross escaped the level of scrutiny and penalty that hailed down on other German publishers. The regime's tolerance of Albatross was, literally, calculated. Within the Literary Chamber and the Propaganda Ministry, books might be suppressed or tolerated depending on where they fell on competing scales of value: financial, cultural, and political. A book might be culturally offensive but financially advantageous, selling well abroad; or it might be financially insignificant but politically useful.[20] When cultural authorities weighed these factors, Albatross generally came out ahead: the regime earned foreign currency from the roughly 70 percent of the books that Albatross exported; and books in English reached smaller, more educated audiences in the Reich and so were deemed less dangerous to the Volk. So Albatross ended up with a strange sort of protection in the cultural realm; the English language functioned as an invisibility cloak, allowing Albatross books to slip by the watchful eyes of Nazi censors. Their public protestations against "un-German" literature aside, officials from both the cultural and the economic sectors had agreed on one thing, at least: English-language books printed in Germany were less culturally troublesome than they were economically useful.

The Nazi authorities' complicated assessment of Albatross reflected a deeper struggle within the Reich. Historians of Hitler's Germany have long wrestled with the question of the National Socialists' motivations: to what degree was the Nazi state able to make decisions driven primarily by National Socialist ideological and political goals, and to what degree were these goals circumscribed by economic realities? In Albatross's case, initially at least, authorities decided they could not afford to take their own moral high ground against Albatross's cosmopolitan tendencies. Financial authorities, in particular, were frantic for foreign currency, and by selling its German-produced books abroad, Albatross folded neatly into the grand plan of Reich Economic Minister Hjalmar Schacht, who had since 1931 put his weight behind exports. Increasing exports and decreasing imports, he argued, was Germany's best hope of accumulating foreign currency surpluses to stabilize the economy. As Albatross later explained, "All our production was subject to German law. One of the provisions of the law was that every penny received from the sale of our books abroad had to pass through Germany."[21]

For tactical reasons, then, Nazi officials took a the-more-the-merrier approach to producing English-language books within its borders. In a stronger economy, they might have taken sides, favoring Tauchnitz over Albatross. But the German economy remained paralyzed by foreign currency shortfalls. Despite stricter surveillance, its gold and foreign currency reserves had dropped: from roughly 980 million RM in 1932 down to 530 million RM in 1933. Since 1931, when Germany abandoned the gold standard, the Reichsmark had not been competitive with other foreign currencies. This made German goods proportionately more expensive than others abroad. The Nazis' political repression exacerbated this grim economic plight; groups of foreign consumers protested Nazi violence and showed their support of German Jews by boycotting German goods. Month by month throughout 1933, exports slowed. Yet Germany still needed currency to pay off 8.3 billion RM of debt to the United States. And the regime was chomping at the bit to rearm its military, a feat that officials knew would require massive expenditures for raw materials, such as iron and oil, that Germany lacked.[22]

Albatross entered Germany, then, at a time when all exports were good exports. As the economic historian Adam Tooze has underscored, "The livelihood of thousands of firms and millions of workers depended on finding customers abroad." By the middle of 1934, Germany's foreign currency reserves had dropped from 530 million RM to a mere 77 million RM—barely enough to cover a week's worth of imports. Exports by summer 1934 were 20 percent lower than they had been twelve months earlier. Germany's trade balance declined into negative numbers. Officials kicked into emergency mode, as they had done in the 1931 summer crisis. On 14 June 1934, Schacht suspended all payments on Germany's international debt. On 23 June, he did away with foreign currency rations to German importers. Shortages were so extreme that the Reichsbank held its remaining reserves close: it would grant money on a daily, rather than a monthly, basis, paying out only as much foreign currency per day as it received. German travelers abroad could count on an exchange ration of no more than 50 RM per month, and could not even take bank bills out of the country, which officials feared would launch a black market trade in German currency.[23]

The Nazis' tolerance for Albatross, seen in this context, sounds a cautionary note about how we approach the topic of censorship itself. "The games themselves are different," notes the cultural historian Robert Darnton, of the rules of censorship from one state and context to the next. And in this way, Albatross's story illuminates a hidden dimension to Nazi censorship: it was, in some cases, as much economic as moral. Historically, censorship has been enacted on moral and often religious grounds by powers ranging from the Catholic Church and kings to governments, both Communist and democratic. And while Nazi officials banned many works on ideological grounds, as Literary Chamber archives attest, officials from the Economics and Finance Ministries also determined which cultural productions should be tolerated on financial grounds. One major goal was not to endanger relationships with Germany's foreign trading partners, the United States and Britain being among the most important. In short, the regime compromised its ideals to preserve its foreign currency income, as it had done before and would do again. As the music historian Michael Kater has pointed out, "If German records of Beethoven symphonies . . . were to be marketed abroad, then British Decca or American Vocalion jazz records featuring the black Louis Armstrong and the Jewish Jean Goldkette had to be allowed into Germany." The regime's readiness, too, in later years, to seize and mock "Degenerate art" but then auction it off to the highest foreign bidders to generate foreign currency fits a similar pattern.[24] The Reich Economics Ministry viewed Albatross, in this light, as a necessary evil and encouraged the company to keep selling English-language books right alongside its German rival.

It is important to note that Albatross gained one critical advantage over German publishers specializing in English-to-German translations, precisely because the Nazis' surveillance of its books was, in the end, so swayed by economic considerations. Nazi authorities wanted Albatross to produce its books in English. In fact, they wanted Albatross to print and sell as many of its books as possible. Abroad, the books reaped foreign currency. Domestically, too, Albatross's need to print four new titles per month, with print runs of between six thousand and eleven thousand copies, kept Brandstetter presses in Leipzig rolling.

Yet if the regime profited from Albatross, it also paid a certain price. The regime's need to privilege money over ideology ultimately elevated Albatross's importance as a publishing house. In much of continental Europe, Albatross was known as the firm that sold modern paperbacks for reasonable prices; in Hitler's Germany, the hefty, and often arbitrary, penalties the regime brought down upon German publishers made Albatross one of the last remaining voices for literary innovation. In tolerating Albatross—albeit for their own financial gain—Nazi authorities paradoxically opened up one space in which the democratic ideals of the Anglo-American literary tradition could still flourish, along with the experimental forms of international literary modernism which the regime had already extinguished.[25]

The Albatross Modern Continental Library was thus, by the end of 1934, stacked with as many contemporary titles as ever. Next to Mansfield's *Letters* were E. M. Forster's *A Passage to India,* whose protagonist sought to develop friendships across race and class, and Charles Morgan's *The Fountain,* billed as one of the best novels of 1932 in British papers. Richard Aldington's *All Men Are Enemies,* banned in Australia for its graphic discussions of sexuality and life in the trenches in World War I, and D. H. Lawrence's *The Rainbow,* banned in England and the United States, also joined Albatross's ranks. With its economic weight, Albatross had turned the knife on its side, walking the blunt, rather than the sharp, edge.

SEVEN

A Tale of Two Publishers

SIX
GOOD POINTS
concerning the
TAUCHNITZ EDITION
and the
ALBATROSS LIBRARY

BY JUNE 1934, THERE was no pretending that Hitler's regime was becoming less tyrannical. Random attacks against Jews continued, largely unchecked. Hitler had done little apart from issuing half-hearted calls for discipline when Nazi Brown Shirts and other thugs assaulted Jews in the streets or attacked their businesses and homes. In a killing spree on 30 June, the regime even massacred its own leaders. In what become known internationally as the Night of the Long Knives—what Germans called the Röhm Purge—Hitler, encircled by members of his entourage, personally raided the hotel in Bad Wiesee, near Munich, where his top S.A. leaders were meeting, pulled some out of their beds, and hauled them into custody at Munich's Stadelheim prison. Ernst Röhm, head of the S.A., had made no secret of his wish to merge the S.A. with the German army and run both divisions. Hitler, wanting the army under his control, claimed to have uncovered a plot against himself, and had six of the S.A. leaders shot without trial. He briefly kept Röhm alive before giving him the option of killing himself or being killed. Hermann Göring authorized hits on other leaders, using the occasion to settle old scores and eliminate Hitler's rivals, whether part of the S.A. or not: among them former chancellor Kurt von Schleicher and Gregor Strasser, former propaganda leader for the NSDAP, both of whom had tried to weaken Hitler's hold over the party.[1]

Hitler justified the killings to the Reichstag on 13 July as his way of protecting the state from traitors and decadents. In a speech reprinted in newspapers around the world, he argued, "Mutinies are broken according to eternal, iron laws. If I am reproached with not turning to the law-courts for sentence, I can only say: in this hour, I was responsible for the fate of the German nation and thereby the supreme judge of the German people. . . . I gave the order to shoot those most guilty of treason, and I further gave the order to burn out down to the raw flesh the ulcers of our internal well-poisoning and the poisoning from abroad."[2]

Many Albatross authors reacted to this violence with revulsion. Two days after the mass killings, Virginia Woolf summarized her conversation with Osbert Sitwell, whose satirical novel *Miracle on Sinai* appeared as Albatross Volume 208. "After hopping & jumping about publishers, Holroyd Reece, lunches dinners & teas, he comes out with 'And can't anything be done about this monstrous affair in Germany?'" Woolf complained bitterly of

> these brutal bullies [who] go about in hoods & masks, like little boys dressed up, acting this idiotic, meaningless, brutal, bloody, pandemonium. In they come while Herr so & so is at lunch: iron boots, they say, grating on the parquet, kill him; & his wife who rushes to the door to prevent them. It is like watching a baboon at the Zoo; only he sucks a paper in which ice has been wrapped, & they fire with revolvers. And here we sit, Osbert I &c, remarking this is inconceivable. A queer state of society. If there were any idea, any vision behind it: but look at the masks these men wear—the brutal faces of baboons, licking sweet paper. And for the first time I read articles with rage, to find him called a real leader.[3]

Other Albatross authors, too, were appalled that the horrific and the everyday existed side by side. In August 1934, Richard Aldington warned his agent not to drive through Germany because Nazi authorities had taken to shooting at cars which did not immediately stop in reaction to their signals. Huxley continued to express his dismay. To one relative, he took some small pleasure in repeating his German friends' description of the propaganda minister: "P.S. the official description of Goebbels is:—nachgedunkelte Schrumpf-Germane—an after-darkened shrink-German. I have tried to find out where it was made, but without success: still, my German friends here swear it's genuine." But for Huxley, Goebbels's propaganda was ultimately no joke. He proposed to his agent in September an article to expose this "new instrument of government of which increasing use is being made in all countries, especially dictatorial ones."[4]

Aldington indicated he would not set foot in Germany, expressing the sentiments of many who deplored the escalation of Nazi inhumanities. Yet in the midst of this outcry, Albatross further solidified its ties to the German economy by finally snatching the prize that had previously eluded it. As Holroyd-Reece exulted, Albatross had taken over "effective control of the now century-old firm of Tauchnitz." In an about-face, Albatross and Tauchnitz promotional materials suddenly presented a united front to continental booksellers and readers. The brochure "Six Good Points Concerning the Tauchnitz Edition and the Albatross Library," for instance, told a new tale that Albatross repeated throughout the 1930s: two once warring publishers working in harmony for the good of Anglo-American literature. A modernized Tauchnitz insignia held sway above the brochure's title, while Albatross's logo floated peacefully just below.[5] With this marriage of convenience, Albatross won strategic control over continental English editions, presenting an optimistically apolitical facade in increasingly dark political times.

Few Tauchnitz or Albatross readers knew the reasons behind the near demise and resurrection of Tauchnitz, or the machinations behind its sale. Word on the street in London was that German currency restrictions had made it difficult for Tauchnitz to reimburse British publishers and that this obstacle had led to the "slowing down" of the esteemed German firm. In book trade circles in Leipzig, another rumor circulated: Sir Edmund Davis, the financial weight behind Albatross, wanted to purchase Tauchnitz. As the publisher Wolfgang Brockhaus remembered, one question cycled through the trade: "Would the old

German firm Bernhard Tauchnitz fall into Jewish hands, and this in the second year after the National Socialist takeover?"[6]

How the various parties resolved this conundrum made a more convoluted story than they cared to tell the public. Strangely enough, the Reich Literary Chamber, charged with oversight of all publishing matters in Germany, had not only approved but also officiated over this international union. Yet its officials had done so more out of necessity than design. They still viewed Albatross as too foreign and too Jewish to be allowed to purchase Tauchnitz outright; however, in the midst of an economic crisis, they could find no German publisher willing to mount enough capital to revive Tauchnitz from its ailing state. With Tauchnitz three years shy of its hundredth anniversary, and the marvelous propaganda opportunities such an occasion promised, the Literary Chamber needed the firm alive and well. A vigorous Tauchnitz, internationally visible, not only projected abroad the image of a more tolerant Germany in intolerant times but ensured ongoing export returns for the Reich. For both propagandistic and financial reasons, then, the Reich Literary Chamber prompted the Brandstetters to purchase Tauchnitz.[7]

In this way, the Tauchnitz heir who had backed out of selling Tauchnitz in 1933 for fear of Nazi retribution had reappeared in mid-1934, as Holroyd-Reece explained, "anxious to sell to us, provided the shares were not passed into British hands." Holroyd-Reece, master of grand schemes, had merely needed to respect the letter of the law to find a more "purely" German partner. The Brandstetter firm was a logical choice. Brandstetter printed Albatross books as well as Tauchnitz books and dictionaries—contracts it stood to lose if Tauchnitz went under.[8]

Since the early 1930s, the Brandstetters had worked the German trade as aggressively as Albatross had plied the continental market. Their firm held a reputation for high-quality printing on cutting-edge machines, and the Brandstetter brothers were risk-taking businessmen. In 1932, the Dresdner Bank noted what a lucrative client the firm had become. Between its printing business and other firms that Brandstetters had recently "acquired," it had posted returns of 6.7 million RM in 1930, rising to 8.4 million RM in 1931. It was also a major Leipzig employer, with 997 employees on average in 1930 and 1,014 in 1931. Brandstetter forcefully sought large contracts and had just won a lucrative five-year bid for the Leipzig telephone and address book.[9]

Holroyd-Reece thus caught the Brandstetters in a phase of expansion, when they were predisposed to say yes. As one Brandstetter associate recalled, Oscar "Willy" Brandstetter and his brother Justus were quite taken with Holroyd-Reece's plan when they met with him at a Basel hotel in summer 1934. Holroyd-Reece poured on the charm, staging "simulated telephone conversations" with the hotel porter to play up his contacts with the best-known Anglo-American authors. His proposal relied upon a division of labor: the Brandstetters would serve as legal owners of Tauchnitz, leaving Albatross to manage and edit the Tauchnitz series, in exchange for a fixed percentage of sales. Remaining evidence suggests that Literary Chamber officials pressured the Brandstetters to accept these terms. Yet since the Brandstetters were, by the assessment of at least one bank, overextended, Holroyd-Reece sweetened the deal. "I lent a sum of money to Messrs Brandstetter of Leipzig," he explained. "Messrs Brandstetter bought the firm of Tauchnitz for their own account and liquidated it the day it was bought, transferring the assets and liabilities to a new [Tauchnitz] firm." On 3 August, four members of the Brandstetter firm—Willy and Justus, their brother-in-law, Raymund Schmidt, and an associate, Karl Krameyer—purchased the entire capital stock.[10]

In late September, Holroyd-Reece and the Tauchnitz owners signed the agreements that would guarantee Albatross a role in the German economy for years to come. On 29 September 1934, a two-page *Börsenblatt* notice announced that the Brandstetters had purchased Tauchnitz and that as of 1 October the Oscar Enoch firm in Hamburg would take over Tauchnitz distribution. The old Tauchnitz was transformed into the new, in a ludicrous jumble of words: "Bernhard Tauchnitz Successors Oscar Brandstetter." Justus Brandstetter defined for the Reichsbank the contracts they had signed: one whereby Albatross would "take over the entire management of the Tauchnitz firm"; and the second, a three-way Albatross-Tauchnitz-Brandstetter contract, which promised "a profitable management of Tauchnitz through Albatross." Holroyd-Reece's description, in contrast, more sharply suggests how much power the Brandstetters ceded to Albatross: "The management of the new firm of Tauchnitz was exclusively in the hands of the Albatross to such an extent that Branstetter [*sic*] were not allowed except through the intermediary of the Albatross, to use the name of Tauchnitz in any shape or form." Holroyd-Reece and Wegner would henceforth decide the content of Tauchnitz books, sign up authors, and pay royalties. Enoch would handle Tauchnitz sales, promotion, and export documentation, as he did for Albatross, with his contract specifying, "Tauchnitz is not allowed to undertake sales without the involvement of Enoch."[11]

So it happened that the Albatross leaders, and the foreign, Jewish capital behind them, became the hope of Tauchnitz's future. Wegner was called back to the Tauchnitz helm, a triumph after being cast off less than four years earlier. Holroyd-Reece presided over the realm of continental English editions. And perhaps most unexpected of all for the German book trade professionals who had aligned their businesses with National Socialist restrictions, the Literary Chamber had engineered a deal that put Enoch, a Jewish publisher-distributor, in sole charge of distributing the books of the venerable Tauchnitz enterprise.

Initially, Literary Chamber officials willingly ignored the incompatibility between Nazi ideology and the Albatross-Tauchnitz-Brandstetter partnership. They had gotten what they wanted: the chance to preserve Tauchnitz's legacy for the German firm's centenary. On paper, for propaganda purposes, the well-respected Brandstetter printers, a fully German firm, controlled Tauchnitz. Full stop. As long as Albatross and Tauchnitz kept up sales abroad, officials left the firms to run much as the directors would.

Still, inconsistencies abounded. While Albatross-Tauchnitz matters in Germany fell under Nazi jurisdiction, the contracts with the Brandstetters left Holroyd-Reece free to promote Tauchnitz as he wished abroad, a situation he used to good effect. One tell-tale sign of his intervention in Brandstetter affairs appeared in a letter to the editor of the *Observer* in October 1934, presumably penned by Holroyd-Reece, in which the new, improved Brandstetter-Tauchnitz firm justified the cultural-political importance of English editions for readers in Hitler's Germany. "At present," the letter reminded British readers, "owing to the difficulties in Germany, which practically prevent the importation of English books, the only means which buyers in Germany have of acquiring the most important English fiction is by buying it in the Tauchnitz and Albatross editions. The value of this commerce is not limited to its purely commercial aspect, because nothing is calculated to foster abroad an understanding of the Anglo-American literary mind better than the study of the literary output of the English-speaking world."[12] Needless to say, Nazi cultural officials would not have endorsed this mission statement, which so closely echoed the agenda of the British Foreign Office and British Council; they cared only about the commercial benefits Albatross-Tauchnitz exports might win them.

Yet if Holroyd-Reece gained control of Tauchnitz's public image in the deal he had struck with the Brandstetters, he also gambled when he yoked Albatross and Tauchnitz operations across national lines and divergent political systems. National Socialist attitudes had insinuated themselves into the Albatross-Tauchnitz-Brandstetter partnership. Early in 1933, Willy Brandstetter had joined the NSDAP, ostensibly to put himself and his firms on the right side of government intervention. On 4 February 1934, the German Labor Front leader of Sachsen and the director of the National Socialist Factory Organization toured the Brandstetter print works, the event hitting a festive ideological note. At the end of the seventy-five-minute tour, the German Labor Front leader spoke to the personnel, twelve hundred strong, the *Börsenblatt* reported. "Brief thanks from the head of the firm and a threefold 'Sieg Heil!' to the People's Chancellor wrapped up the impressive tour, which contributed to the tying of an even tighter bond between the leadership and the workers."[13]

Such was the reality that Albatross leaders knowingly accepted. And that reality was only to become more circumscribed by regulation in the autumn of 1934, when the Literary Chamber delivered a strong message: the state and the book trade would henceforth speak with one voice. On 21 September, in the very week that Albatross celebrated its "effective control" over Tauchnitz, the Literary Chamber engineered a takeover of the German Publishers' and Booksellers' Association, the official book trade organization that had operated independent of the state since its founding in 1825. Although the association had succumbed to the regime's wishes regarding the book burnings and the "Jewish question," its former president had rejected the Literary Chamber's plan for the government to subsidize and control exports. Angered, the chamber installed its own vice president at the head of the Börsenverein to ensure unity between the two organizations. On 15 October, to further minimize potential dissent, the Literary Chamber forged a new organization, the League of Reich-German Booksellers, which all book trade professionals were obliged to join. Whereas the German Publishers' and Booksellers' Association had had 7,700 members, the league centralized its power over 25,000 individuals. Four days later, on 19 October, the Literary Chamber announced that the League of Reich-German Booksellers would henceforth direct book trade policy; in this maneuver, the once influential German Publishers' and Booksellers' Association was essentially reduced to a handmaiden for business the Literary Chamber did not care to handle.[14]

In the midst of such power plays, Albatross remained the strange bird it had always been. Along with all German publishers, it was required to join the league to keep its doors open in Germany; yet at the same time it was not allowed to do so because of its foreign ties. Nazi officials improvised. While the Publishing Holding Company, which owned Albatross, was British, the Albatross Verlag had legal status as a German firm, a fact confirmed in the *Address Book for the German Book Trade* since 1933. Its contract with Tauchnitz made Albatross indispensable to the Brandstetter conglomerate, and the regime wanted both English-language series to flourish and to generate foreign currency. The Albatross-Tauchnitz partnership handed the regime a way out of its conundrum: the two firms would share a membership.[15]

Enoch also improvised, waiting to see how National Socialist policy would seep into his business affairs. He attended the first meeting of the League of Reich-German Booksellers, curious to hear Goebbels give the keynote address. Writing even-handedly years later, Enoch noted that "many of my colleagues including some Party members went out of their way to be friendly or at least polite to me." But his very understatement—as if politeness were the most he could hope for—suggests the strained atmosphere. Since 1921, he had immersed himself in the traditions of the trade, attending book trade meetings, publishing *Börsenblatt* articles, and joining the German branch of the international PEN club.[16] It must have been disturbing to stand among formerly trusted colleagues and encounter nothing more than cordiality.

What it meant to be a German publisher—or a publisher tied to Hitler's Germany—had changed inestimably since Albatross had first settled into the German market. On 5 November 1934, in his speech for the opening of Book Week Berlin's stadium, the Sportpalast, Goebbels set forth his vision of the German book trade's responsibility to the Volk. Urging German publishers and writers to turn German books away from the trendy intellectualism of the Weimar era, he argued that Germany needed a new language: "We [want] to turn toward the broad mass of the Volk, . . . and we [need], therefore, also to speak another language than that which was fashionable in the realms of so-called intellectuality." The German book should engage with the problems of its day.

"Everywhere, one hears the complaint, the Volk no longer have a relationship to the Book!" Goebbels said. "The sentence would be truer in reverse: the book no longer has a relationship to the Volk!" It was now the job of each and every publisher and writer to ensure that culture served the state. "In the National Socialist state it is quite unthinkable that art belongs to the artist," proclaimed Goebbels, "and that the artist holds the privilege of leading a lonely and unknown existence in the rarified atmosphere of the aesthetic or of literature above the Volk." Instead, "the book must return to the Volk." Goebbels left his listeners with one final principle: "Hold tightly to the German book, and you protect therewith the priceless treasure of the German spirit!" His speech was met with thunderous applause.[17]

Albatross had outmaneuvered Tauchnitz, to be sure. Yet what this partnership would mean under the Nazi regime was still a mystery. For all that Albatross had driven its stakes deeper into the German book trade, neither Albatross nor Tauchnitz books fit the definition of the "good books" or the "new language" Goebbels had in mind. Enoch operated in an uneasy stasis, diligently working in Hamburg in a trade that had declared itself inhospitable to his presence and to the books he sold.

Holroyd-Reece, sage enough to understand the precariousness of Albatross's new position in the German economy, hedged his bets to protect Albatross assets. The Paris Registry of Commerce records that on 11 November 1934, three years after Wegner had signed the Albatross Verlag into being in Hamburg, Holroyd-Reece launched a French company called Continenta with the modest sum of twenty-five thousand French francs. Two weeks later, on 26 November, he added another firm, La Société les Éditions Albatros. Up until this time, the Paris Albatross office had merely been an offshoot of the home base in Hamburg. Now, by legally incorporating a French Albatross, Holroyd-Reece was building Albatross's infrastructure to accommodate a host of eventualities. Éditions Albatros could act as a shell company to receive payments on the German Albatross firm's behalf, or, in more dire circumstances, to host Enoch's operations should it be necessary to move them from Germany. Holroyd-Reece also took steps to incorporate an Albatross Ltd. in England.[18] For a time each of these new companies would slumber, poised to awaken when the need and opportunity arose.

Yet with the Nazis' awareness of Albatross slowly growing, it was a risk for

Albatross leaders to trust that winning Tauchnitz—and gaining more control over Anglo-American books in the Reich—would be worth the political fallout. The new Tauchnitz CEO and part owner, Karl Krameyer, left no doubt that National Socialism would play a guiding role in the Brandstetter enterprises. On 2 January 1935, he greeted his assembled employees to celebrate one Herr Kaden, retiring after five decades of service. Krameyer bade adieu to the old year and greeted the new by telling workers the bad news (they would not receive Christmas bonus checks) and the good (the Brandstetters had made investments to increase their printing contracts). Everyone needed to pull together, guided by National Socialism. "However, it takes more comradeship, more discipline, more mutual trust, and more positive collaboration," Krameyer proclaimed. Wishing Herr Kaden well, Krameyer closed his speech with his hopes for the New Year: "To you, my comrades in work, may our old Kaden's loyal performance of his duty be a shining example. And now, onward, with cheerful courage to work in a hopefully successful 1935. Heil Hitler!"[19]

EIGHT

The Center Will Not Hold

WHILE ALBATROSS HAD gotten its wish—control over Tauchnitz—Enoch had little to celebrate as 1935 began, though he was probably relieved to consign 1934 to the past. His father had passed away in July after a long illness, making his mother dependent on him. His wife, Hertha, had died from tuberculosis at a sanatorium in Davos. They had been separated for years, but had, in his words, "remained close" and planned to emigrate to France "for a new life as a reunited family." Her death dashed these plans and left him truly responsible for the well-being of his children, Ruth and Mirjam, age twelve and almost eleven, for the first time, a task he was not well equipped to take on.[1] That he lived surrounded by anti-Semitism in the book trade to which he had devoted much of his life was one more loss among many.

Jeanne Holroyd-Reece sympathized with Enoch's plight. Like Annemarie Wegner, she worked alongside her husband in Paris and so absorbed the shocks to the firm she had helped build. Sensing that Albatross's success could not offset Enoch's personal losses, she sent him an encouraging New Year's letter. "We are very near 1935 and it is always the unexpected that happens. I wish you from the depths of my heart such a lot of good unexpected," she wrote. "There are times in life when the shocks one has to bear are such that one wonders why and how one can go on. It seems to me that you have gone through a period of this kind and that is when friends are needed and should come forth."[2]

Enoch was not, it must be said, an easy man to know well, even in good times. He was socially charming but also brusque and bossy, a man who assumed he was right and brushed off criticism. Like many German men of his generation, he kept his feelings to himself and pushed forward with the tasks at hand, making it hard to read beneath the surface. Yet it was this quality, too, that made him an asset to Albatross in general and to John Holroyd-Reece in particular. "You have been to him the one great help in the last year and a half," wrote Jeanne, "your incredible and alive interest, your sense of responsibility, your human and straight view of our problems in such a great and dignified manner, has helped him more than anything." She thanked him not just for seeing through the chaos to a possible order, but for seeing beyond his troubles to validate her husband's contribution. "You know, dear Mr. Enoch, in all John's business experience, it is the very first time that someone working with him has been gallant enough to recognize the immense pains and work he has done for others. . . . I think it has filled him with more courage and gladness than getting the whole T[auchnitz] business!"

Enoch would have little time to relish Albatross's accomplishments. The unexpected was about to happen, but not the "good unexpected" that Jeanne Holroyd-Reece wished for him. On 12 March 1935, he received a letter from the Reich Press Chamber declaring that non-Aryans were not "sufficiently suitable or reliable to carry out its laws" and ordering him to sell his distribution business to an "Aryan" or liquidate it. Most Jewish owners of art galleries and bookstores in Hamburg had received the same letter with its professional death sentence. Enoch realized that he would have to find a way out of the impasse or leave the country.[3]

Structurally, the outlines of Enoch's story appear familiar. Like many Jews who emigrated early in Hitler's regime, he could have paid the so-called Reich flight tax and left at any time. The regime would have been only too glad to see such a prominent Jewish publisher cross its borders. Yet Enoch did not just want to leave; he wanted to take his business with him. His extended family depended on him. His mother did not work, and his sister had worked for him ever since she had been barred from her position as a chemist. "[It] was imperative for me to maintain this resource of income either as long as possible in Germany or to find a substitute abroad," he recalled. Like other German Jews, he calculated his level of risk. He was no stranger to precarious times and might have felt he could survive them once more. He had published few books that would bring the censors down upon him. And for a time, his status as a decorated World War I veteran granted him exemptions from the regime's anti-Jewish laws.[4]

The Albatross-Tauchnitz venture could not shelter Enoch from the humiliations of being Jewish under Hitler. But Enoch's story departs from well-trodden ground because these business ties did offer him a protection most German-Jewish publishers could not claim. The fruits of the Albatross-Tauchnitz partnership had shown themselves by the end of 1934. Combined, the firms reported sales of 452,983 volumes abroad—500,000 RM of sales, which, even after foreign currency transfers to pay for the French Albatross-Tauchnitz office, yielded a surplus of 264,000 RM for the Reich. In 1935, this surplus rose to 293,000 RM. In March 1935, Tauchnitz alone reached monthly sales of 28,000–30,000 copies between Germany and markets abroad. These figures were promising; Germany was still strapped for foreign currency. Reichsbank demand in 1935 far exceeded intake, with 520 million RM estimated in foreign currency needs per month, and only roughly 370 million RM available.[5] And so Enoch was caught between two chairs, as the German expression goes. The Reich valued his earning power; yet he also held a letter from the Press Chamber that had abruptly shut it down. Being the sort of man who took charge, Enoch appealed his case to the Hamburg Economics Department.

Enoch's appeal, like Albatross books themselves, inadvertently forced the question of National Socialist priorities. Where Albatross books were concerned, officials had suspended their literary ideals for the foreign currency Albatross titles might bring in. Yet the stakes were different when it came to Jewish businesses. The Nazi bureaucracy split neatly into factions. In fact, Jewish professionals who challenged the system found themselves caught in the crossfire between the cultural bureaucracy headed by Goebbels (Reich Propaganda Minister, as well as president of the Reich Chamber of Culture) and the financial bureaucracy headed by Hjalmar Schacht (Reichsbank president and Reich Minister of Economics). By the end of 1934, the two men were disagreeing fiercely over whether to "purify" the book trade of Jews—Goebbels's priority—or to protect their earning power, as Schacht wished.

There was certainly ample political will to oust Jews from the market. In 1933, especially in rural areas, a "sometimes creeping, sometimes galloping" process of "Aryanization" had already been set in motion. Midway through 1935, 20 to 25 percent of the hundred thousand Jewish businesses listed in the 1933 census had been pressured into closing shop. Yet the Reich Economics Ministry urged caution, maintaining until the end of 1937 that Jews were not to be banned from private industry. Schacht had gone to the very top to get Hitler's backing, arguing that with the German economy on the rocks, it was critical to avoid changes in ownership that could spark further job losses. Reich Interior Minister Wilhelm Frick had also passed a decree on 17 January 1934 that forbade authorities to apply Aryan Paragraphs—which excluded Jews—to private industry. Under this decree, Enoch's enterprises should have been protected. Perhaps no one articulated the contradiction better than Hermann Göring. In May 1932, he ranted that Germany should pull Jews "out of every position in which they could exert a corrosive, anti-national, international, or at best, a-national influence to the detriment of the German Volk." He left, however, one exception open: "The reputable Israeli businessman, who wants to remain in Germany as a foreigner, will be allowed to ply his trade and will suffer no damages at all."[6]

Enoch counted on the fact that the regime would put economics over ideology, as it had in tolerating Albatross books. Firms like Albatross and Tauchnitz that specialized in exports and enjoyed international visibility had the best chance of fitting through the narrowing tunnel of government sanctions; even Goebbels demanded special treatment for enterprises whose closure would cause "grave artistic, domestic or international political or economic disadvantages that could impinge on communal life." Enoch's appeal, sent to Goebbels—as president of the Reich Chamber of Culture—thus stressed his value to Germany, as a veteran but primarily as a foreign currency earner. His business is "predominantly an export business," summarized one report, "with direct, evidently family-like connections to Paris and other places. Allegedly, his operation is so strongly dependent on his personal role that it is not possible to sell the business because no buyer even begins to have at his disposal the necessary personal relationships to the purchasers."[7] If Press Chamber officials forced him from the helm, Enoch implied, they would forfeit the export returns that his connections afforded them.

But Goebbels had other ideas. He wanted all Jews out of the German cultural economy, and indeed, in waves throughout 1935, the Literary Chamber, like the other divisions of the Chamber of Culture, had driven Jews from its ranks. In March 1935 it had winnowed out Jewish authors; in the fall, it visited the same grim ostracization on Jewish publishers. "This spiritual and national side of an activity must, however, in the National Socialist state, take priority over the economic," Goebbels insisted to Schacht in December 1935, justifying his course of action. Unable to ignore Schacht's position altogether, though, he snaked a course between extremes, clarifying, somewhat disingenuously, that his mission was not about "liquidating firms" but instead about "eliminating" Jews "*as people* from cultural life." Goebbels vowed to "avoid as far as possible the destruction of economic assets . . . and to show constant consideration for the economic implications of [such] decisions." These distinctions pointed in one direction: Jews would be discreetly forced to sell their firms to "Aryans."[8]

Enoch and Wegner had discussed selling as a last-ditch solution two years earlier, raising the idea that Enoch could, in an emergency, sell his firm to Wegner. Yet Enoch fought this. So did the Hamburg Economics Department, which interceded on his behalf, declaring "unreserved support for the Jewish business owners and argu[ing] that the professional disqualifications that had been issued contradicted all of the declarations of fundamental principle of the highest levels of the Reich." Local officials passed Enoch's case up the ladder to the Hamburg State Office, which requested that the Hamburg Legation in Berlin present the case to the Reich Press Chamber and, ultimately, to the Reich Chamber of Culture—to Goebbels himself. The Hamburg Legation, too, had typically prioritized "economic stabilization over an unregulated policy of displacing Jewish businesses." In Enoch's case, the legation wrote to the Economics Ministry to garner support for his appeal.[9]

The higher Enoch's claim went, the clearer it became that he had launched his appeal into a system that was making up the rules as it went along. Months of conflicting responses filtered back, raising hopes and dashing them, until May 1935, when Enoch received a definitive answer: his appeal was denied. No surviving documents exist to detail the reasoning behind the ruling. Yet success would have been an anomaly. Max Amman, president of the Press Chamber, would have needed to endorse Enoch's appeal—an unlikely action for the head of the official NSDAP publisher, who produced the rabidly anti-Semitic weekly *Das Schwarze Korps.* The Economics Ministry had also taken no forceful action on Enoch's behalf. And when Schacht wrote again to Goebbels in November 1935, sending a copy to Hitler himself, to argue that the well-being of the economy should be put ahead of Goebbels's goal of "purifying" the Reich Chamber of Culture of Jewish influence, it was too late.[10] What Enoch and Wegner had feared on the eve of the boycotts had come to pass. Enoch would need to leave Germany.

*

The documents that detail this phase of Enoch's negotiations with the Nazi regime are densely written in uninspired prose, mired in legalities and minutiae. Yet one fascinating tension emerges, page after page: Albatross's slow (and successful) maneuvering with the Nazi bureaucracy. Holroyd-Reece, in particular, had a knack for leading Nazi authorities away from what he did not want them to see—that Albatross had a cultural mission at odds with National Socialism—toward what he wanted them to believe: that Albatross and its foreign ties worked to Germany's economic and ideological advantage. In May 1935, for instance, he practiced an interesting sleight-of-hand when the Foreign Exchange Office (Devisenstelle) in Hamburg threatened to deny the exorbitant transfers in French francs that the Albatross Verlag sent to Paris each month to fund its French office. To protect Albatross's power base abroad from German intervention, Holroyd-Reece convinced Nazi authorities that the French office did important German propaganda work sub rosa. "At present, with the difficult conditions that persist for every German firm abroad," he wrote, "the worth of foreign representation and an administrative office which can directly meet resistance abroad, is not to be too highly estimated." Albatross and Tauchnitz books were, as he described them in this instance, "goodwill" representatives of German culture in an international market where many consumers refused to buy German goods. They offered proof that Germany remained open to foreign cultures. And they served German financial interests. This logic evidently struck home. As one scholar has noted, "Goebbels's staff seemed to appreciate the degree to which literary prestige was tied to the appearance of relative autonomy from direct political control." Nazi cultural and economic power brokers continued to approve transfers of payments to Paris—leaving Holroyd-Reece free to make many decisions free of Nazi oversight. And they even agreed to ongoing concessions for Albatross, including a special tax break in Germany for Albatross and Tauchnitz authors in May 1935.[11]

To get Enoch out of the country with his distribution operation would require precisely this tactic: persuading naysayers that Albatross was not a negative, Jewish, foreign influence on Tauchnitz but an integral force in an alliance advantageous to the Reich—and that Enoch was critical to its earning power. One longtime friend described Enoch as a "shrewd negotiator and dealmaker, a strong organizer with a sharp financial mind." In December 1935, he made a bold move—probably engineered with his partners to force the issue of his emigration. Albatross met with Brandstetter-Tauchnitz interests on 19 and 20 December to find a way to minimize heavy Tauchnitz losses of 170,000 RM, which the Brandstetters blamed on Albatross management. All were assembled as planned. All were to sign away at least 10,000 RM to restore Tauchnitz's financial health. And then, without warning, Enoch refused to pay. He declared that he would only pay his portion of the Tauchnitz debt if Nazi officials allowed him to relocate his Albatross-Tauchnitz distribution business to Paris.[12] In Hitler's Germany, this gesture carried symbolic weight: a Jewish publisher thwarting a flagship German publisher and printer.

With this maneuver, Enoch and his partners set the stage. Holroyd-Reece and Wegner each played a part. On 21 December, Holroyd-Reece handed Literary Chamber officials a sweet offer. They had long complained that the Parisian Albatross-Tauchnitz office required higher transfers than other export publishers to cover its costs abroad. If Enoch were allowed to emigrate, Albatross proposed, the French office would reduce its fees. Monthly payments would drop from 11,600 to 10,000 RM when Wegner returned to Germany, taking on responsibilities the French office had traditionally handled. It would trim payments another 2,000 RM "as soon as Herr Dr. K. Enoch had transferred his foreign distribution operation for A[lbatross] and T[auchnitz]" to Paris. And once Enoch's operations were fully integrated with the French office, transfers would rest at a monthly low of 6,000 RM. This offer was designed to whet the appetites of the financial, as well as the literary, powers-that-be. The Reich Center for Foreign Exchange Control in Berlin, which oversaw Albatross's immense transfers each month, had pressured its Hamburg office to force Albatross and Tauchnitz to curb their expenditures. Now, overnight, the French office had offered to halve the monthly payments, saving the regime nearly 70,000 RM in foreign currency transfers each year—and all for the removal of one Jewish publisher whom the Literary Chamber wanted to see disappear anyway.[13]

Albatross dangled the lure, but hooking the Nazi bureaucracy would require a far more involved legal process. For this second appeal, Enoch did not just build a defense; he forged a defense team. Albatross enlisted the Brandstetters, along with a team of "Aryan" experts who finessed his emigration strategy. "Fitting all pieces of this plan together took a very long time," Enoch wrote, "filled with intricate negotiations, removal of stumbling blocks, frustrations and also fear of stirring up unfavorable curiosity within the bureaucracy. . . . But risks had to be taken." As an exporter, Enoch needed approval from cultural and financial ministries to exit Germany with a stock of books to launch a distribution operation abroad. To this end, Albatross hired a well-connected lawyer, Dr. Hans Schöne, to secure the support of higher-ups from the relevant bureaucracies, and to drop their names at appropriate moments: Karl Heinrich Bischoff, one of the two section heads of the Literary Chamber division monitoring the book trade; Paul Hövel, charged with "German Literature: Abroad" in the Reich Literature Office (Reichsschrifttumsstelle) of the Propaganda Ministry; and the Reichsbank vice president, Fritz Dreyse. Hövel was an especially important link between factions; his dissertation on the economics of cultural products argued for the Economic Ministry's position that increasing exports was the best way to offset Germany's foreign currency crisis.[14]

Even with these formidable resources, the odds were against Enoch. By the end of January 1936, when he launched his second appeal, the Literary Chamber had shut out 273 Jewish publishers and distributors, leaving 179 cases to be settled. Enoch's account of his emigration, written years later, downplayed the ambiguity of his case. In one page, he outlined his plan. In another, he summarized its obstacles. Of his own emotions in a time of great duress, he made little note. "The thought of immigration, of leaving all that had meant 'home' for soul, body, and mind, to cut one's self off from roots and traditions deeply imbedded for many generations, was an extremely painful one," he admitted. "But it was necessary."[15] Enoch elaborated neither on the reaction of authorities nor their demands. The remaining Literary Chamber files are also silent—a not unusual lacuna, since the seventy thousand files of the "Book Trade Group" were destroyed in the Allied bombing of Leipzig in 1943. What survive are other threads, from other ministries, documenting how close the regime came to denying his appeal.

On 17 January 1936, Schöne sent to the Literary Chamber and foreign exchange authorities in Hamburg and Berlin a ten-page letter crafted around an issue close to the regime's heart: money. In exchange for leaving Germany, Enoch wanted to purchase roughly 60,000 RM's worth of Albatross and Tauchnitz books—ninety thousand books, as the Literary Chamber had suggested—to launch his Parisian distribution business. The trick, for Schöne, was convincing officials that Enoch was not covertly smuggling Jewish assets across Reich borders. He based his appeal on Nazi logic. A fourth-generation German, Enoch had been decorated for fighting for the homeland in the Great War, Schöne argued, and had become an enterprising businessman who benefited the German economy. As 65 percent of Tauchnitz books and 75 percent of Albatross books were sold abroad, Albatross and Tauchnitz had forged a lucrative partnership earning foreign currency for the Reich. This merger, in which Enoch had played a critical role, had saved Tauchnitz from demise and increased export returns.

In essence, Schöne made Enoch's emigration into the means for giving sparring Reich bureaucracies what they wanted. It would cut nearly in half Reich outlays to the French office, while silently removing Enoch from the German book trade, appeasing both financial and cultural officials. Enoch's mass purchase of books would be a boon to the Brandstetters. Too, while Enoch would distribute Albatross-Tauchnitz books outside Reich borders, a Brandstetter-owned firm would win business distributing them in the Reich. Economically, Enoch's emigration would allow him to match or even to surpass "a foreign sales turnover from the Albatross and Tauchnitz concerns with a existing value, already, of RM 500,000–." His ability to work foreign markets more directly would help Albatross and Tauchnitz protect its market share "against the strong appearance of foreign [British] competition and foreign boycott endeavors." German foreign currency restrictions continually threatened to destabilize these firms; each time the French office lacked currency to fund its own expenses or travel and royalties, it endangered the ability of Albatross and Tauchnitz to conduct business and maintain their reputations abroad. And finally, Enoch had agreed to transfer his publishing house and his newspaper distribution business in Hamburg "into Aryan possession."[16]

The Reich Center for Foreign Exchange Control in Berlin—the supreme office policing the movement of foreign currency across national borders—was still suspicious and requested additional documentation. Officials needed reassurance that Albatross would not pull up stakes and leave Germany altogether. The Literary Chamber, having helped to craft the deal, offered no resistance. In a letter of 16 May 1936, its president, the poet Hanns Johst, explained to the Reich Center for Foreign Exchange Control that he had no reservations about Enoch's application, but that he was not sure that Albatross and Tauchnitz earned enough hard currency for the Reich to make them worth the trouble. Still, Enoch had won Literary Chamber approval, enough to get him halfway on the road to France.[17]

As Enoch waited for approvals from financial authorities, he coordinated the back end of his emigration: French permissions. If in Germany he was too Jewish, he found that in France he was both too Jewish and too German. An "often heard axiom was: . . . 'Mistrust all foreigners, but particularly the Germans,'" he wrote. "Also anti-Semitism was traditional and widespread." The French government, generally sympathetic to refugees from Nazi Germany, carefully policed applications for residence and working permits. Enoch's travels to Paris and London, preparing the way for his hoped-for move, were "hectic and strenuous," he wrote. "It was difficult to deal with an alien and often hostile bureaucracy, a different body of law and regulations with people who did not speak my language and had life habits which were quite different from those I was used to. At the same time it was exhilarating to breathe, even if only for a few days at a time, the air of a free country, to feel the independence of spirit of the people, the *joie de vivre* of youth in the sidewalk cafés, to enjoy the absence of uniforms, marches, demonstrations, banners, and other reminders of the police state."[18]

Returning to Hamburg, Enoch adapted again to the world of Nazi restriction, disdain, and surveillance. His only truly pleasant outlook, he admitted, was the "spectacular view" from his apartment, "of several mile-wide waterways with their traffic of small and large boats, freighters and ocean-liners carrying flags of many nations, which for me provided a symbolic contact with the outside world." He watched and waited, tending his Albatross-Tauchnitz sales and preparing to sell his Hamburg businesses to the "Aryan" who knew them best: Wegner. In January 1936, Wegner had moved back to Hamburg from Paris.[19] The two worked in tandem at Enoch's headquarters, the man who owned the businesses next to the one who would soon take them over—one more disconnect in a disconnected world.

*

Between its Brandstetter-Tauchnitz partnership and Enoch's intolerable position, Albatross's lines of affiliation were stretched taut by political pressures, the day-to-day reality of being a multinational firm caught between National Socialism and democracy. Its leaders still played with the firm's pliant international connections, as they always had. Yet they played for different stakes from those of the heady days before Hitler had claimed power. With the British and German governments eyeing one another suspiciously, each slowly gathering its forces against the other, it was necessary to take sides.

Against this backdrop of mounting international tensions, Enoch walked the wire between British capital and German production. His entire future depended on authorities in Hamburg and Berlin believing the core of his carefully calibrated appeal: that Albatross and Tauchnitz worked for the financial and cultural benefit of the Nazi regime and that he, despite his Jewishness, was the best man to move these interests forward. Holroyd-Reece, too, walked the wire, but in the other direction. In times of growing anti-German sentiment in Britain, he needed to keep Albatross's pro-British message before the right eyes. As Albatross rounded out its first year of partnership with the Brandstetter-Tauchnitz concern, Holroyd-Reece met with the British Foreign Office. The Foreign Office has since destroyed the file, leaving only a trace, a tantalizing reference in its correspondence index for 1935: "Publication of British books in Germany by the Albatross Library: scheme of the Publishing Holding Company and activities of Mr. J. Holroyd-Reece in connexion with: support of H[is] M[ajesty's] G[overnment] for: negotiations."[20]

By the summer of 1936, Enoch wanted to be out of Germany, ironically, at the same time that others wanted to come in. Preparations for the Berlin Olympics were in full swing, one more confirmation for Enoch of the world's apathy toward the political situation there. Tourists poured into Germany, down streets where the Olympic flag, with its five interlocking rings, commingled with the swastika-laden circle on the Nazi flag, circles of opposing meaning competing on the same stretch of road. "It was outright disgusting," remarked Enoch," to see . . . visitors to the Olympic Games of 1936 deceived by the temporary removal of anti-Jewish posters and banners and the suspension of other unsavory manifestations of Germany's real face."[21]

Enoch crossed and recrossed Hamburg in June and July, tolerating a humiliating array of intrusions, as he gathered documents from multiple divisions attesting that they had no objections to his leaving. On 19 June, Enoch finally received word from the Reich Center for Foreign Exchange Control that he could purchase his proposed 60,000 RM's worth of books. But there were two conditions: "The books must be purchased and paid for before emigration. It is also to be ensured that only a partial shipment worth 5,000 RM be transferred each month." These conditions kept him at the mercy of the regime. If Reich officials balked at any aspect of his work for Albatross and Tauchnitz abroad, they needed merely to hold his books hostage to destabilize his entire financial foundation. On 7 July, the Hamburg Foreign Exchange Office approved his preliminary emigration pass. Enoch became a number: F V/91/36. Weeks later, on 28 July, he waited for confirmation from the regional finance president (Oberfinanzpräsident) in Hamburg who would seal Enoch's fate. "I ask of you now to grant me the final authorization with greatest haste," Enoch wrote, knowing that his " preapproval" for taking books out of the country was good only until 1 October 1936. With each day squandered, his escape hatch closed another fraction. Still, the finance president dragged out his response another week, finally granting approval on 6 August for the monthly book deliveries to Paris. The very next day, 7 August, Enoch handed over to the Hamburg Foreign Exchange Office the receipts proving he had purchased 37,878 Albatross and 53,030 Tauchnitz books. Enoch now owned, but did not yet truly possess, the raw materials with which he would build his new life in Paris—if and when authorities transported them to France as promised.[22]

Travels abroad, takeoffs and landings: tourists spilling into Germany for the Olympics; Enoch preparing, finally, to set foot on the plane that would carry him away. So many leave-takings carried the promise of return curled up inside them, except that in Enoch's case, when he gathered his belongings on 8 August 1936, he knew he could not and would not return. For each item he had gathered —each document, each stamp on each passport, each Reichsmark to pay for each vibrantly colored Albatross book—he had closed off another part of his world. A week of lasts: the last train ride from the quiet suburb of Blankenese to his office at the bustling city's core, the last step from the creaking elevator after a long day of work, the last glimpse outside his windows onto the Elbe, where day sailors circled the harbor, ceding passage to the freighters determinedly making their way northwest until the river widened at Brunsbüttel, breaching the mouth of the river near Cuxhaven, to spill out into the expanse of the North Sea.

On his last day, Enoch relinquished the final vestige of his professional life in Germany. He wrote to the Literary Chamber, resigning his membership in the League of Reich-German Booksellers. "I have, today, given up my German residence, because of negotiations known and encouraged by the Reich Literary Chamber for me to move my base abroad," he reported. "As the Reich Literary Chamber also knows, I have transferred my businesses in Hamburg to the Albatross managing director to date, the publisher M. C. Wegner, now in Hamburg." In this matter-of-fact way, Enoch reminded officials that he had followed their protocols. He ended with a strangely conciliatory gesture, perhaps born of his nervousness at the magnitude of the shift before him or his desire to show officials a spirit of cooperation so they would not withhold his books. "From my foreign residence, I hope to work with success, promoting exports of the Tauchnitz and Albatross Edition, but also the products of other German publishers."[23]

Enoch left no account of his farewell to his friends and family remaining in

Germany, or to his employees at the businesses he had worked so hard to build. This is not surprising. Many of his Jewish employees had received clearance to work for him in Paris, so the break with the past would not be complete. But there is also the fact of Enoch himself. A friend of thirty years described him as an "emotional man who kept his emotions under discipline."[24] What in his lifetime could have prepared him for such a departure? The Jewish publisher Bermann Fischer, whose emigration plan had provided a model for Enoch's own, put into words the bleak scene of his farewell from the business he had tended and built, the homeland he had loved and was forced to flee: "How can I portray my farewell from Germany? How can I say what I felt when I stood opposite my colleagues in the publishing house for the last time? For the last time! That there was a last time, an end! It was like a death that I experienced alive."[25]

Rather than focusing on the moment of farewell, Enoch saved his most vivid description for his moment of departure, his "great relief when finally, for the last time, on the 8th of August 1936, I boarded an Air France plane to Paris, only after every piece of my clothing including the lining of my hat had been turned inside out in search for possibly hidden money or other valuables." Suspended in the air, he was suddenly freed from the lines of distinction that had kept him bound. "Viewing the peaceful looking landscape slowly moving by, thousands of feet below, it was hard to believe that there was an invisible line not designed by nature but drawn by man, which meant the difference between tyranny and liberty," he reflected. "I do not remember in detail all thoughts which went through my mind when we approached that line, but I do know that the question of a possible future return to a Germany reborn in liberty and decency was not among them. I had made a complete break with the past and all my concerns and energies now belonged to the future in which I was resolved to build again a happy and successful life."[26] Enoch's wide expanse lay ahead, he hoped, on the other side of the invisible line that had too long circumscribed his choices.

NINE

The Shell Game

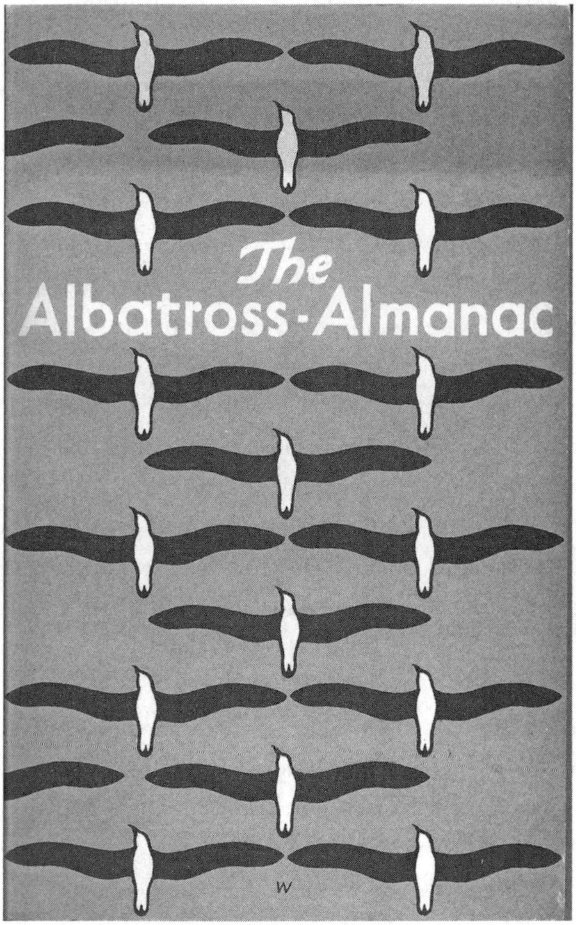

THE COVER OF *The Albatross Almanac* for 1936 featured a flock of birds—all, in a clever visual play, the Albatross logo. The image was captivating in its simplicity. How composed and elegant were these avian hosts in their transit, how free, too, of encumbrances. It was an apt image. Despite the incursions of the Nazi bureaucracy on Albatross's way of doing business, the firm continued to flourish, sending four new titles per month, twelve months per year, across national borders. The cover delivered a timely fantasy, too, of free-spirited flight at a time when flight had become politically laden. Enoch became one of twenty-five thousand Jews to emigrate from Germany in 1936.[1] Wegner made the more unusual journey in the opposite direction, back to Germany, which was spiraling each year into greater unpredictability.

In Nazi math, the switch from Enoch to Wegner meant one Jewish head of Albatross-Tauchnitz distribution in exchange for one "Aryan" managing director. Wegner purchased Enoch's publishing and distribution businesses on 1 September 1936, three weeks after Enoch stepped aboard his flight. The next day a *Börsenblatt* announcement noted the purchase. No mention was made of Albatross. Under the "Aryanization" that Goebbels had pushed forward, this type of announcement had become commonplace. Forced to sell their firms, many Jewish publishers turned, quite naturally, to existing business partners. According to one prominent historian, roughly 20 percent of firms were purchased under fair monetary terms by "Aryan" partners who took over the firm, while Jewish partners started over somewhere out of reach of Nazi policies. Yet in most cases, Jewish firms were sold for a fraction of their actual worth.[2]

The question of whether Enoch got a fair deal is fraught. No matter how sincerely the Albatross partners had agreed that Wegner should purchase Enoch's firms, no matter how much each side gained through agreed-upon terms—negotiated by Enoch's personal and trusted accountant—this transaction remained only the best solution in an abominable situation. "Was this exchange, however, more freighted with conflict?" wondered Christian and Annemarie Wegner's son, Matthias, years later. "One can at least assume that Kurt Enoch took a reserved stance toward the voluntary return of his partner to *this* Germany, even if he himself benefited from it."[3]

Christian Wegner was, in fact, not a likely candidate for return to the rabid state Germany had become. He and Annemarie had adored Paris. They had poured everything into building the Albatross office just south of the Cimitière Montparnasse. They were in love, and Paris was the place where their love had flourished. Annemarie later referred to this period as "the lovely Paris years," and Christian considered Paris his spiritual home. So why not stay when they had had the chance? Christian held himself apart from National Socialism, crossing boycott lines and signing his professional correspondence, "With German greetings," rather than "Heil Hitler." He helped a Jewish friend, one of many former lovers, get out of Germany. A younger Tauchnitz colleague, Wolfgang Krause-Brandstetter, who worked with Christian in the early years of the Albatross-Tauchnitz merger, described him as "always a pronounced anti-Nazi," as well as "a good linguist and a cosmopolitan." One desire seems to have propelled him back. "He must have believed in a propitious career opportunity," reflected Matthias. Hans Otto, Christian Wegner's nemesis at Tauchnitz, had once rightly said that Wegner would never work for Holroyd-Reece long. "We cannot allow ourselves to draw a glib judgment over [what was] a complicated transaction for both sides," concluded Matthias, "yet one thing stands firm: Enoch displayed far-sightedness, C.W. [Christian Wegner] short-sightedness."[4]

This personnel exchange raises another unavoidable question, too: why did Albatross not seize the moment of Enoch's emigration to spirit the entire Albatross operation out of Germany? Enoch had been Albatross's German center, the "Hamburg" listed on every Albatross book cover. Albatross's network radiated out from Paris, too, and as of January 1935, Holroyd-Reece had incorporated Albatross London.[5] That Albatross did not choose to restructure its business outside of Hitler's Germany, whose regime was so hostile to the spirit of the press, seems, on the surface, entirely counterintuitive.

Indeed, authorities from the Reich Center for Foreign Exchange Control in Berlin posed a similar question in the spring of 1936, when they grew suspicious of the financial logic behind Enoch's emigration. With Enoch moving his distribution operation to Paris, next to the existing editorial office, they feared that Albatross might simply pull up stakes in Germany and establish Paris or London as a new base for production. At the Economics Ministry, Schacht viewed the book trade as a pillar of economic stability, one now threatened by the racial policies of the Reich. In February 1936, while Enoch's application was in process, Schacht wrote Hitler, concerned that Aryanization would weaken the export book trade because "the foreign connections are so strongly tied to the person of the former owner that precisely these connections could be torn asunder through an exchange." Watching Enoch board a plane for France, therefore, was not inherently a cause for celebration in the financial bureaucracy. Jewish publishers who left Germany might then set up shop abroad, and Germany would lose these export possibilities altogether.[6]

In fact, the Nazis' fears about Albatross were not realized—not entirely, anyway. For many reasons, it did not serve Holroyd-Reece's interests to dissolve Albatross's German ties. A move across Reich borders would have destroyed Albatross's "takeover" of Tauchnitz, putting at risk Albatross's assets. Specifically, Albatross might lose 450,000 books—"almost the entire production to date"—stored at the Brandstetter printing firm. And while it would be cheaper to produce books abroad, Albatross would never get its foreign-produced books back into Germany, its largest market. "Such a loss of sales is prohibitive for a publishing house," insisted Albatross's lawyer, Dr. Hans Schöne. Albatross also had a binding obligation to print its books with the Brandstetters. Breaking this contract would launch an expensive legal battle, as well as renewed competition between the two firms, which would cost Albatross dearly. Staying in Germany while retaining its French office gave Albatross the best of both worlds, Schöne argued to Nazi officials; it could preserve its partnership with the Brandstetters yet reduce its dependence on monthly German foreign currency transfers—which, when they were delayed, jeopardized the Albatross-Tauchnitz reputation and the stability of both firms abroad.[7]

Yet ironically, the biggest reason that Albatross stayed in Germany was Nazism itself. Precisely because Hitler's Germany was anathema to a humanist vision of books, the cultural mission of Albatross—now one of the sole arbiters of Anglo-American ideas in the Reich—took on heightened importance. As Wegner pointed out to literary agents, it had become increasingly difficult for British publishers to get their books into Germany, less from cultural resistance than because of economic necessity. The Economics Ministry circumscribed "non-vital" imports into Germany wherever possible; in so doing, the regime increased its chances of keeping exports higher than imports so as to accumulate trade surpluses that were essential for purchasing raw materials abroad. As Holroyd-Reece saw it, Albatross functioned as a Trojan horse in this context. It presented a German facade, but held Anglo-American culture at the ready, unleashing it within Reich borders, where it could disarm German nationalism. As long as Albatross kept a presence in Germany, however small, it could continue, as Holroyd-Reece repeated to audiences unsympathetic to Nazi Germany, "to distribute in Germany the literature which was progressively forbidden by the Nazis and which the Albatross alone was continuing to issue abroad."[8]

All seemed as it should be, then, to Nazi authorities as Enoch flew to Paris. They were soon to realize, however, that the Albatross that remained within

Reich borders did not take the shape they had envisioned. While Wegner indeed bought Enoch's firms, he was already planning to leave Albatross altogether. Wegner signed off on Enoch's purchases of Albatross and Tauchnitz books on 7 August, the day before Enoch's departure, and purchased Enoch's firm on 1 September. By then, Enoch and his family had safely made it to Paris. Then, a mere two weeks later, on 15 September, Wegner resigned his post as Albatross managing director. He continued to run Enoch's distribution business under its original name, yet after decades of working for others, Wegner converted Enoch's publishing business into something else entirely: the publishing house in his own name of which he had always dreamed.[9]

While it might seem unlikely, Albatross, too, gained by this arrangement. Albatross lived on in Germany as a distribution center so it could still sell its books in Germany unhindered, yet it had simultaneously consolidated its power and capital in Paris, just out of reach of the Reich. In short, Albatross had not swapped managers or offices so much as it had engineered a bait-and-switch under the noses of Reich authorities in Hamburg and Berlin. Whatever Wegner's level of self-interest in taking over Enoch's firms, his return to Germany was also a critical feature of the unusual emigration deal that Albatross negotiated for Enoch. Numerous documents make clear that Nazi authorities allowed Enoch to emigrate with his livelihood—those ninety thousand books—only because they believed that Wegner was returning to Nazi Germany to lead Albatross forward.

The bait-and-switch was, fortunately for Albatross, not apparent at first to Nazi authorities. Wegner had acted out his part. He moved to Hamburg in January 1936 to work alongside Enoch. In the spring of 1936, he adapted the stationery from the Paris office; next to the phrase "Head Office," he typed a string of x's through the Paris address and replaced it with Enoch's address in Hamburg. As far as officials could tell, Albatross's managing director had come home to run the firm for good, bringing the editorial office from Paris with him. "These negotiations," the Literary Chamber president wrote in May 1936 of Enoch's emigration plan, "have led to a plan to relocate the distribution agency currently in Hamburg and to transfer the Paris agency to Hamburg." He was pleased at this thought. He believed that the Enoch-Wegner switch would yield an immediate monetary gain, since Albatross's Parisian office had cost Germany hundreds of thousands of Reichsmarks in transfers since 1931. By August, he had approved another round of expensive transfers to Paris, but he grew impatient.

"At long last, the relocation should finally be brought off," he noted. "With that, [we] can drop the payments [to Paris]."[10] Only after Wegner's resignation did the truth hit home: Enoch had not just left for Paris, he had taken up leadership at the French office, which had stayed there, still requiring transfers every month.

Holroyd-Reece also gained in other ways from this arrangement. To continue his cultural mission, he moved the remaining "shell" of Albatross headquarters from Hamburg to the Brandstetter premises in Leipzig. It made sense to streamline Albatross operations by relocating closer to its German business partners. Since 1934, Albatross had managed the editorial side of Tauchnitz business for the Brandstetters. And since Enoch's emigration, VAG, a distribution firm owned by the Brandstetters, had also taken over the portion of the Albatross-Tauchnitz business Enoch had been forced to leave behind: distribution inside Reich borders, a task the regime had not wanted to leave in the hands of a Jew.[11]

In an unexpected way, Wegner's departure from Albatross also allowed Holroyd-Reece to dilute the power he accorded to others. Wegner had always been a strong leader, a cofounder of Albatross willing to butt heads with Holroyd-Reece over its fate. On 15 September 1936, to fill Wegner's shoes, Albatross had installed two new managing directors, both trusted and highly capable Albatross associates who were less likely to buck at Holroyd-Reece's dictates: one in France, Jean-Louis Bricaire, and one in Germany, Erich Kupfer.[12] As Albatross director, Holroyd-Reece maintained full power of attorney, with his signature alone being enough to adapt the contracts or structure of Albatross as a whole. In this way, Holroyd-Reece rigged Albatross's structure in Germany to protect it from coming under full-scale German control in the event of war. Holroyd-Reece had won his shell game, at least for the time being.

*

In the mid-1950s, a German graphologist interpreted a sample of Holroyd-Reece's handwriting without knowing to whom it belonged. The writer might be a doctor, or a professor, or perhaps a lawyer, the graphologist speculated, but certainly someone who was "a good talker and highly skilled in negotiation, [and] also in covering up and bending [the truth], when necessary."[13] In finessing Enoch's emigration and Wegner's return, Holroyd-Reece had shown himself to possess all these qualities. Albatross had, for instance, never promised in writing to move its French office back to Germany; it only offered to reduce the fees for the French office once Enoch and Wegner switched places. Albatross let the authorities believe what they wanted to believe—let them overinterpret the written terms of the agreement—until Enoch's emigration was secured. In the end, in fact, the Albatross leaders owed their success as much to the incoherence of the Nazi bureaucracy as to their own cleverness. They exploited the inner workings of German law, to be sure, yet they had an unwitting ally: the fragmentation of the Nazi bureaucracy, characterized by too many talking heads, in too many branches of government, not communicating about the long-term impact of their authorizations.

At many levels, Albatross's interactions with the regime offer an unusual case study showing, up close, how the myth of centralized control and efficiency traditionally associated with the Nazi regime breaks down when we look at actual behavior. Historians have generally come to agree that the Nazi state was characterized by chaos and fragmentation underneath its sheen of ruthless law and order. Jeremy Noakes, a historian of the Nazi Party and administration, succinctly pinpoints a cause of this underlying bedlam: "Because the Nazis had hitherto been concentrating all their efforts on acquiring power, they had made few preparations for government." This disconnect meant that when Hitler seized command there was no coherent plan for integrating the party hierarchy with the existing state bureaucracy. Through the *Führerprinzip*—the so-called leadership principle —Hitler concentrated power in his own hands and delegated responsibilities to his followers, who owed him absolute obedience. Hitler took and granted authority as he wished. He abolished parliamentary procedure, giving the state no say over his decisions. He created new ministries, which were arbitrarily granted jurisdiction over numerous responsibilities— for instance, who oversaw censorship? who could control the police?—that were already regulated by existing institutions. The Nazi Party inserted its own people, many of them untrained, into positions previously held by career civil servants, losing, in the process, years of accumulated experience. What resulted was a kind of functional irrationality, which Jane Caplan, a historian of the Nazi bureaucracy, has termed a "government without administration," replete with contradictions. "The conflict between long-term planning and improvisational opportunism was only one of the fault lines that ran through the Nazi regime from its earliest weeks," Caplan confirms; "equally early to surface were conflicts between centre and periphery, between the institutions of leadership and of execution, and more generally, among the plurality of government institutions, as it became clear that collegial and hierarchical structures of decision-making were breaking down and collapsing into their atomic parts."[14]

These limitations of the regime's so-called polycratic governance quickly made themselves felt when Albatross moved its own center from Hamburg to Leipzig and fell under the oversight of a new regional hierarchy populated by new bureaucrats. To be fair, the confusion that ensued might eventually have arisen in Hamburg, as well. Albatross's structure, stretching across national lines and myriad enterprises, was so intricate that it seemed intentionally designed to thwart understanding; one might say that Holroyd-Reece, in his own elaborate fashion, adapted the Führerprinzip, wanting people to do as he wished rather than to understand why they were doing it. So when Albatross moved its base from Hamburg to Leipzig, the foreign exchange authorities in Hamburg only added to an inherently bewildering situation by dropping the Albatross and Tauchnitz export situation created by Enoch's emigration into the laps of their Leipzig counterparts with little explanation. Holroyd-Reece had created a web whose complexity rivaled that of the Nazi bureaucracy and Leipzig officials wriggled, stuck within it.

For with everything in place and a slew of written reassurances to prove it, the most important piece of the deal for Reich officials failed: the money did not flow from Paris as they had anticipated. Leipzig Reichsbank officials calculated by mid-December 1936—wrongly, as it later turned out—that Enoch owed the Reich 121,400 RM. In short, Albatross was costing the Reich ever more, with the expense of Enoch's book shipments layered atop exorbitant transfers to Paris, while authorities waited, in vain, for Albatross to replenish these outlays. Leipzig authorities panicked. Had their peers in Hamburg blindly let Enoch leave the country with thousands of books? And how had this Jewish publisher been allowed to spirit Albatross and its affiliated firms out of the country, resulting in foreign currency losses Germany could ill afford?[15]

The explanation was simple: Leipzig officials did not understand Enoch's emigration deal. And it was no wonder. Holroyd-Reece had hidden the details of the Wegner-Enoch bait-and-switch within such a thicket of import-export declarations that no one—not even the Hamburg Reichsbank that had overseen Enoch's emigration—had grasped its implications. Only after reviewing Enoch's paperwork three weeks after his departure did a Hamburg Reichsbank official spy reason for concern. Generally, all wares that left Germany to be sold abroad generated revenues—either goods or currency—that came back to the Reich, completing the export circle. As of 1 December 1931, the regional and national foreign exchange watchdog agencies had, in fact, ratcheted up their surveillance over exports to ensure that exporters did not exploit this system. Exporters were required to list all wares shipped outside Germany on Export Valuta Declaration forms; authorities then policed whether the value of goods sold abroad by a particular firm was matched by an equivalent value in goods or currency that flowed back to Germany. A discrepancy in the numbers might indicate that exporters had skimmed profits off the top abroad, to pay their own accounts with foreign suppliers or to invest outside Germany.[16]

Enoch, however, had not been held to these rules. Instead, he had been approved, free and clear, to bring his ninety thousand books to Paris and to keep the revenues from sales of these books abroad for himself, as capital to help him launch his business in Paris. At a time of foreign currency shortfall, a deal of this nature—which cost the Reich tens of thousands of RM in either goods or currency—was shocking. "This transaction was supposedly implemented with the approval of the Reich Literary Chamber and with the authorization of the local Foreign Exchange Office," wrote the Hamburg Reichsbank official to the Hamburg finance president. "We request quick notification, whether the details . . . are accurate." The finance president confirmed that he had, indeed, supported Enoch's application "on account of the decision of the Reich Center for Foreign Exchange Control in Berlin"—the ultimate decision maker in such matters—"*with an addendum of a copy for the Reichsbank.*" He underscored this last phrase, implicitly chastising his underling, as if to say, "Have you people at the Hamburg Reichsbank been paying attention at all?"[17] Here was one price for Hitler's top-down system of government in action: higher-level commands often went unquestioned, even when they did not make sense to the institution in question, leaving lower-level officials with little recourse.

Leipzig authorities, far less schooled in Albatross minutiae than their Hamburg equivalents, knew nothing of such arrangements and unleashed their suspicion on anything and everything Albatross. Leipzig Foreign Exchange Office (Devisenstelle) investigators Gerhard Brueder and Wilhelm Lucke pored through account books, bank statements, correspondence, export forms, foreign debtor accounts, and registry of commerce documents. "The relationships between these firms," they wrote, "are incredibly murky." Enoch's success in establishing himself in exile appalled them even more. "We're talking about a Jew!" they protested, charging that Enoch had "emigrated without authorization, and had illegally brought assets abroad." They were no less stunned that the well-respected Brandstetter concern trusted foreigners and Jews as business partners, and threatened "measures against the firm" if the Brandstetters did not collect the debts and documents which the French Albatross-Tauchnitz office held beyond their reach in Paris.[18]

Despite their attention to detail, Brueder and Lucke were wrong about one thing. "It cannot be presumed," they concluded of Enoch's emigration, "that the authorities would grant their approval to a stealthy relocation of a firm, as is here the case." Yet of course higher officials in both Berlin and Hamburg had been extremely well informed: the Literary Chamber and the Literature Department of the Propaganda Ministry, and the Reich Center for Foreign Exchange Control in Berlin, along with the Hamburg Reichsbank and the Hamburg finance president, not to mention all the offices in and around Hamburg, where Enoch had collected a stack of verifications that he was allowed to leave with his family and livelihood, were all party to the deal.[19]

What Brueder and Lucke took to be bureaucratic incompetence was, in fact, a weakness within the bureaucracy itself. Multiple and overlapping layers of Nazi regulations—administered by agencies that did not accurately communicate the details to one another—had created misunderstandings that would affect Albatross and Enoch for months to come. Brueder and Lucke sought answers at the new address of the Albatross Verlag at the Brandstetter headquarters in Leipzig, only to find the most jarring surprise of all: Albatross, with all its books, papers, and personnel, had seemingly disappeared. "No firm exists at this address," they reported with alarm. "There exist neither business premises, nor a managerial staff . . . , nor are personnel in Leipzig being employed, nor are account books kept." On 4 January, with zero tolerance for a firm with no real office, they urged their superiors to "file for the liquidation of the Albatross Verlag." They froze Albatross assets. They hauled Kupfer—the newly minted German Albatross managing director—back from Paris, where he had spent four months helping Enoch launch Continenta. One week he was in the City of Lights and the next deposited at the token Albatross office in Leipzig—his passport confiscated—while he stood accused of the serious offense of aiding and abetting his Jewish boss to smuggle assets out of the Reich and made responsible for all the ills of his employers.[20] In fact, Kupfer was Albatross's *only* German presence left, the one Albatross asset—apart from its books in Brandstetter warehouses—not dangling out of German reach. What had happened to Albatross in Germany? It had taken Nazi officials several months to articulate this question. It took them years to answer it to their satisfaction.

*

As Germany boiled, Paris remained calm, even for the man who was at the center of the Albatross scandal. Having endured what he called "the fight for survival in the catastrophe of the Nazi era," Enoch was stunned to land in Paris and be treated like any other traveler—with no baggage searches or clamoring over paperwork. He carried only his personal belongings, walking through French customs a regular traveler in a routine world.[21]

The trouble "belonged now to the past," he wrote, "and the hour of a total new beginning was at hand." But the first phase of his life in Paris was lonely; he felt cut off from the past but not yet lodged in any meaningful present. Letters home had to pass the "unfriendly fence" of censorship, making it hard to stay connected with friends and relatives. Having put Nazi Germany behind him, Enoch strove to re-create a sense of home in his new land. "I had the deep desire to grow new roots," he wrote in his memoir, "to regain the feeling of belonging and of identification with the land in which I had found refuge." He remarried, a younger German-Jewish woman, Marga Heinemann, who had emigrated with him. Probably through Holroyd-Reece's connections with the Parisian demimonde, they secured an apartment at 49 quai Bourbon, on the Île Saint-Louis, in a gawky, seven-story building just two windows wide, built centuries earlier and owned by the art patron Princess Bibesco. Walking home along the quai, Enoch could not miss Notre-Dame cathedral arcing up toward the sky or the vines growing riotously over the yellow-white stone walls of the embankment. He had traded his river view in Hamburg for his glimpse of the Seine, "with large French windows giving a view of the other island with the Cathedral and in between the river with its traffic of long convoys of 'péniches,' its sightseeing boats, its quaies with their large old trees." After the indignities of life under Hitler, he was grateful to have landed in this landscape fit for an urban fairy tale. Perhaps, after all, he could belong here, too.[22]

From his new pied-à-terre, Enoch had an enviable commute to the equally impressive offices of Continenta at 16 place Vendôme in the first arrondissement. Cutting north across the Seine, he could catch the Métro from the Hôtel de Ville, disembarking several stops later at the Tuileries Gardens, a few blocks from his office. Or he could walk along the Seine, a brisk half hour, veering north of the quai to pass by the Louvre and through the Tuileries: through the majestically ordered formal allées, past parterre gardens bordered by low plants, and circular pools that dotted the garden's expanse to what Enoch called "one of the most attractive old squares in the center of Paris."[23] Planned by Louis XIV in 1702 to commemorate his armies, place Vendôme was a jewel box of a square. Its rectangular plaza suggested a well-regulated world, with neoclassical house fronts stretching up one side and down the other, as if the entirety were one grand palace. Enoch shared this illustrious plaza with an array of imposing names: Charvet, the high-end shirt maker and tailor, and Van Cleef and Arpels, the toney jeweler. Coco Chanel rented a suite at the Ritz on the opposite side of the square, while the designer Elsa Schiaparelli established her store—nicknamed the "Schiap Shop"—at 21 place Vendôme. Albatross settled into its new home, an up-and-comer in high society.

Behind the well-ordered facade of place Vendôme, Enoch started over, throwing himself into Continenta. While his work "required a great deal of stamina," Enoch relished his travels to and from London. He remembered with fondness his jaunts across the Channel on the "huge biplane 'Hercules,' where a lavish British breakfast was elegantly served." Or on one occasion he tucked into his berth on the night ferry, only to find when he awoke in the morning that the boat remained stuck there, "still in the same fog-bound harbor," in waters too choppy to make the crossing.[24] Metaphors of departure and return, leave-taking and homecoming: Enoch awoke in Paris each morning, but in ways he could not yet fathom he had not fully left Hamburg.

TEN

Suspicion

FROM HOLROYD-REECE'S perspective, there was much to celebrate in Paris. Albatross had decreased its dependence on Germany; Enoch's emigration had pulled control over most Albatross-Tauchnitz distribution beyond Reich borders and increased book stocks in Parisian warehouses. Albatross and Tauchnitz had moved up in the world, trading the rue Boulard for the prestigious place Vendôme. And the coming Tauchnitz centenary gave Holroyd-Reece the perfect platform for selling books and promoting Anglo-American culture. Working side by side with Enoch's distribution operation, his Albatross-Tauchnitz editorial office launched a spirited campaign for the grand occasion of Tauchnitz's hundredth birthday, knowing that readers across Europe would be watching.

The two commemorative volumes that Holroyd-Reece produced for the Tauchnitz centenary—*The Harvest: Being the Record of One Hundred Years of*

Publishing, 1837–1937 and *The Centenary Catalogue of the Tauchnitz Edition*—betrayed his sympathies. Both praised the German innovation behind Tauchnitz, yet neither ultimately embraced Germany as the scene of Tauchnitz's future. The gallery of photos midway through *The Harvest* opened with the first baron von Tauchnitz staring out austerely, decorated with a heavy military cross at his neck and holding a leather-bound book. The second baron von Tauchnitz followed, more professor than nobleman, with his shock of white hair, sweeping mustache, black suit, bow tie, and pince-nez—a German incarnation of Mark Twain. Next came the two-story neoclassical mansion that had served as the original Tauchnitz headquarters, followed by the ornate Jugendstil Brandstetter print works, six stories high, dotted with bas relief images and decorative arches. From this point, Albatross images carried the day: Enoch's former Hamburg headquarters, which the Nazis had forced him to vacate; the demure Paris office where Albatross had been born; and finally, the foyer of the stately Paris head office at place Vendôme, a Grecian affair, with broad stone steps rising between four massive columns. If ever Nazi officials had worried where their transfers of French francs had gone, this array suggested in pictures what Holroyd-Reece did not say in words: Germany was Tauchnitz's origin, but Paris was its future.[1]

Yet if Holroyd-Reece and his partners had outmaneuvered the Reich in the short term, Albatross, Enoch, Tauchnitz, and the Brandstetters were already paying the price. Leipzig authorities could see into the workings of the Paris office little more than readers of *The Harvest:* waiting in the foyer, left to imagine what happened upstairs. Numerous investigators worried that Albatross was being presented as German in the Reich while actually following secret agendas abroad. All Holroyd-Reece's plotting to bolster his French base of operations was, inadvertently, putting his grand office, and the grand plans it embodied, in great peril.

*

From Leipzig, Nazi authorities were closing in on Paris. Investigator Lucke needed no convincing that Albatross was a foreign imposter. A mere three days of rifling through Albatross files in December 1936 had convinced him the regime should shut Albatross's doors forever. Much to his frustration, this had not happened. Instead, in February 1937, Albatross's lawyer, Dr. Hans Schöne, had brilliantly come to the firm's rescue with portfolios of evidence demonstrating that Albatross worked in the regime's interest, financially and—in this year of the

Tauchnitz centenary—culturally, as well. Leipzig authorities had suspended Enoch's book shipments for one month as a warning. Yet otherwise Lucke's Leipzig superiors—taking the lead from their Berlin superiors at the Reich Center for Foreign Exchange Control—had restored to Albatross all its privileges: its assets, Kupfer's passport, and most important for Holroyd-Reece, the monthly transfers to keep Albatross and Tauchnitz from financial ruin in Paris.[2] It is hard to say whether Lucke was more aggravated with Albatross for skirting Reich demands or with Berlin authorities who continued authorizing massive transfers to the Paris office despite his pleas to the contrary.

Against the backdrop of foreign currency shortages that continued to plague the Reich, this whole incident left Lucke and other Leipzig authorities wrestling with grave misgivings and one lingering question: "What importance does the publishing group Albatross-Tauchnitz have for German culture and especially for the German domestic economy?" In the year prior to Enoch's emigration in 1935, Albatross and Tauchnitz had yielded nearly 300,000 RM in foreign currency accruals for the regime, even after paying royalties and office expenses abroad. In the interim, combined Albatross and Tauchnitz sales had slightly increased, as authorities had hoped, from 201,276 copies in the seven months from October 1935 through April 1936, to 215,183 copies from October 1936 through April 1937. Yet in the twelve months following Enoch's departure, Leipzig authorities observed much diminished returns to the Reich of between 30,000 and 75,000 RM, depending on their calculations. Vexed at the thought that Albatross might be returning less than expected to German coffers because of higher foreign expenditures since Enoch's relocation, Lucke pushed this outsider firm to conform to standards like those the Literary Chamber had imposed on Tauchnitz in 1934: German firms should be in German hands, with a German office that truly controlled operations. The Paris office was an unnecessary luxury, he concluded. "There are enough capable booksellers in Germany who could accomplish at least as much."[3]

Inspector Mundt, a senior inspector at the Reichsbank Leipzig, took up Lucke's argument and strove to convince higher-ups at the Reich Center for Foreign Exchange Control in Berlin that Albatross was a malevolent virus eating away at German resources. "Paris holds the management of the domestic [German] firms Albatross and Tauchnitz fully in its hands," he protested, "since, as [I have] repeatedly mentioned, the Albatross-Continenta-Éditions du Pégase constellation of firms represent a purely foreign organization, whose only goal is to transfer money and material assets." He recommended that authorities reject transfers for Albatross, yet approve them for Tauchnitz, "which is, of course, in German hands." "Right!" scribbled one colleague, in the margin, approving a move to strong-arm all Albatross-Tauchnitz business—including Enoch's share of it—back to Germany.[4]

Were it not for the stultifying pace of change in the Nazi bureaucracy, this line of attack could have been devastating for Albatross. Yet for months, nothing happened—nothing, that is, until Lucke fought the matter from below, an unusual move in the top-down system of command that defined Nazi administration. On 29 October, he appeared in person at the Reich Center for Foreign Exchange Control to confront assessors Dr. Hipp (the Regierungsrat, or legal adviser) and Dr. Grabow, only to find that they knew little of Albatross. They had simply rubber-stamped Albatross transfers based on recommendations from two book trade experts: Wegner—lo and behold! still watching over Albatross-Tauchnitz affairs from afar—and Dr. Paul Hövel, the staunch pro-export bureaucrat who had endorsed Enoch's emigration deal and backed Albatross-Tauchnitz at the Propaganda Ministry. Extending his investigations in Leipzig, Lucke was astonished to find that "the 'Albatross' case is very well known in book trade circles. Everyone apparently wonders why the authorities don't step in to take action against the [illegal] transfer of assets abroad." The book trade typically reaped three to four times as much currency as it transferred to cover foreign costs, he discovered; by these calculations, Albatross should be earning "a foreign currency accrual amounting to roughly 400,000 RM, that is, eleven times more than with Albatross." As his coup de grâce, he said what he had only previously hinted: "[Let it be] noted, too, that the director of the agency (Reece), is also a Jew," he reminded his superiors. To condone the Paris office, he implied, was to privilege Jewish interests; he argued instead for a German Albatross purged of its foreign, Jewish taint and worthy of a place in an Albatross-Tauchnitz-Brandstetter triumvirate.[5]

*

If Nazi authorities had truly understood Holroyd-Reece's operations, they might not have deliberated as long or hard over the merits of the Paris office. There were ample clues to suggest that Albatross was not working for German interests as much as it claimed. One was the elegantly typeset change-of-address card Holroyd-Reece sent to business associates in November 1937. The card stated that he would be moving to 12 rue Chanoinesse with all of his publishing enterprises. He had accumulated quite a list of them, six in all. Four were allied: Albatross, Tauchnitz, Pegasus Press (whose French name, Les Éditions du Pégase, he used in this context), and the Publishing Holding Company, which funded Albatross. But the office also housed two other publishers, Les Éditions des Bibliothèques nationales de France and Les Éditions de la Nouvelle revue critique.

In Leipzig, the persistent Lucke came across this announcement in March 1938 in files his office had confiscated from Albatross defender Dr. Schöne during its latest round of invasive investigation into Albatross-Tauchnitz-Brandstetter affairs. In black and white, the list confirmed his suspicion that Albatross was playing Nazi authorities for fools, using Reich monies "to pay for other operations." "It must be characterized as an unworthy and untenable situation that a German firm has fallen into such a dependent relationship," he complained, questioning Brandstetter's ties to its shadowy foreign partner and, to some degree, Brandstetter's loyalties to Germany itself. He still could not ascertain who stood behind the Publishing Holding Company that owned Albatross. Putting these pieces together, Lucke painstakingly arrived at an insight that only Hans Otto before him—Wegner's nemesis at Tauchnitz—had come to years earlier: "When Reece has his hand in the game, the whole thing must be viewed right from the start with exceeding caution."[6]

Holroyd-Reece had, indeed, reached his hand into new games in 1937, and he was not about to leave Paris. Even as the Nazis' debates about Albatross escalated in late October, he was moving his Albatross-Tauchnitz editorial office to his august new abode on the Île de la Cité just a block from Notre-Dame. Traditionally claimed by blue-blood French families and church canons, the street was stamped with history. His own sixteenth-century residence had housed Archdeacon Louis du Bellay; Racine was said to have lived at number 16, while numbers 18 and 20 were tied to more sordid types: a barber and butcher who had made a nefarious business transaction reminiscent of *Sweeney Todd* in the 1380s, for which they were burned at the stake. Holroyd-Reece, once a German boy of modest means educated into British customs, would now swing open the massive, carved entry door to wander into his still, private courtyard, listening to the bells of the cathedral and replenishing number 12 with stories of his own.

One publicity photograph depicts him conducting business at an imposing Spanish desk, at least eight feet in length, with carved urns, thick as a man's leg, bearing the weight of the table top. It is a scene of earnest luxe: the sooty velvet of the chair from which he tilts forward to pick up the phone, the Renaissance-era tapestry draping the wall behind him, the fringe of his brass desk lamp, files in their baskets, papers in plentiful disarray fanning out across the dark wood.[7] From this sanctuary, with its aura of medieval quietude, Holroyd-Reece would set Albatross on its modern course.

Yet Holroyd-Reece's move itself reflected the cost his many schemes exacted from others over time. By 1937, he and Enoch were embroiled in such a quarrel that they could no longer work together. Their experiment at place Vendôme had lasted little more than a year, even its expansive accommodations too cramped to hold two sizable egos each used to running the show. Like Wegner before him, Enoch blamed their rupture on Holroyd-Reece's fiscal irresponsibility. Holroyd-Reece was "most effective in his role as a kind of roving ambassador among authors, publishers, and literary agents," Enoch contended, but "less at home in matters of organization, planning and disciplined business control." Evidence suggests, too, that their breach was also born of personality clashes. Accustomed to the role of advice giver, Enoch gave advice the way others delivered ultimatums, growing resentful when recipients failed to follow his lead. In 1934 he had urged Holroyd-Reece, in "a very thorough and friendly talk," to be more responsible. "It was this meeting," he later concluded, "that became the origin of a gradual cooling, repeated serious clashes and the eventual end of our relationship." By the end of 1937, each was pouring his energies into Albatross and Tauchnitz from his own address, more or less ignoring the other, unless business matters made communication necessary.[8]

Ironically, the fissure that had opened between them—much like Wegner's decision to leave Albatross—left Holroyd-Reece free to pursue whatever games he wished without oversight. And he played and spent abundantly in that year of his final falling out with Enoch, probably one cause of Enoch's alarm. In 1937, in the name of the Publishing Holding Company that owned Albatross, Holroyd-Reece had purchased all shares in the Éditions des Bibliothèques nationales de France, which published art books based on collections of the French National Library. In August 1937, he had infused the Éditions de la Nouvelle revue critique with 400,000 francs.[9] With Albatross and Tauchnitz already struggling to pay advances and royalties to Anglo-American authors—their money was too often tied up in cumbersome delays of foreign currency from Germany—Enoch seems to have felt increasingly that his own future would be jeopardized by Holroyd-Reece's financial hocus-pocus, the shifting of money from one firm to the next to feed an expanding empire. Having fought so hard to get to Paris, this was not a risk Enoch was willing to take.

Enoch and Nazi authorities were not the only ones to look askance at Holroyd-Reece's acquisitions. French intelligence found it suspicious that this Albatross-Tauchnitz representative kept accumulating more publishing houses. Yet if Nazi authorities worried that Holroyd-Reece was following foreign agendas, the French Secret Service came to a wildly different conclusion. "My attention has just been called to the intrigues of a certain REECE," wrote one agent looking through the fledging file the French Secret Service had opened on Holroyd-Reece the year before. "REECE, said to have recently bought the Maison d'Édition 'Nouvelle revue critique,' is suspected of being an agent of the German Information Services."[10]

The idea that Holroyd-Reece was a German agent was not, given the circumstances, untenable. He was German born, and Albatross and Tauchnitz were both legally based in Germany. The Éditions de la Nouvelle revue critique had existed since 1923 as a small, literary review run by two brothers, Alfred and Fernand Keller, out of their bookshop on the rue de Sèvres; in 1932 they had launched a collection of inexpensively produced detective novels that included some of the leading Anglo-American mystery writers. It was not Holroyd-Reece's purchase of the firm that made the French Secret Service wary, but his comments about it. "This little story here does not interest me. It's a cover," he had boasted to someone who turned out to be a government informant. A few days before Christmas, the agent on the case requested that the Prefecture of Police investigate Holroyd-Reece.[11]

What, exactly, Holroyd-Reece was hiding, French intelligence could not discern. Documents show that at a more practical level he was doing more or less what Lucke had suspected, though not for the reasons Lucke believed. With Nazi officials closing in on Albatross, Holroyd-Reece was expanding the Publishing Holding Company's stake in Anglo-American books. On the surface, he gained in the Nouvelle revue critique what he had not possessed since Albatross began printing its books in Germany: a Parisian venture entirely free from German interference. He crowed over the accomplishment to French publishers and agents. "Our new French firm," as he called it, would develop "a French Albatross" and, early in 1938, a German Albatross. "It should therefore be possible on frequent occasions to buy the Continental rights, the French rights and the German rights of an author," he noted, and Italian translation rights would follow "almost automatically," since Mondadori "want[s] to buy . . . everything that we publish in the Continental, the German and the French Albatross."[12] With this new vision of one-stop shopping—a truly radical innovation to which war would put a halt—Holroyd-Reece sought to expand Albatross's reach across national borders and languages, even as these boundaries were politically getting harder to cross.

The French Secret Service followed in his wake. In mid-May 1938, the prefect of police sent the Ministry of National Defense his report on "Hobroyd-Reece"—a humorous misspelling that persisted in further documents. The report declared the investigation inconclusive—though it did note the suspicious flow of traffic in and out of the rue Chanoinesse: "[We have been unable] to obtain any details on the personal relationships of Hobroyd-Reece, because of the many people who visit him for professional or other reasons." Yet interestingly, the writer recorded other information whose significance he evidently did not understand. Holroyd-Reece had listed two references when he renewed his French identity card: in 1934, M. Philippe Bertelot, the former French ambassador to Britain, and in 1937, Lord Tyrrell, the former British ambassador in Paris. The file did not specify how Holroyd-Reece knew the men. Yet given Albatross's self-proclaimed British agenda, it is of interest, in retrospect, to note Tyrrell's role in developing Britain's propaganda apparatus abroad. In the early 1920s, he had served as head of the British Foreign Office News Department—a center for propaganda activities—and in December 1934, on his return from his ambassadorial duties in France, he had been named the first head of the British Council.[13] French intelligence might well have asked, as the Germans had before them, for whom, exactly, Holroyd-Reece was working. It was, in the end, his inscrutability, as much as his purchases, which kept both French and German doubts about him alive into the war.

*

It cannot have eased the suspicions of the French that Holroyd-Reece had gained a new associate in the spring of 1937, even as his relationship with Enoch soured. To assist Holroyd-Reece in this centenary year—and, probably, to keep an eye on him—the Brandstetters sent to the Paris office one of their own: twenty-four-year-old Wolfgang Krause-Brandstetter, appointed the year before to manage Tauchnitz. From April to July 1937, he worked at place Vendôme under Holroyd-Reece's tutelage, learning the business of continental English editions from the inside out. Perhaps nothing, in fact, illustrated the ambiguity in Albatross-Tauchnitz operations better than Krause-Brandstetter's presence in Paris, so close to Enoch. Though the two men were technically allied in boosting Albatross-Tauchnitz sales, the differences between them could not have been more striking. For while Enoch had spent February to August 1936 suffering a host of indignities to escape the Nazi regime, Krause-Brandstetter had just begun working for it; in exchange for a visa to travel to the United States on Albatross-Tauchnitz business, he had agreed to gather information for the German Foreign Office.[14]

Whether Holroyd-Reece knew of Krause-Brandstetter's connection in this regard, the two were kindred spirits across the generations, German-born men who had immersed themselves in British culture and thrilled to wear a mask others might not readily perceive. Unlike Holroyd-Reece, Krause-Brandstetter came by his hyphenated name through family circumstance rather than invention. The biological son of a deceased physicist, Ernst Krause, he acquired the Brandstetter name after his widowed mother married Justus Brandstetter. With this name, the young Wolfgang was also ushered into a secure position in Brandstetter operations. He could have stayed at the University of Leipzig. Yet when Albatross began printing its books with the Brandstetters, he found himself showered with opportunities. With Holroyd-Reece's support, he transferred to Caius College at the University of Cambridge. As he later described this phase of his life, his "close personal friendship" with Holroyd-Reece had opened up a whole new world for his view: "It was due to his encouragement and cosmopolitan outlook that I stayed away from Germany for some years, studying English and literature at Cambridge and later working in the U.S. for both firms."[15]

The relationship took on professional weight when Krause-Brandstetter began work with Tauchnitz on 1 September 1935. He was rather green—six weeks shy of his twenty-third birthday—but Holroyd-Reece had ensured that he would possess skills his Brandstetter elders lacked: fluency in English and an intimate knowledge of Anglo-American literature and culture. In sending Krause-

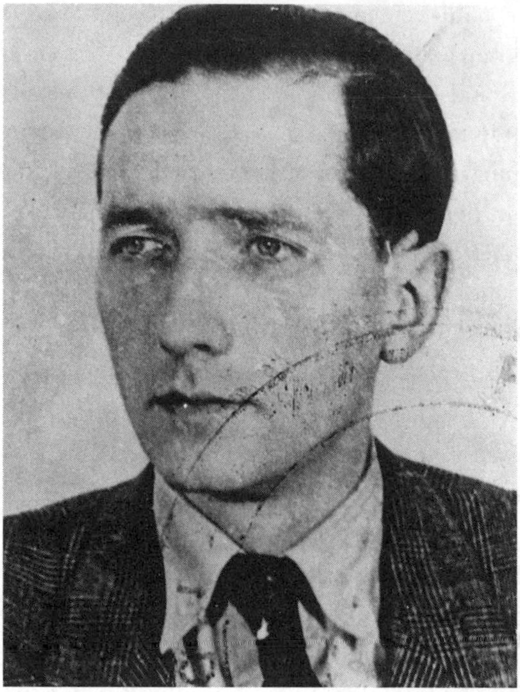

Wolfgang Krause-Brandstetter circa 1939 (Courtesy of John S. Hill)

Brandstetter to England, and later to Paris, the Brandstetters won for their side a publishing insider who could check to see that Holroyd-Reece's brilliant ideas did not land Tauchnitz-Brandstetter operations in deeper financial trouble. Yet Holroyd-Reece had simultaneously groomed Krause-Brandstetter with a broader aim in view. Who better than the symbolic offspring of the Albatross-Tauchnitz marriage to represent the interests of the two publishing houses at a time of international dissent? Krause-Brandstetter had traveled the globe in 1936, drumming up new Albatross-Tauchnitz contacts: from February to August he was in the United States, returning to Germany via a two-month stopover in Japan. He only stayed a matter of weeks in New York, describing this visit as "a failure due to opposition of Jewish interests." California, where he lived for months, was more forgiving.[16]

Tall and handsome, with aquiline features and a ready smile, Krause-Brandstetter had a man-about-town quality, and an ease with new situations that made him stand out. One military superior in 1942 would give him high marks: "He is a mature man of straightforward, open character, reliable, with calm deliberation. He is quick on the uptake and has versatile interests with great open-mindedness. Through his world travels he has acquired an intellectual flexibility with maturity and certainty in his judgments. He is convincing in his [self]-expression."[17]

In other words, Krause-Brandstetter bore a striking resemblance to Holroyd-Reece—cutting a more dashing figure, but schooled in the same charismatic ways. Holroyd-Reece had, too, educated him in the art of being a German in England. In May 1935, Krause-Brandstetter shared these lessons with the newspaper, the *Leipziger neueste Nachrichten* [Leipzig's Latest News], throwing the gates of Cambridge open so German readers could glimpse the English style of education. "Nothing is worse than to engage oneself as an active propagandist and to go like a bull at a gate," he reflected. "The more one conforms to their ways on the surface . . . , the better chance one has to leave behind an effective and positive impression."[18] This critical art of adaptation would serve Krause-Brandstetter well. He would wind his way through Albatross's future, determining its path, though perhaps not quite as Holroyd-Reece had intended.

*

Meanwhile, Nazi authorities had decided that Albatross could have a future in Germany only if it left Paris behind. It seemed that Lucke, finally, would get his wish. On 4 November 1937, not even a week after he challenged assessors in Berlin, a Dr. Schultze-Schlutius took up the paper trail. Charged with oversight of foreign exchange decisions at the Reich Economics Ministry, Schultze-Schlutius skimmed reports, talked with Hövel at the Propaganda Ministry, and made up his mind: Albatross-Tauchnitz distribution should be forced back to Germany by the end of the year; the future of the French office would be reassessed early in 1938 if Albatross "realized, by that point, a satisfactory sales outcome." Schultze-Schlutius's declarations carried weight. He moved in high political circles, and on 24 November, Goebbels endorsed his plan.[19] This course of action meant a death blow to Enoch's distribution business, with Holroyd-Reece's Paris office a close second in line. The Nazi regime wanted its Anglo-American books back.

On 25 November, the day after Goebbels gave his imprimatur to this plan, Holroyd-Reece suddenly appeared in Berlin. With Albatross's financial spin doctor, Dr. Hubert Breitenfeld—partner to Dr. Hans Schöne—by his side at the Reich Center for Foreign Exchange Control, he protested the regime's dictates.

Continenta and the French agent would have to liquidate, the two insisted, if Continenta were forced back to Germany and the agent fees slashed. Breitenfeld asserted that Lucke and his Leipzig superiors had skewed figures. Sales were on the rise, he insisted; the Reichsbank could, in future, count on a net annual currency gain of 100,000 RM. Berlin assessors granted them nothing, noting that only the Brandstetters could advocate on their behalf. The same day, all four Tauchnitz owners signed a letter to the regional finance president of Leipzig—sent on to the Reich Center for Foreign Exchange Control in Berlin—declaring their "burning interest" in preserving the French office. If authorities pulled the plug on Paris, they would cause "heavy injury" to Brandstetter-Tauchnitz interests; the issue was a "question of life or death" for Tauchnitz and the workers who printed Albatross and Tauchnitz books.[20]

The Brandstetters actually did have reason to protest. The Paris office had nurtured Tauchnitz's good reputation abroad and remained its best hope of international visibility and financial success. "It is commendable that the publisher [Tauchnitz] has an already established branch in Paris," remarked one Dutch paper for the Tauchnitz centenary, "which lays emphasis on the values of its work, the brotherhood of all nations." Seen from this angle, Nazi authorities were threatening to pluck Albatross's finest feathers, its cosmopolitan ethos in an era when many readers outside the Reich looked with fear and distaste on its repression, violence, and self-glorification. "Every attempt to save the 6,000 RM [per month]" by closing the French office, declared the Brandstetters, "would lead, to the best of our belief, to irreparable losses . . . not only for our firm, but also for the foreign exchange economy."[21] For if there was no Paris, Holroyd-Reece threatened, Albatross would dissolve its alliance with Tauchnitz and produce its books abroad, driving Tauchnitz into the ground. The biggest loser, then, would be the regime itself.

In truth, Albatross was saved—and Lucke and his associates foiled—not merely by the wizardry of Holroyd-Reece but by the Nazis themselves. It was no accident that Leipzig authorities were far more obsessed with Albatross's worth to the Reich than their colleagues in Hamburg had been. By late 1936, when they first grew skeptical of Albatross, Hitler had declared his Four-Year Plan to accelerate military production for war. On 4 April, he had charged Göring with the task of maximizing foreign currency and raw materials. In the summer of 1936, Göring ruthlessly increased foreign currency reserves by authorizing Reinhard

Heydrich of the S.S. to raid Germans' private accounts. This incursion was, it must be said, launched against the wishes of the economic minister, Schacht, who worried it would weaken confidence in the Reichsmark. Yet such was the tenor of decisions to come. On 18 October 1936, Hitler named Göring plenipotentiary of the Four-Year Plan, an "economic dictator" whose decisions would trump Schacht's, though he lacked Schacht's full understanding of the economy.[22]

Berlin authorities were thus deciding Albatross's fate at a time when Hitler's ambitions were far bigger than his budget. In 1933, Schacht had helped engineer an eight-year rearmament plan, costing 35 billion RM, or 4.3 billion RM annually, on average. Yet under the Four-Year Plan, Major General Friedrich Fromm requested a budget of 9 billion RM per year for the following three years for the army alone. In his annual report for 1938, the Finance Ministry representative within the Reichsbank anxiously pointed out that the Reich suffered under a deficit of 2 billion RM from its radically increased expenditures.[23]

The regime's economic hunger, then, once again won for Albatross a small piece of ground on which to maneuver. In the six months between 1 October 1935 and 31 March 1936, Albatross alone had sold 184,308 books abroad, Kupfer argued; between October 1936 and March 1937, 191,651 books. Sales would be higher were it not for factors beyond Albatross's control. The Spanish and Portuguese market had "completely fallen by the wayside due to the Civil War," he explained, while turnovers elsewhere had "extraordinarily suffered, . . . in Italy in connection with the Abyssinian War and . . . on the Côte d'Azur owing to the flight of tourists." In September 1937, Albatross again played the economic card. Apart from cultural-political benefits abroad, it claimed to offer the Reich a surplus of at least 100,000 RM, roughly 1 million RM's worth of printing contracts for the Brandstetters over time, and a foreign currency bonus, due to the fact that Albatross and Tauchnitz protected the Reich from having to import English-language books to fill the strong demand for them. Albatross also reminded Berlin authorities that the new trade arrangement with France, activated on 1 August 1937, would let the Reich recoup two-thirds of its trade surplus from France in hard currency; this meant that Albatross-Tauchnitz books sold in France, their second-largest market, would now reap more valuable currency gains than before.[24] Leipzig authorities had long since rejected these arguments out of hand. Yet for all their zeal, their Berlin superiors were not sure they could afford to drop Paris from the Albatross-Tauchnitz payroll. They wanted to cut out Paris; the question was how to do so without losing, in the process, the goose that laid the golden eggs.

While Nazi officials deliberated, slowly, for months into 1938, over what to do with the Paris office, Holroyd-Reece had already exacted his own price. Throughout 1937, he had defended Tauchnitz, and by association Albatross, as beacons of free thought in an age of fascism. In his "Prefatory Letter" for the Tauchnitz centenary volumes, he not only stressed that continental English editions "[revealed] the mind and opinion of England and America," but suggested that this was an ever more critical task given new "difficulties" in Europe—an oblique reference to political constraints in Germany, Italy, and Spain. "To describe the change here would tax the reader's patience too heavily," he wrote, "but in the circumstances it is true to say that what the book-reading public outside the British Empire and the United States of America reads of modern English literature is determined to a large extent by the editorial department of this firm. This is a solemn thought, a great privilege and a magnificent opportunity." For readers, the message was that Tauchnitz—and by implication, Albatross—brought Anglo-American culture to the rescue of those living under political repression. "We believe that the present day is a period of great English and American literature," Holroyd-Reece wrote, "and we believe that in the midst of the European turmoil our services are beneficent and perhaps more necessary than ever. We are here to serve all that the English language has to convey to the world and there is joy for us in the serving." He signed this statement "for and on behalf of Bernhard Tauchnitz," christening Tauchnitz with the same nickname he himself was rumored to use when he signed into hotel ledgers on illicit business: The Merchant of Dreams.[25]

ELEVEN

Dear Reader

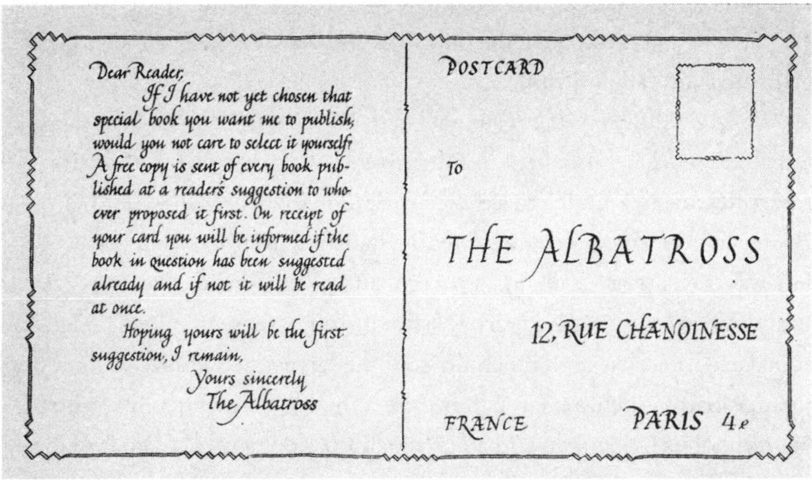

DESPITE THEIR DIVERGENT philosophies, Albatross and the Nazi regime had one thing in common as the 1930s advanced: their scrupulous attention to readers. Ever since its early days as a fellowship of common-minded publishers at the rue Boulard, Albatross had enclosed cards in its volumes to encourage readers to send feedback. "Dear Reader," each card read, "If I have not yet chosen that special book you want me to publish, would you not care to select it yourself? A free copy is sent of every book published at a reader's suggestion to whoever proposed it first. On receipt of your card you will be informed if the book in question has been suggested already and if not it will be read at once. Hoping yours will be the first suggestion, I remain, Yours sincerely, The Albatross." The back of the card left room for readers to join the Friends of the Albatross, steadfast customers who received seasonal catalogues. It also provided space for readers to list their favorite books, and why they were worth publishing with Albatross.[1]

Yet by the late 1930s, "Dear Reader" cards also gave Holroyd-Reece another way to think through a question key to Albatross's survival: Who were its readers? And what *did* they most want to read? In Paris, answers to these questions swayed the fate of the books Albatross published. In Leipzig and Berlin, where Nazi authorities scrutinized sales to see if Albatross was matching its promised levels of foreign currency deposits, they shaped nothing less than the company's future. Not all readers were alike in the eyes of these authorities: there were German consumers, who contributed nothing to the trade balance, and foreign consumers, who generated foreign currency each time they purchased an Albatross or Tauchnitz title.

So when the *Börsenblatt* summarized the June 1937 *Publishers Weekly* article that offered hard numbers on Albatross-Tauchnitz sales, authorities at the Leipzig Reichsbank Office saved the article for Albatross's file. As their pencil markings reveal, they were interested in statistics from national markets. Germany was the largest—with 39.55 percent and 31.07 percent of sales for Tauchnitz and Albatross, respectively. For Nazi authorities, these numbers boiled down to one fact: Albatross and Tauchnitz sold the largest percentage of their books abroad, Albatross being even slightly more valuable than Tauchnitz, with nearly 70 percent of its books sold abroad to Tauchnitz's 60 percent.[2] But for Holroyd-Reece the flip side of this statistic was far more interesting: the largest audience for Albatross and Tauchnitz's books—constituting 30 percent and 40 percent of the roughly five hundred thousand titles it sold annually across Europe—read these books in English under the shadow of the swastika. And Holroyd-Reece wanted to keep it that way.

If not for Hitler's rise to power, 1930s Germany would have been, by numbers alone, the ideal market for Albatross: a nation of readers, with six times as many bookshops per capita as the United States. Germany prided itself on being a cultured nation. *The World of the Book* (*Die Welt des Buches*), a 1937 publication by Nazi authorities that revealed the inner workings of the book trade, applauded Germany's six thousand bookshops, ten thousand "book trade affiliates" and twenty-five hundred publishing houses. It also included an impressive chart, visually representing book production per capita in twelve nations with stacks of books. Germany's stack towered over all others; England came in second, while the United States mustered a pathetic sixth place.[3] Germany was also a nation of book buyers. By 1937, the domestic book trade had recovered from the recession that had killed book sales in the early 1930s. Yet it had also gained a new kind of reader: the cultural bureaucrats who weighed in on which books German readers were authorized to read.

For the Nazi cultural elite, Germans' love of reading remained one of the country's best defenses against foreign accusations that Germany had descended into brutality. In December 1933, for example, the editor of the National Socialist journal *Die neue Literatur* (The New Literature), Will Vesper—whom Thomas Mann had described to fellow author Herman Hesse as "one of the worst of the nationalist buffoons"—touted the book week held in cities across the Reich as a way to "show the world abroad how things stand in the new Reich and what little truth there is in all the buzz about [our] supposed barbarism." The Literary Chamber president also wrote with pride that "the German Volk, like none other in the world, feels itself bound to the book."[4]

Albatross and Tauchnitz books were, of course, not exactly the spiritual anchors that such leaders had in mind. Holroyd-Reece's oft-stated desire to imbue the hearts and minds of German readers with Anglo-American ideals ran against the regime's diatribes, which rose to heights of pro-German religiosity. In *The World of the Book,* Literary Chamber high priest Karl Bischoff—one of the officials who had helped craft Enoch's emigration deal—euphemistically framed Nazi control of the book trade as the state's benign protection of German literature and the Volk. Bischoff incited German readers to realize that the future of the nation rested on their reading habits. "The book is more than a volume in the library," he intoned. "It is, even more than that, the mirror of that which a Volk thinks, creates, works for, suffers; it is the carrier of the fate of the nation." He urged German readers to read German books—"the sword of the spirit and the propaganda of the heart"—to nourish their German souls.[5]

To "help" German readers toward this end, the regime had sharpened censorship measures in 1935 and 1936, with Goebbels handing authorities a new tool for policing books: the *Index of Damaging and Undesirable Literature.* In April 1936, Hitler vested the power over books in Goebbels alone, ending months of internecine struggle for control. Thereafter, books could be confiscated or banned only if they first appeared on Goebbels's list. After July 1936, the Propaganda Ministry gathered a host of authorities periodically to expand the list's content: representatives from the Literary Chamber, the Gestapo, the S.S. Security Service (S.D.), the Party Examination Commission for the Protection of National Socialist Writings, and the Reich Education Ministry. By the end of 1937, the Literary Chamber had also enacted censorship by another name; purging almost all Jewish authors and publishers from the chamber, it barred them from publishing altogether.[6]

To understand how Albatross titles fared under Nazi censorship, it helps to understand one of the lies Goebbels, the German master of truth and lies, spread far and wide: that the Nazi regime did not need censorship to police the book trade. The *Reich Literary Chamber Handbook* proclaimed the regime's official stance: "We do not want censorship. . . . We want publishers who are loyal helpers in our shared task and who are genuinely capable of fulfilling their service to German literature on their own responsibility." This veiled approach became one of the mainstays of Nazi literary politics. For all that it was hushed up, The *Index of Damaging and Undesirable Literature* and its effects were very real indeed. The first list contained 3,601 individual titles and 524 bans on the entire corpus of particular authors, most of them Jewish, German, Communist, or modernist; it also targeted political works aimed against the regime or its leaders, as well as those undercutting National Socialist moral tenets. Bearing the warning "Strictly confidential!" the top-secret list was explicitly *not* available to the publishers, distributors, and booksellers whose economic well-being it threatened. So important was its confidentiality that officials accessing the volume had to sign a notarized contract stating they would keep the book under lock and key, even if they temporarily left the room; they were forbidden to bring it to their lodgings, or even other government offices, under pain of dismissal from their posts.[7]

Despite the obvious contradictions in its policy, the regime maintained it had no need of censorship because it had weeded out the harmful influence of the "unreliable"—that is, Jewish—publishers and booksellers; the remainder should possess the "healthy Volks-sensibility" that would guide them instinctively to the right books. In *The World of the Book,* the book trade expert Horst Kliemann urged booksellers to take seriously their "charge as cultural-political intermediaries and guardians of spiritual creation," and encouraged German readers to see books as food for spiritual health. "Just as one makes the doctor he trusts his family doctor, so, too, should the book lover have his family book dealer." As *Der Buchhändler im neuen Reich* (The Bookseller in the New Reich) of February 1937 explained, booksellers needed no published black list to work from, "for whoever has his heart in the right place will not be in danger of violating the laws of National Socialist Germany, even without such lists."[8]

Such secret censorship was oxymoronic, for without a master list, neither booksellers nor readers could know if they were trading in illicit works. The case of Koehler and Volckmar, the largest distributor in Leipzig, best illustrates the chaos the regime's lock-and-key policy created. A mainstay of the distributor's business was a catalogue circulated to German bookshops. But when its 1935–36 catalogue inadvertently contained titles from Goebbels's list, the firm ran afoul of the Literary Chamber. It was advertising banned literature without knowing it and was instructed to recall all catalogues and print new ones. When the distributor protested at the expense of this punishment, authorities compromised: the firm could black out forbidden titles instead. Koehler and Volckmar pleaded for a copy of the confidential list. But the Literary Chamber did not bend. Nor would it provide a chamber employee to monitor requests, even when the company offered to take on the expense. Finally, midway through 1936, came a cumbrous solution. Koehler and Volckmar sent order forms from Leipzig to the Literary Chamber in Berlin each day, paying a chamber employee to cross off newly banned titles.[9]

Many police and party officials, too, remained especially bewildered about how to handle foreign authors, because the regime so heavily militated against foreign influence, swaying German readers to buy German. The preface to *The World of the Book* offered one typical tirade when it praised the National Socialist takeover of the book trade for eliminating its "sick, the un-German, and foreign elements," to "serve the Volk, intrinsic and bound to the blood." The Literary Chamber's managing director similarly obligated the trade "to maintain and promote the unity of German literature and to wipe out anything that could disrupt or endanger it." Within this logic, foreign literature might erode the health of the German body politic. Translations were treated as "an insidious channel of dangerous ideas or a failure of patriotism on the part of German readers," to the point where librarians, advised to steer patrons away from foreign books, rarely included translations in new purchases.[10]

That such officials sometimes overreacted, overreporting suspicious passages to cultural authorities, was proof enough that the censorship apparatus was having the effect Goebbels wanted. Several Albatross authors were, in this way, pulled into the fray of hidden censorship—including, most prominently,

Sinclair Lewis. Since the book burnings, Lewis had enhanced his reputation as an anti-Nazi renegade with his 1935 novel *It Can't Happen Here,* which depicted a fascist party takeover of the United States, an ugly facsimile of Nazi Germany. In the same month, the Party Examination Commission for the Protection of National Socialist Writings wondered if all of Lewis's works were on Goebbels's list and if the chamber knew anything "prejudicial" about him. The Gestapo in Elbing, too, sent a copy of *Dodsworth* to the Literary Chamber president, who forwarded it to the Propaganda Ministry—expressly because the book contained two pages in which Lewis was proclaimed guilty of "a glorification of Jewishness."[11]

Like any black list, Goebbels's was arbitrary in its judgments. Keeping it restricted encouraged overreaction, heightening paranoia. Despite the many inquiries about Lewis, Goebbels did not, in the end, censor *Dodsworth.* And as the Literary Chamber informed the Party Examination Commission in July 1938, a year after its initial request, all of Lewis's books could be sold in the Reich except the German translation of *It Can't Happen Here.* Lewis did eventually have two other titles banned, both from the Humanitas Verlag: "Let's Play King"—a manuscript which the Literary Chamber had refused to review for the publisher, giving the rather paradoxical excuse that it did not review manuscripts —and *The Prodigal Parents.*[12] Yet despite Lewis's rabble-rousing writing, the bulk of his work remained available for sale in German within Reich borders. And in 1937, Albatross launched new print runs of its entire Lewis corpus for sale in Germany and abroad. All of these titles reached their second print run—with *Ann Vickers* reaching its third in 1938 and *Dodsworth* its fourth—showing that demand for Lewis's works continued.

It was not just publishers and police who sought clarification from higher authorities, but German readers themselves; many were developing scissors in their own heads and some, at least, were proud to show it. In the fall of 1937, one reader wrote to the editor of the rabidly National Socialist weekly *Der Stürmer* denouncing the Albatross edition of Louis Golding's *Five Silver Daughters.*[13] Golding, born in Manchester to Ukrainian-Jewish parents, had reprinted three novels with Albatross: *Magnolia Street* (1932), *The Miracle Boy* (1933) and *Five Silver Daughters* (1935). *Magnolia Street,* a saga of working-class Jewish life in Manchester, had become a best seller in England. *Five Silver Daughters* picked up this theme in following the ups and downs in the lives of a Jewish tailor and his five daughters. In 1937, Albatross undertook its third print run of *Magnolia Street* and its second of *Five Silver Daughters.*

Given the book's Jewish subject matter, the editor of *Der Stürmer* (literally, "The Attacker"), a journal best known for its crass and virulent anti-Semitism, complained to the local police and, for good measure, the Literary Chamber, in late November. Chamber officials requested a copy from Kupfer, who explained that Albatross had already pulled Golding's book from circulation. One official then informed the editor of *Der Stürmer* to pass on word to his concerned reader that the book was no longer on the market but would be subject to review. The correspondence cut off at this point until the end of 1938, when Golding surfaced on the *Index of Damaging and Undesirable Literature* with not just one work but his entire oeuvre banned.[14] Whether this ban included Albatross editions, the list did not specify. It did not need to. Albatross had already complied with the regime's desires by quietly removing Golding's work from view. The episode illustrates that books did not have to appear on Goebbels's list to be suppressed. Their voices could be silenced through sidebar deals, which allowed publishers to avoid the censure of being named to the black list, and further helped authorities justify why the regime had no need of censorship at all.

*

With such practices dominating the German book trade, the idea that foreign books, in English or in translation, could have any legitimate presence in Hitler's Germany by the late 1930s defies received wisdom. Yet if Nazi authorities wanted German readers to buy German, they had also pushed them into a corner. Nazi censorship had ruthlessly, and often quietly, eradicated most of the liberal, modern authors beloved by so many readers—among them world-renowned Jewish authors and thought-provoking authors declared too Communist or anti-Nazi. National Socialist rhetoric made reading a duty rather than a pleasure. Books were selling. Yet instead of choosing German titles, many German readers looked to foreign books to delight and instruct them as the 1930s wore on.

Various accounts, each with its own slant, indicated that many German readers snapped up the opportunity to read foreign. "Granted, there appears today, now and again, worthwhile literature in the Reich of the Swastika: foreign translations or erstwhile books in which the author could still say how he saw the world," stated the monthly report of the German Social Democratic Party in exile in November 1937. "These books are preferred by a considerable portion of the German readership." *Westermanns Monatshefte* (Westermann's Monthly), a cultural journal that had been in existence since 1856, commented in 1938, "Foreign countries are again the big literary vogue. The virtue of being German, of wanting to be German, is only accomplished by some with difficulty." An article from the S.S. weekly *Das Schwarze Korps* (The Black Corps) in June 1938 bemoaned the fact that foreign books were more visible than their German counterparts. "One merely glances at the display windows of the leading bookshops of our big cities. Foreign names, foreign names, foreign names." The number of translated fiction titles, in fact, rose from a low of 342 in 1933 to 543 in 1937, with reprint numbers also suggesting heightened demand. "Our public," recalled a Berlin bookseller, Hans Benecke, "had built up a pronounced mistrust of the recommended blood-and-soil literature." When the Reich Office for the Promotion of German Literature—one of many such official organs—sent out its first list of 100 recommended books in October 1934, Benecke dismissed the list as "books that did not even come under consideration for sale." For Jews in particular, banned from theaters, concerts, movie theaters, and public gathering places after November 1938, Benecke noted that foreign books were perhaps the last means of imaginative escape.[15]

German experts stepped into this maelstrom to educate the public about which foreign authors merited their attention and which to avoid. Hans Franke, in *Die neue Literatur* (New Literature), lambasted critics who had lauded Thomas Wolfe, arguing that they were encouraging an "undesirable import" of nihilism and a heightened subjectivity that readers were best to stay away from. Vesper, the journal's editor, blasted Wolfe's writing and the ludicrous notion that "German ways, German spirit, German national traditions" could ever be surmounted by "the gray liquid manure of the universal civilization that overruns America."[16] For readers who wanted such guidance in less inflated prose, Professor Karl Arns offered his *Index of Anglo-Jewish Authors* in 1938. Ranking authors by the degree of danger they presented, Arms included many more foreign authors than Goebbels had singled out for his *Index of Damaging and Undesirable Literature.* In 1939, Arns produced a second edition devoted to American authors—and British authors overlooked in the first volume—keeping readers up to date on the latest in discouraged reading.

Despite such tools of scrutiny, British and American novels remained highly popular; in 1937 and 1938, they made up close to half the total number of translated fiction titles. The craze for Anglo-American detective novels helped tilt the scales. Dorothy Sayers was so sought after that the *Deutsche Allgemeine Zeitung* (German Public Gazette) serialized her novel *The Unpleasantness at the Bellona Club* (1928) in German between November 1938 and January 1939. Agatha Christie and Edgar Wallace were all the rage; Wallace's publisher, the Goldmann Verlag, published eighteen reprints of his books in 1938 and 1939 alone. At the more rarified end of the spectrum were volumes like the Fischer Verlag's *New America: Twenty Storytellers of the Present* (*Neu Amerika: Zwanzig Erzähler der Gegenwart*), which introduced German readers to a range of contemporary American authors, including Sherwood Anderson, Conrad Aiken, William Faulkner, Thomas Wolfe, Erskine Caldwell, and Katherine Anne Porter. Editor Kurt Ullrich's introduction offered an inspired defense of American culture, which had been, he felt, reflected in a "distorted fun house mirror" in Germany, creating an inaccurate view—all greedy materialism and navel-gazing frivolity—that he hoped his collection would correct.[17]

Anglo-American works were also heatedly discussed in those journals and newspapers that had not been squelched or annexed by Nazi editors. Many journals advertised foreign books under the heading "New Books from Abroad," and the literary sections of urban newspapers regularly commented on Anglo-American authors.[18] Until the start of the war, the well-known literary journal *Die Literatur* offered a regular "English Letter" and "American Letter" discussing new books. Translations of Thomas Wolfe and William Faulkner had quite a presence in the German press, along with those of Thornton Wilder, William Saroyan, John Steinbeck, Katherine Mansfield, Evelyn Waugh, and others. New D. H. Lawrence translations regularly appeared, with the Rabenpresse in Berlin publishing a volume of his letters as late as 1938.

By 1938, foreign literature had grown so popular that it caught the attention of the Security Service (S.D.), the intelligence-gathering wing of the S.S. Its annual report on the literary realm complained of "the appallingly high number of translations from other languages." It observed that translations tended to feed readers' desires for escape from political realities, citing Margaret Mitchell's *Gone with the Wind* as a case in point. Through such translations, the report argued, publishers placed "economic considerations" over their cultural and political responsibilities. But it also conceded that the translations filled a need that German books were not filling. "To some degree, translations help offset the obvious lack of good, entertaining reading."[19] In essence, the regime was losing the war of the good German book, even on its own soil. And Nazi literary authorities knew it.

*

Albatross and Tauchnitz fell both within and beyond the regime's suspicion of foreign books. Their sale in Germany saved the Reich some foreign currency, argued their financial adviser, Schöne, since without them, Germany would have to import such books from foreign publishers, further eroding its trade balance. In fact, among the books the Paris office sought for its Dear Readers was none other than the opus that the Security Service had maligned: *Gone with the Wind.* In October 1937, Assistant Editor Sonia Hambourg put her all into securing it for Tauchnitz. The book had sold 1.5 million copies in the United States and 110,000 in England, and would certainly help Albatross-Tauchnitz export returns to Germany if it caught fire in Europe. But Mitchell had cabled her Paris agent, William Bradley, not to sign with Tauchnitz. Hambourg renewed her efforts: "As our readers are extremely anxious that we bring out GONE WITH THE WIND if humanly possible, would you be good enough to get on to Miss Mitchell again as soon as possible. . . . Perhaps you would also point out to her again that unless she is published in Tauchnitz there is no possibility for GONE WITH THE WIND being sold in Germany, where a large and enthusiastic public is waiting for an opportunity to read it."[20]

Unfortunately for the Paris office, Mitchell would not change her mind; her publisher, Macmillan, was "absolutely opposed to the publication of an English continental Edition," probably more on financial than political grounds. Mitchell stood fast, and so within Germany the book came out only in German. The National Socialist editor Will Vesper launched his anti-Mitchell diatribe in October 1937, asking superciliously, "What does this clever, headstrong, garish and bloodily painted American history have, in reality, to do with us Germans?. . . . Are this semisweet American Lulu and this flippant, ach so noble, ach so deeply cagey cinema hero and noble criminal Rhett really fantasies of our

Volk?" Apparently, many readers were unswayed. The German translation with Goverts Verlag sold 366,000 copies between 1937 and 1941, despite the exorbitant sales price of 12.5 RM—triple the average book price for the day. One young bookseller at the Amelang bookshop in Berlin, Peter Weber, remembered the sensation *Gone with the Wind* had caused among employees when the bookseller got his hands on an unbound version in English that was passed hand to hand in sections before the German translation appeared.[21]

Within the Reich, Albatross sold its books in English to hundreds of bookshops; sales figures show that Kupfer sold roughly 98,544 RM of Tauchnitz books, and 92,260 RM of Albatross books in the Reich—so just under 190,000 books in the eight prewar months of 1939.[22] How these figures relate to actual readers is impossible to say. Some German readers of English probably bought multiple copies; others may have passed them hand to hand, sharing them with friends to save money. Some Albatross volumes, scribbled full of German translations in the margins, show that German readers were using Albatross books to improve their English.

The Reich and Prussian minister for science, education and public instruction, Bernhard Rust, may have inadvertently boosted Albatross-Tauchnitz sales in the Reich when he mandated at the start of 1937 that English would become the first foreign language taught at "all higher schools, with the exception of schools for the young." Albatross and Tauchnitz titles were priced right for German classrooms. In fact, the journal *Englische Studien* encouraged German teachers and professors to turn to Albatross and Tauchnitz titles by offering lists of roughly forty Albatross and Tauchnitz books in each edition, each title reviewed in the journal that year. Albatross titles were featured far more than Tauchnitz's, perhaps because they were more current. Among those listed in the 1938–39 volume were William Faulkner's *The Unvanquished,* Robert Graves's *Count Belisarius,* Freya Stark's *Baghdad Sketches,* Richard Aldington's *Seven Against Reeves,* Louis Bromfield's *The Rains Came,* and D. H. Lawrence's *The Man Who Died* and two volumes of his letters.[23] Albatross and Tauchnitz were well advertised, then, among those readers best poised to encourage their dissemination: German educators with access to young, fertile minds.

*

To say that Albatross books made Anglo-American culture available to German readers, however, is not to say what that culture was. Some reviews suggest that Albatross and Tauchnitz filled the void that Holroyd-Reece claimed: promoting the "mind and heart of England and America" in foreign climes. In 1937, the reviewer Muska Nagel surveyed a host of volumes for *Die Literatur,* which had long specialized in reviews of world literature and had a circulation of roughly thirty thousand. She conveys a reader's joy at seeing the volumes displayed before her, each a miniature doorway to the English-speaking world: "When one has a number of Tauchnitz and Albatross volumes standing in front of one—red, blue, purple, yellow volumes," she begins, "one gets the feeling that one must, through such multi-facetedness, penetrate not only in the literary, but especially the spiritual movements of the English-speaking Volk." She reads, not with Vesper's spite, but with a curiosity to understand the best and the worst of the cultures to which the books offer entry; her review, which included summaries of Aldington's *Very Heaven* and Graves's *Antigua, Penny, Puce,* encourages readers to embrace mind travel to see daily life abroad.[24]

Albatross and Tauchnitz books might well build bridges between cultures. Yet these bridges might support German, rather than Anglo-American ends, as in Hans Effelberger's 1939 tribute to D. H. Lawrence in *Die neueren Sprachen* (The Newer Languages), a journal targeted at German teachers. Effelberger, like many German critics, portrayed Lawrence as a rebel child of England who undermined class expectations by working his way up from a coal-mining family to become a celebrated author. Like many German critics, too, Effelberger read Lawrence through the lens of Nietzsche, declaring that both men "share the will to triumph." If only German readers read more Lawrence works, he argued, they would "discover how near Lawrence often comes to our current völkisch spirit of the age." For support, he quoted the Albatross edition of *Apocalypse,* which Holroyd-Reece had prodigiously fought to win on the heels of Lawrence's death: "Power is there and always will be. As soon as two or three men come together, especially to do something, then power comes into being, and one man is a leader, a master. It is inevitable. Accept it, recognize the natural power in the man, as men did in the past, and give it homage." Such passages, stated Effelberger, defined Lawrence as "a witness that even in England there were personalities, outside the conventional [mindset], who understood the meaning of our historical turning point."[25]

Albatross had always put its readers at the center of its decision-making process. Its "Dear Reader" cards were just one way of taking their literary pulse, finding out what readers read and why. Yet if Albatross books could be used to justify Anglo-American democratic impulses as much as the National Socialist "will to power," readers were also key in another, more unpredictable way. For much of the 1930s, Nazi officials had not only determined much of *what* German readers might read, but sought to tell them *how* to read it. The literary bureaucracy promulgated the ideal of reading as a social act, a membership pass into the *lesende Volksgemeinschaft*—a larger reading community whose interpretations were to reaffirm the value of the National Socialist collective. Bureaucrats in the realms of education and culture actively warned against *Lesewut,* the "reading rage" that could lead individual readers astray, to books or interpretations of books contrary to the National Socialist agenda. Yet in the end, no publisher or government official could determine how Albatross or Tauchnitz books would fare in German readers' hands—whether readers would embrace the collective or seek to preserve reading as an "uncontrollable private act." Books in English could be used to condemn Anglo-American culture as much as to create a yearning for it.[26]

Even in his role as the official figurehead of Nazi censorship, Goebbels was willing to take the risk. As both Reich Propaganda Minister and president of the Reich Chamber of Culture, he could have banned foreign literature at any time. But from a cultural-political angle, he deemed such a decision unwise. Open censorship would potentially endanger Germany's relationships with foreign trade partners. Instead he policed foreign books and left open a modest "depoliticized sphere" where Germans could distract and amuse themselves, the better to solidify their loyalties to the regime. In his diary, he asserted that the regime needed to provide the Volk with sources of relief to avoid the mistakes of the Great War.[27]

Still, accumulated evidence suggests that Albatross faced a smaller risk by staying in Germany than the regime did in tolerating its presence. The British Council certainly thought so. In the late 1930s, it was more preoccupied than ever with how to smuggle "smart" propaganda into Germany. In a November 1938 report, its leaders toyed with, among other projects, a British Library in Germany stocked with British books and periodicals; increasing exchanges of young people; radio news programs, in German, with a reputation for truthfulness ("Veracity, even to the point of dullness, is essential," stated the report, to win German trust). In early December 1938, one British official pressed the council for quick action. "As the Nazi attitude towards Britain, . . . in the party, in the home and in schools, is a strange mixture of admiration and jealousy, bound up with curiosity, it might perhaps be politic to satisfy this curiosity ourselves before it begins to decline or is fed by irresponsible German propagandists." For him, the solution was obvious: "Again, cheapness and excellence of Tauchnitz and Albatross books place English (and American) literature within reach of any who are interested and the most we could do would be to present a small number of carefully chosen books to institutions which are training younger people."[28]

In the end, it is ironic that the Literary Chamber, a critical voice in the censorship apparatus, was one of Albatross's best defenders in the Reich. One case in point involves the chamber's response to the German reader who complained about Golding's Albatross volume. "As a caution, I would like to communicate that the Albatross-Verlag in Hamburg predominantly sells its products in English- and French-speaking countries," the chamber official informed the editor of *Der Stürmer.* "In order to stay competitive against non-German firms abroad, it is forced to publish books that in terms of their content and in view of their authors cannot always be endorsed for German readers. In general, the Albatross-Verlag has hitherto occasioned no objections regarding the distribution of such books in Germany."[29] Whatever his misconceptions about Albatross's market, he parroted the official stance of the Literary Chamber: Albatross was to be treated as a special case, its books to be given greater leeway than others in Germany. In an emergency, "undesirable" Albatross books could always be shipped abroad, with authorities waving their hands to make them disappear.

TWELVE

Allegiances

EACH CHRISTMAS, Holroyd-Reece indulged his love of fine production by designing a special card. For Christmas 1938, he moved into the realm of tasteful excess. His holiday greeting, printed on weighty paper, ran to thirty pages; the fortunate recipients could unfold the concertina-style card like the pleats of an accordion, stretching it across the width of a side table or chimney mantle. Perhaps it was more important to Holroyd-Reece than ever in the last days of 1938 to make a statement.

There was optimism in Holroyd-Reece's designs, as always, or perhaps a measure of defiance. The card spun a holiday fairy tale that flew in the face of the political and economic fluctuations that shaped Albatross's fate. For this extravaganza, Holroyd-Reece had commissioned Gunter Böhmer to create charcoal sketches of life at the rue Chanoinesse. Realism met fantasy as the bespectacled Böhmer drew himself into various tableaux, a stand-in for other viewers. Life at number 12 was, through Böhmer's eyes, many things. It was full of industry: one employee sat hunched over paperwork near an elaborately arched window with a tornado of papers swirling over his head; a lithe assistant climbed a ladder in a lofty ceilinged room bounded by bookcases; John and Jeanne Holroyd-Reece read in the stillness of their private living room upstairs, lit by Chinese lamps. It was mundane: Jeanne wrapped herself up against the weather as she walked their two little black terriers or lounged on a chair on the upper terrace with a view over the pont Louis-Philippe spanning the Seine. It was festive: guests chatted convivially alongside a buffet table against a tapestry-hung wall. It was exciting: John Holroyd-Reece stood at the center of a collage-like maelstrom of negotiations, his back to viewers, swinging his pocket watch—or perhaps his monocle—behind his back, as was his habit. He leaned forward to exchange words with the earnest artist, who had in his time at the rue Chanoinesse sprouted the single horn of that most mythical of creatures, the unicorn. Here life moved. Deals were broken and made. Magic happened.

In the pages of this card, Holroyd-Reece presented a more gracious, less fractured universe than the one that defined his days: a world untainted by Nazi officials in which Christmas cards mattered enough to spare no expense, one, too, in which the rue Chanoinesse and its businesses and inhabitants were flourishing. Yet reality lagged not far behind legend. Talk of war made the rounds of European cafés and dinner tables. Holroyd-Reece held Albatross close, ready to pull it out of harm's way should war occur. The orb swung behind his back, a pendulum, marking time.

*

In the spring of that year, the landscape of Europe had swiftly changed. On 12 March 1938, Hitler's troops marched into Austria. The Austrian president,

Kurt Schuschnigg, resigned, and an astonished Europe watched as German soldiers paraded into city centers and town squares, waving the new, swastika-laden flag of Austria, hanging it on public buildings and monuments.

Germans in exile were devastated. "There is no more Austria," wrote Franz Werfel to his publisher, Ben Huebsch, on 14 March from Capri. Stefan Zweig, an Austrian, later wondered in dismay, "How unimportant are, even now, all our books and what we are doing." For Kurt Enoch, too, the Anschluss put everything else in question. "The invasion of Austria came as a tremendous shock," he later remembered. "Glued to the radio and listening to reports of the rapidly unfolding events, I was filled with rage and terror when I heard the hateful sound of goose-stepping soldiers marching into Vienna and the roar of the 'Heil Hitlers' which 'greeted' the invaders. This event and what followed also changed my latent unease into increasing concern about our personal future." Virginia Woolf made a prediction in her diary for 26 March 1938: "When the tiger, i.e. Hitler, has digested his dinner he will pounce again."[1]

Enoch shared this fear. He was, for the moment, personally safe. But Nazi authorities had been plotting another Anschluss of his economic interests. Early in 1938, around the time the Reich consumed Austria, the Leipzig finance president ratcheted up the pressure on Albatross and Tauchnitz "to dismantle the distribution of both publishers via the Jewish firm Continenta in Paris." If, as financial authorities had repeatedly heard, Albatross and Tauchnitz depended on the French Albatross-Tauchnitz office, they would have to pay a price to keep it: Enoch.[2]

Months in the making, this quid pro quo left Kupfer, the Albatross managing director in Germany, in an uncomfortable spot. He had worked in so many tiers within Albatross that he could trace better than anyone the inner workings of its offices. Kupfer's actions reveal him to be a dedicated employee; his dense, typically single-spaced letters are packed with sales figures and statistics. He put in his hours. But he was not a man who boldly or eagerly chose sides. At thirty-seven, he had a family to support—his wife and two children—and a job to do. To Wolfgang Krause-Brandstetter, who valued brashness and flair, he was the epitome of the cautious paterfamilias—"a timid character, and afraid of committing himself."[3] So Kupfer found himself in the right job at the wrong time when, in January 1938, Lucke and other financial authorities drilled him for answers:

Was Holroyd-Reece's 6,000 RM monthly fee "appropriate" or a scam? How and when might Enoch be excised from Albatross-Tauchnitz operations without damage to the firms' overall interests?

Based on the documents at hand, we can infer that Kupfer's allegiance was less to a particular cultural or political ideal than to Albatross itself. He had followed Wegner from Tauchnitz to Albatross. For five years, he had worked under Enoch, helping him establish Continenta in Paris. Since his precarious start as Albatross's German managing director in 1936—when Nazi authorities had accused him of illegally helping Enoch emigrate—Kupfer had worked directly under Holroyd-Reece, with a distinct division of labor: Holroyd-Reece took the eagle-eye, aerial view of Albatross affairs from Paris, and Kupfer served as Albatross's man on the ground in Germany. The agendas Kupfer pushed through the hoops laid out by the Nazi bureaucracy were, then, Holroyd-Reece's agendas: defending Albatross from the aggressive suspicions of the Leipzig financial authorities; proving that Albatross and Tauchnitz sales numbers were on the rise; and most of all, justifying to authorities why it would be financially and politically unwise to dissolve the French office. Kupfer was, in other words, the perfect company man.

So it was no wonder that in Reichsbank file notes Kupfer appears alternately self-possessed and nervous. Working for Albatross interests as the Nazi authorities defined them suddenly meant working against Enoch. It was one thing for Kupfer to give his opinion on Albatross matters, as authorities had periodically asked him to do, and another to agitate, personally, for Enoch's excision from Albatross-Tauchnitz business. He feared reactions from Enoch and Holroyd-Reece in Paris, certainly, but also repercussions in Leipzig and Berlin if he did not comply. Somewhere between the hovering threat of Albatross being subjected to yet another round of investigations in Germany and the fact that he now officially worked for Holroyd-Reece, Kupfer distanced himself from Enoch. Perhaps he had also grown resentful that he was held responsible in Germany for what Holroyd-Reece and Enoch did abroad. In February 1938, he told Reichsbank inspector Dietrich in confidence that he held "considered it possible to relocate the operation to Germany and [believed], too, that there [would be] no backlash against Albatross Verlag or the alliance with Tauchnitz and Brandstetter." He also implied—to Enoch's detriment—that Continenta had underreported its sales, which allowed it to send lower export revenues back to Germany and to preserve the difference in gains in France.[4]

In March, having second thoughts about how much Enoch stood to lose, Kupfer adapted his stance. He would travel to Paris soon, he told Dietrich, "to negotiate with Enoch over the transfer of distribution to Germany and the liquidation of [his] contract" with Albatross and Tauchnitz books by 31 July. Yet he also requested that "at least a portion of the distribution could be left in Enoch's hands." Dietrich denied this request, demanding instead that Kupfer verify whether Enoch had been fulfilling his contractual agreement to spend a third of his bookseller rebate on promoting Albatross-Tauchnitz books abroad. And so Kupfer was dispatched to Paris to trace an uneasy path as part negotiator, part compliance officer, while Nazi authorities pressed full force to reclaim Leipzig as the center for Albatross-Tauchnitz distribution. "Negotiations over this point should, according to Kupfer, already be under way," recorded Lucke. "Supposedly, too, the Paris factions agree in principle with the transfer."[5]

Sticking out awkwardly from Lucke's assertions is his offhand remark that the deciding powers in Paris "agreed in principle" with Nazi authorities. Here was an uncomfortable truth: Holroyd-Reece had sold Enoch out to preserve his own stake in Albatross. "The wish on the German side to dissolve the relationship with Continenta corresponded to the wish of Herr Holroyd-Reece, who, for other reasons, fiercely wanted to detach himself from Dr. Enoch," wrote Kupfer in one report. "In the last years before the war, the original friendship nearly turned hostile. . . . It is no wonder, then, that Holroyd-Reece, as it later turned out, was already driving the breach with Enoch on his own [account]."[6]

Much as Kupfer presented Holroyd-Reece as the instigator, the ensuing negotiations indicate that both men were agents of this change. Evidence suggests that they broke off their business partnership in the passive-aggressive manner in which some couples end romantic relationships: Holroyd-Reece did not kick Enoch out so much as he made the situation so intolerable that Enoch chose to leave. In Enoch's account decades later, he states it was he who had severed ties, choosing to divorce his financial interests once and for all from Holroyd-Reece's "continued largesse in financial matters" and, more important, from decisions beyond his control in Nazi Germany. Enoch cited "a sharp deterioration of the position of the Jews still remaining in Germany which increased my misgivings and aversions to continue, even if only indirectly, a business relationship with Nazi Germany. . . . Consequently, I proposed to Reece and he agreed to work out terms for our separation."[7]

Fortunately for him, Enoch had diversified his business interests midway through 1937, when he and Holroyd-Reece were becoming increasingly at odds. He had established two firms, both based at 1 Bloomsbury Street in London: Imperia Ltd. to distribute French and English books in England and Enoch Ltd. to launch "English-language publishing activities." Freed from the censorship restrictions of Nazi Germany, he teamed up with Jack Kahane of the Obelisk Press, the Paris-based publisher of Henry Miller's *Tropic of Cancer* and other suppressed books. Kahane charged Enoch with distributing his books in England—at least those that could legally cross borders. Enoch also used Imperia to transport French classics into English hands. He had been "impressed by the success of Penguin Books," and developed a similar series of French books—presented as a "uniform library"—to sell inexpensively abroad. Enoch was "quite satisfied" with these developments.[8] With Nazi authorities bearing down on his Albatross-Tauchnitz business, these ad hoc ventures were proving to be more important to his future than he had imagined.

Only when Enoch had finally declared his intent to divorce his interests from those of Albatross and Tauchnitz did Nazi authorities unexpectedly do an about-face: Paris would remain the hub for all foreign distribution of Albatross-Tauchnitz books after all, they declared. The lure of foreign currency had again trumped ideology: keeping distribution in France, explained one official, would funnel higher percentages of hard currency back to Germany than moving French Albatross-Tauchnitz operations back to Leipzig. This strange and sudden change of direction can be discerned only in fragments, yet its endpoint is clear. Midway through 1938 Enoch rescinded his Albatross-Tauchnitz worldwide distribution rights. For a certain price, he would transfer these rights not to the Brandstetters back in Leipzig, as Nazi authorities had originally planned, but to Holroyd-Reece's French firm, Les Éditions Albatros—the empty shell that had stood at the ready since November 1934.[9]

That Holroyd-Reece could convince Nazi authorities that he, of all people —that same shadowy head of the French office—should take over Enoch's rights suggests quite an effective game of brinkmanship. In fact, the sequence of events seems too neat, the growing enmity between Holroyd-Reece and Enoch fitting almost too smoothly the time frame when the Nazis pressured the Brandstetters to pull Paris operations back to Leipzig. It is as if Holroyd-Reece, knowing the Nazis would force a choice, exacerbated an existing difference of opinion as deftly as an experienced woodcutter slides the awl into the crack in a log. His success is all the more astounding since authorities demanded one condition for his takeover of distribution that he, as the son of a Jewish father, could not entirely fill: "that this enterprise [Éditions Albatros], in line with German regulations, can be characterized as Aryan."[10] Nazi authorities had delivered into Holroyd-Reece's hands exactly what he wanted: separation from Enoch, a promise to keep the French Albatross-Tauchnitz office open and to continue transferring the foreign currency installments that paid its costs, and, finally, distribution of Albatross-Tauchnitz books outside the Reich. With Wegner out, and now Enoch, Holroyd-Reece stood to centralize control over Albatross-Tauchnitz affairs in his hands, all while convincing Nazi authorities that the maneuver worked to their interest.

To Enoch, these negotiations can only have borne echoes of being stripped of his businesses two years earlier. He had sold to Wegner, and would now sell to Holroyd-Reece, a second wave of "Aryanization" no less destabilizing than the first except that it took place on the banks of the Seine rather than beside the docks of Hamburg. "The negotiations took a long time and were not concluded until 1938," Enoch wrote. "They were difficult and complicated by the fact that Reece did not have capital to cover . . . the transition of the distribution to his own organization." Dr. Hubert Breitenfeld, the accountant mastermind behind Enoch's emigration, came to Paris several times, devising an "agreement on the basis of which the transitional finances were provided in the form of a loan from the international banking house of Warburg and Company with which [Enoch] had connections."[11]

Here was a kind of solution. Yet with complex financial negotiations complicated by personality conflicts, the transfer of distribution was easier in theory than in practice. This was no longer 1936, when Enoch had been forced to tamp down on his own outrage, being careful of what he said and did so as not to upset the delicate negotiations to get himself, his family, and his business out of Germany. From Paris, he could make demands rather than concessions. He demanded a high payoff. On 6 October, Kupfer requested on behalf of Albatross in Germany that Nazi financial authorities release 60,000 RM to pay Enoch for ceding his distribution rights to Holroyd-Reece at Éditions Albatros—the sum equivalent to that which Enoch had paid for the Albatross and Tauchnitz titles he had taken to Paris. The first days of November found Kupfer consulting with Nazi authorities in Berlin and waiting for approvals.[12]

Then, within days, the anti-Jewish ferment brewing in Germany boiled over. On 8 November, a young Polish Jew shot Ernst vom Rath, the Third Secretary at the German Embassy in Paris. When news of vom Rath's death was confirmed the following day, the Nazi regime banned Jewish publications and dissolved cultural and educational organizations. Hours later, in the early morning of the 10 November, Germans' resentment of the Jews erupted across the land. The boycotts of Jewish shops in April 1933, the Civil Servant Statute of April that same year that banned Jews from state-funded positions, the Nuremberg Laws of 1935, appalling as they were, paled in comparison with the fury and hatred that everyday Germans, encouraged by S.A. forces, unleashed upon Jews in their midst. In Berlin, the Hitler Youth were on the prowl, some wielding axes, crying out "Germany Awake! Perish Judah!" "Wrecking gangs in civilian clothes" smashed windows of Jewish stores on the prestigious shopping avenues, Friedrichstrasse and Kurfürstendamm, in Berlin, reported the *Chicago Tribune* correspondent Sigrid Schultz, one of the best-informed American journalists in Germany; mass looting ensued, and "the occupants of some shops were dragged into the street and carried off."[13]

The Berlin bookshop owner Hans Benecke—one-quarter Jewish by Literary Chamber definition—arrived at his store on the Kurfürstendamm to see the "appalling image of shattered windowpanes at almost all of the shops located there. The shop windows were cleared out and the sidewalk strewn with glass shards." Word had spread that the S.A. had set ablaze the synagogue in the Uhlandstrasse. "We were faced with a gruesome sight. The synagogues were ablaze with bright flame, which darted from the windows." Yet "the many fire trucks standing by were not permitted to extinguish the flames," deploying their equipment solely to prevent neighboring houses from catching fire.[14]

Nine of Berlin's twelve synagogues were looted and set ablaze, along with synagogues in Stettin, Frankfurt-on-Main, Constance, Cologne, Lübeck, and Leipzig. In Munich, the Gestapo arrested over four hundred Jews in their homes. From Nuremberg came reports of particularly vicious attacks. In one case, storm troopers raided a Jewish home, beating the man and wife, pulling children out of bed, and destroying the apartment. Writing from Berlin, Schultz described "mobs" who "gloated over the smashed stores of Jews. They helped themselves to clothes, furs, and toys, and scattered the goods in the streets for their friends to pick up." She estimated that twenty thousand Jews had been arrested in Germany and Austria in the rampage that came to be known as Kristallnacht, a reference to the splintered shards of glass littering the sidewalks.[15]

While Enoch and his family were safe, his mother, Rosa Enoch, lived in Hamburg until late 1938. Enoch had always planned for her to emigrate and live with his sister in Paris, yet the riots made it newly imperative. On 21 November, she sold her home, and then paid 36,000 RM for the Reich "flight tax" plus 10,800 RM cash to cover her portion of the 1 billion RM tax that Göring levied on Jews for "provoking" the damages of Kristallnacht: in all, she paid 46,800 RM for the privilege of leaving Germany—equivalent to two years of Wegner's starting salary with Albatross.[16]

Enoch grew more recalcitrant; the sheer inhumanity of German violence may have annealed his resolve not to be pushed aside too easily. For in effect, with each phone call from Kupfer to authorities in Berlin, with each small piece of the negotiations locked into place, Enoch's shop windows at the place Vendôme were closer to being smashed at the hands of the Nazi bureaucracy. In Leipzig, Kupfer had been operating on the premise that Enoch would accept the foreign currency equivalent of 60,000 RM. Yet just three days into the New Year, he reported to the Economics Ministry that negotiations had stalled. Enoch would not be rushed. "It is not clear, whether Dr. Enoch will accede to this [amount]," wrote Kupfer, "but we see no other way to come to negotiation, since we have not been successful in getting Dr. Enoch to [make] a legally binding statement." As Kupfer informed the Economics Ministry, "In the first discussions, Dr. Enoch named higher sums."[17]

When negotiations dragged on, some allegiance in Kupfer seems to have snapped; he was tired of being caught in the middle with no resolution in sight. "The entire matter is urgent," he declared to the Economics Ministry in the first days of January 1939, complaining that Enoch was intentionally dragging his feet. In his mind, Enoch owed a debt to his Albatross-Tauchnitz connections, which he blithely disregarded when he put off their request for closure. Kupfer noted that Enoch's relationship with the Scottish publisher Collins, for instance, was "entirely dependent on the goodwill of the Albatross and Tauchnitz firms."

He worried, too, that Enoch might sell only the Albatross-Tauchnitz books he already owned outright so as to curtail the flow of foreign currency back to Germany.[18]

Having expressed his irritation with Enoch, Kupfer aligned Albatross and Tauchnitz with the German economy; both would pay the cost of disentangling Enoch from Albatross-Tauchnitz operations. "In addition, [we] must consider that the financial settlement not only costs the German economy foreign currency, but that it also brings with it an immediate, substantial loss for the Albatross and Tauchnitz publishing houses." In exchange for the financial hit the Reich would take in paying Enoch off, Kupfer granted Nazi authorities the promise they had long wanted: "after paying off Dr. Enoch not even the slightest, most indirect collaboration of the publishers Albatross and Tauchnitz with Dr. Enoch will take place." As for the details of Enoch's settlement, Kupfer noted, "Albatross is prepared to submit completely to the wishes of the German authorities."[19]

This rhetorical stance—head down, submissive, dutiful—arises often in stories of individuals' dealings with the Nazi authorities. Yet if Kupfer took the position to advance Albatross interests, Enoch was not prepared to adopt it himself. In mid-January 1939, Lucke and Herr Römer of the Deutsche Industriebank met with Kupfer and Albatross's lawyer Hans Schöne. All present reached agreement: "The removal of the Jew, Dr. Enoch, is bound up with a foreign currency sacrifice. The suggestion of the Albatross Firm in this regard can be characterized as appropriate and therefore approved." The Economics Ministry, too, "declared itself in agreement."[20] Pragmatism had won the day, as the coldly rational language typical of such meeting notes reflected. The Reich would buy its freedom from this Jewish publisher. Everything was settled—that is, everything except for the fact that Enoch still defended his interests with intractable cool. He would not accept the proposed sum. He would not leave Albatross's story easily.

*

On 16 March 1939, a year after taking Austria, German troops invaded Czechoslovakia. The rumblings of war were too loud to ignore. For Enoch, Hitler's power play was a turning point. "When the drama of Czechoslovakia began to unfold I had become convinced that only a war could put an end to Hitler's regime, which now clearly had become an international calamity and menace of the first order," he wrote. "And I must confess that, closely following the turns and twists of the crisis, I began to wish that war would happen—a war not against a Germany as I had known it and whose heritage I carried with me, but a war against its perversions and a war for the protection of other nations from threats to their security and independence in their affairs." Enoch felt so strongly that he volunteered for the French army.[21]

In the midst of such political threats, allegiances mattered. Yet it is doubtful, as Europe crept toward war, whether even Holroyd-Reece's closest associates knew exactly for what—or for whom—he was working. Perhaps the best way to survive in a world falling apart was to become a cipher whom no one could fully read. The French Secret Service continued to suspect him of working for German intelligence. Its informants had intensified their investigations and turned up a number of intriguing inconsistencies. In June 1937, he had been cited for possessing unauthorized carrier pigeons. The charge had been dismissed, the birds discovered to be "domesticated Biset" pigeons. Still, who knew? In October 1938, the French had uncovered Holroyd-Reece's actions for a British banking group that was brokering a deal with the government of Burgos, in northern Spanish territory held by Franco's nationalist armies. Holroyd-Reece's group was trying to purchase the Société Anonyme Commerciale Italo-Espagnole. If it succeeded, the British group stood to gain offices in important Spanish locales, 4 million pesetas of blocked active and passive assets, and—most important, given visions of a pending war—a stake in the market for hard metals: molybdenum, tungsten-wolfram, bismuth, nickel, and iron. While this endeavor spoke to Holroyd-Reece's British loyalties, he had chosen as his liaison with the Burgos government an unsavory type who piqued the French's suspicions: one Monsieur Henri Pourverelle, a well-connected former French commercial attaché to Guatemala and Peru, described as "a very intelligent man, possessing great talents for financial organization, but *devoid of all scruples.*" Rumor had it that he had drowned his wife. He bragged that in the event of war he would become the head of the French Deuxième Bureau in Portugal. French agents worried about the company Holroyd-Reece kept.[22]

In December 1938, Holroyd-Reece came to the attention of the French minister of labor when subscribers at Lloyd's in London requested that another of Holroyd-Reece's Parisian firms—Sédouy Reece et Cie—handle their automobile insurance in France. As protocol demanded, the minister requested a background check on Holroyd-Reece with the Ministry of National Defense and War, only to receive a rather unusual answer: Holroyd-Reece might be working for German intelligence. When the minister of labor quickly reneged on the deal, the British Embassy in Paris came down upon his head, demanding to know why the French had damaged British interests for no apparent reason. Caught in a bind, the minister wrote once again to the président du conseil at the Ministry of National Defense and War in May 1939: was Holroyd-Reece a German agent or was he not? The president sent a tentative response. In April 1938, he affirmed, one source had depicted Holroyd-Reece as a German agent. But as of December, the Prefecture of Police had communicated that "no piece of information confirms the suspicions that might have been brought against Mr. Reece." Without more evidence, he concluded, "until further notice, I do not consider him as a suspect of being bankrolled by a foreign power."[23]

One month later, a source labeled "certain" offered information to the contrary—information that would have made Hans Otto feel vindicated since he had made the same claim years earlier. In sloping handwriting on an almost empty page stretched a most titillating assertion: "Reece declares himself to be an agent for British Intelligence."[24]

The idea that Holroyd-Reece was, and always had been, a British agent, dovetailed nicely, in fact, with his next maneuver: trying to spirit Albatross assets out of Germany. The previous months had brought a spike in international tensions. On 31 March, Prime Minister Neville Chamberlain announced to Parliament that Britain would support Poland in the case of German aggression, infuriating Hitler. In April, Mussolini invaded Albania, prodding Britain to offer protection to Greece and Yugoslavia if Mussolini pushed beyond their borders. Politically, things were heating up. Holroyd-Reece needed to remedy Albatross matters in Germany before it was too late.

With so many across Europe echoing these fears, Holroyd-Reece needed to safeguard Albatross's assets in case of war. The Brandstetters had turned unpredictable. They had long complained that Holroyd-Reece was not running Tauchnitz profitably, and on 4 March 1939, just before Hitler annexed the Sudetenland, they articulated a threat that snapped Holroyd-Reece to attention: they would no longer work with Albatross on the previous basis and would nullify their contract if Holroyd-Reece did not accept their terms. The Brandstetters' resistance gave Holroyd-Reece pause. Albatross might have "controlled" Tauchnitz for years, as he had always put it, but without Tauchnitz, Albatross stood exposed in Germany. So in April 1939, Holroyd-Reece agreed to run "Tauchnitz business for the calendar year 1939 at his own risk" and "to take on himself any losses that might arise."[25]

Perhaps Holroyd-Reece calculated that this gamble, however unlikely to work in his favor, offered something Albatross desperately needed: Brandstetter-Tauchnitz protection. If the Brandstetters turned against him, he could lose access to Germany, endangering what he had often portrayed as the cultural mission of the two English-language series: to keep readers in Hitler's Germany exposed to Anglo-American ideals. Albatross was also being menaced from other quarters. Three weeks earlier, on 31 March, the Literary Chamber had established Regulation 133, which banned all anonymous capital from any firms under its jurisdiction. This ruling was a death warrant for Albatross, with its shares tied up in the capital of the Publishing Holding Company in Luxembourg and the British holding companies behind it.[26] It would also sound the death knell to Holroyd-Reece's finances. If the regime forced the Albatross Verlag to liquidate, then Holroyd-Reece would lose all the funds that he and other Albatross investors had "loaned" Albatross to cover its first three years of operation. The loan itself was a fiction; the money was hidden start-up capital Holroyd-Reece had presented as a loan. Still, the money was real enough, amounting to 300,000 RM between the original debt and interest on it over time. Holroyd-Reece needed his German partners for the moment, to buy himself time to turn these liabilities into opportunities.

As it turned out, Regulation 133 gave Holroyd-Reece the perfect chance to exploit vagaries in German law. Albatross had been poised to receive fresh capital from British investors, Kupfer explained to the chief finance president of Leipzig on 3 June 1939, yet "the new situation makes collaboration in its existing form impossible." Kupfer proffered an alternative—a plan to reorganize Albatross that resembled a more elaborate version of the Enoch-Wegner exchange. In its simplest outlines, the plan entailed liquidating the existing Albatross in Leipzig and establishing two new Albatross firms in its place: one in Stuttgart that would contain no anonymous capital and another in Switzerland. The Stuttgart Albatross would absorb the debts of the original Albatross. To help pay back this substantial debt, the Stuttgart Albatross would deliver the equivalent value in

Albatross books from Brandstetter warehouses to the Swiss Albatross office; receiving these assets, the Swiss Albatross would, in turn, reimburse Pegasus the appropriate amount in foreign currency.[27]

Whenever Holroyd-Reece started pushing assets across national borders, it paid to look twice at them. What Kupfer did not clarify—perhaps because he was not in the know—was the sleight-of-hand behind the proposed exchange. Having the Stuttgart Albatross "pay" the Swiss Albatross in books was nothing more nor less than Holroyd-Reece's attempt to get Albatross books out of Brandstetter warehouses into his possession. Even if Albatross Leipzig had access to 300,000 RM, the Reich would never be willing to transfer such exorbitant sums in hard currency; in that case, books would suffice. Wegner had mentioned the possibility of a Swiss Albatross in a letter on the eve of the boycotts against Jewish-owned stores in the spring of 1933.[28] Yet this idea had an entirely different resonance in 1939. With the possibility of war lurching ever closer, Switzerland offered not just an out from an anti-Semitic Germany but Holroyd-Reece's last best hope of a continental base likely to remain neutral during wartime.

To sway the regime to accept this books-for-foreign-debt arrangement, Kupfer played up its advantages. First, he argued, the deal would allow the regime to cover Albatross's massive foreign debt to Pegasus by offloading thousands of books in English. This Albatross debt had mounted during the 1930s because Germany could not muster enough foreign currency to send the money that the German Albatross office was prepared to transfer each month. So in the tally sheets of international trade, the Swiss Albatross plan would save the Reich from having to transfer hundreds of thousands of Reichsmarks in hard currency to cover this debt. Second, the Swiss Albatross planned to take up foreign distribution and production of Albatross titles. This might seem a disadvantage, since the books sold abroad would no longer bring in currency for the Reich; yet it would free the Nazi bureaucracy from having to transfer any more funds for Albatross. "Payments for agency costs, for propaganda legwork or for royalties would no longer come into question"—an annual savings of over 100,000 RM—"yet, on the other hand, the German [Albatross] firm will be guaranteed the right of selection over the books." As so often with Albatross proposals, there was ostensibly only one obstacle: Albatross needed time. It would have to keep its existing enterprise afloat while pouring new funds its new Swiss operation. With that, Kupfer made his last request: that the authorities approve monthly transfers of 6,000 RM to the French Albatross-Tauchnitz office "just a little longer until the reconfiguration had been finalized." Six months more, at most, he argued, and the Swiss Albatross would be positioned to cover its costs forevermore.[29]

And so Holroyd-Reece waited: on Enoch, on the Leipzig finance president, on the possibility of war. The Leipzig finance president, astonishingly, signed off on Albatross's proposal. On 15 June, he approved a payment of 36,000 RM over six months, 6,000 RM per month until December, supporting Albatross's Swiss solution, with one caveat: "*Under no circumstances* can you reckon with the granting of a further authorization after 31 December." That Albatross was issued this extension after the years of kerfuffle it had caused regional financial authorities—and when Enoch's emigration had not, as promised, enhanced the flow of foreign currency into the Reich—defies belief. But there it was in writing: Nazi officials were willing to continue transferring precious foreign currency for a deal that would essentially allow Holroyd-Reece to pull Albatross entirely out of German control into his safekeeping in Switzerland. Two weeks later, on 30 June, another piece of Holroyd-Reece's plan slipped into place. Enoch signed over his worldwide Albatross-Tauchnitz distribution rights to Holroyd-Reece's Les Éditions Albatros for a "pay-off" of £5,000, or 60,000 RM. As of 1 July, Holroyd-Reece controlled the Albatross-Tauchnitz books warehoused in Paris, and was poised to unlock a new Albatross future.[30]

*

Yet the bubble was about to burst. There was little time for wishful thinking as the summer of 1939 wore on. On the last day of July, Holroyd-Reece told the British publisher Stanley Unwin that he had just returned from "an unexpected visit to Germany." To smooth matters in Leipzig, he spoke to Albatross and Tauchnitz employees, and to the Brandstetters half a mile up the road from the Albatross office in the Göschenstrasse. He also greased the wheels of the Nazi cultural machinery in Berlin, meeting with Bischoff, the managing director of the Literary Chamber, to talk about Albatross and Tauchnitz. "On this occasion," Bischoff noted, "Reece conveyed that he was still meeting with understanding everywhere."[31]

In August 1939, back in Paris, Holroyd-Reece wrote to his employees in Leipzig, anticipating war. "Tauchnitz has survived four [wars] and we will survive the fifth," he declared, with the aplomb of a captain rallying his crew. He then went about trying to ensure that his optimistic prediction would come true. Even as he prepared for war, he signed new business for the Modern Continental Library. George Orwell was next on the docket, with *Coming Up for Air,* a satirical rendering of the ways capitalism was eroding rural England. "Naturally, I'm delighted about the Albatross business," wrote Orwell to his agent on 4 August. "I've always wanted to crash one of those continental editions." It would, however, require some changes to get the book past German censors, as Orwell recorded in his diary: "Albatross Press arranging for publication of my last book, require excision of certain (though not all) unfriendly references to Hitler. Say they are obliged to do this as their books circulate largely in Germany. Also excision of a passage about a page suggesting the war is imminent."[32]

In early August 1939, such advance censorship was, uncannily, almost a hopeful gesture, suggesting that all that stood between Albatross and its German readers were a few targeted references to Hitler—as if the likelihood of war could be whisked away by careful editing.

THIRTEEN

Faces of War

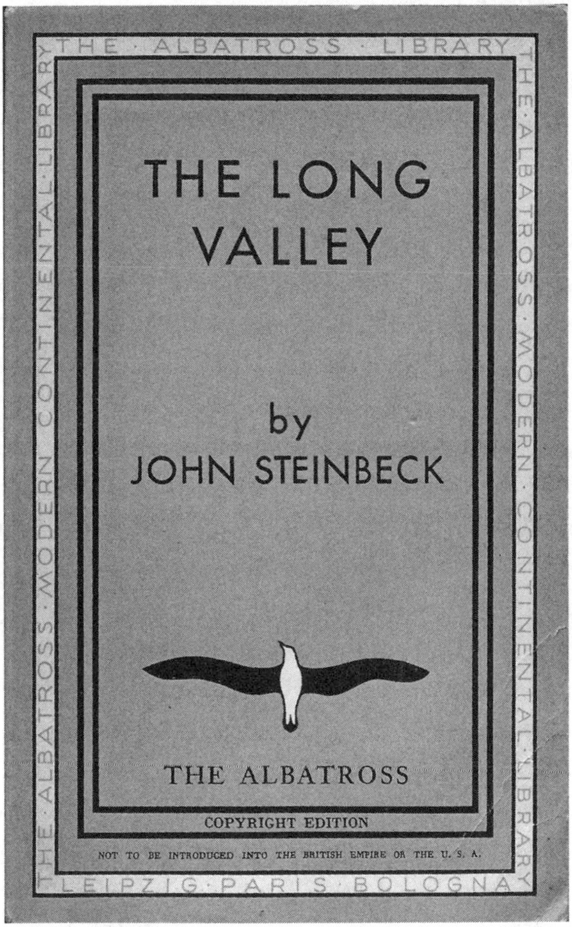

BY AUGUST 1939, rumors of war swirled around Europe. Enoch was enjoying a seaside vacation with his family in Brittany when he learned, on 23 August, that the Russians and Germans had signed a nonaggression pact. Driving through the night to Paris, he returned to a city flush with preparations. "Everything was in turmoil," he recalled. "Roads were filled with military convoys, stations with soldiers or mobilized reserves joining their units; streets, marketplaces and restaurants in the towns and villages I passed were full of excitement." On 1 September, Germany invaded Poland. On 3 September, Britain and France declared war against Germany. In the first hours of war, the French government plastered posters across its capital city declaring mandatory blackouts after dark and designating block wardens to keep order.[1]

On the first evening of the war, the Germans made their presence felt. "German airplanes appeared over the city," wrote Enoch, provoking French antiaircraft fire. "Wailing sirens ordered everybody down into the air raid shelters," he remembered, "which in my case was a large cellar under our old apartment building said to be connected to parts of the vast labrynth [*sic*] of caves and tunnels supposedly stretching underneath the whole city. As it became known later, the bombs did not contain explosives, but leaflets bearing the inscription 'Parisiens, Parisiennes, préparez vos cercueils' (men and women of Paris, prepare your coffins'), a devilish propaganda trick which did not fail to make a strong impression."[2]

The onset of aggressions had an immediate impact on Albatross. With allegiances British, French, and German, the firm and its operations were lodged in a thorny position on both sides of the war. Its leaders found themselves not just on opposite sides of national lines, but at cross-purposes. Holroyd-Reece ran Albatross with a trusted staff who supervised affairs at 12 rue Chanoinesse. Yet the French government had interned his right-hand man, Wolfgang Ollendorff, as a German national—though Ollendorff, half-Jewish, had sought refuge in France with Enoch in 1936 to escape Hitler's racist policies. To make matters worse, the Trading and Communication with the Enemy Acts, which forbade Britons to have contact with Germany, meant that Holroyd-Reece could no longer keep tabs on Kupfer in Leipzig. The Brandstetter presses had eked out Volume 509 of the Modern Continental Library just two weeks earlier: John Steinbeck's story collection *The Long Valley*. Albatross had "lightened" the volume by eliminating one story, "The Raid," which showed Communist sympathies. With war upon them, Albatross editors need not have bothered. Holroyd-Reece could expect this to be the last title he would receive from Leipzig for a long time to come.[3]

The war drew lines, and Albatross would be cut in two, with the Albatross that sympathized with Allied armies cleaved from its German Doppelgänger. All three of the original Albatross leaders had experienced such divisions in the First World War, and they understood too well the cycle depicted by Erich Maria Remarque's *All Quiet on the Western Front:* war made certain men into enemies until the end of war granted them once more a human face and form. "But now, for the first time, I see you are a man like me," Remarque's narrator realizes, as he looks upon an enemy soldier he has killed. "Forgive me, comrade. We always realize it too late."[4] Now, with battle freshly under way, such perilous distinctions would arise all over again. In the Great War, Holroyd-Reece had fought for the British, and Enoch and Wegner for the Germans; now Holroyd-Reece and Enoch stood on the same side, facing Wegner on the other.

*

Much to the chagrin of the French Secret Service, Holroyd-Reece was nowhere to be found when war broke out. A file note of 29 September reported with alarm that he "had left his residence some time ago to accomplish a secret mission, without anyone knowing where he might have gone." His disappearance ran counter to French plans. In the last week of August, the président du conseil at the Ministry of National Defense and War had insisted, "I have learned that John Holroyd-Reece, said to be authorized by British intelligence, is not known to this service, and that . . . he is supposed to have gone to Germany very recently. His activities should be surveilled." Higher military figures were also keen to know the truth. Scored by red pencil for emphasis was one comment from late September: "L[ieutenant] Col[onel] de Mierry would be grateful to the [French] Secret Service to tell him if Mr. Holroyd-Reece is truly suspect." De Mierry, highly esteemed, had been present in the private train when Marshal Ferdinand Foch had signed the Treaty of Versailles. In response to his query, Paul Paillole, a prominent leader of counterespionage for the Fifth Bureau in the French Secret Service, ordered yet another investigation into Holroyd-Reece and his associates.[5]

The British, too, wanted confirmation of Holroyd-Reece's movements. In fact, he was right beneath their noses—in London, where the population was trying on gas masks "for the dress rehearsal," preparing itself for attack. "On 31 August—the eve of the German invasion of Poland—he had traveled to London, leaving his wife and his stepdaughter in Paris," one French agent finally reported in mid-October.[6] Half-Jewish, and more than half wondering how the war might turn out, Holroyd-Reece had taken precautions. He had reoriented

Albatross operations from a Paris-Leipzig axis to Paris-London. He guided the Paris office from afar, nestled into an emphatically British perch, at 7 Paternoster Row in the heart of London's publishing district, to wait out the war.

Yet in wartime, where clear allegiances were everything, such unexplained comings and goings aroused speculation. The "Leipzig-Paris-Bologna" stretching across the bottom of Albatross covers now struck a dissonant chord rather than the cosmopolitan note of the early 1930s. To be sure, Holroyd-Reece's attempts to make Albatross belong to all worlds—as at home in the many capitals of Europe as he was himself—had always caused mild confusion. London agencies tended to frame the firm as British, while Parisian agents like William Bradley referred to it as French or German. The French government, not treating such fluctuations kindly, seized both Albatross and Tauchnitz books as spoils of war; on 28 October, it put the stock of 62,500 Tauchnitz books at the distributor Gaulon et fils under sequester, followed a few days later by "all the goods and assets that the publishing house Tauchnitz successors Brandstetter and Co. possess in France." With Albatross financially yoked to Tauchnitz, Albatross books were also seized and blocked from sale.[7]

This decision was economically disastrous for Holroyd-Reece. War had cut him off from Albatross's most reliable customers, its German readers, as well as from hundreds of thousands of books trapped in Brandstetter warehouses. Overnight, France, Albatross's second-largest market, was locked against him, too, claiming his last resource: the books in Parisian warehouses. On 26 October, Holroyd-Reece's firm Sédouy Reece, with its original capital of 500,000 francs, declared bankruptcy.[8] Albatross might be next.

Holroyd-Reece poured his energies into convincing French authorities that Albatross was indeed British. This negotiation was quite a feat. His name was nowhere on the Albatross Verlag documentation; Albatross had always listed Wegner and after him Kupfer as the German managing directors, and in wartime their names argued against Albatross's Britishness. The Publishing Holding Company, which owned Albatross, was British, but based in Luxembourg. In addition, Holroyd-Reece's urgent appeal that French authorities acknowledge Albatross as British contradicted the message he had been broadcasting far and wide on joint Albatross-Tauchnitz stationery since the mid 1930s: that the firms were happily intertwined.

But war pushed Holroyd-Reece to pry Albatross loose from its German partner. So in mid-November 1939, while French authorities punished Albatross for being German, Holroyd-Reece publicly declared he had been fighting the war of the book for the British in a *Daily Telegraph* article titled "Modern Baron Tauchnitz." "Mr. J. Holroyd-Reece, who is well known in the world of publishers, is suffering more than most of them from the war," the article began. "So successful was [Albatross] that in 1934 he brought its hundred-year-old rival, founded by Baron Bernhard Tauchnitz, under British control." The writer clarified that Albatross was "entirely British-owned," though it "operated from Leipzig, with editorial offices in Paris," and also that Albatross had printed its books in Germany because "Germany constitutes about half the Continental market for English books, and to obtain sales there they had to be printed in the Reich." Most important, the article declared that the war had put Albatross at the mercy of German authorities, making Holroyd-Reece a "victim" of the Nazis. "Since the outbreak of war the German authorities have seized the Albatross stocks and are selling them for their own account. Mr. Holroyd-Reece, therefore, sees his work in Europe for the moment held up. But he hopes the war means only a temporary dislocation of his business."[9]

In late November, Holroyd-Reece returned to Paris to rescue what remained of that business. However flamboyant his return—he was spotted on the rue Royale, sporting a bright-red waistcoat, an ostentatiously tall fur hat, and a glass walking stick—he made a serious enough impression on French officials to convince them to overturn their rulings. On 29 December, a new ordinance released for "friendly sale" the stock of Albatross books at Gaulon et fils. Holroyd-Reece announced this victory to Albatross-Tauchnitz authors, noting that French authorities had decided that "the stocks—unfortunately limited—of Albatross and Tauchnitz books kept in France are British-owned property and as from January 3, 1940, their sale has begun again." With Albatross and Tauchnitz books returned to his care, Holroyd-Reece adapted, as he had done before. He returned to London, leaving his skeleton staff to sell Albatross and Tauchnitz books from Paris to the readers Albatross could still reach. From London, he staved off Albatross authors clamoring for royalty payments tied up in German bank accounts. Through a vote of the Publishing Holding Company board before the onset of war, he had already divested Albatross's German branch of power.[10] Yet his powers were severely limited. Albatross's German branch had always overseen book production, and in wartime it controlled the majority of Albatross's stock of books. Even as Holroyd-Reece laid new plans, Albatross's day-to-day operations spiraled out of his control.

*

Enoch's struggles were of a different order. Though a Jewish refugee, he remained a German national who had, overnight, become an enemy alien. On the second day of war, the French government pasted up posters ordering German and Austrian men to present themselves at the Stade de Colombes so officials could examine their status. With several friends, he appeared at the stadium, bringing a blanket and enough food for a couple of days.[11]

The scene at the stadium showed "every sign of disorganization," according to the American State Department's Intergovernmental Committee on Refugees. Two dozen French soldiers tried to register roughly forty-five hundred men herded together waiting to be admitted, a process which stretched over five days. Anxiety reigned. According to Enoch, he and his friends were treated "with obvious hostility." The French police and army guarded the stadium gate, ordering everyone to empty his pockets before he entered. Internees were allowed to keep eyeglasses or toothbrushes and handkerchiefs; the authorities took watches and money, offering a receipt for recouping these items at their release. As Enoch noted, "The question of when that would be remained unanswered."[12]

The stadium became a giant holding pen, plagued by what the Intergovernmental Committee on Refugees described as "notoriously bad" conditions. With showers and toilets reserved for guards, interned men relieved themselves in tin pails, which overflowed every day. Food rations were inadequate and sleeping quarters rudimentary, either the stadium's hard, narrow benches or the stone floor between them. On the second day, French authorities sprinkled a light layer of straw on these "beds," a thin gesture that added little comfort. As Enoch complained, the stadium was not designed to house crowds for days on end. The men's blankets and coats offered them little protection against the cold September night air. And after several days, the "sanitary conditions defied any description, people got sick and clamored in vain for a doctor. Others became hysterical and had to be restrained and the cries of those awakened by nightmares interrupted the evening quiet which settled after dark over our strange crowd."[13]

Perhaps the greatest insult to Enoch, however, was the political obliviousness of French authorities. The stadium was "filled to capacity with thousands of people thrown together, only because of the one criterion of their nationality, whether they were Nazi officials, ordinary Nazis, Germans of no political color, [or] Jewish and political refugees," triggering brawls among different factions. Finally, officials set up field kitchens that supplied coffee to the stadium's inhabitants, and divided people into groups to prevent fighting. As the days wore on, Enoch distracted himself by playing chess with one German-Jewish friend and walking around the track with a professor who explained his work deciphering old Roman tombstones. Round and round, they strode in their closed circle, waiting for news.[14]

After eleven days, they were told they would leave. "Where to, for what purpose, nobody knew," Enoch remembered. They were loaded on buses, then "on trains that carried us through a long dark night to a new unknown destiny." Daylight revealed an internment camp for German civilians near Mesley-du-Maine, near the English Channel. Here, too, conditions were poor. Though food rations improved, there was a mere pint of water per day per person. Most of the nearly two thousand inmates slept on the bare ground; Enoch secured a coveted spot in a tent—a six foot by fourteen inch allotment where a man could sleep and place his belongings. The camp ran under a quasi-military routine, where a commander "frequently [treated] the men . . . as though they were schoolboys." The one boon was the mail, however sparse; internees could write one letter and receive one package weekly. Enoch got news from his family, along with supplies: warm clothes, boots, and a rubber mattress to protect him against the cold. Yet it remained challenging, Enoch recalled, "to be subjected to orders from others who were often hostile and arbitrary and not only without any human compassion but without even the slightest understanding of the difference between the German enemy—the real enemy alien—and the German refugees, Jewish or political, who were themselves victims of the common foe. But what could one expect when it took such a long time for even the French government to recognize that distinction and to take remedial action?"[15]

The French government had, in fact, begun to realize its mistake. After its knee-jerk reaction, interning all German men and women over the age of sixteen, France's nascent Commissariat général à l'information (General Commissariat of Information)—founded in July 1939 and transformed into the Ministry of Information in April 1940—realized it might have cordoned off precisely those who could help France most: anti-Nazi German refugees possessing a wealth of information. As early as 18 September 1939, the head of the French Service of Propaganda in Enemy Countries wrote to the commissioner general of the Ministry of Information requesting that he "draw up a list of Germans currently detained at the Stade de Colombes who appear to be owed the benefit of a measure of preference because of the loyalty of their attitude during the past few years and for the service they might eventually be able to render to the Commissariat." Appearing on the "List of German Internees at the Stade de Colombes Eligible for a Measure of Favor" were prominent authors such as Lion Feuchtwanger and Fritz von Unruh whose works had been burned in 1933. Enoch's name did not appear, but he was brought to the attention of Georges Mandel, France's minister of the interior, through a Mrs. Braun, whose husband had led the separatist movement for the Saar region, and who had contacted authorities to make them aware of the plight of Jewish and political refugees.[16]

When Enoch was finally released, on 4 December, nearly three months after he entered the Stade de Colombes, his homecoming was bittersweet. "My feelings of relief and joy were tempered by anxiety of what I might find on arrival and by feelings of melancholy and almost guilt at leaving my many comrades and new friends behind." He returned to a different home from the one he had left. "Paris seemed to have aged. Many of the young were gone. The City of Light had become dark. The blackout was strictly observed. Street lights were dimmed and car lights painted over black, making driving after dark hazardous. British uniforms had become part of the street scene, in restaurants and offices. The mood of the people was subdued. Many did not understand what France was fighting for and were puzzled and nervous by the lack of action."[17]

He himself was relieved to tackle his business again, which had "shrunk to almost nothing." Exports to most of Europe and South America "came to a complete halt" and, ousted from his lucrative Albatross-Tauchnitz trade, only his two-way export business between England and France gave him any way forward. When Albatross and Tauchnitz books were sequestered in the fall of 1939, it had opened up a new possibility: to create a French firm to sell English-language books in France. Enoch met with the head of the foreign language department of Hachette, which was "looking for a substitute for their business with Albatross and Tauchnitz, the loss of the tourist market for Obelisk Press and other editions which they used to import from England and the United States." With Maurice

Girodias—son of Jack Kahane, who had run the Obelisk Press until his death at the outbreak of war—Enoch formed the Unicorn Press, supported by Hachette's distribution network. Enoch and Girodias signed Steinbeck's *Grapes of Wrath* and launched discussions with authors such as Somerset Maugham and Elizabeth Bowen, but were held up by paper shortages and lack of access to printers and binderies.[18]

More than anything, Enoch's experience in the camp accentuated his awareness of his own foreignness. He had, in fact, applied for French citizenship in April 1939, but had not yet received it. Now he sought to bolster his ties to France, offering his publishing relationship with Hachette as proof of his allegiance. In March 1940, he wrote to the General Commissariat of Information, noting, "I left Germany definitively in 1936 and transferred the exclusive right of sale for the Albatross and Tauchnitz editions and a large part of the considerable capital that I succeeded in getting out of Germany to this [business], whose headquarters is located in Paris." He declared his intention of using his new business, Imperia, to put his "special experience to work for the publication and exportation of books . . . to the good of French industry."[19]

Then, on 9 April 1940, the Germans invaded Norway and Denmark. With German troops pressing westward toward France, books were the least of Enoch's concerns, his hope of French citizenship just one more foundation crumbling under the weight of the advancing war.

*

If Wegner, for his part, had spent much of the Great War in the air above the battlefields, the new war put him back on the ground. In the fall of 1939, he ran the businesses he had purchased from Enoch from a temporary office in Hanover, where he was stationed, having been called up on 24 July. Wegner soon found that the skills that served him well in publishing also put him ahead in the war. He quickly won a position of authority, orchestrating provisions and supplies for troops belonging to Anti-aircraft Transport Division 11. In February 1940 his superior, Major Cranz, submitted a glowing review to promote him to first lieutenant, praising him for being "assertive, animated, highly adroit, [with an] outstanding knack for organization."[20]

Wegner's military file credits him with having taken part in battles in Flanders and Artois and the push to the English Channel in the first spring of the war.[21] The Maginot Line on which the French so relied had been circumvented, and on May 10 German armies broke into the Netherlands, Belgium, and France, surprising the Allies with a three-pronged attack. The most effective breach was achieved by Army Group A under General Gerd von Rundstedt, forty-five divisions strong, seven of them armored tank divisions. Roughly fifty miles north of the point where the Maginot Line ended, the tank divisions rumbled through the Ardennes forest, penetrating the hilly, densely forested terrain which the French had deemed impenetrable and thus had not bothered to defend.

On 13 May, German troops negotiated the steep cliffs along the Meuse River and crossed over its wide expanse into France. With German troops closing in on Allied troops in Belgium from the north, and sweeping up from the south, the Allies were surrounded and disarmed near the border of France and Belgium. Here was the prize German military leaders had hoped for, the reason they had codenamed this advance Operation Sickle Cut (*Sichelschnitt*). The German scythe was poised, arcing around Allied troops, pushing them up toward the Channel, waiting for the moment to cut them down.[22]

Wegner's organizational talents had landed him behind this front rather than at it. Still, the war made itself felt. "Pentecost Monday. Cold and sunny," he wrote on 12 May 1940, two days into the German advance into Belgium. "The war has now begun—with fresh sacrifices—and no one knows how it will end." He worried about his son Ezard, from his first marriage, stationed near an airport where "danger lay in wait." He was horrified by the Allied bombing of a town in which civilians and children had been killed. "The killing of children already is sickening," he wrote his wife. "Overall, I am in a desolate mood; can't imagine that it will be successful." The next week he traveled home to Hamburg to shore up his business before the German army's surge forward. "On Friday evening late, I was in Hamburg," he wrote on 19 May, "where I experienced the first air raid . . . and was extremely glad that you are away from there." Worried that Hamburg would be an early target of Allied bombers because of its critical port, Wegner and his wife had decided that she and their two young children should relocate to a small town outside Munich, near her family. Missing them, he made the rounds in his own family, seeing his mother, his brother Ekhard, and his daughter from his first marriage. Two days later, he wrote from Cologne, reporting his change in attitude, perhaps helped by the fact that he had received a promotion to first lieutenant on 18 May: "36 hours without sleep, . . . with [lots of] work, but the mood is good." He visited his "very old and mumbling" Aunt

Leni, and enjoyed a "charming reception from friends of Major Cranz." But the next round of troop movements lay just ahead. "Our battalions are already over the border. . . . I think affectionately of you and the children."[23]

As the weeks wore on, Wegner elaborated less on the destruction he saw. Perhaps he wrote with censors in mind; perhaps he wanted to keep the war from seeping into his letters home. By the time he next wrote, in the last week of May, he was ensconced back in Belgium, where Major Cranz not only relied on him but appreciated his savoir-faire: his fluency in French from his publishing days with Albatross in Paris, his fine palate and quick humor. Though Wegner was beneath Cranz in rank, they had whiled away spare hours in and around Brussels in the intervening weeks, playing Ping-Pong, going to a movie; one night he headed to Cranz's for asparagus, a springtime delicacy, which the major was going to cook himself. Wegner had hung the embroidered cat from his five-year-old daughter, Silvia, over his bed and wrote to Annemarie that his "own bathroom with gas heat is certainly the most comfortable luxury." On 25 May, he reported wining and dining in style to fête his promotion: "Yesterday glutted [myself] with the Doctor in the Palast Hotel in Br[ussels]; for each of us a whole lobster, and on top of that, Vouvray!"[24]

This sounded less like war than vacation, one of the perks of being a first lieutenant in a victorious army; it was his task to manage supplies, and so he could access the best of them. Still any respite promised to be brief. The Netherlands had surrendered on 16 May. Belgium had lasted only nine days longer. Between 26 May and 4 June, Allied troops raced to the coast, escaping in any conveyance that could negotiate the English Channel.

On 30 May, Wegner alluded to the next phase of his war. "The Belgian war will now soon be over; we naturally don't know how [the war] will continue, yet I don't think we will stay here too much longer." Ever the material provider, he had sent home a number of packages filled with luxuries no longer easily available in Germany: coffee, clothes for their daughter Silvia, chocolate, nylons.[25] He would not write again for several weeks, too busy with the German army's surge into France, heading Enoch's way.

FOURTEEN

Enemy Books

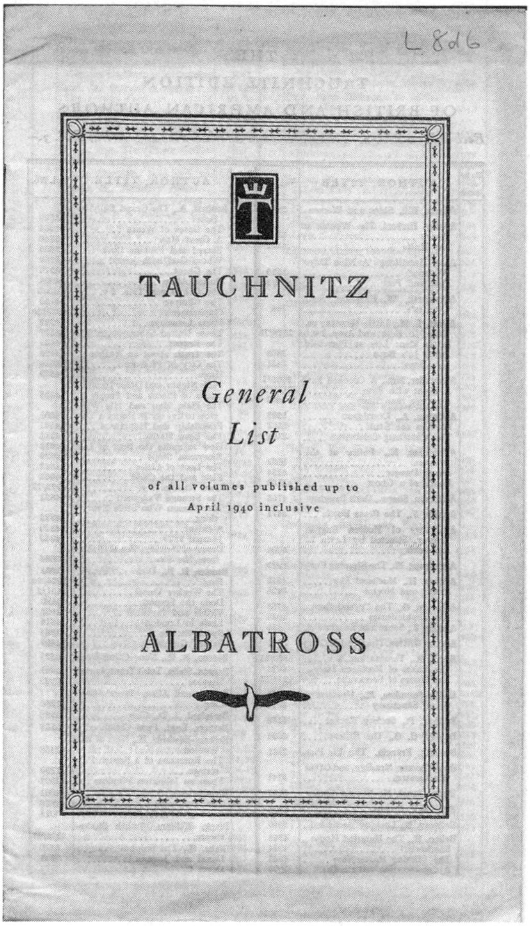

IN A FRAGMENTED WORLD, only Albatross and Tauchnitz books themselves had the distinction of belonging to both sides. From Paris and from Leipzig, which seemed now more than ever two different universes, Holroyd-Reece and Kupfer sent their books flying across Europe in the first few months of the war. In fact, the "General List" of Albatross and Tauchnitz volumes that

Holroyd-Reece circulated to booksellers suggested, on the surface, that the war had changed nothing. It contained "all volumes published up to April 1940 inclusive," as if production had never been disrupted. The regal Tauchnitz "T" still held sway above the title on the cover, with the elegant albatross hovering below.[1] Yet if this brochure implied that Albatross and Tauchnitz still worked together in harmony, the reality was otherwise; Holroyd-Reece and Kupfer—each running half an operation—faced off in a bizarre competition to sell their English-language titles to continental readers as war raged on around them.

That Albatross and Tauchnitz books could be deployed by both sides in the war, rather than being maligned as "enemy books" by one or the other, seems astonishing. This was especially true of the German side, where the Nazi regime, already suspicious of Albatross as a source of pro-British propaganda, had little patience with British political warfare. Anyone watching events in Germany would have thought Albatross's days were numbered. For when Britain declared war on Germany, the German Propaganda Ministry declared war on British books. On the first day of war, the regime immediately banned two publications—the underground anti-fascist newspaper *Germany To-day* and the book *Lord of Terror* by Sydney Horler, a Tauchnitz author—an announcement that one Leipzig official deemed relevant to Albatross's status and tucked into his Albatross file. More regulations followed. A Propaganda Ministry ordinance of 15 October 1939 outlawed crime and adventure novels "that do propaganda for English institutions and the English nature." By November, officials had established a student movement which had as its goal "to search the history and culture of all peoples and every scientific branch [of inquiry] for material and arguments against England." Booksellers were ordered to pull translations of British books from display windows, and in December 1939 new translations were banned.[2]

Surprisingly, though, Nazi officials did not take the simplest solution of banishing Albatross books outright. Nor did they penalize the Brandstetters by suppressing Tauchnitz volumes. Albatross and Tauchnitz books continued to roll off Brandstetter presses, their pace slowed, but not stopped, by the war. *The Flashing Stream,* by the British author Charles Morgan, was the first Albatross title printed in wartime Germany—an unlikely choice, given Morgan's reputation as a Francophile and an ardent anti-fascist. Yet his play was advertised as Volume 510 on 25 September in the daily insert to the German book trade newspaper, along with an Albatross Crime Club book by Agatha Christie, *Appointment with Death.*[3]

How long Albatross would survive in the prevailing climate of animosity toward British books depended on how authorities in different branches of the regime interpreted its usefulness. In one sense, the war had delivered to financial authorities the result they had long desired: Albatross and Tauchnitz enterprises that operated independent of the whims and expense of their Paris owners. And officials from the Literary Chamber, the Propaganda Ministry, and the Foreign Office eyed Albatross's astounding distribution network with envy and hope, debating how they could enlist it in service of German culture—a vision of books in German overtaking the continent as surely and swiftly as Hitler's armies.

*

There was one reason, however, that Nazi officials did not simply seize Albatross as enemy property when war broke out: as of November 1939, there was no official policy on how the Reich would accomplish such a thing. Nor was there consensus among Nazi elites. The Economics Ministry and Hermann Göring—commander-in-chief of the Luftwaffe and Hitler's minister (plenipotentiary) of the Four-Year Plan—pushed for financial action: to liquidate foreign firms for German gain. The regime had already seized private firms, both Jewish and non-Jewish, with no regard for the law, and wartime offered, in their minds, a justification beyond all others. Yet the Foreign Office vociferously resisted. It worried that if the Reich liquidated enemy property, other nations would retaliate against German firms. Above all, the Reich needed to maintain civil relationships with its remaining international trading partners to retain access to the raw materials that fed its war machine. Thus the Foreign Office advocated less invasive maneuvers. Throughout the first fall of war, each wing of the Nazi bureaucracy fought for its own interests, trying to win control over this all-critical policy: whether foreign firms would be plundered outright or placed under German stewardship.[4]

While the Nazi elite remained stalemated, Kupfer was expected to continue with business as usual, if anything could be said to be "usual" about running the highly specialized export of English books when Germany was at war with Britain. With Leipzig cut off from Paris—and Holroyd-Reece marginalized —Kupfer was left with the responsibility of running the whole show with access to only half its functions. Paris had always been the place from which Holroyd-Reece, fluent in several languages, had cultivated relationships with authors. Since 1936, Paris had been the hub from which Enoch nurtured his relationships with European distributors. Over time, Paris had also become Albatross's financial saving grace; had Holroyd-Reece not paid honoraria from Paris to authors on the verge of launching costly lawsuits, Albatross and Tauchnitz might long since have crumbled. Kupfer, used to taking Holroyd-Reece's lead, overnight inherited Holroyd-Reece's day-to-day tasks; at the same time Nazi authorities expected him to reestablish Leipzig as the Albatross-Tauchnitz export center. In short, despite himself, Kupfer once again became Albatross's most strategically placed employee.

Kupfer's struggles can only have been intensified by the fact that more threatening authorities had stepped into Holroyd-Reece's place—each plucking Albatross from its German roots and debating whether to destroy it or to replant it more firmly in German soil. In early November, Kupfer reported that "the Reich Ministry for Popular Enlightenment and Propaganda and the Economic Ministry are taking up the question" of what to do with Albatross. But while Kupfer waited on these powerful authorities in Berlin, regional officials insisted that Albatross, with its foreign ties, stood in violation of the law. In fact, in December 1939 the Leipzig Chamber for Industry and Commerce declared that it would bar Albatross from selling its books if Kupfer did not recuse himself and appoint an absentee custodian. Bandied back and forth between regional and national levels of bureaucracy, Kupfer did what he knew how to do: he soldiered on, requesting a custodian and waiting for approvals, selling the books he was expected to sell.[5]

Kupfer's impasse reveals both a deficiency in the Nazi bureaucracy—obsessed with regulations but overloaded with more urgent dilemmas in wartime—and the sheer chaos that war imposed on the German book trade. The Propaganda Ministry demanded he "purify" the Albatross and Tauchnitz series of objectionable titles. With account books, author contracts, and royalty records located in Paris, now enemy territory, he was also forced to re-create many documents. The only accountant familiar with the Paris accounts had quit for personal reasons, and a new accountant caused such a hurricane of numerical disaster—"an unholy disarray"—that he was quickly fired. Adding to the challenge of managing Albatross was an acute labor shortage. Many employees had been drafted, including Kupfer himself, who was expected to direct the firm from the front, and replacement personnel were hard to find. "Although Private First Class Kupfer was still able to attend to the most important matters of the operation," wrote Kupfer of himself in the third person, "he found, however, after his release [from the military] at the end of October 1939 an operation that barely functioned."[6]

Apart from the overarching question of whether Nazi authorities would dismantle Albatross, Kupfer faced a host of practical, urgent dilemmas. He was highly capable, yet spoke only faltering English, as is evidenced by a statement he sent one editor with the unintentionally humorous postscript: "Please excuse our retard discount by cause of war, but we could not make it up at an earlier date, as our former Editorial Department of Paris had always done this for us." And more critically, Kupfer did not hold full power of attorney because Holroyd-Reece had restructured Albatross after Enoch's emigration to protect it from legally falling under German control; any decisions to change Albatross's partnership with Tauchnitz or the Brandstetters, to sign new contracts, or to alter foreign trade agreements needed signatures of both Kupfer and his equivalent, the French managing director. Lucke had once wryly commented that Holroyd-Reece "clinches all even passably important decisions." Now, Holroyd-Reece loomed large, even in his absence. Kupfer could not, alone, legally compel foreign booksellers to pay Leipzig rather than Paris; many were hesitant to alter previous agreements, some fearing legal trouble, and some mistrusting the Nazi regime.[7]

It is intriguing to see Nazi authorities forced into such a stand-off. Until enemy property guidelines were put in place, investing power over foreign firms officially in German hands, authorities were bound not by the regime's wishes for Albatross but instead by a force exterior to the Reich: the international law that determined business dealings—and Albatross-Tauchnitz sales—in the continental market. In early December, still lacking enemy property protocols, Nazi bureaucrats improvised. They blocked Albatross from producing new titles, which had appeared every two weeks throughout the fall. And the Literary Chamber launched its own "professional and political" investigation of the Albatross-Tauchnitz-Brandstetter relationship. "The Albatross situation has naturally never been quite in order, but it was difficult to do anything about it here [in Berlin], since at a purely formal level everything seemed to be above board," explained Karl Heinrich Bischoff, a leading bureaucrat in the chamber, explaining why the regime had not only tolerated Albatross but had cut into its own foreign currency reserves to support it. "I rather explain it to myself this way: a nod to foreign sales, [and] emphasis from here that there is no cultural-political interest [in the series], because it revolves around English-language literature." With mingled resignation and sarcasm he added, "The royalty applications (foreign currency) are still naturally rolling in."[8]

Only in April 1940 did the Propaganda and Economics Ministries officially decide to preserve Albatross. The Economics Ministry had determined that Albatross sales were useful to the war effort; they generated trade credits in particular national markets which the regime could use to purchase raw materials it needed. And so, during the war, as before, Kupfer pushed Albatross and Tauchnitz sales in English from Germany. Between September 1939 and the end of July 1940, he sold 128,770.14 RM of books for Albatross and 169,732.42 RM for Tauchnitz to readers in the Reich and neutral countries. These figures were roughly 50 percent lower than those in peacetime for Albatross and 25 percent for Tauchnitz.[9] Still, the numbers were striking; for most of this time period, Kupfer had lost access to France and the Netherlands, Albatross's second- and third-largest markets.

Yet if the Propaganda Ministry tolerated Albatross for its sales, not all titles were created equal. So-called Jewish books were the first to fall. On 1 December 1939, the Literary Chamber required publishers to report any books by Jewish authors or about Jewish subjects. Nine weeks later, Kupfer sent an inventory of the fifty-nine titles Albatross and Tauchnitz had pulled from sale, along with one copy of each book. Included in the Albatross list were only two authors. One was G. B. Stern, a Britisher famous for her five-volume series *The Radowitz Chronicles,* a matriarchal, somewhat feminist depiction of upper-class Jewish life. Albatross had published two of her titles, *Little Red Horses* (Volume 50) and *Pelican Walking* (Volume 236). The second was Humbert Wolfe, an Italian-born British poet who worked his way from the Board of Trade to the Ministry of Labour and was created a Commander of the Most Excellent Order of the British Empire (CBE) for his service; his *PLM: Peoples, Landfalls, Mountains* was Volume 338 of the Albatross Library. Tauchnitz volumes made up the bulk of the list, with authors including Gilbert and Joanna Canaan, Fannie Hurst,

G. H. Lewes, Maarten Maartens, Leonard Merrick, Ludwig Lewisohn, E. Phillips Oppenheim, the essayist Paul Cohen-Portheim, and the World War I poet Siegfried Sassoon. Kupfer followed up with officials to determine whether the books should be stamped as unsalable, or whether he could fall back on the 1930s solution for "undesirable" titles—shipping them over the border to pad the trade balance.[10]

On 10 June 1940, with the Germans on the verge of seizing Paris, *Confidential Announcements for the Book Trade*—a periodical informing booksellers of new regulations that affected book sales—offered a provisional answer. All books by authors considered Jewish or pro-Jewish were to be removed from sale, among them Tauchnitz titles by Frank Swinnerton and Israel Zangwill, and a host of Albatross titles: Graham Greene's *Brighton Rock,* three titles by Rosamond Lehmann, two by G. B. Stern, two by Rebecca West, three by Michael Arlen, and one by Michael Joseph. *The Albatross Book of Living Verse* was also banned outright, presumably because it would be too hard to remove Jewish authors from its pages, as was the accepted protocol for "purifying" anthologies so they could be resold. Ernest Hemingway's two Albatross titles—*The Sun Also Rises* and *Men Without Women*—also appeared on the list; officials considered *The Sun Also Rises* defeatist and pacifist, not qualities they wanted to promote in wartime. Intriguingly, the list made calculated allowances for other titles banned in Germany—such as Huxley's *Brave New World* and *Brief Candles*—that might be popular abroad.[11] Since the Germans were about to conquer France, Nazi authorities apparently viewed Albatross titles less as enemy books to be banned and more as enemy spoils to be exploited.

*

A world away, Holroyd-Reece turned his attention to selling the Albatross and Tauchnitz books he could reach, and to ensuring that whichever way the war turned out, these English-language series might have a postwar future. With Germany and Austria out of reach, the war had cost him nearly half of his market, as well as precious time and money when the French government locked down his warehouses. These trials aside, between September 1939 and the end of May 1940, he sold slightly more than half the Albatross and Tauchnitz holdings in Paris: roughly 150,000 of the ostensibly 280,000 volumes that remained at the start of war.[12] Yet such success, as he knew, would lead to its own undoing.

The Brandstetters controlled the entire production wing: the printing apparatus, hundreds of thousands of Albatross books, and the costly original plates necessary for reprinting existing titles.

Unlike Kupfer, however, Holroyd-Reece stood on the right side of the war to build upon a different cornerstone of Albatross and Tauchnitz's future: the British and American authors on whom the two series depended. This freedom was both a luxury and a liability. He wrote, telegraphed, and phoned his way throughout the so-called phoney war—the British nickname for the early phase of the war in which the Western Front remained still—placating anxious authors. Some wondered how they might get their royalties out of Germany, while others voiced the more threatening question Holroyd-Reece hoped to keep at bay: At what point did the war void their Albatross contracts, leaving them free to sell their titles elsewhere? A letter from George Orwell to his agent in December 1939 offers one indication of the authors' confusion. "Do you know what has happened to the Albatross people? . . . Have they gone west, I wonder?"[13] Hardly. Orwell's agent had to clarify that the war had changed everything.

With the onset of war, Holroyd-Reece cast off the menacing oversight of Nazi officials for the scrutiny of Allied intelligence. British and French agents clearly wondered whether his publishing activities were masking some vein of undercover work. Yet as one British agent monitoring his correspondence confirmed with his French contacts in February 1940, Holroyd-Reece's letters "did not reveal anything suspect, but [instead] a lot on the subject of financial complications. . . . The impression that one takes from this is that this group of publishing companies, working in different continental countries with Holroyd-Reece at its head, is struggling not to go bankrupt."[14]

War also plunged Albatross into a public relations nightmare. Rumors abounded in the London *Evening Standard* and certain continental journals that Albatross was in league with the Nazi regime. Holroyd-Reece eloquently staged his defense in a four-page, single-spaced "Note for the Information of British Albatross and Tauchnitz Authors" in January 1940. Albatross had printed its books in Leipzig not because of any allegiance to Germany, he explained, but because it wanted to "secure for the authors and the publishers the large German market." He decried anti-Albatross statements as "slanderous and highly prejudicial . . . because it is made to appear as though the Albatross were a German government or Nazi concern whereas in fact the British owners of the venture together with the authors are victims of the war." Albatross was friend, not foe, to British authors, he argued, and had been for years nearly the only means of securing a German audience for British books. "Except for his organization," as he rightly contended, "the German market has been closed, either almost completely or entirely."[15]

Trusting in the strength of the Maginot Line to protect Albatross's French office from German interference—or at least acting as if he did—Holroyd-Reece sent a follow-up letter on 30 April, requesting that Albatross authors stay as loyal to Albatross in hard times as Albatross had been to them. Authors continued to barrage him with complaints; their books were selling on the continent and they wanted their royalties. Yet their books had become wartime pawns—a fact beyond his control—and, Holroyd-Reece implied, beyond that of Albatross's German branch, as well. He could, he explained, launch an injunction to bar German Albatross-Tauchnitz sales in neutral countries. Yet he painted the absurdity of this ploy, involving legal battles in over thirty countries, and foreign booksellers faced with the same titles in German-produced and Anglo-French-produced editions confused about which to sell. Lest authors assume he had passively surrendered to these exigencies, he ended with sugar-spun images of a brighter future. The Anglo-French Albatross planned to reprint titles, and with authors' help the Anglo-French Albatross might not just survive the war but grow: "The fact that Mr. Holroyd-Reece is now residing in London should make collaboration even easier than it was before."[16]

These were sweet words in a dark time. On 30 April, the day Holroyd-Reece crafted his letter to Albatross authors, the British had begun evacuating troops from Norway, ceding control to the Germans just three weeks after they invaded. In this context, there is something by turns foolhardy and admirable in Holroyd-Reece's persistence. It was his birthday, the beginning of his forty-third year. It was also day 253 of a war that showed no sign of ending soon, a war that had already stripped him of so much control and that might soon pull from his hands the publishing endeavors into which he had poured so much of himself for the previous decade. What did he need to muster in himself to pretend otherwise? With German armies on the march, the time of illusions was nearing its end. Churchill had developed his own nickname for these early months of the war: the "twilight war." This phoney war was soon to get real for Albatross, the twilight to fade to black.

*

True control of Albatross books in wartime was about to be passed into other hands altogether: those of the Reich Commissioner for the Handling of Enemy Property, former bank commissioner and minister-president Dr. Friedrich Ernst, appointed in late December 1939. After months of agitated negotiation, the regime had decided how to handle Albatross and other firms with "significant enemy influence." Under no circumstances could they be seized at will; instead, they would be sequestered and run by German custodians. Each custodian would take on power of attorney, dissolving the decision-making power of the existing management and board, and determine how to use the firm for German ends. Each custodian also had a second, equally important responsibility: to preserve, as much as possible, the firm's assets for the postwar world so that Germany could not be held financially responsible for a firm's demise in the event of war reparations being demanded.[17]

The Reich's concern with the legal postwar liabilities of bookselling seems at odds with its rampant disregard for the law in other quarters. Ever since Hitler had abolished parliamentary procedures, he had headed a regime where lawlessness ruled, the Führer's decision being the ultimate law of the land. Throughout the 1930s, authorities had seized Jewish property, and Jews themselves, justifying all manner of ill-gotten gains and torture on the grounds that Jews no longer counted as citizens. Abroad, in the first months of war, German Einsatzgruppen (mobile death squads) had decimated swathes of Poland—its land and its people—and then unrestrainedly taken what remained. Yet when it came to enemy property regulations, the regime had decided—as in earlier years, when it tolerated Albatross books—that it could not follow its inclinations without unduly harming the German economy. The Foreign Office worried about repeating the mistakes of the First World War, in which Germany had arbitrarily liquidated foreign property but then been forced to reimburse foreign companies at great expense after the war. In short, the regime's willingness to flout the law had its limits, especially when it came to international trade. The caution of the Foreign Office won the day.[18]

As a result, Reich Commissioner Ernst proved to be less tractable to carving up Albatross than Albatross's foes in Germany might have expected. Indeed, reported to have been "a remarkable able and active man," he also turned out to be the unlikely defender of Albatross in its first wartime challenge: a takeover attempt by the Brandstetters. They were tired of taking orders from Albatross. Their alliance—so full of promise in 1934—had earned them little but suspicion and debt. Reich officials had cast aspersions on them and ransacked their files. Albatross owed them at least 30,000 RM, and Tauchnitz far more.[19] With Paris and Holroyd-Reece cut off by war, they envisioned Tauchnitz in the seat of power and themselves winning back the trust of the regime.

In fact, had the timing of Wegner's military appointment been different, he might have experienced much of the spring of 1940 from a desk chair in Leipzig rather than from a supply truck on the Belgian front. The Brandstetters wanted Wegner to lead the charge, granting Tauchnitz—and Germany—the upper hand once again over English books on the continent. The Literary Chamber agreed with this solution, and on 2 February prodded Ernst to accept Wegner as the most qualified candidate for Albatross custodian, since he already had the backing of the Chamber of Commerce and Industry, the municipal court, and the governmental president of Leipzig.[20]

Yet instead of appointing Wegner outright, the commissioner took time to familiarize himself with Albatross's case. He worried that Wegner, occupied with his own publishing house, might let Albatross business languish; he also intuited that Wegner stood close to the Brandstetters and so might privilege their interests over those of Albatross. The commissioner's Albatross file grew fatter, as pressing appeals arrived from various quarters to appoint Wegner. Kupfer begged for a decision. His delay was stalling "important negotiations and agreements" with foreign vendors, and the Brandstetters were pressuring him to get Albatross on the right side of the law. In April 1940, in fact, fed up with the status quo, Willy Brandstetter sent Albatross an ultimatum: if Kupfer did not get Wegner appointed by the end of April, the Brandstetters would no longer release books from their warehouses. Willy Brandstetter also nullified Tauchnitz's longstanding contract with Albatross. "I myself strongly regret that I have been forced today to write you this type of letter," he wrote with seeming honesty. "But you must also admit that I have really exercised extraordinary patience and have waited months for the appointment of an absentee custodian."[21]

Back at the Office of Enemy Property, this threat raised the hackles of the

Reich Commissioner, who quickly called Brandstetter to explain that he considered his letter a personal affront. Albatross came under *his* jurisdiction, and he would not allow Tauchnitz to dissolve its contract with Albatross—a decision of enormous magnitude—without his say-so.[22] The Brandstetters might want to seize Albatross for German interests—their own—to reimburse themselves for the time, money, and hassle Albatross had cost them. A host of Nazi authorities endorsed their plan. Only the Reich Commissioner stood in the way. The war had apparently changed many things, but not one: somehow, Albatross wriggled through, despite its questionable status, finding a higher protector—this time one chosen by the Reich itself—with a higher plan for the firm.

The following day Justus Brandstetter had recourse to the kind of argument Otto had invoked nearly a decade earlier. Brandstetter wound up his six-page report detailing the rocky Albatross-Tauchnitz marriage with one supreme rationale for why Tauchnitz should be allowed to sever ties from Albatross: "Tauchnitz, as a pure German firm, can no longer be expected to tolerate [a situation] in which it continues to leave its management in the hands of a firm exclusively financed with foreign capital, which on top of everything is without adequate legal representation, and whose spiritual leader, Herr Reece, bragged after the outbreak of war that he had succeeded in bringing the 100-year old Tauchnitz under British control as of 1934." Branstetter added a flourish to stress his allegiance, feigned or otherwise, to Nazi ideology: he penciled in "Jude" next to Holroyd-Reece's name, and added, for good measure, that Albatross stood "under Jewish influence." In short, Justus Brandstetter put it to Nazi authorities as baldly as he could: German ministries were continuing to privilege the interests of a foreign, Jewish firm over those of a loyal German enterprise.[23]

After another round of discussions on the subject, the Reich Commissioner ultimately conceded that Wegner might be a viable candidate after all. Yet at first no one could track him down. And then word finally arrived that he was at the Belgian front. With Wegner otherwise occupied—or rather, about to become a German occupier—Ernst sought someone else to lead Albatross into a wartime future that could serve German ends. In late May 1940, Kupfer, the Brandstetters, and the Literary Chamber settled on a custodian with ties to neither Albatross nor Tauchnitz: one Walter Osbert Gey, forty-six years old, from Liebertwolkwitz, just outside Leipzig. A grainy photograph attached to an application for the Institute of Certified Accountants (Wirtschaftsprüfer) shows the man who became responsible for Albatross affairs for the duration of the war. Gey was, like Kupfer, a family man, married with two children. In his photograph, he projects a stolid, earnest presence, with a roundish face, balding head, and glasses.[24] Ernst deemed Kupfer—whose efforts he seems to have estimated highly—indispensable to the daily running of Albatross, but Gey would be the man in charge: Holroyd-Reece's double, driving Albatross-Tauchnitz sales from the German market Holroyd-Reece had been so loath to lose.

FIFTEEN

Return and Departure

NAZI MILITARY MANEUVERS were quickly redrawing the map of Europe and with it the fates of the former Albatross leaders. On 25 May 1940, General Maxime Weygand acknowledged at a War Cabinet meeting that France might need to admit defeat. In a last-ditch effort, he ordered troops to hold fast on the defensive line north of Paris along the Somme and Aisne Rivers; yet even he doubted that these much diminished forces could succeed against Germany's largely intact military. On 5 June, Germans launched Operation "Code Red," pushing into France. On 10 June, realizing that the Germans had broken the Somme-Aisne line and were beginning their march toward Paris, top French officials fled for Poitiers.[1]

While waves of German troops crossed the Belgian border into France, Wegner followed behind with supply trucks for his enormous army division. To return to France was to cross over the lines of memory, reaching back to the time, almost a decade earlier, when he had first moved to Paris to launch his Albatross dream. He seemed eager to discover the fate of old friends, using his little free time to track them down. "I was in Rohaix yesterday," he wrote to Annemarie on 9 June, "& after a long search found the printing house Georges Frère. The available personnel are French and touchingly loyal to their families. [They] recounted that Marcel's parents are well with one daughter in Paris-Plage, that is, on the German side. The three sons are French soldiers."[2]

Before he returned to Paris, Christian was hoping to enjoy his last days in Belgium with his superior, Major Cranz. "Tomorrow we are moving into an updated castle belonging to the duke von Cranz," he explained to Annemarie. "The family is there, speaks impeccable German. We will have guestrooms with sheets. . . . Heat is great, accommodations good, wines top-notch! Aperitifs, too. I have been speaking a lot of French to the friends of my commander." Wegner knew such luxuries were fleeting. "Yet it won't last long, since we'll certainly follow behind. Here [we are] already almost behind the lines. At night the front drones on over here: until now, we've been protected from bombs, but of course they've already been in Munich." He worried about his wife and children, who had moved near Munich precisely to avoid this danger. "Did you have to go into the cellar?" Five days later, on 14 June, he wrote again. "We've got to get moving again already, [we] pull [out] today or tomorrow to northern France, where the conditions for accommodations will be arguably less good than here." He reflected that "the military success of the recent weeks has been astounding," and planned a detour to see if the paint factory owned by one of his friends was still standing. "Probably, everything is destroyed in France, just as the nutritional status of the people [here] seems far worse."[3]

More than anything, Wegner's letters reveal his awareness of war as a time of contrasts. Families split along national lines. Aperitifs at the castle owned by Major Cranz's family. Bombed-out villages on the drive south. He took photographs of his friends. He took photographs of emptied-out landscapes. He savored the good things that came his way. "We are oozing with strawberries, eggs, butter, and cheese," he admitted to Annemarie. Aware that she, like most other Germans, suffered from shortages, he sent packages home, numbering each one and its contents, waiting for confirmation she had received the goods wartime had rendered precious. He felt cut off from home, complaining to Annemarie that his unit had "still not received any mail, it is truly foul."[4]

While Christian Wegner prepared to occupy France, Kurt Enoch prepared to defend it. He had joined the 99th regiment of the "prestataires," a branch of the French army open to refugees forty years or older. He was transferred to Camp du Ruchard, near Poitiers, for training. "I departed with a heavy heart," he wrote. "The beginning of the German offensive was also the beginning of one of the most trying times for me personally, for my family and for others in a similar situation." His elder daughter, Ruth, seventeen years old, had been at an American boarding school in Normandy, and he worried that she might be cut off by advancing German troops. Instead, she made her way to Paris only to be interned by the French government as an enemy alien. A new decree mandated that all German and Austrian women over sixteen—apart from mothers with younger children or women over seventy—had to report to the Vélodrome d'hiver in Paris, a gathering point for transfer to the Camp de Gurs near the border of Spain. Ruth and Enoch's sister Ilse were both sent to Gurs; Enoch's wife, Marga, was allowed to stay in Paris to take care of his younger daughter, Mirjam, who was sixteen.[5]

At Camp du Ruchard, Enoch was appointed group leader of his barracks. For a time, life progressed normally, with the men doing roadwork, loading ammunition, and eating army rations in the mess hall under a sign that read, "Here, one does not eat; one dines." Then came word of the German advance. "From the scattered news that came over the command post radio and from occasional newspapers that found their way to us," Enoch later wrote, "we knew that the war had gone from bad to worse."[6]

Inside the French capital, it was obvious the Allies were not faring well. A British Parisian, Ninetta Jucker, described the refugees pouring into the city: first came wealthy Belgians, in luxurious cars, "crowded with children and luggage and surmounted by the inevitable mattresses which we were coming to recognize as the symbols of flight"; then several days later, refugees on "farm carts . . . full of children and bedding, household utensils, and even livestock, drawn up by the side-walk in the Avenue Friedland." Out of packed trains, too, spilled "fugitives, who had lived through days of terror, bombed and machine-gunned on the roads, often after abandoning ruined homesteads."[7]

Then, as the French realized the Germans were truly invading, they, too, joined the ragtag procession. Sylvia Beach recalled, "Day and night, people streamed through the rue de l'Odéon. People camped, and slept, in front of the railway stations in the hope of getting on a train. Some left in their cars—which had to be abandoned along the roadsides for lack of gas. Most of them fled on foot, carrying babies and baggage, or pushing baby carriages or wheelbarrows. Some had bicycles." "Why flee?" she asked, resolute to stay with her French friends. "Only about 25,000 people were left in Paris." She and her longtime companion, Adrienne Monnier, watched refugees stream from one side of Paris to the other: "cattle-drawn carts piled with household goods; on top of them children, old people and sick people, pregnant women and women with babies, poultry in coops, and dogs and cats. Sometimes they stopped at the Luxembourg Gardens to let the cows graze there."[8]

Marga waited in Paris with Kurt's daughter Mirjam and his mother; as enemy aliens, they could not leave without a permit. "Everyone who possibly could had left for the south of France," she remembered. "The invasion . . . was imminent." Then on 13 June, they could wait no longer. They put on their knapsacks filled with extra shoes, canned food, and blankets, and rolled their bicycles into the street, leaving their lovely apartment on the Île Saint-Louis. "We joined the general exodus: tens of thousands marched along the highway," wrote Marga. "The entire sad mass of humanity moved in a southerly direction." The first night they slept in an abandoned cinema, mustering their forces for the long march south with civilians and retreating French soldiers, past abandoned automobiles lining the road. When Italian planes machine-gunned the lines of refugees, they scattered. "Everybody threw himself flat on the ground; many did not get up when the raid was over," Marga recalled. "It got so bad that we had to change our routine: we could no longer walk during the day but had to hide in the woods and only proceed after dark." As the day wore on, a bus requisitioned for army use offered Enoch's mother, visibly struggling with the long walk, a ride to the next town. This seemed like a gift until Marga and Mirjam arrived to find the town in flames. They searched everywhere but could not find her. They had no choice but to rejoin the parade south. Hoping that French soldiers had kept her safe, they held fast to the slips of paper their concierge had pressed into their hands: the address of her family in the south of France, a chance of refuge.[9]

*

The stories of those who remained in Paris are filled with the weight of loss as they saw the Paris they knew and loved stripped of the sights and sounds that had made it real to them. "June 13 was the last day," wrote Jucker. The city was suspended. "Nothing moved, except near Montparnasse, where the last refugees were still camping outside the station, in the hope of getting onto a train." Time literally stood still for her; Jucker relied on the enormous clock on the side of the Renault factory she could spy out her apartment window, yet the workers who usually wound the clock had fled, leaving its hands frozen. Peter de Polnay, a Hungarian-born writer with ties to England, was struck most by the eerie silence. "The noise of Paris was gone. . . . Paris had its own noise, which belonged to her like the Eiffel Tower or the Métro station of Réaumur-Sébastopol." Before the Germans marched into Paris, too, a "weird black fog" and then a "downpour of black rain" settled upon the city, as if it were some stage set, the fog and rain trick effects to announce the arrival of an enemy in an evening at the theater. While some Parisians blamed it on "devilish machinations of the Germans," the French Command had, in fact, set the oil deposits of the Basse Seine on fire, to keep them from the Germans. The Métro ran, but there were no buses. The gas barely flickered. On the Champs-Élysées, Jucker and her husband, Marco, sat in an otherwise abandoned cinema, watching a film.[10]

Sylvia Beach met her friend Dr. Thérèse Bertrand-Fontaine at the American Hospital, where they watched out the window. "An endless procession of motorized forces: tanks and armored cars and helmeted men seated with arms folded. The men and the machines were all a cold gray, and they moved to a steady, deafening roar." Nazi officials quickly seized on the symbolic gestures their victory afforded them. For Jucker, who lived two hundred yards from the Eiffel Tower, the occupation began with the sound of German boots. The French had disabled the elevators, so a French policemen guided German soldiers to the tower, where they raised a Nazi flag so large that it ripped in the wind and had to be replaced. De Polnay noticed other ironies. German troops marched past war posters plastered across the city to buoy French morale. One proclaimed, "We will defeat [the enemy] because we are the strongest." Another held the heading "Deuxième Bureau Contre Kommandatur," with "a frightened Hitler visible on the poster." All such bolstering had been for naught. French prisoners in rags marched alongside German troops. "The music shrieked and the swastika fluttered in the breeze, coming up from the Champs Élysées, and then I saw a large wreath, with the same swastika, on the tomb of the Unknown Soldier," remembered de Polnay. "I thought I would vomit. The crowd was silent and watched. Nobody spoke." Within two days, the French surrendered. On 16 June, Premier Paul Reynaud resigned and Marshal Philippe Pétain, who had achieved incredible reverses against the Germans in the Battle of Verdun in the First World War, was installed in his place. On 17 June, Pétain requested an armistice.[11]

By this time, Christian Wegner, who had driven into Paris on the heels of invading German forces, was ensconced in his hotel, across from the Opéra. He wrote to Annemarie of his mixed feelings on his return to the place he still loved: "I am sitting at the open hotel window, see the opera in front of me, & write. The [people of the] city must be home at 9 p.m. There are no buses or taxis, so it is a sad scene. Nevertheless full of memories for me. I was in the Alb[atross] office." Christian repeated news, some accurate and some not, that he had gleaned of his Albatross colleagues. "The Reece family gone. Ollendorf & Alex & E[noch] in concentration camps. Sonia's husband and Bricaire soldiers!" Sonia Hambourg, assistant editor, "told of harrowing days." The wife of one Albatross colleague, he elaborated, "point-blank flung her arms around my neck; she went through terrible things with the children, yet remained, thank God, whereas almost all others have fled. Jeanne [Holroyd-Reece] and Mother E[noch] had unfortunately fled, whereto, no one knew to say."[12]

Journeys backward and forward in time, a homecoming, but a laden one: all the old, familiar places void of so many old, familiar people, and Wegner part of the occupying army they had fled. "You can hardly measure the distress of the people and then the joy, when the news of the end of the fighting came through this afternoon," he wrote to Annemarie. Still, he was aware of this new Paris as a city almost haunted. "In the fourteenth arrondissement none of our neighbors was there—everything closed, offices, pharmacy, etc. Tomorrow morning early I am expecting my major, to show him Paris; in the afternoon we drive back [to northern France]; a *fully* forlorn land between P[aris] and St. Quentin. In the abandoned houses is not one human soul. It seems like a hell." His letter ended awkwardly between flippancy and concern, hastily wrapping up experiences too vast to fit in an envelope: "Otherwise nothing new! How much longer, the war? Who knows!"[13]

The occupation of Paris meant different things to different people. Albatross continued to exist, but in a changed world. Sylvia Beach protected her community and sold her books in English from the rue de l'Odéon as long as she could get away with it. "Parisians who survived the exodus came back," she remembered, "and my French friends were delighted to find Shakespeare and Company still open. They fairly stuffed themselves on our books, and I was busier than ever." In a hardcover black notebook with "1940" stamped on the front in gold, Beach inadvertently offered an alternate history of the invasion. If for Jucker the Renault clock stood still and for de Polnay the city lost its noise, for Beach there was another sign of German intrusion: the days she sold no books. On 4 June, she had sold Rosamond Lehmann's *Dusty Answer* (Albatross), on 5 June D. H. Lawrence's *Lady Chatterley's Lover* (Odyssey), on 8 June, Virginia Woolf's *To the Lighthouse* (Albatross). A span of empty pages marks the days of exodus and conquest. Only on 20 June did Beach resume sales, with two reviews, followed by a copy of the *New Yorker* the next day. During the summer months, with Paris under German occupation, she sold, among others, Joyce's *Ulysses,* Steinbeck's *The Long Valley,* Wilder's *The Bridge of San Luis Rey,* Lawrence's *The Woman Who Rode Away,* and Huxley's *Beyond the Mexique Bay.* Simone de Beauvoir, who had some trouble with arrears from Beach's lending library, checked out a number of Albatross titles, among them Faulkner's *The Unvanquished,* Hemingway's *To Have and Have Not,* William Saroyan's *Inhale and Exhale,* and E. M. Forster's *Passage to India*—and a non-Albatross title, Richard Wright's *Native Son.*[14]

Christian Wegner, the cofounder of the publishing house whose books Beach sold and loaned from her modest storefront, stood on the other side of this experience. From somewhere outside Paris, he wrote Annemarie on 24 June. He had finally received two of her letters, in reverse order. He was sad to hear of friends fallen in battle. He was concerned that her radio did not work, and that "fruit is so difficult to get." Ever the provider, he pressed her for what he might send: "I have, you know, sent infinite amounts of tea, coffee, choc[olate]. You should have it soon enough. I would still like to get you shoes. Size 38? Will that do? And what type and color? Do you have enough clothes? Children's shoes, scarves, gloves?"[15]

The soldier in Wegner waited anxiously along with the provider to hear news of the war. "The scene in the boxcar at Compiègne, where I was eight days ago, is over," he remarked. "We are waiting hourly for the armistice; and then we will probably be deployed against England. Hopefully!" The *hoffentlich* strikes an odd note, as if he has been swept up in victory, hungry for the next *Sieg.* His son Matthias later expressed disbelief: "The man who had so often visited his business associates in London, wanted, of all things, to participate in the invasion of this country. He was, after all, by now a man of no less than fifty years who had at his disposal a talent for organization lauded by many as perfectly brilliant —yet for political injustice, for the repulsiveness of the system that he served or had to serve, he lacked every instinct. The most important thing for this passionate entrepreneur was his business." Wegner's sympathies crossed national boundaries. "Poor Sonia!," he declared of the British editor who had been with Albatross since its beginning, and who who had been so happy to see him back in Paris. "All of her cousins and so forth are English soldiers or with the marines. I will only head back to Paris when I see, overall, more clearly. Otherwise, we're fine; at the moment, the enemy is leaving us in peace."[16] The war had put him on this side and not the other. What, exactly, would it mean to see more clearly?

*

While Wegner sought news of his friends and explored old haunts, Enoch tried to convince his French officers to let him go. "The misconception of our commanding officer," wrote Enoch later, "was such that when he announced to us on the 16th of June that France had asked for an armistice, he admonished us not to show our pleasure too openly. This lack of understanding could have had much more serious consequences for us." Hearing on the radio that the Germans could easily reach their location, Enoch and his fellow émigré soldiers "found it very difficult to make it clear to our command that it was a question of life and death for us to move away." The French officers held their ground. "Only after we threatened to revolt," Enoch remembered, did they agree to vacate the camp. When Italian planes bombed the road, they sought shelter in the dugout, where they waited for an "all clear" signal that never came. The French officers had abandoned them.[17]

With some of the men, Enoch marched south, his sights on Limoges. On 1 July, he arrived in Montauban, which like many other towns in the Vichy zone was "overflowing with refugees." The city provided cots, blankets, and field kitchens. It was nearly impossible to find a place to sleep. Enoch settled down in the attic of an old villa, with half a roof. "Nothing dramatized more poignantly the tragedy and misery which had befallen millions than the inscriptions on every available space—on house walls, sidewalks, pavements—asking for information about people who were lost, and giving names and addresses of those who were looking for them. I had no hope that the inscriptions would give me news of the whereabouts of my family." He sent word to his brother Otto, who had emigrated to Detroit, to see if he could organize visas for the family. But the situation seemed nearly hopeless.[18]

And then the miraculous happened: a soldier, hearing Enoch say his name at the post office, handed him a slip of paper with information about his sister Ilse and daughter Ruth. French soldiers guarding Gurs had released them shortly before the armistice; after a failed escape attempt from the coast, they had found shelter in a church basement in Oloron-Sainte-Marie, near Gurs. By day, they diligently handed out pieces of paper listing their whereabouts. It was one of these slips that the soldier passed to Enoch, who sent a secretary by train to find them. Marga and Mirjam found them in similar fashion. Enoch heard, too, that his mother had returned to Paris.[19]

Relieved that his family was alive, Enoch turned his attention to getting them to safety. "Most countries had closed their borders to us," he recalled. "Moreover, the armistice agreement forbade the issuing of exit permits to German refugees, leaving illegal border crossing as the only way out. Last but not least, we needed passports which none of us had at that time." But then came another stroke of luck. Eleanor Roosevelt had secured entry permits for anti-Nazi refugees trapped in Vichy France who might be "assets" to the United States. Enoch's brother Otto, who had worked as a research engineer in Detroit since 1937, wrote the State Department of Enoch's plight, and even contacted Thomas Mann, who sent a letter of support from the United States, to which he had immigrated at the outbreak of war. Enoch was given a tentative spot on the list of the so-called Emergency Rescue Committee, and made his way to the American consulate in Marseilles to present his case. "Until now the world had seemed closed to us and the future nebulous without anything firm on which to pin realistic hopes," wrote Enoch. "Now there was the vision of an open door to a new beginning in the most desirable, most exciting, and most powerful country in the world."[20]

Still, this vision was just that: a vision. The obstacles were intimidating: "how to move the family to Marseilles in order to pick up the U.S. entry permits"; how "to obtain the Spanish and Portuguese transit visas—which would necessitate an extended illegal stay in Marseilles"; how "to leave France without valid exit permits"; how "to somehow reach Lisbon and find passage to the United States." Each checkpoint brought a new threat, especially for Enoch's daughters. While he, his wife, and his sister had resident permits, Ruth and Mirjam had no identity papers at all. So worried was Enoch, and so little did he trust French authorities that when they were on the train he had instructed the girls, if the police came to check papers, to open the door—these being the days when each compartment had its own exit to the outside—and jump out. And there remained "the most agonizing problem": how to get his mother out of France.[21]

Enoch sought help from the "underground grapevine" that had sprung up to aid refugees. Yet even with this guidance, the quest for visas and the journey between Marseilles and the Spanish border were plagued by danger and detours. They had learned of a secret escape door at the train station at Marseilles leading from the station coffee shop into the kitchen of the neighboring hotel that enabled those without papers to circumvent the heavily guarded exits to the station. Enoch arrived to find this door had been locked and had to improvise; only later, when the door opened, could he and his family wind their way safely from the coffee shop through the hotel kitchen and out to the street. At the Spanish consulate, where a throng of refugees waited for visas, the Enoch family's plans were again temporarily threatened when the concierge suddenly declared the numbers that held their places in line invalid. "Pandemonium broke out, everybody rushed forward to storm the door; my wife was knocked down, trampled and kicked so that she fainted." The incident proved a blessing, as the concierge, alarmed, took Enoch and his wife inside. "We were now treated with special consideration and visas for the entire family were handed us without delay."[22]

Still, they lacked exit visas for Vichy France, and moved from one contact to the next in search of a way across the border into Spain. They traveled to Perpignan—at the advice of Varian Fry, the human face of the Emergency Rescue Committee—only to find the escape operation that might have covertly gotten them across the border into Spain had been shut down. Moving on to Cerbère, a Mediterranean town where they had heard that the station restaurant owner might help them, they joined a line for tourists departing the station to escape scrutiny of their documents. The restaurant owner discouraged them from attempting to cross the mountains with "so many women," and suggested that they throw themselves on the mercy of the local police commissioner. With Marga beside him and cash to bribe the commissioner, Kurt walked into his office. "Our first reaction was one of shock: sitting there behind his desk, stony-faced and unsmiling, was the same official whom we had told only moments before that we had come to Cerbères [*sic*] for a seaside holiday." They apologized, telling the truth and trying to bribe him, to little avail. "After all, you have your legs," he retorted, unmoved.[23]

And so they used them, driven by the hope of a safer future on the other side of the imposing, craggy mountains that stood between them and Spain. One road led up the French side to a high plateau and border guard station, winding down on the Spanish side to a guardhouse and a walled cemetery. They should hide there, the restaurant owner had told them, until they heard French guards leaving their shifts, and then continue on the road until they reached an old fig tree close to the Spanish guardhouse. There, since they had valid Spanish visas, the guards would take them into custody and guide them to the border post.

Little worked as planned. Ruth's shoes were far too large, and made noise "clearly audible to unwelcome ears." Kurt grew stressed, impulsively raising his voice at her to quiet her down. He could not find the start of the shortcut. He fell into a ditch, sending an avalanche of stones hailing down. "There was only one thing to do: to leave the road at once and to climb—sometimes on all fours—straight up the slope as fast as everyone could manage. It was terrible," he remembered. "The sharp cactus spikes which we grabbed for support lodged deep under our skin, the tumbling rocks struck our hands and legs, and the steep, hurried ascent made us breathless. But worst of all, we made a terrible noise." Luckily, no one heard them, and they arrived, "bleeding and exhausted," at the top. On the Spanish side, they followed bright lights to a false hope: the illumination of ships in the harbor that led them in the wrong direction to a high cliff overlooking the water. Ilse collapsed and refused to go on. Only when the moon came out could they see the guardhouse up the hill. They walked toward it, where they were confronted by guards at gunpoint. The moment could go one way or the other. They handed the guards cigarettes. The guards gave them water to wash off blood, telling them they should say they came by the road if they were stopped. When the commandant arrived to examine their papers, they were, finally, allowed into Spain.[24]

A car brought them to Portbou and a bustling location set up to help refugees; there a man brought them train tickets to Barcelona and took them to their next train. Kurt grew nervous when a Spanish official took their papers, worried he might be turned over to the Germans. But their papers were returned and they found their next contact, a station porter, a former government interpreter whom the Spanish fascist regime had dismissed because he was Jewish. This porter, Mr. Kaplan, showed them around Barcelona, establishing enough trust that Enoch gave him money to help his mother if she made the journey that far.

Their respite was brief. The train to Madrid was slow, and the view outside disheartening: "Civil War prisoners with chains on their legs worked on the roadbed, sadly staring into the car windows." The compartments were squeezed full. Marga had sat still for so long by the time they arrived that she had to be carried out of the train on a stretcher. A small boon awaited: a room at a large hotel, where they rested up for the last phase of their European journey, the train to Lisbon. "After so many months of blackout, signs of decay and destruction, and sights of an uprooted, harassed and deeply troubled humanity, I was struck by the bright lights, clean white buildings and the relaxed look on people's faces," wrote Enoch. In Lisbon, the kindness of near strangers once more brought them relief. A friend of his secretary rented them rooms in a small town outside the city to protect them from the intrigues—crime, political intelligence, secret diplomatic exchange—which ran rampant in Portugal's capital. The Emergency Rescue Committee sought passage for them on a steamer to the United States. It also offered something far more mundane, yet valuable enough that Kurt, dressed in shabby clothes from a French relief agency, recalled it years later: a new, warm overcoat, the hope of protection against the elements to come.[25]

The American Export Line was booked solid. The only passage available was a Greek ocean liner, the *Nea Hellas*—a risky option, since rumors abounded that Greece was about to enter the war and many feared the boat might become a target. Enoch secured two cabins. Among the 678 passengers were celebrated German émigrés who, like the Enochs, were being spirited away from Hitler's occupying forces: Franz Werfel and his wife, Alma; Heinrich Mann, brother of Thomas Mann; Golo Mann, son of Thomas Mann; Frederike Zweig, first wife of Stefan Zweig, with her two daughters; and Hans Jacob, an esteemed journalist and interpreter. Red Cross flags flew at the masts.[26]

Finally, came the moment of first sight. "It was on the 12th of October 1940 when the skyline of New York—so often seen in pictures—appeared over the horizon and the pilot's boat became our first contact with the new world," wrote Enoch. At 9 A.M. on 13 October, the ship docked at Fourth Street, in Hoboken, New Jersey. *New York Times* reporters rushed on board to interview the famous writers. For Enoch, it was all a blur. "The *New York Times,* the image of abundance and our sudden move into the spotlight came almost as a shock to me." It was a day of reunions. "Of the emotional reunions that I witnessed all around us," Enoch recalled, "one stands out in my memory: Thomas Mann and Heinrich Mann, the two brothers, divided and often in bitter feuds on philosophical and political positions dating back to pre-World War I days, greeting each other in passionate embrace."[27]

For Kurt Enoch, the arrival, with all its complexities, was difficult to comprehend. "After more than a year of a defensive battle for survival all my energies had now to be concentrated on the reconstruction of our future, and there was no time to be lost to spring into action," he reflected years later. His situation "was not a very pretty picture." He was forty-five years old, with a wife and two teenaged daughters and an elderly mother who was still back in France. His assets remained in Europe, inaccessible and perhaps lost for good, and he owed his brother several thousand dollars for the cost of passage. "My knowledge of English left much to be desired and our legal status was uncertain. Except for some business contacts I had had no personal connection with Americans. My only assets were my professional knowledge and experience, a certain reputation in the publishing world and an unbroken confidence in myself."[28]

SIXTEEN

Albatross Under the Occupation

IN THE FIRST YEAR OF THE WAR, Holroyd-Reece must have done an exceptionally good job convincing French authorities that Albatross and Tauchnitz were under British control, for by the time Erich Kupfer and Wolfgang Krause-Brandstetter arrived at 12 rue Chanoinesse, on 25 October 1940, Occupation officials had a lot of questions for them to answer. As Kupfer later reported, "As a result of misinformation on the part of Herr Holroyd-Reece, the opinion persisted [in Paris] that not only Albatross, but also Tauchnitz, was English property." In wartime, assumptions about national affiliation, true or not, had consequences. Bruno Conrad, the German custodian of Hachette—a longtime French book distribution giant—was on the verge of confiscating Albatross and Tauchnitz books when Kupfer and Krause-Brandstetter arrived on the scene. And that was the least of the two men's troubles.[1]

Kupfer and Krause-Brandstetter were allied on Albatross-Tauchnitz business and had come together to seize and inventory the Albatross and Tauchnitz books in the Paris warehouses that had been lost to the Reich for the first year of the war. Yet they also worked for different masters. Kupfer, by authority of the Reich Commissioner, Ernst, was to claim Enoch's Parisian firm, Continenta, as enemy property so that Albatross in Leipzig could legally usurp Enoch's contracts with foreign booksellers. Krause-Brandstetter was embarking on a more ambitious project. The Propaganda Ministry and Foreign Office were launching a joint campaign involving Albatross and Tauchnitz, a secret mission of great importance to spread German books abroad. And he had been sent to Paris to begin quietly laying the groundwork.[2]

Yet before they could advance these tasks, Kupfer and Krause-Brandstetter had to prove to military Occupation authorities precisely what Holroyd-Reece had spent months disproving: that Albatross and Tauchnitz were, despite French claims, firms with legitimate German ties. Holroyd-Reece had not made their task easy. The war had forced him to abandon Paris. But his octopus-like reach into numerous publishing houses meant he maintained some hold, even after fleeing to London. Something did not smell right. And until German propaganda officials could determine what it was, and how Holroyd-Reece's firms were tied up with it, they treated everything he had touched with suspicion.[3]

In the office at 12 rue Chanoinesse, which had once bustled with the activity of multiple publishing houses, the high-ceilinged library stood quiet; no one was present in the tidy curtained office to check a file or to race up the stairs to the back terrace and its expansive view over the Seine. What would happen next to this seat of Holroyd-Reece's power over Anglo-American books—and who would savor his outlook on the pont Louis-Philippe sweeping across to meet the Île Saint-Louis—depended on the whims of sparring German officials.[4] For Krause-Brandstetter, who had stepped into Holroyd-Reece's position as the front man for Albatross-Tauchnitz operations abroad, it was not a peaceful trip.

*

Krause-Brandstetter must have expected a more favorable reception. It was, for him, an exciting time. He had been wooed for a post in the Information Section of the Foreign Office (Deutsche Informationsstelle), which handled publishing, propaganda, and radio abroad. As the historian Frederic Spotts frames it, the Information Section was a fast-paced men's club with a clandestine edge: "To buy off journalists, publishers and anyone else who was useful, it could draw on secret funds of a billion francs, which were charged to Occupation costs." With a staff of no less than six hundred, it managed six dailies, eleven weeklies, four bi-monthlies and seven monthlies while also issuing four daily press bulletins.[5] Because this section was part of German Embassy operations in Paris—though set up, for propaganda reasons, to seem a separate entity—Krause-Brandstetter's affiliation also promised to open up to him the social world of the Nazi cultural elite, among them Dr. Otto Abetz, the German ambassador, and Dr. Karl Epting, head of the embassy's German Institute (Deutsche Institut), a propaganda center disguised as a cultural institute that offered German language classes and hosted elaborate parties to promote German music and thought.[6]

This combination of information gathering and intrigue perfectly suited Krause-Brandstetter, already primed for such a role by his travel around the world on Albatross-Tauchnitz business. Not to mention that it was a far sight less dangerous than his first wartime assignment, rolling over the border into Poland on 1 September 1939 with his anti-artillery gun battery. Krause-Brandstetter had milked his family connections to leap from the battlefield into the cushier confines of the Foreign Office. He first became a member of the Nazi Party in April 1940—this late date suggesting he joined more from opportunism than ideological conviction.[7] By the time he arrived in Paris, things were, personally speaking, looking up.

Unfortunately for Krause-Brandstetter, officials from the military Propaganda Division (Propaganda-Abteilung) in Paris, overseen by Colonel Heinz Schmidtke, were oblivious to the Foreign Office's secret mission and his leading role in it. On arriving, he was ordered to report to the headquarters of the German military high command at the Hotel Majestic at 19 avenue Kléber. There Walther Schulz, the operating head (Arbeitsführer) of the Propaganda Division, interrogated him at some length. Krause-Brandstetter was "'from the same clan and related by [the Albatross-Tauchnitz] marriage' with an English Jew, namely R. [Holroyd-Reece]," railed Schulz, so "German authorities could not, therefore, consider B[randstetter] as acting bona fide (in connection with Tauchnitz property)." Since September, Schulz had been among the officials who had tried, haltingly, to follow the convoluted trail left by the "English Jew." They had gradually gathered enough crumbs to realize that Holroyd-Reece held shares in myriad firms, some technically French, some English, and that he played some mysterious but critical role in Albatross and Tauchnitz. Over time, Schulz had turned tetchy, his outrage growing in proportion to his lack of clarity. Krause-Brandstetter's close kinship to Holroyd-Reece so incited Schulz's ire that he even made him "swear on oath that Tauchnitz was German property, and that Albatross, though closely connected, did not belong to Tauchnitz."[8]

In this manner, Krause-Brandstetter experienced firsthand a reality that historians of the Occupation have reconstructed after the fact: "the Nazi Occupation was dysfunctional from its outset to its demise." In France, no less than in the Reich, competing authorities jostled for control, spawning what the Occupation historian Allan Mitchell describes as "a welter of titles, acronyms, ill-defined prerogatives, and overlapping duties as the German bureaucracy struggled to adapt itself to the particular circumstances of Occupied France." The realm of propaganda was no exception. German officials took propaganda more seriously than ever when it came to winning over foreign peoples to the superiority of German culture. In Occupied France, two offices fought for the chief role: the Foreign Office, for which Krause-Brandstetter was to be employed, and the military Propaganda Division, which reported to Goebbels's Propaganda Ministry in Berlin. The professional rivalry between the two was fierce. Foreign Office operations in Paris—the German Embassy and German Institute—were run by educated men who had lived in France before the war and prided themselves on a superior awareness of cultural matters in France. Not surprisingly, they wanted to wrest control over propaganda away from the military Propaganda Division, whose affiliates they viewed as boorish newcomers to the French scene. Ambassador Abetz even appealed to Hitler—successfully—to limit the power of military propaganda officials to censor, preserving for Foreign Office and embassy bureaucrats the more exciting role of "positive propaganda"—cultural events and political propaganda designed to sway the French to embrace German culture and the German cause.[9]

Whether the Foreign Office had intentionally held Krause-Brandstetter's mission close or forgotten to communicate its scope to the military propaganda wing, Kupfer and Krause-Brandstetter—along with Albatross and Tauchnitz—were caught between these divisions in a bureaucratic comedy of errors that had stakes for Albatross and Tauchnitz books abroad.[10] Krause-Brandstetter found himself in an especially awkward position. Schulz, who spearheaded censorship of the French book trade, was not a man he wanted to irritate. He belonged to an elite six-member group called the Permanent Circle for Literary Questions, which had met every Thursday since August to generate strategies for squelching anti-German elements in the book trade: two S.S. Oberstürmführers; Dr. Bernard Niggemeyer, the captain of the German Secret Field Police (Geheimefeldpolizei), units of military police supporting Occupation forces in France; Epting, the head of the German Institute; and Dr. Friedhelm Kaiser, head of the Literature Section (Gruppeschrifttum) of the military Propaganda Office for Greater Paris, known as the Propaganda-Staffel for short. Books with Communist sympathies or Jewish ties, critical of Nazism or German culture (known as *Hetzliteratur,* or "heckling literature"), but also Anglo-Saxon books had all fallen prey to the censorship and seizure machinery these officials had put in place. And there stood Krause-Brandstetter, presiding over a vast warehouse of Albatross and Tauchnitz books—at last count, 280,000 strong—all in English, housed at 11 passage Charles Dallery in the eleventh arrondissement of Paris, with up to another 170,000 such books dispersed among French booksellers.[11]

Shortly after marching into Paris, military propaganda officials had clamped down on the French book trade. They quickly seized the Éditions Denoël and Éditions Sorlot, accusing them of publishing anti-German books; the same day, they appeared at the cutting-edge Gallimard and Grasset publishing houses. By the end of June, they had requisitioned Hachette; a few days later, they installed Bruno Conrad at its offices on the boulevard Saint-Germain, putting the circulation of books in France under German control. In early August, the regional military propaganda office, the Propaganda-Staffel, settled into luxurious quarters at the prestigious address of 52 Champs-Élysées, claiming four floors and 150 well-furbished offices. From these headquarters, propaganda officials consulted with higher-level authorities in Schulz's Propaganda Division to decide which firms had significant Jewish influence or objectionable ties and should be "Aryanized" or closed. In another gesture that left little to interpretation, the Wehrmacht requisitioned the best-known English bookstore in Paris—W.H. Smith, at its extravagant quarters on the rue de Rivoli—confiscated its books, and turned the space over to the Frontbuchhaendler Herbst, which supplied books to German troops.[12]

Only as summer rolled into fall did Occupation officials take the more systematic actions against books that led them to Holroyd-Reece's door. Schulz's Propaganda Division and beneath him, the regional Propaganda-Staffel, had published two censorship lists, the Liste Bernhard and the more comprehensive

Liste Otto. On 27 August 1940, in the Occupation's first widespread book-confiscation action, secret police and French police descended on the city's bookstores, equipped with flyers warning booksellers to hand over publications from the lists or risk punishment. Between 8 A.M. and the end of the day, the operation hit 2,350 bookshops and sales venues and gathered over 20,000 books, all deposited at 77 avenue de la Grande Armée. It was Conrad at Hachette—the same Conrad poised to confiscate Albatross and Tauchnitz books—who extended confiscation efforts by pointing out 80 booksellers who doubled as publishers. From their warehouses, French police gathered over 100 tons of "rabble-rousing content" and expected to be busy the rest of the week gathering more. "One hundred prisoners of war will unload daily roughly ten to eleven lorries of inflammatory literature."[13]

Kupfer and Krause-Brandstetter had the bad fortune to arrive in Paris one month after Schulz and his propaganda cronies had flooded the city with thirty thousand copies of the new and improved Liste Otto—which tagged Holroyd-Reece's Éditions de la Nouvelle revue critique, housed at 12 rue Chanoinesse, as objectionable Hetzliteratur. Both men knew this judgment could endanger Albatross-Tauchnitz interests in France, as well as the regime's secret plans for their publishing houses in Germany. Indeed the consequences were already evident. Two weeks before their arrival, Kaiser, the head of the Literature Section for the regional Propaganda-Staffel, had written to the German military high command advocating immediate closure of the Nouvelle revue critique and three other firms: Nathan and Calmann-Lévy, for being Jewish owned, and the Éditions de la Nouvelle revue française, a review owned by Gallimard, for being too risqué. When it came to Holroyd-Reece's firm, Kaiser and his underlings at the Propaganda-Staffel's Literature Section had turned up nothing, from their perspective, at all redeemable. "The publisher has shown extremely anti-German influences in its production," the letter opened. "The owners, the two Keller brothers, are not Jewish, however a sinister, smooth-talking German emigrant, a certain Herr Riis [Reece], who has the majority of shares at his disposal, has understood how to make his influence count [using] the manner of the Jewish-emigrant smear campaign." All in all, officials culled forty-two objectionable titles from Holroyd-Reece's list by authors whom they deemed "the most infamous dirty rats of the Jewish-emigrant slander movement."[14]

Krause-Brandstetter moved quickly to clear the Tauchnitz name, meeting with Conrad, the new German kingpin of French book distribution, the day after he arrived in Paris. Conrad was happy to detach Tauchnitz from Holroyd-Reece's sphere of influence. He had nursed a disdain for Holroyd-Reece ever since Albatross had taken over Tauchnitz management in 1934. "At the time, the change in ownership disconcerted me, as a German bookseller abroad," he explained to Schulz, "since I heard here more about how a foreign Jewish clique was bothering Tauchnitz." More recently, in April 1940, Conrad had come across a London *Bookseller* article in which Holroyd-Reece had bragged that he had personally taken over Tauchnitz, "thus bringing the firm with the greatest and most distinguished list of general books, English and American, under the sole control of the Albatross concern."[15]

This proclamation had struck a nerve with Conrad, who had shared it with superiors, as if to justify why he contemplated shutting down Albatross-Tauchnitz in France. For if the British-owned Albatross controlled the German-owned Tauchnitz, there was only one logical consequence. "Since after this the English ownership of the enterprise seemed to be definite, I had started to request from the military administration the confiscation of the books from local wholesaler dealers." Only when Krause-Brandstetter confirmed in writing that he was the "proxy holder" of both the Brandstetter printing firm in Leipzig and the Tauchnitz publishing company did Conrad relax his guard. Not a man to take things at face value, Conrad cross-checked Krause-Brandstetter's statements by verifying Tauchnitz's German status in the *Address Book for the German Book Trade.* Having satisfied himself, Conrad sent Krause-Brandstetter's testimony through the military propaganda hierarchy in Paris to Kaiser's Literature Section and higher up the chain of command to Schulz at the Propaganda Division, vouching that Tauchnitz was and had remained "a pure German enterprise."[16]

In the end, Conrad seemed relieved that he did not have to sequester the books of a publisher which had, for most of its hundred-year existence, presented a distinguished German face to literary Europe. "I did not need to take umbrage at letting the volumes of this series [Tauchnitz] be put back on the market and ordering some more," he reflected, "since they are well introduced in schools and universities here, and continually needed; it is from the German standpoint right and important that German editions are still read and sold rather than French." Little matter, for Conrad, that the books were in English, or that Enoch and the British half-Jewish Holroyd-Reece had helped expand this market in the late 1930s. He swept past such inconsistencies, caring only that the books were produced in Germany—serving the German economy—and framing Tauchnitz as the German victim of a crafty foreign Jew. "I am now convinced," he wrote to Schulz's Propaganda Division, "that the Tauchnitz Verlag is still German owned and I have learned that the Jew Riese had lied and owed the [Firm] Brandstetter in Leipzig roughly 300,000 [RM]."[17]

*

With Conrad on their side, Krause-Brandstetter and Kupfer averted a debacle: both Albatross and Tauchnitz books were cleared for sale. On 6 November 1940, two days before he returned to Leipzig, Kupfer appeared, under orders, at Kaiser's office on the Champs-Élysées to report on his findings in Paris. As the head of the Literature Section for Greater Paris, Kaiser needed "insight into the multifarious entanglements of the firms Albatross, Tauchnitz, Continenta, and so forth." If his records offer any indication, Kaiser was so ill-informed that Kupfer spent most of his visit getting him up to speed on Albatross's personalities and the tortuous history of the Albatross-Tauchnitz-Brandstetter-Continenta-Enoch-Wegner-Holroyd-Reece alliances. He walked Kaiser through the challenges of his Paris trip: a distribution war created by Holroyd-Reece and the diffuse legal issues swirling around Continenta. He shared with Kaiser that Albatross was only the most visible of Holroyd-Reece's publishing endeavors, and admitted that he knew little of Holroyd-Reece's Parisian nexus of firms.[18]

The Continenta piece of Kupfer's account was complex enough in its own right to send Kaiser reeling. Some months before Kupfer and Krause-Brandstetter arrived in Paris, Enoch had disappeared from place Vendôme—going who knew where?—and as far as Occupation officials could discern, he was not coming back. His absence and that of Holroyd-Reece opened up an opportunity that the Reich Commissioner for the Handling Enemy Property in Berlin did not want to miss. Throughout the entire first year of war, Continenta had partially impeded Albatross-Tauchnitz distribution from Leipzig. On paper, Enoch had transferred his distribution rights to Holroyd-Reece on 1 July 1939; yet war had erupted before Holroyd-Reece finalized his negotiations with the Nazi officials who regulated monies from exports. De facto, then, the deal hung in limbo; most foreign booksellers still held contracts with Enoch's Continenta, rather than with

Holroyd-Reece's Éditions Albatros. So once the Germans reached Paris, the Reich commissioner saw his chance to take over Continenta, which sat abandoned, ready for the taking, all the more easily because Enoch was Jewish.[19]

Yet not even this takeover turned out to be simple. Enoch had, in fact, left almost everything behind, including something Kupfer quickly discovered and bemoaned: a financial obstacle course to rival that of Holroyd-Reece. Just as Albatross shares belonged to the Publishing Holding Company in Luxembourg, Continenta shares were owned by the Continenta Publishing Holding Company. Just as there was not one, single Albatross, Enoch had created Continenta-Amsterdam, ostensibly to handle distribution in the Netherlands, but more likely to help him convey funds to or from the Warburg Bank in Amsterdam.[20] Enoch might have resented Holroyd-Reece, and with good reason, but he had learned a trick or two from him along the way. Each offshoot of each publishing venture required its own enemy property custodian, so Kupfer and his superiors soon came to see Continenta, like Holroyd-Reece's holdings, as akin to monsters from ancient legends that sprouted more heads when they sliced one off.

Kaiser summarized his discussion with Kupfer, sending copies to other powerful Occupation officials, among them Schulz, from the military Propaganda Division, and Epting of the German Embassy. Even after this long debriefing, Kaiser remained befuddled. He noted that "a certain Holroyd-Reece played a role in the beginnings of the Albatross Press that could not exactly be assessed." As to Holroyd-Reece's other endeavors, Kaiser kept his analysis vague enough to be unchallengeable. Of the "array of other publishing houses . . . assembled around Holroyd-Reece and the Continenta business of Herr Enoch," he concluded only that "their exact influence and interlocking relationship could not yet be ascertained."[21]

One critical point did emerge from this meeting: someone above Kaiser in the chain of command had informed him, finally, that the regime had larger plans for Albatross and Tauchnitz, linked to Krause-Brandstetter's relocation to Paris. As Kupfer confirmed in his official report, if it proved possible to "acquire" the French firms linked with Enoch and Holroyd-Reece so as "to eventually infuse them with new tasks, Kaiser will give full consideration to the interests of both German publishers [Albatross and Tauchnitz], which are now known to him." If Kaiser reassured Kupfer on this score, Kupfer in turn reassured Kaiser on another: "[Kupfer] and the Brandstetter house are desirous of merging the Albatross and Tauchnitz houses to run them *as a pure German publishing house.* They have no interest in Paris and also no interest in the survival of Continenta."[22] Kupfer's intentions are difficult to read. Yet whether he wanted to protect what he had helped build in Albatross and saw a Brandstetter takeover as the best means to that end or whether he was just telling Nazi authorities what they wanted to hear, his statement helped solidify in authorities' minds that Albatross worked for German ends. Forged nearly a decade earlier to disseminate Anglo-American books across continental Europe, Albatross was about to be enlisted for a radically different cause.

SEVENTEEN

The Deutsche Tauchnitz

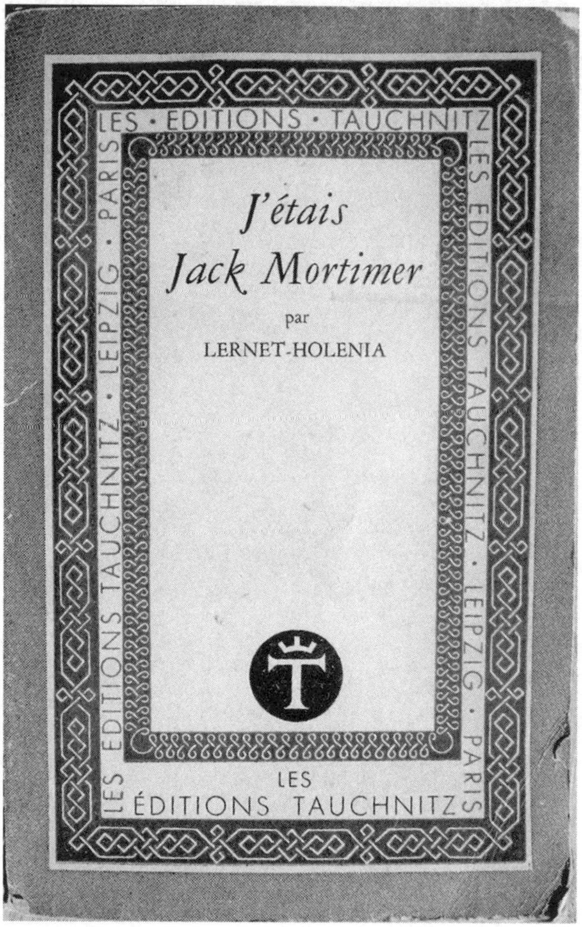

SMALL PRIVATE BOOKSHOPS had long been the intellectual lifeblood of Paris, and Adrienne Monnier owned one of them—the Maison des Amis des Livres, at 7 rue de l'Odéon, around the corner from Shakespeare and Company, run by her one-time lover and lifelong friend Sylvia Beach. To express the love of reading that characterized her circle of friends, Monnier created a newsletter, *The*

Gazette of the Friends of Books. "The French love books. They are always ready to love them," she observed in 1938, urging her readers, "Tell us the books you love and for what reasons."[1]

When the Nazis occupied Paris, they, too, wanted to know what books French readers loved and for what reasons. Early in the war, the German book trade had plenty of books to sell. The problem was how to make foreign readers want to read them. Few among the occupied peoples of Europe were in the mood for anything German. In Denmark, Allied sympathizers responded in English when German soldiers posed questions in German. Some wore bullseye hats—knitted berets with three concentric circles in the colors of the Royal Air Force—so British pilots might see from the air that the Danes were on their side. The Dutch specialized in underground newspapers, a few reaching circulations of a hundred thousand. Yet nowhere was resentment against the Germans higher than in Paris, where German troops had paraded so triumphantly down the Champs-Élysées in a flag-waving, boot-stomping display designed to humiliate the French. The Germans had seized the most luxurious accommodations for their Occupation bureaucrats and imposed a curfew on a people used to staying out well past midnight. They instituted food rationing in September 1940, forcing the French to pay for keeping some three hundred thousand German occupiers fed and housed. For the Germans to think that the French would spend their hard-earned francs on German books was pushing expectations too far.[2]

Goebbels and his staff were well aware of this resistance, and hatched plans to overcome it. While they and propaganda officials in the Foreign Office ideally wanted foreign readers to bow to the superiority of German culture, they saw that forcibly breaking down the cultural doors—especially in France, which boasted of Paris as the seat of French and European culture—would only exacerbate opposition. Instead, they launched what scholars have since called "an international soft power campaign" that could quietly take its place in occupied nations to convince inhabitants that National Socialism held the "key to a broader European renewal." Their goal was to maintain German control of culture while creating the illusion of a "New European Order" in which varied national cultures coexisted in a climate of autonomy and free choice. To this end, propaganda officials created "a web of new, German-dominated, trans-European institutions of cultural and intellectual exchange," including the German Institute in Paris. They invested in exchange programs, welcoming writers and students from other nations into the fold with German language and literature. And in October 1940, the Propaganda Ministry and the Foreign Office jointly decided it was time for German publishers to think internationally, as Albatross, and Tauchnitz before it, had done to such great effect.[3]

Wolfgang Krause-Brandstetter—and the Albatross and Tauchnitz books at his disposal—were the German Foreign Office's answer to the question of how to insinuate German books across national borders without the taint of propaganda. He had family ties to Tauchnitz, whose name was renowned across Europe. He was well educated and, though only twenty-eight, well acquainted with the mind of the enemy, having lived in England and France. He crossed linguistic boundaries easily and suavely. Perhaps most important, his work with Holroyd-Reece on Albatross-Tauchnitz matters at the Paris office in 1937 made him privy to the inner workings of an operation which the Propaganda Ministry and Foreign Office wanted to be involved in: inexpensive books in a single language, sold across Europe.

Little matter that Albatross and Tauchnitz sold books in English. The Occupation made it critical for the Nazi regime to win foreign peoples over to the German message, and the Foreign Office realized that Albatross and Tauchnitz were doing something right. Their books sold, war or no war. Indeed, they sold so well that Krause-Brandstetter and Kupfer had quickly discarded their original plan to confiscate Parisian stocks of Albatross-Tauchnitz books and transport them back to Leipzig. The books were simply too much in demand. Why bother with an expensive fleet of fifty trucks to cart thousands of books back to a central distribution point in Leipzig when, as Kupfer reported, "the demand per se for books of both collections in Paris is great." Hachette had already placed a substantial order: thirty-five hundred Albatross-Tauchnitz volumes selected from the series as a whole, plus a thousand copies of each title that had appeared since September 1939. In mid-December, Hachette secured roughly five thousand more volumes. Thousands more were scattered among Parisian bookshops waiting for sale, or were housed with Hachette or the smaller distributor Gaulon et fils.[4]

The Information Department of the Foreign Office looked with avidity at this scene, envisioning readers in occupied countries lining up to purchase a German-language series created in the Albatross-Tauchnitz image. It was only a matter, they imagined, of grafting German books onto the Albatross-Tauchnitz business model. So when Kupfer took the train back to Leipzig in November

1940, Krause-Brandstetter stayed behind to establish local contacts and enlist a French printer. Albatross and Tauchnitz had made Anglo-American culture accessible to continental readers; now the Deutsche Tauchnitz series would dish up German culture instead. With access to Tauchnitz's well-respected name and Albatross's international infrastructure, Krause-Brandstetter could play the cards much as he wished.[5]

*

The decision to form Deutsche Tauchnitz had been several years in the making. Even before the war, Nazi officials were dismayed that Germany was losing the war of the book to Anglo-American and French influence. The S.D., charged with both intelligence gathering and the monitoring of public opinion, was perplexed in its annual report for 1938 that German readers would turn for "instruction and relaxation" to foreign books and concluded that they had been forced into these reading patterns because of "the obvious lack of good, entertaining reading" in German. The first quarterly report of the S.D. for 1939 had fixed on the same question. Rather than acknowledging that Nazi literary taste was out of step with continental readers, the report blamed German book prices for lower than desired exports. It proposed, in fact, that the regime develop its "own series of well-known German literature at the least expensive price" to minimize the influence of emigrant publishers and give the regime more control over German books abroad.[6]

Culling entertaining German literature for export became a major agenda item at both the Literary Chamber and Foreign Office, where Krause-Brandstetter was gearing up for a full-time post. The problem German authorities faced within Reich borders—a national literature without enough "fun"—proved a huge obstacle abroad. Early in 1940, Karl Heinrich Bischoff, Albatross's Literary Chamber contact, pondered this dilemma. Germany needed two things, he concluded: first, to appoint a "translation agent" who understood diverse continental markets and could promote German translations abroad (ironically, Holroyd-Reece possessed the perfect skills for this position); and second, to fight the hold of English books over continental readers. Even in Scandinavia, where many readers could read German fluently, Bischoff was forced to admit that "for some time the German book has been systematically driven out by the English [book], particularly in the North."[7]

Nazi officials were not the only ones to notice that "good, light fiction" from Germany was flagging in the face of foreign competition. One pro-Nazi Dutch book distributor stressed the dire fate of German books to Werner Klatten, head of the Information Department, in May 1940, shortly after Germany occupied the Netherlands. Before 1933, wrote the Dutch distributor, "the German book was dominant in almost every arena." Since Hitler came to power, however, German book sales had radically decreased. He attributed this partly to anti-German sentiment—which he blamed on German exiles and Jewish slander campaigns—but also to "the absolute lack of good sales organization and well-centralized propaganda." German books were dying on the vine, he noted, and Anglo-American books, in translation and in English, clambered over and around them. "The English book has been edging up [in sales], supported by Jews and Jew-friends, and has achieved a record turnover. This has happened, too, through the very inexpensive series Penguin, Albatross, and so forth, that one finds everywhere in Dutch bookshops in large numbers. A German series in this or a better model in the same price class did not come out and has not yet appeared." Klatten highlighted this last point in red, suggesting that it hit a nerve.[8]

The Deutsche Tauchnitz series was designed to change all this, propelling Germany into the cultural lead in Europe. The series was to consist of "special editions of modern German novels, to be disseminated for propaganda purposes only in countries outside Germany that Hitler occupies." The books maintained the design elements of their English-speaking cousins: the bright colors, one for each genre, and the sparse use of print on the cover, with the title floating above the author's name. To draw on readers' existing loyalties to the Tauchnitz series, the German series specifically mimicked the updated Tauchnitz covers Holroyd-Reece had instituted in 1938: the circular logo, with the strong Tauchnitz "T" embedded in the center of a white circle, topped by a small, modern-looking crown. To appeal to French readers not yet fluent in German, Krause-Brandstetter also instituted a smaller series of titles translated from German into French; these imitated the familiar look of the Albatross volumes, with their rectangular borders. To sweeten the appeal, the Deutsche Tauchnitz cost only the equivalent of 1.20 RM, undercutting the 2 RM charged for standard Albatross and Tauchnitz volumes in English. In France, the books cost 24 francs, still not inexpensive in a world where sausage with a side of potato salad cost 20 francs on the upscale boulevard Montparnasse.[9]

The Information Department realized that the challenge was one of marketing as well as availability and price, the task as much psychological as practical. In Occupied Europe, lively prose and suspense were the order of the day. In fact, there were to be no overtly political titles. Although the Propaganda Ministry and Foreign Office bore the start-up costs, they wanted to mask their role entirely, as if the Brandstetter concern on its own had decided to launch a German series to capitalize on the wartime market. By 1941, the Foreign Office had come up with a new slogan: "Propaganda sold is better than propaganda given." This catchy phrase captured Goebbels's feeling that propaganda often failed because it bludgeoned readers with a message, leaving them feeling deadened. The best propaganda, for Goebbels, worked under the radar, as the Deutsche Tauchnitz series was carefully crafted to do.[10]

By December 1940, Krause-Brandstetter's planning was in full swing, in anticipation of its debut in spring 1941. He had found printers in the French provinces to produce the series more economically than German printers. He was ready to begin production "as soon as [he received] the blessing of the [Propaganda Ministry] regarding the authors." And he was plotting not only a series in German books but "an edition translated into English or French" to extend the reach of German culture in Occupied France—or, if the military war should move forward—in Britain.[11]

Still, to succeed, Deutsche Tauchnitz needed one thing neither the Brandstetters nor Tauchnitz possessed: Albatross's infrastructure. Even the most alluring titles would do the regime no good if they could not get the books into the hands of readers. Here, the Albatross-Tauchnitz office on the rue Chanoinesse came in handy. Before its partnership with Tauchnitz, Albatross had built up exactly the "good sales operation" and "well-centralized propaganda" that the Dutch book distributor had pinpointed as critical to the success of any continental series. In the early 1930s, Holroyd-Reece, Wegner, and Enoch had created an astounding network of roughly six thousand venues across Europe to outsell Tauchnitz. But war created its own opportunities. These distribution pathways, once part of Tauchnitz's undoing, would now become the routes allowing Deutsche Tauchnitz to reach across Europe, selling books for the German cause. Here was the Brandstetters' chance to make this glorious infrastructure—from the largest distributors to the tiniest bookshops in Europe—work for them, and for German culture as a whole. Kupfer was also called upon to handle "a significant part of the editorial work . . . which was originally to have been accomplished by the Bernhard Tauchnitz Nachfolger firm itself."[12] The balance of power had shifted: the Brandstetters and Tauchnitz now, finally, had the upper hand.

After much preparation, the series was launched, with some fanfare in propaganda circles, in the last week of April 1941. The weekly report from the Literature Section in Paris proclaimed its merits: "[This week] appeared the first volumes of the Deutsche Tauchnitz edition, which has as its goal to promote German literature abroad." Instead of enhancing French stereotypes of German books as too heady or stuffy, "There appeared books from the most varied arenas: novels, novellas, dramas, poetry, travel writing, adventure stories, and so forth." Despite the hype, the monthly report for June 1941 noted that "the turnover of the Deutsche Tauchnitz Edition was not as good as expected. It probably has partly to do with the fact that large troop squadrons have been withdrawn." The Librairie étrangère of Hachette even reduced its orders because "sales of the first six titles did not yield the expected results."[13]

Deutsche Tauchnitz faced the same obstacles as other Foreign Office attempts to lure French readers—namely, the reluctance of the French to accept the culture of their occupiers. While the German Institute, funded by the Foreign Office, showed rising attendance at German courses and musical evenings, many commentators later claimed that the free food was more alluring than the cultural offerings. Another Foreign Office endeavor, a Franco-German bookshop called the Librairie Rive Gauche that featured the Deutsche Tauchnitz line, fared no better. Situated at a prominent spot near the Sorbonne, it became a symbolic target for anti-German antagonism. The Literature Section of the Propaganda-Staffel in Paris reported in November 1941 that the bookshop had suffered a rash of small attacks in its early days, with perpetrators spilling acid over the books on the shelves. On 21 November, an aggressor had gone to more violent extremes, throwing two grenades, set on timers, through the windows, "which, on exploding, destroyed the windowpanes, the roof, and a large number of books."[14]

Only time would tell whether Deutsche Tauchnitz, tied up in this broader push-pull with German culture, would fulfill the vision of the Propaganda Ministry and Foreign Office: a German book in the hands of every foreign reader. With Deutsche Tauchnitz designed on the Albatross-Tauchnitz model for producing Anglo-American books—a model that remained popular even in wartime—they had, they thought, every reason for hope.[15]

EIGHTEEN

English Books Abroad

THE NAZIS HAD PUSHED Holroyd-Reece firmly off the Île de la Cité and onto the British Isles. Having lost Albatross strongholds in Germany and then France, he reassessed the firm's prospects from his office at 7 Paternoster Row in London. The street, its tightly packed brick and stone buildings overlooked by the majestic dome of Saint Paul's Cathedral, had ostensibly earned its name from the priests who had once paced back and forth murmuring the Lord's Prayer in Latin. Charles Dickens described it as "the literary heart of London, . . . its history bound up with that of the great publishing firms and great literary enterprises." Holroyd-Reece might have welcomed a Paternoster or two on Albatross's behalf. On 2 July 1940, not yet two weeks after the French armistice, he wrote to a British literary agency, spreading word that though Albatross had lost access to the bulk of its books, it had not entirely succumbed to the German invasion of France. "While our programme will be somewhat reduced in scope," he admitted, "we are starting the business again from London, where we are unfettered from foreign currency regulations and restrictions of any kind, and can revert to the happy long-forgotten days when advances can be paid in the ordinary course of business."[1]

Yet Holroyd-Reece had little time to relish his literary locale, Albatross's potential, or freedom from German red tape. On the Sunday following Christmas 1940, German planes dropped bombs over London. The American journalist Ernie Pyle described it as a "night when London was ringed and stabbed by fire." Watching from a balcony, he looked in awe at the eerie glow. "Flames seemed to whip hundreds of feet in the air. Pinkish-white smoke ballooned upward in a great cloud, and out of this cloud there gradually took shape—so faintly at first that we weren't sure we saw correctly—the gigantic dome of St. Paul's Cathedral . . . like a picture of some miraculous figure that appears before peace-hungry soldiers on a battlefield." Paternoster Row burned brightly, with over a million books from seventeen publishers feeding the flames.[2]

Albatross had lost yet another home to military aggression. And war had rendered Holroyd-Reece powerless with regard to Albatross and Tauchnitz books; the Germans would do with them what they would. He had tried to diminish the power of Albatross's German branch in the courts of international law before the war, when he and other shareholders had transferred the rights of the Albatross Verlag to Albatross London. As he repeatedly attested, however, the war made it impossible for him to monitor production and sales in Occupied territories; in his words, "Our statistics were kept in Germany and being an entirely British firm, we are unable to communicate with our German subsidiary."[3]

Ironically, losing his toehold on the continent aligned Holroyd-Reece more strongly with other British publishers. German military success had placed him with the publishing and propaganda establishment on the same side of a sticky question: how to get British books into the neutral markets remaining. At the crossroads where trade, books, and political warfare converged, a plethora of government offices—the British Council, the Ministry of Information, the Export Credit Guarantees Department, His Majesty's Stationery Office, the Publishers Association, and the National Book Council—avidly discussed this issue, explains the publishing historian Valerie Holman. "The absence of British books from the bookshops and libraries of neutral countries had been the subject of much adverse comment since the outbreak of war," commented the historian E. H. Carr from his post at the Ministry of Information, seeking funding from the Treasury in December 1939 for a book export scheme. The Foreign Office championed higher paper rations for the British Council, arguing in June 1942 that "to increase such reading is in the national interest to a very high degree" to counter "the very dangerous extent" of Nazi propaganda. The Government Sub-Committee for the Supply of Books pleaded for an array of books, among them "cheap reprints of the classics, books on British Life and Thought, . . . reprints of outstanding contemporary fiction, poetry and criticism, [and] text books for the teaching of English." By 1943, the British Council and Ministry of Information were airlifting such books to neutral countries at considerable expense, all to keep "British Life and Thought" alive.[4]

In this context, Holroyd-Reece's problem—that his books were trapped behind enemy lines—opened up unusual possibilities, chances that the British government could not even consider for its own efforts. It had no means or hope of smuggling its books into German-occupied zones on a widespread scale. The ambassadors best positioned to do British cultural work in Occupied Europe, therefore, were precisely the books that Holroyd-Reece had been forced to leave behind.

*

Albatross and Tauchnitz stood at the ready, in war- as in peacetime, to fill readers' desires for diversion. Yet by order of the Reich Commissioner for the Handling of Enemy Property, Friedrich Ernst, the German auditor, Walter Gey, now spearheaded their sale, or, as Holroyd-Reece called it, "the illicit sale of our books in neutral countries and/or in Germany." Gey turned out to be, however, a rather more licit enemy property custodian than Holroyd-Reece might have imagined. He earnestly took up his responsibilities, as is evident from his reports for the Reich Commissioner, a treasure trove of information about Albatross finances, production, sales, and political conditions from year to year. He set a high bar for himself. "I am busy," he wrote to Ernst on his first day, "getting a general idea of the state of the firm. That is, all things considered, associated with some difficulties."[5] This was an understatement, given how much confusion Albatross had already engendered for the Nazi bureaucracy, yet it was also characteristic of Gey's persistent management approach.

Gey's voluminous correspondence and meticulous records paint a portrait of a man who dutifully took the lead of the Reich Commissioner, yet who also claimed his own authority—even-handedly advocating for Albatross interests, for instance, even when his position clashed with the Brandstetters' wishes. In turn, he was measured enough to appreciate that Kupfer, and not he, had the publishing expertise necessary to reach decisions about the firm. The two men appear to have forged a good relationship as they navigated Albatross through wartime contingencies and power plays. In short, Gey's mission to preserve the firm's well-being—one of his prime responsibilities under enemy property guidelines—eventually seemed to be in alignment with his own loyalties, as if he gradually identified with the firm over the regime.

Once Gey took over Albatross sales in tandem with Kupfer, he soon realized that there was ample demand for Albatross's books, abroad and at home. Sales from August to December 1940 of 80,400 RM climbed past those of 62,200 RM for the same months in 1939. "The favorable sales situation has also held in the first months of 1941," he explained to Ernst in March 1941. "The only difficulties emerge from the fact that the inventories are shrinking and that new production cannot yet be effected on a sufficient scale due to the heavy strain on the graphic trade." Gey quickly discovered, in fact, that sales were limited by wartime conditions rather than demand. "A stronger dispatch [of books] than we have achieved in recent months can hardly be facilitated, given the lack of a sufficiently suitable work force." Yet again in June 1941 he noted an uptick, and by the end of July sales had leapt to 95,000 RM. The year 1941 closed with sales of 165,000 RM, slightly outpacing those of 155,000 RM the previous year.[6]

Gey's report from December 1940 also reveals who was purchasing Albatross books, with a list of over 70 foreign clients, stretching from Madrid to Istanbul, from Athens to Oslo. Within the Reich, clients included over 250 bookshops, not merely in urban centers such as Berlin, Hamburg, and Munich, but also in university towns and regional centers across the heartland, from Aachen and Bremen down to Wuppertal and Zwickau. The demand for Albatross books was indeed so consistent that Gey adjusted his formula for assessing their worth; he no longer discounted older stock, because "the decrease in production throughout the book market" meant that "even older stock reaches a better turnover than in normal times with customarily full production." Albatross books sold on. Yet Gey had already ascertained that Albatross's "full-blown turnover" would create its own undoing. In his quarterly report for June 1941, he yoked this good and bad news. "The demand for the published works of the firm is so great today that sales for the near future are absolutely assured," he concluded. "Larger, in contrast, is the danger that the possibility of [filling] deliveries will keep shrinking, owing to the impossibility of new printing and reprinting."[7]

Back in Paris, at Shakespeare and Company, Sylvia Beach inadvertently confirmed Gey's fears. One of her notebooks for 1941 included a wish list of titles: one copy each of Lawrence's *Sons and Lovers,* Louis Bromfield's *The Rains Came* and *The Farm,* Hemingway's *The Sun Also Rises,* and Rosamond Lehmann's *Invitation to the Waltz,* as well as three copies of her *Dusty Answer.* By the time Beach wrote this short list, half its titles had been banned by the Nazis, in and outside the Reich. Another well-worn notebook with "Orders 1941" written at the top in red block letters, contained a running list of "Orders & Books Out of Stock," including many by authors whose work she had sold well into 1940: William Faulkner, Virginia Woolf, Katherine Mansfield, and James Joyce, along with titles such as Huxley's *Brave New World,* Steinbeck's *Of Mice and Men,* and Forster's *A Passage to India.*[8] Albatross books were disappearing more quickly than they could be replaced.

*

Just in time for Christmas 1941, Wolfgang Krause-Brandstetter wrote to Werner Klatten, his boss at the Information Section, with best wishes for the New Year. He had chosen a fitting gift for Klatten to mark the end of his own first year at the Foreign Office: six enlargements of cartoons from the British comic journal *Punch,* featured in Albatross Volume 400, *The British Character.* Albatross had first published the volume in 1939, before the war. Through 120 pages, it offered readers a romping satire of the traits that others typically mocked in the British and the British mocked in themselves. One doggerel poem in the first pages set the tone:

The British with their tidy minds,
Divide themselves up into kinds.
The common kind they call the masses,
The better kind—the upper classes.
In either case it's really not
A specially inspiring lot.
The common ones play darts in pubs,
The others slowly die in clubs.[9]

This self-deprecating humor threaded its way through the volume's cartoons. Each sketch represented a British quality: the Importance of Breeding, the Tendency Not to Know What to Do on Sundays, Political Apathy, Failure to Appreciate Good Music, and—what Hitler approved most in the English—Aptitude for Building Empires. One illustration on the Importance of Tea showed two men and two women huddled in the pounding rain lighting a small stove to make tea, while one man futilely held a dinky black umbrella over the group. More to the point in wartime, the cartoon on Refusal to Admit Defeat revealed one British explorer with his tiny sled, fists raised in hopeless bravado against rings of polar bears closing in on him. Klatten welcomed the gift. "The splendidly drawn figures have been very well received . . . by all acquaintances to whom I have shown them, and have earned a place of honor in my library."[10]

Sketched by the English for the English, yet now repurposed with care for Nazi officials, the cartoons illustrated not just the British Character, as it were, but Albatross's position in wartime Germany: born elsewhere but deployed for the Nazi cause. For beyond providing Krause-Brandstetter with an apt gift, *The British Character* was notable for being one of numerous titles Albatross reprinted in Leipzig during the first two years of war. It is one thing to imagine the Reich commissioner authorizing sales of Albatross back stocks to reap foreign currency. Yet it is another to realize that the regime allowed Albatross to reprint many titles until midway through 1941. In a wartime economy, this meant that Albatross was granted paper that could have been diverted to other German publishers or propaganda aims. It was an odd conundrum. The regime had flatly banned trade in all British authors in German translation in the first months of war, but still sanctioned production of Albatross titles. Albatross lived on in Germany against the grain.[11]

The British Character inadvertently illustrated a blind spot in Nazi thinking about wartime publishing. Parodies of British culture, to Goebbels's mind, were exactly the sort of thing that should be encouraged. Holroyd-Reece acknowledged as much in a postwar interview when he noted that Goebbels had "ordered that this book should be published . . . and exported to all German-occupied countries, so as to show the peoples there how degenerate the English were." In his introduction, the British satirist E. M. Delafield spoke slightingly of the English, though tongue in cheek, asserting that "every Englishman is an average Englishman: it's a national characteristic. . . . He can therefore enjoy himself *without having to think.*" And in truth, taken out of context, these comments were not far off Goebbels's caustic renderings. "English films are indescribably naive," he remarked in his diary. "But I think they are good enough for the English, who are themselves enormously stupid, unenlightened, and primitive. We should take this more into account in our propaganda aimed at England." Missed in this analysis was the fact that *The British Character* and other satires were self-parodies, generated by a culture capable of introspection and self-criticism. As Holroyd-Reece remarked, "Goebbels did not understand Pont's irony." From the Nazi perspective, *The British Character* confirmed Germany's upper hand. No matter what happened, as one cartoon suggested, the British had a Love of Keeping Calm; even when their ship was sinking, they sat in the dining room, smoking their cigarettes and exchanging gossip, blissfully unaware of the waist-high water creeping up to seal their doom.[12]

Whatever misguided reasons lay behind the regime's promotion of this volume, few Albatross titles reprinted between 1939 and 1941 so neatly fit Nazi agendas. To some degree, the choice of what to reprint was probably determined by plates the Brandstetters held in stock. Yet to increase exports and domestic sales alike, Kupfer may also have studied reader demand. Many of the Tauchnitz offerings reprinted between 1939 and 1941 were schoolroom classics: the poetry of Robert Browning, *Treasure Island* by Robert Louis Stevenson, dramas by Oscar Wilde—including *The Importance of Being Earnest*—and *The Four Pleasant Plays of George Bernard Shaw,* which had its twenty-sixth printing in 1940. Most Albatross offerings, too, featured authors who had won continental success. Albatross had published *Of Mice and Men* in 1938 and reprinted it in 1940 and 1941. Katherine Mansfield's *The Garden Party and Other Stories* reached its sixth printing in 1941.

Two of Albatross's most intriguing wartime selections, however, were books by Charles Morgan. Ironically, while Albatross was reprinting his *Portrait in a Mirror* (1940) and *Sparkenbroke* (1941) from Leipzig, Morgan was working for British Naval Intelligence and drafting anti-Nazi essays for the *Times Literary Supplement,* published later in the war under the moniker "Menander's Mirror." His lecture "France is an Idea Necessary for Civilization" was particularly critical of Hitler's regime. Passionately, Morgan laid out why "the life and spirit of France constitute an idea the death of which would be the death of civilization" and why the Germans, in contrast, were "more dangerous to us than a barbarous people" because they had "rejected the fundamental ideas upon which is based our view of civilization, our hope for mankind." He urged Britons and Americans to stand together with French ideals against their German foe: "If we are divided, the world is lost."[13]

It seems a striking incongruity that Nazi officials tolerated Albatross and Tauchnitz production and sales to this degree. There was, as Holroyd-Reece ascertained, the fact that the Germans "[needed] all the foreign currency that they [could] get." Gey noted this reason along with others in August 1941 that made Albatross worthy of protection: that Albatross and its foreign networks were essential to the Deutsche Tauchnitz mission and that the Brandstetters still wanted to "Germanize" Albatross by taking over its shares; but he needed more time to assess whether this was legally possible under wartime constraints.[14]

Yet, seen more globally, Albatross books also advanced one part of the war effort critical to Goebbels: they sated the sheer, unstoppable, unfillable demand of German readers for books that could engross them enough to help them forget the war. "There is no doubt that a very strong need for pure entertainment is currently present in the German people," he mused in his diary, "and not only at home but also at the front, and for this reason we are right, while giving the war its due, also to ensure that the nation can find the necessary relaxation in art, theater, film, and radio." His diaries between 1939 and 1941 are sprinkled with references to how to keep readers happy despite the dearth of paper—by reducing newspapers, stopping production of unnecessary journals, or collecting used books for the front. Goebbels made his priorities clear in paper-rationing guidelines for fall 1941, which specified "entertaining and relaxing fiction in all categories" as important, along with books "of beneficial influence on our Volk's struggle for survival."[15]

German readers' hunger for diversion escalated with the privations of war. The S.D. reported soaring book sales in Christmas 1939, a trend which accelerated as war continued. One Berlin bookseller saw his profits skyrocket from 47,500 RM in 1939 to 123,600 RM in 1941. One Stuttgart bookseller similarly more than doubled his sales in three years, with a daily average of 459 books in 1939 and 891 books in 1941. In Hamburg, one bookseller helped over 1,000 clients in one day. In August 1940, Christian Wegner exclaimed to Annemarie, "The turnover without the war would not be as ample—and for that reason: all publishers are faring similarly!"[16]

Book shortages were inevitable. In August 1940, the S.D. complained that booksellers could fill roughly 40 percent of readers' orders. Publishers could not fill Christmas orders received later than July; in the hierarchy of needs, military print orders took precedence over entertainment. Rumors of shortages sent readers into a buying frenzy: "everyone is now already trying to secure all the books that they want to give only at Christmas." From a host of cities came the ringing cry in the last days before the holidays: "Everything is sold that looks like a book." Price played little role. Many booksellers sold out even their old, slow-selling "shelf warmers," unloading everything but the most obscure specialist publications. "Many well-educated readers never received the books they valued, despite ordering them early," the S.D. noted, while new readers drawn to new releases "because of discussions in the press, determined with some annoyance, that the books . . . were not to be had." One Freiburg bookseller deemed his clients book-crazy: "Who could have believed that the desire for a book could one day soar into the illimitable!" Wegner was relieved at his "insane Christmas sales," yet identified a lurking threat: "We hardly have any books in stock. . . . Whether we receive any more is questionable given current production difficulties." The S.D. expressed similar worries, noting that book suppliers had exchanged their "profits for empty shelves."[17]

This scene was a far cry from the idealistic picture the Nazi official Horst Kliemann had painted in *The World of the Book* in 1938. In prewar days, he had reassured readers that "every bookseller is in the position to procure every book for which the client could wish." In wartime, this proclamation rang hollow. By Christmas 1941, the old world in which German booksellers advised their clients "with love and devotion" had been supplanted by a new reality, summed up best by one Stuttgart bookseller: "Formerly, at the opening of the shop doors, His

Majesty the Client entered the shop. Today [enters] the 'Enemy,' who must be hindered from mindlessly robbing our stocks."[18]

In this context, the regime's vision of books as powerful carriers of political meanings fell prey to the shortages spawned by its military ambitions. As the S.D. opined, "politically responsible" booksellers could hardly steer readers to "desirable" reading when "there was simply nothing more there to recommend." Officials postponed the opening of new libraries, and the ordering of new books reflecting National Socialist aims. Libraries—German readers' cheapest mode of acquiring books that might reflect the regime's ends—were as plagued by shortages as the rest of the book trade. With coal rationed, the book binder for the Hamburg Public Library complained that binding materials would not stick in the cold. With gasoline rationed, deliveries were allowed only twice a week, and one library director from a more remote area was told to use his bicycle to retrieve books for his public.[19]

Ironically, then, the National Socialist state had created exactly the opposite reading habits it wanted to engender. The books German readers craved, according to S.D. insiders, were the genres that Albatross published—precisely, too, those produced by Deutsche Tauchnitz and sold only beyond Reich borders. "People want books with action and suspense . . . the craving for lighter, more cheerful reading, is described as quite large," claimed the S.D. in November 1940. "Political-ideological writings of an educational character and N[ational] S[ocialist] writings in a narrower sense are, at the moment, hardly read." In January 1941, the same news echoed back from different markets: "Good novels and good books are being emphatically demanded by our comrades in the Volk." The demand for such books might seem superficial, but it had deeply emotional stakes; one German woman in the summer of 1940 pleaded for "a suspenseful, entertaining novel," as the S.D. reported, "so as not to wait up nights with worry about the airplanes and then afterward be forced to cower mindlessly in the cellar."[20]

*

In one sense, the regime gradually clamped down on Albatross for the same reason it had allowed it to survive so long: its books were popular. Yet if authorities had once wanted to increase Albatross sales for German economic ends, the climate of the Occupation—and their desire to see the Deutsche Tauchnitz and other German books take hold—made them worry that Anglo-American books in general, and Albatross and Tauchnitz books in particular, might have become too popular among foreign readers for Germany's good. The regime's ideological imperatives in this case finally began to outweigh its economic need. Directive 119 concerning the "export of English literature," from the Propaganda Ministry's 1 October 1941 *Confidential Announcements for the Book Trade,* for example, forbade German publishers to export their translations of British books to neutral or occupied territories for foreign currency gains. Once the United States entered the war in December 1941, American authors were subject to similar oversight. On 10 March 1942, the Reich Literature Office in the Propaganda Ministry told book trade members that initiating conversations and contracts with foreign firms and authors was "undesirable."[21]

Kupfer, who more than anything did not want Albatross to be driven out of business by the war, had often wondered how long its luck would last. "On the basis of his preliminary talks with the Reich Propaganda Ministry and Reich Literary Chamber," Gey reported, Kupfer had "long nursed the fear that, given cultural-political considerations, [they] would have to reckon with restrictions on sales of English-language literature." In the second half of 1941, after German troops invaded the Soviet Union, full-blown paper rationing took hold, and Gey was told not to bother to apply for any. On 31 October 1941, Albatross also inherited a new Reich Commissioner for the Handling of Enemy Property—Johannes Krohn, a former Secretary of State, called in to take over when Ernst retired from the position—who was not initially well-versed in the minutiae of Albatross's case. Finally, on 27 April 1942, with Deutsche Tauchnitz on the march through Europe, the Propaganda Ministry leveled the blow: "The distribution of the collections of British and American authors, the Tauchnitz Edition and Albatross Books, in neutral countries abroad and in territories occupied by German troops, is undesirable." Export of both series from Germany was "to cease immediately," and Albatross and Tauchnitz could expect "further instructions" about the fate of their books within Reich borders.[22]

This crackdown posed a dilemma for Gey, certainly, but more immediately for Oskar Möhring, the enemy property custodian for Enoch's Continenta and Holroyd-Reece's Éditions Albatros back in Paris. Heaped in the warehouse at 11 passage Charles Dallery were no less than 8,028 Albatross mysteries, veritable piles of murder and mayhem, that he hoped to unload, including J. V. Turner's *The Homicide Haven,* H. Adam's *Death on the Fairway,* and J. M. Walsh's *Spies*

Never Return. All but 3 of the 35 titles derived from the Albatross Mystery and Crime Club. French readers were not the problem; they would snap them up. With the climate of occupation tense and French adults reduced to a diet of 1,200 calories per day, why not be drawn into a battle of wits between Agatha Christie's mastermind detective, Hercule Poirot, and the murderer of the mysterious Mr. Shaitana in *Cards on the Table*? How would Poirot ever narrow down the culprit when he had, at the time of the murder, been engrossed in his own rubber of bridge? There was something to be said for the diversions of print in hard times.[23]

Unfortunately for Möhring, however, none of these rippingly suspenseful books had been produced in Germany, but "had been directly imported from England." Möhring was stuck with the one Albatross series printed by Collins in Edinburgh. In his view, a book was a book, a commodity to be sold for whatever gain it yielded, regardless of where it was printed or whose cultural ideals it espoused. On 7 August he sent a query to the military Propaganda Division, requesting that he be allowed to sell the books in a one-time deal to earn money to offset costs associated with overseeing the firms. Yet he knew that Nazi financial authorities, their eyes still riveted on the international trade balance, would probably refuse to let him sell British-produced books that would in any way contribute to British gain.[24]

Beyond the legal issues at stake, Möhring faced an ideological wall. The Anglo-American books officials objected to most were precisely the crime and mystery novels he wanted to sell. The Literature Section of the Propaganda-Staffel in Paris had already articulated its bias against such novels. Its "Report Concerning the State of Light Fiction" from July 1941 regretted that too many French readers "[contented] themselves with the reading of crime, adventure, and romance novels." To reach these readers, the Germans would have to become competitive in exactly the suspenseful genres they belittled. "It is a singularly regrettable fact," concluded the report, "that adventure and crime novels play out most notably in English and American milieus. Thereby, the perception that all the threads of world affairs run together in London and New York has become deeply impressed [on people]. This perception must be changed. Not London, but Berlin, not England, but rather Germany must, in the imaginations of the French public, become the future location for all important world events.

The Anglo-American subject matter of popular literature must, then, finally be replaced by German subject matter."[25]

It is unclear whether the early, disappointing returns for Deutsche Tauchnitz propelled the German propaganda machine in France to come down harder on Anglo-American books. Yet the timing is certainly suggestive. A report from the Literature Section of the Propaganda-Staffel in May 1941, just weeks after the Deutsche Tauchnitz release, set the tone for the coming months when it ruled that French publishers were too engaged with Anglo-American books. Translations from the English outnumbered those from the German. English-language sources cited in French scientific articles outpaced German sources. Even textbooks for teaching French readers German included practice sentences such as "If you had departed last week for America, you would already be there today." The report noted the irony: "It would make far more sense, in this context, to at least mention a trip to Germany!" In the summer of 1941, German cultural officials aggressively acted on their conviction that German books could flourish only if Anglo-American literature were cut off at the root. "The many translations from English and American [authors] must vanish," proclaimed one report in late June, "letting instead the translations of German poets and authors take their place." In mid-July, the Literature Section enacted a new ban which it blamed on paper shortages: "to eliminate new releases and printings of English and American literature." Though French booksellers were allowed to sell existing stock, many were unsettled by the prohibition, counting translations from the English among their top sellers. On 5 September 1941, the Committee for the Organization of the Book further informed booksellers that "translations of works from the English language are to be removed from exhibition sites and are no longer allowed to be displayed in shop windows."[26]

Having relegated Anglo-American books in translation to the dustbin—and no longer replenishing Albatross and Tauchnitz stocks—Nazi cultural officials were eager to put Deutsche Tauchnitz to its true test. As the series started its second year, joyous reports proliferated. "German-language books are appearing more and more in the display windows of French bookshops," declared the Literature Section in March 1942. "The demand for our literature is, according to some booksellers, very brisk. A lot of German is being learned and thereby, naturally, [people] are reaching for the German book. The Deutsche Tauchnitz series, especially appealing to readers given its deliberately low price, is being eagerly bought." By August, the series had sold more than a million copies. Kurt Metzner—a leader within the Cultural-Political Division of the German Foreign Office, who doubled as the Propaganda Ministry liaison for the Deutsche Tauchnitz series—celebrated the success of the series at a workshop for "Literature Promotion" at the Foreign Office. To a crowd of expectant case officers, he concluded, "On average, Deutsche Tauchnitz, which of course has not been around long at all, has already implemented itself so well that it can no longer be pushed out of the saddle, and multiple European countries are already demonstrating a demand to such an extent that the bookstores and sales venues are incessantly requesting newly produced volumes."[27]

What Metzner did not stress was how hard he and his colleagues had worked to spur the growth of the series. His original version of his speech suggested a more uneven success; it stated that Deutsche Tauchnitz "has, by and large, already implemented itself so well," but he had crossed out the "by and large." The Foreign Office seems to have remained dissatisfied. In April 1942, it adapted its strategies to make the series more visible. Klatten, Krause-Brandstetter's boss, took personal responsibility: "We want to design a Tauchnitz display window for Brandstetter, [and] to talk through the marketing plan again." At a workshop on 12 August 1942 for young, ambitious cultural bureaucrats, Metzner put his full force behind the series. "German will, to an increasing extent, be the world language," he proclaimed, "and the Deutsche Tauchnitz is called upon, in this regard, to achieve pioneering work." He had recently sent volumes to Germany's diplomatic missions in different countries but asked his listeners to help with their promotion by "educating the public authorities, institutes, and associations," and setting up book reviews to broaden the series' influence. Klatten regularly filled orders for officials, who requested the complete line for their bookshelves, or for German propaganda outlets abroad, which often ordered thousands of copies in one fell swoop. Willy Brandstetter also listed German soldiers as a large subgroup of Deutsche Tauchnitz readers.[28]

Yet it was not enough just to replace New York or London with Berlin. Metzner had reason to be concerned: if the books' primary consumers were, as Foreign Office documents suggest, German soldiers, officials, and booksellers already biased toward the regime, it would be a stretch to say that Deutsche Tauchnitz was accomplishing "pioneering work" for German culture abroad. Deutsche Tauchnitz had built itself on the model for continental editions in English, yet it faced for the first time the hurdle that Albatross and Tauchnitz had overcome by the late 1930s: reaching an audience beyond the native speakers it already held in its fold.

It was a particularly high hurdle for the Germans. The French had long tipped ideologically toward Anglo-American culture, their educated class favoring English over German as a second language. As the Propaganda-Staffel admitted in a September 1941 report, French readers were clearly hungry for books—literally reading while eating to distract themselves from insufficient rations—but only hungry, apparently, for certain foreign delicacies. Sending undercover investigators into bookstores to gauge bookseller and reader sentiment, propaganda officials determined that French booksellers were not displaying the pro-German brochures they had provided—an act of refusal that reflected the "reigning state of mind of its clientele: a wait-and-see attitude and a more and more pronounced hostility toward all that is German or thought to be of German inspiration." They learned that there remained across Paris "a very robust sale of *foreign translations,*" yet "the French book is not selling well and translations from English seem more than ever to be favored by the public, which finds here an opportunity to express their Anglophile sympathies." French readers remained, in short, more enamored of Britain and the United States than ever. In time it also became clear that Krause-Brandstetter's attempts to reach out to French readers through Deutsche Tauchnitz titles translated into French were falling flat, not making it beyond a handful of titles. In the terse climate of Occupation, Deutsche Tauchnitz, in whatever language, resonated as little more than "an arrogant gesture, not joyously accepted, it seems."[29]

*

Möhring received no immediate response to his question about selling Albatross books, partly because there *was* no straightforward answer. Goebbels had established different regulations for distinct markets. The Propaganda Ministry had banned Albatross exports. Yet in the summer of 1942, most Albatross titles still sold freely within Reich borders with the sanction of the Literary Chamber and Propaganda Ministry. In France, officials wavered. On 15 September 1942, Möhring received the official verdict of the Occupation government: his request to sell the Albatross Crime Club books to a wholesaler at a discount "had been rejected by [the office of] the Occupation commander in France, since it was categorically forbidden to sell English works."[30]

Yet as in so many cases regarding books in wartime, there was room for interpretation. Unsure of what to do with its Albatross-Tauchnitz titles—those produced in Germany rather than the British Isles—Hachette had gone straight to one of the top military authorities over propaganda: the same Schulz who had cornered Krause-Brandstetter two years earlier. He ruled that the remaining Albatross and Tauchnitz books *could* be sold in France because they were, for the time being, to be treated as German. Albatross sales continued to be permitted even after the third edition of the Liste Otto was published on 10 May 1943, ten years to the day after the book burnings in Germany, with its warning: "The sale of works in English, Polish, and Russian is absolutely forbidden. Exception is made for the English classics [and] the works of the Tauchnitz Edition, as well as for books used in schools for the study of language." In late November a small note in the book trade newspaper *Bibliographie de la France* made this exception official: "Sales of the Albatross Edition are permitted in France." In fact, as late as February 1944, when one regional propaganda official complained that many shops still sold Anglo-American books, higher propaganda officials continued to set Albatross and Tauchnitz apart. "As far as books from the Tauchnitz and Albatross publishing houses go, their sale is not to be hindered, since they function as a special kind of German propaganda," explained one official. "All remaining books in the English language are to be confiscated, and, where appropriate, booksellers should hand them over to the S.D. [to determine] the penalty."[31]

It is surprising that Nazi authorities took the risk, "special propaganda" or not, especially when the British government—through the British Council and Ministry of Information—was simultaneously airlifting books in English to the few remaining neutral countries in Europe. Albatross had outlived its financial usefulness to the Reich. It could not pretend to advance the marketing aims of the Foreign Office and Propaganda Ministry. Nor could it do the symbolic work Metzner demanded of Deutsche Tauchnitz, to make "the book and the sword appear in indivisible oneness." If anything, Albatross books undermined this Nazi agenda directly. As the British publisher and minister Harold Macmillan begrudgingly acknowledged to Pearl S. Buck, "It is true, of course," he wrote, "that the [British] Government's purpose in having English books in circulation is just as much satisfied by the circulation of a Continental edition [as by one produced in Britain]."[32]

Yet if Albatross had the books, it no longer had a sword left in the fight. As for Albatross's wartime readers—those who actually cracked open Albatross books to get drawn into the foreign worlds within—Gey's sales figures cannot tell us who they were or what they made of these books: whether they, like some French readers, understood their reading as a form of political action and the books as reflections of English and American cultures that undermined German ideals, or whether they simply grabbed what was available in a market of paper and book shortages, failed book deliveries, and too much time needing to be filled. Reading was an unpredictable act, at best. As Kate Sturge has suggested, "Reading remained a private activity in a society which had refused the possibility of privacy; and in that private space foreign literature surely had at least the potential to move its readers beyond the narcissistic mirror of translation, to take on a momentum of its own and begin to offer a window on the outside world."[33] Seen in this light, the fact that Albatross books stayed in demand during the war suggests that Albatross may, in the end, have encouraged continental Europe to become part of the "English-speaking world," even as its colorful books and cosmopolitan ideals receded into the distance.

NINETEEN

Rivals

ABROAD, TAUCHNITZ'S DECISION to "go German" spurred astonishment and regret. In a July 1942 article, "Exit Tauchnitz," *Time* magazine reported that "the Nazis have decreed that the century-old Tauchnitz Library must cease publishing works of U.S. and British writers," and concluded, "No longer will homing U.S. tourists shiver as they smuggle cheap, paperbound, Tauchnitz classics . . . past uninterested U.S. customs officers." A *New York Times* journalist more personally lamented the demise of the English Tauchnitz. "One remembers with a kind of homesickness those modest, neutral-colored little books," he began. "On shipboard, on rainy days, in trains, in pension gardens, they were a comfort. It brings back a vanished world to think of them, of reading, . . . while the steamer gently rocked and the reader was happier than he can be now."[1]

Holroyd-Reece had little time for such wistfulness. After the Germans bombarded his London office, he took up his defense of Albatross from a new location: 13 New Square, a road near Chancery Lane, Lincoln's Inn Fields, and the Royal Courts of Justice that enclosed a large green courtyard. A Gothic Revival entrance gate, replete with turrets and arches, gave way on the left and right to spare, four-story, flat-fronted brick buildings, with only the chimneys jutting up from the roof at intervals to distinguish one from the next. Yet from his new office, as from his old, Holroyd-Reece was losing ground. In England, Albatross was yoked in readers' minds with Tauchnitz, and Holroyd-Reece was the only one visible enough to take the blame. Journalists were spreading word that the mighty Tauchnitz had been pulled under Nazi influence. Albatross might well go down with it. The continental market for English books was open to competition, and Holroyd-Reece saw rivals rising up over the horizon, as Hans Otto had once spied Albatross so many years before.

*

Unfortunately for Holroyd-Reece, the rivals he feared were not imaginary. In April 1942, the Swedish publisher Albert Bonnier opened a New York office expressly to win American rights for his own continental English edition: Clipper Books. Since the Nazi regime had banned Albatross and Tauchnitz from exporting books to Sweden, Bonnier planned to fill the gap. Books in English were ever more in demand. His was a respected house, in operation since 1804, even longer than Tauchnitz. His selling pitch to authors and agents rang sweetly on American ears. "Sweden is one of the oldest democracies in the world and self-government and other democratic ideals have deep roots in the Swedish soil," he asserted. "At the present time, when Sweden is practically cut off from the Western world, German publishers—without the restrictions of a sea-blockade—can pour their literature into the Swedish bookstores, and thereby gain an advantage, which we are very anxious to counteract. One of the best and most effective ways of fighting this infiltration of Nazi ideas into Sweden is of course the uninterrupted publishing of translations of good books from the democratic, English-speaking world." Clipper Books would take up this charge, acting as a Swedish Albatross or Tauchnitz that stood for "the cause for which all the democracies fight," as did Bonnier's popular Zephyr series, which followed it.[2]

As war dragged on, publishers became bolder about encroaching on Albatross-Tauchnitz terrain. By fall 1942, Pearl S. Buck and Lewis Bromfield had signed with Bonnier for one novel each, new releases for which Albatross or Tauchnitz might, in peacetime, have sought copyright. Late in 1942, Laurence Pollinger—a British literary agent who had once demanded that Albatross purchase all D. H. Lawrence titles or it would get none—crossed a more delicate line when he handed over to the Jan Foerlag rights for English editions of *Lady Chatterley's Lover* and *The Rainbow* in Sweden held by the Odyssey and Albatross Presses. His logic? His legal counsel claimed that the publishers were German, so their standing contracts did not hold under the British Trading with the Enemy Act. Wartime dictates trumped Albatross's contractual rights, or at least it served Pollinger's interests and those of the Lawrence Estate to say so.[3]

Holroyd-Reece resented such incursions, especially when they threatened the only asset Albatross had left: copyright. Most contracts stated that Albatross was obligated to publish a given work, or to reprint a sold-out title, within six months of the signing date in either the Albatross or Tauchnitz series, or the rights would revert to the author. Wartime constraints rather than outright negligence had kept Albatross from meeting these conditions. Yet authors nonetheless scrutinized the moral line, wondering how long they were obligated to tie up their rights with these firms when they could not even get their royalties out of Germany. Buck, for instance, took up the question with the British lawyer C. D. Medley, an expert in book trade legalities, when Bonnier requested exclusive rights to all her former Tauchnitz titles. "There certainly was an arrangement of some sort [with Albatross]," he noted, "and the arrangements with the Tauchnitz company were, I feel sure, kept alive." He recommended that Buck's agent write Holroyd-Reece directly, offering one caution: "He is not a gentleman who is likely to relinquish his rights."[4]

Holroyd-Reece responded to Medley weeks later from Windermere, in the Lake District of northwest England, where he was ostensibly "[catching] up with arrears of work." "Needless to say, I am only too pleased to assist you in any way I can," he wrote with his characteristic veneer of openness. His position was straightforward. "The buyer and owner of the copyrights or licenses was Albatross," he insisted, for all Tauchnitz and Albatross titles signed after September 1934. Yet he admitted that the war had caught Albatross up in "a terrible tangle of rights" involving "a very difficult problem of international law," which he and the Publishing Holding Company could sort out only in enemy property proceedings after the war. In the meantime, he invoked historical precedent: "As

Germany has perpetrated five wars since Tauchnitz began, I can only say that . . . in the past the Tauchnitz authors have been content to treat their contracts as just having been suspended by hostilities."[5]

Holroyd-Reece, a spectacular manipulator of the law by trade, did not enjoy being at the mercy of others' legal interpretations in a tussle with Swedish publishers and others who were, in his words, "no doubt contemplating publishing books on the lines of Albatross and Tauchnitz after the war." He requested Medley's help. "I would be grateful . . . if you would take the opportunity of telling [your Albatross and Tauchnitz clients] that no expense and no pains will be spared by the owners and managing agents . . . to see that the interests of our authors are fully safeguarded and protected. One of the agents has taken the view that, because I am the largest individual shareholder in this country, I should have paid authors their royalties at any rate up to the war, but I need hardly explain to you that, firstly I am not allowed to do so under the Defense Regulations, and secondly it is impossible because I have not got the particulars which are either in Germany or in occupied France." Holroyd-Reece was protected, in this one sense, for the moment, but left vulnerable in another, as he made abundantly clear. "In conclusion may I ask you to use your own discretion about the information contained in this letter, because there are in London and elsewhere, potential rivals as far as Albatross and Tauchnitz are concerned."[6]

*

The most dangerous of these rivals, Allen Lane, Holroyd-Reece knew all too well. In fact, in a manner of speaking, Holroyd-Reece had schooled Lane in paperback production. On 30 July 1935, Lane launched his famous Penguin Books into the British market. Like Albatross, Penguin dressed different genres in different colors; like Albatross, Penguin offered a brand rather than just a product. Selling at sixpence (6d) each, Penguins were far cheaper than the so-called "cheap" hardcovers that sold for 3s/6d or 2s/6d. They could be "bought as easily and casually as a packet of cigarettes," remarked Edward Young, the artist who brought Penguin's charming icon into the world. And Lane also cleverly sold his Penguins outside traditional bookshops, winning a critical contract with Woolworth's stores. If the British publishing establishment had been resistant to Albatross and Tauchnitz editions because they undermined the more lucrative hardcover market, it was even more put off by Penguins, which transgressed not only traditional price points but the sacrosanct walls of bookshops themselves. Lane argued, against the traditional grain of the trade, that his mass market approach would enhance profits by "converting book-borrowers into book-buyers." And he appeared to be right. With the help of low prices and spirited marketing, he sold 3 million copies in his first year.[7]

While Lane deserves credit for taking this risk, he had taken lessons from Holroyd-Reece. The British book trade of the early 1930s was immersed in speculation about what Stanley Unwin called the "New Reading Public": to what degree did it exist? And if, in fact, it did—with a growing middle class and the expansion of reading in the working classes—how might publishers best reach it? Some time late in 1933 or early in 1934, Holroyd-Reece had invited Lane to capitalize on this market by co-publishing a "Modern Library" series in England on the Albatross model. For Holroyd-Reece, such a series, like Albatross Crime and Mystery Club books already produced by Collins in Edinburgh, would increase Albatross's stake in the British economy. In a confidential memo, Holroyd-Reece set the terms for this more truly British Albatross: Lane would produce and sell the books in England, Holroyd-Reece would sell them on the continent, and Holroyd-Reece would "assist [Lane's] production department to work out and lay down minutely the principles governing the production of this series." Negotiations solidified to the point where Holroyd-Reece indeed shared with Lane Albatross's economies of scale—how it produced the most books for the least money—and set the series launch for the fall. Then, in spring 1934, Lane backed out, due to copyright difficulties and financial risk.[8] Initially, this was little more than a failed deal, yet it became a harbinger of trouble to come. Lane pilfered the insights he had gleaned from Holroyd-Reece, severed ties with his directors at the Bodley Head, and created his own company.

Outcry against Penguin was fierce. Jonathan Cape, who had sold Lane rights for the first Penguins only because he was sure Lane would fail, later told him, somewhat tongue in cheek, "You're the b[astard] that has ruined this trade with your ruddy Penguins." George Orwell loved Penguins as a reader, yet noted that they were such a "splendid value . . . that if the other publishers had any sense they would combine against them and suppress them." Years later, Holroyd-Reece ribbed Lane: "With the greatest skill and charm you blunted the attack against yourself by claiming that it was all my fault since your brilliantly successful efforts were derived from the instigation and impetus of the Albatross." Holroyd-Reece had, in good faith, shared his production secrets with Lane, only to pay the price down the line. Sylvia Beach's purchase logs for 1937 show that she purchased a Penguin edition of *A Passage to India* for 4 francs, rather than the 1934 Albatross edition, more than thrice the price at 14 francs.[9]

In Penguin, Lane achieved what Holroyd-Reece had envisioned nearly a decade earlier: a British publishing house which held rights to sell its books across more markets than ever. This was the way of the future. American publishers caught on: Robert de Graff started Pocket Books on the cusp of war in 1939, the American News Corporation launched Avon Books in 1941. One reason that Buck, among other authors, hesitated to commit her continental English rights to Bonnier or any other publisher was that the old model was breaking down. As her husband, the publisher Richard Walsh, noted to her agent in May 1943, "I think we are all agreed that we don't want to give away any exclusive Continental rights in English, and that in general we look forward to the possibility that American cheap editions may be sold on the Continent after the war." With governments and publishers hoping for an end to the war, reaching a mass readership also had other, more political implications. Young, Penguin's graphic designer, noted that Lane's motives were both "missionary and mercenary"; he was certainly in it for the money, yet it was also "very important that books should be mass-produced if there is to be any meaning in liberty of opinion, and if knowledge is to be accessible to everyone." The threat to Holroyd-Reece's market, in other words, was immense. Governments and publishers would all want to get English-language books into continental Europe at war's end.[10]

For the moment, however, roughly thirty blocks south of Bonnier's New York office, at 245 Fifth Avenue at 28th Street, one of Lane's chief American allies lay in wait. This foe was familiar to Holroyd-Reece, though dressed in new American clothing: Kurt Enoch, working for a nascent American branch of Penguin Books. In the way an action leads to a reaction, this turn of affairs resulted from Enoch's falling out with Holroyd-Reece in the late 1930s. No longer able to rely on Holroyd-Reece to represent his businesses, Continenta and Imperia, in England, after their rift in 1937, Enoch had hired a young British publisher, Charles Pick. Pick knew Lane, and shared with him Enoch's attempt to import French classics into England; Lane was sufficiently intrigued to visit Enoch in Paris and discuss publishing French and German translations of his Penguin Specials series. In the end, the war shattered these plans, yet the seeds of Enoch's future lay in this failure. By late 1941, Enoch was working for Penguin, Albatross's biggest prewar rival in Europe. "I started on my new task with great enthusiasm and anticipation," he remembered, "happy at the end of my first year in the United States to resume my career as a publisher once again."[11]

It had been a long way from the place Vendôme, over a daunting route. On Enoch's arrival in New York, his English had been rudimentary, and he was unable to provide for his family. "I left behind in Paris everything that I still possessed," he explained to U.S. officials. "We arrived in the USA only with that which we had on our bodies and a few pieces of luggage." He sent his elder daughter, Ruth, to Iowa to work as a nanny and housekeeper—work for which she was unsuited and which left her deeply unhappy—while his younger daughter, Mirjam stayed with relatives in New Jersey to finish high school. Much to his relief, his mother arrived from Europe early in 1941 and was living with his sister Ilse, first in New York and later in San Francisco. His brother Otto in Detroit, urged him to take any work he could find. Enoch bucked at the thought. "I had never been an employee before and was used to acting on my own initiatives and decisions," he later wrote.[12]

He borrowed more money from his brother and spent weeks networking. He tracked down German émigré publishers: Fritz Landshoff, former owner of the Kiepenhauer Verlag in Berlin, and Kurt Wolff, with whom Holroyd-Reece had launched the Pantheon series. He met with American publishers: Bennett Cerf of Random House and B. W. Huebsch of Viking. With another émigré, Henry Koppell, he found his first toehold; Enoch could use Koppell's address, a desk phone, and secretarial assistance in exchange for half of the profits. Enoch Publishing Company was born, and Enoch exported scientific textbooks and reference books for fellow German émigré publishers Maurice Dekker and Eric Proskauer.[13]

Then, late in 1941, the past came to greet him in the form of Lane, who confessed he was on the verge of closing down his American branch of Penguin. The enterprise had begun in the summer of 1939, when twenty-one-year-old Ian Ballantine left England with crate loads of Penguins and an immense task: to create a market for British Penguins in the United States. Within months, the war had killed the effort. Between low sales, paper shortages, and production and transportation slowdowns, Lane saw little reason to continue—that is, until Enoch seconded Ballantine's idea that Penguin produce books for the American market in the United States. When Enoch offered to raise start-up money—

circumventing wartime restrictions on transferring funds from England—Lane agreed. With a loan of $3,000 from Kurt Wolff, Enoch became vice president of the fledging Penguin operation, in charge of production and design, with Ballantine responsible for sales and distribution. "We'd split all profits, but I'd assume all losses," Enoch later explained, wagering his all on Penguin's success.[14]

Enoch's work at Penguin offered him the professional camaraderie he had lacked in his last years in Paris. "Especially in the beginning, when money and staff were at a minimum," he wrote, "Ballantine, myself and others often joined to pack, ship or do menial jobs until late into the night, in order to get the work done or to save money." Enoch was grateful, and took advantage of the opportunities in New York, as he had in Paris. Yet he did not relish starting anew for the third time. "I could not know whether the anchor dropped here could or would be permitted to hold," he admitted. "For the time being we were physically safe—guests of the most powerful nation of the world. I could again provide for myself. People were mostly friendly, helpful and generous. But we did not really belong."[15]

Enoch's feeling of not belonging might have been his sharpest weapon. He was determined to make a life for himself and his family, to hold on to his vision of himself as a publisher, to belong once again. His application for American citizenship included a passionate plea for this opportunity. He had fled Germany "because of racial persecution and strong opposition to the Nazi system," he explained. "I have been expatriated and do not owe allegiance to any country." Now what he wanted most was the luxury of staying in one place. "May I finally point out that after having succeeded a third time to reestablish myself I hope to find a final refuge and to be relieved from the fear to be forced again out of the country when the war is over and to start again to resettle myself," he wrote.[16] Enoch never fully lost this feeling. Being forced out, leaving everything behind: these drove him forward, making of him a formidable rival who would, soon enough, face Holroyd-Reece once again.

TWENTY

When the Bombs Fell

TO CELEBRATE THE TENTH anniversary of Hitler's reign, the Nazi elite gathered with thousands of party loyalists on 30 January 1943 for an evening of rousing speeches at the Berlin Sportpalast. Goebbels had originally planned an inspirational paean around one theme: "The victory of the National Socialist movement" and its struggle "for a more just order of life, for freedom, and for their daily bread." Yet by the time the anniversary arrived, news of German reverses after six months of heavy fighting at Stalingrad had filtered back into the Reich. The Sixth Army was being crushed by the Soviet Red Army. The Luftwaffe had stopped dropping relief packages of food, medical supplies, and ammunition, which meant that by the time Göring and Goebbels stepped to the podium to deliver their rallying cries to the Volk, German soldiers were scared, ill, slowly starving, and unable to defend themselves. Goebbels ordered that no flags be flown. Hitler declined to appear, saying he was "with his soldiers" and asking Goebbels to deliver his statement.[1]

Drained of some of its intended glory, the celebration became a political diversion to inspire the party faithful to look the other way, past Stalingrad. Hitler's speech described the dedication of German soldiers as the example for the German people. "'Battle' was the slogan in those days of the National Socialist movement from its very inception, and 'battle' has remained our slogan to this very day," Goebbels exhorted the crowd. Only victory was admissible.[2]

Allied forces commemorated Hitler's tenth anniversary quite differently: by sending uninvited guests—Royal Air Force Mosquito light bombers—on a daylight air raid on the German capital. The London press reported that British bombs had forced Göring and Goebbels to interrupt their broadcasts. The *New York Times* played up the attack's symbolic significance: "There was drama at the Nazis' celebration of the tenth anniversary of their rule—high drama surpassing anything that these past masters of showmanship had ever staged or seen before. But it was drama in reverse—drama provided by their enemies who now direct the play." For Prime Minister Winston Churchill, President Franklin Roosevelt, and the Joint Chiefs of Staff, this attack marked the beginning of the "strategic bombing" campaign they had agreed upon at the Casablanca Conference days earlier, a campaign that would, they hoped, incrementally halt Germany's ability to muster the munitions, men, and morale it needed to wage war.[3]

The next day, German radio played the somber, haunting Adagio of Anton Bruckner's Symphony No. 7 in E Major. The strings rose above the ominous resonance of the tuba and brass to set the stage for the announcement many Germans expected: their troops in Russia had surrendered. Two weeks later, on 18 February, Goebbels took up where the persistently rising tone of the strings had left off, inciting the German people to move beyond the devastation on the Eastern Front. "Total war is the demand of the hour," he exclaimed; "In this hour of national reflection and contemplation, we believe firmly and unshakably in victory. . . . Now, people rise up and let the storm break loose!" These were the standards of the war going forward, measures of absolute loyalty and self-denial against which soldiers and civilians alike would be judged. They were to touch the lives of more than one in the Albatross-Tauchnitz fold. Wegner would be the first.[4]

*

There are letters no one wants to write home, and on 2 November 1943, Christian Wegner wrote one of them. "My dear Annemarie!" he began, "It looks as though even after all the hardship lately, another storm is preparing itself. I am sitting—please don't be frightened—in detention, awaiting trial, because an officer whom I had reprimanded denounced me out of revenge, saying that on the 30th of July, I had made seditious statements. I hope I will succeed in bringing the truth to victory." He had to wait at least two weeks for a decision, but urged his wife to take hope. "Please don't give yourself any unnecessary worry. I think I will manage it." With these reassuring words, Wegner covered over what was, in fact, a dire situation. He had been accused of "Zersetzung der Wehrkraft," the crime of "subverting the war effort" or "undermining military morale," which, at its worst, carried the death penalty. German soldiers had arrested him in Paris on 30 October, when Wegner and his friends gathered to celebrate the baptism of the new son of a close Albatross associate, Wolfgang Ollendorff. Climbing the steps to the party, Wegner saw soldiers waiting higher up the spiral stair. As Wegner wrote to his wife, "Happiness and unhappiness could not live closer to one another." The soldiers waited at their posts, allowing Wegner to claim his last hours with his closest friends before being locked away. He uncharacteristically broke down in tears. Some of his friends encouraged him to slip out the back. He could hide and wait out the war, they urged. Wegner refused, walking out the front door to his arrest.[5]

Until this point, Wegner had received nothing but accolades in his military career. By summer 1940, his regiment had broken through to the English Channel and emerged victorious from battles in Flanders and Artois, earning him the War Merit Cross First and Second Class with Swords for bravery critical to German success but not connected with the front lines. In February 1940, he was promoted from lieutenant to first lieutenant, and in June 1940 to captain. On 1 June 1943, less than six months before his arrest, he received a glowing evaluation of his work as commander of the Transport Section of the 16th Flak Division that recommended he be promoted to major. His superiors valued him as a man of astounding talents and reliable loyalties: "direct, open, upright character . . . versatile personality . . . unflagging commitment." The court-martial faced a conundrum. They had little idea what had driven this fifty-year-old, twice-promoted, well-rounded leader to behavior that warranted his arrest. While the court-martial gathered evidence, Wegner waited alone in his cell. Apart from a fifteen-minute discussion with one longtime friend who was present at his arrest, he was allowed to talk with no one in the first seventeen days—a stark punishment for one so gregarious.[6]

In any such conflict, there is the search for the true note in the reverberation between what happened and how it is portrayed. Wegner framed his downfall in starkly simple terms. Late in July 1943, he had returned to his post after vacationing near Munich, where Annemarie and their two children were waiting out the war, trying to avoid the bombs Christian feared Allies would drop on the strategic port of Hamburg. Shortly after his return to duty, on 30 July, he received news too unsettling to fathom. The Allies had indeed bombed Hamburg, flattening the homes of his mother and brother and perhaps his business. Cutting deeper, the Wehrmacht reported the Allies were accelerating attacks on Sicily, where Ezard, his oldest child, a son from his first marriage, was fighting. In the late spring, wrought up after a devastating break-up with his fiancée, Ezard had left his position as a police constable of the 16th Flak Division—where Christian could more or less monitor his safety—to volunteer for Göring's regiment in Sicily. It had been three weeks since Christian had heard from his son, who was only twenty-two, which had left him "almost desperate with fear and anxiety." And on 24 July, Mussolini surrendered, leaving German soldiers in Italy vulnerable. Under this duress Wegner had unleashed a stream of bitter words upon whoever would listen.[7]

On weighing the factors in his case, it seems fair to say that, whatever the effect of the bombing or his sincere angst for his son, Christian Wegner also landed in prison for the same reason Hans Otto had fired him from Tauchnitz so many years earlier: he said and did what he wanted to when he wanted to. He had never kept his opinions to himself, nor had he adjusted his behavior when he traded his well-tailored business suits for a military uniform. The court-martial acknowledged that his career had made him "intellectually very spry" and given him "an extensive knowledge and worldview." He respected his superiors, who admired his confidence and his "established love of engagement" with the war effort. But it also noted a shadow side of his personality. Wegner did not notice the limits of his own one-man show; he "mostly monopolized the conversation " and brooked no disagreement, creating resentment among his subordinates.[8]

Put differently, Wegner liked to be on the winning side; and the longer the fighting wore on—and Wegner saw his own interests jeopardized by choices of the German high command—and the higher the death toll, the more his narcissism put him at odds with the very men on whose side he fought. When the Allies occupied North Africa in November 1942, for instance, he had declared to one senior lieutenant that "from now on, [we] could not count on a German victory." Pointing at theaters of war on a map spread before them at the mess hall, he "spoke of the winding up of Italy and the Balkans and depicted further adverse developments." On 6 April 1943, Wegner ended up similarly locked in argument with one Captain Stiegler, during a late night full of lively discussion in which "the twelve men involved drank twelve bottles of burgundy and twelve glasses of cognac, as well as twelve bottles of sparkling wine." Wegner became heated over Stiegler's contention that National Socialism was equivalent to a religion. He disagreed, not wanting to mix religion and politics. "The parley ended with discord," Wegner creating the enemy who would later denounce him.[9]

The court-martial determined that Wegner was already unhinged when he returned to duty in July 1943. "He became highly agitated, since he saw his life's work completely annihilated," claimed the report. On running into Stiegler, Wegner let loose. "Well now, Mr. Optimist, what do you have to say now?" Wegner taunted. "[The Allies] have now destroyed Hamburg through bombing raids, next month they will destroy Berlin, and that is how it will continue." When Stiegler invoked the rhetoric of "total war"—that war demanded sacrifices—Wegner grew enraged. "If I had not become a poor man through the bombing of Hamburg, I would bet you that events will play themselves out as I've predicted to you." Stiegler told Wegner he was "ripe for a sanitarium," and took his leave. Wegner ended the evening with a military equal, who talked him down from his "completely hysterical state," and got him to promise that he would hold to his "mission to make clear to his men that they had the duty, whatever the setbacks, to endure." As far as Wegner knew, the story ended there.[10]

That a charismatic, decorated leader could give way to such extreme flights of uncensored criticism suggested, among other things, that the Allied bombs had met their mark. The engineers of the Hamburg bombing had not called it Operation Gomorrah for nothing. It was the first round-the-clock campaign either side had undertaken, with British pilots targeting the city by night and American bombers hitting industrial targets by day, to prevent civilians from recovering between raids. The Allies had a new weapon to embolden them, code-named "Window": paper strips coated with foil that squadrons dropped by the sackful to render German radar systems useless. The British air chief marshal, Sir Arthur "Bomber" Harris, not mincing words, envisioned nothing less than the destruction, on a biblical scale, of this lively port: a purgatorial cleansing by fire that would decimate industrial and military targets and, in his words, "[undermine] the morale of the German people to a point where their capacity for armed resistance is fatally weakened." As he told his men in cold military parlance, "At least 10,000 tons of bombs will have to be dropped to complete the process of elimination."[11]

Elimination was an accurate word. The first British raid, on 25 July 1943, was the largest attack to date on a city in modern warfare. Seven hundred seventy-one Royal Air Force bombers dropped 2,300 tons of explosives on western quadrants of the city and the city center between one and two o'clock in the morning, including roughly 350,000 "incendiary" bombs that fanned existing fires and started new ones. What began as a gorgeous fireworks display—a series of yellow, red, and green flares to help bombers distinguish targets—became, as the historian Keith Lowe properly calls it, an inferno. The Allies had also bombed water mains and electrical lines, rendering futile German attempts to fight the flames.[12]

The weather made the city blaze up quickly—the kind of hot, dry, summer days that drew Hamburg's citizens out to the parks ringing the Alster Lake, walking, riding bicycles, or savoring whatever wartime approximation of Kaffee und Kuchen they could find at waterside cafés. Many were tired of false alarms and avoided the shelters, narrow tunnels packed with sweaty, anxious humanity, and sometimes cats, dogs, and chickens. But this time, by the time they had stumbled out of their beds, many had to run through burning courtyards into streets completely ablaze. The fires grew so hot that even tarmac melted; inside buildings, the fires "melted cutlery, glass bottles and burned bricks to ash." Many families died in their cellars of smoke inhalation or in public shelters, designed to save their lives, that became their coffins. The death toll was all the more devastating because Hamburg's Gauleiter, Karl Kaufmann, worried about creating floods of refugees, had forbidden people from leaving the city after the first raid.

The writer Hans Erich Nossack described the lurid scene on his return to the city: "Mile after mile, there was not a single living house. . . . In areas I thought I knew well, I lost my way completely." Scenes of contradiction lived on in his mind: "Children cleaning and raking a small front yard" amid downed buildings, and "inside a house that stood alone and intact in the midst of a vast expanse of rubble, a woman cleaning her house." The city stank and oozed with filth, as rats and flies took over, "lords of the city." Yet more than anything, Nossack stressed the emotional disorientation. "The horror of it made it hard to take note of details." Operation Gomorrah killed forty-five thousand residents of Hamburg—a death toll ten times greater than in any previous raid—and sent nearly a million refugees, more than half the population, straggling out of the city to find relief with friends or relatives.[13]

For Christian Wegner, unable to confirm or deny his losses, August began with agonizing waiting. He had heard nothing of his son. News from Hamburg was slow to arrive. Finally, in mid-August, Annemarie wrote. "Our office has also been destroyed," she reported. "There was, of course, not much else to expect . . . , nevertheless, one always holds out that tiny spark of hope. . . . It must have been unimaginably horrific in Hamburg. . . . The city is simply demolished, systematically, bit by bit. And so it continues, everywhere. And what is it all for?" She worried about her husband and his son and longed for a reunion that would not come any time soon; she did not yet know that Ezard had, indeed, fallen in the line of duty in Italy on 14 July. "How unfathomably far away are the normal times," she concluded. The foil chaff that had outwitted German radar still littered the ground. Though the *Hamburger Zeitung* proclaimed it harmless, children were told not to touch it; it could be poisonous.[14] The world had indeed become surreal.

*

What effect the Allied bombing had on Wegner's outbursts became a critical question for the court-martial. Did his defeatist proclamations result from an accumulation of losses that culminated in his not being fully sound of mind? Or were they born of personal weaknesses just coming to light? The report never excused him. But the dense document, which ran just over sixteen single-spaced pages, offered an unusually detailed—and perhaps strategic—explanation of how a man with Wegner's immaculate record found himself incarcerated in the fifth year of the war. As Wegner's son Matthias later mused, it was as if the judge subtly crafted his narrative to spare Christian the harshest punishment.[15]

Wegner's defense turned on the question of intent. At one level, the sheer number and the seriousness of his tirades were damning. Well before the bombing of Hamburg, he had unthinkingly mouthed off. Yet at another level, the tribunal acknowledged that his "acute uneasiness and worry" had made him "see the situation black on black," and "that he did not act with the idea that his actions had a subversive effect." It also worked in his favor that he was a decorated soldier with "50 years of an honorable life behind him." Nonetheless, there were limits to the court-martial's sympathy. "The severity of the time demands severe measures," stated the report. "In the current fight for survival, . . . it cannot under any circumstances be tolerated that unreflective blatherers go unpunished, when they send into the world subversive opinions . . . without thinking through the consequences of their actions."[16]

The evidence was in, and the court-martial deliberated. Wegner waited on his sentence, not in prison, but at a deluxe hotel in Brussels, thanks to his general's goodwill. Perhaps this privilege, or his habit of landing on his feet, had led him to expect that his name would be cleared. So it was with anger that he learned of his sentence on 23 November. "I must make a very difficult and awful disclosure, that will horribly affect my whole life and above all, also that of our firm," he wrote to his loyal associate, Walther Platz. "Yesterday, because of an accusation made against me out of revenge, I was sentenced to *four* years in prison and loss of [military] rank!" He had been kicked out of the Literary Chamber, destroying his economic stability. "Besides which my poor head is still so full of these frightful experiences that I am not at all close to being able to anticipate all the consequences," he declared to Platz, who would have to run his business with Annemarie. "For you, it is, for the time being, as if I were dead."[17]

Wegner did not rest with this verdict, and on 3 December shared with Annemarie his plan: his friend Kurt Ezart knew the sculptor Arno Breker, a favorite of Göring's, and would entreat him to commute Christian's sentence. In the next weeks, Wegner sat in his cell, restlessly planning a future over which he had no control. Christmas found him still waiting. He knew his brother Ekhard was advocating in Berlin on his behalf, and his friend interceding with Breker, yet it took so long to get information that he found it futile even to contact his lawyer. "One always has the feeling of speaking into the void." On New Year's Day, as in days before, he practiced chess problems, exhausting the lines of offense and defense suggested by his chess book. He sought anything to occupy his mind, the puzzle book Annemarie had sent him already "fully cracked." "Naturally, I have learned patience," he confessed, "but this uncertainty torments me."[18]

Finally, in early February 1944, Christian learned his sentence had been reduced to eight months in the Wehrmacht prison in Germersheim, after which he would be sent to the Eastern Front. In any other context, this would hardly seem news to celebrate. Yet for Wegner, being sent back into battle was better than the alternative. He urged Annemarie to share his hopes: "Believe in a better time and such a one in which we can stand across from one another again in freedom and in peace. We will all bite our way through until then." He worked in the prison library, "gratified" for the moment, repairing the shabby books, much as he hoped to restore his own good name, whatever that might mean in the years ahead.[19]

Before leaving for the Eastern Front, Wegner was permitted a day's leave to see his family. Then six-year-old Matthias was shocked to see his father "wearing a heavy, field-gray coat, reaching almost to the floor, and a steel helmet. The sad sight left its mark on me," he remembered, "because we had seen our father until that point only in his, for us, quite imposing officer's uniform. On his back, he lugged a massive soldier's knapsack, over which he had slung his gun. With this load he drew forward, hunched over yet without showing even the slightest whiff of fear, in our company to the train station of G., to climb into the train for the East, already completely overstuffed with soldiers. Yet what did it mean—'to climb in'–those trying to board could not force their way into the interior of the train, but had to cling tightly to the running boards along the side, out in open air. It was a highly dangerous journey into the unknown. We stood, as the train swung into action, waving from the platform, until the contours of the train melded into a tiny point on the horizon." On the way to Danzig, as they later learned, Wegner had pushed through to the inside of one of the wagons to protect himself, a feat at which he had apparently grown quite practiced.[20]

*

Goebbels's call for "total war" propelled government offices and ministries to determine what sacrifices they, too, might make for the Reich. In the spring of 1943, the Literary Chamber and Propaganda Ministry ordered the closure of most publishing houses, except those "of absolute necessity to the war effort." Both Tauchnitz and Oscar Brandstetter made the short "list of warranted firms." Between Deutsche Tauchnitz and the Brandstetters' military printing contracts, they had won a secure spot in the regime's esteem. Albatross, in contrast, was selected for closure, pending a decision by the Leipzig Chamber of Commerce and second Reich Commissioner for the Handling of Enemy Property, Johannes Krohn.[21]

This judgment came as no surprise to Walter Gey. He had steered the firm through increasingly restrictive regulations: by August 1941, no paper rations; in April 1942, no exports. Erich Kupfer had been called up to the Norwegian front in March 1942, and Gey himself only narrowly escaped military service when the Foreign Office suddenly declared a renewed interest in Albatross and the Reich Commissioner interceded on his behalf. Perhaps most important, Albatross no longer stood under Brandstetter protection. The Brandstetters took their cue from the Propaganda Ministry's message that books in English were out of favor. In mid-June 1942, they announced that they were severing their contracts with Albatross at the end of the year. They no longer needed Albatross. Not only had the firm paid back most of its debt to Tauchnitz, but the commissioner had finally declared that the Brandstetters could not take over Albatross shares.[22] Since they could not seize control of Albatross, the Brandstetters grasped the other shining prize before them: only in wartime could they cancel their contract without argument from the British interests that usually drove Albatross's agenda, so they might emerge from the war free and clear of Holroyd-Reece's maneuvers.

Gey had tried, at each turn, to make the best of Albatross's ever-shrinking terrain. Being a man who dutifully pursued his mandate to protect Albatross interests, he had staged an earnest defense of the Albatross-Tauchnitz partnership in the fall of 1942. Kupfer, who continued to advise Gey from the front, seemed initially resigned to Albatross's separation from Tauchnitz. Yet in late November, he suddenly sent an uncharacteristically ardent appeal. "Albatross cannot let itself be pushed aside," he declared. "What could O.B. [Oscar Brandstetter] have started with Tauchnitz without us? We were the keys to Tauchnitz for these men, and I cannot give it all up. I, personally, have, without exaggeration, accomplished tremendous work for Tauchnitz. You should have lived through the transition phase in the fall of 1934. . . . Indeed, it is too cheap and does not correspond to the principle that the war should not be used to exploit business goals, to push the managing director into a dead-end track and to let the publishing house go to the dogs. So let's wait and see what the Herr [Reich Commissioner Krohn] says." But this appeal was too little, too late. Krohn agreed that the separation was too far along to fight. The Brandstetters ended on a conciliatory note, evidently wanting to avoid competition after the war. "When English-language production is once again revived," their letter stated, "we would see it as desirable if both firms seek one another's counsel to . . . prevent a rivalry disadvantageous to both sides."[23] At the end of 1942, the once rivals turned partners became two entities once again: not quite enemies, rivals in waiting, marking time to the day the war would end.

In the first months of 1943, Gey thus recalibrated Albatross operations on the small piece of ground left to him. With one accountant, one office worker, and two stockroom workers on half days—one of them a seventy-year-old man—he sold the Albatross books that remained. In one small act of defiance, he refused to cede Albatross distribution to the Brandstetters, noting, instead, that it would be "valuable as far as prestige is concerned" for Albatross to preserve its name and its independence wherever possible. Only at the end of April, nearly four years into the war, did the Propaganda Ministry enact the regulation Gey had long feared: the ban of Albatross sales in the Reich, with the exception of schools and ministries. By the end of September, Gey had—even in the face of this ban—nonetheless sold 170,000 RM's worth of books. He concluded, "1943 will yield a quite unusually high profit, namely because of the large volume of sales in the first months [of the year]." He also won one other modest victory. Authorities at the Leipzig Chamber of Commerce declared that they had no interest in formally closing Albatross; it was at a standstill, anyway, as they saw it.[24] So Gey continued to sell Albatross books, and to report sales to the Reich Commissioner, until a higher authority dictated otherwise.

In the end, however, forces more powerful than the Nazi bureaucracy decided the question of what to do with Albatross. On 4 December 1943, in the two hours between the air raid warning at 3:39 A.M. and the all clear at 5:39, 442 Allied bombers unleashed 1,400 tons of explosives and fire bombs on Leipzig, the sixth-largest city in Germany, with 700,000 inhabitants. Since half of Leipzig's own firefighters had been sent to Berlin to put out fires after a bombing two days earlier, the city's defenses were weakened. The city burned.

After the raid, the Allies gathered eyewitness accounts from German prisoners of war to verify the damage. One thirty-seven-year-old railway-yard worker recounted that bombs had shattered the glass roof of the train station, blown out all the windows, and decimated "three trainloads of soldiers on furlough, which had just pulled into the station." Another soldier described the city center as "utterly in ruins," to the point "that he did not see a house that was not completely gutted." A former grade school teacher on furlough from the front reported massive destruction in other parts of the city, too. "A hospital in the western part of the city was heavily damaged, killing many new born infants and mothers, and the Messehallen in which aircraft were assembled were heavily hit. . . . Often one could see that in a whole city block, just one house stood, seemingly undamaged."[25]

Casualties were far lower than in Hamburg, with roughly two thousand killed. Apparently, many had disobeyed the directive to stay in air raid shelters and fled instead, saving themselves from being roasted in the heat. Still, statistics told a grim tale. Over 1,000 commercial buildings had been flattened, along with 472 factory buildings. The book trade took an especially large hit. "For more than half-a-century, Leipzig was the most important city in the world for German language publishing," explained a postwar report by the American Office of Military Government for Germany. "Special railroad cars left Leipzig daily or from two to three times each week, loaded with publications for every German language city in Europe." The bombing had destroyed the largest book distributor, along with many smaller printing houses. One prisoner of war returned home astonished to find that "no books or periodicals are printed anymore."[26] Millions of books were destroyed, and with them the raw materials for diversion and instruction on which the Propaganda Ministry depended to cultivate the proper morale among its depleted citizens.

This phase of total war won Albatross little but total damage. On 13 December, Gey wrote to Reich Commissioner Krohn from his home in Liebertwolkwitz. "The entire contents of the office and storerooms is gutted by fire," he confirmed, and he had no idea whether the unbound volumes at the Brandstetter printing works had been saved. To some degree, it did not matter. There was no way to get them bound, since the Brandstetter plant had also been heavily hit. Gey faced the inevitable conclusion: "The publishing house will probably, therefore, remain completely dormant from now on."[27]

Since Albatross had no real present, Gey looked to the future. His reports to Krohn and his associates at the Office for the Handling of Enemy Property suggest that Gey took a certain pride in this work: in fighting to preserve Albatross's contracts with the Brandstetters, in seeing it sell enough books to pay off its debts, and now, in keeping with enemy property guidelines, in rescuing what assets he could. Gey gathered for safekeeping the archives of all published volumes stored elsewhere, as well as author contracts stored in deposit boxes at the bank. The rest would have to wait. Every last book, sheet of paper, pencil, and paper clip had fed the flames or was buried under layers of debris. With Kupfer's help—he had received leave in January—Gey explored the former Albatross headquarters. Even the safe had done little good against the heat generated by the fires, its contents "largely burnt to cinders." Their entire stock of books was annihilated: what turned out to be 12,830 banned books, 47,672 books ready for sale, and 70,550 unbound books, along with Holroyd-Reece's prized collection: a Tauchnitz archive of 5,250 volumes, one copy of each volume from Tauchnitz's century of publishing.[28]

Though faced with little more than remnants, neither Kupfer nor Gey showed the Reich commissioner any sign of faltering. Gey had kept copies of financial statements at his home office and had insisted that certain logbooks from 1943 be kept off the premises. From these statements, the two men were determined to reconstitute their accounts. They also hoped to decode the card index, to calculate book losses and monies they owed for royalties. They had lost nearly 150,000 books, but had thankfully discovered 30,000 unbound copies at a neighboring storage space in the Senefelderstrasse. In these they saw raw materials to keep Albatross alive. "After my discussion with Herr Kupfer, we are agreed," wrote Gey, "that we should do everything possible to push through the sale of these volumes. There remains, doubtless, the need for English literature for the purposes of teaching and study, for which the volumes available [to us] are suitable and intended." They would bind these volumes however they could and sell them to cover costs. A glimmer of Gey's allegiance to Albatross shone through the lines of his report. "Through such a continuation, if also only limited, of sales, the name Albatross will also remain upheld in book trade and readerly circles and thereby doubtless contribute to the preservation of the ideal worth of the publishing house," he concluded. He then added, "It might well also be advisable in order to maintain the equilibrium with Tauchnitz."[29]

Gey's afterthought is a striking commentary on his own loyalties and on his ability to envision what must have seemed unimaginable as he made his way through a haunted landscape pockmarked with skeleton buildings to the rubble of the former Albatross office: that the war would end and that one day in peace the old rivalry with Tauchnitz might be rekindled. In the first half of 1944, no Albatross books were sold from Leipzig. Yet Gey pressed on. He was unhappy that the bombings had made Albatross more dependent on the Brandstetters; Albatross could sell none of its forty-five thousand unbound volumes—he and Kupfer had unearthed a bonus of fifteen thousand at another site—until Brandstetter's binding machines got to work. Fortunately, the Brandstetters seemed inclined to help, though Gey noted, somewhat cynically, that they might be operating "out of the egotistical motive to free up the space that has, until now, been taken up with Albatross's unbound volumes." Gey's tensions with the Brandstetters aside, he was glad that they had had the foresight to store paper and certain machines outside Leipzig. "In any case, the first volumes are meanwhile in the works. In a short time, [we] can reckon with delivery."[30]

Gey had no doubt that the roughly forty-five thousand volumes could be sold when they were bound. His confidence is, in retrospect, rather bold. The bombing had forced Albatross into an even more restrictive framework, but his words read as those of any businessman savoring robust sales in a healthy economy. "With regard to the sale of the prepared volumes, there exist no difficulties at all," he remarked. "Inquiries for the Albatross volumes come in continually and preliminary work has been done so that in each case shipments can begin right after individual volumes are complete." By July 1944, he had eleven thousand bound titles ready for sale, and had sold over half by the end of September.[31]

Then, just as suddenly as Albatross had almost been forced to close its doors because of total war, it was mandated to keep them open. The Germans had abandoned Paris on 25 August. The next day, the Literary Chamber president imposed upon "the Albatross Verlag the continuation in total war." What this meant was, initially, little. Gey kept Albatross running as ordered. Almost a year to the date of the bombing that had obliterated three-quarters of its volumes, he recorded heightened sales. Between the beginning of October and mid-December 1944, he had sold 13,000 RM of Albatross books in the Reich, bringing turnover to 21,000 RM for the year. After the sales vacuum of the first half of the year, he had, in the second half, delivered easily "half" of the twenty-nine thousand volumes he had prepared for print. Albatross stores of books were dwindling, with each new sale, perhaps down to the last books of all.[32]

Gey closed 1944 with a modest gain: 519.99 RM, added to a profit of 59,952.79 RM in 1943. In his last report to the Reich Commissioner's office, in early February 1945, he described these gains as "extraordinarily modest," but seemed happy, "since first and foremost, what matters is preserving the assets of the firm."[33] All the rest—all those future battles over copyrights and royalties, the legal clashes over restitution of damages, the attempt to revive Albatross fully—belonged to another day and place and person, in an as yet unfathomable peace.

TWENTY-ONE

Making Peace

"I HAD THOUGHT THAT for me there could never again be any elation in war," wrote Ernie Pyle. "But I had reckoned without the liberation of Paris." Rumors of a pending Allied invasion had swirled through Paris since early August, and the city was on the edge. Wolfgang Krause-Brandstetter, stationed in Paris since January under the Luftwaffe's General Friedrich-Carl Hanesse, was preparing to evacuate. On 15 August, he traveled northeast to Reims under orders to secure lodging for the staff of one Generalmajor von Buttlar. That same day Nazi occupiers packed twenty-six-hundred political prisoners into trains to Buchenwald, and the next day the Gestapo gunned down thirty-five French

Resistance fighters in the Bois de Boulogne. Over the next few days, much of the city went on strike—Métro workers, police, and postal workers included—resulting in a general shutdown on 18 August. Resistance fighters rose against the Germans. In small groups, they reclaimed city buildings and sabotaged German outposts and communication lines. The movement's leaders and the German military governor of Paris, General Dietrich von Choltitz, met to divide the city into zones safe for each side. German tanks and soldiers threaded out of the city. On 24 August, the 2nd French Armored Division, under General Philippe Leclerc, moved in, clearing western Paris, while American forces bore down from the east. The next day, von Choltitz formally surrendered, leaving General Charles de Gaulle to address the French public in a victory speech from the Hôtel de Ville.[1]

The true celebration began on 26 August, as General de Gaulle strode down the Champs-Élysées, reclaiming France for the French. He sauntered, dignified and erect in his uniform, his long face set in an opaque and serious expression, a staid counterpoint to the exuberant throngs. Ten and twelve deep, people filled the sidewalks, overflowing into the streets. Some chanted "Vive la France" in emphatic staccato. Others danced and sang the "Marseillaise," while still more held aloft massive banners in block letters with "Vive les Alliés."

The place de la Concorde swelled with "almost hysterical" crowds, recounted Pyle. "As our jeep eased through the crowds, thousands of people crowded up, leaving only a narrow corridor," he remembered, "and frantic men, women and children grabbed us and kissed us and shook our hands and beat on our shoulders and slapped our backs and shouted their joy as we passed." To capture the whole was impossible; "it was so big I felt inadequate to touch it." Only scenes rose out of the fray: "one funny little old woman, so short she couldn't reach up to kiss men in military vehicles, who appeared on the second day carrying a stepladder"; a French tank commander rolling into the city "with goggles, smoking a cigar, and another soldier in a truck playing a flute for his own amusement"; pet dogs perched, bewildered, atop tanks and trucks. "And in the midst of it all was a tandem bicycle ridden by a man and a beautiful woman, both in bright blue shorts, just as though they were holidaying, which undoubtedly they were." For many, the liberation brought joyous reunions. Ernest Hemingway swept into the rue de l'Odéon with four British Broadcast Company cars to visit one of his favorite Parisian haunts: Sylvia Beach's Shakespeare and Company. Beach, who had closed her bookshop in 1941 and been interned for six months by the Germans, raced downstairs, where she crashed into Hemingway, who, as she remembered, "picked me up and swung me around and kissed me while people on the street and in the windows cheered." With unnecessary drama, he and several soldiers clambered up onto the roof to "liberate" the building, as the last remnants of the German army cleared the 14th arrondissement.[2]

These accounts, like others of this celebratory day, are infused by ebullience. As the *Life* magazine photographer Ralph Morse articulated it, the day meant something quite particular to those who cheered in the streets. "One thing that really stands out," Morse recalls, "is the feeling of certainty in the air. *Everyone* knew it was over. And I don't mean the battle for Paris. I mean the war. . . . When the Germans surrendered Paris, we all sensed it was now only a matter of time, and not much time, before we took Berlin."[3]

Krause-Brandstetter knew this, too, and knowing it, he was nowhere to be found among his partners-in-arms who fled to Reims to regroup. Instead, he hid out at 9 rue Condé, one block from Shakespeare and Company. There, at the home of his French friend Comte Gérard de Brion, he pondered his options as Paris caroused around him.[4]

Krause-Brandstetter's whereabouts were a pressing question on the German side. Following his stint developing Deutsche Tauchnitz for the Foreign Office and Propaganda Ministry, he had received training with the Abwehr, the German intelligence branch. Two weeks after the liberation of Paris, British agents picked up a transmission indicating that the Germans were looking for him: "Oblt. Krause Brandstetter is required for urgent and important special assignment." Later that day came the response: "Oberstlt. Brandstetter missing in Paris since 19/8." By this point, only Allied intelligence knew that Krause-Brandstetter had spent the day of the German surrender giving himself up in civilian clothes to British officers of the Air Intelligence Section of the T-Force, part of a joint British-American campaign to seize German scientific and industrial targets. Within a week he had been flown to England and interned at Camp 7 Beaconsfield, known as No 1. D.C.[5]

*

On 29 January 1945, Holroyd-Reece appeared at the London headquarters of the Combined Services Detailed Interrogation Centre, located in three mansions on the grounds of Kensington Palace Gardens. The British National

Archives remain largely silent on his comings and goings during the last years of the war, leaving a mysterious gap. Yet Krause-Brandstetter's choice to defect and face interrogation by the British brought Holroyd-Reece back into view, lured by the possibility of fresh information about Albatross and Tauchnitz from an important source whose loyalties he had spent years cultivating. And so he dropped by "The London Cage," nicknamed for the barbed wire surrounding the premises," telling Krause-Brandstetter he "just wanted to see how [he] was."[6]

Holroyd-Reece had, in fact, reached out to British intelligence after receiving a postcard from Krause-Brandstetter, which he had somehow smuggled out of his POW camp. Each must have been curious to see the other; yet it is hard to say who outperformed whom at this first meeting in years. Krause-Brandstetter saw Holroyd-Reece as an ally: someone to get him cigarettes and help him gain employment on British propaganda broadcasts for Germany. Holroyd-Reece, for his part, had been instructed by British intelligence "to find out whether [Krause-Brandstetter] had been working for the Brandenburg Division . . . and whether he was doing intelligence work while he was in Paris." For nearly two hours, Holroyd-Reece talked with his protégé—or, rather, Krause-Brandstetter talked at him. "The prisoner talked volubly and very confusedly," wrote Holroyd-Reece in his report for British intelligence, "partly because he was surprised and probably very pleased to see the Writer." British agents listened in, their transcripts recording this strange reunion.[7]

The obvious topic was Albatross-Tauchnitz. Holroyd-Reece said he had gleaned news from Paris through "round-about diplomatic channels." Krause-Brandstetter filled in the gaps. He claimed that "he protected the Paris office of Albatros from German interference" by testifying on its behalf, so that "Albatros property in Paris was not touched by the Germans." He informed Holroyd-Reece that the "Leipzig branch of Albatros still exists on paper, but has in fact been broken up." He presented Deutsche Tauchnitz as a "great success, 3,700,000 volumes sold from 1941 to 1944." Perhaps most critical of all, he noted that "in return [for editing the German series], the Propaganda Ministry turned a blind eye to the 'English series' which was sold under the counter in neutral countries and in France and published by both Tauchnitz and Albatros." The "English classics" reached sales of 200,000 to 300,000 RM per year, he recalled, with Tauchnitz's profit for 1943 reaching 400,000 RM; Deutsche Tauchnitz had finally pushed Brandstetters' returns on this investment into the black.[8]

The transcripts offer an intriguing portrait of Holroyd-Reece that exists nowhere else. He comes to life not as his usual, hard-driving, garrulous self but as a restrained presence who poses questions and settles back to listen. Krause-Brandstetter, in contrast, seems nervous, spilling words. To Holroyd-Reece, he confided his fear that his business dealings might get him in trouble. He confessed he had earned monies in Paris "which . . . he should have remitted to Germany"—including profits from Albatross and Tauchnitz sales in France—that totaled 2.7 million francs. He had, meanwhile, begun to entice one of his British interrogators into helping him transfer funds to England, to ground an Anglo-German publishing firm. He was still on the make, it would appear, even in his internment camp.[9]

British intelligence officers let Holroyd-Reece run this show. Yet they eavesdropped with keen attention. They had planned for this day. One week earlier, MI-5's Section B.1.b—responsible for "special research," such as analyzing transmissions from Germans to their agents or handlers—had met with other intelligence sections to discuss the two men. Their discussion remains classified in documents that MI-5 withheld at the release of Krause-Brandstetter's file in 1999, evidently concerned, decades later, that they might expose something better concealed. What remains are preliminary notes, in which neither Krause-Brandstetter nor Holroyd-Reece comes out entirely clean. Intelligence officers noted that Krause-Brandstetter had revealed to Holroyd-Reece information that he had concealed from his British captors: he had interrogated for the Germans a number of downed Allied pilots who fell into Occupied territory, and he was currently still hiding military information from the British. More surprising to intelligence officers was, they noted, "Mr. Reece's approval of P/W Brandstetter's withholding of military information from Interrogation officers." Which was worse, their comments implied, the Abwehr officer trying to get in good with his captors, or the naturalized British citizen who condoned his German friend's hiding potentially critical military information from the Allies?[10]

Interrogators already found Krause-Brandstetter's allegiances hard to place. "P/W is highly intelligent; speaks perfect English and French; is well acquainted in the U.K., U.S., and France," remarked a report of 29 August 1944. "States that he was never in sympathy with Nazi party and that he had made up his mind several months ago to remain in Paris; that his motive was to disassociate himself from the Nazis and to be able to resume his business occupation directly after the war." Another report attested that he had turned himself in "to help the Allies from the propaganda point of view, for which he felt that he was well equipped." Interrogators took his statements at face value, judging him "a weak character" who saw that his "personal comfort would be greater here than in Germany." Still, they initially honored his request to be kept separate from other German prisoners, treating him as a source who probably knew "a great deal more than he has thus far divulged." Krause-Brandstetter claimed ties with the Resistance. In a list of his belongings was also a label with the name "Soldat Rolf Brandstetter," perhaps a means of reducing his rank and changing his identity. Yet he had not convinced British intelligence that his sentiments were sincere. On 21 October, he was transferred to an "anti-Nazi" camp, with a not exactly ringing endorsement: "He gives the impression of being very calculating in a cold, intelligent sort of way, very serious and very nationalistic."[11]

Over months, British officials picked apart Krause-Brandstetter's testimony to determine when he had joined the Abwehr. As MI-5, responsible for domestic surveillance, exchanged intelligence with MI-19, charged with interrogating enemy prisoners of war, British agents realized that he possessed far greater intelligence skills than he had admitted. One source proved especially illuminating: double agent Ronny Seth, a Special Operations Executive agent trained by the British for a mission in Lithuania who had been captured by the Germans, turned to their side, and then recaptured by the British. By Seth's account, he dined at Claridge's in January 1944 with a German by the code name of "Braun," who hoped to get him drunk so he would talk. Yet after a bottle of red wine, two bottles of champagne, and two cognacs, it was "Braun" who broke his own cover: "He told me that his real name was Brandstetter of Tauchnitz Books, and that he was hoping to get to England himself as an agent." As a later report also clarified, Krause-Brandstetter had not just acted as Seth's interpreter, as Krause-Brandstetter had claimed to British intelligence; instead, he had instructed Seth for weeks, "in military, naval, and air force intelligence, viz: the meaning of British Army flashes; tank, aircraft, and ship recognition; troop movements; and the composition of messages."[12]

In the weeks following Holroyd-Reece's visit with Krause-Brandstetter, agents requested information on the hard-to-assess relationship between the two men. Krause-Brandstetter submitted an account outlining the association between Albatross and Tauchnitz, Holroyd-Reece's mentorship, their "close personal friendship," and the older man's role in helping him study abroad and remain outside Nazi Germany in the 1930s. It was only "upon the occupation of France in 1940," he said, that "Mr. Reece went back to England and we lost track of each other." Hoping to be employed for British propaganda, Krause-Brandstetter also played up Holroyd-Reece's connections in this domain, mentioning not only Selfton Delmer, responsible for propaganda radio broadcasts to Germany, but Brendon Bracken, the British minister of information, whom he named as "a personal friend" of Holroyd-Reece's.[13]

While Krause-Brandstetter accentuated his connection to his former mentor, Holroyd-Reece was at pains to distance himself in his own report. "The prisoner tried to convey that it was not quite clear to him whether the British authorities realized that he was not a 'regular prisoner,'" he explained. Krause-Brandstetter inflated his importance, Holroyd-Reece argued, describing himself "as an important publisher" to his captors—"the reference being to the Albatross and Tauchnitz Editions which he claims to own by virtue of war-time contracts." Holroyd-Reece was dismissive. "The general impression of the character and nature of the prisoner is deplorable. He told endless stories in a mock modest vein to suggest the importance of his functions during the war: his journeys to Rome; to Paris; the business he had done and the difficulties he had had in persuading his friends of the futility of the Nazi cause and so forth."[14] Holroyd-Reece was on the victor's side of the barbed wire. Yet these dual accounts, side by side, open as many questions about Holroyd-Reece as they did about Krause-Brandstetter. It was odd, and, indeed, illegal, that the two men were supposedly in contact during the first year of the war, since the Communicating with the Enemy Act explicitly forbade such exchanges. And either Krause-Brandstetter was name-dropping, or Holroyd-Reece had a more intimate connection with propaganda circles in England than he openly acknowledged.

MI-5 continued to treat Krause-Brandstetter with suspicion. Its Lieutenant Colonel V. H. Seymer declared Krause-Brandstetter "unsuitable for any employment in the Allied war interest," and reflected on his motives. "Whether or not he intended to penetrate that organization [Political Intelligence Department], and whether or not he was sent over to our lines for that purpose," Seymer wrote in early March, "I regard him as a calculating Nazi only suitable for close custody." D. I. Wilson, of MI-5 section B.1.b., felt that Seymer was overstating Krause-Brandstetter's deception. All the same, he agreed that Krause-

Brandstetter "should not be treated as an anti-Nazi case. In my view his motives were purely personal and financial." Other ulterior motives for his surrender became clear only months later, when the war's end brought new information to light. In mid-August 1945, British intelligence received confirmation that Krause-Brandstetter had served as the "English expert" who helped the Germans infiltrate French Resistance networks that rescued Allied pilots who had fallen in German territory. Several surviving airmen had identified him, by photograph, as their interrogator, recalling that "he claimed to have been raised and educated at Pasadena, California," and to have worked at the Lockheed aircraft plant there. This German counterespionage operation had ultimately sent more than 150 British and American pilots to Buchenwald—where 2 died—rather than to prisoner-of-war camps. In mid-November 1945, Agent D. J. Barnes of MI-5's renegade investigation unit concluded that Krause-Brandstetter had played "a major part" in questioning pilots and "should be treated as a war criminal." In early December, the French office of Prisonniers de guerre de l'Axe made a formal request to MI-19 to hand Krause-Brandstetter over. He had made his way to England, only, perhaps, to be returned to a France that was prepared to take revenge on its former occupiers.[15]

Renegade investigation units typically handled individuals considered outliers: British citizens who might have collaborated with the enemy or been used as stool pigeons planted in enemy circles to gather information, or, more generally, those suspected of subversive activities. Investigator Barnes of this unit had reviewed Krause-Brandstetter's documents and forwarded Holroyd-Reece's report on Krause-Brandstetter to a colleague, requesting that he in turn pass them to another agent "dealing with the case of Holroyd-Reece." Clearly Barnes wondered whether there was one renegade in this case, or two. Krause-Brandstetter might still be just innocent enough not to be guilty, but for Barnes, at least, Holroyd-Reece was perhaps just guilty enough not to be entirely innocent either. One other detail is worth noting. While most undercover agents chose a pseudonym close to their own names, Krause-Brandstetter had selected, instead, the name of the "English expert" he knew best: John.[16]

*

On 30 April 1945, the day of Hitler's death, which happened to be Holroyd-Reece's forty-eighth birthday, Holroyd-Reece worked at 13 New Square, Lincoln's Inn, toying with possibilities. He had Aldous Huxley on his mind. The war had boxed him in, leaving him just enough room to defend Albatross interests. The end of the war freed him to take the more offensive stance that was instinctively his and that made his heart thrum. He could finally build the international Albatross conglomerate that the war had put on hold. He wanted to bring Albatross back to life not only in English but in a host of languages, including German, French, Spanish, and Italian: to offer a super-selection of Albatross titles in translation. This time he planned to partner with one publisher in each national market to spur sales and circumvent the sticky problem of national loyalties. And for his birthday, Holroyd-Reece wanted Huxley. He needed Huxley's name, as one of a select group of internationally visible authors, to set Albatross aloft again over postwar Europe, lither and more vibrant than ever.[17]

Yet his dream faced a stubborn obstacle: getting British publishers to think beyond their national interests for their authors. And so Holroyd-Reece appealed to Huxley's publisher at Chatto and Windus, Harold Raymond. Persuading Raymond would not be easy. He had been a lead agitator against Albatross since its inception and still criticized Huxley's former agent for having acted "high-handedly and crazily in selling Aldous's continental rights at such early dates that he lost the sale of hundreds of copies of the English edition." Raymond had, in fact, already joined with the British publishers Jonathan Cape and Heinemann to mount a rival to Albatross, Star Editions. "Such a company would at any rate enable the English publisher to keep control of the situation," he noted, showing his anti-Albatross bias, "and not let a foreign firm undercut them in one of their most important markets." Huxley had also recently asked Raymond to manage his foreign rights.[18] In short, Raymond was a one-man police force for Huxley's rights. And he was just one of the publishers and agents Holroyd-Reece needed to win over if his Albatross International Series were to become anything more than his brainchild.

In a densely written letter that rode the line between bravado and innuendo, Holroyd-Reece ended the war as he had begun it, crafting his next mighty sales pitch. Albatross offered authors something no British publisher could match, he argued: a true and deep knowledge of the continental market. Partly through Albatross's influence, Anglo-American books had grown more popular before the war, and continental booksellers had come to value Albatross's quality control. Trying to persuade his British competition to back off, Holroyd-Reece argued that only Albatross was "intellectually and politically independent enough" to offer the continental trade the "priceless protection" they sought against partisan British interests. Foreign booksellers trusted Albatross because "Albatross has always been 'unpolitical' and never 'anti' anything or any ism," Holroyd-Reece explained. In fact, Albatross had become rather a champion for the side of good: "The fact moreover that we sold in many countries with the permission (however unwilling) of the local authorities books and authors which were in translation forbidden, strengthened our reputation—sometimes into what became almost a legend. We have on record 'blanket orders' for large quantities of unspecified titles, on the sole condition that any book by that particular author was forbidden in the particular market."[19]

From Holroyd-Reece's point of view, he was offering Huxley no less than the world: publication across continental Europe in all the major languages, all for one signature. He would agree to whatever royalties Raymond suggested, with a stunning addition: an unheard-of 50 percent of profits on books whose royalties exceeded the advance. "The Albatross imprint has a service to offer," Holroyd-Reece concluded, "which cannot be rivaled by any combination of English publishers."[20]

Raymond remained unimpressed by this display, and put Holroyd-Reece back in his place. Did Albatross have continental rights to all or only some of Huxley's works? And what had Huxley's books earned with Albatross, anyway? While he waited for answers, he privately dismissed Holroyd-Reece's plan as "a grandiose scheme," and drafted a counter plan of his own. Holroyd-Reece wanted to expand Albatross's roster of international affiliations. Fine and good. Raymond wanted to pin it down. Most Albatross contracts from the 1930s had been sealed with the Albatross Verlag in Germany. To his lawyer, he wondered, Might Albatross's nationality be the linchpin that could be tugged at, a little at a time, to finally take Albatross down?[21]

*

The last months of the war found Kurt Enoch facing equally trenchant worries in New York. "Kurt, in six months, you'll be broke," predicted Ballantine, Enoch's partner in Penguin Incorporated. The two partners had spent the last years of the war using Ballantine's military connections to keep the fledgling Penguin in paper rations and income. Then, without warning, Ballantine announced his plan to jump ship and found his own publishing house: Bantam Books. Enoch was "totally surprised," not having been party to a tense meeting between Allen Lane and Ballantine late in 1944 that had set Ballantine on this course. All three men wanted to get paperbacks to more readers. Yet Ballantine wanted to focus on popular titles that would sell themselves, whereas Enoch sought "fiction and non-fiction with more selective appeal." This distinction was enough to make the young Ballantine waltz out the door and to keep Enoch, more aligned with Lane, in the Penguin fold. Enoch was left with a skeleton staff and Ballantine's message of doom ringing in his ears. "Again I would have to fend for myself," he concluded.[22]

Yet staying with Lane posed its own problems. Enoch's preference was to run Penguin alone, but Lane had control and liked to exercise it. The first "man on the ground" whom Lane temporarily dispatched to Manhattan to fill Ballantine's role was a woman: his trusted associate Eunice Frost, nicknamed "Frostie." In the summer of 1945, Frostie met her task with a determination that matched Enoch's own, yet they worked at odds. While Enoch later claimed "it was not difficult to develop a constructive working and harmonious personal relationship between her and myself," Frostie had few nice things to say in return. She called Enoch "the most lugubrious and depressing person to work with," and noted–unthinkingly, given his forced flight from the Nazis—that working with him was "like living with the Gestapo. There is something about his 'Pardon me' and his pale little stare which brings out the worst in one," she reported back to Lane.[23]

In late summer 1945, Lane sent an emissary to replace Frostie: Victor Weybright. Raised on a farm in Maryland, Weybright had met Lane when he worked at the American Embassy in London, handling American lend-lease agreements with England during the war. His first meeting with Enoch—whom Lane had neglected to inform of his arrival—was far from ideal. "Enoch not only had never heard of me but was determined not to see me," Weybright recalled later. "It was not an auspicious commencement of my new incarnation, but I resolved that, having endured a good many German bombs and burnt my bridges behind me I could endure a bit of German rudeness in New York."[24]

By September, Enoch and Weybright had agreed to work together by working apart, each granted an "absolute parity" of decision making in his zone of responsibility. Enoch became managing director, president, and treasurer of American Penguin, while Weybright became editorial director, chairman, and secretary. This was a wise move. Editor Marc Jaffe, who worked under both men for eleven years beginning in the late 1940s, recalled them as "the most unlikely couple in publishing." Enoch came off very much as a "serious working publisher," a "distinguished slender gentleman with a pipe in his mouth," who "moved with calm assertiveness pretty fast around the office." Weybright was, in contrast, a "theatrical character" who "loved the flair." As Jaffe remarked, "he created this persona out of his smarts and good taste in literature and a desire to really get ahead in the world and to present himself not just as a boy who grew up in a farming family in Maryland." He threw lively cocktail parties and cultivated a vaguely British accent and a habit of weaving archaic phrases into his letters—a favorite being his use of "from my coign of vantage" rather than "from my point of view." His son-in-law, Truman "Mac" Talley, described him as "portly," wryly noting that "he loved port" and that "he was always very demanding of himself."[25] In short, Weybright was the American version of Holroyd-Reece.

In this way, Enoch met the peace by taking up the work he had left behind in Europe: sending English-language paperbacks out into the world, with a new partner. Yet for Enoch, the end of the war would always mean something different from what it meant to the Americans with whom he forged a new sense of belonging. "T]he now assured victory of our side had lifted the fears and agonies over the ongoing war which had remained my steady preoccupation," he wrote years later. "Although Germany had been my country, I could not help being deeply satisfied with its humiliation and destruction. . . . I was not able to draw a line between what its people had become when they embraced the Nazi regime and what they had been before they succumbed to the Nazi myth. The cancer had spread too widely and the evil become too satanic." He recognized, he admitted, that his reaction "was more emotional than rational," and that within Germany there must have been many "who had suffered silently or in revolt." "But at that time, I could not make allowances or feel sympathy with such victims. How could one be sure who and where they were? I was not ready—perhaps never will be—to forget or forgive."[26]

*

In Hamburg, on one of the very last days of the war, fifteen-year-old Thomas Wegner spied a forlorn figure on the front steps of his family's house. "A bum stood before me, a homeless guy, filthy, so wiped out, with metal-rimmed glasses," he remembered years later. This apparition was, in fact, his uncle

Christian. The young Thomas had never before seen his uncle except in well-polished dress: smart suits, intellectually stylish glasses, crisp shirts in summer, a white officer's uniform festooned with medals. Out of nowhere, Wegner appeared before him and his family on their elegant street several blocks west of the Alster Lake, with its Jugendstil villas largely spared from Allied bombings. He looked like a furniture mover in borrowed black pants, too short for him, with broad suspenders and a blue and white striped shirt.[27]

That Wegner should appear on the doorstep was—there is no other way to put it—an impossibility. In the fall of 1944, he had traded four years in prison for a ticket to the Eastern Front—a ticket that for hundreds of thousands of German soldiers ended up being a death warrant. For the fifty-two-year-old Wegner, little else might have been expected. He had been degraded to the position of gunner in the anti-aircraft unit, a rank that would not only put him in harm's way, but was guaranteed to keep him there. Yet Wegner was lucky—or made his own luck. On the train journey east, he met up with a greenhorn first lieutenant by the name of Enders who had just been promoted and was being farmed off to the east to manage troops. This young man had a title but little military know-how; Wegner had experience but had been stripped of his title. As Thomas Wegner recounts the story that Christian repeated to his father, the two men teamed up, becoming partners in a *Zweckbündnis,* a marriage of convenience that would serve both sides. "You will be my manservant," decided the first lieutenant. "You will direct the artillery battery and I will sign off on the orders."[28]

Christian Wegner arrived in the Courland Pocket, the peninsula jutting out from present-day Latvia, in time to face the winter weather—"freezing, [with] a strapping eastern wind," as he put it in one of his letters home to Annemarie. In January 1945 the Russian offensive approached, and Christian painted for Annemarie the beginnings of the retreat in which he did not want to believe. "We have packed up, yet since we have no vehicles, it is seemingly illusory," he acknowledged. It was critical to stop the Russians, he said, "otherwise it's going to go badly for all of Germany. I have never yet witnessed a retreat, [and] find the whole thing appalling, especially the absence of leadership." He alluded to the possibility of his death. "Cross your fingers for me, yet if something happens, don't let it get you down, and preserve for me, despite everything and my many transgressions, a loving remembrance." His son Matthias later read these accounts with disbelief: "The German troops find themselves everywhere in retreat, yet this soldier still believes he can hold off the Soviet army!" Christian Wegner existed on a plane somewhere between folly and arrogance. Yet this combination helped him survive the last battles in early April at Pillau (now Baltyisk), near Königsberg. He also escaped the fate of the 189,112 German soldiers carted back to labor camps by the Russians, and repatriated only years later.[29]

How Wegner made it home was another astonishing tale. He squeezed his way onto one of the last four ships retreating via the Baltic Sea with the Russians in pursuit. Three were hit by torpedoes. Wegner had, incredibly, landed a spot on the fourth ship, which made its escape west toward Kiel, sixty miles north of Hamburg. Only when the ship docked did the German soldiers packed aboard learn of Hitler's death on the last day of April. The war could not last much longer. On 25 April, Allied and Russian forces had celebrated Elbe Day, the momentous meeting of their troops at Torgau, on the Elbe River east of Leipzig, after they had driven German forces into retreat. The British had just captured Kiel, with all its German scientific bases and shipyards.[30]

Wegner had landed at an opportune moment and made the most of it. He secured civilian clothes for himself and made his way into newly British-occupied territory, where British troops took him prisoner. "Bring me to the division staff," he requested of an officer, in impeccable English, honed through years of Tauchnitz and Albatross experience. When delivered to a higher officer, he talked of his time in England, dropping names from the publishing world. It turned out they had friends in common. Wegner told the officer he was returning from the Eastern Front after being sentenced at the hands of the Nazis, imprisoned, and stripped of his rank. His fortunes quickly turned. He might have been seized as an enemy, but instead was invited to hop into the military jeep, catching a ride to the city limits of Hamburg. Hungry and exhausted, he made the rest of the way on foot, appearing in the misfit ensemble that made him almost unrecognizable to his nephew. There he waited out the last days of war in his brother's basement.[31]

In the first days of peace, Wegner presented himself to the British cultural authorities occupying Hamburg. Yet in the aftermath of war, with the daily revelations about the Nazis' inhumanities, German publishers faced new hurdles: denazification hearings, licensing applications, applications for paper rations for publishing endeavors most in line with British cultural and propaganda goals. Wegner had one distinct advantage over most of his peers: the Nazis had thrown him in prison for treasonous behavior, proof enough for British authorities that

Wegner had not been fully captivated with their cause. Overnight, what had been the bane of his existence became his gold card.[32]

Wegner returned to a publishing scene governed by the British authorities' scorched-earth policy toward pro-Nazi propaganda. To prohibit the dissemination of such reading material, authorities had enacted Ruling 191, which forbade "all forms of printing, publishing, distribution [and] sale" of a host of printed materials without permission. Still, the British permitted German publishers to reorganize within weeks. On 21 June the British Occupation government approved the founding of a booksellers association, which held its first meeting on 10 July in Hamburg. On 21 July, the Publishers' and Booksellers' Association reopened its doors in Wiesbaden. By the end of July, registration for booksellers and libraries began, along with the "weeding out of undesirable literature" by the British military authorities. On 9 August, the Northern German Booksellers' Association was founded, with Wegner as head of the board. On 31 October, the Christian Wegner Verlag was granted license number C 86 B, making Wegner one of the first six publishers in Hamburg to clear his name in the denazification process and to receive a license under the British occupation.

The first official postwar book of the Christian Wegner Verlag was a memoir in German by Isa Vermehren, a rebellious spirit who was expelled from high school in 1933 when she refused to give the Nazi salute. Vermehren became a local celebrity when she channeled her protest into political cabaret, singing satirical sea chanteys that caricatured the Nazi elite at Werner Finck's famous Katakombe theater in Berlin until the Nazis punished Finck, sending him to Esterwegen concentration camp in 1935. Vermehren continued to perform, both in films before the war and onstage with the Red Cross for the troops during the war. Her memoir, *Journey Through the Last Act, Ravensbrück, Buchenwald, Dachau: A Woman Reports* (1946), described the ultimate cost of her family's tendency for revolt: the Nazis threw Vermehren's family into concentration camps, after her brother, an Abwehr officer, defected to the British side early in 1944. In publishing this book, Wegner thus quickly showed himself willing to cast a critical eye on the recent Nazi past, allying himself in this way, too, with the British postwar agenda.[33]

In Hamburg, in London, in New York, the three former Albatross leaders turned their attention to books in peacetime: each charting a course of his own, at odds with one another in a new publishing world that looked little like the old.

TWENTY-TWO

Rising from the Ashes

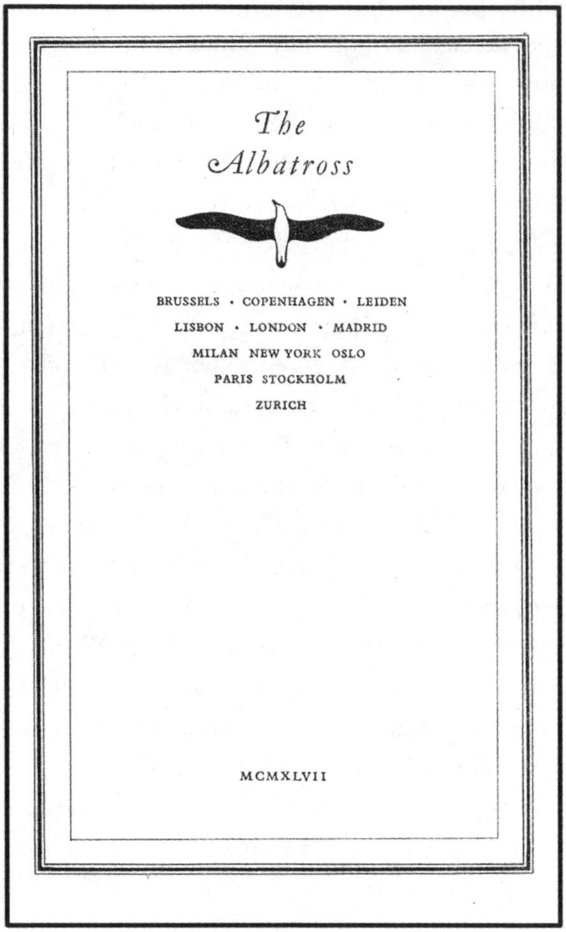
The Albatross

BRUSSELS · COPENHAGEN · LEIDEN
LISBON · LONDON · MADRID
MILAN NEW YORK OSLO
PARIS STOCKHOLM
ZURICH

MCMXLVII

ALBATROSS'S PROMOTIONAL brochure of 1947 suggested that it had friends everywhere. "If it has been the fortune of The Albatross to find in many places and different climes willing imitators," the brochure opened, "it has been our far more important privilege to have gained the support of the most eminent publishers in many of the countries on the Continent of Europe." Holroyd-

Reece's vision was an idea for its time: an Albatross with more international ties than ever to liberate a continent held captive by nationalism. In this new Europe, Albatross had forged partnerships with one publisher in each market, an array of joint imprints bearing the Albatross logo: in Brussels and Paris, Librairie Marcel Didier; in Copenhagen, Steen Hasselbalchs Forlag; in the Netherlands, A.W. Sijthoff's Uitgeversmaatschappij N.V.; in Madrid, Ediciones Albatross; in Milan, Arnoldo Mondadori; in Oslo, H. Aschehoug and Company; in Lisbon, Portugalia Editora; and in Stockholm, P.A. Norstedt & Söner.[1]

Yet even Albatross's expanded ties could not protect it from the "Kriegspsychose [war psychosis] and prejudice against German firms" that Holroyd-Reece had predicted. This sentiment reinforced the British book trade's longstanding resentment toward Albatross and Tauchnitz. It was not, to say the least, a grand time to have German ties in England. For this reason, Holroyd-Reece came to the end of one war only to begin another. He was, as he had confessed to Harold Raymond, recovering from overwork, "rising to the surface, however, steadily though slowly." His wife, ill from cancer through the last months of the war, passed away in late June, and his doctor had ordered him to take it easy, a state constitutionally foreign to him. Rivals hovered around him: Swedish, British, American. He had suffered exorbitant, perhaps irreparable, financial damages.[2]

The end of war allowed him to set into motion, like a film reel whirring forward, business that the war had frozen in time. Yet it also brought him under the light of scrutiny. During the hostilities he could not access sales information or legally pay back royalties—or so he claimed. He could not easily reprint books when the plates had been seized as enemy property or melted down for Nazi bullets. In peacetime, such explanations no longer held. Clients wanted their royalties. They wanted their literary rights. The moment of reckoning had arrived.

An *Observer* article from mid-September 1944, a month after the German retreat from Paris, put its finger on a movement stirring among British publishers: to get their own books onto the continent before Albatross and Tauchnitz could regroup. The anonymous article quoted Stanley Unwin, a pillar of the British publishing establishment, who stressed that "one potent form of the Germans' aggression was book-selling; everywhere their book trade followed the flag and the Front Bücherei even came close behind the tank." The British, he implied, should learn a thing or two from their opponents. Taking his lead, the article concluded: "Further ahead, with the British Council, the Book Council, and our progressive publishers assisting, we must organize far better than before the dispersion of British books over Europe. Why leave so much to Herr Tauchnitz?"[3]

And so in peace, no less than in war, the matter that Holroyd-Reece had pondered for well over a decade became anew the question of the hour. The British book trade and government propaganda organizations portrayed readers in war-ravaged Europe as so many hungry birds tilting their heads up, mouths agape, starving for the intellectual nourishment England might provide. Germany was the most obvious target. "Opinion is forming now in Germany," wrote the British military governor in Berlin in October 1945, "and the demand for enlightenment about Britain, its political institutions, its culture, its way of life, etc, cannot be greater." He urged the British Council to intervene. "There are not means at all of bringing British books, gramophone records or other material into Germany at the present," he complained. And the Germans' attempts to fill the vacuum themselves at "British evenings" held in various locales were, as he put it, "so tragically inadequate and misleading that it looks almost like an act of cultural sabotage." The Germans needed better, and more, British culture, quickly, he concluded. "What we are giving them now is far worse than a stone and more like a very stale doughnut."[4]

The council had already developed a solution to this "stale doughnut" problem: the Book Export Scheme (BES), a plan to make British books available in weak-currency countries that lacked British sterling. The council had launched BES in the first year of the war. Under this scheme, the council paid British publishers for books sold in a particular foreign market; it then collected payment in kind in the local currency, which it funneled into local improvement projects that met the agendas of the Foreign Office and Ministry of Information. All parties won: foreign readers got their books, British publishers increased sales abroad, and the British government gained an opportunity to publicize British culture and create international goodwill.[5]

If any publisher was poised to infuse continental markets with British thought in peacetime, argued Holroyd-Reece, it was he. He understood distinct national markets from their political concerns down to nitty-gritty questions of production capacity, marketing venues, infrastructure, and foreign currency limitations. Albatross was, by any account, an old hand. "Before the war, as I think you know, the Albatross Modern Continental Library was the principal means of disseminating the best British Literature on the Continent of Europe," asserted Lieutenant Commander Maury Meiklejohn, a new director in Holroyd-Reece's ever-widening Albatross constellation, putting Albatross's name forward for BES in October 1946. The firm was ideally suited to continue this work, he argued. It had built up "a considerable market before the War" in precisely the weak-currency countries served by BES: Yugoslavia, Bulgaria, Romania, Greece, Hungary, and Poland. It was reprinting books in Italy and the Netherlands, and in six weeks would launch its new series: ten prewar and five new titles each month until fifteen hundred of its six thousand (combined Albatross-Tauchnitz) titles were circulating. Royalties and profits would return to England, yet because Albatross got paper from its international partners, it could publicize British culture without eating into Britain's limited paper rations.[6]

Yet if the British Council had deemed Albatross books good enough to represent British culture before the war—and had been especially grateful for their presence in Hitler's Germany, where hardly a British publisher had been able to tread—the postwar world raised a new question: Could Albatross, with its German ballast, still serve as an effective postwar cultural ambassador? The official BES Committee held its first meeting on 19 December 1946, with an impressive roster of experts from the Board of Trade, the Foreign Office, the Central Office of Information, and the British book trade. Yet rumblings against Albatross had started a full two months earlier. Harry Paroissien, representing Penguin Books, expressed mixed feelings. On the plus side, Albatross already served the continent and would have fifteen titles ready every month. On the minus side, he felt—not surprisingly, given his allegiances—that "the books in that form do not offer such a good value as the Penguin Library." Not wanting to appear biased, perhaps, he noted that the Pan Books series to be produced by Collins were also "well-worth encouraging," because they sold at roughly a quarter of Albatross's price and were thus better designed to "meet the competition of the American Pocket books." If the British were to come out ahead in continental Europe, where most readers had little money to spend, he implied, pricing might be enough to rule publishers in or out. He tabled his decision, waiting to hear from others on the board.[7]

The debate spread quickly to the Central Office of Information. In mid-October, Ellis Charles Raymond Hadfield, the director of publications for the office—and author of *English Rivers and Canals* (1945) and *The Pilot Guide to*

Political London (1945)—brought his thoroughness to the topic of whether Albatross fit the Book Export Scheme. British literary agents and the British Publishers Association were railing against contracts set by the "new Albatross," as he had learned from a report Unwin had prepared for Lord George Lloyd, a former governor of Bombay who became chairman of the British Council in 1937. Albatross was also laden with heavy cultural baggage. "It seems undoubted that Mr. Holroyd Rees, the moving spirit, is of German origin," Hadfield reported, "and I am told that before the war the company was German, while its employees were of German origin. It was therefore associated in the minds of Continental people with Germany." His worry? "That many Continentals will . . . have a feeling that Britain is encouraging German enterprise." On its initial merits, he felt that "the background of Albatross is too doubtful for their products to be actively assisted by the government through BES." He ordered investigations of Albatross with the Treasury and of Holroyd-Reece with MI-5.[8]

On 27 January 1947, the Central Office of Information took over the British Export Scheme—to be renamed British Book Exports (BBE)—and decided that Albatross could, indeed, be excluded on the basis of its German ties if committee members so decided. The Department of Overseas Trade representative listed "objections both on cultural grounds and in relation to the export trade." One Treasury official had drummed up troubling news from the Foreign Office: "that, at least in France, this firm were known as German collaborators during the war, and that certain book shops in Paris have had to withdraw their books at public request, and we agree that, in the circumstances, it would not be wise to include them in the scheme." N. G. Thompson of the Central Office of Information worried, further, that Albatross still ran with dicey company. After establishing Ediciones Albatros in Madrid in May 1946, it had gotten cozy with the fascist Spanish government; rumor had it that Albatross had secured paper at nearly half the price demanded of other publishers in exchange for supplying the government with Swiss francs. For Thompson, such decisions walked too close to the moral edge.[9]

Hadfield felt uncomfortable excluding Albatross because of its political background. He reminded Thompson that "there are only two grounds on which we might have excluded Albatross: (a) that it is not really a British firm . . . [and] (b) that BBE does not handle books printed abroad." He also noted that such distinctions blurred the more British publishers modeled themselves after Albatross. As of January 1947, the Foreign Office German section reported a possible "scheme to print and issue in Germany and Austria editions of Penguin Books in English." And as he knew, a swathe of the British book trade was following Albatross's lead: "Guild Books and Star Books (groups of British publishers), Pan Books (British) and Penguin, are producing and planning similar editions for the Continent, some of which will also be produced there."[10]

In essence, Hadfield understood that Albatross was becoming a victim of its own success. In the 1930s it had stood nearly alone in selling English-language paperbacks on the continent, with Tauchnitz by its side, and Penguin slowly invading its terrain—as Albatross had crept up on Tauchnitz years earlier. Suddenly, with the end of the war, British publishers, with the backing of the British government, wanted to get in on the game. Hadfield was faced with a conundrum: no one on the committee wanted Albatross included in BBE, yet its members would appear no better than snitty schoolchildren if they cut Albatross out. "Personally I would rather not handle Albatross books through BBE," he admitted, "but after careful consideration I feel we have little sound reason for imposing a censorship on grounds of prejudice." The editor C. R. N. Routh, also installed at the Central Office of Information, concurred. "There seems to be quite insufficient basis for saying that Albatross is not a British firm, and there is no other ground for excluding all the Albatross activities (other than the publishers' dislike of Albatross)." He granted his approval. On 19 September 1947, Hadfield confirmed that "we shall now buy Albatross books under the B.B.E. scheme." From one Austrian distributor alone, Albatross expected an initial order of twenty thousand books.[11] This was a victory when Holroyd-Reece needed one.

It is striking, in retrospect, that this victory was so narrowly won. Despite Holroyd-Reece's nearly decade-long success in flooding the continent with modern Anglo-American books that advanced British propaganda agendas, he had remained an outsider, with few defenders after the war. The British book trade had reasons to be angry at Albatross. The firm owed back royalties for the entire war, which Holroyd-Reece claimed he could not recover except through the sluggish process of German enemy property proceedings. The literary agent David Higham felt he had waited long enough. "No fault of John's that everything came to a standstill," he wrote. "But after the fighting stopped, there was John again, parading his usual airs of splendor, full of new plans, but not, it seems, for paying old debts."[12]

Yet British publishers, who did not like Holroyd-Reece personally, also wielded the question of Albatross's national allegiance as a tool to get what they wanted, though their interpretations varied wildly. One month after the end of the war, Higham hammered home one legal interpretation of Albatross's ties: "Albatross in England is legally as well as morally responsible for the fulfillment of all Albatross obligations no matter with which of the four companies the agreements were made." On the idea that one could not legally separate one Albatross branch from the other, he delivered an ultimatum: either Holroyd-Reece immediately pay all royalties or he would consider the Albatross contracts terminated and resell the continental rights of his authors' books. Huxley's publisher, Raymond, invoked the opposite logic when he wanted to reclaim Huxley's rights for his own venture, Star Books. He sought—and received—confirmation from the Trading with the Enemy Department that the German Albatross counted as an "enemy" corporation. For Raymond, the Britishness of the holding company that owned Albatross was distinct from the German firm, leaving open a means to invalidate Albatross contracts.[13]

More telling than the particulars, however, is the fact that such discussions were taking place—that the Committee for the BBE actively sought to prohibit Albatross from participating as soon as it advanced its name, that Raymond and Higham exchanged Holroyd-Reece files, sharing new information as it came in. Albatross had won more enemies than friends. Holroyd-Reece had too often talked big and delivered less than he promised. Yet he was also paying a price for being foreign, for breaching the implied etiquette of those in the British trade. "I must admit that I find Holroyd-Reece's project altogether too Germanic for my taste," noted Raymond of Albatross's International series, professing himself "uneasy" at the thought of Albatross holding "the combined control both of English continental editions and of the translation rights in several countries." Higham described Holroyd-Reece as a "strange figure" in "dark clothes and black stock" who "gave off a sinister vapour" and had a "strange trick of speech," adding "un" to certain words in his sentences. The literary agent Graham Watson, who had attended the same properly British public school as Holroyd-Reece, noted that the Teutonic in Holroyd-Reece won out over the Anglo-Saxon.

Like the actor Peter Ustinov or the publisher George Weidenfeld, Watson claimed, Holroyd-Reece "possessed . . . a physical aura of well-being which appears to arise from too much indulgence in goose-liver and other European delicacies. None of the three could be mistaken for an Anglo-Saxon with his gaunt complexion and Puritan mien."[14]

One anecdote adroitly pinpoints Britons' discomfort with Holroyd-Reece's manner. Late in 1940, Holroyd-Reece introduced the multimillionaire F. F. A. Pearson to the British minister of health, hoping to garner support for "the raising of a large loan in the United States for settlement of evacuees after the war, the money to be raised and to be lent by the Ministry of Health to His Majesty's Government for general war purposes." The Foreign Office naturally checked the bona fides of both men before getting involved, reporting that "Mr. Holroyd-Reece used to be active in Paris in connexion with the Albatross Press, which . . . is *au fond* a German Konzern," and that "He & his wife are both rather odd & he gives an unsatisfactory impression." This negative impression derived, in the end, from very little, and the writer pressed on, seeking another, more illustrative example. He settled on Holroyd-Reece's evening garb: "The impression of 'loucheness' conveyed by both Mr. & Mrs. Holroyd-Reece was enhanced but not occasioned by the fact that his tails were lined with red satin & that he wore a cloak of blue with silver tassels in the evening. I sh[oul]d mistrust anything he has to do with."[15] Holroyd-Reece had maneuvered abroad, across national boundaries, in four languages, wearing all manner of cloaks to fight the German enemy outside, when all the while his biggest enemies were preparing his downfall from within.

*

If Albatross remained ostracized, de facto, from the British book trade, it had business to attend to elsewhere. Like the rest of the British publishing world, Albatross wanted to get back into the German market; the question was how to thread its way through the snare of occupation bureaucracy to get there. There was a conspicuous lack of a German partner in Albatross's expansive list of international allies. This omission was not for lack of desire or effort on Holroyd-Reece's part. If anti-German bias stood in Holroyd-Reece's way in England, postwar logistics blocked his progress in Germany. Since the Potsdam Conference in late July 1945, the former Reich had been divided into French, British, American, and Russian zones. The British Occupation government strictly policed lists of books allowed to be published in northwest Germany, all titles needing approval from the Control Commission for Germany. In short, for Holroyd-Reece, all roads to Germany led through the British government. By late fall 1947, he had visited Germany at least twice, talking with the chief of command, the head of the Publications Section of the Control Commission for Germany, and Sir Cecil Weir, the president of the Economic Sub-Section in Germany. Holroyd-Reece saw the opportunity just out of reach: Germany had been Albatross's largest market before the war and held the promise of surpassing this mark with postwar readers hungry for new sustenance.[16]

Wegner, of course, was already where Holroyd-Reece wanted to be—on the ground in Hamburg, priming the pump for new business. Remnants of the war were everywhere, two years after its end. Each day, Wegner walked into an angular brick building at 1 Speersort, whose roof had collapsed in Operation Gomorrah. Originally built in 1938 for the National Socialist newspaper the *Hamburger Tageblatt,* the "Pressehaus," as it was known, housed multiple publishers after the war. Standing under the first floor arcades looking west, Wegner faced piles of rubble: shells of buildings, empty-eyed, windows blown out, standing guard over heaps of bricks and mortar and whatever fragments of furniture and former lives lingered once the fires had burnt out. All around, what remained recalled what did not, like the Nikolai Church a half mile down the road. The tallest building in the world before the cathedral at Rouen was finished in 1876, the church, with its almost five-hundred-foot tall Gothic Revival spire, presided over its own lost walls and stained-glass windows, an appropriate symbol for the city of remnants through which Wegner moved to reach his destination.[17]

In these surroundings, Wegner worked around what he had lost to what he might gain. The occupation of Germany by the four powers made one type of reading more desirable than ever: bilingual dictionaries. Fortunately, Wegner knew a thing or two about the genre. In 1930, during his early days at Tauchnitz, he had partnered with Allen and Unwin—Stanley Unwin's firm—to produce a two-volume English-Russian/Russian-English dictionary for the British market. Fast forward fifteen years to the British occupation of northwestern Germany. In August 1945, the Christian Wegner Verlag revived the *Englisch-Deutsch und Deutsch-Englisch* Tauchnitz pocket dictionary with the backing of the Control Commission for Germany.[18]

Whether he held the official rights is unclear. Perhaps he was still jumping the gun, as in days gone by. In any case, Wegner's affiliation with Tauchnitz was only as straightforward as postwar conditions allowed. Just as the war had split Albatross in two, the occupation of Germany had fractured the publishing trade across zones. In the end-of-war roulette, Leipzig had landed in the Russian Zone, along with the Brandstetter printing and publishing empire. So when the Allen and Unwin publisher C. A. Furth, stationed in Germany with the British military government, approached Wegner about joining forces to produce additional Tauchnitz dictionaries, answers were not at hand. Furth got Wegner special clearance and funds to cross into the Russian Zone to negotiate rights with the Brandstetters.[19]

Wegner arrived just when the Brandstetters needed a solution to their postwar dilemma. The end of war had not been kind to them. Willy Brandstetter had earned a healthy profit on Deutsche Tauchnitz, only to spend the last nine months of the war imprisoned on charges of Wehrkraftzersetzung (the same charge levied against Wegner) and *Feindbegünstigung*—the latter one of those impressive German compound words that means "treating one's enemies well." The Brandstetters' housekeeper, embittered by the condescending treatment she felt she received at the hands of the family, had denounced him for reckless comments after the failed attempt on Hitler's life on 20 July 1944. Brandstetter had remarked, without irony, "It is only good that nothing happened to the Führer, because this death would have been far too easy for him."[20]

Brandstetter was released from prison in mid-April 1945, straight into the uncertainty plaguing many Germans. Like many in Leipzig, the Brandstetters had hoped the Americans would keep control of Sachsen; when they instead retreated in July 1945, leaving Sachsen to the Russians, the Brandstetters found themselves at risk, accused of being Nazi sympathizers. Wegner arrived in Leipzig just in time. On 20 May 1946, the Brandstetters established a new Tauchnitz Edition Company, based at Wegner's office address in Hamburg, with Wegner as the director, to protect this distinguished name in German publishing from Russian interference. Six weeks later, the Russian military government seized the entire Brandstetter holdings. By the end of 1948, there were 247 publishing-related businesses in the Russian Zone; before the war there had been 735. Some had been destroyed in the war, while others, not wanting to face still more nationalist oversight after the mind-numbing restrictions of the Hitler years, had fled to the West. Willy and Justus Brandstetter were among the émigrés, who "left the Eastern Zone by night." On 1 December 1947, they relocated to Wiesbaden in the American Zone, leaving behind multiple firms—Oscar Brandstetter, Jacob Hegner, Linden Verlag, W. Moeser, Bernhard Tauchnitz Nachfolger, and VAG—yet determined to reopen their strongest printing and publishing businesses in the Western Zone.[21]

By this point, Wegner had also gained a critical ally: Krause-Brandstetter. British intelligence had returned him to Germany in 1946, after lengthy investigations into his wartime activities. More than a year later, the thirty-five-year-old still awaited a publisher's license. With no prospects in the Russian Zone, he had moved to Hamburg, where he listed Wegner's office as his address. On 9 October 1947, the Book Section of the Public Relations/Information Services Control in Hamburg requested that his case be expedited, "as it is proposed that he should enter into partnership with Herr Wegner in the firm of Tauchnitz." In October and November 1947, the Book Section claimed he had been "exonerated," yet the Personnel Office demanded further clearance. Eventually authorities granted him a provisional permit, and on 12 February 1948, Wegner named Krause-Brandstetter as joint chief executive, winning back, as it were, the Brandstetter heir apparent to secure his Tauchnitz Edition rights. Only on 22 October 1948 did the door to Krause-Brandstetter's future as a publisher officially reopen. The Licensing Advisor had found no evidence against him, either overlooking his name in Nazi Party rolls or determining that he had joined out of expedience—to keep his job at the Foreign Office—rather than out of ardent conviction. In either case, Krause-Brandstetter received a small card with his name misspelled—"Brandtstetter"—and the decision: "no objection."[22]

With this partnership sealed, Wegner projected confidence all around, reporting to Allen and Unwin that he was leading Tauchnitz back to its roots as a publisher of books in English. "The first volumes of the new Tauchnitz series will appear in the next weeks," he wrote in early June 1947, with a roster including John Galsworthy's *The Forsythe Saga,* Shaw's *St. Joan,* Huxley's *Brief Candles,* Hugh Walpole's *Jeremy at Crale*—and even an Edgar Wallace thriller, *The Ringer.*[23] Tauchnitz was making its way, a contender in the world of books in English, however hobbled its return.

There was, however, one major problem: both the Wegner-Brandstetter alliance and Holroyd-Reece laid claim to the Tauchnitz rights, and in 1947 Holroyd-

Reece wanted the German market back. Wegner unambiguously justified his claim to Furth at Allen and Unwin in January 1947: "Since [the Brandstetter Tauchnitz firm] had no prospect of receiving a publishing license in the Russian zone, a new firm, 'Tauchnitz Edition G.m.b.H.' was grounded [in Hamburg] last year, whose shares are in my possession. This firm has taken over all rights to their publications." Furth was suspicious. He penciled in a skeptical note. "*Not* shown as licensed in the list dated Aug. 1946." A week later, he registered a more powerful reservation: "I have since heard that Albatross claim to be the successors to Tauchnitz; that is to have acquired all Tauchnitz' copyrights before the war. Holroyd-Reece is *apparently* now seeking to establish the claim, which directly contradicts Wegner's claim." And indeed, Holroyd-Reece was, quite vehemently, repeating the arguments he had honed during the war. Under the 1934 contract between the Brandstetters and Albatross, he asserted, "Brandstetter were not allowed except through the intermediary of the Albatross to use the name of Tauchnitz in any shape or form." And the contracts also specified, he declared, that Albatross, and not the Brandstetters, owned Tauchnitz's rights, and that "the war has not cancelled or invalidated the existing agreements at all, but has, in certain rather complicated legal forms, suspended their execution."[24] Sixteen years after they had so optimistically forged an entirely new vision for books in English on the continent, Holroyd-Reece and Wegner faced off against one another, and it was not the war, this time, that placed them on opposing sides.

*

Despite Wegner's bold strides to put Tauchnitz back on the map, and Holroyd-Reece's to reclaim Tauchnitz and smuggle Albatross into Germany along with it, they and all other publishers eager to infuse Germany with English-language books faced one obstacle more daunting than any other: the massive devastation of postwar Germany. British Zone authorities were full of convictions about "reeducating" Germans under the Potsdam Agreement, which specified that "German education should be so controlled as completely to eliminate National Socialist and militarist doctrines and to make possible the successful development of democratic ideas." They were passionately prepared to cultivate the "4 Ds: denazification, democratization, demilitarization, decentralization." In this context, books in English could, they hoped, "project Britain," shining the light of democracy on a Germany darkened by Nationalism Socialism for over a decade.[25]

Yet authorities were still determining what it meant to "project Britain" into Germany, which lacked basic materials and where morale was low. Germany had been shamed before the world. It had lost 11 percent of its population, 7.5 million people, to the war, not counting those missing or taken prisoner. In most urban centers, half of the housing stock had been destroyed, leaving 20 million people homeless, not to mention millions of displaced persons created by refugee crises in the east. With businesses not yet rebuilt, there was massive unemployment and the poverty that followed in its wake. And as one scholar of war and hunger has aptly noted, "The aftermath of the Second World War was a hungry world." During the war, Germany had seized food resources from occupied territories to cover its needs; the end of the war, in contrast, left Germans to suffer hunger themselves, overseen by Allied authorities. American Zone rations were 1,135 calories per day, raised to 1,550 in January 1946, while in the British Zone, the ration remained at just over 1,000 calories in March 1946—the equivalent of two slices of bread with margarine, a couple of potatoes, if they were available, and a spoonful of porridge. Women and teenage girls prostituted themselves for food. The black market for food spiked, as did the number of patients who appeared at hospitals suffering from hunger edema. The mortality rate rose, and no wonder: in Hamburg, some people lost about two pounds a day in weight.[26]

What role books could play, or how Germans could afford the luxury that books had become when they were struggling for survival, remained unclear. The British-Jewish publisher Victor Gollancz experienced this tension all too keenly during his six-week stay in the British Zone in fall 1946. He wrote widely about the physical problems plaguing postwar Germany, especially childhood malnutrition, publishing articles in numerous British newspapers to rally the British people to improve Germany's quality of life. Yet he acknowledged, too, "There were times during my visit to Germany when I thought the intellectual and spiritual starvation to be even worse than the physical." He recounted the story of one German professor who sold his precious law books for a pound of butter. He spoke with schoolteachers who complained of the difficulties of educating children when there was at times a 50 percent rate of absenteeism because so many children lacked shoes. "German after German, when they learned that I was a publisher, begged me to send them English books," he wrote, "this or that book if obtainable, but, if not, any books of any kind." He proposed that "everybody with a friend in Germany should send him good English books of any kind" through the "Save Europe Now" venture he had founded the year before.[27]

Gollancz turned to the British public in this quest rather than to British authorities because authorities faced material challenges of their own. With only two paper mills operating in Germany, paper was tightly rationed. Hamburg's regional commissioner received only 41 sets of English newspapers and magazines for his region of 3 million people. Even the officially sponsored newspaper, *Die Welt,* was in short supply, with one paper for every 4.5 people in the British Zone. By the end of 1947, authorities had stocked 64 special information centers and libraries—all carrying the name *Die Brücke,* "The Bridge," to imply the cultural exchange that took place within their walls—with reading materials in English; the Hamburg information center cited 1,000 visitors per day by February 1948, yet the majority were already well educated and semi-fluent in English, leaving authorities with few means to reach other sectors of German society. Beyond these practical concerns, the Nazi era had also left its psychological mark. Many readers of the younger generation, weaned on traditional National Socialist ideals, had learned a "fear of modernity" that stayed with them after the fall of the regime. Years under Nazi authorities also left many Germans suspicious of information they received through newspapers and radio, both of which had previously served as mouthpieces for the regime.[28]

In this regard, books were actually the British authorities' best hope for the future, in that they were less associated in the minds of German readers with official propaganda than the print press and radio. Yet ironically, of course, the Control Commission authorities who monitored publications sought to provide German readers with propaganda all over again—the best, they argued, that Britain could offer. They carefully monitored which publishers and which books would best "project Britain" to prepare Germany for the new era. And whether Albatross would be among the publishers allowed to play this role remained an open question. As N. G. Thompson from the Central Office of Information explained to his BBE colleagues, the "Tauchnitz-Wegner-Albatross wrangle" was making difficulties for them all. "Holroyd-Rees has two objectives," he noted, "namely to get Albatross re-established in a big way in Germany and to bring Wegner to heel over the Tauchnitz rights." Yet the Control Commission for Germany, which was in the position to choose between them, was not enthusiastic about Holroyd-Reece. British authorities had, instead, "flirted with Bonnier for a long time," remarked Thompson, "and would probably like to see a Tauchnitz-Bonnier tie-up in Germany." In this context, then, Wegner held a distinct advantage. "The C.C.G. [Control Commission for Germany] . . . has consistently backed Wegner as an able and co-operative publisher," confirmed Thompson. He, too, tacitly admired Wegner, describing him as "a sharp-witted man, . . . and an adept at business-political manoeuvre[s]."[29]

The matter would ultimately be decided in London under most unusual circumstances during the Christmas season of 1947. Wegner's acumen had, this time, earned him a great prize: an invitation from Unwin and other British publishers to return to London as a "visiting leading publisher." Yet Wegner's trip did not unfold as anticipated. In his years away from England, he had lost the instinct for negotiating London's streets, where drivers raced down the left side. In a perilous moment, perhaps lost in thought, he strode into the street and was blindsided by a car. His injuries were serious, a broken clavicle and cranial trauma. Instead of spending his sojourn retracing the steps of his younger years or courting British publishers at the clubs of their choice, Wegner spent his visit recuperating in the hospital.[30]

Such were the stakes of getting the right publishers into the German market for Britain that a race to Wegner's hospital bed ensued. The German section of the Foreign Office wanted to reach Wegner before Holroyd-Reece got his chance. British authorities were concerned that Holroyd-Reece might pressure Wegner to partner with Albatross to put himself on a fast track to licensing approvals in the British Zone. Yet Holroyd-Reece had already beaten his opponents to the punch. "Holroyd-Rees of course seized this opportunity to see Wegner and bring him to heel," Thompson wrote. "According to Wegner they 'have now come to an amicable agreement.'" Presumably this meant a deal by which Wegner would retain an interest in Tauchnitz in exchange for some sort of connection to Albatross. Curtis Brown, after visiting Wegner, confirmed to Thompson that it was probably too late to overturn the decision. As Thompson relayed, "Apparently Albatross have 'taken possession' of Wegner to the extent of paying [for] his hospital bed."[31]

Thus it happened that Wegner returned to Hamburg shortly after Christmas 1947 with a mended clavicle and a renewed Albatross-Tauchnitz partnership. Wegner and Holroyd-Reece had begun the year opposed, but ended it reunited in common cause. As they joined forces again, they were their own best illustration for the Albatross myth Holroyd-Reece was reviving for the postwar world. "The real significance of the Albatross, according to ancient mythology, is to carry living souls across the water. That is why we adopted the sign of the Albatross as our trademark," mused the Albatross brochure for 1947. "Today the need for the friendly intercourse and fruitful understanding among the peoples of the postwar world is as great as ever and therefore the Albatross is resuming its old task of answering this deep need." Holroyd-Reece did not pretend that nothing had changed. The brochure acknowledged the challenge of meeting former standards of "accuracy, good paper and careful binding" in a continent plagued by shortages—yet he pledged to hold true to prewar principles: to sell high-quality books, "made without pretence," offering a "true cross-section of what is new in form and content in modern literature in the English language."[32]

Behind the alluring tale spun in its brochure, Albatross fended off challenges that Holroyd-Reece kept tightly under wraps. Production was running behind schedule. He had planned an ambitious relaunch of the series early in 1947: fifteen titles per month—five new and ten existing titles—in editions of fifteen thousand to sell for the equivalent of 5 shillings each, with two-thirds of the books produced in Italy and one-third in the Netherlands. Yet by the end of March 1947, only twelve titles had been reprinted in Italy, and the first five titles from the Netherlands were not ready for sale until June. In the interim, the perils of running a postwar business stretched across national lines made themselves felt: shortages of wood-free paper, difficulties in securing import licenses authorizing shipments of books from one national market to another, and foreign currency quotas that limited transfers between the British mothership and Albatross's foreign partners. Each delay cost Albatross precious time, leaving a void which British and American publishers were happy to fill. "The competition of the cheap Pocket-Books, Penguins, Collins' White Circle Pocketbooks, Trianglebooks, Modern Library a[nd] o[ther] series is very strong; these series often contain the same titles as Albatross," complained one report of November 1947 from Albatross's Dutch partner. "The Albatross books are too expensive."[33]

More critically, Holroyd-Reece had evidently sketched for Wegner a glowing portrait that masked Albatross's deteriorating financial health and these many pending threats to it. By October, the minutes of the Collins board meeting were sounding a note of alarm. Board members talked of the "gloomy situation" in

Europe. The Pan paperbacks that sold on the continent for one-third to one-fourth the price of Albatross titles were "paying their way"; Albatross, in contrast, was not. Collins had already advanced Holroyd-Reece £20,000 and given a guarantee for £15,000. Yet this had not sufficed, and he now wanted another loan of £35,000. After much debate, "it was finally decided that this could be granted, but only on the following conditions: the matter must be referred to the Bank of England; a time-table for repayment must be drawn up; balance sheets must be produced; all assets must be fairly in our name; we must hold all shares and ensure that we have a lien on all stocks; our own auditors should be brought into the picture." And the starkest, most final condition of all: "This to be the last loan to Albatross."[34]

Holroyd-Reece knew well the art of successful wooing. Some time after the death of his second wife, Jeanne, in June 1945, he had married a beautiful, red-headed American named Eileen, whose family money ostensibly helped line the Albatross nest. And so, into 1948 Holroyd-Reece lived much as before, in a milieu of rarified luxury, still projecting a self-possessed air, as the author John Brophy recalled of their meeting in late July. "A strong character, with a manner, but I like him," wrote Brophy of Holroyd-Reece. "Holroyd-Reece's office might be a suite of rooms owned by a nineteenth-century gentleman with eighteenth-century tastes, and when he takes me to his flat in Old Square, to meet his wife and drink iced vermouth, it is even more charming. . . . The corner of the Square where he lives is the oldest part of the fabric, and, pointing to a couple of small windows in the brick wall, he tells me that it was behind them that Sir Thomas More—'your colleague, my dear Brophy'—wrote *Utopia.*"[35] Holroyd-Reece, that "nineteenth-century gentleman with eighteenth-century tastes," was about to come up against a harsh twentieth-century reality that More would have understood: there are dangers to holding firm while the earth shifts beneath one's feet.

TWENTY-THREE

Homecoming

THE WORD *HOMECOMING* suggests closure, a return to a place of belonging in which one's emotional restlessness might have hope of being stilled. So it is inappropriate for Enoch's return to Germany. "On March 17, 1949 I entered Germany by train," he wrote, "almost 13 years after I had boarded a plane for a flight to freedom but also to a very uncertain future. At that time I had no idea if or when or under what circumstances I would ever return, and certainly could not anticipate or visualize a Germany as I was about to find [it]." He arrived in Frankfurt after nightfall. "The darkness did not conceal the lack of a roof and other destruction of the railway station," he noticed. "The dim light inside, the quietness of the place where no other trains seemed to move and . . . the slow motion of the few people who moved around gave the place an almost eerie atmosphere."[1]

Enoch was entering a divided world, where Germans used one set of taxis and Allied personnel another. And so, a German no more, at least by official categories, he hailed a cab reserved for Allied use and was driven to the Frankfurter Hof, a once illustrious hotel reduced to a "partly reconstructed building, . . . standing in the middle of what looked like . . . bulldozed empty building sites." In the morning he saw the true devastation the war had wrought: "streets with totally or partly ruined buildings, little traffic consisting of mostly dilapidated cars, downtrodden and starved looking pedestrians, . . . the city . . . still in a state of daze from which it had not started to recover." Four years after the war, Germany was barely making do.[2]

Practical rather than personal reasons had compelled Enoch to return. He and Victor Weybright, his partner in the American Penguin, had proved a formidable team in New York, and like so many other British and American publishers they were looking to expand their European horizons. A photograph depicts the two men, side by side, puffing their pipes, perusing a book Enoch holds out before them. It was this common purpose—the book held always metaphorically before their eyes—that united them when their wildly divergent personalities might sooner have driven them apart. In their first months working together for Allen Lane, Enoch and Weybright had set themselves apart from British precedent. The United States was no England. Bookstores were concentrated in the Northeast, with few venues elsewhere. To reach American readers in the hinterlands, they turned up the volume on their marketing and book covers—at which Lane took umbrage—and restructured their distribution. By 1947, their disagreements with the head office had grown profound enough that Enoch and Weybright severed ties with Lane and founded their own venture: the New American Library. On 25 February 1948, they launched their series under the slogan "Good Reading for the Millions," positioning books at eighty thousand newsstands and bookstores in the United States and Canada—Signet Books for fiction, and Mentor mostly for nonfiction. "The offices were small and dark, and yet out of them came an energy which Kurt inspired," recalled the New American Library editor, Marc Jaffe. "I remember him, very often dressed in a gray flannel suit, rushing from office to office in that typical, slightly bent forward pose of his, involved in everything from production to sales to covers." After a decade of false starts, of gauging political and economic threats, Enoch had fenced off his own piece of ground.[3]

In 1949 Enoch zeroed in on a familiar project: getting books in English onto continental bookshelves. "Traditionally, American business was not very export oriented," he explained. "The domestic market was huge and dealing with foreign countries too complicated and burdensome." For Enoch, in contrast, exports were the stuff of his life—what had made Albatross-Tauchnitz valuable to the Nazi regime and paved the way for his emigration. "Encouraged by my previous success with Albatross and Tauchnitz . . . ," he wrote, "I always had visions of the potential of world-wide activities. Now I felt that postwar conditions in many countries offered a golden opportunity for the book industry, especially for our product, the inexpensive paperback book, as the ideal means to satisfy a great present need."[4]

He was in good company, perhaps too good. British publishers like Pan and Penguin had made inroads in the continental market, aided by the British government. The American government, as the historian John Hench documents, followed suit, looking to "use books to 'disintoxicate' the captive people after years of fascist propaganda and to generate goodwill for the United States." The American paperback market had exploded, with books aplenty for the task: Pocket Books was founded in 1939, Avon in 1941, Dell in 1943, Bantam in 1945. The American government was also sponsoring cheap overseas editions to advertise the American way of life to Europeans fed up with years of Nazi domination. And Albatross and Tauchnitz were jockeying for position alongside continental editions from Sweden and England.[5]

Enoch's cause was greatly aided by the Economic Cooperation Administration (ECA), launched in 1949 by American and allied governments. Just as the Book Export Scheme helped British publishers sell their titles in weak-currency countries, the ECA came to the rescue of American publishers. European importers could pay for American books in their local currency, and the ECA, in turn, paid American publishers the appropriate amount in U.S. dollars. There was, however, one condition: titles had to "reasonably reflect American cultural and intellectual life and reading habits and convey a well-balanced picture of American institutions." With this in mind, Enoch stacked a committee with literary experts to propose 150 titles that might, in this sense, double as American propaganda. Enoch was planning on succeeding where Deutsche Tauchnitz had failed—combining cultural propaganda, ideally not recognizable as such, with strong sales.[6]

Without even waiting to hear the results of his application, Enoch flew to

Amsterdam on 5 March 1949, "well-armed" with catalogues and samples to pave the way for the New American Library abroad. His agenda was ambitious. In a matter of weeks, he was to travel through the Netherlands, France, Denmark, Norway, Sweden, Austria—and Germany. "The reasons for me to undertake this trip myself were: my special knowledge of the markets, my old personal relationships with the important personalities involved and the advantage of being able to make decisions, work out and sign agreements on the spot." While he was under way, the New American Library won its bid to distribute $100,000 of its titles in countries working with the ECA. Having made it in the new world, Enoch was ready to face the old.[7]

In this postwar world, Albatross's former asset—its experience on the continent—was fast becoming its greatest liability. Compared with the New American Library and other British and American publishers who had more recently jumped into the business of paperbacks, Albatross was burdened by its past. Its association with Hitler's Germany in the minds of so many continental readers clearly hurt its possibility of resurgence after the war. Yet Enoch's rushed trip to Germany also suggests that Albatross was done in by the Allies, too—all those publishers who had once sold Albatross their rights were now claiming the continent for themselves.

*

In late March 1949, Enoch ventured back to Hamburg. It was a sobering return. There were no family members to greet him; all had either emigrated or gone to their deaths in concentration camps. As for former acquaintances or colleagues, he wondered, "In what mental or physical state would I find them? Who was now in charge of whatever was left of the once flourishing Hamburg book trade?" He revisited his family gravesite and the "landmarks of my former life, the school, University, my last home at the Elbe River." He made his way to the Atlantic Hotel, one of two hotels where he, as a "foreigner," was permitted to stay. Positive memories nested next to negative. "I often enjoyed tea or dinner on its terraces or public rooms with a view over the lake," he recalled, "a boat race or just pleasant sights of the goings on on the lake (and where shortly before the final Nazi takeover, Goering with a number of his cohorts, had spoiled my pleasure by noisily sitting down at a table next to mine)."[8]

Enoch knew from experience that he needed one reliable distributor in each country to handle all promotion, distribution, and sales, and to manage inventory. In Hamburg, he sought a familiar face from years before. "I had learned that Kupfer had survived the war and lived now in Hamburg, but I had no idea what he was doing," Enoch recalled. "From my years of association with Kupfer, from conversations with him and from his action and behavior during the trying time of our work under the Nazi régime and in exile, I was absolutely sure that he never was one of them and that their ideology was alien to him. I hoped that I would find him unchanged and otherwise still suitable to do the job I had in mind."[9]

Enoch's timing was impeccable. Kupfer was indeed in Hamburg, working for the new Albatross-Tauchnitz endeavor. Like all German publishers, however, its ambitions had been cut short by postwar realities: shortages of paper and ink, decimated back stocks from repeated bombings, damaged infrastructure that slowed communication and distribution, and too few printers to handle surging demand. To put a fine point on it, while Enoch had books ready for sale, Kupfer had been halted at every turn by occupation bureaucracy. He had been trying to secure a license in Leipzig since 1946; if granted, Albatross could open a "branch" in Hamburg, a strategy publishers used to spirit assets away from Soviet interference. Yet while Russian Zone authorities had weighted the Albatross application by mid-1948 as "urgent," given demand for books in English, they made the company wait in line behind other, mostly state-occupied publishers. In June 1948, a frustrated Kupfer changed tactics, simultaneously seeking a license in Berlin, where the four occupying powers operated under the Russian-influenced Magistrat for Gross-Berlin and British authorities might have some power. Yet Berlin authorities would grant no license until Kupfer assured them Berlin would become the seat of Albatross's activities. This he could not do, given the volatility of Berlin, torn between zones. Such was the impenetrability of doing business in a bifurcated Germany—and the situation only worsened once the Soviets blocked Allied access to the roads and trains between the West zones and Berlin on 28 June 1948.[10]

By March 1949, with the blockade still in effect, Kupfer remained mired, with an unpredictable future, ready to meet Enoch on whatever ground he proposed. Germans were not permitted at his hotel, so Enoch met Kupfer at "one of the old good restaurants" that was back in business. "I was quite moved when I saw him again," wrote Enoch, "and most of the evening was, of course, taken up with the story of his personal experiences and situation." Kupfer's own life was split across zones; he had moved to Hamburg for business, while his wife and family remained in Leipzig. His youngest son had died in the war, after being recruited for "one of the youth defense groups which under the insane orders of Hitler were engaged to defend every village or little town." Kupfer was depressed, low on funds, and struggling to revive his separate endeavor to produce travel guides—not exactly a viable proposition in war-ravaged Germany, where tourism was at a standstill. Yet he had experience and a work space. He had rented part of an enormous building called "The Bunker," a structure with a fortress-like tower in the center of the city. Enoch extended Kupfer credit so he could purchase the necessary books, promising that Kupfer could manage the enterprise, christened "Transatlantik," to get New American Library books on continental shelves. And so Enoch entered back into business with the man who had once played a role in cutting him out of his Albatross-Tauchnitz business in Paris.[11]

His business settled, Enoch wandered around the old city. He visited a former Jewish publishing house, Glogua, to seek out its former owner's fate. He met with Ernst Rowohlt—former publisher of Sinclair Lewis and Ernest Hemingway—who had turned wartime deprivations to his advantage with his "Ro-Ro-Ro" editions. With printing presses, binding machines, and paper in short supply, he reprinted whole books on rotary presses on newsprint, like newspapers. Hamburg was coming back to life. Enoch did, in the end, allow himself some "sentimental journeys into the past" along the avenues of the "Little Alster" bordered by cafés, fine hotels, and banks. Yet one location he assiduously avoided. "I had no desire to visit the offices of my former business, which after the takeover by Wegner now carried his name." Had he sought out Schauenburgerstrasse 14, he might have been shocked to see that it, too, belonged to the casualties of war. After seeing his office twice bombed out, and twice relocated, Wegner had set up his postwar publishing house at the Pressehaus at Speersort and his distribution business at Alstertor 21, a short side street that led to the small Alster Lake around which Enoch strolled. Yet none of this was any longer Enoch's concern. His one sentence, with no decoration or elaboration, said all he needed to say.[12]

Still, nothing was to be so simple. Wegner remained eminently practical, and in the postwar turn to restitution, he sought Enoch out. Wegner had bought Enoch's firm under the duress of the Hitler era, and under postwar regulations he had questions to answer. It is hard to imagine the scene of this first face-to-face meeting. Enoch chose not to describe it in his memoirs. Whatever his feelings, Enoch confirmed in writing to Wegner "that I can assert no claim for restitution for the sale of the Oscar Enoch Firm, Hamburg, effected in 1936, and that I forgo any eventual legally entitled claims for restitution, since I was fully paid at the time for the sale to you."[13]

Wegner was reassured on the one hand but unsettled on the other. Enoch had appeared at a critical juncture, just when the Albatross-Tauchnitz team had mustered enough resources to think concretely about production. Wegner had won the Brandstetters over, despite their long-nursed distrust of Holroyd-Reece, but in mid-April 1949, he pressed for results. "We need to make up our minds without delay to begin in Germany," Wegner declared to Holroyd-Reece. "Hopefully the questions of credit regarding the production and paper credits have been satisfactorily resolved; on this, naturally, much depends." Wegner basked in the dream of new books. "I'm very curious, naturally, about the important book that you have in view for Albatross and me," he noted, hoping it was Huxley's newest, *Ape and Essence.*[14]

Enoch's journey to Hamburg, however, dealt the nascent Albatross-Tauchnitz partnership a hard blow, since in its aftermath Kupfer revealed, as Holroyd-Reece wrote to Wegner on 21 April, that "he has decided to throw in his lot with Enoch." Kupfer's decision—or as Holroyd-Reece and Wegner saw it, his defection—made urgent action necessary. Wegner would get his old job back, becoming once more the Albatross Verlag managing director, to "get the firm formally registered or re-registered in Hamburg." Getting a new license would cost precious time. They had not selected titles or decided how to price the volumes. They had not sent plates from Italy and the Netherlands to expedite production. Nor had they established a clear budget. Holroyd-Reece asked them to calculate costs "within the means at our disposal, or to be more precise within the means that will be at our disposal at any moment"—his "at any moment" indicating that the promised cash infusion of 100,000 deutsche marks and the 100,000 DM's worth of paper was not yet firmly in hand. All the while, Enoch and a cohort of other American publishers were on the brink of flooding the German market with books ready-made, ready to sell, ready to drive them under.[15]

The new Albatross-Tauchnitz venture, like Albatross a decade before, was being pieced together as they wrote, with more than one disagreement to be resolved. More strongly than his partners, Holroyd-Reece veered away from "the lighter type of fiction," insisting that their brand should distinguish them from the new breed of American paperbacks. "Where the modern books are concerned, we want not only to keep the standard up, but to keep it as high as possible." He would not be moved. "Naturally, I attach a certain amount of publisher's vanity to the name of Albatross," he admitted to Wegner. But more than anything, he wanted their books in German bookshops quickly. "Please remember that it is necessary in view of the American competition to get out as many titles as possible," he noted. He also worried that the price of 3.50 DM was too low. "I would sooner sell less in quantity and give the market a first class product at a reasonable price than try to publish where . . . I know beforehand that we cannot make any money. Remember that I am older than I was, and I am not prepared to go and re-establish the business in Germany, unless it is on the basis of sound finance."[16]

Wegner and Krause-Brandstetter watched British and American paperbacks stream across German borders, while Holroyd-Reece continued to cast aside their worries about pricing. "[Your] fear about the up-tick in price given the competition from Pan and other cheap books, I cannot share," he insisted. "Our experience shows, that the best wholesale dealers in Europe do not regard the Albatross-Tauchnitz product as cheap books, but rather as the best selection from Anglo-American literature, and on top of that, a good value." Holroyd-Reece claimed to embrace the future, yet the principles he held aloft were those from days of old: "One says to the bookdealer: 'Support the series on which you and we earn, and if the level of sales increases, then our prices will get cheaper.' I am somewhat afraid to limit ourselves to the best-selling authors. Our tradition is that the Albatross-Tauchnitz author of today is tomorrow's classic."[17]

Albatross and Tauchnitz did indeed have a tradition—and they had, in fact, helped transform many an up-and-coming 1930s author into a classic. Yet economic conditions on the ground in Germany militated against both such high ideals and such high prices. Wegner and Krause-Brandstetter worried that holding onto tradition too tightly would squeeze the life out of the new venture. On 27 April, Wegner proposed that they temporarily follow the lead of their competitors, importing Albatross titles produced in Italy and the Netherlands, while they built up their Tauchnitz repertoire in Germany. Over a month later, he waited for a response. "I have still heard nothing from you about the Tauchnitz-

Albatross matter," he wrote to Holroyd-Reece on 30 May. "The situation is beginning to get critical, if we don't come out with a certain program of production soon." As weeks had stretched on without news, Krause-Brandstetter seems to have gotten nervous. On the sly, in mid-May, he sought out Raymond Pagan, chief of the Publications Branch for the American Zone, to see whether the Brandstetters might win Tauchnitz rights away from both Wegner and Holroyd-Reece for the family firm in Wiesbaden.[18]

Meanwhile, Holroyd-Reece claimed to have answered Wegner's concerns from Paris in a timely fashion in mid-May, but the letter had gotten waylaid. On 5 June, he reassured Wegner that all was well. The money had come through —100,000 DM. "This money will be used *in toto* to pay . . . for the import of, say, 50,000 copies," wrote Holroyd-Reece. "Reckon that we have 100 titles. If you import 50,000 this means an average of only 500 per title and this is of course far too little. Then remember that we will have ready in the next three months over 30 new titles and we must get to the position in which we get ongoing orders."[19]

While this letter sounded promising, for Krause-Brandstetter it was too little, too late. In the interim he followed the one piece of advice Pagan had offered him: "to engage in as much activity as possible whereby the Tauchnitz name would appear frequently before the public eye." In response, Krause-Brandstetter planned a trip to England and Sweden for Tauchnitz interests, a fact that sent Holroyd-Reece reeling. On 8 June, he insisted that Krause-Brandstetter cancel his trip. "I surely don't need to explain the whole story to you anew," explained Holroyd-Reece's lawyer to Wegner, in what became a record of Albatross's woes. "The agents have subscribed to the stance that all earlier contracts with Albatross and Tauchnitz are terminated, owing to the war. It has cost a year-long battle to discourage them from this." One publisher was still threatening a lawsuit. Others pressured Albatross to reprint their titles within six months or lose the rights altogether. "Here, too, there are great difficulties to overcome. How would it look, for God's sake, if emissaries of the Tauchnitz Editions G.m.b.H. in Germany appear here, and on their own account carry on negotiations with the agents with reference to the earlier Tauchnitz rights. That would, of course, result in hopeless confusion, since Tauchnitz rights cannot be claimed by two different firms, namely Albatross Ltd and Tauchnitz Edition G.m.b.H." He urged Wegner to keep Krause-Brandstetter focused on the task at hand.[20]

As this letter made clear, Holroyd-Reece still called the shots. Yet despite his efforts, he was increasingly firing these shots, as the German expression "ein Schuss ins Blaue" would have it, "into the blue," reacting, rather than acting, never knowing where they would land.

*

The beginning of Albatross's end was, by this point, lodged deep in its tissue, in the way that Rainer Maria Rilke speculated that "you had your death *inside* you as a fruit has its core." On 15 June 1949, Wegner wrote to Holroyd-Reece with alarm. "The cheap American editions have begun to flood the book trade," he reported. "The result is a very strong decline in orders for the Tauchnitz Edition, which is all around seen as too expensive." To have any "prospect of success," he insisted on reducing the price from 3.50 DM to 2.50 DM. "If that is not possible," he argued, "then it makes no sense, in my view, to promise anything at all from the German trade." Wegner also worried that Holroyd-Reece's financial calculations were off—not from carelessness, but because the costs of doing business had changed so radically. An Albatross Limited list of "Advances Paid on Non-Published Titles" from 31 May 1949 verifies that Wegner's fears about money were on target. The list, containing hundreds of titles in English, French, German, Portuguese, and Spanish, documented more than £7,000 of advances paid for books that never materialized—a gross indulgence in times when money was so tight. "We must pull ourselves together and precisely examine your calculations," Wegner urged Holroyd-Reece, "to see whether under the current production ratios it is possible to import Albatross books to Germany. You see that your coming is urgently required, since sealing an agreement is futile, without clarifying these fundamental issues."[21]

Though Holroyd-Reece was all too aware of what he called "the terrible time factor," his time was locked up. May had been spent in London, and then Florence, where he set up his temporary office for his new Italian company, Edizione Continentale, which was to bolster Albatross operations. June he was in London again, and only after that Germany, too little, too late. Holroyd-Reece had a longtime habit of reorganizing companies when their finances were strapped. As Wegner pushed him to act, his attention was diverted, more focused on Italy than Germany.[22]

There was one last small flurry of activity around the Hamburg Albatross-Tauchnitz that summer. On 28 June 1949, Kupfer took his final action as Albatross managing director. He wrote to the Civil Court in Leipzig to announce that Albatross Leipzig was opening a branch in Hamburg at the address of the Christian Wegner Verlag. Two weeks later, Holroyd-Reece signed his name before a London notary granting his lawyer the power of attorney to make decisions for him on behalf of the Publishing Holding Company in Luxembourg, "in all matters . . . concerning the firm, The Albatross Verlag G.m.b.H." Notes from the managing directors meeting of Collins publishers held in Glasgow on 1 September 1949 further suggest that Albatross was being reorganized to allow Collins—as Albatross's longtime creditor—a stronger hand in managing its strategy and finance. That Holroyd-Reece had ceded anyone this much decision-making power over his affairs was a sign that the firm no longer had much lifeblood in it. The minutes for a later directors meeting held in Glasgow on 24–25 October 1949 contain merely a cryptic comment: "*Albatross:* . . . Holroyd Reece has returned to Italy and no information was available on production and sales progress. His life had been insured for £50,000."[23]

In a *Publishers Weekly* article that appeared at the end of 1946, Holroyd-Reece had, with characteristic bravado, warned other publishers away from Albatross's market. He had named his firm Albatross, he noted, both because "he had wanted a name that would look the same in many languages" and because, "according to tradition, it is exceedingly dangerous to try to shoot down the Albatross." Yet as the postwar market developed, it was Albatross that faced new dangers. In July 1949, Albatross's Dutch partner, Sijthoff, offered pessimistic projections for Albatross sales, partly because of the very series which Enoch had helped create abroad: "Now, with the Marshall-Aid, large quantities of cheap little American books are being imported, with the support of a huge advertising campaign in Western Europe. These are the 'Signet' and 'Mentor' series, which offer really good titles. . . . The import of these books means tough competition for all other English series." In fact, Albatross could not sell enough of its ample back stocks to cover its even ampler debts: by the early 1950s, Albatross owed British distributor W.H. Smith over £3,000, and Sijthoff nearly £7,000, a mere fraction of Albatross's entanglements across national lines. In March 1950, Holroyd-Reece sold his interest in Albatross for 275 million lire (£150,000), as he explained to Sijthoff, "chiefly because it gave me the chance to pay everybody in full and at once." Yet when the buyer broke the contract, the result was yet another restructuring of Albatross's organization. An Italian firm,

I. Krachmalnicoff in Milan, became general agents for the sale and distribution of the remaining Albatross stocks. The organization's letters, filled with cheery plans for reorganization, reflected a misplaced optimism. "The sale has come completely to a standstill," remarked Albatross's Dutch partner. "The public that reads English has passed on to the cheap English and American series." The French Albatross subsidiary declared bankruptcy late in 1950.[24]

It was not just Albatross that carried its death within it by this point. All publishers specializing in continental editions shared the same fate: Bonnier's Zephyr Editions and the Ljus Editions from Sweden; Star Editions, forged by Harold Raymond and several other British publishers; and also a new Tauchnitz firm in Milan, started in July 1950, in which Krause-Brandstetter had a stake. This new Tauchnitz, like Albatross, made a feverish attempt to restore the Tauchnitz name to its former glory. Even Huxley's publisher, Raymond, who openly resisted continental editions, was prepared to let his authors sign with it. Yet his reasons echoed Sijthoff's predictions. "It looks as if either the war or American and English paper covered 'cheaps' has been steadily putting an end to [continental editions]," he noted to the British Society of Authors in January 1951, "for both Zephyr and Albatross seem to be in difficulties, and Star Editions has given me first-hand experience of the problem." He took a now-you-see-it-now-you-don't approach to the Tauchnitz contract proposed to him because the advance was unusually high—£75—and a boon for the author. He did not, evidently, expect the new Tauchnitz to last any longer than Albatross or his own Star Editions. As he put it, "The money is payable on signing the contract, so let's go while the going's good."[25]

The going would not be good for long, despite Krachmalnicoff's efforts to push Albatross sales throughout 1951. In October 1951, Holroyd-Reece was still sending letters using his Albatross Ltd. stationery at 13 Lincoln's Inn. He sometimes cut off the "Albatross Ltd." at the top; he sometimes revived the Albatross name. As late as December 1952, Richard Aldington mentioned to Holroyd-Reece that he hoped to publish his memoir of T. E. Lawrence—*Lawrence of Arabia*—in the Albatross series. The volume, which revealed Lawrence as the illegitimate child of a British aristocrat, risked bringing libel suits down upon it unless Holroyd-Reece could convince well-heeled Brits related to this aristocrat to see the book's merits. "I'm no hand at the younger women, but I fancy my chances with my Mother's generation," he remarked to Aldington, of his abilities to bring one of the aristocrat's elderly daughters around. "And don't forget that notably in this country my appearance and manner are considered so extremely odd that what would seem inconceivable from a black-coated lawyer has before now been found quite plausible on my lips." Yet the "Lord High Romantick" and his powers of persuasion had finally come up against the realities of market change. After repeated and failed attempts to sell Albatross, Collins dealt the firm its death blow in 1955.[26]

In this one sense, it might be said that Albatross ended as it had begun. In the more hopeful years of Albatross's youth, back in January 1934, Holroyd-Reece had once written to Osbert Sitwell about his incessant travels. "I feel rather like my own bird, the Albatross," he wrote with self-deprecating humor, "who by habit, spends most of his time in the air, without alighting on firm ground."[27]

CONCLUSION

Longing

TODAY, THE ENTRY to 12 rue Chanoinesse looks much as it did in the sketch that Gunter Böhmer presented to Holroyd-Reece for his Christmas card in 1938—though Böhmer invests it with more personality than it projected when I rounded the corner that March day in 2009, turning my back on Notre-Dame to take a look at Holroyd-Reece's French pied-à-terre for the first time. The address is select, but the house is unostentatious, what the French call "brave" (pronounced "brahv"), well-behaved. Böhmer imbues it with a far more expressionistic surge of feeling. His rendering is redolent with motion, astir, as if the house is shaking itself loose from its foundations, about to take flight. This is a place where life happened, his sketch seems to say. The door is slightly ajar, inviting viewers in.

There are many paths to any door. And indeed, many people made their way to and from 12 rue Chanoinesse, from divergent factions, with differing intent. British and American authors, publishers, and agents were welcomed into the inner sanctum as part of the courteous ritual of publishing, the wooing that might lead to a contract. In the late 1930s the French Secret Service watched that door, noting the flow of foreigners—so many Germans!—venturing to and from the premises. During the Occupation, Krause-Brandstetter used this address to sell Albatross and Tauchnitz books in France; German enemy property custodians, too, investigated here what Holroyd-Reece's French office had taken from the Reich and whether anything remained. After the war, Holroyd-Reece returned to claim what was his—that is, until his debts caught up with him and the belongings from his living and office quarters were seized, leaving him, like me, standing on the outside looking in.[1]

Other passers-by have also sought out this door, trying to imagine what happened there. One—a woman Holroyd-Reece met in Florence in March 1949—made her way to the rue Chanoinesse because she could not forget him. Years earlier Katherine Strelsky had journeyed from the United States to Italy to make a new life for herself after her husband of twenty years, a Russian émigré scholar at Vassar, suffered a fatal heart attack. She had been hired for one of Holroyd-Reece's many ventures, an Italian villa converted into a finishing school for girls. Like Holroyd-Reece, she knew what it was to translate one culture for another—she was writing a book about Fyodor Dostoyevsky's *The Idiot*—and she was immediately smitten by her employer. "[You and I] talked about French poetry and Browning and the Bible, and your beautiful sorrel shirt, that shouldn't be stained," she wrote of the day they met, "and in the end as you were leaving you took my hand and said, with a look that heartened me in my deepest uncertainty that you wished me success and all good things, and I felt I had had a benediction. . . . I was in Florence, about to live in a castle, and to do work which should have been a joy and an easy challenge, among friends and colleagues. And I had seen you."[2]

Strelsky fell too hard and too fast, being neither the first nor the last to trust too much in Holroyd-Reece's promises. By the time he met her, he had married his third wife, whose family money he purportedly squandered in bad investments—Albatross probably among them, given the timing. While the German Albatross-Tauchnitz partnership was dissolving in May and June 1949, he built up his Italian office and stole away for passionate tête-à-têtes. Strelsky's typed account offers an intimate portrait of him unlike any other I have found. They met at a moment when his business dealings were foundering, and his promises to his lover were hardly constant. In one breath, he fervently declared their indestructible connection. Yet in the next, he set this passion against reality. "I can't see ahead," he admitted. "I can't ask you to share my life. (Shudder.) It looks insoluble." Still, he held out hope: "Someday I'll come and say, 'It's very interesting what you are doing, but now you are coming with me.'"[3]

Then, after fifteen months, he abruptly ended their relationship. Strelsky was hard hit, and typed up lengthy segments of their conversations—adding phrases in blue pencil as they occurred to her later—to remind herself that she had not been mistaken in his love. Reading through her voluminous notes years later, I found it a little embarrassing to be a voyeur of their love talk, all their private feeling with no outlet but the page. Was he merely heartless, ruthless? Or was he sincere, I wondered, but in the manner of an actor, believing what he said as he said it? His manner with Strelsky suggests one thing above all: in love, as in business, Holroyd-Reece practiced a well-honed amorality. The tangible pleasure or gain before him enticed him more than commitments at some distance of time or space, as Annemarie Wegner observed elsewhere, damning him on these grounds as a *Halunken*—a scoundrel or reprobate. This glimpse into Holroyd-Reece's romantic life suggests, in part, how he justified his dealings with the Nazi regime to keep Albatross operating. His truth was tied up with his need; he said what he needed to say, convincing himself while he convinced others. The private man and his public face were, in the end, perhaps not so far apart.[4]

For years after he ended their relationship in 1951, Strelsky toiled in the aftermath of her emotional upheaval. She gathered a mass of materials, as if writing a biography of Holroyd-Reece. She drew up lists of his many addresses. She reprinted his articles from the *Christian Science Monitor* in the early 1920s. She collected first-person accounts of battle in World War I—those clashes in which his unit had seen action. She drew elaborate battle maps on transparent sketching paper, as if to follow his footsteps through the war. She verified his record, writing to the British military to see if he had, in fact, served in the Dorset Yeomanry; she received an answer in 1953 stating that no trace of him could be found in the regimental lists. And she visited the house in the rue Chanoinesse, standing outside and watching as a man opened the weighty door and went in; Strelsky caught a glimpse of a small cobblestoned court with a great tree in one corner and on the far side the massive stone arch of the inner door, before the concierge shot her a menacing look and closed the door with finality.[5]

*

In research, as in life, it matters who guards the gate. Like Strelsky, I have put together what I can of John Holroyd-Reece and his world, digging through whatever information I could find. There are still so many questions. He was unbelievably shrewd when it came to getting ventures funded; yet there is little sign that Albatross turned a profit on his watch. Nor did a French firm in which he had heavily invested, Éditions arts et métiers graphiques, though it boasted an array of wealthy Jewish financiers—Henri and Philippe Rothschild among them. Was Holroyd-Reece using his wheeling and dealing to help these Jewish families transfer money safely to England, as an economist friend posited to me one day? Or was he, as MI-5's suspicious reaction to him suggests, passing information to the Germans?[6]

Weighing the evidence, it seems at least plausible that Holroyd-Reece provided information in some capacity to British intelligence, as he claimed to the French. He spoke at least four languages. His constant travels across national lines on publishing business gave him legitimate reason to linger in the political hot zones of Italy and Germany in exactly the years that fascism enflamed their populations with its fervid passions and promises. Wolfgang Krause-Brandstetter's contention in 1945 that he was "not a regular prisoner" of war sticks with me, too. If Holroyd-Reece worked for British intelligence, it is not inconceivable, nor would it be unprecedented, that he built up his younger associate as a German insider who could pass him information, first from the Foreign Office, and then from the Abwehr.[7] In this scenario, it is also possible that Holroyd-Reece delivered low-level information to Nazi officials on his trips to Germany, making concessions to keep Anglo-American propaganda in the form of Albatross books before German eyes. In my mind, I turn over the possibility that Holroyd-Reece and Krause-Brandstetter were both renegades, working in some small part of their lives for the same cause.

Following the twists and turns of Albatross's entanglements with the Nazi regime is, finally, to run up against the question of collaboration. Albatross books, like others of their time, cannot be held aloft as inherently subversive forces under National Socialism just because they were in English or associated with Anglo-American culture. In multiple artistic realms, most prominently radio, film, and literature, Goebbels called for "light entertainment," treating it as another tool of war. By allowing *Wirklichkeitsflucht*—the flight from reality—by legitimizing escapism, Goebbels encouraged German soldiers and civilians alike to nourish themselves and regather their forces for the demands of total war. In this sense, as Christian Adam, a historian of reading habits in Nazi Germany has pondered, "the light reading [that held itself far from politics] potentially had, in the balance, a more stabilizing effect on the system than politically polemical texts." The trenchant comment of one journalist who emigrated from Germany in 1938 also comes into sharp focus here: "Everyone who worked under Goebbels, regardless of any self-bestowed anti-Nazi credentials, played an instrument in Goebbels' orchestra. All those romances, those old-fashioned tales, everything that was part of so-called normal life, without directly challenging the Third Reich, was part of the grand scheme."[8]

We must ask the same question, too, of the Albatross managers. The years since the Second World War have brought evolving standards of judgment to bear on those who supervised decisions about culture in Hitler's Germany, or who wrote and published books there—most famously embodied in Thomas Mann's stinging critique that "a stench of blood and criminality clings" to books published in Germany between 1933 and 1945. Albatross leaders certainly had before them an admirable goal, endorsed by the British government in the mid-1930s: to keep Anglo-American books in German hands. Yet in retrospect we cannot avoid the realization that they, in varying degrees of choice and necessity, also tuned their instruments in Goebbels's orchestra, opening themselves up to self-censorship and compromise, to realize their personal, economic, and propaganda goals. Enoch sold Albatross and Tauchnitz books that profited the German economy until the late 1930s, when the regime forcibly excised him from this trade. Holroyd-Reece negotiated with Reich Literary Chamber officials until the last month before the war. Wegner bought Enoch's firm, participating in the Reich's "Aryanization," and later became an army officer, advising Albatross's enemy property custodian about the firm's international networks. Krause-Brandstetter, with his Foreign Office ties, argued that Albatross books should be allowed for sale under the Occupation in France even after they had first been banned, leaving Nazi officials to justify their sale as a "special kind of German propaganda" that advertised the regime's tolerance.

Carrying forward these contradictions, Albatross enters broader conversations about National Socialist literary politics and censorship—though, as a long-forgotten bearer of Anglo-American culture, it may do so through the side door. Jan-Pieter Barbian has written at length of the "failure of state literary policy" in Hitler's Germany, evidenced by the "rapidly widening discrepancy between its propaganda and the everyday realities of writers, publishers, booksellers, librarians, and readers." His groundbreaking research demonstrates from a number of angles that Nazi literary policy was far from the well-organized, lean, efficient machine of popular stereotypes; instead, "except in its destructive measures against books and people . . . extensive and hectic activity revealed neither coherent planning nor a unified objective."[9]

Albatross's story both affirms and extends our understanding of these dynamics, precisely because it crossed so many lines. Within Germany, the firm and its leaders inhabited what one scholar has called "the grey zone occupying the vast space between vocal opposition and full collaboration."[10] Reaching beyond Germany, Albatross's infrastructure, market, and operations inherently crossed national borders and interests. Precisely because Albatross offers—so to speak—a bird's-eye view of cross-national dynamics of publishing and censorship surrounding the Second World War, its story yields different insights: that demand for Anglo-American culture remained strong across Nazi-occupied Europe, especially in Hitler's Germany; that censorship of Anglo-American books was idiosyncratic, shaped as much by international trade and political infighting as by ideological measuring sticks; and that the Nazi cultural elite not only envied Anglo-American literature its success with continental readers but actively harnessed Albatross and copied the English edition's model for its German-language wartime series with its secret ties to the Propaganda Ministry and Foreign Office. Placing Albatross in its historical context, then, ultimately illuminates something Nazi propaganda officials admitted only among themselves: the Germans were losing the war of the book.

In the end, though, there is this fact, too: the more that the Nazis cracked down on Anglo-American culture but tolerated Albatross, the more Albatross became one of the last voices for Anglo-American culture in Nazi-occupied Europe. Perhaps someday, through the recovery of still other documents, we will come to a better understanding of what its brightly bound books meant to the readers who reached for them in times of duress. Annemarie Wegner gives us one glimpse, in a letter of early March 1943, to her husband. The war was wearing her down. Like all other civilians, she faced shortages. She shared stories of those who had been injured or killed in the war. Her *Hausmädchen*—part household help, part nanny to her two children—was on the verge of getting called up to work in the factories. And she wrote with relief of the books Christian had sent her. "I am stocked up on books for at least a year," she wrote, as one might write of food stuffs or other provisions essential to life. "I am immensely grateful. At the moment, I am reading Katherine Mansfield again with great joy. She writes so subtly, I love her so much." While she does not describe her reading as an act of resistance, neither does it seem merely an escape. I like to read in these words, as I believe she may have meant them, her remembrance of other days and the preservation of hope in another, less restrictive world to come.[11]

These and other speculations live on in me, such dead ends unavoidable. I tried to locate the children of Erich Kupfer and Walter Gey, and to request information about Krause-Brandstetter from the family firm in Wiesbaden, to no avail. Sadly, too, the women of the Albatross Press remain largely beyond my reach. I know they and their efforts were critical to its success: Annemarie Wegner, managing the rue Boulard office; Jeanne Holroyd-Reece, ensuring that her husband cross-checked accounts and attended to the conflicts bubbling, always, just underneath the surface; editor Sonia Hambourg Bassarab, reviewing manuscripts, patiently addressing authors' complaints, and picking up the pieces after the war.

Some traces remain of the players, major and minor, who shaped Albatross and its fate. According to sources who knew the family of the Albatross enemy property custodian, Osbert Walter Gey, he remained in Liebertwolkwitz just southeast of Leipzig after the war. In 1949, he was "denounced . . . on negligible grounds" to the Soviets and fled with his wife and two children to West Germany. Erich Kupfer settled in Hamburg. As the head of the Transatlantik-Buchhandels-Gesellschaft, he maintained a decades-long association with Enoch, importing New American Library books to postwar Germany. For Enoch's seventieth birthday, Kupfer published a tribute in the German book trade journal. "Whenever I happen to speak of [Kurt Enoch] with a Hamburg colleague of the older generation, a pair of eyes spontaneously light up and the memory of him is awakened. 'How is it going with our old friend from America?'" Kupfer made a point of acknowledging Enoch's losses. "Success lies in his nature, in his weighing [things out], in taking action. . . . It is decidedly a mark of his being that the pogroms did not throw him off, but instead called him, 'despite the odds,' to new deeds in other lands."[12]

Krause-Brandstetter turned his attention to Tauchnitz as Albatross collapsed, following the path for books in English that had shaped his beginnings as a publisher. In July 1950, he dissolved his contract with Wegner and sold Tauchnitz rights to Dr. Erhard Aeschlimann, a Swiss-born book dealer who headed the Antiquarian Department of the Hoepli firm in Milan. The Tauchnitz scholars Ann Bowden and William B. Todd read this contract as evidence that "Brandstetter alone previously had exclusive rights to all original Tauchnitz publications, and that Holroyd-Reece's arrogant pretensions, however often asserted from 1934 to 1950, were completely invalid." Krause-Brandstetter served alongside Aeschlimann while building up his family firm in Wiesbaden, which specialized in bilingual dictionaries. He died on 7 December 1963, just barely fifty-one. "In Wolfgang Brandstetter the Oscar Brandstetter KG has not only lost a model head of operations," read his obituary. "He was, beyond that, a friend to everyone and a good companion. The enterprise will carry on, in keeping with his vision." The Oscar Brandstetter Verlag does, indeed, continue printing its multilingual scientific and technical dictionaries today.[13]

The three Albatross leaders traced divergent paths through publishing landscapes in the postwar years. Kurt Enoch built a reputation for himself as a pioneer in paperbacks, crossing a threshold of success neither Wegner nor Holroyd-Reece ever reached. In 1957 alone, the New American Library sold 40 million books, its arsenal ranging from Mickey Spillane to William Faulkner, from Tennessee Williams to Thomas Mann, Margaret Mead, and Plato. Until 1960, Enoch remained president; then he and Weybright sold the firm to the Times

Mirror Company, where Enoch initially served on the board of directors and later as vice president, developing a new book division. He resigned in 1968, yet continued to work as an independent publishing consultant from his office at 680 Fifth Avenue. On 2 December 1957, he applied for restitution from Germany under a 1953 law to reimburse those persecuted by the Nazi regime. For the loss of his income between 1936 and 1941, he received 45,370 RM or 9,074 DM. His growing awareness that millions of Jews, including his own family members, had died at the hands of the Nazis led him to donate millions of dollars to Jewish organizations and causes, including a major hospital and medical school in Israel and the Einstein Medical School in New York.[14]

In the United States, as elsewhere, Enoch showed a stubborn streak. When town officials planned a road too close for his liking to his vacation house in upstate New York, he tried to get the road diverted. When that failed, he sold the home and bought another. He continued, too, to be a risk taker and world traveler. In his mid-seventies he remained as taken with flying as he had been as a boy, and on one occasion, under supervision of an expert pilot, he gave the eighteen-year-old son of his first cousin the ride of his life. "He pointed the nose of the plane upwards, which meant it lost speed and stalled, and headed straight down to the ground, until he pulled it out of the dive a few long seconds later." The photo essay from Enoch's commemorative seventieth-birthday book shows him traversing worlds: robed in a Japanese kimono, standing before the turrets of Red Square in Moscow (part of the first book industry delegation to the Soviet Union in 1962), and perched atop an elephant, led by a turbaned guide, in Ceylon.[15]

"I know that I have to be thankful—and I am thankful—that fate permitted me to be here tonight, in good health, among my family and good friends," Enoch remarked on his eightieth birthday. "But I must confess that in my later years it has not been easy for me to accept the fact that the best is *not* still to come, and that reflections on the past have replaced the looking forward." He acknowledged the trials of his past: "I have lost precious time wasted by wars and political upheavals which forced me to make three fresh starts in my professional career and cut short the transition from youth to adulthood." Yet he also stressed that "one can find a compensating good for the 'bad' things in one's life"; above all, he noted, his past rendered his present "more precious." Enoch died on vacation in Puerto Rico at eighty-six. His funeral featured tributes from numerous publishing luminaries. Peter Mayer, chief executive of Penguin Ltd., who had been with him on his last birthday, offered a final classic anecdote of his determination. "When the cake with candles came to the table (and my mother put eighty-six candles into the cake), Kurt could not blow them all out at once," Mayer recalled. "So he asked that they be lighted again. And *then* he put them out in one great breath. That was Kurt, he never gave up." The inside cover of his funeral book featured a saying by Horace: "Pluck off and enjoy each single day."[16]

Like Enoch, Christian Wegner never stopped looking ahead. What a friend had once said of his performance in military drills—"It was almost always Christian Wegner who took the lead"—remained true in his postwar career. His resourcefulness and shrewd pursuit of his own interests stood him in good stead in a postwar Hamburg beleaguered by shortages. He got access to paper, though it was heavily rationed, and to printers, though those not destroyed in the war were few and far between. One colleague later fondly remembered how Wegner, ever the material provider, had saved a literary event by zooming up in his car—when few private vehicles were granted licenses—to provide a bag of coal to heat the freezing room. True to form, amid the economic uncertainty of 1948, Wegner began to publish the first of a fourteen-book series of Goethe's works and letters. His colleagues later praised him for dreaming big when postwar conditions had not encouraged dreaming. Other classics included newly edited volumes of Friedrich Hölderlin, Georg Büchner, and Heinrich von Kleist. There were few huge sellers in the Wegner Verlag arsenal—Pierre La Mure's novel *Moulin Rouge* being one exception. But the distribution business bolstered his income, leaving Wegner the freedom for which so many publishers long: to publish the books of their choice. When he played the memory game "What did I bring on vacation?" with friends on the island of Sylt in the years directly after the war, in the list of things to remember was always one item: "a good book from the Christian Wegner Verlag."[17]

Wegner also put his innovative thinking to work for the new book trade organization, the German Publishers' and Booksellers' Union; in 1950 he became chairman of its Committee for Publishers. So visible was he, in fact, that the U.S. State Department invited him as one of a handful of German publishers for a lengthy visit in the fall of 1950—where he saw Enoch again in New York. Over the next two decades, he organized more than thirty German book exhibits around the world. He became a member of the Anglo-German Club and the German branch of the international PEN organization of authors. He orchestrated the return of Thomas Mann to his home city, Lübeck, in 1953. He frequented plays, concerts, and the opera, his love for culture leading him to positions with the Hamburg Deputation for Culture, the board of the Thalia Theater, and the Advisory Board of the Hamburg Public Libraries. Such engagement speaks to the very best of Wegner's impulses and talents. "When I think back on my father," wrote his son Matthias, "I think of his lively zest for life, of his unbelievable talent for organization and of his . . . great care-taking of others and me."[18]

In late October 1950, when Wegner returned to Germany from the United States, he found a claim from the Jewish Trust Corporation waiting for him, requiring that he pay Enoch restitution for the two businesses he had purchased in 1936. Wegner countered that Enoch's accountant had set the terms of the sale and that Enoch himself "had explicitly explained. . . . that he did not feel himself harmed by the then sale of his firm, and therefore was disinclined to levy a claim for restitution." Enoch, indeed, sent a letter supporting Wegner's case, and the story of Enoch and Wegner might have found its end there. Yet in 1951, Wegner teamed up with the German émigré publisher Gottfried Bermann-Fischer to create a German paperback series, the Fischer Bücherei, which, for Enoch, too closely resembled the format of the New American Library. On 14 March 1952, he sued the Fischer Bücherei for plagiarizing his design. The German courts ultimately decided against Enoch, who could, or would, not offer a bank guarantee of over 150,000 DM. In the end, *Der Spiegel* offered its own implicit verdict by placing images of the series' covers side by side. As the title noted, they could "hardly be told apart."[19]

For Wegner's seventieth birthday in September 1963, his colleagues produced a book in his honor. "May you, who lived through the hard years of bleakness," wrote one colleague, "long be able to play a role in building up what a publisher in a free world can bring about for good." Yet Wegner would not have much time to do so. In the same year he was diagnosed with cancer and died on 14 January 1965. A colleague purchased his distribution business, and the Christian Wegner Verlag closed in 1970.[20]

As for the most elusive of the three Albatross founders, John Holroyd-Reece, he seemed to disappear from sight after the war. "There were reports from Milan that he was running a dancing school," the literary agent Graham Watson wrote. "Then rumours circulated about his buying a castle in Kent. Later a small press report gave news of some entanglement with the police when he arrived in England unannounced in a small aeroplane at a remote airfield. And then, a few years later, his death was reported. I have always felt that some author should emulate A.J.A. Symons whose brilliant *Quest for Corvo* set a new fashion in investigative biography. *Quest for Holroyd-Reece* might throw a little light into the dark corners of the life of this mysterious man."[21]

Watson was not far off. When Albatross was limping to its end in 1949 and 1950, Holroyd-Reece did help run a finishing school for girls at the Torre di Bellesguardo, a villa just outside Florence, where he had his affair with Katherine Strelsky. The castle rumor also contained some truth. After the war, Holroyd-Reece lived in "the Keep"—the tower and last remnant of the medieval fortress—on the estate of Chilham Castle in Kent, formerly owned by Sir Edmund Davis, Albatross's first and largest benefactor, who had passed away on the eve of the war. During the war, the government had billeted soldiers at the Keep. Holroyd-Reece moved in thereafter, trading one set of medieval lodgings in the center of Paris for this other, ensconced in the British countryside near Canterbury. Built in the 1170s and surrounded by fourteen-foot-high walls, it played to Holroyd-Reece's medieval sensibilities. From the tower roof, which offered a lovely view of the surrounding countryside, Holroyd-Reece might perhaps imagine himself lord of all he surveyed.[22]

In the 1950s, Holroyd-Reece married the poet Gitta Deutsch, a Jewish refugee from Austria, whom he had met years earlier when she was a typist in his office. It was his fifth marriage. Deutsch's daughter, Lady Elisabeth Schiemann—a teenager when they married—thought Holroyd-Reece at first "the weirdest person her mother had ever met," but "a fascinating personality." She remembers him as a "portly" man six feet tall, with a gentle voice, who "looked like a character from Mr. Pickwick." He had not lost his gift of gab, or his ability to charm. He loved to play the "grand seigneur," recounting amazing stories, often with seemingly far-fetched twists, as he stroked the long scar on the side of his face. "I don't know how much he built himself up as an imaginary person," Schiemann mused, years later. She found him to be a stickler for propriety. When she and her mother stood with him in the elevator one day, a man entered but did not remove his hat, as was the custom. Holroyd-Reece plucked the stranger's hat from his head. Another time, when his stepdaughter acted inappropriately at the table, he levied a challenge: if she did not stop, he would throw his soup at her. She did not stop, and he indeed threw his soup.[23]

Schiemann remembers him as a man of immense willpower, who smoked a hundred cigarettes a day for years, and then one day simply stopped. He never lost his luxe tastes or his penchant for the grand. He remained, as she remarked, "very good at playing the British gentleman." As visitors entered the domain of the Keep, they passed through a wrought-iron gate topped by his three initials regally intertwined. Typical of his manner of being, if he could not inherit a crest, he would create it—and he did, reproducing it on the gorgeously produced Christmas cards that he sent friends and acquaintances each year.[24]

In the late 1950s, Holroyd-Reece sought restitution in Germany for damages Albatross had suffered in the war. His case was denied. Not only was his name not listed anywhere on Albatross documentation in Germany; he had ensured that it would not be to veil British involvement when Albatross was founded. But authorities in Bonn claimed that damages could be legally paid only from the city where a business had held its last official seat in Germany. With Leipzig claimed by the Soviets and folded into East Germany, Holroyd-Reece had no recourse. Though he kept a lower profile after Albatross's demise, Holroyd-Reece remained full of schemes—what Schiemann called "his mad ideas." In 1950, he was involved in a plan to distribute milk in Italy. He continued to broker literary contracts, a habit that most spectacularly went awry in his attempt to help Richard Aldington publish his book on Lawrence of Arabia with Collins in the 1950s. As Schiemann noted, Holroyd-Reece "made a lot of money and lost a lot of money" in his later years.[25]

On 7 March 1969, he died suddenly of a heart attack. A plain ivory card announced his funeral service at the Church of Saint Mary, Chilham. The organist played Johann Sebastian Bach's cantatas "Who only lets God rule" and "All men must die." The graphic designer Hans Schmoller, who had fled Germany in 1937 and become the typographer for Penguin in London, wondered, two weeks after Holroyd-Reece's death, why the London *Times* had remained silent. "Surprisingly the death of John Holroyd-Reece on March 7 has gone unnoticed in your columns," he wrote. "Though he had lived in retirement . . . of late, his contribution to publishing was remarkable in the twenties and thirties." Among

Holroyd-Reece's achievements, Schmoller listed the Albatross Library, "whose meticulously edited, fastidiously chosen and excellently designed and printed paperbacks—with their entirely new colour-coding for the different subjects—were the forerunners of Sir Allen Lane's Penguins."[26]

Holroyd-Reece had perhaps exhausted in life all the attention he did not receive at his death. In some respects, both personal and financial, he had barely made it across the finish line. Because he had not adequately provided for his wife, leaving huge debts at Lloyds, she had to auction off his many beautiful collections each Friday over the course of seven weeks in the summer of 1969.[27] Yet the bronze head he had once had cast of himself still stands at watch in the garden of his stepdaughter, Lady Schiemann, surrounded by ivy.

*

In closing the book on Albatross, I must confess that when I initially perused the outside of its offices at the rue Boulard, place Vendôme, and rue Chanoinesse, I envisioned writing from an entirely different perspective: that of Sonia Hambourg, the young British editor who had come to Paris after graduating in history from Somerville College, one of the first women's colleges at Oxford. What I knew of her was evocative. As the daughter of celebrated Russian-Jewish pianist, Marc Hambourg, she had grown up in a milieu that ensured her a thoughtful education and solid social contacts. She was the first of a generation of British women officially encouraged to cultivate their minds, rather than just their families—grasping for that "room of her own" that Virginia Woolf urged female graduates to demand in her address to them in 1928. The more I learned of the coterie of brash, often self-absorbed men who headed the Albatross Press, the more I wondered how Hambourg would describe them if I could drop by to visit her for tea. What strategies had she developed to inure herself to their quick-changing moods and the flashes of criticism visited upon her and others? She must have had a bold streak to stay with Albatross for so long. In 1935, she married the Romanian artist Mircea Bassarab, who mysteriously disappeared during the war, perhaps for supporting the Resistance, as Hambourg herself had done. She remained in Paris for the remainder of the war, despite the fact she was half-Jewish; like Sylvia Beach, she did not want to abandon her friends. After the war, she took up again with Tauchnitz, staying until 1951, when, worn down by publishing, her life took a surprising turn. In 1953, she joined a contemplative Russian Orthodox order of nuns, becoming a strong support to its founder and eventually becoming the abbess herself. She died on 20 November 1980.[28]

In 2009, with the help of my artist friend of three decades, Virginie L'Homme Fontaine, I climbed into a borrowed car on a quest to discover Sonia Hambourg's story. We left the highway ninety minutes outside Paris, following winding roads into terrain that became suddenly hilly. In the small town of Bussy-en-Othe, we drove on narrow streets lined with low stone walls to the Convent of the Protective Veil of the Mother of God. Sister Elisabeth, stately and thin, graciously greeted us in perfect British-accented English for our scheduled appointment in a small courtyard lined with pollarded trees. She had been a novice under Mother Mary, the religious name Hambourg took when she joined the order. We talked for some time about Hambourg. She was devoted, said Sister Elisabeth, but quite a taskmaster in the convent's printing shop. In later life, she had brought her love of publishing to the Church, translating Russian Orthodox liturgies into English for use abroad. Farmers in the area sometimes recounted how Mother Mary had delivered messages for the Resistance, Sister Elisabeth informed us, but other than that she knew little of her earlier life. All the nuns had destroyed their worldly belongings before taking their vows. Then, out of nowhere, she offered an aside: "Her sister is still alive, you know. I have her number somewhere. Would you like me to call her?" I felt my voice tremble, as I said yes. Yet it was already too late. We called; but we had reached her in her last days, when she could not speak.

More than anything, my sojourn into the world of Albatross has left me filled with humility and awe. The events I have recorded played out over a relatively short period of time, in an era increasingly remote to us. As the last eyewitnesses to this era die out, we lose access, daily, to one critical way we have of knowing this past. Sonia Hambourg Bassarab, like the other women who shaped the Albatross Press, does not have a voice here because history has, largely, not preserved the voices of enough women. In the greater moral questions, too, Albatross's story leaves me at a loss. Its trajectory offers us no hero in the older tradition of the "Great Man" history, nor does it reveal its protagonists to be mere victims of institutions or events beyond their control. We can look back and tell what happened to whom and when. We can track how the Albatross leaders chose to react to various circumstances. Yet it is harder to convey the unpredictability of their choices—for good or ill—and the tenaciousness of their hope that small adaptations would bring safety for themselves, for their families, and, through the Albatross Modern Continental Library, for democratic ideals in Europe, as it was gradually smothered by totalitarianism.

When I think about the process of researching and writing this book, and the many detours I took en route, I am brought back to comments the sculptor Alberto Giacometti made to Henri Matisse in 1947, the sculptor conveying to the painter his experience of working with clay. Giacometti confessed to finding it "impossible to capture the entirety of a figure (we were too close to the models, and if we started from a detail, from a heel or from the nose, there was no hope at all of ever attaining a whole)." He elaborated, "One could spend one's entire life without achieving any result. The shape dissolves, it merely appears in the form of grains moving around in a deep dark void."[29]

Suspended between the detail and the whole, too, the writer writes, crafting shapes out of words, building something out of nothing—the opposite of the sculptor, who works in negative space, tearing away the excess from a block of clay, bit by bit, until a whole is revealed. "Details enthrall me, small details like an eye in a face or the moss on a tree," Giacometti reflected to an interviewer years later. "Yet no more than the entirety, for how can we tell the difference between the detail and the whole? It is the details that form the entirety. . . . They afford beauty to shapes." Suspended between the detail and the whole, the writer writes, trying to "afford beauty to shapes," and one hopes, truth, too. Yet the more I write, the more I see the wisdom in this sculptor's words: "The closer I get, the more it grows and further away it moves."[30]

Notes

Unless otherwise indicated, or quoted from an English-language source, all translations are mine.

INTRODUCTION

1. Dr. Willy Hoffman, Gutachten, 30 June 1941, 20206, File 1681, SAL. Hoffman was appointed custodian for a French firm, Les Éditions Pégase, owned by the Albatross director and fully enmeshed in Albatross finances. Yet because Albatross listed Leipzig as its seat after 1936, the regional finance president in Leipzig (Oberfinanzpräsident) remained involved in wartime investigations of Albatross directed by the Reich Commissioner for Enemy Property in Berlin.
2. Dr. Friedhelm Kaiser, Aktenvermerk, 6 November 1940, AJ40/1006, ANF.
3. Propaganda-Staffel to Chef des Militärverwaltungsbezirks Paris, 9 October 1940, AJ40/889; Bruno Conrad to Chef der Militärverwaltung in France, Abteilung Schrifttum, 26 October 1940, AJ40/1006, both ANF.
4. Le Préfet de Police to Monsieur le Président du Conseil, Ministre de la Défense Nationale et de la Guerre, 14 October 1939, CHA Fonds Moscou dossier 42834, SHD.
5. Dr. Willy Hoffman, Gutachten, 30 June 1941, 20206, File 1681, SAL.
6. Wyndham Lewis to Stuart Gilbert, 19 June 1934, quoted in McCleery, "Tauchnitz and Albatross," 303.
7. For an early challenge to stereotypes of Nazi censorship, see Schäfer, *Das gespaltene Bewusstsein.* On the need to recalibrate our assumptions about censorship under fascism by research into the political and economic realities that defined its parameters, see also Barbian, "Literary Policy," 157; Steinweis, *Art, Ideology and Economics,* 1–7, Bonsaver, *Censorship and Literature,* 2–4; Adam, *Lesen unter Hitler,* 24–5. Two recent works on censorship in a more international context are also of note: Darnton, *Censors at Work;* and Moore, ed., *Censorship and the Limits of the Literary.*
8. Geoffrey Faber, Editorial in *Publishers Weekly,* referenced by Faber in his letter to the chancellor of the exchequer, 18 July 1940, quoted in Holman, *Print for Victory,* 3.

9. This loaded language is best exemplified by the Reichsbank Leipzig: 20133, File 1363, SAL.
10. "Tauchnitz Marks 100th Year," 2317; Walter Gey to the Reichskommissar for Enemy Property, 20 June 1941, R87/1192, BAL; Anonymous, File Note, 24 June 1941, AJ/40/701, ANF.
11. There are remarkable national histories of publishing and censorship, yet recent scholarship has called for more research into cross-national dynamics that historically operated in the book trade. See, for instance, Shep, "Books Without Borders," 29–32; Renders, "Hitler's European Publishing Ambitions," 232–33; Adriaan van der Weel and Peter Verhaar, "Book Trade Archives to Book Trade Networks," *Bibliologia* 1 (2006): 151–66.
12. Penguin's story, told elsewhere in great detail, will not be my focus here. See Lewis, *Penguin Special,* 75–79, 91–92; McCleery, "The Paperback Evolution," 11–14.
13. For articles on Albatross, see Pressler, "The Tauchnitz Edition" and "Tauchnitz und Albatross," Schmoller, "The Paperback Revolution," McCleery, "Tauchnitz and Albatross" and "The Paperback Evolution," and Troy, "A Modern Press for Modern Times" and "Books, Swords, and Readers." For an illustrated bibliography of all prewar and many postwar Albatross titles, contact Alastair Jollans at his blog: https:/papcrbackrevolution.wordpress.com/.
14. Ayçoberry, *The Social History of the Third Reich,* 11. For discussion of why we need to understand individuals to understand book historical dynamics, see Spiers, *Serious About Series,* and McCleery, "The Return of the Publisher to Book History."
15. W. G. Sebald, *Austerlitz* (New York: Random House, 2001), 24.

CHAPTER ONE. TAUCHNITZ HAS A RIVAL

1. Dr. Hans Otto, "Rundschreiben," 4 November 1931, 21056, File 17, SAL.
2. Nowell-Smith, *International Copyright Law,* 43–44; Pressler, "The Tauchnitz Edition," 66; Todd and Bowden, *Tauchnitz International Editions in English,* 3–46, 609.
3. D. H. Lawrence to Arthur McLeod, 17 September 1912, in Lawrence, *The Cambridge Edition of the Letters and Works of D. H. Lawrence,* vol. 1, *1902–13,* ed. James T. Boulton (Cambridge: Cambridge University Press, 1979), 456; Sinclair Lewis to the Tauchnitz firm on the occasion of its centenary, quoted in Holroyd-Reece [attrib.], *The Harvest,* 68.
4. Holroyd-Reece (attrib.), *The Harvest,* 31; Todd, "Firma Tauchnitz," 8; *Die neue Rundschau* quoted in *Kleiner Führer,* 21; Bruno Conrad, "5000 Bände Tauchnitz Edition," *Börsenblatt der deutschen Buchhandel,* 14 July 1931, 665.
5. Pressler, "Tauchnitz und Albatross," A2.

6. Hans Otto, "Rundschreiben," 4 November 1931, 21056, File 17, SAL.
7. Ibid. Dr. Otto to Dr. A. Lee Gobert and Dr. Pinckernelle, 4 November 1931, Gobert to Otto, 7 November 1931, all 21056, File 17, SAL; Hamburg Registry of Commerce, Albatross Verlag, 231-7, Number 8499, SAH. Albatross was incorporated in Hamburg on 6 November 1931, but entered in the registry only on November 12.
8. Todd and Bowden, *Tauchnitz International Editions,* 610.
9. Hans Otto, "Rundschreiben, Eilt!," n.d. [probably 15 January 1931], 21056, File 15, SAL; Dr. Otto, "Rundschreiben," 11 December 1931, 21056, File 17, SAL.
10. Matthias Wegner, Email to author, 8 November 2009.
11. Brown, *Contacts,* 209; Hans Otto to Dr. Bruno Hauff, 4 September 1930, Freiherr von Tauchnitz to Otto, 22 September 1930, both 21056, File 20, SAL; Otto to Walter Jäh, circa 10 February 1932, 21056, File 17, SAL.
12. Saucke, "Christian Wegner zum 60. Geburtstag," 449; Markus Wegner, Interview, 7 May 2012, Hamburg, Germany; Markus Wegner, "Max Christian Wegner als Flieger im Ersten Weltkrieg," n.d. MEW.
13. Max Christian Wegner, Johanneum and University Transcripts, Ernst Wegner, "Dem Bücheronkel: Mit einem Bild der jüngeren Söhne," *Ernst Wegner zum Gedachtnis* (Privately printed: Weihnachten 1921), 15, both MEW; Saucke, "Christian Wegner zum 60. Geburtstag," 449.
14. Hans Otto, "Rundschreiben," 18 September 1930, Otto to Max Christian Wegner, 25 September 1930, both 21056, File 20, SAL.
15. Hans Otto to Professor Schöffler, 8 September 1930, Otto, "Rundschreiben," 18 September 1930, both 21056, File 20, SAL; Markus Wegner, Interview, 7 May 2012.
16. Matthias Wegner, "Offener Brief an einen Enkel," n.d., MW.
17. Brown, *Contacts,* 209–10; Pressler, "Tauchnitz und Albatross," A4.
18. Announcement: "The Albatross," *Börsenblatt für den Deutschen Buchhandel,* 3 December 1931, 7037.
19. Ibid.; Hans Otto to Dr. Franz Sester, 10 December 1931, 21056, File 17, SAL.
20. John Holroyd-Reece to Bernhard Tauchnitz Verlag, 9 November 1931, Hans Otto to his board, "Streng Vertraulich!," 10 November 1931, John Holroyd-Reece to Otto, 14 November 1931, 18 November 1931, 21 November 1931, all 21056, File 17, SAL.
21. Hans Otto, "Rundschreiben," 11 December 1931, 21056, File 17, SAL.
22. Hans Otto, "Rundschreiben," 14 October 1930, 21056, File 20, SAL.
23. Fiona Brewster, Interview, 3 May 2013, Le Breuil-Rouillac, France; see Herbert S. Gorman, "Bizarre Career of a Mad French Painter: Vincent van Gogh," *New York Times,* 22 April 1923, BR5; John Holroyd-Reece, "The Rise of Modern Czech Art," *Christian Science Monitor,* 8 June 1925, 10; John Holroyd-Reece, "Glassware of R. Lalique," *Christian Science Monitor,* 25 July 1931, 9; Barker, *Stanley Morison,* 215; "Holroyd-Reece, John," in *Who Was Who, 1961–1970* (New York: St. Martin's, 1972), 546.

24. "Harcourt, Brace Gain Pegasus Press Rights," *New York Times,* 3 June 1928, 21; Wolfram Göbel, *Der Kurt Wolff Verlag, 1913–1930* (Frankfurt am Main: Buchhändler Vereinigung, 1977), 907–10. Wolff, *Briefwechsel eines Verlegers, 1911–1963,* xliv–xlv.
25. Radclyffe Hall, *Your John: The Love Letters of Radclyffe Hall,* ed. Joanne Glasgow (New York: New York University Press, 1997), 143–44; Watson, "More Sketches from Memory," 2559.
26. Hans Otto, "Rundschreiben," 17 March 1932, 21056, File 16, SAL.
27. Enoch, *Memoirs,* 42.
28. Lowe, *Inferno,* 6–12.
29. Enoch, *Memoirs,* 49–50; Jaeger, "Kurt Enoch," A289, A292; Enoch, *Memoirs,* 53–54.
30. Graham, "Kurt Enoch: Paperback Pioneer," 44; Enoch, *Memoirs,* 12–15.
31. Enoch, *Memoirs,* 24, 32–33.
32. Lowe, *Inferno,* 16–17; Enoch, *Memoirs,* 46.
33. Enoch, *Memoirs,* 48–49, 59; Ruth Gruenthal, Interview, 10 August 2009, Westport, Connecticut.
34. Tooze, *Wages of Destruction,* 318.
35. Karl Wiegand, quoted in Nagorski, *Hitlerland,* 71; Kershaw, *Hitler: 1889–1936,* 333; Nagorski, *Hitlerland,* 71.
36. Tooze, *Wages of Destruction,* 17–19; Enoch, *Memoirs,* 57.
37. Ebi, "Devisenrecht und Außenhandel," 183–86; Radio von Radiis, *Deutsche Aussenhandelspolitik,* 10; Ebi, *Export um jeden Preis,* 19–21; Tooze, *Wages of Destruction,* 20.
38. C. Kearton [Curtis Brown Ltd.] to Messrs The Hogarth Press, n. d. [shortly before 28.8.31], Hogarth Press 219, UR; Wilhelm Lucke, Aktennotiz, 19 March 1938, 20133, File 1363, SAL; John Holroyd-Reece to Hans Mardersteig, 27 September 1931, Archivio storico Arnoldo Mondadori editore, Arnoldo Mondadori, John Holroyd-Reece File, FM.
39. Ruth Gruenthal, Interview, 10 August 2009; Lowe, *Inferno,* 19–22; Enoch, *Memoirs,* 59.
40. Enoch, *Memoirs,* 60. Enoch became Albatross's sole client, purchasing its books and selling them to distributors and booksellers for a percentage of sales.
41. Mühlberger, *Hitler's Voice,* 31–32; Evans, *The Third Reich in Power,* 14; Kershaw, *Hitler: 1889–1936,* 355; Lowe, *Inferno,* 22–23.

CHAPTER TWO. SPIES FOR ENGLAND

1. [Kurt] Gundermann, "Leseland: Handbuch für Reisende," *Die literarische Welt* 7, no. 49 (4 December 1931): front cover.
2. "Trip to England and America," *Die literarische Welt,* 7, no. 49 (4 December 1931):

16; Dr. Hans Otto, "Rundschreiben," 11 December 1931, 21056, File 17, SAL.

3. William A. Bradley to Sinclair Lewis, 4 October 1933, William A. Bradley Literary Agency, Sinclair Lewis, File 37.5, HRC; Dr. Franz Sester to Hans Otto, 14 December and 19 December, 1931, 21056, File 17, SAL.
4. Hans Otto, "Rundschreiben," 11 December 1931, 21056, File 17, SAL.
5. Hans Otto to Dr. Franz Sester, 10 December 1931, 21056, File 17, SAL; "In eigener Sache!" *Börsenblatt für den Deutschen Buchhandel,* 12 December 1931, 7329.
6. "In eigener Sache!" *Börsenblatt für den Deutschen Buchhandel,* 29 December 1931, 7495.
7. Rainer Hering, "Academics and Radical Nationalism: The Pan-German League in Hamburg and the German Reich," Jones, "Introduction," both in Jones, *The German Right in the Weimar Republic,* 108–33, 1–9, quotation on p. 1; Among the most powerful voices in this array were the Stahlhelm, a paramilitary veterans organization, half a million strong, which promoted military training as the means to a stronger national community; the Pan-German League, whose fifty thousand members, many from the educated elite, sought to expand the German empire and suppress the infiltration of foreign ideas and races; and the German National People's Party, the most prominent conservative nationalist party until the rise of the NSDAP, which increasingly wielded anti-Semitic and "völkisch" rhetoric in the 1920s to consolidate its base. See Jackisch, *The Pan-German League;* Eley and Palmowski, eds., *Citizenship and National Identity;* Weitz, *Weimar Germany.*
8. Brian Crim, "Weimar's 'Burning Question': Situational Anti-Semitism and the German Combat Leagues, 1918–1933," in Jones, *The German Right in the Weimar Republic,* 194–219; Hering, "Academics and Radical Nationalism," 114.
9. "Wer English liesst, kauft Tauchnitz!" *Der Querschnitt* 12, no. 2 (February 1932): 149; Hans Otto, "Rundschreiben," 4 November 1931, Dr. Franz Sester to Otto, December 13, 1931, both 21056, File 17, SAL.
10. Hans Otto to Walter Jäh, circa 10 February 1932, Jäh to Otto, 16 February 1932, 21056, both File 17, SAL.
11. Hans Otto to Herr Dr. Kärcher et al., 13 February 1932, Otto to Tauchnitz Vorstand, 18 February 1932, both 21056, File 17, SAL.
12. Hans Otto to Herr Braune, March 18, 1932, Otto, "Feststellung über die Nationalität des Herrn Johann Hermann Riess," n.d., both 21056, File 16, SAL.
13. Hans Otto, "Rundschreiben," March 18, 1932, Otto to Dr. Karl Silex, 24 March 1932, Otto to Minckwitz, 11 April 1932, all 21056, File 16, SAL.
14. Hans Otto to the German Embassy in Paris, n.d. [probably April 1932], 21056, File 16, SAL; John Holroyd-Reece Citizenship Announcement, *London Gazette* (8 August 1919): 10107; Divorce—Petition, in *Times Law Reports,* ed. J. Ferguson Walker, vol. 41, 7 November 1924 (London: G.E. Wright, 1924), 24; Otto to Tauchnitz Board, 28 January 1932, 21056, File 17, SAL.

15. Pressler, "Tauchnitz und Albatross," A7; Watson, "More Sketches from Memory," 2559. Hans Schmoller also called Holroyd-Reece "brilliant and incorrigibly ambiguous," in Hans Schmoller, *Two Titans: Mardersteig and Tschichold, a Study in Contrasts* (New York: The Typophiles, 1990), 44; Metropolitan Police, 6 May 1919, HO 144/1411/275893, NAK. His guardian was Percy Ingham, the director of the London School of Dalcroze Eurhythmics.
16. K. A. Woodward, Letter, 19 June 1916, G. F. Fisher, Repton Headmaster, Letter, 13 June 1916, Percy Broadbent Ingham, Letter, 1 April 1919, all HO 144/1411/275893, NAK.
17. Anonymous handwritten note, n.d., John Holroyd-Reece to Mr. Scott, 1 May 1919, both HO 144/1411/275893, File 21, NAK.
18. Fiona Brewster, Family Album, FVB.
19. Hans Otto to the German Embassy in Paris, n.d. [probably April 1932], 21056, File 16, SAL
20. Mr. Frentzel to Hans Otto, 7 April 1932, 21056, File 16, SAL.
21. Michael S. Howard, *Jonathan Cape: Publisher* (London: Jonathan Cape, 1971), 104–7; John Holroyd-Reece to Richard Aldington, 18 November 1932, Richard Aldington Papers, Collection 68, Box 1, Folder 1, SIUC.
22. Scc Ford and Balmès, *Published in Paris.*
23. "The Modern Continental Library," n.d. 20206, File 1681, SAL; Dr. Franz Sester to Hans Otto, 19 December 1931, 21056, File 17, SAL.
24. Van der Weel, "The Rise of the English Book," 280–81; A. P. R. Howatt with H. G. Widdowson, *A History of English Language Teaching* (Oxford: Oxford University Press, 2004), 232–41.
25. Enoch, *Memoirs,* 60–61;"Tauchnitz Has a Rival," 1643–44.
26. Kingsford, *The Publishers Association,* 119; Abel Chevalley, *The Modern English Novel,* trans. Ben Ray Redman (New York: Knopf, 1925), p. xi. Originally published as *Le Roman anglais de notre temps* (London: H. Milford, 1921); Bernhard Fehr, *Die englische Literatur des 19. und 20. Jahrhunderts* (Berlin: Akademische Verlagsgesellschaft, 1923), and *Die englische Literatur der Gegenwart und die Kulturfragen Unserer Zeit* (Leipzig: Bernhard Tauchnitz, 1933); *Kleiner Führer.*
27. Fritz Schlawe, *Literarische Zeitschriften: 1910–1933* (Stuttgart: J. B. Metzlersche Verlagsbuchhandlung, 1973), 20, 59; Schlösser, *Die englische Literatur in Deutschland,* 2–3, 166–67. Schlösser's numbers include first and new editions, and new print runs.
28. Fouché, "L'édition française depuis 1945," 216; Fitch, *Sylvia Beach and the Lost Generation,* 401–2; Beach, *Shakespeare and Company,* 51, Beach, Notebook 1935–1941, Sylvia Beach Papers C0108, Box 68, PUA; Fitch, *Sylvia Beach and the Lost Generation,* 401–2.
29. "Tauchnitz Has a Rival," 1643–44.

30. John Holroyd-Reece to Arnoldo Mondadori, 30 March 1932, Archivio storico Arnoldo Mondadori editore, Arnoldo Mondadori, Holroyd-Reece File, FM; "The Modern Continental Library," n.d. 20206, File 1681, SAL; Rundle, "Translation in Fascist Italy," 16–17. Holroyd-Reece did, indeed, "plumb" the Italian market, especially through his partnership with Mondadori, whom Rundle describes as "one of the most enterprising publishers of translations" in 1930s Italy (20). Holroyd-Reece agreed to vet novels and pass the cream of the crop on to Mondadori for translation into Italian (John Holroyd-Reece to William A. Bradley, "Memorandum: Albatross Activities in France," 14 September 1937, William A. Bradley Agency, Series II: Publisher Correspondence, File 129.9 Albatross, HRC).
31. John Holroyd-Reece to Laurence Pollinger, 11 March 1932, D. H. Lawrence Collection, Series IV: Curtis Brown, Ltd., Folder 37.1, HRC; Letter from C. Kearton [Curtis Brown Ltd.] to Joseph Hergesheimer, 16 June 1931, Alfred A. Knopf Inc. Records, 1873–1996, Series IVA: Author Files, Joseph Hergesheimer, Folder 715.6, HRC. So in league were Brown and Albatross that in January 1933 Brown's French agent moved into the Albatross office on the rue Boulard, sharing space at Albatross's Parisian addresses until the war broke out. See Curtis Brown, Ltd., Change of Address Card, William A. Bradley Literary Agency Records, Curtis Brown Correspondence, File 223.5, Margareta Scialtiel, HRC.
32. Taylor, *Projection of Britain,* 127–28.
33. Taylor, *British Propaganda,* 6–8; Taylor, *Projection of Britain,* 129–32; Norton quoted in Taylor, *Projection of Britain,* 138; Taylor, Projection of Britain, 143–45, 151.
34. Taylor, *Projection of Britain,* 144, 153.
35. Ibid., 141–42; John Holroyd-Reece to Hans Mardersteig, 27 September 1931, Archivio storico Arnoldo Mondadori editore, Arnoldo Mondadori, Holroyd-Reece File, FM.
36. Fiona Brewster, Interview, 3 May 2013, Le Breuil-Rouillac, France; Alan Marshall, "Marius Audin, Stanley Morison et la publication des *Livrets typographiques* et de la *Bibliographie des De Tournes,*" *Bulletin du bibliophile* 2 (November 1994), reprinted by the Musée de l'Imprimerie Lyon at http://www.imprimerie.lyon.fr/imprimerie/sections/fr/documentation/fonds/audin/?aindex=2#not43; Stanley Morison to Jan van Krimpen, 20 February 1931, quoted in Barker, *Stanley Morison,* 319.
37. Taylor, *Projection of England,* 164–65. Taylor lists British Council funding as follows: January 1935, £5,000; 1936–37, £15,000; 1937–38, £30,000; 38–39 to £110,000.
38. Contract between Les Éditions Pégase, Paris (The Pegasus Press), and the Albatross Verlag, Hamburg, 15 November 1931, 20206, File 1681, SAL. As security, Pegasus held a stock of Albatross books in Paris. For its efforts, Pegasus demanded high fees: the equivalent of 6,000 RM or 25 percent of sales, plus a potential 10

percent surcharge. To ensure fluid cooperation, Wegner, technically employed by Pegasus, also signed as managing director for Albatross in Germany.

39. Pressler, "Tauchnitz und Albatross," A4; for Holroyd-Reece's status in the Publishing Holding Company, see Dr. Willy Hoffman, Gutachten, 30 June 1941, 20206, File 1681, SAL; Les éditions du Pégase [list of shareholders], n.d. [received 21 February 1941], R87/1192, BAL; Oskar Möhring to Militärbefehlshaber in Frankreich, Verwaltungsstab Abteilung Wi. I/3, 7 August 1942, AJ 40/701, ANF. The list of Pegasus shareholders indicates that Holroyd-Reece owned 445,000 francs of the 700,000 francs of shares. Möhring, appointed wartime custodian for Pegasus, clarified that of the 374 shares at 1,000 francs and the 3,260 shares at 100 francs, Holroyd-Reece owned 1,848 shares, with the next largest shareholder owning only 620.

40. Fiona Brewster, Family Album, FVB; Stanley Morison to Jan van Krimpen, 20 February 1931, quoted in Barker, *Stanley Morison,* 319.

CHAPTER THREE. WINNING THE CONTINENT

1. Advertisement: "The Albatross Modern Continental Library," *Börsenblatt für den Deutschen Buchhandel,* 1 March 1932, n.p.

2. Isabelle Olivero, *L'Invention de la collection: de la diffusion de la littérature et des savoirs à la formation du citoyen au XIXe siècle* (Paris: Éditions de L'Imec, 1999), 224; Albert Boni and Horace Liveright's Modern Library, founded in 1917 in New York, and Chatto and Windus's Phoenix Library in 1920s England, are two examples of hardcover series with which Albatross would have been in competition. See Bourdieu, *Rules of Art,* 148, for the factors delimiting the literary field.

3. "The Modern Continental Library," n.d., 20206, File 1681, SAL; Beach, *Shakespeare and Company,* 21; Max Meyerfeld, "Enter D. H. Lawrence," *Das literarische Echo* 25 (1923): 581–84, quote on 581; James Joyce to Harriet Shaw Weaver, 14 August 1927, quoted in Richard Ellmann, ed. *Selected Letters of James Joyce* (New York: Viking, 1978), 327 (Wegner has been credited with discovering the Joyce volume, but Curt Otto approved it in 1928. Yet in 1930 alone, Wegner introduced twenty-one new authors for Tauchnitz, pushing far beyond its previous average of four per year. Schlösser, *Die englische Literatur in Deutschland,* 34); Charles Prentice to Richard Aldington, 7 July 1931, Richard Aldington Papers 68, Box 6, Folder 3, SIUC.

4. Beach, *Shakespeare and Company,* 21; Fouché, "L'édition littéraire, 1914–1950," 209; Beach, Notebook: 1932, n.p., C0108 Sylvia Beach Papers, Box 25, PUA. The cost for German books in the category for poetry and fiction ranged from 2.56 RM in 1933 to 2.71 in 1935; see Horst Kliemann, "Die Welt des Buchhandels," 176. "Die

neuen Bücher aus dem Insel Verlag," in *Das Inselschiff,* Christmas 1933. This catalogue lists titles from 1932, bound in linen: Huxley's *Brave New World* for 6 RM, Woolf's *To the Lighthouse* for 7 RM, and Lawrence's *Sons and Lovers* and *The Rainbow* for 8 RM and 6 RM, respectively. "Nun Hören Sie den Rat . . . ," *Die literarische Welt* 49 (25 November 1932): 1.

5. "Tauchnitz Has a Rival," 1645.
6. Fiona Brewster, Interview, 13 December 2013, Le Breuil-Rouillac, France; Lady Elisabeth Schiemann (stepdaughter of Holroyd-Reece), Telephone Interview, 22 September 2013.
7. "Tauchnitz has a Rival," 1645.
8. Max Christian Wegner to Annemarie Wegner, 11 March 1932, MW.
9. Max Christian Wegner to Annemarie Wegner, 12 March 1932, MW; Matthias Wegner, Interview, 3 October 2009, Hamburg, Germany.
10. Max Christian Wegner to Annemarie Wegner, 13 July 1932, MW.
11. Paul Léon to James Joyce, 14 July 1932 and 28 September 1932, Joyce to Léon 25 September 1932, all James Joyce–Paul Léon Papers, 1930–40, NLI; Max Christian Wegner to Annemarie Wegner, 19 October 1932, MW; the Odyssey Press printed only two titles, *Ulysses* and D. H. Lawrence's *Lady Chatterley's Lover.* See also McCleery, "The Reputation of the 1932 Odyssey Press Edition of *Ulysses,*"; and Luca Crispi, "*Ulysses* in the Marketplace: 1932," *Joyce Studies Annual* (2012): 29–65. The Odyssey Press editions sold for 5.6 RM (two volumes in paper boards) and 9 RM (one volume cloth-bound edition on India paper).
12. Max Christian Wegner to Annemarie Wegner, 19 October 1932, Max Christian Wegner to Annemarie Wegner, 22 May 1932, both in MW. On Holroyd-Reece and Wegner's different strengths, see McCleery, "Tauchnitz and Albatross."
13. "Tauchnitz Marks 100th Year," 2318; see Fischer and Füssel, eds., *Geschichte des deutschen Buchhandels,* 300, on the governmental emergency declaration of 8 December 1931 that ordered publishers to reduce prices of German-produced books by 10 percent as of 1 January 1932 to help stimulate the economy; Jean-Louis Bricaire [on behalf of John Holroyd-Reece] to Arnoldo Mondadori, 5 March 1932, Archivio storico Arnoldo Mondadori editore, Arnoldo Mondadori, Holroyd-Reece File, FM; Holroyd-Reece's correspondence to Mondadori makes it seem he would have been willing to keep Mondadori as printer while Wegner insisted on switching to a German printer. However, I am not convinced by Holroyd-Reece, since he later vociferously fought to keep Albatross books in Germany.
14. John Holroyd-Reece to Arnoldo Mondadori, 30 March 1932, Holroyd-Reece, Telegram to Mondadori, 6 May 1932, Mondadori, Telegraph to Holroyd-Reece, 28 May 1932, all in Archivio storico Arnoldo Mondadori editore, Arnoldo Mondadori, Holroyd-Reece File, FM. Thanks to Joachim Gerdes for the translations.

15. Barbian, *Literaturpolitik im Dritten Reich,* 40.
16. "L'Albatross Continental Library concurrente della Tauchnitz," *Avvisatore settimanale* (5 June 1932): 699.
17. "Goede en goedkoope Engelsche boeken," *Het Vaderland,* 17 March 1932, 9.
18. "The Albatross Modern Continental Library," *Allgemeen Handelsblad,* 12 April 1932, 5; Fritz Bieber, "Albatross," *Die literarische Welt* 8, no. 17 (22 April 1932): 6.
19. Rudolf Imelman, "Albatroß," *Frankfurter Zeitung,* 18 September 1932, 6.
20. K.B. "Das englische Buch auf dem Kontinent," *Die literarische Welt* 36–37 (2 September 1932): 9.
21. "Rule Britannia!" *Die literarische Welt* 49 (25 November 1932): 15–16; Wilhelm Lucke, Report of 19 March 1938, 21033, File 1363, SAL.
22. John Holroyd-Reece to Laurence Pollinger, 11 January 1933, Pollinger to Max Christian Wegner, 26 January 1933, both D. H. Lawrence Collection, Series IV: Curtis Brown, Ltd., Folder 37.4, HRC.

CHAPTER FOUR. UN-GERMAN LITERATURE

1. Enoch, *Memoirs,* 63–64.
2. Evans, *Third Reich in Power,* 158; Barbian, *The Politics of Literature,* 13; Adam, *Lesen unter Hitler,* 28; Lowe, *Inferno,* 24.
3. "Albatross Modern Continental Library," *Börsenblatt für den Deutschen Buchhandel,* 1 March 1933, 154.
4. Kershaw, *Hitler, 1889–1936,* 460–68; Lowe, *Inferno,* 24; Barbian, *Literaturpolitik im NS-Staat,* 81–83; Adam, *Lesen unter Hitler,* 19.
5. Max Christian Wegner to Annemarie Wegner, 1 April 1933, MW.
6. Barkai, *From Boycott to Annihilation,* 25–31; Bajohr, *"Aryanisation" in Hamburg,* 58–69; "EN" file, SWA; Enoch, *Memoirs,* 70; Charles Enoch, Interview, 11 July 2011, Washington, D.C.; Charles Enoch, Email to author, 10 October 2014.
7. Enoch, *Memoirs,* 66.
8. Max Christian Wegner to Annemarie Wegner, 31 March and 4 April 1933, MW.
9. Max Christian Wegner to Annemarie Wegner, 31 March 1933, MW.
10. Max Christian Wegner to Annemarie Wegner 4 April 1933, MW.
11. Rosamond Lehmann, *The Swan in the Evening: Fragments of an Inner Life* (New York: Open Road Media, 2015), 59.
12. "Topics of the Times," *New York Times,* 20 December 1933, 20, quoted in Mark Schorer, *Sinclair Lewis* (New York: McGraw Hill, 1961), 592.
13. Dorothy Thompson, *I Saw Hitler!* (New York: Farrar and Rinehart, 1932), 13–14; "Hitler Power Seen in Middle Class," *New York Times,* 12 May 1933, 12.
14. Ann Watkins to A. C. Peters, 28 July 1931, YCAL MSS 268 Sinclair Lewis, Box 50,

Folder 642, BL; "New Lewis Novel Published Today: 'Ann Vickers,'" *New York Times,* 25 January 1933, 11.

15. Sinclair Lewis, *Ann Vickers* (New York: Doubleday Doran, 1933). Dorothy Thompson Diary Entry, 5 January 1933, quoted in Vincent Sheean, *Dorothy and Red* (Boston: Houghton Mifflin, 1963), 225.
16. Anne Springer, *The American Novel in Germany* (Hamburg: Cram/de Gruyter, 1960). One German book club chose *Main Street* as an early selection in 1922; Kurt Wolff's Transmare Verlag produced *Babbitt* in a print run of twenty thousand copies—relatively large for translations; and between 1928 and 1931, Ernst Rowohlt published *Elmer Gantry, Mantrap, The Man Who Knew Coolidge,* and *Dodsworth* in runs of eleven thousand each. William A. Bradley to Sinclair Lewis, 20 September 1932, William A. Bradley Literary Agency, Sinclair Lewis, File 37.4, HRC; Daniel Longwell to Lewis, 27 December 1932, YCAL MSS 268 Sinclair Lewis, Box 46, Folder 484, Doubleday & Doran, BL; "Book Notes," *New York Times,* 14 February 1933, 13; Bradley to Lewis, 19 August 1933, William A. Bradley Literary Agency Collection, Sinclair Lewis, File 37.5, HRC.
17. Dorothy Thompson to Sinclair Lewis, 15 March 1933, quoted in Sanders, *Dorothy Thompson,* 187.
18. Barbian, *Literaturpolitik im NS-Staat,* 29.
19. Ibid., 31–37; Dahm, *Das jüdische Buch,* 27–28; Lowe, *Inferno,* 24.
20. Dorothy Thompson to Sinclair Lewis, 13 March 1933, quoted in Sanders, *Dorothy Thompson,* 185.
21. *Völkische Beobachter,* 14 April 1933; Barbian, *Literaturpolitik im NS-Staat,* 39–41; Dahm, *Das jüdische Buch,* 18.
22. Frederick T. Birchall, "Nazi Book-Burning Fails to Stir Berlin," *New York Times,* 11 May 1933, 1; for a transcript of Joseph Goebbels's speech of 10 May 1933, as printed in the *Völkische Beobachter* of 12 May 1933, also translated into English, see the University of Arizona Library's web exhibit, "Goebbels's Speech," Speeches, May 10, 1933, at http://www.library.arizona.edu/exhibits/burnedbooks/goebbels.htm.
23. Birchall, "Nazi Book-Burning Fails to Stir Berlin," 1.
24. Goebbels's Speech to Buchkantate, *Börsenblatt der deutschen Buchhandel,* 16 May 1933, 353–56, quoted in Barbian, *Literaturpolitik im NS-Staat,* 44; Dahm, *Das jüdische Buch,* 28–29. The *Börsenblatt* had aligned itself with the regime by this point, so it was biased in Goebbels's favor; see Wolfgang Hermann, "Prinzipielles zur Säuberung der öffentlichen Büchereien," *Börsenblatt für den Deutschen Buchhandel,* 16 May 1933, 356, quoted in Dahm, *Das jüdische Buch,* 18; List of Authors, *Börsenblatt der deutschen Buchhandel,* 13 May 1933, 1, quoted in Barbian, *The Politics of Literature,* 25. The listed authors were Lion Feuchtwanger, Ernst Glaeser,

Arthur Holitscher, Alfred Kerr, Egon Erwin Kisch, Emil Ludwig, Heinrich Mann, Ernst Ottwalt, Theodor Plivier, Erich Maria Remarque, Kurt Tucholsky, and Arnold Zweig.

25. Sheean, *Dorothy and Red,* 263; "Nazis Pile Books for Bonfires Today," *New York Times,* 10 May 1933, 1; Sinclair Lewis, "Let America Honor Books Nazis Burn," *Jewish Telegraphic Agency,* 14 May 1933.
26. Sinclair Lewis to Ernst Rowohlt, 2 November 1933, YCAL MSS 268 Sinclair Lewis, Box 48, Folder 598, BL.
27. Ernst Rowohlt to Lewis, 19 October 1933, YCAL MSS 268 Sinclair Lewis, Box 48, Folder 598, BL. Rowohlt included the article "Literarische Emigrantenzeitschriften" from *Börsenblatt für den Deutschen Buchhandel,* 10 October 1933.
28. Sinclair Lewis to Ernst Rowohlt, 2 November 1933, YCAL MSS 268 Sinclair Lewis, Box 48, Folder 598, BL; Lewis to William A. Bradley, 4 November 1933, William A. Bradley Literary Agency, Sinclair Lewis, File 37.5, HRC.
29. Max Christian Wegner to William A. Bradley, 6 October 1933, William A. Bradley Literary Agency, File 129.9 The Albatross, Bradley to Sinclair Lewis, 14 November 1933, Lewis to Bradley, 21 December 1933, William A. Bradley Literary Agency, Sinclair Lewis, File 37.5, all HRC.
30. Albatross royalty reports of 21 September 1933, 23 March 1934, 30 July 1934, 27 September 1934, 31 December 1934, 16 May 1935, 30 August 1935, all William A. Bradley Literary Agency, Sinclair Lewis, Files 37.5–37.6, HRC.
31. Enoch, *Memoirs,* 65–67, 70–71.
32. Belke and Zeller, eds., *In den Katakomben,* 66; Barbian, *The Politics of Literature,* 26–27.
33. Barbian, *Literaturpolitik im NS-Staat,* 100–105; Dahm, *Das jüdische Buch,* 29–32; Steinweis, *Art, Ideology and Economics,* 32–39.
34. Enoch, *Memoirs,* 62; John Holroyd-Reece to C. D. Medley, n.d. [but probably September 1943], David Lloyd Agency for Pearl Buck (C0060), Box 28, File 21, PUA; Wilhelm Lucke, Aktennotiz, 19 March 1938, 21033, File 1363, SAL.

CHAPTER FIVE. MADE IN BRITAIN?

1. Ezra Pound to Olga Rudge, 24 September 1933, Olga Rudge Papers, YCAL MSS 54, Box 114, Folder 358, BL; Advertisement for *The Albatross Book of Living Verse, Albatross Almanac 1935* (Hamburg: Albatross, 1934), 172; Max Christian Wegner to Pound, 8 November 1932, Box 23, Folder 997, W. Keller to Pound, 5 March 1931, Box 51, Folder 2315, Pound to T. C. Wilson, 30 October 1933 and 3 December 1933, Box 23, Folder 997, all Ezra Pound Papers, Series I–IV, YCAL MSS 43, BL.
2. Ezra Pound to John Holroyd-Reece, 13 January 1934, quoted in Holroyd-Reece to Pound, March 4, 1934, Ezra Pound Papers, Series I–IV, YCAL MSS 43 Box 23,

Folder 997, BL; Pound to Ford Madox Ford, 11 October 1933, in *Pound/Ford: The Story of a Literary Friendship* (New York: New Directions, 1971), 129. See also the correspondence between Pound and former Tauchnitz director Curt Otto from 1924, for Pound's invective against Tauchnitz's editorial decisions: Curt Otto to Pound, 11 December 1924, Ezra Pound Papers, YCAL MSS 43, Box 51, Folder 2315 Bernhard Tauchnitz, BL.

3. John Holroyd-Reece to Ezra Pound, 18 September 1933, Holroyd-Reece to Pound, 27 December 1933, both Ezra Pound Papers, Series I–IV, YCAL MSS 43, Box 23, Folder 997, BL.
4. John Holroyd-Reece to Ezra Pound, 4 March 1934, Ezra Pound Papers, Series I–IV, YCAL MSS 43, Box 23, Folder 997, BL.
5. Alma Louise Olsen, "Scandinavia Considers Some New Regimes," *New York Times,* 6 August 1933, BR8; "Books of the Year: Poetry in 1933," *The Observer,* 31 December 1933, 4.
6. "The Albatross: An English Tauchnitz," *Times* (London), 1 March 1932, 10; Henryk Fleischer, "Why Tauchnitz?" *The Observer,* 23 July 1933, 23.
7. "British Books Abroad," *Publisher and Bookseller,* 13 May 1932, 953–54, 953.
8. Kingsford, *The Publishers Association* 48, 119–20; Thomas Lauffer, Bookseller, Budapest, to Messrs. Chatto & Windus, 25 January 1932, Buchhandlung Karl Buchhholz, Berlin, to Messrs. Chatto & Windus, 26 January 1932, both CW 48/11, RHGA.
9. "Continental Editions. Views of the Publishers' Association." *The Author* 43, no. 3 (Spring 1933): 80–82; Harold Raymond to Laurence Pollinger, 17 November 1931, AUC 27/8 Curtis Brown, UR.
10. Harold Raymond to K. B. Potter, 1 March 1932, CW 48/11, RHGA.
11. Paul Léon to Ralph Pinker, 8 December 1933 and 3 January 1934, James Joyce Collection, Gen MSS 112, Box 2, Folders 72–73, BL. Léon had granted Albatross the right of first refusal but created a bidding war, hoping another British publisher would outbid Albatross.
12. Sinclair Lewis to William A. Bradley, 27 June 1934, William A. Bradley Literary Agency, Series I: Author Correspondence, Sinclair Lewis, File 37.5, HRC; Jonathan Cape to Ralph Pinker, 13 December 1933, Pinker Files as agent for James Joyce, the Henry W. and Albert A. Berg Collection of English and American Literature, the New York Public Library, Astor, Lenox and Tilden Foundations, New York.
13. "The Albatross" Printed Statement, n.d. but 1945 or 1946, sent by Herberth Herlitschka to Isabel Wilder, 14 May 1946, YCAL MSS 108 Thornton Wilder, Box 13, Folder 302 Albatross, BL; Sinclair Lewis to William A. Bradley, 2 August 1933, William A. Bradley Collection, Sinclair Lewis, File 37.5, HRC.
14. "The Albatross: British Authors on the Continent," *The Observer,* 31 December 1933, 12.

15. Evidence suggests that Holroyd-Reece had developed this plan by March 1932. See CW 100/16, RHGA.
16. "The Albatross: British Authors on the Continent," 12.
17. Arthur Chichester, "Letters to the Editor: Continental Editions," *The Author* 44 (Autumn 1933): 21–22, 21.
18. John Holroyd-Reece to Ezra Pound, 11 January 1934, Ezra Pound Papers, Series I–IV, YCAL MSS 43, Box 23, Folder 997, BL.
19. Advertisement: "The Albatross Crime Club," *Börsenblatt für den Deutschen Buchhandel,* 29 March 1933, 21056, File 21, SAL.
20. Sturge, "Flight from the Programme," 58; Neil Clark, *Stranger Than Fiction: The Life of Edgar Wallace* (London: History Press, 2014), 27; Schlösser, *Die englische Literatur in Deutschland,* 174–76; Sturge, "Flight from the Programme," 58.
21. Sturge, "Flight from the Programme," 77–78.

CHAPTER SIX. THE SCISSORS IN THEIR HEADS

1. Dahm, *Das jüdische Buch,* 26; Maria Huxley to Roy Fenton, 1 July 1933, quoted in Huxley, *Letters,* 371; Huxley to Naomi Mitchison, 13 August 1933, quoted in Huxley, *Letters,* 372–73.
2. *The Albatross Almanac, 1933* (Hamburg: Albatross, 1932). This volume was prepared in 1932, to advertise Albatross authors before Christmas, yet remained on sale throughout 1933.
3. Bahr, "Nazi Cultural Politics," 14–17.
4. Barbian, *Literaturpolitik im NS-Staat,* 81–83, 250–54; Adam, *Lesen unter Hitler,* 15–28; Cuomo, *National Socialist Cultural Policy;* Leonidas Hill, "The Nazi Attack on 'Un-German' Literature: 1933–1945," in Rose, *The Holocaust and the Book,* 12; Dahm, *Das jüdische Buch,* 6; Bahr, "Nazi Cultural Politics," 13. Bahr argues that the polycratic governance that defined the Nazi bureaucracy was especially evident in the cultural realm. The Austrian journalist Walter Petwaidic is credited with the phrase "authoritarian anarchy" to describe how different centers of power grew up around Hitler, competing for his attention. See Martin Kitchen, *Nazi Germany at War* (London: Longmans, 1995), 4. See also Chapter 9, below, for this term's place in a historiographic debate about Hitler's power.
5. Barbian, *The Politics of Literature,* 317; Adam, *Lesen unter Hitler,* 33–36; Sturge, "Flight from the Programme," 53–59; see also Barbian, "Die doppelte Indizierung," in its entirety.
6. Circulars in R55/684, BAL, quoted in Barbian, *The Politics of Literature,* 29–30.
7. Herberth Herlitschka to Messrs. J. B. Pinker and Sons, 10 January 1934, Aldous Huxley Papers M0107, Box 1, Folder 8, SU; Sturge, "Flight from the Programme," 55.

8. Hall, *Der Paul Zsolnay Verlag,* 262. See especially pages 254–80 for marvelous case studies of German publishers who paid a price for publishing Anglo-American books in translation. Barbian, *Literaturpolitik im NS-Staat,* 408.
9. Sturge, "Flight from the Programme," 61; Hall, *Der Paul Zsolnay Verlag,* 205.
10. Herberth Herlitschka to Messrs. J. B. Pinker and Sons, 10 January 1934, Aldous Huxley Papers M0107, Box 1, Folder 8, SU; see also Lewis, *Penguin Special,* 78, which references the British publisher Stanley Unwin's remark that British authors "resented having to sign a form declaring that they were of suitably Aryan descent."
11. Robert Graves to J. B. Pinker, 4 March 1934, J. B. Pinker and Sons, Robert Graves File, the Henry W. and Albert A. Berg Collection of English and American Literature, The New York Public Library, Astor, Lenox and Tilden Foundations, New York; Herberth Herlitschka to J. B. Pinker and Sons, 14 May 1934, Katherine Mansfield Papers Additions, NL.
12. Aldous Huxley to Robert Nichols, 9 October 1933, in Huxley, *Letters,* 374.
13. Herberth Herlitschka to J. B. Pinker and Sons, 2 August 1934, Aldous Huxley Papers M0107, Box 1, Folder 6, SU.
14. Huxley, *Beyond the Mexique Bay* (New York: Vintage, 1960), 146. All passages from the 1934 original are taken from this reprint.
15. Ibid., 85, 87.
16. Ibid., 149–50.
17. McCleery, "Tauchnitz and Albatross," 307–8. These are all Tauchnitz books published post-1934, after Albatross took over editorial control of Tauchnitz.
18. Huxley, *Beyond the Mexique Bay* (Hamburg: Albatross Verlag, 1935), 10.
19. Schlösser, *Die englische Literatur in Deutschland,* 33–34.
20. Linthout, *Das Buch in der Nationalsozialistischenpolitik,* especially 345–84.
21. The accepted shorthand for this debate is the "primacy of politics" versus the "primacy of economics." The British Marxist historian Timothy Mason is credited with launching the debate by arguing that Nazi political actors outweighed German industrialists and the economic elite in driving their agendas home. See Mason, *Nazism, Fascism and the Working Class,* and for the "primacy of economics," see Tooze, *Wages of Destruction.* For a nuanced overview of both sides, see Ian Kershaw, "Politics and Economics in the Nazi State," in his *The Nazi Dictatorship,* 40–58. "The Albatross" Printed Statement, n.d. but 1945 or 1946, sent by Herberth Herlitschka to Isabel Wilder, 14 May 1946, YCAL MSS 108 Thornton Wilder, Box 13, Folder 302 Albatross, BL.
22. Ebi, *Export um jeden Preis,* 24; Tooze, *Wages of Destruction,* 20–27, 50–51; Radio von Radiis, *Deutsche Aussenhandelspolitik,* 13.
23. Tooze, *Wages of Destruction,* 27, 69–72; Ebi, *Export um jeden Preis,* 24; Radio von Radiis, *Deutsche Aussenhandelspolitik,* 13; Tooze, *Wages of Destruction,* 69.

24. Darnton, *Censors at Work,* 15; Kater, *Different Drummers,* 49; Nicholas, *The Rape of Europa,* 23–25. See also Ebi, "Devisenrecht und Außenhandel," 185–86, for an explanation of why exporters like Albatross held a critical financial advantage over most other German firms. In short, by mid-1934, to keep foreign currency outlays as low as possible, the regime granted German importers only 10 percent of their original foreign currency needs from 1931. This severely limited their purchasing power of raw materials and their ability to produce goods. In contrast, the regime readily approved Albatross's monthly foreign currency transfers to fund its expenses abroad.
25. On the fate of literary modernism in Nazi Germany, see Sturge, "Flight from the Programme," 59.

CHAPTER SEVEN. A TALE OF TWO PUBLISHERS

1. Kershaw, *Hitler, 1889–1936,* 512–17; Evans, *The Third Reich in Power,* 31–33.
2. Adolf Hitler, Speech to Reichstag on 13 July 1934, quoted in Kershaw, *Hitler: 1889–1936,* 519; "Points in Hitler's Speech," *New York Times,* 15 July 1934, 14.
3. Woolf, *The Diary of Virginia Woolf,* vol. 4, 223.
4. Richard Aldington to Charles Prentice, 4 September 1934, Ralph Pinker Collection of Richard Aldington Papers: Collection 72, File 20, SIUC; Aldous Huxley to Julian Huxley, 22 July 1934, Aldous Huxley to Mr. Sagar, 12 September 1934, both in Huxley, *Letters,* 383.
5. Richard Aldington to Charles Prentice, 4 September 1934, Ralph Pinker Collection of Richard Aldington Papers: Collection 72, File 20, SIUC; John Holroyd-Reece, "Note for the Information of British Albatross and Tauchnitz Authors," January 1940, David Lloyd Agency for Pearl Buck (C0060), Box 28, Folder 19, PUA.
6. "Tauchnitz Changes Hands: Bought by a Leipzig Firm. A Grateful Public," *The Observer,* 7 October 1934; Pressler, "Tauchnitz und Albatross," A5.
7. Wilhelm Lucke, Aktennotiz, 19 March 1938; Reichsbankoberinspektor [probably Heppner, but signature illegible], Albatross-und-Tauchnitz Verlag bezw. Oscar Brandstetter u. Dr. Enoch, Paris, 16 November 1931, both 21033, File 1363, SAL. The Reich Literary Chamber also continued to endorse Albatross's partnership with Tauchnitz because it made it possible for Tauchnitz to pay its royalties abroad and thus keep its good name alive; see Dr. Hans Schöne to the Reichstelle für Devisenbewirtschaftung, 2 April 1937, 20206, File 1681, SAL.
8. John Holroyd-Reece to C. D. Medley, n.d. [probably September 1943], David Lloyd Agency for Pearl Buck (C0060), Box 28, Folder 21, PUA
9. Internal Memo from the Board of Dresdner Bank, 21 August 1932, 21018, File 257, SAL.
10. Pressler, "Tauchnitz und Albatross," A6; Internal Memo from the Board of the

Dresdner Bank, 14 July 1933, 21018, File 257, SAL; Holroyd-Reece to Medley, n.d. [probably September 1943], David Lloyd Agency for Pearl Buck (C0060), Box 28, Folder 21, PUA. According to bank figures, the four men purchased 200,000 RM of Tauchnitz shares for 150,000 RM, with the total cost, including books and assets, mounting to 400,000 RM: see Dresdner Bank Report, 10 December 1934, 21018, File 257, Deutsche Bank Tauchnitz Balance Sheet, 31 December 1934, 21017, Brandstetter File 286, both SAL.

11. J. B. [Justus Brandstetter], "Die Entwicklung des Verhältnisses der Firmen Tauchnitz-Albatross," 16 April 1940, R87-1192, BAL; Holroyd-Reece to Medley, n.d. [probably September 1943], David Lloyd Agency for Pearl Buck (C0060), Box 28, Folder 21, PUA; Gestionsvertrag, 21 September 1934, 21056 Bernhard Tauchnitz Verlag, File 4, SAL.
12. Letter to the editor, *The Observer,* 28 October 1934, 13. This language echoes, nearly word for word, Holroyd-Reece's formulations elsewhere about the value of English editions, and the Brandstetters were not fluent in English.
13. Wolfgang Krause-Brandstetter, CSDIC Report, PW Paper 31: "Printing and Publishing in Germany," RG 165 Records of the War Department General and Special Staffs, Captured Personnel and Material Branch, Reports Relating to POW Interrogations, 1943–1945, CSDIC SIR to CSDIC POW Papers, Box 642, NACP; "Betriebsbesichtigung," *Börsenblatt für den Deutschen Buchhandel,* 4 February 1934, 139.
14. The new president of the German Publishers' and Booksellers' Association, Wilhelm Baur, was young but had behind him Max Amann, the head of Eher Verlag—the National Socialist Party publisher—who had Hitler's ear. The association was left to produce the *Börsenblatt,* update the bibliography of German publications, maintain the address book for the German book trade, and nurture relationships between German and foreign book trade organizations. See Barbian, *Literaturpolitik im Dritten Reich,* 46–48; Dahm, *Das jüdische Buch,* 60; Barbian, *Literaturpolitik im NS-Staat,* 116.
15. Both firms used the number 15478, as indicated on both Tauchnitz and Albatross letterheads for 1936. See the Albatross to Kurt Enoch, 31 July 1936, and Tauchnitz to Kurt Enoch, 31 July 1936, Series 314-15, File F464, SAH.
16. Enoch, *Memoirs,* 65.
17. "Woche des deutschen Buches: Reichsminister Dr. Goebbels zur Eroeffnung der Buchwoche," *Börsenblatt für den Deutschen Buchhandel,* 8 November 1934, 973.
18. Continenta Registry of Commerce Entry, Series D34U31239, 264514B, AVP; Les Éditions Albatros Registry of Commerce Entry, Series D33U31237, 264016B, AVP; Pressler, "Tauchnitz und Albatross," A4; Memorandum and Articles of Association, Albatross Ltd., 22 January 1935, Albatross Verlag, File 1: General, HRC.
19. Karl Krameyer, Speech for Herr Kaden, 2 January 1935, 21033 Reichsbankhauptstelle, File 918, SAL.

CHAPTER EIGHT. THE CENTER WILL NOT HOLD

1. "Todesanzeige: Oscar Enoch in Hamburg," *Börsenblatt für den Deutschen Buchhandel,* August 1934, 652; Enoch, *Memoirs,* 56; Ruth Gruenthal, Interview, 10 August 2009, Westport, Connecticut.
2. Jeanne Holroyd-Reece to Kurt Enoch, 26 December 1934, CE. Jeanne Holroyd-Reece was Belgian by birth, and her English was sometimes unidiomatic.
3. Mr. Köhn, Hamburgisches Staatsamt, Verwaltungsabteilung, to the Reich Press Chamber, 28 March 1935, Series 131-6, File 106, SAH; Bajohr, *"Aryanisation" in Hamburg,* 74.
4. Enoch, *Memoirs,* 72–73. Jewish veterans were initially allowed to work for the state, even after the Civil Servant Statute of 7 April 1933. For the Reich flight tax see Barkai, *From Boycott to Annihilation,* 99–100, Evans, *The Third Reich in Power,* 389. It was created by Brüning in 1931 to stop the loss of capital. The Nazi regime adapted the statute to its own ends; originally it taxed assets above 200,000 RM at 25 percent, yet after May 1934 it levied taxes on assets above 50,000 RM. The Reichsbank also culled monies by paying only half the market rate for Reichsmarks until the beginning of 1935. At the time Enoch wanted to leave, the Reichsbank had reduced the exchange rate to 30 percent, so he would have had to pay far more than 25 percent on his assets to emigrate, unless he cut a deal.
5. Enoch, *Memoirs,* 67; Dr. Hans Schöne to the Reich Literary Chamber (to be forwarded to the Devisenbehörde), 17 January 1936, Series 314-15, File F464, SAH (Reich officials henceforth pushed to reduce Albatross-Tauchnitz foreign transfers to increase the surplus for the Reich); Schöne to the Reichsstelle für Devisenbewirtschaftung, 2 April 1937, 20206, File 1681, SAL; Karl Krameyer to Allgemeine Deutsche Creditanstalt, 29 March 1935, 21006, File 1052 Bernhard Tauchnitz Nachfolger, Brandstetter & Co, SAL; Ebi, *Export um jeden Preis,* 25.
6. Evans, *The Third Reich in Power,* 382–91; Barkai, *From Boycott to Annihilation,* 54–63 (on Schacht's position), 69–77 (on "Aryanization"). The census figure represented only those who declared their Jewishness as a religion, not those whom the Reich later identified as Jewish only by race. Dahm, *Das jüdische Buch,* 48; Barbian, *The Politics of Literature,* 173–74; "Hauptmann Görings Judenprogramm," *Jüdische Rundschau,* 31 May 1932, quoted in Dahm, *Das jüdische Buch,* 33; see also Bajohr, *"Aryanisation" in Hamburg,* Helmut Genschel, *Die Verdrängung der Juden aus der Wirtschaft im Dritten Reich* (Göttingen: Musterschmidt, 1966); Uwe Dietrich Adam, *Judenpolitik im Dritten Reich* (Düsseldorf: Droste, 2003).
7. Dahm, *Das jüdische Buch,* 65; Bajohr, *"Aryanisation,"* 74; Herr Eiffe [Vertretung Hamburgs in Berlin] to the president of the Reichskulturkammer, 6 April 1935, Series 131-6, File 106, SAH.
8. Dahm, *Das jüdische Buch,* 48–49. The Literary Chamber sent Jewish publishers

the first round of letters in early fall 1935 stating that they would soon be barred from membership, and the second between October and December, ordering them to liquidate their firms or sell to an "Aryan."

9. Bajohr, *"Aryanisation,"* 74–75; Herr Klaun to Vertretung Hamburgs in Berlin, 4 May 1935, Series 131-6, File 106, SAH.
10. Bajohr, *"Aryanisation,"* 76; Dahm, *Das jüdische Buch,* 68–69.
11. Albatross Verlag to Herrn Präsidenten des Landesfinanzamts Hamburg (Devisenstelle), 8 May 1935, 21033, File 1363 Albatross, SAL; Martin, " 'European Literature' in the Nazi New Order," 503; Max Christian Wegner to William A. Bradley, 13 May 1935, William A. Bradley Agency, File 129.9 The Albatross, HRC. As of May 1935, Albatross and Tauchnitz authors were allowed to pay 3 percent rather than 10 percent tax in Germany. This deduction was not offered to British and American authors who published with other German firms, and was probably a variation of the book subsidy agreement (*Buchausgleichsverfahren*) under which the regime paid German firms additional monies in the Reich to compensate for demanding that they keep their prices abroad as low as possible to increase exports.
12. Graham, "Kurt Enoch," 45; J. B. [Justus Brandstetter], "Die Entwicklung des Verhältnisses der Firmen Tauchnitz-Albatross," 16 April 1940, R87/1192, BAL. Albatross was to contribute 20,000 RM, Enoch 10,000 RM, and the Brandstetters an unspecified portion.
13. Albatross Verlag to the Herrn Präsidenten des Landesfinanzamts Hamburg (Devisenstelle), 21 December 1935, 21033 Reichsbankhauptstelle Leipzig 1363, SAL. Because Enoch's distribution business earned him more than his publishing business, he belonged to the Reich Press Chamber. However, the Literary Chamber was drawn into his appeal because Enoch was so critical to Albatross-Tauchnitz exports; see Bajohr, *"Aryanisation" in Hamburg,* 77. See also Bermann Fischer, *Bedroht—Bewahrt,* 112–13, for an emigration "deal" of another prominent Jewish publisher that may have provided a model for Enoch's own.
14. Enoch, *Memoirs,* 73–75. Note that Enoch calls Schöne an accountant, but Schöne advocated for him and Albatross as a lawyer. On Hövel and Bischoff, see Barbian, *The Politics of Literature,* 64 and 88; see also Hövel, *Grundfragen deutscher Wirtschaftspolitik* (1935).
15. Enoch, *Memoirs,* 64, 73.
16. Dr. Hans Schöne to the Reich Literary Chamber (to be forwarded to the Devisenbehörde), 17 January 1936, Series 314-15, File F464, SAH.
17. Hanns Johst, President of the Reich Literary Chamber, to the Reich Foreign Exchange Control Office, 16 May 1936, Series 314-15, File F464, SAH. Johst did not dispute that Albatross earned a solid sum for the Reich; he felt, however, that Albatross earned more "clearing currency," which the regime had to spend on goods in particular national markets because of its agreements with particular govern-

ments, than "hard currency," which the regime could spend as and where it wished. That Johst endorsed Enoch's application is interesting in that he was appointed on 1 October 1935, after the ouster of the more liberal Hans Blunck, in part because he was willing to enforce the expulsion of Jews from the chamber. Highly sympathetic to the regime's aims, he was appointed an SS Oberführer under his protector, Heinrich Himmler, who placed Johst on his personal staff. See Cuomo, "Hanns Johst und die Reichsschrifttumskammer," 110–14.

18. Enoch, *Memoirs,* 75–76.
19. Ibid., 71; see, for instance, Max Christian Wegner to the Reichsschrifttumskammer, 6 April 1936, Captured German and Related Documents on Microform, A3339 RKK Z011, NACP.
20. "Publication of British Books in Germany by the Albatross Library," *Index to the Correspondence of the Foreign Office,* volume for 1935 (Nendeln: Kraus Reprints, 1969).
21. Enoch, *Memoirs,* 68.
22. Mr. Utermöhle to the Devisenstelle Hamburg, 19 June 1936, Der Präsident des Landesfinanzamts Hamburg (Devisenstelle) to the Reichsbankhauptstelle Hamburg, 7 July 1936, Zollfahndungsstelle an den Herrn L.F.A. Präsidenten Devisenstelle Hamburg, 9 July 1936, Reichsbankhauptstelle Altona (Elbe) to the Herrn Präsidenten des Landesfinanzamts Hamburg (Devisenstelle), 11 July 1936, Kurt Enoch to the President of the Landesfinanzamt Hamburg (Devisenstelle), 28 July 1936, President of the Landesfinanzamt Hamburg to Dr. Kurt Enoch, 6 August 1936, Albatross Verlag, Abschrift unserer Rechnung vom 31 Juli 1936, Bernhard Tauchnitz Nachfolger Brandstetter & Co, Abschrift unserer Rechnung vom 31. Juli 1936, Enoch to President of the Landesfinanzamt Hamburg (Devisenstelle), 8 August 1936, all Series 314-15, File F464, SAH.
23. Kurt Enoch to the Reichsschrifttumskammer, 8 August 1936, 21765 Boersenverein der Deutschen Buchhändler zu Leipzig, File 11142 Continenta, SAL.
24. Graham, "Kurt Enoch," 49.
25. Bermann Fischer, *Bedroht—Bewahrt,* 122.
26. Enoch, *Memoirs,* 76.

CHAPTER NINE. THE SHELL GAME

1. Kershaw, *Hitler, 1936–1945,* 858n228; as Kershaw notes, the Reich Advocacy Office for German Jews (Reichsvertretung der deutschen Juden), which was created in 1933 to represent the interests of the Jewish community, calculated the number of Jews emigrating from Germany as 37,000 in 1933, 23,000 in 1934, 21,000 in 1935, and 25,000 in 1936.
2. Evans, *The Third Reich in Power,* 392–97.

3. Matthias Wegner, "Offener Brief an einen Enkel," unpublished manuscript, MW.
4. Matthias Wegner, Interview, 6 May 2012, Hamburg, Germany; Wolfgang Krause-Brandstetter, CSDIC Report, PW Paper 31: "Printing and Publishing in Germany," RG 165 Records of the War Department General and Special Staffs, Captured Personnel and Material Branch, Reports Relating to POW Interrogations, 1943–1945, CSDIC SIR to CSDIC POW Papers, Box 642, NACP. This might be the assessment of someone hesitant to point the finger, except that Krause-Brandstetter readily labeled certain leaders in his own family firm as pronounced Nazi sympathizers. Hans Otto, "Rundschreiben," 11 December 1931, 21056, File 17, SAL; Matthias Wegner, "Offener Brief an einen Enkel," unpublished manuscript, MW.
5. Memorandum and Articles of Association, Albatross Ltd., 22 January 1935, Albatross Verlag Records, 1: General, HRC.
6. Dr. Hans Schöne to the Reichsstelle für Devisenbewirtschaftung, 20 March 1936, Series 314-15, File F464, SAH; Schacht to Hitler, 13 February 1936, quoted in Dahm, *Das jüdische Buch,* 70; Barbian, *The Politics of Literature,* 173–74.
7. Dr. Hans Schöne to the Reichsstelle für Devisenbewirtschaftung, 20 March 1936, Series 314-15, F464, SAH. New competition would involve Albatross in price wars and would cost the firm the substantial fees of 80,000 to 100,000 RM that the Brandstetters paid Albatross to manage Tauchnitz each year.
8. Importers of "unnecessary luxury goods" were granted no foreign currency allocations and those of "somewhat necessary goods" were limited to 10,000 RM annually. See Ebi, *Export um jeden Preis,* 22. See Max Christian Wegner to William A. Bradley, 14 February 1934, William A. Bradley Agency, File 129.9 The Albatross, HRC; "The Albatross" Published Statement, n.d. but 1945 or 1946, sent by Herberth Herlitschka to Isabel Wilder, 14 May 1946, YCAL MSS 108 Thornton Wilder, Box 13, Folder 302 Albatross, BL.
9. Albatross Verlag, Abschrift unserer Rechnung vom 31 Juli 1936, Bernhard Tauchnitz Nachfolger Brandstetter & Co, Abschrift unserer Rechnung vom 31. Juli 1936, Series 314-15, F464, SAH; Christian Wegner Verlag Announcement, *Börsenblatt für den Deutschen Buchhandel,* 2 September 1936, 3876. Wegner continued, however, to import the Albatross Crime and Mystery Club series produced by Collins in Edinburgh.
10. Max Christian Wegner to the Literary Chamber, 22 April 1936, Captured German and Related Documents on Microform, A3339 RKK Z110, NACP; President of the Reich Literary Chamber to the Reich Foreign Exchange Control Office, 16 May 1936, Series 314-15, F464, SAH; President of the Reich Literary Chamber, August 1936, quoted in Aktennotiz 19 June 1937, 21033, 1363, SAL.
11. Dr. Hans Schöne to the Reich Literary Chamber (to be forwarded to the Devisenbehörde), 17 January 1936, Series 314-15, File F464, SAH.
12. Hamburg Registry of Commerce, Albatross Verlag, 231-7, Number 8499, SAH.

13. Dagmar Nick, Handwriting Analysis of John Holroyd-Reece, Frühjahr 1956, LES.
14. Noakes, "Hitler and the Nazi State," 74–75; Caplan, *Government Without Administration,* 137. This discussion of the Nazi bureaucracy fits within a larger debate about power in the Reich. Hitler actively thwarted Interior Minister Wilhelm Frick's attempts to create a functioning, centralized bureaucracy, since he was paranoid about others' power. "Intentionalists" privilege the idea that Hitler was a strong dictator whose intentions strongly defined the Nazi state, while "structuralists" see Hitler as a weaker dictator whose own resistance to organized bureaucracy created chaos and competition and, in fact, ultimately thwarted certain Nazi goals. For a succinct overview, see Kershaw, "Hitler: 'Master in the Third Reich' or 'Weak Dictator'? in his *The Nazi Dictatorship,* 59–79.
15. Reichsbankhauptstelle Leipzig to den Herrn Präsidenten des Landesfinanzamts Leipzig—Devisenstelle, 19 December 1936, 21033, File 1363, SAL.
16. Ebi, *Export um jeden Preis,* 22.
17. Reichsbankhauptstelle Hamburg to President of the Landesfinanzamt Hamburg (Devisenstelle), 3 September 1936, Note from President of the Landesfinanzamt Hamburg, 12 September 1936, both Series 314-15, File F464, SAH. Officials seem to have approved this arrangement so Enoch could use the monies from sales abroad to pay royalties and other costs for Albatross, cutting back on foreign currency transfers from Germany.
18. Gerhard Brueder and Wilhelm Lucke, Bericht, 4 January 1937, 21033, File 1363, SAL. The comments about Enoch derive from a slightly earlier report: Schreiben der Reichsbankhauptstelle Leipzig vom 19. Dezember 1936 an den Herrn Präsidenten des Landesfinanzamts Leipzig, 21033, File 1363, SAL.
19. Gerhard Brueder and Wilhelm Lucke, Bericht, 4 January 1937, 21033, File 1363, SAL; Oeffentliche Auskunfts- und Beratungsstelle für Auswanderer in Hamburg, Bescheinigung, 9 July 1936, Series 314-15, File F464, SAH.
20. Gerhard Brueder and Wilhelm Lucke, Bericht, 4 January 1937, Reichsbankhauptstelle Leipzig, 21033, File 1363, SAL. Kupfer had done nothing but follow protocol: he had secured the proper permissions from the Devisenstelle Hamburg for a travel permit and 500 RM to cover expenses.
21. Enoch, *Memoirs,* 77.
22. Ibid., 77, 84–86.
23. Ibid., 77.
24. Ibid., 84.

CHAPTER TEN. SUSPICION

1. Holroyd-Reece [attrib.], *The Harvest; Centenary Catalogue of the Tauchnitz Edition.*

2. Gerhard Brueder and Wilhelm Lucke, Bericht, 4 January 1937, Dr. Hans Schöne to the Reichsstelle für Devisenbewirtschaftung, 1 February 1937, Reichsoberinspektor [name illegible], Aktennotiz, 10 February 1937, all 21033, File 1363, SAL. Enoch naturally felt the suspension of his book shipments as an injustice. He essentially paid the price for Albatross to stay open in Germany. Leipzig documents suggest that he was pegged by authorities both because he was Jewish and because they wrongly viewed him, rather than Holroyd-Reece, as the driving force behind Albatross until 1938.
3. Inspektor Mundt (Reichsbank Leipzig), Aktennotiz, 19 June 1937, Walter Beyer and Wilhelm Lucke, Bericht, 3 July 1937, both 21033, File 1363, SAL.
4. Inspektor Mundt (Reichsbank Leipzig), Aktennotiz, 19 June 1937, Albatross und Tauchnitz—Absatz in Exemplaren Ausland, n.d. [approximately May–June 1937],Inspektor Mundt (Devisenstelle Leipzig), "Agenturspesen," 3 September 1937, all 21033, File 1363, SAL.
5. Diplomkaufmann Lucke, Bericht, 31 October 1937, 21033, File 1363, SAL. Hövel's economic screed, *Grundfragen deutscher Wirtschaftspolitik* [*Fundamental Questions of German Economic Policy,* 1935], resonated with the logic that exports of any kind were the saving grace of the German economy; see Diplomkaufmann Lucke, Notiz betr. Albatross Leipzig, 31 October 1937, Diplomkaufmann Lucke, "Ergebnis bei der Firma The Albatross Verlag . . . ," 27 October 1937, both 21033, File 1363, SAL.
6. Wilhelm Lucke, Bericht, 19 March 1938, 21033, File 1363, SAL.
7. Jetta S. Wolff, *Historic Paris* (London: John Lane, 1921), 91. See also the photograph of 12 rue Chanoinesse at "Rue Chanoinesse. 4th," Virtual Tourist, http://members.virtualtourist.com/m/p/m/1e43ab; "John Holroyd-Reece, Managing Director: Publishing Holding Company," Holroyd-Reece File, Katherine Strelsky Papers, 2010-M4, SL.
8. Enoch, *Memoirs,* 61, 80; Ruth Gruenthal, Interview, 14 August 2013, Westport, Connecticut.
9. Wolfgang Ollendorff to OKVR Dr. Rinke, 14 January 1941, AJ/40/701, ANF; Les Éditions de la Nouvelle Revue Critique, Series D33U31341, 274478B, AVP.
10. File Note, 23 April 1938, CHA Fonds Moscou dossier 42834, SHD.
11. Endrèbe, "Le Roman policier," 263–64; File Notes, 10 December and 21 December 1937, CHA Fonds Moscou dossier 42834, SHD. Boyle Somerville, the first officer to head the Naval Section of the British Secret Service, recommended that no agent should "set forth on S.S. [Secret Service] without 'cover,' that is to say, a fictitious cloak for his real activities;—some open and legitimate pursuit, business or calling under which he can operate without detection," quoted in Jeffery, *The Secret History of MI6,* 63.
12. John Holroyd-Reece to William A. Bradley, "Memorandum: Albatross Activities

in France," 14 September 1937, William A. Bradley Agency, Series II: Publisher Correspondence, File 129.9 Albatross, HRC.

13. Report of April 1938 sent from Le Préfet de Police à Monsieur le Président du Conseil, Ministre de la Défense Nationale, 14 May 1938,CHA Fonds Moscou dossier 42834, SHD; Taylor, *Projection of Britain,* 13–14, 150–51. Between 1916 and 1919, Tyrrell had occupied an important post in the Political Intelligence Department in the British Foreign Office—a fact that was probably unknown to the Préfecture de Police. This dovetails with the period when Holroyd-Reece was rumored to have worked for British intelligence.
14. Appendix 1. PW's Career up to 1943, n.d., and M.I. 19 Internal Memo, 24 February 1945, both KV2/160 (PF Series): Wolfgang Krause-Brandstetter: Based in Paris, NAK.
15. Krause-Brandstetter to Major Steed, 8 February 1945, KV2/160 (PF Series): Wolfgang Krause-Brandstetter: Based in Paris, NAK. Krause-Brandstetter completed three semesters at Caius College from 1933 to 1935.
16. Appendix 1. PW's Career up to 1943, KV2/160 (PF Series): Wolfgang Krause-Brandstetter: Based in Paris, NAK.
17. Beurteilungsnotiz über den Oberleutnant (Kr.O.) und Adjutanten Wolfgang Krause-Brandstetter, 30 September 1942, Pers 6/243270, BAF.
18. Wolfgang Krause-Brandstetter, "Cambridge—wie es heute ist: Erziehungsstätten für Englands kommende Generation," *Leipziger neueste Nachrichten,* May 1935.
19. Dr. Schultze-Schlutius (Reichsstelle für Devisenbewirtschaftung) to the Herrn Präsidenten der Reichspressekammer—Propagandaministerium—z. Hd. Von Herrn Dr. Hövel, 4 November 1937, Dr. Schultze-Schlutius to Herrn Oberfinanzpräsidenten Leipzig, 7 December 1937, both 21033, File 1363, SAL.
20. Dr. Hipp, Aktenvermerk, 26 November 1937, Dr. Hipp, Aktenvermerk, 26 November 1937, Die Inhaber der Firma Oscar Brandstetter an den Oberfinanzpräsidenten Leipzig (Devisenstelle), 26 November 1937, all 21033, File 1363, SAL.
21. "Honderd Jaar Tauchnitz Edition," *Het Vaderland,* 8 June 1937, 9; Die Inhaber der Firma Oscar Brandstetter an den Oberfinanzpräsidenten Leipzig (Devisenstelle), 26 November 1937, 21033, File 1363, SAL.
22. Tooze, *Wages of Destruction,* 214; Evans, *The Third Reich in Power,* 357–61; Noakes and Pridham, *Nazism,* 2:291; Overy uses the term "economic dictator" in *War and Economy in the Third Reich,* 202.
23. Tooze, *Wages of Destruction,* 207–13; Walter Bayrhoffer, Annual Report for 1938, quoted in Aly, *Hitler's Beneficiaries,* 47; Overy, *War and Economy in the Third Reich,* 183, 203. See also Noakes and Pridham, *Nazism,* 2:277–300, for an overview of the conflict between "guns and butter" caused by the privileging of rearmament: German civilians suffered shortages, and businesses could often not surmount shortages on raw materials they needed to produce their goods.

24. Albatross Verlag to the Devisenstelle des Landesfinanzamts Leipzig, 12 May 1937, Dr. Schöne to the Reichsstelle für Devisenbewirtschaftung, 18 September 1937, both 21033, File 1363, SAL. When the government of France's prime minister Léon Blum fell to Camille Chautemps on 22 June 1937, it offered Schacht a chance to arrange a clearing (trade) agreement between Germany and France. See Carine Germond and Henning Türk, eds., *A History of Franco-German Relations in Europe: From Hereditary Enemies to Partners* (London: Palgrave Macmillan, 2008), 130–32. Albatross reminded authorities that under this agreement, the Reich would receive two-thirds of its trade surplus from France back as either hard currency or "free Reichsmarks," with one-third as "clearing currency" they could spend on French goods.
25. Holroyd-Reece [attrib.], *The Harvest,* 11–14; Fiona Brewster, Interview, Le Breuil-Rouillac, 13 December 2013. The volumes reprinted testimonials to Tauchnitz from celebrities over the years, among them Benjamin Disraeli, Robert Browning, William Makepeace Thackeray, H. G. Wells, and Sir Hugh Walpole. The Nazis considered Disraeli a Jewish politician, despite his conversion to the Anglican church, and the regime had banned H. G. Wells in 1935.

CHAPTER ELEVEN. DEAR READER

1. Unfortunately, the filled-out "Dear Reader" cards were probably destroyed during the war. The Albatross collector Alastair Jollans has only found blank cards in his widespread searches for Albatross books and ephemera.
2. "Die Verbreitung der Tauchnitz Edition," *Börsenblatt für den Deutschen Buchhandel,* 28 December 1937, 1019. France stood a far second in line in sales, with Tauchnitz doing 9.75 percent of its business there, and Albatross 13.82 percent. Beyond these markets, Tauchnitz and Albatross readership was split. Australia, Switzerland, and Italy shared third place for Tauchnitz, with roughly 6.3 percent of sales each. But Albatross, with its more cutting-edge books, had a slightly different profile: 9.52 percent of sales in the Netherlands, followed by Switzerland at 6.44 percent and Italy at 5.98 percent.
3. Holman, *Print for Victory,* 227; Kliemann, "Die Welt des Buchhandels," 151.
4. Thomas Mann to Hermann Hesse, 16 February 1936, *Herman Hesse/Thomas Mann: Correspondence,* ed. Otto Basler (Frankfurt: Suhrkamp/Fischer, 1968), 64–65; Will Vesper, "Mitteilungen," *Die neue Literatur* 12 (December 1933): 726; Johst, "Zum Geleit," n.p.
5. Bischoff, "Staat und Buch," 183, 185, 196.
6. Barbian, *Literaturpolitik im NS-Staat,* 253–56; Adam, *Lesen unter Hitler,* 28–29; Dahm, *Das jüdische Buch,* 66–86; Barbian, *Literaturpolitik im NS-Staat,* 218–33.
7. Adam, *Lesen unter Hitler,* 33–36; Ludwig Warmuth, *Reichsschrifttumskammer*

Taschenbuch für den deutschen Buchhandel (Berlin: Otto Elsner, 1938), 61, quoted in Sturge, "Flight from the Programme," 62; Barbian, *Literaturpolitik im NS-Staat,* 255.

8. Kliemann, "Die Welt des Buchhandels," 158; *Der Buchhändler im neuen Reich* (February 1937): 41, quoted in Schäfer, *Das gespaltene Bewußtsein,* 12.
9. Barbian, *Literaturpolitik im NS-Staat,* 281–86.
10. Langenbucher [attrib.], "Vorwort," n.p.; Sturge, "Flight from the Programme," 51, 61.
11. Parteiamtliche Prüfungskommission zum Schutze des NS-Schrifttums to the Reichsschrifttumskammer, 23 July 1937 and 30 July 1937, Geheime Staatspolize Elbing to the Reich Literary Chamber President, 8 March 1938, both Captured German and Related Records on Microform, A3339-RKK-Z020, NACP.
12. Reich Literary Chamber to Parteiamtliche Prüfungskommission zum Schutze des NS-Schrifttums, 13 July 1938, A3339-RKK-Z020, Captured German and Related Records on Microform, NACP; "Sinclair Lewis," at Verbannte Bücher: Online Veröffentlichung der Liste der von den Nationalsozialistischen verbotenen Schriften, http://www.berlin.de/rubrik/hauptstadt/verbannte_buecher/suche.php?page=9&s_jahr=1932&orderby=ort&order=desc.
13. Editor of *Der Stürmer* to Reich Literary Chamber, 25 November 1937, A3339-RKK-Z016, Captured German and Related Records on Microform, NACP.
14. Editor of *Der Stürmer* to Reich Literary Chamber, 25 November 1937, Erich Kupfer to the Reich Literary Chamber, 7 December 1937, Reich Literary Chamber to Editor of *Der Stürmer,* 2 December 1937, Reich Literary Chamber to Editor of *Der Stürmer,* 12 December 1937, all from Captured German and Related Records on Microform, A3339-RKK-Z016, NACP; "Louis Golding," at Verbannte Bücher: Online Veröffentlichung der Liste der von den Nationalsozialistischen verbotenen Schriften, http://www.berlin.de/rubrik/hauptstadt/verbannte_buecher/suche.php?page=9&s_jahr=1932&orderby=ort&order=desc.
15. Bericht vom 4 November 1937, *Deutschland-Berichte der Sozialdemokratischen Partei Deutschlands, 1934–1940,* 7 vols., ed. Klaus Behnken (Frankfurt: Salzhausen, 1980), 1640, quoted in Adam, *Lesen unter Hitler,* 231. Published in Prague, and then in Paris, this semi-monthly report amassed reports from secret sources in Germany and was seen as a reliable source of information for foreign journalists and governments. *Westermanns Monatshefte,* quoted in Schäfer, *Das gespaltene Bewußtsein,* 13. "Wirklichkeitsnähe—unliterarisch?" *Das schwarze Korps,* 9 June 1938, quoted in Benecke, *Eine Buchhandlung in Berlin,* 105; Sturge, "Flight from the Programme," 53; Benecke, *Eine Buchhandlung in Berlin,* 101.
16. Hans Franke, "Unerwünschte Einfuhr," *Die neue Literatur* (October 1937): 501–8, Will Vesper, "Übersetzungen," *Die neue Literatur* 39, no. 8 (1938): 403–4, both quoted in Barbian, "Die doppelte Indizierung," 20.

17. Sturge, "Flight from the Programme," 56; Schäfer, *Das gespaltene Bewußtsein,* 14; Ullrich, ed., *Neu Amerika,* 9.
18. Schäfer, *Das gespaltene Bewußtsein,* 13.
19. "Das Schrifttum im Jahre 1938," in Boberach, *Meldungen aus dem Reich,* 2:155–56.
20. Schöne to the Reichsstelle für Devisenbewirtschaftung, Anlage 2, 18 September 1937, 21033, File 1363, SAL; Hambourg to Mrs. Bradley, 25 October 1937, William A. Bradley Literary Agency, File 129.9 The Albatross, HRC.
21. William A. Bradley to Albatross, William A. Bradley Literary Agency, File 129.9 The Albatross, HRC; Vesper, "Übersetzungen," *Die neue Literatur* 39, no. 8 (1938): 403–4, quoted in Barbian, "Die doppelte Indizierung," 20; Adam, *Lesen unter Hitler,* 238, 324; and see especially Annemarie Wallrath-Janssen, *Der Verlag H. Goverts im Dritten Reich* (Munich: Saur, 2007). Goverts sold so many copies in 1938–39 that this book ensured the publisher sizable wartime paper rations; German publishers were allocated paper based on a percentage of their paper use the year prior to the war.
22. Since the figures listed are for "Umsatz"—overall sales turnover rather than number of volumes sold—I am dividing by 1 RM, the amount Albatross and the regime calculated for its return on each book after production costs, to get this figure. This figure dovetails with Holroyd-Reece's report that Albatross and Tauchnitz sold roughly one-third of their books inside the Reich. For sales outside the Reich, Leipzig authorities calculated, as of early in 1938, "an approximate turnover in recent years of 500,000 volumes" annually; see Wilhelm Lucke, Aktennotiz über die Angelegenheit Albatross-Tauchnitz, 19 March 1938, 21033, File 1363, SAL.
23. "Mitteilungen," *Die neue Literatur* (7 July 1936): 429; see, for instance, *Englische Studien* 72 (1937–38): 439, and 73 (1938–39): 318, 439.
24. Muska Nagel, "Ernte aus England: Zu neuen Albatross- und Tauchnitzbüchern," *Die Literatur* 40 (October 1937): 273.
25. Hans Effelberger, "Zum Gedächtnis von David Herbert Lawrence," *Neueren Sprachen* 47 (1939): 118–20; D. H. Lawrence, *Apocalypse* (Hamburg: Albatross, 1932).
26. Trommler, "Targeting the Reader, Entering History," 121–24.
27. Barbian, *Literaturpolitik im NS-Staat,* 5, 254; Schäfer, "The Young Generation's Non-National Socialist Literature During the Third Reich," 46.
28. D. W. Sawdon to British Council Secretary General, 5 December 1938, BW 32/2, NAK.
29. Reich Literary Chamber to Editor of *Der Stürmer,* 2 December 1937, Captured German and Related Records on Microform, A3339-RKK-Z016, NACP.

CHAPTER TWELVE. ALLEGIANCES

1. Jeffrey B. Berlin, "March 14, 1938: 'Es gibt Kein Oesttereich mehr'; Unpublished Correspondence Between Franz Werfel, Alma Mahler Werfel and Ben Heuebsch," *Deutsche Vierteljahrsschrift für Literaturwissenschaft und Geistesgeschichte* 62, no. 4 (1988): 741–63, 753; Jeffrey B. Berlin, " 'Wie unwichtig sind ja überhaupt jetzt alle unsere Bücher und das, was wir machen!': The Unpublished Correspondence Between Stefan Zweig and Felix Braun During the *Anschluß* Year 1938," *Germanisch-Romanische Monatsschrift* 41 (1991): 322–48, 323; Enoch, *Memoirs,* 93; Virginia Woolf, entry for 26 March 1938, *The Diary of Virginia Woolf,* vol. 5, 132.
2. Walter Gey and Erich Kupfer, Bericht über offene Albatross-Fragen, n.d. [following Paris-Amsterdam trip of 27 October 1941 to 8 November 1941], R87/1192, BAL.
3. Wolfgang Krause-Brandstetter, CSDIC Report, PW Paper 31: "Printing and Publishing in Germany," RG 165 Records of the War Department General and Special Staffs, Captured Personnel and Material Branch, Reports Relating to POW Interrogations, 1943–1945, CSDIC SIR to CSDIC POW Papers, Box 642, NACP.
4. Reichsbankinspektor Dietrich, Aktennotiz, 16 February 1938, 21033, File 1363, SAL.
5. Reichsbankinspektor Dietrich, Aktennotiz, 1 March 1938, 21033, File 1363, SAL; Wilhelm Lucke, Bericht, 25 May 1938, 21033, File 1363, SAL.
6. Walter Gey and Erich Kupfer, Bericht über offene Albatross-Fragen, n.d., R87/1192, BAL. Gey and Kupfer's account contradicts that of Lewis's *Penguin Special,* in which he claims that "Holroyd-Reece took a tearful farewell of his partner," 141. Holroyd-Reece might have acted as though he was upset at splitting from Enoch, but other accounts do not suggest it.
7. Enoch, *Memoirs,* 80.
8. Ibid., 81–83.
9. Aktennotiz, 13 January 1939, 20206, File 1892, SAL. Because Germany was in debt to so many national markets, the sales of German products abroad often earned Germany trade credits, which forced German authorities to purchase goods in individual markets, rather than hard currency they could spend where and as they wished. In this context, the file note explains that Germany could earn a higher percentage of hard currency if it kept Albatross-Tauchnitz distribution in the hands of the French office rather than shifting it to a firm in Germany, garnering for Germany as hard currency roughly 70 percent of the 100,000 RM of foreign currency it earned annually through Albatross and Tauchnitz sales abroad in 1937–38.
10. Ibid.
11. Enoch, *Memoirs,* 81.
12. The Albatross Verlag [Erich Kupfer] to Reichswirtschaftsministerium Hauptabteilung V—Devisenbewirtschaftung [Gerichtsassessor Dr. Wrück], 3 January 1939, 20206, File 1892, SAL.

13. Berlin correspondent, "Nazi Attacks on Jews: Orgy of Hitler Youth: Synagogues Burnt," *Times* (London), 11 November 1938, 14; Sigrid Schultz, "Mobs Wreck Jewish Stores in Berlin," *Chicago Daily Tribune,* 10 November 1938, 1.
14. Benecke, *Eine Buchhandlung in Berlin,* 132.
15. Berlin Correspondent, "Nazi Attacks on Jews," 14; Sigrid Schultz, "Homes Burned; Stores Looted; Terror Reigns: Mobs Run Wild in German Streets," *Chicago Daily Tribune,* 11 November 1938, 1.
16. Kurt Enoch, Widergutmachungsantrag, 2 December 1957, Anlage 1, 27 November 1957, Wiedergutmachungsakte 221195/45317 SAH; Enoch, *Memoirs,* 88–89. The timing of Rosa Enoch's arrival in France is a bit unclear. Enoch says she arrived in "late 1938" and had "narrowly . . . escaped the disaster of the 'Kristall Nacht'"; yet documents from her restitution file suggest she might have arrived later in November. There remains the remote possibility that German authorities granted her a visa to leave for Paris, provided she leave her assets behind, and then she sold her home and paid the flight tax after her arrival in France. Göring used Kristallnacht as an excuse to levy this tax, called the *Judenvermögensabgabe,* on Jews in Germany. Any Jews with assets over 5,000 RM based on tax reports of early 1938 had to pay 20 percent on those assets. Most Jews paid in four installments—later a fifth was added—but authorities made Enoch's mother pay her full amount all at once.
17. The Albatross Verlag [Erich Kupfer] to Reichswirtschaftsministerium Hauptabteilung V—Devisenbewirtschaftung [Gerichtsassessor Dr. Wrück], 3 January 1939, 20206, File 1892, SAL.
18. Ibid.
19. Ibid.
20. Vermerk, 13 January 1939, 20206/1892, SAL; Wilhelm Lücke, Zum Antrag der Firma Bernh. Tauchnitz nachf. v. 25.7.44, 11 August 1944, 20206/1892, SAL.
21. Enoch, *Memoirs,* 93; Enoch, Citizenship Application, n.d., RGA.
22. Intelligence Report from Préfecture de Police to Monsieur le Président du Conseil, Ministre de la Défense Nationale et de la Guerre, November 1938, Renseignement, 8 October 1938, both CHA Fonds Moscou dossier 42834, SHD.
23. On 31 December 1937, Holroyd-Reece had infused an existing firm with 500,000 francs to handle "all brokerage operations, of commissions in all substances and notably in insurance of all kinds, . . . in France as well as abroad": "Confidential: a/s de la Sté Sedouy, Reece & Cie," 17 March 1939, Le Ministre du Travail à Monsieur le Président du Conseil, Ministre de la Défense Nationale et de la Guerre, 8 May 1939, both CHA Fonds Moscou dossier 42834, SHD.
24. Handwritten file note, 20 June 1939, CHA Fonds Moscou dossier 42834, SHD.
25. J.B. [Justus Brandstetter], "Die Entwicklung des Verhältnisses der Firmen Tauchnitz-Albatross," 16 April 1940, R87/1192, BAL; Dr. Georg Schärtl to Herr

Wirtschaftsprüfer Walter Gey, 25 October 1940, R87/1192, BAL. Schärtl lists the date of the new contract as 21 April 1939.

26. The Albatross Verlag [Erich Kupfer] to the Oberfinanzpräsident Leipzig, 3 June 1939, 20206, File 1681, SAL.
27. Ibid.
28. Max Christian Wegner to Annemarie Wegner, 31 March 1933, MW.
29. Erich Kupfer to Oberfinanzpräsident Leipzig, 3 June 1939, 20206, File 1681, SAL.
30. Oberfinanzpräsident Leipzig, Genehmigungsbescheid, 15 June 1939, 20206, File 1681, SAL; Wilhelm Lucke, "Zum Antrag der Firma Bernh. Tauchnitz Nachf. v. 26.7.11 [*sic:* should be 26.7.44], 11 August 1944, 20206, File 1892, SAL.
31. Holroyd-Reece to Sir Stanley Unwin, 31 July 1939, AUC74/10, UR; K. H. Bischoff to Karl Thulke, 14 December 1939, Captured German and Related Records on Microform, A3339-RKK-Z007, NACP.
32. "Books: Exit Tauchnitz," *Time,* 20 July 1942, 86; Peter Davison, *George Orwell: A Literary Life* (New York: St. Martin's, 1996), 113. Full diary entry on Davison's website, Orwell Diaries, 1938–1942, Orwell Prize, http://orwelldiaries.wordpress.com/2009/08/04/4839-2/.

CHAPTER THIRTEEN. FACES OF WAR

1. Enoch, *Memoirs,* 94–95.
2. Ibid., 95.
3. Entry on the Albatross Verlag, *Tägliches Verzeichnis der Neuerscheinungen,* Bearbeitet von der Deutschen Bücherei, 17 August 1939 (Leipzig: Deutschen Bücherei), 1001; John Steinbeck, *The Long Valley* (Leipzig: Albatross, 1939), which includes this note: "One story, namely 'The raid,' included in the original edition, is omitted here with the consent of the author."
4. Eric Maria Remarque, *All Quiet on the Western Front,* trans. A. W. Wheen (New York: Random House, 2013), 164–65.
5. Renseignements, 29 September 1939, Le Président du Conseil at the Ministre de la Défense Nationale et de la Guerre [signed Dentz] to Messr. Le ministre de l'intérieur direction générale de la Sûreté Nationale, 23 August 1939, SR [Service Renseignement], File note, 28 September 1939, Paul Paillole, Renseignements, 29 September 1939, all CHA Fonds Moscou dossier 42834, SHD.
6. Jucker, *Curfew in Paris,* 9; Report from le Préfet de Police to Monsieur le Président du Conseil, Ministre de la Défense Nationale et de la Guerre, 14 October 1939,CHA Fonds Moscou dossier 42834, SHD.
7. Requisitoire, 28 October 1939, Requête, 5 December 1939, both 1258W/0001, AVP; Holroyd-Reece, Note for the Information of British Albatross and Tauchnitz

Authors, January 1940, David Lloyd Agency for Pearl Buck (C0060), Box 28, Folder 19, PUA.

8. Renseignements, 10 April 1940, CHA Fonds Moscou dossier 42834, SHD.
9. "Modern Baron Tauchnitz," *Daily Telegraph,* 16 November 1939. Holroyd-Reece's estimate that Germany made up "about half the Continental market for English books" is higher than the 1937 estimate listed in *Publishers Weekly* because of Hitler's annexations of Austria and the Sudetenland.
10. Fiona Brewster, Interview, 3 May 2013, Le Breuil-Rouillac, France; Holroyd-Reece, Note for the Information of British Albatross and Tauchnitz Authors, January 1940, David Lloyd Agency Pearl Buck Files (C0060), Box 28, Folder 19, PUA.
11. Enoch, *Memoirs,* 96.
12. "The Situation of the German and Austrian Refugees," RG 59 General Records of the Department of State, Lot File No. 52 D 408, Records Relating to the Intergovernmental Committee on Refugees, NACP; Enoch, *Memoirs,* 96.
13. "The Situation of the German and Austrian Refugees," RG 59 General Records of the Department of State, Lot File No. 52 D 408, Records Relating to the Intergovernmental Committee on Refugees, NACP; Enoch, *Memoirs,* 96–97.
14. Enoch, *Memoirs,* 96–98.
15. Ibid., 99–100; "The Situation of the German and Austrian Refugees," RG 59 General Records of the Department of State, Lot File No. 52 D 408, Records Relating to the Intergovernmental Committee on Refugees, NACP.
16. Didier Georgakakis, "Le Commissariat général à l'information et la 'drôle du guerre,'" *Mélanges de l'École française de Rome* 108, no. 1 (1996): 39–54; see also the finding aid for the Ministry of Information at http://www.archivesnationales.culture.gouv.fr/chan/chan/pdf/F41.pdf; Le Chef du Service du Propagande en Pays Ennemis to Monsieur le Commissaire Général à l'Information, 16 September 1939, Personnes Émigrées qui sont utilisées par le Commissariat out peuvent l'être éventuellement, 20 September 1939, both F41/981, File D.V. No. A 21 Émigrés allemands-autrichiens-tcheques, ANF; Enoch, *Memoirs,* 100.
17. Enoch, *Memoirs,* 102–3.
18. Ibid., 104–5.
19. Enoch, Curriculum Vitae for Ministry of Information, F41/981, File D.V. No. A 21 Emigrés allemands-autrichiens-tcheques, ANF. Enoch later told an American journalist that he had briefly worked for the French Ministry of Information on propaganda: Sidney Fields, "Only Human: Proves American Dream," *Chicago Daily News,* 1964, n.p., from Kurt Enoch Scrapbook, CE.
20. Dr. Blasberg, Feldgericht [on Hauptmann Christian Wegner], 26 November 1943, MW; Major Cranz, Vorschlag zur Beförderung eines Offiziers, 17 February 1940, Pers 6/195111, BAF.

21. Dr. Blasberg, Feldgericht [on Hauptmann Christian Wegner], 26 November 1943, MW.
22. Jackson, *The Fall of France,* 30–31.
23. Max Christian Wegner to Annemarie Wegner, 12 May 1940, 19 May 1940, 21 May 1940, MW.
24. Max Christian Wegner to Annemarie Wegner, 25 May 1940; 12 May 1940, 25 May 1940, MW.
25. Max Christian Wegner to Annemarie Wegner, 30 May 1940, MW.

CHAPTER FOURTEEN. ENEMY BOOKS

1. Tauchnitz-Albatross General List of all volumes published up to April 1940, n.d., AJ.
2. Urkundsbeamte der Geschäftsstelle bei dem Amtsgericht Leipzig, Abt. V/118, Begläubigte Abschrift aus der Sonder-Ausgabe des Deutschen Reichsanzeiger und Preußischen Staatsanzeiger Nr. 204, 3 September 1939, 8 September 1939, Registerakten 824/28583 Abt. B, AGL; "Zur Entwicklung im deutschen Schrifttum seit Kriegsbeginn," 13 November 1939, in Boberach, *Meldungen aus dem Reich:* 3:582–83; Barbian, *Literaturpolitik im NS-Staat,* 271; Stieg, *Public Libraries,* 245–46.
3. Entry on the Albatross Verlag, *Tägliches Verzeichnis der Neuerscheinungen,* Bearbeitet von der Deutschen Bücherei, 25 September 1939 (Leipzig: Deutschen Bücherei), 1151.
4. Lindner, *Das Reichskommissariat,* 32–35. See also Imlay and Horn, *The Politics of Industrial Collaboration.*
5. Erich Kupfer to Herrn Regierungspräsidenten Leipzig, 6 November 1939, 20206, File 1681, SAL; Industrie und Handelskammer Leipzig to the Amtsgericht Leipzig Abteilung V, 1 December 1939, Registerakten 824/28583 Abt. B, AGL.
6. Erich Kupfer, Memorandum zur Erklärung der späten Fertigstellung des Abschlusses Albatross und Tauchnitz, 29 August 1940, R87/1192, BAL.
7. Erich Kupfer to Maxwell Perkins, Charles Scribner's Sons (C0101), Series Hemingway I, Box 6, File 41, PUA; Wilhelm Lucke, Aktennotiz über die Angelegenheit Albatross-Tauchnitz, 19 March 1938, 21033, File 1363, SAL; Kupfer, Memorandum zur Erklärung der späten Fertigstellung des Abschlusses Albatross und Tauchnitz, 29 August 1940, R87/1192, BAL.
8. Albatross titles appeared every two weeks throughout the fall of 1939 until December 1939. It is unclear whether the authorities halted production or whether the Brandstetters had run out of contracts for books to print. William Saroyan's *The Way to Be Alive* (Volume 518) earned the odd distinction of being the last new Albatross title to be published by the Germans during the war; Karl Thulke to

K. Bischoff, 5 December 1939; K. Bischoff to Karl Thulke, 14 December 1939, both Captured German and Related Records on Microform, A3339-RKK-Z007, NACP.

9. The Economics Ministry determined that Albatross no longer brought in hard currency, yet reaped "clearing currency" Germany could use to purchase raw materials in national markets where it held debts. From January to July 1939, Albatross sold 157,466.56 RM; from January to July 1940, Albatross sales fell 52.2 percent to 75,292.46 RM. In the first six months of 1939, Tauchnitz sold 145,846.23 RM's worth of books, dropping 24.9 percent, to 109,574.69 RM in the same period for 1940. Calculated differently, Albatross sold 22,500 RM of books per month in 1939 before the war, and roughly half that number in the same period in 1940. It is difficult to determine exact sales, outside of limited reports in which Albatross leaders give number of volumes sold. Albatross leaders did roughly calculate a 1 RM per book profit, but also assessed older books at a lesser value. I have followed the system that Albatross and the Nazi bureaucracy used for assessing value during Enoch's emigration case. See R87/1192, BAL.
10. Documents concerning Albatross and Tauchnitz "Jewish" books, Captured German and Related Documents on Microform, A3339-RKK-Z007, NACP; Nicholas, *The Rape of Europa,* 3–25.
11. *Vertrauliche Mitteilung für die Fachschaft Verlag* [Confidential Announcements for the Book Trade], 10 June 1940, n.p. See Erich Kupfer to the Reichsschriftumskammer, 26 March 1941, Captured German and Related Documents on Microform, A3339-RKK-Z007, NACP, for how the Literary Chamber authorized exports of "Jewish" Albatross and Tauchnitz books in July 1940.
12. Walter Gey to Reichskommissar, 17 July 1941, R87/1193, BAL.
13. George Orwell to Leonard Moore, 8 December 1939, quoted in Davison, *George Orwell: A Life in Letters* (London: Harvill and Secker, 2010), 172.
14. British Secret Service to French Secret Service, 8 February 1940, CHA Fonds Moscou dossier 42834, SHD.
15. John Holroyd-Reece, Note for the Information of British Albatross and Tauchnitz Authors, January 1940, David Lloyd Agency Files of Pearl S. Buck (C0060), Series II: Foreign Translations and Publication Rights of Pearl S. Buck, Box 28, File 19, PUA.
16. John Holroyd-Reece to Pearl Buck, 30 April 1940, David Lloyd Agency files of Pearl Buck (C0060), Series II: Foreign Translations and Publication Rights of Pearl S. Buck, Box 28, File 19, PUA.
17. The Reich Justice Ministry controlled enemy property decisions, with Reichskommissar Ernst under its authority. An ordinance of 15 January 1940 laid down enemy property regulations. See Lindner, *Das Reichskommissariat*, 29–35, and Imlay and Horn, *The Politics of Industrial Collaboration.*
18. Lindner, *Das Reichskommissariat,* 32–35.

19. On Ernst, see SGD Brigadier James Greenshields and SGD Colonel Charles A. Reid, Final Report on Target P. 109 on US Group CC and Control Commission for Germany (British Element), Summary of Dr. Krohn with footnote on Dr. Ernst, 64-65, 11 July 1945, B129/76, BAK; Reichskommissar für die Behandlung feindlichen Vermögens, Aktenvermerk, 30 March 1940, R87/1192, BAL. Over time, the Brandstetters had become Albatross's largest German creditor.
20. Reich Literary Chamber Gruppe Buchhandel to Reichskommissar Ernst, 2 February 1940, R87/1192, BAL.
21. Erich Kupfer to Reichskommissar Ernst, 27 March 1940, Oscar "Willy" Brandstetter to Albatross Verlag, 9 April 1940, both R87/1192, BAL.
22. Reichskommissar Ernst, Aktenvermerk, 17 April 1940, R87/1192, BAL.
23. Justus Brandstetter, "Die Entwicklung des Verhältnisses," 16 April 1940, R87/1192, BAL.
24. Reichskommissar Ernst to Herrn Leutnant Christian Wegner, 19 April 1940, Erich Kupfer to Herrn Reichskommissar Ernst, 30 May 1940, Reichskommissar Ernst, Aktenvermerk, 4 June 1940, all R87/1192, BAL. For photograph see "Reichskammer für Wirtschaftstreuhander" Informationbogen, 11 May 1943, PK D0045, BAL.

CHAPTER FIFTEEN. RETURN AND DEPARTURE

1. Jackson, *Fall of France,* 131–35.
2. Max Christian Wegner to Annemarie Wegner, 9 June 1940, MW.
3. Max Christian Wegner to Annemarie Wegner, 9 and 14 June 1940, both MW.
4. Ibid.
5. Enoch, *Memoirs,* 106–7.
6. Ibid., 107–8.
7. Jucker, *Curfew in Paris,* 37–39.
8. Beach, *Shakespeare and Company,* 213–14.
9. Margaret Enoch to Kurt Enoch, n.d., quoted in Enoch, *Memoirs,* 118–19.
10. Jucker, *Curfew in Paris,* 50; De Polnay, *The Germans Came to Paris,* 36–37; Jucker, *Curfew in Paris,* 46.
11. Beach, *Shakespeare and Company,* 214; Jucker, *Curfew in Paris,* 51–52; de Polnay, *The Germans Came to Paris,* 50; Jackson, *The Fall of France,* 2.
12. Max Christian Wegner to Annemarie Wegner, 17 June 1940, MW.
13. Ibid.
14. Beach, *Shakespeare and Company,* 214; Beach, Black Notebook 1940, Sylvia Beach Papers C0108, Box 72, PUA; "Simone de Beauvoir," Borrowers Card, Shakespeare and Company, Sylvia Beach Collection: III Bookshop, Box 103, PUA.
15. Max Christian Wegner to Annemarie Wegner, 24 June 1940, MW.
16. Ibid.; Matthias Wegner, "Offener Brief an einen Enkel," MW.

17. Enoch, *Memoirs,* 108–9.
18. Ibid., 112–13.
19. Ibid.; Ruth Gruenthal, manuscript corrections to quotations from interview of 14 August 2013 in Westport, Connecticut, in draft of Chapter 15.
20. Enoch, *Memoirs,* 123–24; "One of Ford's Finest Research Men Retires," Engineering Center News, April 1959, Enoch Scrapbook, CE; Enoch *Memoirs,* 126.
21. Enoch, *Memoirs,* 125–26; Ruth Gruenthal, Interview, 14 August 2013, Westport, Connecticut.
22. Enoch, *Memoirs,* 128–30.
23. Ibid., 130–33; Ruth Gruenthal, manuscript corrections to quotations from interview of August 2013 in Westport, Connecticut, in draft of Chapter 15.
24. Enoch, *Memoirs,* 134–36; Ruth Gruenthal, manuscript corrections to quotations from interview of 14 August 2013 in Westport, Connecticut, in draft of Chapter 15.
25. Enoch, *Memoirs,* 138–40; Sidney Fields, "Only Human: Proves American Dream," *Chicago Daily News,* n.d. [probably 1964], Enoch Scrapbook, CE.
26. Enoch, *Memoirs,* 140–41.
27. Ibid.; "Authors Who Fled from Nazis Arrive," *New York Times,* 14 October 1940, 16; Enoch, *Memoirs,* 142.
28. Enoch, *Memoirs,* 142–43.

CHAPTER SIXTEEN. ALBATROSS UNDER THE OCCUPATION

1. Erich Kupfer, Bericht, 19 November 1940, R 87/1192, BAL. Holroyd-Reece had convinced French officials that Albatross held "unsecured claims" against Tauchnitz, presumably for the books held beyond its reach in Leipzig warehouses.
2. Ibid.
3. Ibid.; Fouché, *L'Édition française sous l'Occupation,* 63–67.
4. Kupfer, Bericht, 19 November 1940, R 87/1192, BAL.
5. Spotts, *The Shameful Peace,* 40–41.
6. Spotts, *The Shameful Peace,* 40; see also Eckard Michels, *Das Deutsche Institut in Paris, 1940–1944: Ein Beitrag zu den deutsch-französischen Kulturbeziehungen und zur auswärtigen Kulturpolitik des Dritten Reiches* (Stuttgart: Steiner, 1993).
7. Appendix 1. PW's Career up to 1943, KV2/160 (PF Series): Wolfgang Krause-Brandstetter: Based in Paris, NAK (from March to June 1939, Krause-Brandstetter had served as a sergeant, but from August to December 1939 the war pulled him into Poland, for which he earned a promotion to second lieutenant); Wolfgang Krause-Brandstetter, Party Membership Form, RG242 Foreign Records Seized, Collection BDC Microfilm NSDAP Ortsgruppenkartei, A3340-MFOK-CO15 Captured German and Related Records on Microform, NACP; Oscar William Brandstetter to Herr Klatten, 17 August 1940, Bestand, PA.

8. Fouché, *L'Édition française sous l'Occupation,* 63–67; Top Secret report of conversation between John Holroyd-Reece and Wolfgang Krause-Brandstetter, n.d., KV2/160 (PF Series): Wolfgang Krause-Brandstetter: Based in Paris, NAK. On rivalries between Occupation officials, see Allan Mitchell, *Nazi Paris,* 28–29, 73–74, and Spotts, *The Shameful Peace,* 52–53.
9. Mitchell, *Nazi Paris,* 27–31, 74–75; Spotts, *The Shameful Peace,* 36–40.
10. Mitchell, *Nazi Paris,* xi, 4–5, 27–34.
11. Fouché, *L'Édition française sous l'Occupation,* 17; Oskar Möhring to Militärbefehlshaber in Frankreich, Verwaltungsstab, Abt. Wi. I/3, 15 September 1942, AJ 40/701, ANF.
12. Fouché, *L'Édition française sous l'Occupation,* 15–16; Gruppe Schrifttum Tätigkeitsbericht: 23 to 29 August 1940, AJ40/1005, ANF.
13. The Liste Bernhard was a strictly German affair. Kaiser, the head of the Literature Section (Gruppe Schrifttum) of the military Propaganda Office for Greater Paris (Propaganda-Staffel), had worked with propaganda authorities in Berlin, compiling a pamphlet of 143 politically offensive titles. The French Syndicat des Éditeurs also helped crafted the Liste Otto: see Gez. Niggemeyer Feldpolizeikommissar, "Beschlagnahme von Buecheren und Druckschriften im besetzten Gebeit Frankreichs," 31 August 1940, AJ40/889, ANF; Mitchell, *Nazi Paris,* 30; Spotts, *The Shameful Peace,* 56–57.
14. Fouché, *L'Édition française sous l'Occupation,* 58–76, 110–111; Sonderführer K. [Kaiser] and Staffelführer, Propaganda Staffel Paris, to the Chef des Militaerverwaltungs Bezirks Paris, 9 October 1940, AJ40/889, ANF, also quoted in Fouché, *L'Édition française sous l'Occupation,* 67.
15. John Holroyd-Reece's words come from an article in *The Bookseller* (14 April 1940), quoted in Bruno Conrad to Chef der Militärverwaltung in France, Abt. Schrifttum, 26 October 1940, AJ40/1006, ANF.
16. Wolfgang Krause-Brandstetter, Erklärung, 26 October 1940, AJ40/1006, ANF; Bruno Conrad to Chef der Militärverwaltung in France, Abt. Schrifttum, 26 October 1940, AJ40/1006, ANF. Ironically, Conrad did not realize Albatross was also listed in the *Address Book for the German Book Trade,* and thus counted as a firm with German status.
17. Bruno Conrad to Chef der Militärverwaltung in France, Abt. Schrifttum, 26 October 1940, AJ40/1006, ANF.
18. Dr. Friedhelm Kaiser, Aktenvermerk, 6 November 1940, AJ40/1006, ANF.
19. Dr. Lenz to the Reichskommissar, 24 October 1940, R87/1192, BAL.
20. In his Paris years, Enoch had borrowed additional monies from the Jewish-owned Warburg Bank in Amsterdam through one of the Warburg sons with whom he had grown friendly in Hamburg; see Enoch, *Memoirs,* 81. Some evidence suggests that Continenta-Amsterdam may have been created less to handle Dutch distribution—

which Enoch could have easily done from Paris as he did with other markets—than to shuttle loan money or repayments more easily between Warburg in Amsterdam and Enoch in Paris. Continenta-Amsterdam paid especially low prices for the Albatross-Tauchnitz books it purchased from Continenta-Paris to sell in the Netherlands, rates that were "balanced out" by payments that Continenta-Paris then made to Continenta-Amsterdam. See Dr. jur. Otto Lenz to the Herrn Reichswirtschaftsminister, 3 January 1940, 21033, File 1363, SAL; Walter Gey and Erich Kupfer, Bericht über offene Albatross Fragen, n.d. [report about trip to Paris, 27 October–8 November 1941], R87/1192, BAL.

21. Dr. Friedhelm Kaiser, Aktenvermerk, 6 November 1940, AJ40/1006, ANF.
22. Ibid.

CHAPTER SEVENTEEN. THE DEUTSCHE TAUCHNITZ

1. Richard McDougall, *The Very Rich Hours of Adrienne Monnier* (New York: Scribner, 1976), 151.
2. Hans Hertel, "Armstrong, Bogart, Churchill, Penguin: The Danish Turn to Anglo-American Cultural Values from the 1920s to the 1950s," in *Britain and Denmark: Political, Economic and Cultural Relations in the Nineteenth and Twentieth Centuries*, ed. Jørgen Sevaldsen (Copenhagen: Museum Tusculanum Press, 2003), 448; Gunnar Lestikow, "Denmark Under the Nazi Heel," *Foreign Affairs Journal* (January 1943), available at http://www.foreignaffairs.com/articles/70240/gunnar-leistikow/denmark-under-the-nazi-heel; Allan Mitchell, *Nazi Paris*, 14–19.
3. Martin, "'European Literature' in the Nazi New Order," 488–90; see also Barbian, "'Kulturwerte im Zeitkampf.'" The historian Joseph Nye coined the term "soft power" and brought it into popular use through his *Bound to Lead: The Changing Nature of American Power* (New York: Basic, 1990) and *Soft Power: The Means to Success in World Politics* (New York: Public Affairs, 2004).
4. Erich Kupfer, Bericht, 19 November 1940, R 87/1192, BAL; Exécution des commandes d'ouvrages Tauchnitz-Albatross à Leipzig, 17 December 1940, Deutsche Informationsstelle II, R 66813, PA.
5. Erich Kupfer, Bericht, 19 November 1940, R 87/1192, BAL; Wolfgang Krause-Brandstetter to Werner Klatten, 6 December 1940, Deutsche Informationsstelle II, R 66813, PA.
6. "Das Schrifttum in Jahre 1938," in Boberach, *Meldungen aus dem Reich*, 2:156; "Das Schrifttum im ersten Vierteljahr 1939," ibid., 2:290.
7. Karl Heinrich Bischoff, Vorschlag betreffend die Errichtung einer Übersetzungsagentur, 1 February 1940, R56/V/115, BAL.
8. H. Roskam, "Die niederländischen Buchhandel und das deutsche Buch in den Niederlanden," 9 May 1940, Kult—D IV, R 66810, PA.

9. Karl Buchheim and Isabel F. Pantenberg, *Eine sächsische Lebensgeschichte: Erinnerungen, 1889–1972* (Munich: R. Oldenbourg, 1996), 187; Le Coupole Menu, 1943, Collection Hachette: Messageries Hachette C17 B4 (S2): 41-44, IMEC.
10. Outline of a Speech by Herrn Klatten (Head of the Deutschen Informationsstelle II) vor den Kulturreferenten, 11 July 1941, Deutsche Informationsstelle IV, R 67066, PA. See also Renders, "Hitler's European Publishing Ambitions," 503.
11. Wolfgang Krause-Brandstetter to Werner Klatten, 6 December 1940, Deutsche Informationsstelle II, R 66813, PA.
12. Walter Gey to the Reichskommissar, Betrifft: The Albatross Verlag, 20 June 1941, R87/1192, BAL.
13. Gruppe Schrifttum of the Propaganda-Staffel Paris, Tätigkeitsbericht: 27 April to 3 May 1941, AJ40/1005, ANF; Bruno Conrad [Director of Department Étrangère Hachette], Monatsbericht for DEH, June 1941, Collection Hachette, Messageries Hachette, C17 B4 (S2), Le Directeur des Messageries [Hachette], Librairie Étrangère, to Wolfgang Krause-Brandstetter, 25 June 1941, Collection Hachette, Messageries Hachette, C26 B2 (S2), both IMEC.
14. Pierre Audiat, quoted in Fouché, *L'Édition française sous l'Occupation,* 190; Mitchell, *Nazi Paris,* 80; Gruppe Schrifttum of the Propaganda-Staffel Paris, Tatigkeitsbericht: 28 November 1941, AJ40/1005, ANF.
15. In forging the Deutsche Tauchnitz, the regime did what it had done elsewhere. It took a cosmopolitan model and subverted its liberal purpose for German ends. See, for instance, Martin's discussion in his "'European Literature' in the Nazi New Order" of how the Propaganda Ministry adapted the tradition of inviting international writers to Germany for an "exchange" of ideas—an excuse to get nationalist writers from different nations to come together to solidify nationalist tendencies. In the case of the Deutsche Tauchnitz, officials missed one critical irony: that it might be perceived as a wolf in sheep's clothing—that is, that looking like Albatross-Tauchnitz books might not be enough to mask the new series' distance from Albatross's original cosmopolitan intent.

CHAPTER EIGHTEEN. ENGLISH BOOKS ABROAD

1. Charles Dickens, Jr., *Dickens's Dictionary of London* (London: Charles Dickens, 1882), 215; John Holroyd-Reece to A. P. Watt and Co., 2 July 1940, David Lloyd Agency for Pearl Buck (C0060), Box 28, File 19, PUA.
2. Ernie Pyle, *Ernie Pyle in England* (New York: Macbride, 1945), 31–33; Holman, *Print for Victory,* 30.
3. Dr. Pinner to M.M. [probably Maurice Meiklejohn], 7 May 1947, Frieda Lawrence Collection, Series IV: Miscellaneous, Box 8, Folder 7, HRC; John Holroyd-Reece

to Pearl Buck, 30 April 1940, David Lloyd Agency Files of Pearl Buck (C0060), Box 28, File 19, PUA.

4. E. H. Carr to the Secretary to the Treasury, 14 December 1939, TNA T 160/1340, The British Council, 2 June 1942, TNA BT 96/121 Foreign Office, Government Sub-Committee for the Supply of Books, Minutes of 13 June 1942, TNA BT 96/121, all quoted in Holman, *Print for Victory,* 20, 124, 125, respectively.
5. John Holroyd-Reece to Messrs. A.P. Watt & Son, 2 July 1940, David Lloyd Agency for Pearl Buck (C0060), Box 28, Folder 19, PUA; Walter Gey to Reichskommissar Ernst, 10 August 1940, R87/1192, BAL.
6. Walter Gey to the Oberlandsgericht Dresden, 6 March 1941, Gey to the Reichskommissar, 20 September 1941, Gey, Report for Reichskommissar, 7 January 1942, all R87/1192, BAL.
7. Walter Gey, Anlagen zur Bilanz, 31 December 1940, Gey to Reichskommissar, 20 June and 17 July 1941, all R87/1192, BAL.
8. Sylvia Beach, Orders & Books out of Stock, Sylvia Beach Papers C0108, Box 72, PUA.
9. Wolfgang Krause-Brandstetter to Werner Klatten, 20 December 1941, Deutsche Informationsstelle II, R 66812, PA; Pont of Punch [Graham Laidler], *The British Character,* Introduction by E. M. Delafield (Leipzig: Albatross, 1939), 18.
10. Werner Klatten to Wolfgang Krause-Brandstetter, 30 December 1941, Deutsche Informationsstelle II, R 66812, PA.
11. Dr. Gaupp, Aktenvermerk, 30 August 1941, R87/1192, BAL.
12. "The Albatross Books Re-Appear in Denmark too," *Berlingske Tidende,* 2 March 1949, n.p., English translation of article in Danish paper, LES; E. M. Delafield, "Introduction," in Pont of Punch *The British Character,* 7; Goebbels, *The Goebbels Diaries,* 361; "The Albatross Books Re-Appear in Denmark Too," *Berlingske Tidende,* 2 March 1949, n.p., English translation of article in Danish paper, LES; "The Love of Keeping Calm," in Pont of Punch, *The British Character,* 45.
13. Charles Morgan, "France is an Idea Necessary to Civilization," in Morgan, *Reflections in a Mirror,* Second Series (New York: Macmillan, 1947), 100, 111–12; Victor de Pange, *Charles Morgan* (Paris: Éditions Universitaires, 1962), 24–26.
14. John Holroyd-Reece to A.P. Watt and Co., 2 July 1940, David Lloyd Agency for Pearl Buck (C0060), Box 28, File 19, PUA; Walter Gey to Reichskommissar, 16 August 1941, R87/1192, BAL. Gey was charged with clarifying whether the Brandstetters could take over Albatross. The details are complicated, but, in essence, if Albatross's debts were too high, the Reich Commissioner could authorize a Brandstetter takeover as a wartime necessity, i.e., the only way to "rescue" Albatross from itself. If Gey judged Albatross debts to be reasonable, however, then the commissioner would not grant the Brandstetters the permission they wished. At

this juncture, the question remained undecided because Albatross finances were so complicated and they stretched over several national markets.

15. Goebbels, *Tagebücher,* 2:607, quoted in Barbian, *The Politics of Literature,* 5; Goebbels, *The Goebbels Diaries,* 52 (used books), 115 (newspapers), 246 (journals); R. Erckmann, "Grundsätzlichees zur Papierfrage," *Der Buchhändler im neuen Reich* 7 (1942): 171–75, quoted in Barbian, *Literaturpolitik im NS-Staat,* 278. See also Kater, *Different Drummers,* 47, for Goebbels's call for "lighter music" on German radio stations, including jazz, to which he was ideologically opposed, to help listeners escape the trials of their days.
16. Benecke, *Eine Buchhandlung in Berlin,* 109; "Zur Lage im Schrifttum," February 1942, in Boberach, *Meldungen aus dem Reich,* 9:3317–18; Max Christian Wegner to Annemarie Wegner, 6 August 1940, MW.
17. "Mangel im Gebiet des Schrifttums," 22 August 1940, in Boberach, *Meldungen aus dem Reich,* 5:1492; "Zur Lage im Buchhandel," 19 September 1940, ibid., 5:1585; "Zur Lage im Schrifttum," January 1941, ibid.,6:1926; "Meldungen zur Lage im Schrifttum," February 1942, ibid., 9: 3317; Max Christian Wegner to Annemarie Wegner, 29 December 1940, MW; "Zur Lage im Sortimentsbuchhandel," in Boberach, *Meldungen aus dem Reich,* 8:2951.
18. Kliemann, "Die Welt des Buchhandels," 162, 166–67; "Meldungen zur Lage im Schrifttum," February 1942, in Boberach, *Meldungen aus dem Reich,* 9:3317–18.
19. "Zur Lage im Schifttum Januar 1941," in Boberach, *Meldungen aus dem Reich,* 6:1926; Stieg, *Public Libraries,* 249–50.
20. Adam, *Lesen unter Hitler,* 320. Adams notes that book production rose to 341 million books in 1941, 100 million more than in the previous year, and that fiction outstripped political titles (fiction: 100 million; texts for children and adolescents: 44 million; political titles: 59 million). "Zur Lage in Schrifttum September 1940," in Boberach, *Meldungen aus dem Reich,* 5:1576.
21. "[Anweisung] Nr. 119, Betr. Ausfuhr des englischen Uebersetzungsschriftuums," *Vertrauliche Mitteilungen für die Fachschaft Verlag,* Nr. 116–162 (1 October 1941), 2. Adam Tooze also notes that the Reich's need for foreign currency diminished as Germany claimed more terrain, and more spoils of war, from those it conquered, and imposed a centralized clearing system for currency on western Europe: *Wages of Destruction,* 386–87. "[Anweisung] Nr. 187, Betr. Behandlung des nordamerkanischen und britischen Übersetzungsschriftuums," *Vertrauliche Mitteilungen für die Fachschaft Verlag,* Nr. 187–195 (5 January 1942), 1; "[Anweisung] Nr. 202, "Betr. Unmittelbare Fühlungnahme mit den ausländische Vertretungen fremder Staaten," and "[Anweisung] Nr. 203, "Betr. Hinweise auf das Reichsministerium für Volksaufklärung und Propaganda bei Vertragsabschlüssen mit ausländischen Autoren und Verlagen," *Vertrauliche Mitteilungen für die Fachschaft Verlag,* Nr. 196–236 (10 March 1942), 1–2.

22. Walter Gey, Bericht zur Bilanz per 31 December 1931, 4 July 1942, R87/1193, BAL; Dr. Gaupp [Office of the Reich commissioner], Aktenvermerk, 30 August 1941, R87/1192, BAL; SGD Brigadier James Greenshields and SGD Colonel Charles A. Reid, Final Report on Target P. 109 on US Group CC and Control Commission for Germany (British Element), Summary of Dr. Krohn with footnote on Dr. Ernst, 64-65, 11 July 1945, B129/76, BAK; this report offers the following reason for Ernst's retirement as Reich Commissioner: "It is believed that [Ernst] was never a member of the Party and that he gave up his post because of the political difficulties in which it involved him and because private industry was more attractive to him and offered better remuneration." Dr. Hövel, Schnellbrief, 27 April 1942, Devisenstelle Leipzig, 1681, SAL.
23. List of Albatross Books, n.d. [attachment to Oskar Möhring to the Militärbefehlshaber Frankreich, Verwaltungsstab, Abteilung Wi. I/3, letter of 7 August 1942], AJ/40/701, ANF.
24. Oskar Möhring to the Militärbefehlshaber Frankreich, Verwaltungsstab, Abteilung Wi. I/3, 7 August 1942, AJ/40/701, ANF. In this letter, Möhring mentions that he has just written the Propaganda-Abteilung (Propanda Division) for permission to sell the books to a Herr Neilsen of Messageries du livre who wanted to buy the entire stock at a 55 percent discount off the regular price of 30 francs per book.
25. Gruppe Schrifttum Tätigkeitsbericht, 20–25 July 1941, AJ/40/1005, ANF.
26. Gruppe Schrifttum Lagebericht, 31 May 1941, AJ/40/1005, ANF; Gruppe Schrifttum Tätigkeitsbericht, 21–28 June 1941, AJ/40/1005, ANF; "Bericht über die Lage der Unterhaltungsliteratur," Gruppe Schrifttum Bericht, 20–25 July 1941, AJ/40/1005, ANF; Fouché, *L'Édition française sous l'Occupation,* 27–29. The ban on Anglo-American books, except for the classics, was reiterated in the third edition of the censorship list, released on 8 July 1942.
27. Gruppe Schrifttum at Propaganda-Staffel Paris, Arbeits und Lagebericht, 29 March 1942, AJ40/1005, ANF; Referatsleiter der Kulturpolitischen Abteilung des Auswärtigen Amtes und Ministerialrat Kurt Metzner, "Vortrag zur Kulturreferentenbesprechung am Mittwoch den 12. August 1942," Deutsche Informationsstelle IV, R 67066, PA.
28. Werner Klatten to Metzner, 28 April 1942, Bestand, PA; Metzner, Vortrag zur Kulturreferentenbesprechung, 12 August 1942, D IV, R 67066, PA; Explanation of Annual Statement for Tauchnitz to the Commerz-Bank, Leipzig, 31 December 1942, 21016, File 336, SAL; See, in the context of reading material for soldiers, Manning, *When Books Went to War.* Deutsche Tauchnitz books were intended to have a similarly inspiring effect on German soldiers—although this was not their primary target audience—as Molly Guptill Manning claims English-language books did for Allied soldiers.
29. Spotts, *The Shameful Peace,* 67; "Enquête dans les Librairies des 20 Arrondisse-

ments de Paris," 8 September 1941, AJ40/1006, ANF; Todd and Bowden, *Tauchnitz International Editions in English*, 747.

30. Oskar Möhring to Verwaltungsstab Abteilung Wi I/3, 15 September 1942, AJ/40/701, ANF.
31. W. M. Schulz, Aktenvermerk, 15 March 1943, 21765 Börnsenverein Bestand, F101, SAL; Announcement, *Bibliographie de la France* 46–47 (19–26 November 1943), n.p.; Monatsübersicht der Gruppe Schrifttum der Propaganda-Abteilung Frankreich, Paris, 21 February 1944, AJ/40/1005, ANF.
32. Metzner, "Vortrag zur Kulturreferentenbesprechung am Mittwoch den 12. August 1942," Deutsche Informationsstelle IV, R 67066, PA; A.P. Watt and Sons to David Lloyd, 10 November 1942, David Lloyd Agency for Pearl Buck (C0060), Box 28, File 23, PUA.
33. Sturge, "Flight from the Programme," 80. Sturge is summarizing a point made by Helga Geyer-Ryan in her "Trivialliteratur und Literaturpolitik im Dritten Reich," *Sprachen im technischen Zeitalter* 67 (1978): 267–77.

CHAPTER NINETEEN. RIVALS

1. "Exit Tauchnitz," *Time,* 20 July 1942; "A Library Closed," *New York Times,* 23 June 1942, 18.
2. Albert Bonnier to "Gentlemen," April 1942, David Lloyd Agency for Pearl Buck (C0060), Box 28, Folder 23. PUA.
3. Buck signed with Bonnier for *The Dragon Seed,* and Bromfield for *Wild Is the River.* In 1938, the Nazi regime had suppressed Buck's Tauchnitz editions, for which Albatross held most of the rights, and in 1940 Bromfield's Albatross titles. So Bonnier offered such writers a continental outlet otherwise denied to them: see Laurence Pollinger Ltd., Files Concerning D. H. Lawrence's *Lady Chatterley's Lover,* 1931–1979, Series 3, Box 3, Folder 8, PUA. *Lady Chatterley's Lover* quickly sold out, reaching a second printing in its first year.
4. C. D. Medley to A. S. Watt, 24 August 1943, David Lloyd Agency for Pearl Buck (C0060), Box 28, folder 21, PUA.
5. John Holroyd-Reece to C. D. Medley, n.d. [probably September 1943], David Lloyd Agency for Pearl Buck (C0060), Box 28, Folder 12, PUA.
6. Ibid. Given rumors that Holroyd-Reece had worked for British intelligence in World War I, as well as his own claim that he did so leading into World War II, it is at least worth mentioning that Grizedale Hall, the main prisoner-of-war camp for German and Italian officers, was located near Windermere. It is not a place to which Holroyd-Reece otherwise seems to have retired, and his linguistic talents would have made him admirably suited to interrogate new arrivals.
7. Young, quoted in Lewis, *Penguin Special,* 87; on the resistance of the British pub-

lishing establishment, see Lewis, *Penguin Special,* 88–89; Allen, quoted in, Silverman, *The Time of Their Lives,* 385.

8. John Holroyd-Reece to Allen Lane, Confidential Memorandum, n.d. but probably March 1934, JL25/1, Correspondence with Albatross Ltd., RHGA; McCleery, "The Paperback Evolution," 12–13.
9. Cape and Orwell quoted in Schmoller, "The Paperback Revolution," 299–300. On 28 February 1938, Holroyd-Reece and Lane defended paperbacks at the dinner of the Double Crown Club, a bibliophile society. Some years later, Holroyd-Reece made the comment in the text, quoted in Lewis, *Penguin Special,* 141. Sylvia Beach, 1937 Purchase Log, Sylvia Beach Papers C0108, Box 68, PUA. See also Davis, *The Paperbacking of America,* 28.
10. Richard Walsh to David Lloyd, 24 May 1943, David Lloyd Agency for Pearl Buck (C0060), Box 28, folder 23, PUA; Edward Young, quoted in Lewis, *Penguin Special,* 87.
11. Enoch, *Memoirs,* 148–50.
12. Enoch, Eidesstattliche Versicherung, 3 March 1958, State of New York, Restitution File, SAH; Ruth Gruenthal, Interview, 10 August 2009, Westport, Connecticut; Enoch, *Memoirs,* 143.
13. Enoch, *Memoirs,* 144–45.
14. Ibid., 148–49; Sidney Fields, "Only Human: Proves American Dream," *Chicago Daily News,* n.d. [probably 1964], Scrapbook, CE.
15. Enoch, *Memoirs,* 156, 152–53; At this time, Enoch held only a temporary visitor's visa; with German quotas exhausted in 1940, there had been no option for a permanent visa. Ruth Gruenthal, Interview, 14 August 2013, Westport, Connecticut.
16. Kurt Enoch, Application for Citizenship, n.d., RGA.

CHAPTER TWENTY. WHEN THE BOMBS FELL

1. "30 January 1943: The Tenth Anniversary of the Takeover of Power; Guidelines from the Reich Propaganda Leader," German Propaganda Archive, Calvin College, at http://www.calvin.edu/academic/cas/gpa/30jan1943.htm; Kershaw, *Hitler, 1936–1945,* 547–50; Evans, *The Third Reich at War,* 413–20.
2. Joseph Goebbels, "Rede auf der Kundgebung zum 10 Jahrestag der Machtübernahme," in Goebbels, *Goebbels-Reden,* 2:158–71; for a partial English translation see "Excerpts from Speeches by Goering and Goebbels at Party Rally," *New York Times,* 31 January 1943, 39.
3. "Fear-Haunted Anniversary," *New York Times,* 1 February 1943, 14; Lowe, *Inferno,* 61–62.
4. Joseph Goebbels, "Rede auf der Kundgebung des Gaues Berlin der NSDAP," in Goebbels, *Goebbels-Reden,* 2:172–208; for a readily accessible English translation

see the German Propaganda Archive at Calvin College: http://research.calvin.edu/german-propaganda-archive/goeb36.htm.

5. Max Christian Wegner to Annemarie Wegner, 2 November 1943, MW; Fiona Brewster, Interview, 3 May 2013, Le Breuil-Rouillac, France; Michel Ollendorff, Interview, 12 December 2013, Vincennes, France. Both interviewees were struck by Wegner's reaction because they said it was the first time they had ever seen a man cry. Matthias Wegner, Interview, 6 May 2012, Hamburg, Germany; Thomas Wegner, Interview, 5 May 2013, Cologne, Germany.
6. Dr. Blasberg, Feldgericht [on Hauptmann Christian Wegner], 26 November 1943, MW; "Kriegsbeurteilung zum 1 June 1943 . . . über den Hauptmann . . . Christian Wegner," 1 June 1943, Pers6/195111, BAF (woven into the narrative was the rubber-stamp line—also included in Krause-Brandstetter's promotion documents—"shows mastery of the National Socialist body of thought and knows how to convey it"). Max Christian Wegner to Annemarie Wegner, 17 November 1943, MW.
7. Max Christian Wegner to Annemarie Wegner, 2 November 1943, MW.
8. Dr. Blasberg, Feldgericht, 26 November 1943, MW.
9. Ibid.
10. Ibid.
11. Sir Arthur "Bomber" Harris, 24 July 1943, quoted in Lowe, *Inferno,* 62–63.
12. Lowe, *Inferno,* 89–91, 110, 176–77; Overy, *The Bombing War.*
13. Lowe, *Inferno,* 100, 115, 184, 293–94; Lowe's figures indicate staggering losses: 40,385 residential buildings, along with 109,471 homes, 3,785 industrial plants, 7,190 small businesses, 83 banks, 379 office buildings, 112 Nazi party offices, 7 warehouses, 13 public utility premises, 22 transport premises, 76 public offices, 80 military installations, and 12 bridges. Hans Erich Nossack, *The End,* trans. Joel Agee (Chicago: University of Chicago Press, 2006), 41.
14. Annemarie Wegner to Max Christian Wegner, 9 August 1943, MW; Matthias Wegner, Email to author, 18 May 2016; Lowe, *Inferno,* 168.
15. Matthias Wegner, Interview, 3 October 2009, Hamburg, Germany.
16. Dr. Blasberg, Feldgericht, 26 November 1943, MW.
17. Max Christian Wegner to Herr Platz, 23 November 1943, MW.
18. Max Christian Wegner to Annemarie Wegner, 3 and 15 December 1943 and 1 January 1944, MW. Some family evidence suggests that Wegner may have dropped this plan and been pardoned by his division commander. Markus Wegner, Email to author, 19 August 2015.
19. Max Christian Wegner to Annemarie Wegner, 7 February 1944, MW.
20. Matthias Wegner, "Offener Brief an einen Enkel," MW.
21. Wilhelm Baur, "Zur Lage im Buchhandel," *Börsenblatt für den Deutschen Buchhandel,* 110: 82 (17 April 1943): 1; "Liste der stillzulegenden Verlage," T580 961, Captured German and Related Records on Microform, NACP.

22. Walter Gey to Finanzamt für Körperschaften Leipzig, 29 May 1942, 1681, SAL; Dr. Gaupp for the Reichskommissar für die Behandlung feindlichen Vermögens to the Wehrbezirkskommando Leipzig III, 10 March 1942, R87/1193, BAL. Kupfer was ordered to start military service on 30 September 1941; however, the Reich Commissioner got him a three-month extension on the grounds that Albatross was achieving important work for the regime. Werner Klatten, Wolfgang Krause-Brandstetter's boss at the Foreign Office expressed an interest in Albatross in January 1942. There is evidence that Klatten was considering using Albatross's recognized name and format to launch a poetry or literature series promoting the new European order which Hitler envisioned, but it may be that Krause-Brandstetter also intervened; see Gruppe Informationsstelle IV to Herr Geutebrück, Mitteilung für Herrn Geutebrück, 13 August 1942, 66816, PA. The Brandstetters' attempt to take over Albatross shares failed when, in late August 1941, enemy property custodian Willy Hoffman reported to the Reich Commissioner that the Albatross Verlag's debt of roughly 200,000 RM to Pegasus could largely be cleared from its slate. It is simplest to say that Hoffman judged the "loan" Pegasus had granted to Albatross in 1931 to be hidden start-up capital. Holroyd-Reece owned Pegasus; Holroyd-Reece directed the Publishing Holding Company that owned Albatross. This was good news for Albatross's financial bottom line. Yet with Albatross no longer in dire financial straits, the Reich Commissioner could not authorize a Brandstetter takeover of Albatross. For further details on these financial questions, see 20206 (Oberfinanzpräsident Leipzig), File 1681, SAL, and R87/1193, BAL.
23. Erich Kupfer to Walter Gey, 6 and 24 November 1942; Bernhard Tauchnitz Nachfolger, Brandstetter & Co to The Albatross Verlag, 14 October 1942, all R87/1193, BAL.
24. Walter Gey to Reichskommissar, 7 July 1943, R87/1193, BAL.
25. S. J. McCune, Captain AUS NOI Section, "Secret NOI Report on the Leipzig Air Raid," 29 March 1944, RG 165 Records of the War Department General and Special Staffs, Box 653, NACP; General Report, n.d. [but after December 1943] and Confidential, Air Raid Damage in Germany, n.d. [but after April 1944], both RG 165 Records of the War Department General and Special Staffs, Box 658, NACP.
26. Semi-Monthly Report, Publications Branch, Office of Military Government for German (US) Information Services Division, 20 January 1949, RG 260 Records of United States Occupation Headquarters, World War II, Box 1212, NACP; Confidential, Air Raid Damage in Germany, n.d. but after April 1944, RG 165 Records of the War Department General and Special Staffs, Box 658, NACP.
27. Walter Gey to Reichskommissar, 13 December 1943, R87/1193, BAL.
28. Walter Gey to Herrn Oberbürgermeister der Reichsmessestadt Leipzig Amt für Kriegssachschäden als Feststellungsbehörde, 29 June 1944, R87/1193, BAL.

29. Walter Gey to Reichskommissar, 2 February 1944, R87/1193, BAL.
30. Walter Gey to Reichskommissar, 23 March 1944, R87/1193, BAL.
31. Ibid.; Walter Gey, Report to Reichskommissar, 6 October 1944, R87/1193, BAL.
32. Walter Gey to Reichskommissar, 6 October 1944, 12 December 1944, and 8 January 1945, all R87/1194, BAL.
33. Walter Gey to Reichskommissar, Bericht zur Bilanz per 31. Dezember 1944, 5 February 1945, R87/1194, BAL.

CHAPTER TWENTY-ONE. MAKING PEACE

1. Ernie Pyle, *Brave Men* (Lincoln: University of Nebraska Press, 2001), 482; Report, September 29, 1944, KV2/160 (PF Series): Wolfgang Krause-Brandstetter: Based in Paris, NAK. According to a confirming report by the Allies, Krause-Brandstetter served under Hanesse in a unit called the Leitstelle I Luft, where he and other officers did intelligence work while ostensibly serving on Hanesse's general staff; see CSDIC (U.K.) Report, S.I.R. 1162, Organisation and Activities of German Abwehr (France and Elsewhere), Appendix I: Abwehr Personnel, 5 November 1944, RG 165 Records of War Department General and Special Staffs, Captured Personnel and Material Branch Reports relating to POW Interrogations, 1943–1945, CSDIC UK SIR to CSDIC UK SIR, Box 662, NACP; the von Buttlar in question is probably Generalmajor Edgar von Buttlar, who served under the German Military Commander of France as of 7 August 1944. Matthew Cobb, *Eleven Days in August: The Liberation of Paris in 1944* (London: Simon and Schuster, 2014), 253–99.
2. Pyle, *Brave Men,* 483–87; Beach, *Shakespeare and Company,* 218–20.
3. Ben Cosgrove, "LIFE at the Liberation of Paris, 1944: A Photographer's Story," 5 August 2013, at http://time.com/3877719/the-liberation-of-paris-a-photographers-story/.
4. Précis of conversation between John Holroyd-Reece, Esq., and P/W Oberleutnant Wolfgang Brandstetter, German Air Force, 2 February 1945, KV2/160 (PF Series): Wolfgang Krause-Brandstetter: Based in Paris, NAK.
5. Obltn. Krause-Brandsta [*sic*], I Luft Paris, B.1. Folder B, Transmissions 114854 and 115245, 6 September 1944, KV2/160 (PF Series): Wolfgang Krause-Brandstetter: Based in Paris, NAK; Transcript of Conversation between Oberlt. Brandstetter and Mr. John Holroyd-Reece, 29 January 1945, KV2/160 (PF Series): Wolfgang Krause-Brandstetter: Based in Paris, NAK.
6. Krause-Brandstetter to Major Steed, 8 February 1945. KV2/160 (PF Series): Wolfgang Krause-Brandstetter: Based in Paris, NAK.
7. John Holroyd-Reece to O.P. London District Cage, Top Secret Memorandum, n.d., KV2/160 (PF Series): Wolfgang Krause-Brandstetter: Based in Paris, NAK. The Brandenburg Division used its troops' fluency in languages to cross enemy

lines, pretending to be from the local culture, so they could seize critical bridges or assets in advance of a full-fledged German attack. Yet some of its units were also extremely violent. The Division in Poland had been implicated in massacres at Katowice.

8. Précis of conversation between John Holroyd-Reece, Esq., and P/W Oberleutnant Wolfgang Brandstetter, German Air Force, 2 February 1945, KV2/160 (PF Series): Wolfgang Krause-Brandstetter: Based in Paris, NAK. The figures he gives for the "English series" may only include Tauchnitz. Gey kept figures for Albatross.
9. John Holroyd-Reece to O.P. London District Cage, Top Secret Memorandum, n.d., KV2/160 (PF Series): Wolfgang Krause-Brandstetter: Based in Paris, NAK. Among other purchases, Krause-Brandstetter admitted, he also bought shares in the Éditions Cluny when one of its owners, Fernand Hazan, had been driven out by the Nazis, and then sold them back to Jacques de Brion, the other owner, with great gain to himself. Krause-Brandstetter claimed that Brion had ties to the French Resistance and that he himself had sought protection at the end of the war from French people whom he had "saved from death sentences" during the Occupation.
10. "Appendix I: MI5 Organization," in Guy Liddell, *The Guy Liddell Diaries: MI5's Director of Counter-Espionage in World War II,* ed. Nigel West, vol. 1: *1939–42* (New York: Routledge, 2005), 312.; "Minutes Between B.1.B. and Sections re: Holroyd-Reece and Brandstetter," 22 January 1945, C.S.D.I.C., Précis of conversation between Holroyd-Reece and Brandstetter, recorded at London District Cage on 29 January 1945, written up 2 February 1945, both KV2/160 (PF Series): Wolfgang Krause-Brandstetter: Based in Paris, NAK. It is also possible that Holroyd-Reece agreed with Krause-Brandstetter simply to keep him talking.
11. Krause-Brandstetter claimed ties to Father Raymond Bruckberger, a Dominican priest active in the Resistance. While interrogators found the claim "a bit fantastic," Krause-Brandstetter did have among his possessions a fake identity card, which he said Bruckberger had helped him procure. When the S.D. and Sipo issued such cards to Germans in Paris, they used one of the Paris Préfectures; Krause-Brandstetter's card derived, instead, from the Préfecture of Yonne, adding some merit to his story: "Secret" Report, Headquarters "T" Force, Twelfth Army Group, Wolfgang Brandstetter, 29 August 1944; CSDIC Report, Sir 886, Report on Information from . . . Oblt. Brandstetter . . . ; "List of Belongings Sent over with Ober Lt. Krause-Brandstetter, n.d.; Captain M. Hilton, Interrogation Report on PW sent to No. 7, n.d. 5 November 1944. All four sources KV2/160 (PF Series): Wolfgang Krause-Brandstetter: Based in Paris, NAK.
12. Extract from Statement made by "Seth" [from interrogation on 13 September 1944], extract made on 23 September 1944, Extract [from second interrogation report on "Seth" dated 27 April 1945] made on 23 October 1945, both KV2/160 (PF Series): Wolfgang Krause-Brandstetter: Based in Paris, NAK.

13. Krause-Brandstetter to Major Steed, 8 February 1945, KV2/160 (PF Series): Wolfgang Krause-Brandstetter: Based in Paris, NAK.
14. Holroyd-Reece to O.P. London District Cage, Top Secret Memorandum, n.d., KV2/160 (PF Series): Wolfgang Krause-Brandstetter: Based in Paris, NAK.
15. Lt. Colonel V. H. Seymer to P.I.D. Foreign Office, 24 January 1945, Lt. Colonel V. H. Seymer [S.L.B.3] to B.1.B, Notes on Brandstetter, 1 March 1945, D.I. Wilson to S.L.B.3 [probably to V. H. Seymer], 4 March 1945, Appendix B: Personalities of SD Counter-Evasion Service (Paris), Summer of 1944., n.d. probably 17 August 1945], Major John F. White to Brigadier General G. Bryan Conrad, Memo: Betrayal of American Evaders: SD Counter-evasion Service (Paris), Summer of 1944, 17 August 1945, Major C. P. Hope, Paris M.I.5 Liaison Section to M.I.5—S.L.B.3 (Major Patterson), 6 December 1945, all KV2/160 (PF Series): Wolfgang Krause-Brandstetter: Based in Paris, NAK.
16. J. Barnes, SLB3 (Renegades Investigation Unit) to W. Morgan, 8 March 1945, KV2/160 (PF Series): Wolfgang Krause-Brandstetter: Based in Paris, NAK; I thank Professor John Hill at Immaculata College for sharing information from the Interrogation Report on Miodraz Yevremovich (alias "Draga"), n.d., p. 18, KV2/3412, NAK, which revealed that Krause-Brandstetter used the name "John Brandstetter."
17. John Holroyd-Reece to Harold Raymond, 30 April 1945, CW 100/16, RHGA.
18. Harold Raymond to J. C. Medley, 22 May 1945, CW 100/16, RHGA. According to Raymond, Albatross paid only a 7.5 percent royalty on a less expensive book, while hardcover editions paid a 25 percent royalty on a higher priced book. Raymond preferred to pay the higher royalty on hardcover editions, which were expensive enough to leave a stronger profit per book for the publisher. Huxley's former agent, Ralph Pinker, went into liquidation during the war, perhaps partly through nonpayment of Albatross royalties from Germany.
19. John Holroyd-Reece to Raymond, 30 April 1945, CW 100/16, RHGA.
20. Ibid.
21. Harold Raymond to John Holroyd-Reece, 4 May 1945; Raymond to J. C. Medley, 22 May 1945, both CW100/16, RHGA.
22. Enoch, *Memoirs,* 160–62.
23. Ibid., 168; Frost quoted in Lewis, *Penguin Special,* 215.
24. Weybright, *The Making of a Publisher,* 165.
25. Weybright, *The Making of a Publisher,* 17; Marc Jaffe, Phone interview, 29 May 2014; Talley quoted in Silverman, *The Time of Their Lives,* 429.
26. Enoch, *Memoirs,* 163.
27. Thomas Wegner, Interview, 5 May 2013, Cologne, Germany; Matthias Wegner, "Offener Brief an einen Enkel," n.d., MW.
28. The figures for the number of German casualties remain disputed. However, according to Percy Schramm, who kept the official diaries for the OKW (Oberkom-

mando der Wehrmacht) during the war, casualties on the Eastern Front between 1 September 1939 and 31 January 1945 are roughly one million dead and one million missing or POW. See Percy Schramm, *Kriegstagebuch des Oberkommandos der Wehrmacht: 1940–1945,* 8 vols. (Frankfurt am Main: Bernard and Graefe, 1961), 6:1508–11; Thomas Wegner, Interview, 5 May 2013, Cologne, Germany; Markus Wegner, E-mail, 19 August 2015. According to Markus Wegner, Wegner's son from his third marriage, Enders escaped with Wegner on one of the last ships from Pillau, and Wegner showed his gratitude to Enders by financially supporting him when he returned to the university to study law.

29. Max Christian Wegner to Annemarie Wegner, 14 January and 21 January 1945, quoted in Matthias Wegner, "Offener Brief an einen Enkel," MW; Matthias Wegner, "Offener Brief an einen Enkel," MW; Howard D. Grier, *Hitler, Dönitz, and the Baltic Sea: The Third Reich's Last Hope, 1944–1945* (Annapolis, Md.: Naval Institute Press, 2007), 81–88.
30. Matthias Wegner, "Offener Brief an einen Enkel," MW; Elbe Day, https://en.wikipedia.org/wiki/Elbe_Day (accessed 31 May 2016); Appendix H: A Diary of T-Force Operations in Kiel, May 1945, transcribed from TNA FO/1031/49, and available at http://arcre.com/archive/wwii/targetforce/tforceh (accessed 31 May 2016).
31. Matthias Wegner, "Offener Brief an einen Enkel," MW; Matthias Wegner, Interview, 3 October 2009; Hansgeorg Maier, "Verlegerprofil: Max Christian Wegner," *Welt und Wort* 3 (March 1951): n.p.
32. Matthias Wegner, Interview, 3 October 2009, Hamburg; Markus Wegner, Interview, 7 May 2012, Hamburg.
33. Gesine Froese, ed., *Als der Krieg zu Ende War: Ein Lesebuch vom Neubeginn in Hamburg und Schleswig-Holstein* (Hamburg: Norddeutscher Verleger- und Buchhändler-Verband, 1985), 160; *Handbuch der Lizenzen Deutscher Verlage* (Berlin: de Gruyter, 1947), 106; Clipping of Announcement, *Neue Hamburger Presse,* 7 November 1945, n.p.; Isa Vermehren, *Reise durch den letzten Akt: Ein Bericht (10.2.44 bis 29.6.45)* (Hamburg: Christian Wegner, 1946).

CHAPTER TWENTY-TWO. RISING FROM THE ASHES

1. The Albatross, MCMXLVII, Promotional Brochure, 1947, C Rep. 120, File 760, LAB.
2. Précis of conversation between John Holroyd-Reece, Esq., and P/W Oberleutnant Wolfgang Brandstetter, German Air Force, 2 February 1945, KV2/160 (PF Series): Wolfgang Krause-Brandstetter: Based in Paris, NAK; Holroyd-Reece to Harold Raymond, 30 April 1945, CW 100/16, RHGA; Death Announcement for Jeanne Holroyd-Reece, *Times* (London), 2 July 1945, 1; she passed away on 28 June 1945.
3. "Comment: Books into Europe," *The Observer,* 17 September 1944, 4.

4. Military Governor, British Troops, Berlin, B.A.O. R. Personal and Confidential to Michael Grant, British Council Deputy Director, European Division, 31 October 1945, BW32/3, NAK.
5. Hench, *Books as Weapons,* 206; Holman, *Print for Victory,* 162–67.
6. Maury Meiklejohn to Mr. Paroissien, 12 October 1946, INF 12/457, NAK.
7. Minutes of the first meeting of the Official Committee to coordinate the work of BES, Central Office of Information, INF 12/186, NAK. Book trade representatives included Stanley Unwin, who had since become Sir Stanley for his service to His Majesty's Government; Mr. Harry Paroissien of Penguin Books; Mr. F. E. K. Foat of distributor W.H. Smith; and literary agent Curtis Brown, Albatross's "godfather" from days of old; Mr. Paroissien to Miss Aitken, 11 October 1946, INF 12/457, NAK.
8. On Lord Lloyd, see J. M. Mitchell, *International Cultural Relations,* 44; Mr. Hadfield to Mr. Routh, 6 November 1946, INF 12/457, NAK.
9. Memo by Finance Officer referencing comment made by Mr. E. Mercier [Department of Overseas Trade], 20 December 1946, INF 12/457, NAK; M. R. Bruce [Treasury] to Mr. Hadfield [Central Office of Information], 20 March 1947; anonymous report, Albatross in Spain, n.d., Mr. Thompson to Mr. Hadfield, 2 April 1947, both INF 12/457, NAK.
10. Mr. Hadfield to Mr. Thompson, 31 March 1947, INF 12/457, Foreign Office German Section CO 901/208, PMD Section SITREP for January 1947, Mr. Hadfield to Mr. Lees [Treasury], 28 February 1947, INF 12/457, all three NAK.
11. R. G. Davies and Mr. Hadfield, The Albatross Ltd., 24 July 1947; Mr. Hadfield to Miss Bruce [Treasury], 19 September 1947; Agreement between the Albatross Ltd., London, and Rudolf Lechner und Sohn, Vienna, 16 January 1948, all INF 12/457, NAK.
12. Higham, *Literary Gent,* 191–92.
13. David Higham to John Holroyd-Reece, 5 June 1945, J. C. Medley to Harold Raymond, 23 May 1945, Holroyd-Reece to Raymond, 27 June 1945, all CW 100/16, RHGA. To Raymond, Holroyd-Reece maintained that he contractually owned rights "on *all* Huxley's output, past, present and future" and that these rights were protected because it was legally "established beyond doubt that the Albatross concern is in fact 100 per cent British." See also B. G. C. Wright to Mr. Price, 10 August 1945, CW 100/16, RHGA. In this letter, the British Trading with the Enemy Department, which countered Holroyd-Reece's claim, implied that contracts with the "enemy" German Albatross branch were not legally binding.
14. Harold Raymond to Aldous Huxley, 3 July 1945, CW/Huxley 1945 File, RHGA; Higham, *Literary Gent,* 191–92; Watson, "More Sketches from Memory," 2559.
15. J. V. Browne, Handwritten File Note, 9 December 1940, Foreign Office 371: Political/America/United States 1940, A 5075,NAK.

16. Eva A. Mayring, "Control Commission for Germany (British Element)," in Benz, ed., *Deutschland unter allierter Besatzung,* 239–43; Maury Meiklejohn to Mr. R. G. Davies, 6 June 1947, N.G. Thompson to Mr. Hadfield and Mr. Routh, 10 December 1947, both INF 12/457, NAK.
17. For maps documenting the Hamburg bombing, including the section where Wegner's office at Speersort was located, see Lowe, *Inferno,* 164–65, 204–5, 242–43. For the Pressehaus and the Nikolai Church see the Wikipedia articles "Hamburger Tageblatt" (Pressehaus, at de.Wikipedia.org) and "St Nicolas' Church, Hamburg" (at en.wikipedia.org), both accessed 28 July 2016.
18. Max Christian Wegner to Stanley Unwin, 25 January 1930, AUC 27/8 Curtis Brown Ltd., UR; N. G. Thompson to Mr. Hadfield and Mr. Routh, 10 December 1947, INF/457, NAK.
19. Todd and Bowden, *Tauchnitz International Editions,* 891–93; C. A. Furth to Max Christian Wegner, 14 January 1947, AUC, MC Wegner of Christian Wegner Verlag, UR.
20. Report of 27 September 1944, ZC 06483 A 1-3, BAL.
21. Werner Jäckh, *Festschrift zum 125 Jährigen Bestehen der Firma Bernhard Tauchnitz Verlag, 1837–1962* (Göppingen: Buchdruckerei Johannes Illig, , 1962); Todd and Bowden, *Tauchnitz International Editions,* 891; Leipzig Registry of Commerce, Entry 15, HRA 1220 Oscar Brandstetter Leipzig, SAL; Harry Bergholz, "Survey of Book- and Music Publishing in Post-War Germany," *Modern Language Journal* (December 1950): 616–25; VAG to Börsenverein, 4 May 1948, Börsenverein File 9494 VAG; Friedrich Vieweg und Sohn to Firma Oscar Brandstetter, 26 February 1948, 21056, File 8, SAL.
22. "Zum Tode von Wolfgang Brandstetter," *Börsenblatt für den Deutschen Buchhandel,* 17 December 1963, 2327; Book Section, PRISC Regional Staff, Hamburg, Information Control Memo to German Personnel Office of the PRISC Regional Staff, 9 October 1947, Personnel file of Wolfgang Brandstetter, Bestand VBS 243, Aktensignatur: 2703002610, RK Certificate, BAL; Todd and Bowden, *Tauchnitz International Editions,* 891; Jones, "Eradicating Nazism from the British Zone," 149–50.
23. Max Christian Wegner to C. A. Furth, 4 June 1947, AUC, MC Wegner of Christian Wegner Verlag, UR.
24. Max Christian Wegner to C. A. Furth, 19 January 1947, Anonymous handwritten comment on letter from Chatto and Windus to Wegner, 29 January 1947, both AUC, MC Wegner of Christian Wegner Verlag File, UR; John Holroyd-Reece to C. D. Medley, n.d. [probably September 1943], David Lloyd Agency for Pearl Buck (C0060), Box 28, Folder 12, PUA; Holroyd-Reece to Harold Raymond, 27 June 1945, CW 100/16, RHGA. See Todd and Bowden, *Tauchnitz International Editions,* 879–81, 891, for their claim that the Brandstetters retained Tauchnitz rights throughout these various partnerships.

25. Potsdam Agreement, Part III, Paragraph 7, quoted in Welch, "Priming the Pump of German Democracy," 222.
26. Lowe, *Savage Continent,* 34–50; Collingham, *The Taste of War,* 467–68.
27. Gollancz, *In Darkest Germany,* 227–29.
28. Gollancz, *In Darkest Germany,* 227–29; Gienow-Hecht, "Art Is Democracy," 31–32; Clemens, *Britische Kulturpolitik in Deutschland,* 67, 204–9; Welch, "Priming the Pump of German Democracy," 231.
29. N. G. Thompson to Mr. Hadfield and Mr. Routh, 10 December 1947, INF 12/457, NAK.
30. F.O. German Section CO 901/208 PMD section SITREP for January 1947, NAK; Markus Wegner, Interview, 7 May 2012, Hamburg, Germany.
31. N. G. Thompson to Mr. Hadfield and Mr. Routh, 10 December 1947, INF 12/457, NAK.
32. The Albatross, MCMXLVII, Promotional Brochure, 1947, C Rep. 120, File 760, LAB.
33. Maury Meiklejohn to Mr. Paroissien [Book Export Scheme], 12 October 1946, INF 12/457, NAK; for titles printed in Italy see Minutes of the Board meetings, 18–20 November 1946, Collins Archive, 1/1/5, GUL; for Dutch production, see S. G. van Looy to Wolfgang Ollendorff, 5 June 1947, SYT D 27 Correspondentie met Londen m.b.t. The Albatross Modern Continental Library, 1946–49, File Two: January–June 1947, Archief van A.W. Sijthoff's Uitgeversmaatschappij N.V., UL; this file also contains details of the postwar difficulties. Report, "Visit London, 1 November 1947," SYT D 24 Verslagen van besprekingen m.b.t. The Albatross Modern Continental Library, 1946–1951, File 6, Archief van A.W. Sijthoff's Uitgeversmaatschappij N.V., UL.
34. Minutes of the Board meetings, 18–20 November 1946, Collins Archive, 1/1/5, GUL; Minutes of Board meetings, 28 and 30 October 1947, Collins Archive 1/1/5, GUL. When R. G. Davies of the Central Office of Information researched John Holroyd-Reece's connections, he discovered that Collins had loaned £20,000 to Albatross on 18 April 1947, which gave "much ground for speculation." Mr. Davies and Mr. Hadfield, "The Albatross Ltd," 24 July 1947, INF 12/457, NAK.
35. Fiona Brewster, Interview, 3 May 2013, Le Breuil-Rouillac, France; John Brophy, Entry for 28 July 1941, *The Mind's Eye: A Twelve-Month Journal* (London: Arthur Barker, 1949): 167–68.

CHAPTER TWENTY-THREE. HOMECOMING

1. Enoch, *Memoirs,* 200.
2. Ibid., 200–201.
3. Ibid., 160, 173–77; Silverman, *The Time of Their Lives,* 423–24. To bridge the tran-

sition, New American Library books temporarily appeared under a shared imprint with Penguin; Marc Jaffe, Phone interview, 29 May 2014.

4. Enoch, *Memoirs,* 195–96.
5. Hench, *Books as Weapons,* xiii; see Schreuders, *Paperbacks U.S.A.,* for Pocket (18–30), Avon (31–36), Dell (57–62), and Bantam (63–87); Manning, *When Books Went to War,* 59–74, 152–54. See also Manning and Hench for extensive discussions of structures the American government and publishers instituted during the war to provide books for American troops, and, later, for continental readers.
6. Hench, *Books as Weapons,* 253–55; ECA criteria quoted in Enoch, *Memoirs,* 196–97; for the American government's use of modernist literature as postwar, pro-democracy propaganda, see also Barnhisel, "Cold Warriors of the Book," "Perspectives USA," and *Cold War Modernists.*
7. Enoch, *Memoirs,* 197. Enoch contradicts himself in his memoir regarding his travel dates in Europe; at one point, he gives his departure date as 5 April 1949 (197), but several pages later says his first train ride into Germany was 17 March 1949 (200). I assume he left for Europe on 5 March.
8. Ibid., 202–3.
9. Ibid., 202.
10. Erich Kupfer, Beurteilung, n.d., Magistrate von Gross-Berlin Abt. Für Volksbildung, Verlage Buchh Leihb. C Rep 120, Grieben Verlag, File 946, LAB; Albatross Beurteilung, n.d., Magistrate von Gross-Berlin Abt. Für Volksbildung, Verlage Buchh Leihb, C Rep 120, File 760, LAB.
11. Enoch, *Memoirs,* 203–5. Before the war, Kupfer had also been involved in the "Aryanization" of the Grieben Verlag, a publisher of travel guides, owned by the Jewish publisher Viktor Goldschmidt. See Dahm, *Das jüdische Buch,* 92–97, for how the Literary Chamber blocked Albatross from purchasing Grieben in 1938 because it was foreign; instead, Kupfer acted as Albatross's front man for the purchase. Dahm logically interprets this as a mercenary "Aryanization" deal, which depleted Goldschmidt's resources. But documents in the Albatross Verlag files at the HRC suggest that Holroyd-Reece was trying to help Goldschmidt emigrate. He requested that Kupfer purchase the firm in Germany for as little as possible—and provided the funds—so as to pay Goldschmidt as high a sum as possible in England to support him after his emigration. After the war, Kupfer wanted to own the Grieben Verlag outright, separate from Holroyd-Reece's intervention. Given the devaluation of the firm, Holroyd-Reece worried about his ability to adequately restore Goldschmidt's funds: John Holroyd-Reece to Max Christian Wegner and Wolfgang Krause-Brandstetter, 25 April 1949, Albatross Verlag Records, 2: Correspondence, File: Tauchnitz Edition Company 1949, HRC.
12. Enoch, *Memoirs,* 206; Christian Wegner Verlag to Geschäftsstelle des Börsenvereins, 4 July 1944, 21765, File F 2421, Christian Wegner Verlag, SAL.

13. Kurt Enoch to Max Christian Wegner, 13 September 1951, Series 213-13, Z 8326, SAH.
14. Max Christian Wegner to John Holroyd-Reece, 16 April 1949, Albatross Verlag Records, 2: Correspondence, File: Tauchnitz Edition Company 1949, HRC.
15. John Holroyd-Reece to Wolfgang Krause-Brandstetter and Max Christian Wegner, 21 April 1949, Albatross Verlag Records, 2: Correspondence, File: Tauchnitz Edition Company 1949, HRC.
16. Ibid.
17. John Holroyd-Reece to Wolfgang Krause-Brandstetter and Max Christian Wegner, 25 April 1949, Albatross Verlag Records, 2: Correspondence, File: Tauchnitz Edition Company 1949, HRC.
18. Max Christian Wegner to John Holroyd-Reece 27 April and 30 May 1949, Albatross Verlag Records, 2: Correspondence, File: Tauchnitz Edition Company 1949, HRC; Raymond Pagan (chief of the Publications Branch for the American Zone) to Wolfgang Krause-Brandstetter, 13 May 1949, RG 260 Records of United States Occupation Headquarters World War II, Office of Military Govt. for Germany (OMGUS), Records of Office of Military Govt., Hesse, The Informational Services Division: General Recommendations of the Publications Branch: 1946–49, Box 1212, NACP.
19. John Holroyd-Reece to Max Christian Wegner, 5 June 1949, Albatross Verlag Records, 2: Correspondence, File: Tauchnitz Edition Company 1949, HRC.
20. Raymond Pagan to Wolfgang Krause-Brandstetter, 13 May 1949, RG 260 Records of United States Occupation Headquarters World War II, Office of Military Govt. for Germany (OMGUS), Records of Office of Military Govt., Hesse, The Informational Services Division: General Recommendations of the Publications Branch: 1946–49, Box 1212, NACP; Dr. Pinner to Max Christian Wegner, 8 June 1949, Albatross Verlag Records, 2: Correspondence, File: Tauchnitz Edition Company 1949, HRC.
21. Rainer Maria Rilke, *The Notebooks of Malte Laurids Brigge,* trans. Stephen Mitchell (New York: Vintage, 1985), 10; Max Christian Wegner to John Holroyd-Reece, 15 June 1949, Albatross Verlag Records, 2: Correspondence, File: Tauchnitz Edition Company 1949, Albatross Limited, Advances Paid on Non-Published Titles —31st May 1949, both Albatross Verlag Records, 3: Lists, 1948–1950, File: Publication Dates/Owed and Paid Advances, HRC; see also McCleery, "Tauchnitz and Albatross," 314–15.
22. John Holroyd-Reece to Wolfgang Krause-Brandstetter and Max Christian Wegner, 21 April 1949, Albatross Verlag Records, 2: Correspondence, File: Tauchnitz Edition Company 1949, HRC.
23. Erich Kupfer to Amtgericht Leipzig, 28 June 1949, Registerakten 824/28583 Abt. B, AGL; Vollmacht Document, 13 July 1949, Albatross Verlag, AGL; Notes for Collins

Managing Directors Meeting, 1 September 1949, Notes for Collins Directors Managing Meeting, 24–25 October 1949, File, both GUL; see also McCleery, "Tauchnitz and Albatross, 314.

24. "Albatross International Reprints Ready for Expansion," *Publishers Weekly,* 14 December 1946, 3216–17; S. G. van Looy to Wolfgang Ollendorff, 13 and 19 July 1949, both SYT D 28 Correspondentie met Parijs, UL; McCleery, "Tauchnitz and Albatross," 314; S. G. van Looy to John Holroyd-Reece, 3 April 1950, John Holroyd-Reece to S. G. van Looy, 15 February 1951, Albatross to Sijthoff, 14 March 1951, S. G. van Looy to John Holroyd-Reece, 6 September 1951, all SYT D 26 Correspondentie m.b.t. The Albatross Modern Continental Library, File 3: 1951, UL. For Holroyd-Reece's attempt to sell Albatross to Drs. Mattioli and Aeschlimann, who tried to revive Tauchnitz, see SYT D 26, 1950–51 and SYT D 28, 1949–50, UL; for his attempt to sell to Mondadori see McCleery, "Tauchnitz and Albatross," 314–15.

25. Harold Raymond to Denys Kilham Roberts, 23 January 1951, Hogarth Press, 441, UR; McCleery, "Tauchnitz and Albatross," 313.

26. John Holroyd-Reece to Miss Ruth Mandl, 2 October 1951, Katherine Strelsky Papers, John Holroyd-Reece File, SL; Richard Aldington to Holroyd-Reece, 18 December 1952, Holroyd-Reece to Alister Kershaw, 21 December 1952, both Richard Aldington Collection, 1913–1963, HRC; McCleery, "Tauchnitz and Albatross," 314–15. For the story of how Aldington eventually published *Lawrence of Arabia* with Collins, see Fred D. Crawford, *Richard Aldington and Lawrence of Arabia: A Cautionary Tale* (Carbondale: Southern Illinois University Press, 1998).

27. John Holroyd-Reece to Osbert Sitwell, 19 January 1934, Osbert Sitwell Papers, Box 40.1, Recipient File E-L, HRC.

CONCLUSION

1. Fiona Brewster, Personal Interview, 13 December, Le-Breuil-Rouillac, France.
2. Katharine Strelsky, Unpublished Notes, 21 March "two years later" [probably 1951, since they met in 1949], Katharine Strelsky Papers MC 815, John Holroyd-Reece File, SL.
3. Fiona Brewster, Personal Interview, 13 December 2013, Le Breuil-Rouillac, France; Katharine Strelsky, Unpublished Notes, 21 March "two years later" [probably 1951, since they met in 1949], Katharine Strelsky Papers MC 815, John Holroyd-Reece File, SL.
4. Annemarie Wegner to Max Christian Wegner, 7 April 1943, MW.
5. These materials on John Holroyd-Reece can all be found in the Katharine Strelsky Papers MC 815, John Holroyd-Reece File; Capt & Adj. R.A. of the 294th (Queen's Own Dorset Yeomanry) [signature illegible] to Mrs. Katharine Strelsky, 15 Sep-

tember 1953. See also Katherine Strelsky, "The Sign" ["circa 1953?" penciled on the cover page], a thinly veiled autobiographical story, Katherine Strelsky Papers, unlabeled file; all SL.

6. Arts et Métiers Graphiques: Liste des Actionnaires, AJ/40/722, File B1446, ANF.
7. The London *Times* associate editor Ben MacIntyre, among others, offers examples of this type of relationship in his books about intelligence agents.
8. Adam, *Lesen unter Hitler,* 321; Haffner, *Germany's Self-Destruction: Germany from Bismarck to Hitler,* trans. Jean Steinberg (London: Simon and Schuster, 1987), 211, quoted in Barbian, *The Politics of Literature,* 373.
9. Barbian, *The Politics of Literature,* 377–78.
10. Bonsaver, *Censorship and Literature in Fascist Italy,* 3.
11. Annemarie Wegner to Max Christian Wegner, 4 March 1943, MW.
12. Erich Kupfer, Personal- und Firmennachrichten: "Dr. Kurt Enoch wird siebzig," *Börsenblatt für den Deutschen Buchhandel,* 19 November 1965, 2506. According to Klaus Saur, a publisher who has passionately researched twentieth-century German publishing history, in 1954 Kupfer's firm Grieben went bankrupt, and the remains were handed over to the Thiemig-Verlag in Munich.
13. Todd and Bowden, *Tauchnitz International Editions,* 892, 895; "Wolfgang Krause-Brandstetter," *Börsenblatt der deutschen Buchhandel,* 1963, 2327.
14. "Obituary Notes: Kurt Enoch," *Publishers Weekly,* 26 February 1982; Herbert Mitgang, "Kurt Enoch, 86; Pioneer in Paperback Publishing," *New York Times,* 17 February 1982, B6; Enoch, Publishing Consultant Announcement, 29 January 1968, CE; Ruth Gruenthal, Email to author, 16 April 2013. On 18 September 1953, West Germany passed the "Bundesergänzungsgesetzes zur Entschädigung für Opfer der nationalsozialistichen Verfolgung," a law entitling those who suffered under Nazi persecution to financial restitution: Dr. Dietzold, Restitution Document, 2 September 1959, Wiedergutmachungsakt, Series 351-11, File 45317, SAH.
15. Ruth Gruenthal, Interview, 10 August 2009, Westport, Connecticut; Charles Enoch, Interview, 11 July 2011, Washington, D.C.; "Kurt Enoch on the Occasion of His 70th Birthday" [commemorative booklet], 1965, CE.
16. Kurt Enoch, "Kurt Enoch's Remarks to his Guests at the Dinner Given on his 80th Birthday," 22 November 1975, Kurt Enoch, 1895–1982 [commemorative program for his funeral], 1982, both CE.
17. Trunz and Honeit, eds., *Gratulatio,* 9; Markus Wegner, "Christian Wegner," German Wikipedia entry, https://de.wikipedia.org/wiki/Christian_Wegner (accessed July 2009); Matthias Wegner, Email to author, 11 July 2014; Markus Wegner, Interview, 7 May 2012, Hamburg, Germany.
18. Hansgeorg Maier, "Verleger Profile: Max Christian Wegner," *Welt und Wort* 3 (March 1951): 99; "Max Christian Wegner," *Who's Who in Germany,* 3rd ed. (Munich: Intercontinental Book and Publishing Company, R. Oldenbourg Verlag,

1964), 1834; Markus Wegner, "Christian Wegner," German Wikipedia entry: https://de.wikipedia.org/wiki/Christian_Wegner (accessed July 2009); Matthias Wegner, Email to author, 11 July 2014.

19. Jewish Trust Corporation to Wegner, 18 October 1950, Wegner to Wiedergutmachungsamt beim Landgericht Hamburg, 2 August 1951, both Series 213-13 Z 8326, SAH; "Kaum zu Unterscheiden," *Der Spiegel,* 1952, 30, clipping from MEW.
20. Trunz and Honeit, eds., *Gratulatio,* 12; Matthias Wegner, Interview, 6 May 2012, Hamburg, Germany.
21. Watson, *Book Society,* 97.
22. Lady Elisabeth Schiemann, Phone interview, 22 September 2013. On the age of the estate, see "Chilham Castle," Castles and Fortifications of England and Wales, at http://www.ecastles.co.uk/chilham.html; on the Keep, see http://www.chilham-castle.co.uk/the-history-of-chilham-castle/pre-1607-ancient-castle/.
23. Lady Elisabeth Schiemann, Phone interview, 22 September 2013.
24. Ibid.; Holroyd-Reece Christmas Cards, Katharine Strelsky Papers MC 815, John Holroyd-Reece File, SL.
25. For Holroyd-Reece's appeal, see B368/1013, File Cardew-Smith and Ross, BAK; Lady Elisabeth Schiemann, Phone interview, 22 September 2013; on scheme to distribute milk, Fiona Brewster, Interview, 13 December 2013, Le Breuil-Roulliac, France; for the role Holroyd-Reece played in the mishaps that delayed this book's publication, see Fred D. Crawford, *Richard Aldington and Lawrence of Arabia: A Cautionary Tale* (Carbondale: Southern Illinois University Press, 1998); Lady Elisabeth Schiemann, Phone interview, 22 September 2013.
26. Mr. H. P. Schmoller, "Mr. John Holroyd-Reece," *The Times* (London), 22 March 1969, 10.
27. Sotheby's Auction Announcements, *The Times* (London), 10 June 1969, 10; 17 June 1969, 15; 24 June 1969, 15; 1 July 1969, 13; 8 July 1969, 17; 15 July 1969, 15; 22 July 1969, 15.
28. For Sonia Hambourg Basserab's connection to the Resistance, see Jennifer Lash, *On Pilgrimage: A Time to Seek* (London: Bloomsbury, 1998), 53; Kallistos Ware, "Obituaries: Mother Mary," *Sobornost: The Journal of the Fellowship of St. Alban and St. Sergins* 3, no. 1 (1981); Pauline Adams, *Somerville for Women: An Oxford College, 1879–1993* (Oxford: Oxford University Press), 353.
29. Letter from Alberto Giacometti to Pierre Matisse, Late in 1947, quoted in Angel Gonzalez, *Alberto Giacometti: Works/Writings/Interviews* (Barcelona: Poligrafa, 2007), 132.
30. "Why Am I a Sculptor? An Interview by André Parinaud," from the original in French, "Entretien avec Alberto Giacometti: Pourquoi Je Suis Sculpteur," *Arts* (Paris), June 13–19, 1962, 1, 5, quoted ibid., 150.

Selected Bibliography

ARCHIVES

Public

AGL Amtsgericht Leipzig (Municipal Court Leipzig)

ANF Archives Nationales de France (French Federal Archives, Pierrefitte-sur-Seine, France)

AVP Archives de la Ville de Paris (City Archive, Paris)

BAF Bundesarchiv/Militärarchiv, Freiburg (German Federal Archives/ Military Archives, Freiburg)

BAK Bundesarchiv-Koblenz (German Federal Archives, Koblenz)

BAL Bundesarchiv-Lichterfelde (German Federal Archives, Lichterfelde)

BL Beinecke Rare Book and Manuscript Library, Yale University, New Haven, Connecticut

FM Fondazione Mondadori e Alberto Mondadori, Milano, Archivio storico Arnoldo Mondadori editore, Arnoldo Mondadori, File John Holroyd-Reece (Mondadori Foundation, Milan)

GUL Glasgow University Library, Glasgow, Scotland

IMEC Institut Mémoires de l'édition contemporaine, Sainte-Germain la Blanche Herbe

HRC Harry Ransom Center, The University of Texas at Austin

LAB Landesarchiv-Berlin (Regional Archive of Greater Berlin)

NACP National Archives, College Park, Maryland

NAK National Archives, Kew, England

NL Newberry Library, Chicago, Illinois

NLI Department of Manuscripts, National Library of Ireland, Courtesy of the National Library of Ireland, Dublin

PA Politisches Archiv (German Foreign Office Archive, Berlin)

PUA Manuscripts Division, Department of Rare Books and Special Collections, Princeton University Library, Princeton, New Jersey

RHGA Random House Group Archives, permission granted by The Random House Group Ltd., University of Reading, Special Collections, Reading, England

SAH	Freie und Hansestadt Hamburg, Kulturbehörde, Staatsarchiv-Hamburg (State Archive of Hamburg)
SAL	Sächisches Staatsarchiv, Staatsarchiv-Leipzig (Saxon State Archives, Leipzig)
SHD	Service historique de la Défense (Military Archives, Vincennes, France) (© Service historique de la Défense, CHA Fonds Moscou dossier 42834)
SIUC	Special Collections Research Center of Southern Illinois University, Carbondale
SL	Schlesinger Library, Radcliffe Institute, Harvard University, Cambridge, Massachusetts
SU	Stanford University, Courtesy of the Department of Special Collections, Stanford University, Palo Alto, California
SWA	Stiftung Warburg Archive, Blankenese, Germany
UL	University of Leiden, Special Collections, Leiden, The Netherlands
UR	University of Reading, Special Collections, Reading, England

Private

AJ	Alastair Jollans, London, England
CE	Charles Enoch, Alexandria, Virginia
FVB	Fiona Vendredi Brewster, Le Breuil-Rouillac, France
LES	Lady Elisabeth Schiemann, Kent, England
MEW	Markus Ernst Wegner, Hamburg, Germany
MW	Matthias Wegner, Hamburg, Germany
RGA	Ruth Gruenthal, New York, New York

PRINTED SOURCES

Adam, Christian. *Lesen unter Hitler: Autoren, Bestseller, Leser im Dritten Reich.* Berlin: Galiani, 2010.

Aigner, Dietrich. *Die Indizierung "schädlichen und unerwünschten Schrifttums" im Dritten Reich.* Frankfurt am Mein: Buchhändler-Vereinigung, 1971.

———. *Das Ringen um England: das deutsch-britische Verhältnis, die öffentliche Meinung, 1933–1939, Tragödie zweier Völker.* Munich: Bechtle, 1969.

Aly, Götz, *Hitler's Beneficiaries: Plunder, Racial War and the Nazi Welfare State.* New York: Metropolitan Books, 2007.

Andrew, Christopher. *The Defense of the Realm: The Authorized History of MI5.* London: Penguin, 2009.

Arns, Karl. *Index der anglo-jüdischen Literatur.* Bochum-Langendreer: Pöppinghaus, 1938.

———. *Index der anglo-jüdischen Literatur: Amerika und Nachtrage zu England.* Bochum-Langendreer: Pöppinghaus, 1939.

Ayçoberry, Pierre. *The Social History of the Third Reich.* New York: New Press, 1999.

Bahr, Erhard, "Nazi Cultural Politics: Intentionalism vs. Functionalism." In *National Socialist Cultural Policy,* ed. Glenn Cuomo, 5–22. New York: St. Martin's, 1995.

Bajohr, Frank. *"Aryanisation" in Hamburg: The Economic Exclusion of the Jews and the Confiscation of Their Property in Nazi Germany.* New York: Berghahn Books, 2002.

Barbian, Jan-Pieter. "Die doppelte Indizierung: Verbote US-amerikanischer Literatur zwischen 1933 und 1941." In *Verfemt und Verboten: Vorgeschichte und Folgen der Bücherverbrennungen 1933,* ed. Julius H. Schoeps und Werner Tress, 260–90. Hildesheim: Olms, 2010.

———. " 'Kulturwerte im Zeitkampf': Die Kulturabkommen des 'Dritten Reiches' als Instrumente nationalsozialistischer Außenpolitik," *Archiv für Kulturgeschichte* 74, no. 2 (1992): 415–59.

———. "Literary Policy in the Third Reich." In *National Socialist Cultural Policy,* ed. Glenn Cuomo, 155–96. New York: St. Martin's Press, 1995.

———. *Literaturpolitik im Dritten Reich: Institutionen, Kompetenzen, Betätigungsfelder.* Frankfurt am Main: Historischen Kommission des Boersenvereins, 1993.

———. *Literaturpolitik im NS-Staat: Von der "Gleichschaltung" bis zum Ruin* Frankfurt: Fischer Verlag, 2010.

———. *The Politics of Literature in Nazi Germany: Books in the Media Dictatorship.* Trans. Kate Sturge. New York: Bloomsbury, 2013. [Translation of *Literaturpolitik im NS-Staat.*]

Barkai, Avraham. *From Boycott to Annihilation: The Economic Struggle of German Jews, 1933–1943.* Hanover, N.H.: University Press of New England, 1989.

Barker, Nicholas. *Stanley Morison.* Cambridge: Harvard University Press, 1972.

Barnhisel, Greg. *Cold War Modernists: Art, Literature, and American Cultural Diplomacy.* New York: Columbia University Press, 2015.

———. "Cold Warriors of the Book: American Book Programs in the 1950s." *Book History* 13 (2010): 185–217.

———. "Perspectives USA and the Cultural Cold War: Modernism in Service of the State." *modernism/modernity* 14, no. 4 (2007): 729–754.

Beach, Sylvia. *Shakespeare and Company.* New York: Harcourt Brace, 1959.

Belke, Ingrid, and Bernhard Zeller, eds. *In den Katakomben: Jüdische Verlage in Deutschland, 1933 bis 1938.* Marbach am Necker: Deutsche Schillergesellschaft, 1983.

Benecke, Hans. *Eine Buchhandlung in Berlin: Erinnerung an eine schwere Zeit.* Frankfurt am Mein: Fischer, 1995.

Benz, Wolfgang, ed., *Deutschland unter allierter Besatzung, 1945–1949/55: Ein Handbuch.* Berlin: Akademie Verlag, 1999.

Bermann-Fischer, Gottfried. *Bedroht—Bewahrt: Der Weg eines Verlegers.* Frankfurt am Mein: Fischer, 1967.

Bischoff, Karl Heinrich, "Staat und Buch." In *Die Welt des Buches: Eine Kunde vom Buch,* ed. Hellmuth Langbenbucher, 179–94. Ebenhausen bei München: Wilhelm Langewiesche-Brandt, 1938.

Boberach, Heinz, ed. *Meldungen aus dem Reich, 1938–1945: Die geheimen Lageberichte des Sicherheitsdienstes der SS.* 17 vols. Hersching: Pawlak, 1984.

Bonn, Thomas. *Heavy Traffic and High Culture: New American Library as Literary Gatekeeper in the Paperback Revolution.* Carbondale: Southern Illinois University Press, 1989.

Bonsaver, Guido. *Censorship and Literature in Fascist Italy.* Toronto: University of Toronto Press, 2007.

Bourdieu, Pierre. *Rules of Art: Genesis and Structure of the Literary Field.* Stanford: Stanford University Press, 1996.

Brown, Curtis. *Contacts: A Memoir.* New York: Harper and Brothers, 1935.

Browning, Christopher. "Untersttatssekretaer Martin Luther and the Ribbentrop Foreign Office." *Journal of Contemporary History* 12, no. 2 (April 1977): 313–44.

Bühler, Edelgard, and Hans-Eugen Bühler. *Der Frontbuchhandel, 1939–1945: Organisationen, Kompetenzen, Verlage, Bücher.* Frankfurt am Mein: Buchhändler-Vereinigung, 2002.

Bussemer, Thymian. *Propaganda und Populärkultur: Konstruierte Erlebniswelten im Nationalsozialismus.* Wiesbaden: Deutscher Universitäts-Verlag, 2000.

Caplan, Jane. *Government Without Administration: State and Civil Service in Weimar and Nazi Germany.* New York: Oxford University Press, 1988.

Centenary Catalogue of the Tauchnitz Edition, 1837–1937. Leipzig: Bernhard Tauchnitz, 1937.

Clark, Sir Fife. *The Central Office of Information.* London: Allen and Unwin, 1970.

Clemens, Gabriele. *Britische Kulturpolitik in Deutschland, 1945–1949: Literatur, Film, Musik, und Theater.* Stuttgart: Franz Steiner, 1997.

Collingham, Lizzie. *The Taste of War: World War II and the Battle for Food.* London: Allen Lane, 2011.

Cuomo, Glenn, "Hanns Johst und die Reichsschrifttumskammer: Ihr Einfluss auf die Situation des Schriftstellers im Dritten Reich." In *Leid der Worte: Panorama des literarischen Nationalsozialismus,* ed. Jörg Thunecke, 108–32. Bonn: Bouvier, 1987.

Cuomo, Glenn, ed. *National Socialist Cultural Policy.* New York: St. Martin's, 1995.

Dahm, Volker. "Anfänge und Ideologie der Reichskulturkammer: Die 'Berufsgemeinschaft' als Instrumentkulturpolitischer Steuerung und sozialer Reglementierung." *Vierteljahrshefte für Zeitgeschichte* 34:1 (January 1986): 53–84.

———. *Das jüdische Buch im Dritten Reich.* Munich: Beck, 1993.

Darnton, Robert. *Censors at Work: How States Shaped Literature.* New York: Norton, 2014.

Davis, Kenneth C. *The Paperbacking of America: Two-Bit Culture.* Boston: Houghton Mifflin, 1984.

Decleva, Enrico. *Arnoldo Mondadori.* Turin: UTET, 1993.

de Polnay, Peter. *The Germans Came to Paris.* New York: Duell, Sloane, and Pearce, 1943.

Donaldson, Lady Frances Lonsdale. *The British Council: The First Fifty Years.* London: Jonathan Cape, 1984.

Duara, Prasenjit. "Transnationalism and the Challenge to National Histories." In *Rethinking American History in a Global Age,* ed. Thomas Bender, 25–46. Berkeley: University of California Press, 2002.

Ebi, Michael. "Devisenrecht und Außenhandel." In *Wirtschaftskontrolle und Recht in der Nationalsozialistischen Diktatur,* ed. Dieter Gosewinkel, 181–98. Frankfurt am Main: Vittorio Klostermann, 2005.

———. *Export um jeden Preis: die deutsche Exportförderung von 1932–1938.* Stuttgart: Steiner, 2004.

Eley, Geoffrey, and Jan Palmowski, eds. *Citizenship and National Identity in Twentieth-Century Germany.* Stanford: Stanford University Press, 2007.

Endrèbe, Maurice-Bernard. "Le Roman policier." In *Le Livre Concurrencé, 1900–1950,* 257–65. Vol. 4 of *Histoire de l'Édition Française,* ed. Henri-Jean Martin, Roger Chartier, and Jean-Pierre Vivet. Paris: Promodis, 1983.

Enoch, Kurt. *Memoirs of Kurt Enoch: Written for His Family.* New York: Privately printed by his wife, Margaret M. Enoch, 1984.

———. "The Paperbound Book: Twentieth-Century Publishing Phenomenon." *Library Quarterly* (July 1954).

Espagne, Michel, and Michael Werner. *Qu'est-ce qu'une littérature nationale? Approches pour une théorie interculturelle du champ littéraire.* Paris: Maison des Sciences de l'Homme, 1994.

Evans, Richard. *The Coming of the Third Reich.* New York: Penguin, 2004.

———. *The Third Reich at War.* New York: Penguin, 2008.

———. *The Third Reich in Power, 1933–1939.* New York: Penguin, 2005.

Fischer, Ernst, and Stephan Füssel, eds. *Geschichte des deutschen Buchhandels im 19. und 20. Jahrhundert.* Part I: *Die Weimarer Republic: 1919–1933.* Munich: Klaus Saur, 2007.

Fischer, Ernst, and Reinhard Wittman, eds. *Geschichte des deutschen Buchhandels im 19. und 20. Jahrhundert.* Part 3: *Drittes Reich.* Berlin: De Gruyter, 2015.

Fitch, Noel Riley. *Sylvia Beach and the Lost Generation: A History of Literary Paris in the 1920s and 1930s.* New York: Norton, 1983.

Ford, Hugh, and Anne-Dominique Balmès, *Published in Paris: l'édition américaine et anglaise à Paris, 1920–1939.* Paris: Institut Mémoires de l'édition contemporaine, 1996.

Fouché, Pascal. *L'Édition française sous l'Occupation, 1940–1944.* Paris: Bibliothèque de Littérature française contemporaine de l'Université Paris VII, 1987.

———. "L'Édition littéraire, 1914–1950." In *Le Livre Concurrencé, 1900–1950,* 189–241. Vol. 4 of *Histoire de l'Édition Française,* ed. Henri-Jean Martin, Roger Chartier, and Jean-Pierre Vivet. Paris: Promodis, 1983.

Gienow-Hecht, Jessica C. E. "Art Is Democracy and Democracy Is Art: Culture, Propaganda and the *Neue Zeitung* in Germany, 1944–1947." *Diplomatic History* 23 (1999): 21–43.

Glass, Charles. *Americans in Paris: Life and Death Under Nazi Occupation.* New York: Penguin, 2010.

Goebbels, Joseph. *The Goebbels Diaries, 1939–1941.* Ed. and trans. Fred Taylor. New York: Putnam, 1983.

———. *Goebbels-Reden.* 2 vols. Ed. Helmut Heiber. Düsseldorf: Droste, 1971.

———. *Die Tagebücher von Joseph Goebbels.* Ed. Elke Fröhlich. Munich: Saur, 1987.

Gollancz, Victor. *In Darkest Germany.* Hinsdale, Ill.: Regnery, 1947.

Graham, Gordon. "Kurt Enoch: Paperback Pioneer." In *Immigrant Publishers: The Impact of Expatriate Publishers in Britain and American in the Twentieth Century,* ed. Richard Abel and Gordon Graham, 41–51. New Brunswick, N.J.: Transaction, 2009.

Hall, Murray. *Der Paul Zsolnay Verlag: Von der Gründung bis zur Rückkehr aus dem Exil.* Tübingen: Max Niemeyer Verlag, 1994.

Heller, Gerhard. *Un Allemand à Paris: 1940–1944.* Paris: Seuil, 1981.

Hench, John. *Books as Weapons: Propaganda, Publishing and the Battle for Global Markets in the Era of World War II.* Ithaca: Cornell University Press, 2010.

Higham, David. *Literary Gent.* New York: Coward, McCann and Geoghegan, 1978.

Hofmeyr, Isabel. "Introduction." In *The Portable Bunyan: A Transnational History of "The Pilgrim's Progress."* Princeton: Princeton University Press, 2004.

Holman, Valerie. *Print for Victory: Book Publishing in England, 1939–1945.* London: British Library, 2008.

Holroyd-Reece, John [attrib.]. *The Harvest: Being the Record of One Hundred Years of Publishing, 1837–1937.* Leipzig: Bernhard Tauchnitz Successors Brandstetter, 1937.

Hövel, Paul. *Grundfragen deutscher Wirtschaftspolitik.* Berlin: Springer, 1935.

———. *Wesen und Aufbau der Schriftumsarbeit in Deutschland.* Essen: Essener Verlagsanstalt, 1942.

Huxley, Aldous. *Letters of Aldous Huxley.* Ed. Grover Smith, New York: Harper and Row, 1969.

Imlay, Talbot, and Martin Horn. *The Politics of Industrial Collaboration in World War II: Ford, France, Vichy, and Nazi Germany.* Cambridge: Cambridge University Press, 2014.

Jackisch, Barry A. *The Pan-German League and Radical Nationalist Politics in Interwar Germany, 1918–1939.* Burlington, Vt.: Ashgate, 2012.

Jackson, Julian. *The Fall of France: The Nazi Invasion of 1940.* Oxford: Oxford University Press, 2003.

Jaeger, Roland. "Kurt Enoch (1895–1982) und der Gebrüder Enoch Verlag (1913–1936)." *Aus Dem Antiquariat* 5 (2000): A288–99.

Jeffery, Keith. *The Secret History of MI6: 1909–1949.* New York: Penguin, 2010.

Johst, Hanns. "Zum Geleit." *Die Welt des Buches: Eine Kunde vom Buch,* ed. Hellmuth Langbenbucher, n.p. Ebenhausen bei München: Wilhelm Langewiesche-Brandt, 1938.

Jones, Jill. "Eradicating Nazism from the British Zone: Early Policy and Practice." *German History* 8 (1990): 145–62.

Jones, Larry Eugene, ed. *The German Right in the Weimar Republic: Studies in the History of German Conservatism, Nationalism, and Anti-Semitism.* New York: Berghahn, 2014.

Jucker, Ninetta. *Curfew in Paris: A Record of the German Occupation.* London: Hogarth, 1960.

Kater, Michael. *Different Drummers: Jazz in the Culture of Nazi Germany.* Oxford: Oxford University Press, 2003.

Kershaw, Ian. *The End: the Defiance and Destruction of Hitler's Germany.* New York: Penguin, 2011.

———. *Hitler, 1889–1936: Hubris.* New York: Norton, 1998.

———. *Hitler, 1936–45: Nemesis.* New York: Norton, 2000.

———. *The Nazi Dictatorship: Problems and Perspectives of Interpretation.* London, Edward Arnold, 1993.

Kingsford, R. J. L. *The Publishers Association, 1896–1946.* Cambridge: Cambridge University Press, 1970.

Kleiner Führer durch die gute englische und amerikanische literatur der neuesten Zeit. Leipzig: Bernhard Tauchnitz Verlag, 1933.

Kliemann, Horst. "Die Welt des Buchhandels: Werbung, Handel und Leserschaft." In *Die Welt des Buches: Eine Kunde vom Buch,* ed. Hellmuth Langbenbucher, 135–78. Ebenhausen bei München: Wilhelm Langewiesche-Brandt, 1938.

Langenbucher, Hellmuth [attrib.]. "Vorwort." In *Die Welt des Buches: Eine*

Kunde vom Buch, ed. Hellmuth Langbenbucher, n.p. Ebenhausen bei München: Wilhelm Langewiesche-Brandt, 1938.

Lewis, Jeremy. *Penguin Special: The Life and Times of Allen Lane.* London: Penguin, 2006.

Lindner, Stephan H. *Das Reichskommissariat für die Behandlung feindlichen Vermögens im Zweiten Weltkrieg.* Stuttgart: Steiner, 1991.

Linthout, Ine van. *Das Buch in der nationalsozialistischenpolitik.* Berlin: De Gruyter, 2011.

Lowe, Keith. *Inferno: The Fiery Destruction of Hamburg, 1943.* New York: Simon and Schuster, 2007.

———. *Savage Continent: Europe in the Aftermath of World War II.* London: St. Martin's, 2012.

Lubrich, Oliver, ed. *Travels in the Reich, 1933–1945: Foreign Authors Report from Germany.* Chicago: University of Chicago Press, 2010.

Manning, Molly Guptill. *When Books Went to War.* Boston: Houghton Mifflin Harcourt, 2014.

Martin, Benjamin George. "'European Literature' in the Nazi New Order: The Cultural Politics of the European Writers' Union, 1941–1943." *Journal of Contemporary History* 48, no. 3 (2013): 486–508.

Mason, Timothy. *Nazism, Fascism and the Working Class.* Cambridge: Cambridge University Press, 1995.

Mazower, Mark. *Hitler's Empire: How the Nazis Ruled Europe.* New York: Penguin, 2008.

McCleery, Alistair. "The Paperback Evolution: Tauchnitz, Albatross, and Penguin." In *Judging a Book by Its Cover: Fans, Publishers, Designers, and the Marketing of Fiction,* ed. Nicole Matthews and Nickianne Moody, 3–18. Aldershot, UK: Ashgate, 2007.

———. "The Reputation of the 1932 Odyssey Press Edition of *Ulysses,*" *Publications of the Bibliographical Society of America* 100 (March 2006): 89–103.

———. "The Return of the Publisher to Book History: The Case of Allen Lane." *Book History* 5 (2002): 161–85.

———. "Tauchnitz and Albatross: A 'Community of Interests' in English-Language Paperback Publishing, 1934–1951." *Library* 7, no. 3 (September 2006): 297–316.

Michels, Eckard. *Das Deutsche Institut in Paris, 1940–1944: Ein Beitrag zu den deutsch-französischen Kulturbeziehungen und zur auswärtigen Kulturpolitik des Dritten Reiches.* Stuttgart: Steiner, 1993.

Mitchell, Allan. *Nazi Paris: The History of an Occupation.* New York: Berghahn, 2008.

Mitchell, J. M. *International Cultural Relations*. Boston: Allen and Unwin, 1986.

Mollier, Jean-Yves, *Édition, presse et pouvoir en France au XXe siècle*. Paris: Fayard, 2008.

Moore, Nicole, ed. *Censorship and the Limits of the Literary: A Global View*. London: Bloomsbury, 2015.

Mühlberger, Detlef. *Hitler's Voice: The Völkische Beobachter, 1920–1933; Organization and Development of the Nazi Party*. Oxford: Peter Lang, 2004.

Nagorski, Andrew. *Hitlerland: American Eyewitnesses to the Nazi Rise to Power*. New York: Simon and Schuster, 2012.

Nicholas, Lynn H. *The Rape of Europa: The Fate of Europe's Treasures in the Third Reich and the Second World War*. New York: Vintage, 1995.

Noakes, Jeremy. *Government, Party, and People in Nazi Germany*. Exeter, UK: University of Exeter Press, 1980.

———. "Hitler and the Nazi State: Leadership, Hierarchy, and Power." In *The Short Oxford History of Germany: Nazi Germany*, ed. Jane Caplan, , 73–98. Oxford: Oxford University Press, 2008.

Noakes, Jeremy, and G. Pridham, eds., *Nazism: A History in Documents and Eyewitness Accounts, 1919–1945*. 2 vols. New York: Schocken, 1990.

Nowell-Smith, Simon. *International Copyright Law and the Publisher in the Reign of Queen Victoria*. Oxford: Clarendon, 1968.

Overy, Richard. *The Bombing War: Europe, 1939–1945*. London: Allen Lane, 2013.

———. *War and Economy in the Third Reich*. Oxford: Oxford University Press, 1994.

Poulain, Martine. *Livres pillés, lectures surveillées: les bibliothèques françaises sous l'Occupation*. Paris: Gallimard, 2008.

Pressler, Karl H. "The Tauchnitz Edition: Beginning and End of a Famous Series." *Publishing History* 6 (1979): 63–78.

———. "Tauchnitz und Albatross: Zur Geschichte des Taschenbuchs." *Aus dem Antiquariat: Börsenblatt für den deutschen Buchhandel* 8 (29 January 1985): A1–A10.

Pyle, Ernie. *Brave Men*. Lincoln: University of Nebraska Press, 2001.

———. *Ernie Pyle in England*. New York: Macbride, 1945.

Radio von Radiis, Guido. *Deutsche Aussenhandelspolitik unter dem Einfluss der Devisenbewirtschaftung von 1931 bis 1938*. Vienna: Carl Gerolds Sohn, 1939.

Renders, Hans, "Hitler's European Publishing Ambitions: A Plea for an International Perspective." *Quaerendo* 42 (2012): 231–40.

Riding, Alan. *And the Show Went On: Cultural Life in Nazi-Occupied Paris*. New York: Knopf, 2010.

Rose, Jonathan, ed. *The Holocaust and the Book: Destruction and Preservation.* Amherst: University of Massachusetts Press, 2001.

Rundle, Christopher. *Publishing Translations in Fascist Italy.* Bern: Peter Lang, 2010.

———. "Translation in Fascist Italy: 'The Invasion of Translations.'" In *Translation Under Fascism,* ed. Christopher Rundle and Kate Sturge, 15–50. Houndmills, UK: Palgrave Macmillan, 2010.

Sanders, Marion. *Dorothy Thompson: A Legend in Her Time.* Boston: Houghton Mifflin, 1973.

Saucke, Kurt, "Christian Wegner zum 60. Geburtstag." *Börsenblatt für den Deutschen Buchhandel* 9, no. 72 (8 September 1953): 449.

Schäfer, Hans-Dieter. "Culture as Simulation: The Third Reich and Postmodernity." In *Flight of Fantasy: New Perspectives on Inner Emigration in German Literature, 1933–1945,* ed. Neil H. Donahue and Doris Kirchner, 82–112. New York: Berghahn, 2003.

———. *Das gespaltene Bewußtsein: Über deutsche Kultur und Lebenswirklichkeit 1933–1945.* Munich: Carl Hanser, 1982.

———. "The Young Generation's Non-National Socialist Literature During the Third Reich." In *Flight of Fantasy: New Perspectives on Inner Emigration in German Literature, 1933–1945,* ed. Neil H. Donahue and Doris Kirchner, 46–81. New York: Berghahn, 2003.

Schlösser, Anselm. *Die englische Literatur in Deutschland von 1895 bis 1934.* Jena: Verlag Walter Biedermann, 1937.

Schmoller, Hans. "The Paperback Revolution." In *Essays in the History of Publishing in Celebration of the 250th Anniversary of the House of Longman, 1724–1974,* ed. Asa Briggs, 283–318. London: Longmans, 1974.

Schoeps, Julius, and Werner Treß, eds. *Verfemt und Verboten: Vorgeschichte und Folgen der Bücherverbrennungen 1933.* Hildesheim: Olms, 2010.

Schreuders, Piet. *Paperbacks, U.S.A.: A Graphic History, 1939–1959.* San Diego, Calif.: Blue Dolphin, 1981.

Shep, Sydney, "Books Without Borders: The Transnational Turn in Book History." In *Books Without Borders,* vol. 1, ed. Robert Fraser and Mary Hammond, 13–37. Houndmills, Basingstoke, UK: Palgrave Macmillan, 2008.

Silverman, Al. *The Time of Their Lives: The Golden Age of Great American Book Publishers, Their Editors, and Authors.* New York: Truman Talley, 2008.

Spiers, John. *Serious About Series: American "Cheap" Libraries, British "Railway" Libraries and Some Literary Series of the 1890s.* London: Institute of English Studies, University of London, with the Senate House Library, 2007.

Spiers, John ed. *The Culture of the Publisher's Series.* Vol. 1: *Authors, Publishing and the Shaping of Taste.* Houndmills, Basingstoke, UK: Palgrave Macmillan, 2011.

———. *The Culture of the Publisher's Series*. Vol. 2: *Nationalisms and the National Canon*. Houndmills, Basingstoke, UK: Palgrave Macmillan, 2011.

Spotts, Frederic. *The Shameful Peace: How French Artists and Intellectuals Survived the Nazi Occupation*. New Haven: Yale University Press, 2008.

Steinweis, Alan E. *Art, Ideology and Economics in Nazi Germany: The Reich Chambers of Music, Theater and the Visual Arts*. Chapel Hill: University of North Carolina Press, 1993.

Stieg, Margaret. *Public Libraries in Nazi Germany*. Tuscaloosa: University of Alabama Press, 1992.

Sturge, Kate. "Flight from the Programme of National Socialism? Translation in Nazi Germany." In *Translation Under Fascism*, ed. Christopher Rundle and Kate Sturge, 51–83. Houndmills, Basingstoke, UK: Palgrave Macmillan, 2010.

"Tauchnitz Has a Rival: The Appearance of a Well-Organized Competitor in the Continental Market Is of International Interest," *Publishers Weekly* (April 1932): 1643–46.

"Tauchnitz Marks 100th Year," *Publishers Weekly* (June 5, 1937): 2314–18.

Taylor, Philip M. *British Propaganda in the Twentieth Century: Selling Democracy*. Edinburgh: Edinburgh University Press, 1999.

———. *The Projection of Britain: British Overseas Publicity and Propaganda, 1919–1939*. Cambridge: Cambridge University Press, 2007.

Todd, William. "Firma Tauchnitz: A Further Investigation." *Publishing History* 2 (1977): 7–24.

Todd, William, and Ann Bowden. *Tauchnitz International Editions in English, 1841–1955: A Bibliographical History*. Newcastle, Del: Oak Knoll Press; London: British Library, 2003.

Tooze, Adam. *Wages of Destruction: The Making and Breaking of the Nazi Economy*. London: Allen Lane, 2006.

Trommler, Frank. "Targeting the Reader, Entering History: A New Epitaph for the *Inner Immigration*." In *Flight of Fantasy: New Perspectives on Inner Emigration in German Literature, 1933–1945*, ed. Neil H. Donahue and Doris Kirchner, 113–30. New York: Berghahn, 2003.

Troy, Michele K. "Books, Swords, and Readers: The Albatross Press and the Third Reich." In *Moveable Type, Mobile Nations: Interactions in Transnational Book History*, ed. Simon Frost and Robert W. Jensen-Rix, 55–72. Copenhagen: Museum Tusculanum Press, 2010.

———. "A Modern Press for Modern Times: Behind the Scenes at the Albatross Press." In *The Culture of the Publisher's Series*. Vol. 2: *Authors, Publishers, and the Shaping of Taste*, ed. John Spiers, 202–18. London: Palgrave Macmillan, 2011.

Trunz, Erich, and Maria Honeit, eds. *Gratulatio: Festschrift für Christian Wegner zum 70. Geburtstag am 9 September 1963*. Hamburg: Christian Wegner Verlag, 1963.

Ullrich, Kurt, ed. *Neu Amerika: Zwanzig Erzähler der Gegenwart.* Berlin: Fischer, 1937.

Van der Weel, Adriaan, "The Rise of the English Book in the Netherlands, 1840–1900." *Quaerendo* 30, no. 1 (2000): 277–87.

Watson, Graham. *Book Society.* New York: Atheneum, 1980.

———. "More Sketches from Memory." *Bookseller* (22 October 1977): 2558–60.

Weitz, Eric. *Weimar Germany: Promise and Tragedy* (Princeton: Princeton University Press, 2007).

Welch, David, "Priming the Pump of German Democracy: British 'Re-Education' Policy in Germany after the Second World War." In *Reconstruction in Post-War Germany: British Occupation Policy and the Western Zones, 1945–1955,* ed. Ian Turner, 215–38. Oxford: Berg, 1989.

Weybright, Victor. *The Making of a Publisher: A Life in the Twentieth-Century Book Revolution.* London: Weidenfeld and Nicholson, 1968.

Wolff, Kurt. *Briefwechsel eines Verlegers, 1911–1963.* Ed. Bernhard Zeller and Ellen Otten. Frankfurt: Verlag Heinrich Scheffler, 1966.

Woolf, Virginia. *The Diary of Virginia Woolf.* Ed. Anne Olivier Bell. Vol. 4: *1931–1935.* Vol. 5: *1936–1941.* New York: Harcourt Brace Jovanovich, 1982.

Chapter-Opening Illustration Credits

Introduction: The door to 12 rue Chanoinesse (Photo by the author)

Chapter 1: Cover of Tauchnitz edition of *A Portrait of the Artist as a Young Man* (Courtesy of the Collection of Alastair Jollans)

Chapter 4: List of Albatross Modern Continental Library titles, *Börsenblatt für den Deutschen Buchhandel,* 1 March 1933 (Courtesy of the State Archives of Saxony, Staatsarchiv-Leipzig, Bernhard Tauchnitz Verlag 21056, File 21)

Chapter 5: Cover of *The Albatross Book of Living Verse* (Courtesy of the Collection of Alastair Jollans)

Chapter 6: Cover of *The Albatross Almanac,* 1933 (Courtesy of the Collection of Alastair Jollans)

Chapter 7: Albatross-Tauchnitz promotional brochure from 1935 (Courtesy of the Collection of Alastair Jollans)

Chapter 8: Kurt Enoch's Hamburg office (Courtesy of the Yale University Library)

Chapter 9: Cover of *The Albatross Almanac,* 1936 (Courtesy of the Collection of Alastair Jollans)

Chapter 10: John Holroyd-Reece (*left*) at work with colleague Wolfgang Ollendorff and possibly Sonia Hambourg at the Albatross Paris office (Courtesy of Michel Ollendorff)

Chapter 11: Example of the "Dear Reader" card enclosed in each Albatross volume (Collection of the Author)

Chapter 12: Page from John Holroyd-Reece's Christmas card for 1938, which he commissioned from Gunter Böhmer (Courtesy of the Collection of Alastair Jollans)

Chapter 13: Cover of John Steinbeck's *The Long Valley* (Courtesy of the Collection of Alastair Jollans)

Chapter 14: Tauchnitz-Albatross general list of volumes (Courtesy of the Collection of Alastair Jollans)

Chapter 15: Kurt Enoch in France in the late 1930s with his daughter Mirjam, his mother, Rosa, and his wife, Marga (Courtesy of Charles Enoch)

Chapter 16: View over the Seine from the terrace of the Paris Albatross-Tauchnitz office at 12 rue Chanoinesse (Courtesy of the Fiona Brewster Archive)

Chapter 17: One of the handful of German Tauchnitz titles translated into French to try to make German literature more appealing in France (Courtesy of Elisabeth Coutrot)

Chapter 18: Cover of Pont of Punch, *The British Character* (Courtesy of the Collection of Alastair Jollans)

Chapter 19: Kurt Enoch in the early to mid-1940s, after he had begun working for Penguin (Courtesy of Charles Enoch)

Chapter 20: Max Christian Wegner in 1944 (Courtesy of Markus E. Wegner)

Chapter 21: John Holroyd-Reece shortly after the war (Courtesy of the Schlesinger Library, Radcliffe Institute, Harvard University)

Chapter 22: Albatross promotional brochure, 1947 (Courtesy of the Landesarchiv-Berlin, C Rep. 120 Nr. 760)

Chapter 23: Victor Weybright (*left*) and Kurt Enoch (Courtesy of Charles Enoch)

Conclusion: Sketch of 12 rue Chanoinesse, commissioned by John Holroyd-Reece from Gunter Böhmer (Courtesy of the Fiona Brewster Archive)

Index

Page numbers in *italics* refer to illustrations.